D1520589

Legal Issues
in the
Struggle Against Terror

Legal Issues
in the
Struggle Against Terror

Edited by

John Norton Moore

Robert F. Turner

Carolina Academic Press

Durham, North Carolina

Library of Congress Cataloging-in-Publication Data

Moore, John Norton, 1937-
  Legal issues in the struggle against terror / John Norton Moore and Robert F.
Turner.
    p. cm.
  ISBN 978-1-59460-830-8 (alk. paper)
  1. War on Terrorism, 2001---Law and legislation--United States. 2. Terror-
ism--United States--Prevention. 3. National security--Law and legislation--
United States. 4. Civil rights--United States. 5. Habeas corpus--United
States. 6. War on Terrorism, 2001---Law and legislation. 7. Terrorism--Pre-
vention. I. Turner, Robert F. II. Title.

KF9430.M68 2010
344.7305'325--dc22   2009051501

CAROLINA ACADEMIC PRESS
700 Kent Street
Durham, North Carolina 27701
Telephone (919) 489-7486
Fax (919) 493-5668
www.cap-press.com

Printed in the United States of America

Contents

Foreword   vii
R. James Woolsey

Preface   xi
John Norton Moore & Robert F. Turner

Chapter 1   The Legal Regime for Detainees   3
David E. Graham

Chapter 2   Military Commissions as the Forum to Prosecute
Acts of Terrorism and Other Violations of the Law of War   35
Major General John Altenburg

Chapter 3   Habeas Corpus and the Detention of Enemy Combatants
in the Global War on Terror   65
Honorable James Terry

Chapter 4   U.S. Constitutional Issues in the Struggle Against Terror   81
Robert F. Turner

Chapter 5   National Security, Litigation, and the State Secrets Privilege   113
Robert M. Chesney

Chapter 6   Civil Liberties in the Struggle Against Terror   141
Elizabeth Rindskopf Parker

Chapter 7   Hate Propaganda and National Security   171
Robert M. O'Neil

Chapter 8   Civil Litigation Against Terrorism: Neglected Promise   197
John Norton Moore

Chapter 9   U.S. Intelligence and the War on Terror   235
Frederick P. Hitz

Chapter 10 A New Recipe for Renditions and Extraditions 251
A. John Radsan

Chapter 11 Homeland Security, Information Policy, and
the Transatlantic Alliance 277
Stewart A. Baker & Nathan Alexander Sales

Chapter 12 The Relations between Military and Civilian Authorities
within the United States 299
Kurt Johnson, Kevin Cieply, & Jeanne Meyer

Chapter 13 *Jus ad Bellum* in the Struggle Against Terror 333
Walter Gary Sharp, Sr.

Chapter 14 *Jus in Bello* in the Struggle Against Terror 359
W. Hays Parks

Chapter 15 Legal Issues of Outsourcing Military Functions
in Wartime 411
M.E. "Spike" Bowman

Chapter 16 The Role of Immigration Policy in the Struggle
Against Terror 437
Lieutenant Colonel Margaret D. Stock

Chapter 17 Dealing with the Nuclear Threat in the Struggle
Against Terror 463
Robert L. Pfaltzgraff, Jr.

Chapter 18 Bioviolence: Facing the Prevention Challenge 495
Barry Kellman

Chapter 19 Cyberterrorism: Legal and Policy Issues 519
Jeffrey F. Addicott

Index 567

Foreword

R. James Woolsey, Former Director of Central Intelligence

Some twenty-two centuries ago, in 204 B.C., the bitter Second Punic War had finally begun to turn in favor of the Roman Republic. The Romans had launched an attack under their great general, Scipio, against Carthage itself, and on the way to North Africa he had conquered several city-states in Italy that had once been loyal to Rome but had betrayed her some years before and formed an alliance with Carthage. After conquering Locri, Scipio left behind his lieutenant, Pleminius, to occupy the city.

A short while later a delegation of Locrians traveled to Rome and asked to meet with the Roman Senate. The Senators agreed to hear them out, and what they heard was an indignant blast at the behavior of Pleminius and his troops—details of the desecration of Locrian shrines, robbery, torture, and a full list of horrors: "This officer of yours," the Locrians told the Senators, "there is nothing human except his face and appearance, there is no trace of the Roman except in his clothing and speech...."

The Roman Senate's reaction would have been met by stunned disbelief in virtually any other third century B.C. capital, or indeed in most capitals throughout history. The Senators immediately opened an investigation of the Roman troops' behavior, freed the Locrian women and children who had been put in captivity, and not only apologized but restored double the amount of property that had been stolen by the Roman troops.

In telling the story of Locri in his fine book, *Empires of Trust*, Thomas F. Madden stresses the degree to which the American founding fathers saw themselves as recreating the Roman Republic while repairing some of the flaws that had led to its collapse in the first century B.C. into imperial rule. One of many Roman traits that they retained was a commitment to the principle that war does not abrogate the need to observe the law. This is certainly not to say that war and law require no adjustments when they intersect, and sometimes clash. But the Roman way of succeeding in war while honoring the rule of law has become the American way as well—one aspect of this is summed up by the Marines' saying, "We are your best friend, and your worst enemy."

The interactions between war and law have always been complex, but until recent years Americans have generally had little doubt whether or not they were in fact at war. Wars generally began with some use of military force, even if disputed (the sinking of the battleship *Maine*, the Tonkin Gulf incident) and involved either formal declarations or at least some concrete expression of a national decision (a congressional resolution). Guerrilla wars and insurrections, sometimes using terrorism as a major tool, at least ordinarily have had clear-cut sides and objectives (the Basques in Spain, the Tamil Tigers in Sri Lanka).

Today's struggle against terror, however, which provides the war-like context for this excellent collection of essays, is different. The first, and in many ways the dominating, issue with which one is faced is whether we are, predominantly, at war or at peace.

Clearly there are some elements of both in our current circumstances. But I would submit that much of our confusion is spawned by a hesitancy to acknowledge that we are in some key ways definitely at war, but not with the kind of enemy we are used to. Our hesitancy seems to me heavily driven by the religiously-rooted nature of our enemy's ideology. The United States is very substantially a nation of religious refugees and their progeny. Our record of religious tolerance is not perfect but compared with most countries' records it is exemplary. About the last thing most Americans think is proper is to discriminate against someone because of his religion—respect for the First Amendment is, in more than one sense, at the heart of our national identity.

Yet not all totalitarianism is secular—Communism, Nazism, and Fascism are, and we came to understand how to deal with those. But dealing with religiously-rooted totalitarianism is very difficult for us religious refugees, and history unfortunately contains many examples of religious beliefs that have inspired totalitarian ideology and behavior, whether it was Catholic Torquemada's leadership of the Spanish Inquisition, Protestant Thomas Muentzer's drive for a totalitarian society during the Reformation, Puritan Cotton Mather's persecution of the Quakers, Jewish Yigal Amir's assassination of Yitzhak Rabin, Hindu enforcers of suttee, Shinto kamikazes, or Muslim suicide bombers. It may be difficult for Protestants to read about Muentzer or Hindus to read about suttee without wincing, but it is impossible to understand such behavior and movements without understanding their religious roots. Surely we are able to judge today's Hindus and Catholics on their behavior and personal merits without tarring them with the brush of Torquemada or the practitioners of suttee.

But just as surely it is impossible to discuss, much less understand, these cases of religiously-rooted totalitarian behavior without candidly admitting that they were driven by some people's understanding of what their religion required of them. And if one cannot describe, discuss, and understand what motivates such behavior one cannot change it. The Spanish Inquisition would still be with us if Catholics had never been able to discuss and understand that it was a malignant branch of their religion that needed to be eliminated.

So does euphemism advance or detract from our ability to understand? Are we better able to deal with religiously-inspired violence that seeks to move us toward replacing our Constitution with a Caliphate if we must call such incidents "man-caused disasters?" Has Saudi Prince Alwaleed bin Talal aided our understanding of riots by Muslims in France by ordering Fox News (in which he is reported to have a substantial investment) not to call them "Muslim" riots but just "riots"? Would those who halted the Spanish Inquisition have been able to move more quickly if they had called Torquemada and his followers "anger-management-challenged candidates for therapy with pyromaniacal propensities?"

Lawrence Wright, in his definitive work, *The Looming Tower,* tells us that with just over one per cent of the world's Muslims Saudi Arabia controls around 90 per cent of the world's Islamic institutions. The beliefs espoused and taught by most of those institutions are essentially those of the Wahhabis, Saudi Arabia's dominant sect of Islam—they are views that are somewhere between violent and genocidal with respect to Shi'ites, Jews, homosexuals, and apostates and highly repressive of women and many other groups. Their objective is to replace democratic government with a world-wide Caliphate—a theocratic dictatorship. These views are substantively quite similar to al Qaeda's. The principle difference between the two is not a matter of substance but the question of tactics and control, a bit like the difference between Stalinists and Trotskyites in the 1920s and 1930s.

So by all means let us carefully lay out the lines that should guide our behavior, considering carefully those aspects of our lives where we may reasonably say we are at peace and those where we must admit we are at war. This book is a superb guide in that regard. And let us ensure that we are not only the worst enemy of those who are trying to destroy us but the best friend of those who join us—those who will work with us in defending the Constitution and tolerance against hatred and theocratic totalitarianism.

Above all, let us call things, and ideas, and beliefs by their real names so that we can probe, question, analyze, and decide how to proceed and lay out our guidelines based on facts and logic. Orwell, as is often the case, put it best:

"Language ..." he said in his 1946 essay, "Politics and the English Language," should be "an instrument for expressing and not for concealing or preventing thought."

Preface[1]

John Norton Moore & Robert F. Turner

The September 11 attacks focused the nation's and the world's attention on the problem of international terrorism. This focus has in turn raised important new legal questions. When sovereign nations engage in armed conflict, well-established regimes exist to establish the legal rights of belligerents and innocent civilians who may be found on the battlefield. The rights and duties of soldiers—on the battlefield, or if wounded or captured by the enemy—are generally clear. But in this conflict, fought against non-governmental terrorist organizations rather than the armed forces of sovereign nations, the answers to many questions are not that clear.

The nineteen chapters that follow are authored by some of the nation's leading authorities and address core issues in the struggle against terror from a variety of important perspectives. Some of the essays that follow address aspects of constitutional or other domestic United States law, while others focus on concerns of international law. Still other chapters address intermestic blends of domestic and international law. Their common feature is their special relevance to the struggle against al Qaeda and its terrorist allies.

---

1. The University of Virginia takes pride in its pioneering role in the development of the important new field of national security law. The first law school course on national security law was offered in 1969 at the University of Virginia School of Law and was taught by Professor John Norton Moore. In 1981, Professors Moore and Turner co-founded what was originally called the "Center for Law and National Security," the nation's first "think tank" devoted to non-partisan, non-profit, interdisciplinary advanced scholarship and education on legal issues affecting American national security. It was subsequently renamed the Center for National Security Law, http://www.virginia.edu/cnsl/. The Center's *National Security Law* casebook was published in 1990 and a revised edition was released in 2005. Since the attacks of September 11, 2001, the field has exploded, with several new national security law and terrorism law centers emerging and courses being offered at most law schools across the nation. Each summer since 1991 the Center has run a National Security Law Institute to train law professors and government practitioners in this growing new field.

Our first chapter addresses one of the most controversial issues associated with the United States' struggle against terrorism, the treatment and interrogation of detainees. Author David Graham served with distinction as an Army Judge Advocate General (JAG) officer prior to becoming the Executive Director of the Army's Judge Advocate General's Legal Center and School. He is widely recognized as the principal founder of the military law field of "operational law"—a key component of national security law—and he was a natural choice to deal with detention issues. After a brief survey of the pre-9/11 legal regime for detainees, he discusses various detainee-related government decisions following the 9/11 attacks, first in Afghanistan, and then at Guantanamo Bay, Cuba. He next examines a series of relevant Supreme Court decisions and discusses two key statutes enacted by Congress in response to these judicial determinations—the 2005 Detainee Treatment Act and the 2006 Military Commissions Act—together with an important 2007 Executive Order regarding CIA interrogation methods issued in response to this latter piece of legislation. He then concludes by raising a series of significant questions for readers to consider concerning where we are—and where we should be going—in addressing this matter in the future.

Closely related to the issue of treatment and detention of detainees is the question of how to try them for war crimes or acts of terrorism against the United States if such a decision is made. Chapter Two of this volume addresses a variety of issues pertaining to the use of military commissions. Its author is another highly respected former Army JAG officer, Major General John Altenburg, who retired as the Deputy Judge Advocate General of the Army to the private sector in 2001. He returned to government service in 2004 to spend three years as the appointing authority for military commissions covering detainees at Guantanamo. General Altenburg notes that military commissions have a well-established and honorable tradition in the prosecution of war crimes dating back to the earliest days of the country, and speculates that—in addition to public ignorance of this tradition—opposition to the use of commissions may in part have resulted from both the secrecy surrounding the Bush Administration's handling of the issue and broad claims of Executive power that are addressed in Chapter Four. In addition to providing a useful historic review of relevant military law, General Altenburg chastises the government for failing to embrace some necessary technical changes in the regulations urged by military lawyers in general and the Office of Military Commissions in particular. Had these changes been adopted, he speculates that the *Hamdan* case might well have been decided differently by the Supreme Court. He notes that special concerns for the preservation of national security secrets may make some cases untriable, and cautions that "the government should not risk achieving a criminal conviction by employing rules and procedures that reduce a defendant's trial rights in a way that justifies international derision of the legitimacy of the proceedings."

The third key legal issue involving the detention of enemy combatants in the struggle against terrorism involves the rights of detainees to challenge their detention through the historic writ of habeas corpus. During World War II, more than 400,000 German and Italian POWs were transferred to camps within the United States to be detained for the duration of hostilities. Only a very small number were ever charged with criminal behavior or had any contact with domestic U.S. courts. In 1950, the Supreme Court rejected a habeas petition submitted by German soldiers who were being held in a prison in the U.S.-controlled part of Germany pursuant to convictions by military tribunals that they had continued to fight against U.S. forces after the unconditional surrender of their government. In a relatively brief opinion, the Court rejected the petition, denying them any access to U.S. courts. Fifty-four years later, in a trilogy of 2004 cases involving claims by alleged enemy combatants being held at the U.S. naval station at Guantanamo, Cuba, a different Supreme Court reached a different conclusion. These cases and the history of habeas corpus are presented in Chapter Three by Dr. James Terry, a former Marine JAG Colonel and Legal Counsel to the Chairman of the Joint Chiefs of Staff, who currently serves as Chairman of the Board of Veterans Appeal.

Chapter Four addresses a variety of constitutional separation-of-powers issues involving the President, Congress, and the Senate. Co-editor Robert F. Turner examines the views of the Founding Fathers on the proper constitutional role of the legislature in the foreign policy and national security realm, discussing in the process such modern controversies as the authority of the President to authorize warrantless foreign intelligence electronic surveillance and the interplay between the power of the purse and the power to "declare War" given to Congress, and the President's "Executive" power and authority as Commander in Chief.

Closely related is the power of senior executive branch officials to prevent litigation in federal courts on the grounds that going forward would place in jeopardy "state secrets" the disclosure of which would do serious harm to the national security. What is the basis of this by now well-established doctrine? Is it fair? Can it be used to conceal government mistakes or wrongdoing? Should Congress by statute regulate the doctrine? Professor Robert Chesney addresses the history of the doctrine and examines pending legislation on the topic.

Chapter Six provides a broad overview of civil liberties issues related to the struggle against terrorism. Its author, McGeorge Law School Dean Elizabeth Rindskopf Parker, brings an unusual background to the project. After many years as a civil rights attorney working with the NAACP Legal Defense and Education Fund, Inc., she became the general counsel to both the National Security

Agency and the Central Intelligence Agency, in addition to serving as the number two lawyer in the Department of State. One of four former chairs of the American Bar Association's Standing Committee on Law and National Security contributing to this volume, she discusses a series of First and Fourth Amendment issues raised by the special character of the current conflict against terrorism.

The First Amendment is the central focus of Chapter Seven as well. Former University of Virginia President, law professor, and founding Director of the Thomas Jefferson Center for the Protection of Free Expression, Robert M. O'Neil tackles the difficult issue of "hate propaganda." To illustrate the issue, he notes that Saudi Arabia has been funding a school in northern Virginia that uses textbooks that reportedly teach young children to hate people of certain ethnic, national, or religious groups. There are numerous Web sites on the Internet that preach hatred and even promote terrorism against disfavored groups. Professor O'Neil examines the long and often unsatisfying history of Supreme Court jurisprudence in this area, including decisions involving the Communist Party and other alleged "subversive" groups, and discusses as well the constraints that have been adopted by our northern democratic neighbor, Canada, to address this problem.

One of the most innovative issues in the struggle against terror is addressed in Chapter Eight. America has traditionally been a strong champion of the rule of law, and Professor John Norton Moore—the founder of the field of national security law and principal co-editor of this volume—has long argued that an important but often neglected legal tool in the struggle against terrorism and other forms of tyranny is civil litigation. Building on his landmark 2004 text, *Civil Litigation Against Terrorism*, Moore not only makes the case for private lawsuits by victims of terrorism and their heirs, but also proposes a new treaty to promote and make this remedy effective. For more than a dozen years the two co-editors of this volume have taught an interdisciplinary graduate seminar at the University of Virginia on "War & Peace: New Thinking About the Causes of War and War Avoidance." A central premise of this enquiry is that incentives matter, and if we wish to maintain the peace and deter potential aggressors it is important to act in such a manner that they will perceive such conduct as not in their personal self interest. The key values in this process are perceptions of strength and will, and disincentives like being held financially liable for misconduct can be cumulative in effect. For example, lawsuits against the perpetrators of the Libyan attack on Pan Am Flight 103 two decades ago, which ultimately resulted in payments in excess of $2 billion to relatives of the 270 victims of the terrorist bombing, made a difference. In the process, Libya accepted responsibility for the attacks and renounced future acts of terrorism.

One of the many things that separate the current conflict from traditional warfare is the tremendous importance of intelligence in achieving a successful outcome. Traditionally, good intelligence helped identify the location and intentions of an adversary—which facilitated classic military functions like closing with and destroying enemy forces. In the struggle against al Qaeda and the Taliban, identifying and locating the enemy within or outside of our own national borders is by far the most important aspect of a successful outcome, as the function of closing with and neutralizing the enemy could often be accomplished by a small metropolitan police force. Al Qaeda has no armor, artillery, or infantry divisions—it resorts to terrorism because it recognizes it is hopelessly inferior in military power to its adversaries. Intelligence thus becomes arguably the single most important function in this struggle, and to address that issue we have enlisted the considerable talents of Professor Frederick Hitz. Prior to becoming a Senior Fellow at the Center for National Security Law—with teaching responsibilities in both the School of Law and the University of Virginia Department of Politics—Hitz had a distinguished governmental career, including directing CIA operations in Europe and serving as the first statutory CIA Inspector General. Few can rival his expertise in this field.

Chapter Ten is also authored by a former employee of the CIA. Professor John Radsan, of the William Mitchell School of Law, served for eight years in the Department of Justice and as CIA Assistant General Counsel. Like Professor Hitz, he is a graduate of Harvard Law School. He addresses two controversial issues related to gaining control or transferring control of suspected terrorists: rendition and extradition—the former being controversial when American agents snatch suspected terrorists off the streets of other countries, the later when terrorist suspects are sent to countries with dismal human rights records for interrogation.

One of the most significant structural responses to the 9/11 attacks has been the establishment by Congress of the Department of Homeland Security (DHS). We have called upon a dear friend and colleague—another former Chairman of the ABA Standing Committee on Law and National Security, and the first DHS Assistant Secretary for Policy—to discuss some of the more important legal issues in this area. Joined by former Deputy Assistant Secretary and now George Mason University Law School Professor Nathan Sales, Stewart Baker documents how customs and border protection agents at major airports have worked to prevent dangerous terrorists from entering the United States. Particularly interesting is their discussion of differences of opinion between our government and the European Community on airline passenger privacy, and the general issue of the interplay between safeguarding privacy rights and efforts to protect Americans from foreign terrorists.

Prior to the 9/11 attacks, there were four geographic combatant commands within the U.S. military focused upon Europe (EUCOM), the Pacific (PACOM), South and Central America (SOUTHCOM), and the Middle East/Central Asia (CENTCOM). (A fifth, Africa Command [AFRICOM], was established in 2007.) While the North American Aerospace Defense Command (NORAD) coordinated air defense efforts over North America throughout most of the Cold War, the U.S. mainland had not been attacked by a foreign enemy in more than a century and there had never been thought a need for a unified geographical combatant command for North America. That changed following the 9/11 attacks with the establishment in 2002 of Northern Command (NORTHCOM). Chapter Twelve, written by former NORTHCOM Staff Judge Advocate Kurt Johnson, Prof. Kevin Cieply (former NORTHCOM Chief of Land Operations Law), and Lieutenant Colonel Jeanne Meyer (USAF), addresses the role of NORTHCOM and the important issues its establishment raises about civil-military relations and the role of the military within the territorial United States.

Chapters Thirteen and Fourteen address core issues in the law of war/law of armed conflict. For centuries, scholars of international law have debated legal rules governing the initiation of armed conflict (*jus ad bellum*) and the conduct of such conflicts (*jus in bello*). Perhaps not surprisingly, we have turned to the senior levels of the Pentagon to find prominent scholars to address both issues. Dr. Walter Gary Sharp, a retired Marine JAG officer, is an adjunct professor at Georgetown Law Center while serving as Senior Associate Deputy General Counsel at the Pentagon. He provides important historical background on the rights of states to initiate the use of armed force and then focuses especially on actions against terrorists and other non-state actors. His counterpart in that office, W. Hays Parks—a legendary figure who served for two-dozen years as Special Assistant for Law of War Matters to the Judge Advocate General of the Army and has been the Charles H. Stockton Professor of International Law at the Naval War College—provides a general overview of international law governing the conduct of war and its implications for the struggle against terrorism.

The "outsourcing" of traditional military functions to civilian contractors during the struggle against terrorism has been historically unprecedented and is the cause of a great deal of concern. Traditionally, the American military has relied heavily on private industry for *products*: weapons, ammunition, transportation, food for the troops, and the like. Today, we also outsource *services*, some of which have traditionally been viewed as the exclusive province of uniformed combatants. Do these non-governmental personnel have the "combatant's privilege" to engage with and destroy the nation's enemies, or are they limited to using force in self-defense against an imminent threat to themselves or others? What is their status under the 1949 Geneva Conventions or other international agreements governing the law of armed conflict? If they break the law, may they be tried by military courts-martial? If not, are our domestic laws adequate to ensure that wrongful conduct will not escape accountability? To address the many important issues raised by this new practice, we have enlisted the service of M. E. "Spike" Bowman, a Distinguished Fellow at the Center for National Security Law who previously served as a Navy JAG officer before establishing and managing the National Security Law Unit in the FBI's Office of General Counsel. Many of the issues raised by the privatization of traditional military functions have still not been resolved, but Spike does an excellent job of identifying and analyzing many of them.

One of the distinguishing characteristics of all of the perpetrators of the 9/11 attacks was that they were foreign nationals inside the United States as visitors. In the months and years thereafter, a major debate has taken place about U.S. immigration policies. Is it too easy for foreign radicals to enter America? Should our immigration rules be modified to make it more difficult for potential terrorists to enter our country, even if that means excluding promising foreign students, business people, and innocent tourists in the process? In Chapter Sixteen, West Point Professor Margaret Stock, a leading expert on immigration law, addresses a variety of important issues in this area.

In our judgment, the most important single issue facing the nation today in the struggle against terrorism is the danger that terrorists will gain control of nuclear weapons or other weapons of mass destruction. To address the nuclear issue, we have recruited a non-lawyer, Dr. Robert L. Pfaltzgraff, Jr., the founding president of the Institute for Foreign Policy Analysis and Shelby Cullom Davis Professor of International Security Studies at the Fletcher School of Law and Diplomacy, Tufts University. Among the many alarming scenarios he addresses are a relatively primitive Soviet-era SCUD missile launched from off our shores and designed to explode 40–400 kilometers above the Earth's surface. Such a burst could disable the infrastructure on which modern society depends over thousands of square miles, shutting down power grids, information systems, and virtually everything based upon electronics by electromagnetic pulse (EMP), all without a single fingerprint to identify the source. Dr. Pfaltzgraff also discusses a series of other threats, including assembling and detonating an improvised nuclear device, attacking a nuclear power plant, or detonating a radiological "dirty bomb" in which conventional explosives would disburse radioactive waste over a large area. He also addresses a variety of measures that might be taken to reduce the risks of such devastating attacks.

Only slightly less frightening is the risk of a biological attack, and we are pleased to have found Professor Barry Kellman to address this highly technical issue. Director of the International Weapons Control Center at DePaul University College of Law and author of the highly acclaimed 2007 volume, *Bioviolence: Preventing Biological Terror and Crime*, Professor Kellman also chairs the American Bar Association's Committee on International Security of the Section on International Law and Practice. He notes that it would be much easier for foreign terrorists to transport a small vial of biotoxins through airport security and customs inspection than to move a nuclear weapon, and addresses ways in which genomics, nanotechnology, and other microsciences might be used to alter bacterial agents like plague or rabbit fever to increase their lethality or make them resistant to traditional treatments. He notes the importance of international cooperation in addressing this threat, and emphasizes the importance of establishing an effective system for controlling access and accounting for pathogens and biolabs.

The final chapter addresses the important issue of cyberterrorism, the use of cyberspace to cause harm to the nation's critical infrastructure. The author, Dr. Jeffrey Addicott, is a retired Army JAG Colonel and currently Distinguished Professor of Law and Director of the Center for Terrorism Law at St. Mary's University School of Law. He discusses a variety of techniques used under the general heading "cyber attack" to cause harm or harass a target. These include viruses, Trojan horses, worms, spyware, malware, and many others. Some, like phishing, are regularly used by criminals and criminal organizations to trick people into revealing bank account numbers, passwords, Social Security numbers, and the like. Other techniques are often used by teenagers merely curious to see whether they can hack into a Pentagon computer. But a 2007 cyber attack that virtually shut down the nation of Estonia demonstrated that these techniques can be used to great effect during periods of war or heightened tensions. And the potential that hostile states or terrorist groups might use computer attacks to shut down critical infrastructure systems like electrical power grids, transportation systems, or emergency services is a real and serious threat. Dr. Addicott provides a valuable summary of the problem and then discusses a number of important questions related to the prevention or prosecution of cyber attacks, as well as a discussion of whether cyber attacks might in certain circumstances constitute acts of war warranting the use of defensive armed force.

If there is a common theme in this volume, we believe it is excellence. We are particularly pleased with the quality of the contributors who have participated in this enterprise. They represent a diverse range of backgrounds and political viewpoints. Some are primarily academics, others have distinguished careers in government service, and several belong to both groups. They include lawyers, political scientists, and technical experts on such matters as chemical, biological, and nuclear weapons of mass destruction—in our view the most important issue of concern in this struggle, but all of the contributors share in common that they are among the world's top experts on the subjects they are addressing.

Many of the issues being addressed are so new or so unsettled that no one can draw bright legal lines with great confidence. Courts have struggled for more than two centuries over the precise bounds of Executive power in foreign affairs, and able scholars argue passionately on various sides of these issues today. Throughout most of our history Congress made no effort to constrain the President's conduct of foreign intelligence, and post-Vietnam congressional activism in this area has produced great uncertainty about line drawing. All admit that the Fourth Amendment prohibits "unreasonable" searches and seizures, but major differences exist about what conduct is "reasonable" during a period of armed conflict against terrorists who seem willing to slaughter as many Americans as possible.

For more than twenty-seven years, the Center for National Security Law has published literally dozens of books, monographs, and similar publications on a range of important topics. We are proud of this volume, and we are confident that both expert and lay readers will find it of value as they seek to come to terms with these important legal issues.

We would be remiss if we failed to express our grateful appreciation to all of the contributors to this enterprise as well as to Donna Ganoe, Becky Gildersleeve, Judy Ellis and the rest of the staff at the Center for National Security Law for their important roles in bringing this project to fruition. We are also grateful to Dr. Keith Sipe, Linda Lacy, and Tim Colton, of Carolina Academic Press, for their professionalism and wise counsel.

LEGAL ISSUES IN THE
STRUGGLE AGAINST TERROR

Chapter 1

The Legal Regime for Detainees

David E. Graham[1]

Perhaps no legal issues evolving from the 2001 al Qaeda terrorist attacks on the World Trade Center and Pentagon have generated more controversy and judicial scrutiny than those associated with the manner in which the United States government has dealt with certain individuals seized and detained since those attacks. While the law applicable to captured personnel deemed to be "detainees" was generally well settled prior to 9/11, many legal challenges to this governing law, from both an international and constitutional law standpoint, have since arisen. Accordingly, this chapter will focus briefly on the established legal regime for detainees that preceded 9/11, and then move on to a more detailed discussion of the impact on this regime effected by the President's post-9/11 declaration of a "Global War on Terrorism" and the designation of certain

---

1. *Executive Director, The Judge Advocate General's Legal Center and School, U.S. Army.* David E. Graham, a retired Army Colonel, has extensive experience in International Law and played a seminal role in developing the field of Operational Law. He served as Chief of the International/Operational Law Division, Office of the Judge Advocate General of the Army, and as Director of the Center for Law and Military Operations, now an integral part of the Army JAG School. Mr. Graham has a long-standing relationship with the former JAG School and the University of Virginia, where he was a professor, department head, and academic director. He has published articles in multiple law journals and has lectured extensively worldwide. In late 2007, he authored THE US JUDICIAL RESPONSE to POST 9/11: EXECUTIVE TEMERITY AND CONGRESSIONAL ACQUIESCENCE, a policy brief on behalf of The Foundation for Law, Justice and Society, which accurately predicted the outcome of *Boumediene v. Bush*, 128 S. Ct. 2229 (2008). He holds an M.A. in International Affairs from The George Washington University, a J.D. from the University of Texas School of Law, and a Certificate from The Hague Academy of International Law. He is also a Distinguished Graduate of The National War College.

individuals, seized and detained during the course of this "war" as "unlawful enemy combatants."[2]

The Pre-9/11 Regime for Detainees

In examining the pre-9/11 legal regime applicable to "detainees," it is essential to assess the meaning of this term. "Detainees" has often been used as a generic reference to all individuals captured and detained by the U.S. Armed Forces. However, for the purposes of this chapter, and from both a legal and regulatory perspective, the term is used to identify a quite distinct category of captured and confined personnel. This is evidenced in two basic Department of the Army documents: Army Regulation (AR) 190-8, "Enemy Prisoners of War, Retained Personnel, Civilian Internees and Other Detainees" (1 October 1997), and Army Field Manual (FM) 34-52, "Intelligence Interrogation" (28 September 1992).[3]

The very title of AR 190-8 clearly indicates that the category of "Other Detainees" is distinguishable from the other named categories of individuals to whom the terms of the regulation apply. This is reinforced in paragraph 1-1.a: "This regulation provides policy, procedures, and responsibilities for the administration [and] treatment ... of enemy prisoners of war (EPW), retained personnel (RP), civilian internees (CI), and other detainees (OD) in the custody of U.S. Armed Forces." And, in terms of the substantive import of this distinction, paragraph 1-1.b notes that "This regulation implements international law, both customary and codified, relating to EPW, RP, CI, and ODs...." That is, AR 190-8 specifically purports to reflect the existing international law requirements for the treatment of all categories of personnel captured and confined by U.S. forces.

It is essential to note, also, that individuals deemed to be "unlawful combatants" ("unprivileged belligerents") fall within the category of "Other Detainees." "Unprivileged belligerents" are defined as spies, saboteurs, or civilians who participate in hostilities or who otherwise engage in unauthorized attacks

---

2. For the purposes of this chapter, the term "legal regime for detainees" refers to the legal principles applicable to the treatment, interrogation, and potential trial of personnel captured by the U.S. Government and specifically classified as "detainees"—to include those individuals designated as "unlawful combatant" detainees.

3. The U.S. Army is the Department of Defense (DOD) Executive Agent for POW/Detainee matters. Accordingly, AR Reg. 190-8 represents a multi-service regulation that sets forth DOD-wide policy and guidance on this subject.

or other combatant acts against a sovereign State.[4] Again, however, while such personnel are not entitled to Prisoner of War (POW) status and may be prosecuted for engaging in such activities in a regularly constituted judicial forum of the capturing State, they are, nevertheless, ODs, and are to be treated accordingly while in the custody of the U.S. Armed Forces.

As indicated, all individuals designated as "Other Detainees" fall within the context of the protective provisions of AR 190-8, provisions dictated by international law. The more relevant of these provisions are contained in paragraph 1-5.

1-5.a. (1) All persons captured, detained, interned, or otherwise held in U.S. Armed Forces custody during the course of conflict will be given humanitarian care and treatment from the moment they fall into the hands of U.S. forces until final release or repatriation.

(2) All persons taken into custody by U.S. forces will be provided with the protections of the GPW (1949 Geneva Convention Relative to the Treatment of Prisoners of War) until some other legal status is determined by competent authority.

1-5.b. All prisoners will receive humane treatment without regard to race, nationality, religion, political opinion, sex, or other criteria. The following acts are prohibited: murder, torture, corporal punishment, mutilation, the taking of hostages, sensory deprivation, collective punishments, execution without trial by proper authority, and all cruel and degrading treatment.

1-5.c. All persons will be respected as human beings. They will be protected against all acts of violence, to include rape, forced prostitution, assault and thefts, insults, public curiosity, bodily injury, and reprisals of any kind. This list is not exclusive.

FM 34-52, in force until superseded by FM 2-22.3 (Human Intelligence Collector Operations, September 2006), noted that intelligence is gathered through the interrogation of, once again, distinctive categories of individuals: EPW's; Captured Insurgents; Civilian Internees; Other Captured, Detained, or Retained Persons; and Foreign Deserters or Other Persons of Intelligence Interest. The Manual reaffirmed that "detained" personnel whose status was not clear were entitled to EPW protection until their status was determined by a competent authority. And, as in the case of AR 190-8, FM 34-52 spoke specifi-

---

4. U.S. Army Judge Advocate General's Legal Center And School, Operational Law Handbook (2007).

cally to a prohibition against the use of force against all categories of personnel captured by U.S. forces, to include "detainees." In part, it provided:

> The [Geneva Conventions] and U.S. policy expressly prohibit acts of violence or intimidation, including physical or mental torture, threats, insults, or exposure to inhumane treatment as a means of or aid to interrogation.
>
> Such illegal acts are not authorized and will not be condoned by the U.S. Army. Acts in violation of these prohibitions are criminal acts punishable under the UCMJ (Uniform Code of Military Justice). If there is doubt as to the legality of a proposed form of interrogation not specifically authorized in this manual, the advice of the command judge advocate should be sought before using the method in question.
>
> Experience indicates that the use of prohibited techniques is not necessary to gain the cooperation of interrogation sources. Use of torture and other illegal methods is a poor technique that yields unreliable results, may damage subsequent collection efforts, and can induce the source to say what he thinks the interrogator wants to hear.
>
> Revelation of use of torture by U.S. personnel will bring discredit upon the U.S. and its armed forces while undermining domestic and international support for the war effort. It also may place U.S. and allied personnel in enemy hands at a greater risk of abuse by their captors. Conversely, knowing the enemy has abused U.S. and allied PWs does not justify using methods of interrogation specifically prohibited by the [Geneva Conventions] and U.S. policy.
>
> Physical or mental torture and coercion revolve around eliminating the source's free will. Examples of physical torture include: electric shock; infliction of pain through chemicals or bondage; forcing an individual to sit, stand, or kneel in abnormal positions for prolonged periods of time; food deprivation; and any form of beating. Examples of mental torture include: mock executions; abnormal sleep deprivation; and chemically-induced psychosis.
>
> Coercion is defined as actions designed to unlawfully induce another to compel an act against one's will. Examples of coercion include: Threatening or implying physical or mental torture to the subject, his family, or others to whom he owes loyalty; Intentionally denying medical assistance or care in exchange for the information sought or other cooperation; Threatening or implying that other rights guaranteed by the [Geneva Conventions] will not be provided unless cooperation is forthcoming; And specific acts committed by U.S. Army

personnel may subject them to prosecution under one or more ... punitive articles of the UCMJ.[5]

In summary, the pre-9/11 legal regime for detainees, including detainees designated as "unlawful combatants," clearly reflected the fact that these individuals were to be viewed as a category of captured personnel distinct from the several other categories of individuals who might be captured and confined by U.S. forces. Equally clear is the fact that the DOD regulatory and doctrinal guidance applicable to detainees was explicit in terms of the manner in which such individuals were to be both treated and interrogated. Moreover, as noted in this guidance, the specifically articulated requirements contained therein reflected both controlling international law and U.S. policy.

Post-9/11: A Second U.S. Legal Regime for "Unlawful Combatant" Detainees

Framing the Context of a Second Regime

Following the terrorist attacks on the World Trade Center and the Pentagon on September 11, 2001, an almost uniform consensus existed that, though initiated by a non-State entity, these al Qaeda strikes constituted an "armed attack" against the United States. It was reasoned that these acts represented simply the latest al Qaeda action in what amounted to an "ongoing armed attack" against U.S. citizens and property, one dating back to the initial bombing of the World Trade Center in 1993, the bombing of the U.S. Embassies in Kenya and Tanzania in 1998, and the 2000 attack on the *U.S.S. Cole* in Yemen. A very distinct difference of opinion would evolve, however, as to whether this latest al Qaeda strike, even given the scale of its destructive force, served to signal the initiation of a "war" or "armed conflict" between this transnational terrorist organization and the United States.

On September 12, 2001, the United Nations Security Council unanimously adopted a resolution condemning "the ... terrorist attacks" of 9/11, which the Council regarded, "like any act of international terrorism, as a threat to international peace and security."[6] On September 28, the Council also unanimously adopted, under Chapter VII of the UN Charter, a U.S.-sponsored resolution obligating all member states to deny "financing, support, and safe haven to

---

5. Army Field Manual 34-52, Intelligence Interrogation, pp. 1-7 and 1-8 (Sept. 28, 1992).
6. SC Res.1368, para.1 (Sept.12,2001).

terrorists."[7] Additionally, both of these resolutions affirmed—in the context of
the events of 9/11—the inherent right of both individual and collective self-
defense, as well as the need "to combat by all means" the "threats to international peace and security caused by terrorist acts."[8] Note is made, however,
that while these resolutions made repeated references to "terrorist attacks" and
"international terrorism," conspicuously absent was any UN recognition of the
existence of a "war" or "armed conflict" between the United States and al Qaeda,
triggered by the 9/11 attacks.

In the week that followed, President Bush declared a national emergency[9]
and called to active duty the reserves of the U.S. Armed Forces.[10] He also signed
into law, on September 18, a Joint Resolution of Congress that was to become
a pivotal aspect of the coming debate over the manner in which the government
would choose to classify, treat, interrogate, and bring to trial certain detainees
seized in Afghanistan and elsewhere. This Resolution authorized the President
"to use all necessary and appropriate force against those nations, organizations, or persons he determines planned, authorized, committed, or aided the
terrorist attacks or harbored such organizations or persons, in order to prevent
any future acts of international terrorism against the United States by such
persons, organizations or persons."[11] Again, however, this Resolution contained no reference to a congressional declaration or acknowledgement of the
existence of an ongoing "war" or "armed conflict" with al Qaeda, or with terrorism, writ large. Moreover, this authorization for the use of force was limited to only those individuals or entities linked specifically to the 9/11 attacks.

Despite the absence of a recognition of the existence of a "war" or "armed
conflict" triggered by the events of 9/11 in either the UN or congressional resolutions, it soon became evident that the Administration had made the decision to frame all future Executive branch actions taken in relation to 9/11 in
the context of the President's constitutional "war making" powers. And, in
order to validate this approach, a "war" was required. An early indicator of the
decision to move in this direction occurred in the form of a speech delivered
by President Bush to a joint session of Congress on September 20, in which
he declared: "On September 11th, enemies of freedom committed 'an act of
war' against our country."[12]

---

7. SC Res.1373, para.1 (Sept.28,2001).
8. SC Res.1368, pmbl.; SC Res.1373, pmbl.
9. Proclamation 7463, 66 Fed. Reg. 48,199 (Sept.18, 2001).
10. Exec. Order No. 13,223, 66 Fed. Reg. 48,201 (Sept. 18, 2001).
11. Authorization for Use of Military Force, Pub. L. No. 107-40, 115 Stat. 224 (2001).
12. See Address Before a Joint Session of the Congress on the United States Response

A further indication of this strategy was evidenced by a November 13, 2001, Presidential Order Establishing Military Commissions: "Detention, Treatment, and Trial of Certain Non-Citizens in the War Against Terrorism." The title of this order reflects an early use of the term, "War Against Terrorism," and Section 1(a) states:

> International terrorists, including members of al Qaida, have carried out attacks on United States diplomatic and military personnel and facilities abroad and on citizens and property within the United States on a scale that has created 'a state of armed conflict' that requires the use of the United States Armed Forces.

Additionally, Section 2 very broadly defines the term, "individual subject to this order," identifying not only members of al Qaeda, but any person, worldwide, who "... has engaged in, aided or abetted, or conspired to commit, acts of international terrorism, or acts in preparation therefore, that have caused, threaten to cause, or have as their aim to cause, injury to or adverse effects on the United States, its citizens, national security, foreign policy, or economy; or has knowingly harbored one or more [of these] individuals...."[13] Clearly, in the view of the Administration, the United States was now not only at "war" with the transnational terrorist organization, al Qaeda; the United States was now at "war" with "terrorism" worldwide.

Of significance, also, is the fact that the issuance of this Presidential Order clearly evidenced a very early decision that all terrorists seized and detained during the course of this "war on terrorism" would be tried, for offenses allegedly committed, in a U.S. judicial forum—in this case, specifically established Military Commissions. The legitimacy of this choice of forum, in turn, would depend fully on the status the U.S. government would choose to accord the individuals subject to this Order.

The decision to validate all future 9/11-related policy and legal decisions in the context of the President's "war making" powers afforded the Executive branch a degree of governmental control fully in keeping with the Administration's concept of the Unitary Executive, a governing philosophy founded on a belief in the broadest possible exercise of Presidential authority. Very importantly, for the purposes of this chapter, it was a decision that would also ultimately result in the creation of a second, very distinct U.S. legal regime that would be

---

to the Terrorist Attacks of September 11, 37 WEEKLY COMP. PRES. DOC. 1347, (Sept. 20, 2001).

13. Military Order-Detention, Treatment and Trial of Certain Non-Citizens in the War Against Terrorism, 66 Fed. Reg. 57,833 (Nov. 16, 2001).

applied specifically to individuals seized and detained during the course of this ongoing "war." In essence, the United States would, in the future, deal with al Qaeda members, and all other terrorists suspected of conducting or planning acts of international terrorism that threatened U.S. interests, as well as those who supported or harbored these individuals, not as terrorists, but as combatant participants in an "armed conflict" being waged against the United States Accordingly, the United States would no longer apply either the domestic or international law relevant to "terrorism" and "terrorists" to such personnel, but would, instead, apply what it deemed to be the relevant provisions of the Law of War. This approach served as the critical basis for future decisions made in connection with the manner in which the U.S. government would categorize, treat, interrogate, and bring to trial what was to become a very distinct category of "detainees."

Status and Treatment of Personnel Captured in Afghanistan

In response to the sanctuary and support afforded the al Qaeda organization by the Taliban government of Afghanistan, the United States and a number of allied States initiated military action against Afghanistan, and al Qaeda personnel present there, on October 7, 2001. Though the United States had not recognized the legitimacy of the Taliban government, it was assumed by those planning and conducting the military operation that the ensuing conflict would be international in nature, one to which the full range of both the codified and customary Law of War would apply. Accordingly, this relevant law would include, as a matter of course, the 1949 Geneva Conventions and, specifically, the provisions of the Third Geneva Convention Relative to the Treatment of Prisoners of War (GPW).[14] Acting on this premise, the U.S. military was prepared to apply the pertinent provisions of the Third Convention to all personnel captured during the course of the conflict, to include, when necessary, conducting "Article 5 tribunals" to determine whether certain individuals should be accorded POW status.[15] This would not be the case.

---

14. Convention Relative to the Treatment of Prisoners of War, Aug. 12, 1949, 6 UST 3316, 75 UNTS 135. [Third Geneva Convention].

15. Article 5 of the Third Geneva Convention states, in part: "Should any doubt arise as to whether persons, having committed a belligerent act and having fallen into the hands of the enemy, belong to any of the categories enumerated in Article 4 [persons entitled to POW status], such persons shall enjoy the protection of the present Convention until such time as their status has been determined by a competent tribunal."

As the United States began taking captives in Afghanistan, the status and treatment to be accorded captured Taliban and al Qaeda personnel became, somewhat surprisingly, a difficult and unsettled issue. While military Judge Advocates on the ground were prepared to apply the relevant provisions of the Conventions, and had sought a reaffirmation of this approach through existing command channels, they were provided with no clear guidance. As a result, these attorneys advised that, given the lack of such guidance, all captured personnel were to be treated in a manner "consistent" with both the GPW and the Fourth Convention Relative to the Protection of Civilian Persons in Time of War (GC).[16]

Presidential Determinations Regarding Detainee Status and Treatment

Status Determination

Stepping into what had become a prolonged void concerning the status to be accorded captives seized in Afghanistan, President Bush made the first of a number of Administration determinations that would signal a decision to abandon the applicability of the pre-9/11 detainee legal regime with respect to the manner in which it would categorize and treat individuals captured, both in Afghanistan and elsewhere, during the course of the now ongoing "war on terrorism."

Acting on advice contained in a Department of Justice (DOJ) opinion of January 22, 2002, the President initially indicated that the United States would neither apply the Geneva Conventions to the conflict in Afghanistan, in general, nor the GPW to the al Qaeda or Taliban captives, in particular.[17]

The DOJ legal analysis underlying this approach proceeded along these lines. Al Qaeda, as a non-State actor, was said to be incapable of signing and becoming a party to international conventions. Given this fact, it followed that al Qaeda was entitled to no rights or privileges conveyed by these conventions, particularly those of the 1949 Geneva Conventions, in general, or the GPW, specifi-

---

16. U.S. Army Judge Advocate General's Legal Center and School, Center for Law and Military Operations, Legal Lessons Learned from Afghanistan and Iraq 53 (2004).

17. *See* Memorandum from Jay S. Bybee, Assistant Attorney General, U.S. Dep't of Justice, to Alberto Gonzales, Counsel to the President, and William J. Haynes II, General Counsel, Dep't of Defense (Jan.22, 2002).

cally. Additionally, as private citizens, al Qaeda members who had taken up arms against a sovereign State—i.e., the United States—were "unlawful combatants" and, as such, entitled to no protections under the Law of War, to include the rights and protections of the GPW. In sum, al Qaeda personnel captured in Afghanistan were not entitled to POW status; they were simply "unlawful combatant" detainees.[18]

The DOJ opinion also dealt with a legal argument concerning the status of al Qaeda personnel that had surfaced in the preceding weeks—and one that was to later become a critical aspect of a landmark Supreme Court decision dealing with the President's establishment of Military Commissions. This argument revolved around an assertion that the "conflict" under way between al Qaeda and the United States was actually one of a non-international nature. And, as such, Common Article 3 of the Geneva Conventions, that article dealing exclusively with such conflicts and the rights and protections that flow to individuals seized during these conflicts, was said to apply. DOJ summarily dismissed this contention, noting that, by its own terms, Common Article 3 applied to internal conflicts; i.e., to civil wars. The ongoing conflict with al Qaeda, it was said, was international in scope.[19]

The DOJ opinion then moved on to a discussion of the status of the Taliban—and Taliban personnel. In doing so, DOJ opined that, acting under his constitutional Article II authority as Commander in Chief—given the now occurring state of "war" that existed between the United States and terrorists and terrorism, worldwide—the President was empowered to suspend any part, or all of, any international agreement relevant to the conduct of this "war." Accordingly, the President could suspend the applicability of the Geneva Conventions to the conflict in Afghanistan, as a whole, and, more specifically, the applicability of the GPW to Taliban personnel.[20] In speaking to this course of action, DOJ noted several supporting factors: that Afghanistan was a "failed State," possessed of no functioning central government; that it had evidenced an inability or unwillingness to fulfill its international obligations; and that it enjoyed very little international recognition as the legitimate Afghan government.[21]

DOJ also noted that the President might pursue an alternative approach toward this issue, suggesting that he might choose to apply the Geneva Conventions, and particularly the GPW, to the Afghan conflict as a matter of policy, rather than as a matter of law. Having applied the GPW to the captured Tal-

---

18. *See id.* at 9–10.
19. *See id.* at 10.
20. *See id.* at 10–11, 24–25.
21. *See id.* at 18–22.

iban personnel, however, he might then make the determination that these individuals failed to qualify for POW status under the specific requirements of
this Third Convention.[22] In essence, either DOJ approach would produce the
same result: Taliban personnel held by the United States would not be entitled
to POW status. As in the case of the members of al Qaeda, the Taliban captives
would be viewed simply as "unlawful combatant" detainees.

The President's initial indication that the United States would choose not to
apply the Geneva Conventions to the Afghan conflict—or to those seized in
the course of this conflict—met with substantial domestic and international
criticism. Indeed, much of this criticism originated with career U.S. government attorneys who viewed the conflict in Afghanistan as clearly international
in nature—and one to which the full range of the Law of War, to include the
Geneva Conventions, applied. Following several weeks of intense internal governmental debate on this matter,[23] the President issued a February 7, 2002
Memorandum which formally set forth the government's position on the status that would be afforded captured al Qaeda and Taliban personnel, the manner in which they were to be treated, and the legal rationale for these decisions.[24]

Presidential Memorandum: Humane Treatment of al Qaeda and Taliban Detainees

Citing both the January 22 DOJ Memorandum and a February 1 letter from
the Attorney General,[25] the President, in his Memorandum of February 7, is-

---

22. *See id.* at 25, 28.

23. *See* Draft Memorandum from Alberto R. Gonzales, Counsel to the President, to
President George W. Bush, "Decision Re/ Application of the Geneva Convention on Pris-
oners of War to the Conflict with Al Qaeda and the Taliban" (Jan. 25, 2002); Memoran-
dum from Colin L. Powell, Secretary of State, to Alberto R. Gonzales, Counsel to the
President," Draft Decision Memorandum for the President on the Applicability of the Geneva
Convention to the Conflict in Afghanistan" (Jan. 26, 2002); Letter from John Ashcroft, Attorney General, to President George W. Bush (Feb. 1, 2002); Memorandum from William
H. Taft, IV, Legal Advisor, Department of State, to Alberto R. Gonzales, Counsel to the
President, "Comments on Your Paper on the Geneva Conventions" (Feb. 2, 2002); Memo-
randum from Jay S. Bybee, Assistant Attorney General, to Alberto R. Gonzales, Counsel
to the President, "Re: Status of Taliban Forces Under Article 4 of the Third Geneva Convention of 1949 (Feb. 7, 2002), reprinted in MARK DANNER: TORTURE AND TRUTH: AMER-
ICA, ABU GHRAIB AND THE WAR ON TERROR 83–104 (2004).

24. Memorandum from President George W. Bush, "Humane Treatment of Al Qaeda
and Taliban Detainees" (Feb. 7, 2002), reprinted in DANNER: TORTURE AND TRUTH 105.

25. Ashcroft Letter (Feb.1, 2002), *supra* note 22.

sued a formal decision that the Geneva Conventions did not apply to the "conflict" with al Qaeda in Afghanistan or elsewhere, citing the fact that al Qaeda was not a High Contracting Party to these Conventions. Accordingly, he noted, al Qaeda personnel did not qualify as POW. This determination, in effect, resulted in al Qaeda captives now formally taking on the status of "unlawful combatant" detainees.

The President additionally determined that, though he possessed the constitutional authority to suspend the applicability of the Conventions, as a whole, to the conflict in Afghanistan, he would not do so. Instead, as a matter of policy, vice law, he would apply the Conventions to the U.S. conflict with the Taliban. Having done so, however, he stated that, acting on facts supplied by the Department of Defense (DOD) and upon the recommendation of the DOJ[26] he had concluded that, under the relevant provisions of Article 4, GPW, the Taliban did not qualify for POW status. As a result, they, too, would be deemed "unlawful combatant" detainees.

An appreciation for the DOJ legal analysis resulting in the President's somewhat controversial decision regarding the status of captured Taliban personnel requires a brief look at the relevant provisions of Article 4, GPW:

Article 4: Prisoners of War
A. Prisoners of War, in the sense of the present Convention, are
Persons belonging to one of the following categories, who have
Fallen into the power of the enemy:

(1) Members of the armed forces of a party to the conflict, as well as members of militias or volunteer corps forming part of such armed forces.

(2) Members of other militias and members of other volunteer Corps, including those of organized resistance movements, belonging to a Party to the conflict..., provided that such militias or volunteer corps, including such organized resistance movements, fulfill the following conditions:

(a) that of being commanded by a person responsible for his subordinates;

(b) that of having a fixed distinctive sign recognizable at a distance;

(c) that of carrying arms openly;

(d) that of conducting their operations in accordance with the laws and customs of war.

---

26. Bybee Memo to Gonzales (Feb. 7, 2002), *supra* note 22.

Article 4(A)(1) deals with the regular armed forces of a State and militia and volunteer corps members who are incorporated into, and become an integral part of, such armed forces. Article 4(A)(2) speaks to militia and volunteer corps members, as well as members of resistance groups, who may fight on the side of a Party to a conflict, but who are not incorporated into the armed forces of that Party. While the militia and volunteer corps members identified in 4(A)(1) automatically qualify for POW status, those referenced in 4(A)(2) must meet the four specific requirements of 4(A)(2). In its analysis, DOJ summarily dismissed any consideration that Taliban personnel would qualify for POW status as members of the Afghan armed forces, focusing, instead, on whether the Taliban fighters qualified for such status under the requirements of 4(A)(2). DOJ concluded that they did not. As a result, these individuals became "unlawful combatant" detainees.[27] While this legal analysis concerning the status of Taliban captives is debatable, it was, nevertheless, accepted and acted upon by the President.

A concomitant issue associated with the status determination of, particularly, members of the Taliban was that of whether Article 5, GPW, imposed an obligation on the United States to conduct "Article 5 tribunals" in order to make valid status determinations regarding captured Taliban personnel. The relevant portion of Article 5 provides:

> Should any doubt arise as to whether persons, having committed a belligerent act and having fallen into the hands of the enemy, belong to any of the categories enumerated in Article 4, such persons shall enjoy the protection of the present Convention until such time as their status has been determined by a competent tribunal.

The Commentary to this article reflects that it was to apply in very limited situations—to deserters and persons accompanying the force who had lost their identity cards.[28] Moreover, it is clear, as well, that the "doubt" in issue must occur in the collective "mind" of the Capturing Power, not that of any other entity. And, in this case, there was no doubt on the part of the United States, as reflected by a presidential determination, as to the status of the individuals concerned. They were not entitled to POW status and were, accordingly, "unlawful combatant" detainees.

This presidential determination to designate both al Qaeda and Taliban detainees as "unlawful combatants," under the Law of War, was essential to the

---

27. *See id.* at 4–7.

28. COMMENTARY ON THE GENEVA CONVENTION RELATIVE TO THE TREATMENT OF PRISONERS OF WAR 77 (Pictet ed. 1960).

government's evolving decision to formulate a second legal regime applicable exclusively to such detainees—one that would differ substantially from the pre-9/11 regime in terms of the manner in which these "unlawful combatants" would be treated and interrogated. It was a determination that was also of particular importance with respect to the judicial forum in which these individuals could lawfully be tried. Had they been accorded POW status, specific provisions of the GPW would have required their trial by military court-martial, pursuant to the procedures of the Uniform Code of Military Justice (UCMJ).[29] As "unlawful combatants," however, they could be tried, instead, in a U.S. judicial forum of choice—in this case, the Military Commissions specifically constituted under the previously referenced Presidential Order of November 13, 2001.

Finally, having articulated his reasoning for declaring al Qaeda and Taliban personnel to be "unlawful combatants," the President addressed the previously noted contention that Common Article 3 of the Conventions should be deemed applicable to the U.S. "conflict" with al Qaeda. Drawing, once again, upon the advice of DOJ, he stated that Common Article 3 applied to neither the al Qaeda nor Taliban detainees, as the relevant conflicts[30] were international in scope— and Common Article 3 applied only to "armed conflicts not of an international character."

Detainee Treatment

Turning from the issue of the status that would be accorded captured al Qaeda and Taliban personnel, the President next spoke to the manner in which these individuals were to be treated: "As a matter of policy, the United States Armed Forces shall continue to treat detainees humanely and, to the extent appropriate and consistent with military necessity, in a manner consistent with the principles of Geneva." Note that the President characterized his decision to afford humane treatment to the detainees as an issue of "policy" rather than as one required by either domestic or international law. Also important are the caveats placed on this policy requirement. Treatment was to be "consis-

---

29. Uniform Code of Military Justice, 10 U.S.C., Sections 801–946.

30. Memorandum from President (Feb. 7, 2002), *supra* note 23 at 2. Note the President's use of the term, "relevant conflicts." This was in keeping with the government's position that two distinct conflicts were at issue—one that had been waged with the Taliban government of Afghanistan, and a second, ongoing, conflict with "international terrorists," to include al Qaeda, worldwide.

tent," rather than in accordance with, the Conventions. And even this level of treatment was not mandatory. It was to be provided these detainees only to the "extent appropriate and consistent with military necessity."[31]

This largely ambiguous "standard" of treatment deemed applicable to captured al Qaeda and Taliban personnel represented a significant departure from the established pre-9/11 detainee legal regime. In sum, the President had determined that al Qaeda and Taliban captives were not POWs; they were "detainees." And not simply detainees, but "unlawful combatant" detainees—an evolving category of detainees to whom a newly conceived and unilaterally implemented standard of treatment would apparently now be applied.

Guantanamo Bay: A New Legal Regime for "Unlawful Combatant" Detainees

Following the military operation in Afghanistan, hundreds of captured al Qaeda and Taliban personnel were transported to the U.S. Naval Base at Guantanamo Bay, Cuba, a site selected specifically for the reason that U.S. courts had consistently viewed Guantanamo as beyond the reach of their judicial jurisdiction. An immediate question arose: Declared to be "unlawful combatant" detainees, devoid of any Geneva Convention rights and protections, what legal principles dictated the manner in which these individuals were to be treated and interrogated? The U.S. regulatory and policy guidance comprising the pre-9/11 legal regime for detainees—set forth in AR 190-8 and FM 34-52—was still in place[32] and, initially, these precepts were applied. The adherence to this established regime would be short lived, however.

On October 25, 2002, the Commander, U.S. Southern Command, forwarded a memorandum to the Chairman of the Joint Chiefs of Staff, in which he noted that a number of Guantanamo detainees had successfully resisted interrogation practices then in use (techniques contained in FM 34-52). Accordingly, he forwarded a number of proposed "counter-resistance" techniques for DOD and DOJ review and approval, as, in his words, he was "... uncertain whether all the techniques ... are legal under U.S. law, given the absence of judicial interpretation of the U.S Torture Statute...."[33]

---

31. *Id.*

32. AR 190-8 and FM 34-52, *supra* notes 2, 4.

33. Memorandum from General James T. Hill, Commander, U.S. Southern Command, to General Richard B. Myers, Chairman, Joint Chiefs of Staff, "Counter-Resistance Techniques," (Oct. 25, 2002), reprinted in DANNER: TORTURE AND TRUTH 179.

The exclusive reference to the U.S. Torture Statute[34] appeared to reflect a conclusion drawn from a legal analysis conducted by a limited number of U.S. government attorneys of the law applicable to the treatment and interrogation of all "unlawful combatant" detainees captured in the "war on terrorism" and held outside the United States, to include those detained at Guantanamo. In their view, the President had determined that, as "unlawful combatants," these detainees were not entitled to Geneva Convention protections. It followed then that, as the requirements of AR 190-8 and FM 34-52 were driven exclusively by U.S obligations under these Conventions, a continued application of the regulatory and doctrinal requirements at issue was now simply a matter of policy, not law. And policy could be changed. Indeed, it was argued, the President had already made this change, previously determining that the level of treatment accorded al Qaeda and Taliban detainees need only be "consistent" with the Conventions—and that even this requirement was subject to the demands of "military necessity." Thus believing it to be relieved of its international obligations, the government apparently felt that it was now free to concern itself with the requirements of only one aspect of U.S. law, the Torture Statute.

Apparently lost in this legal analysis of the law applicable to "unlawful combatant" detainees was an awareness of the existence of other substantive provisions of international law that seemingly had a direct bearing on the treatment and interrogation of the detainees held at Guantanamo and elsewhere: the International Covenant on Civil and Political Rights, the UN Universal Declaration of Human Rights, the fact that Common Article 3 of the 1949 Geneva Conventions is almost universally viewed as the customary international law baseline standard of treatment to be afforded individuals captured in any form of "conflict," an argument relating to the continued application of the Fourth Geneva Convention to the detainees in issue, regardless of their designation as "unlawful combatants," and the fact that the United States has long viewed, as customary international law, those minimal protections to be accorded any individual taken captive in a conflict, set forth in Article 75 of Protocol I Additional to the 1949 Geneva Conventions.[35] In brief, it was far from certain

---

34. The Torture Statute, 18 U.S.C., Section 2340, 2340A (1994), is the U.S. statutory implementation of the Convention Against Torture and Other Cruel, Inhuman or Degrading Treatment or Punishment, Dec. 10, 1984, S. TREATY DOC. No. 100-20 (1988), 1465 UNTS 85.

35. International Covenant on Civil and Political Rights, Dec 19, 1966, 999 UNTS 171; Universal Declaration of Human Rights, G.A. Res. 217A, at 71, U.N. GAOR, 3d Sess., U.N. Doc. A/810 (Dec.12, 1948); Convention Relative to the Protection of Civilian Persons in Time of War, Aug 12, 1949, 6 UST 3516, 75 UNTS 287; Protocol Additional to the Geneva

that the United States was free to base its legal analysis regarding the legitimacy of the proposed detainee treatment and interrogation techniques forwarded by U.S. Southern Command, for DOD and DOJ review, solely on an interpretation of the meaning of the U.S. Torture Statute. Nevertheless, this was the case.

The process through which a significant number of the interrogation techniques proposed for use at Guantanamo were approved by the Secretary of Defense, the subsequent withdrawal of a portion of these techniques, and the later re-issuance of modified techniques by DOD, on the recommendation of a DOD Working Group constituted by the Secretary of Defense, has been detailed elsewhere. So, too, has the reasoning contained in an August 2002 Memorandum issued by the Office of Legal Counsel, DOJ, that essentially served as the legal basis for the use of a number of these interrogation practices.[36] The significance of this process is highlighted, however, by the fact that an investigation later revealed that it was the migration of a number of these practices from Guantanamo to Iraq, where the Law of War clearly applied in its entirety, which at least partially accounted for the occurrence of U.S. detainee abuse at Abu Ghraib prison.[37] It was only after this abuse became public in 2004 that the 2002 DOJ Opinion and the 2003 DOD Working Group Report were withdrawn.[38]

Conventions Of 1949, And Relating to the Victims of International Armed Conflicts (Protocol I), art. 75, June 10, 1977, 16 I.L.M. 1391.

36. *See* David E. Graham, "The Treatment and Interrogation of Prisoners of War and Detainees," 37 GEORGETOWN J INTL LAW 73–80 (2005). In addition to the 1 August 2002 DOJ Office of Legal Counsel Memorandum that dealt with this subject, OLC issued a second, still classified, 14 March, 2003 Memo to the DOD General Counsel, entitled, "Military Interrogation of Alien Unlawful Combatants Held outside the United States." The OLC legal analysis contained in these two Memos served as the "controlling authority" for—and was reflected in—an April 2003 DOD interrogation Working Group Report to the Secretary of Defense that spoke to the legitimacy of specifically identified interrogation techniques.

37. INDEP. PANEL TO REVIEW DEPT OF DEFENSE DETENTION OPERATIONS, FINAL REPORT 14 (Schlesinger Report) (2004).

38. The 1 August DOJ Opinion was withdrawn on 30 December 2004: Memorandum from Daniel Levin, Acting Assistant Attorney General, Office of Legal Counsel, to James B. Comey, Deputy Attorney General, "Legal Standards Applicable under 18 U.S.C. Sections 2340–2340A," *available at* http://www.usdoj.gov/olc/18usc23402340a2.htm. The DOD Working Group Report was withdrawn on 17 March 2005 in a Memorandum from William J. Haynes, DOD General Counsel, for The Judge Advocates General and the Staff Judge Advocate to the Commandant: "Department of Defense Interrogation Policy". In this Memorandum, the DOD General Counsel stated: "I agree that, in light of the Justice Department's modi-

Clearly, however, as of 2004, the pre-9/11 legal regime in place for all detainees held by U.S. Forces had been replaced by a second U.S. detainee regime
applicable to any individual now declared by DOD to be an "unlawful combatant" in the "Global War on Terrorism." And, this second regime, which included detainee treatment and interrogation practices directly at odds with those
sanctioned under the pre-9/11 regime, extended not only to those al Qaeda and
Taliban captives held at Guantanamo, but to any terrorist deemed to be an "unlawful combatant" by—and held under the control of—the U.S. government.

A Trilogy of Detainee-Related 2004 Supreme Court Decisions

In the summer of 2004, as reports of the abusive treatment of detainees by
U.S. personnel were making worldwide headlines, the Supreme Court issued
three decisions directly impacting both legal and policy decisions previously made
by the Administration regarding the manner in which it would classify, treat,
interrogate, and bring to trial "unlawful combatant" detainees.

In *Rumsfeld v. Padilla*, the Court considered the government's assertion that
it possessed the authority to seize a U.S. citizen in the United States, designate
him an "unlawful combatant," without affording him an opportunity to contest this designation, and confine him, indefinitely, in a Navy brig in Charleston,
South Carolina.[39] While the Court dismissed Padilla's *habeas* action challenging such Executive authority, it did so on purely technical grounds and declined to accept the asserted Executive power, leaving this matter for
consideration in a clearly available *habeas* plea that might later be filed in an
appropriate U.S. District Court. Two years later, as the Court was determining whether to consider a *habeas* challenge to the legality of Padilla's continued military detention, he was transferred to civilian custody, no longer declared
an "unlawful enemy combatant" by the government, and later tried and convicted of "conspiracy to commit terrorism" in a U.S. District Court in Miami.

In *Hamdi v. Rumsfeld*, the Court considered the due process protections to
be afforded a U.S. citizen, of Saudi Arabian origin, seized in the Afghanistan

---

fication of its earlier legal analysis, the legal portion of the 2003 DOD Working Group Report on Detainee Interrogations does not reflect now-settled executive branch views of the
relevant law.... I determine that the Report of the Working Group ... is to be considered a
historical document with no standing in policy, practice, or law to guide any activity of the
Department of Defense."

39. *Rumsfeld v. Padilla*, 542 U.S. 426 (2004).

theater of war, declared an "unlawful combatant," and, again, indefinitely confined in the Navy brig at Charleston.[40] During over two years of confinement, Hamdi had been denied access to an attorney, as well as the right to have the validity of his status determination reviewed. In an 8–1 decision, the Court ruled that, though, under the 2001 Authorization for Use of Military Force, Congress had impliedly "... authorized the detention of combatants in the narrow circumstances alleged ..." due process demanded that a U.S. citizen held in the United States as an "enemy combatant" be afforded access to an attorney and the right to contest the factual basis for his status determination before a "neutral decision maker."

Following the *Hamdi* decision, the U.S. government initiated the conduct of "Combatant Status Review Tribunals" (CSRTs) at Guantanamo, using procedures ostensibly based on what the Court, in *Hamdi*, had stated the Due Process Clause required in the way of procedural safeguards for an American citizen held as an "enemy combatant" detainee in the United States. However, the sufficiency of these CSRT procedures, in terms of affording a Guantanamo detainee with an adequate opportunity to challenge his designation as an "enemy combatant," would later prove to be an issue that would also find its way to the Court.[41] Additionally, the government avoided further judicial rulings on the specific judicial procedures to be afforded Hamdi, given his certain return to the courts, by reaching an agreement that, in return for the forfeiture of his U.S citizenship, he would be released and returned to Saudi Arabia.

Finally, in *Rasul v. Bush*, a case involving a British citizen captured in Afghanistan and held as an "enemy combatant" for over two years at Guantanamo, the Court, in a 6–3 decision, ruled that U.S. courts did, in fact, possess the jurisdiction to consider *habeas* challenges to the legality of the detention of foreign nationals captured abroad in connection with "hostilities" and incarcerated at Guantanamo Bay.[42] An essential aspect of the Court's ruling centered on its view that the United States exercised complete and exclusive jurisdiction and control over the Guantanamo base. The Court's decision resulted in the government's rationale for the choice of Guantanamo as the site

---

40. *Hamdi v. Rumsfeld*, 542 U.S. 507 (2004).

41. *Boumediene v. Bush*, 553 U.S.(2008). The Petitioners in this case cited numerous structural flaws in the CSRT process, to include a ban on counsel for individuals appearing before CSRTs, the lack of an independent decision-maker, and the failure to provide detainees with notice of the factual basis for the government's claim or any meaningful opportunity to present evidence of their own.

42. *Rasul v. Bush*, 542 U.S. 466 (2004).

for its indefinite detention of foreign national "enemy combatant" detainees; i.e., the belief that these individuals would be unable to file *habeas* writs in U.S. courts, as no longer being valid.

The 2005 Detainee Treatment Act: Legislatively Sanctioning a Second Legal Regime for "Unlawful Combatant" Detainees

Shortly following the issuance of the 2004 Supreme Court decisions dealing with detainee-related issues, and reacting to the recently revealed abuse of detainees held at Abu Ghraib, Congress passed the 2005 Detainee Treatment Act (DTA), legislation that dealt directly with the treatment, interrogation, and trial of U.S.-held detainees.[43]

Very significantly, the DTA mandated a finite standard of treatment and interrogation for all detainees held in the custody or under the effective control of DOD, or under detention in a DOD facility. This was accomplished through a statutory declaration that no such person could be subjected to any treatment or technique of interrogation not authorized by and listed in Army FM 34-52.[44] Given this mandate, an intense U.S. inter-agency debate surrounding the desirable content of a revised FM 34-52 followed, and a new FM, FM 2-22.3, Human Intelligence Collector Operations, was published in September, 2006.[45] With the publication of this FM, there was, in essence, a legislatively required return to the pre-9/11 legal regime for detainees held by DOD—a regime that once again reflected the applicable requirements of international law.

Often overlooked, but just as importantly, however, the DTA also clearly sanctioned a parallel U.S. standard of detainee treatment and interrogation. This occurred in the form of a somewhat obtuse legislative endorsement of the second detainee legal regime that had been established by the United States since 9/11, and one that would now apply to only those "unlawful combatant"

---

43. Detainee Treatment Act of 2005, Pub. L. No. 109-148, 119 Stat. 2739 (to be codified at 42 U.S.C. Section 2000dd).

44. *Id.* at Section 1002.

45. FM 2-22.3 sets forth 19 approved interrogation techniques. 16 of these techniques were contained in FM 34-52. The three additional interrogation practices require special approval, prior to their use. All of these techniques are valid under U.S. law and meet U.S. obligations under international law.

detainees held in the custody or under the physical control of a non-DOD U.S. agency. This was accomplished in the following way: While the DTA prohibits the "cruel, inhuman, or degrading treatment or punishment" of such detainees, this provision is deceiving. This section of the DTA then goes on to define such treatment as only that form of "cruel, unusual, and inhumane treatment" prohibited by the Fifth, Eighth, and Fourteenth Amendments to the Constitution.[46] And, as reflected in U.S. case law, this definition embodies a treatment standard that poses a very basic question: "Given the totality of the circumstances surrounding the treatment in issue, does this treatment actually 'shock the conscience' of the court considering the conduct in question?" This very broad and circumstantially dependent standard is subject to an interpretation that arguably enables non-DOD agency representatives to engage in detainee treatment and interrogation practices specifically prohibited for use by DOD personnel.

Additionally, in direct response to the recent Supreme Court decisions adversely impacting the process through which the government had designated captives to be "unlawful combatant detainees" in the "war on terrorism," subjecting them to indefinite detention and trial by Military Commission, Congress legislatively prohibited U.S. courts from entertaining writs of *habeas corpus* filed by such detainees.[47] And finally, in a related matter, Congress chose to imbue the U.S. Court of Appeals for the District of Columbia Circuit with the exclusive jurisdiction to review the validity of any decision made by a CSRT in adjudging whether an alien detainee was, in fact, an "enemy combatant" who the United States might then indefinitely detain and prosecute.[48]

The 2006 Military Commissions Act: Reaffirming a Second Legal Regime for "Unlawful Combatant" Detainees

The legal issues surrounding the Military Commissions established for the purpose of trying "unlawful enemy combatants" for certain crimes committed in the "war on terrorism" are dealt with elsewhere in this publication.[49]

---

46. *Supra* note 42, at Section 1003(d).

47. *Supra* note 42, at Section 1005(e)(1).

48. *Supra* note 42, at Section 1005(e)(2).

49. As has been noted, the U.S. may lawfully try "unlawful combatants" in a domestic judicial forum of its choice. Accordingly, the controversy surrounding the use of Military Commissions to try such individuals has not centered on the use of these Commissions,

However, it is noted that it was the Supreme Court's 2006 decision in the *Hamdan v. Rumsfeld* ruling[50] that the Military Commission process constituted by the President violated both the U. S. Armed Forces Uniform Code of Military Justice and Common Article 3 of the 1949 Geneva Conventions, that resulted in the passage of the Military Commissions Act (MCA).[51]

Most significantly, the MCA clearly reaffirmed the existence of two very distinct U.S. legal regimes for detainees. The Act's definition of "unlawful enemy combatant" is so sweeping in nature that it potentially subjects many individuals who have never committed belligerent acts against the United States on a battlefield to seizure, indefinite U.S. confinement, and trial before a Military Commission. The Act also reaffirms the ability of non-DOD U.S. personnel to engage in "enhanced" interrogation techniques—as long as these practices, given the prevailing circumstances surrounding their use, do not "shock the conscience" of a U.S. court.[52] Additionally—and surprisingly—the MCA also authorizes the use of a detainee's coerced testimony before a Military Commission, a provision that arguably reflects a Congressional intent to specifically sanction the use of coercive measures against "unlawful combatant" detainees in the custody of a non-DOD U.S. agency.[53] Finally, while reaffirming the prior DTA legislative stripping of the jurisdiction of federal courts to hear *habeas* appeals from individuals declared to be "enemy combatants," subject to in-

---

per se, but on whether these Commissions, as structured under the MCA, afford those subject to their jurisdiction with adequate due process protections under both U.S. and international law. A concomitant issue—beyond the scope of this chapter—has also been that of whether individuals seized for the commission of terrorist acts can lawfully and realistically be viewed as "unlawful combatants." Some commentators have argued that such individuals should continue to be viewed—and tried—as "terrorists," subject to trial in U.S. District Courts—pursuant, perhaps, to specifically modified Federal procedures, or, if necessary in a specially constituted Federal court that deals exclusively with cases of terrorist activities.

50. *Hamdan v. Rumsfeld*, 126 S. Ct. 2749 (2006).

51. Military Commissions Act of 2006. Pub. L. No. 109-366, 120 Stat. 2600 (to be codified at 10 U.S.C. Sections 948a–950w and other sections of titles 10, 18, 28, and 42).

52. 10 U.S.C. Section 948a(1)(a)(i). The definition of "unlawful enemy combatant" contained in this provision of the MCA removes any requirement of proximity to the battlefield—and includes persons who are deemed to be supporting hostile actions against any "co-belligerent" State in the "Global War on Terrorism", not just the U.S. Section 6(c) of the MCA again defines "cruel, inhuman, or degrading treatment or punishment" as only that "cruel, unusual, and inhumane treatment or punishment prohibited by the Fifth, Eighth, and Fourteenth Amendments to the Constitution"—a restatement of the "shocks the conscience of the court" standard.

53. *Supra* note 50, at sec. 3, 10 U.S.C., Section 948r.

definite detention and trial by Military Commission,[54] the MCA also amends the 1997 War Crimes Act (WCA).[55]

This amendment of the WCA is of particular significance. Previously, this Act had provided federal courts with the jurisdiction to prosecute any U.S. national, to include a member of the U.S. Armed Forces, for the commission of a "war crime." "War crimes," in turn, were defined as including, among other violations of the Law of War, violations of Common Article 3 of the Geneva Conventions. And, among those acts prohibited to be taken against persons covered by this article are those noted in 3(1)(c) "outrages upon personal dignity, in particular, humiliating and degrading treatment...."[56] While it was evident that the detainee treatment and interrogation practices mandated for DOD detainees in AR 190-8 and FM 2-22.3 clearly did not violate this Article 3 provision, far less clear was whether this held true for those treatment and interrogation procedures now sanctioned under the second statutorily authorized U.S. legal regime for non-DOD "unlawful enemy combatant" detainees.

Faced with this uncertainty, Congress chose to amend the WCA by legislatively creating the concept of "grave breaches" of Common Article 3. In doing so, it specifically identified certain crimes it deemed to be such "grave breaches"—and mandated that only the commission of these offenses would now constitute "war crimes" for the purpose of WCA prosecution.[57] In using this approach, Congress was thus able to "legislatively airbrush" Common Article 3(1)(c) offenses from existence in terms of the WCA—and effectively pre-

---

54. *Supra* note 50, at sec. 7.

55. Pub. L. No. 104-192, Section 2(a), 110 Stat. 2104 (1996) (codified at 18 U.S.C. Section 2441), as amended in 1997.

56. *Supra* note 13, at art. 3(1)(c).

57. *Supra* note 50, at sec. 6(b). The concept of "grave breaches" is common to all four of the 1949 Geneva Conventions. All Parties to these Conventions are obligated to enact any legislation necessary to provide penal sanctions for persons committing, or ordering to be committed, any of the grave breaches defined in the respective Conventions. Article 130 of the GPW lists, as grave breaches, the following acts "if committed against persons ... protected by the Convention": willful killing, torture or inhuman treatment, and willfully causing great suffering or serious injury to body or health. It is the U.S. position that "unlawful combatant" detainees are not protected by the GPW. However, as a result of the Supreme Court's ruling in *Hamdan v. Rumsfeld* that Common Article 3 of the Conventions applied to the "conflict" with al Qaeda, Congress originated the concept of Common Article 3 "grave breaches" in order to legislatively define—and limit—those specific Article 3 violations subject to prosecution under the War Crimes Act. This Congressional interpretation of Common Article 3 is controlling only in terms of U.S. law; it has no effect internationally.

serve the ability of non-DOD U.S. personnel to continue to function within the second U.S. detainee legal regime.

Still another significant aspect of the MCA was its authorization of the President to interpret, on behalf of the United States, both the meaning and application of the 1949 Geneva Conventions—and to issue, in the form of an Executive Order, "higher standards and administrative regulations" for violations that do not constitute "grave breaches" of these Conventions.[58] While not apparent on its face, this provision, in essence, reflected a Congressional decision to require the President to issue guidance concerning non-DOD detainee treatment and interrogation practices he deemed to be compliant with the provisions of Common Article 3—to include Article 3(1)(c).

Executive Order 13440: "Interpretation of the Geneva Conventions Common Article 3 as Applied to a Program of Detention and Interrogation Operated by the Central Intelligence Agency" (July, 2007)

On July 20, 2007, the President issued Executive Order (EO) 13440: "Interpretation of the Geneva Conventions Common Article 3 As Applied To A Program Of Detention And Interrogation Operated By The Central Intelligence Agency."[59] In its preface, the President reiterated the now familiar basis for the approach taken by his Administration in connection with the classification, treatment, interrogation, and trial of "unlawful enemy combatant" detainees.

> The United States is engaged in an armed conflict with al Qaeda, the Taliban, and associated forces.... On February 7, 2002, I determined for the United States that members of al Qaeda, the Taliban, and associated forces are unlawful enemy combatants who are not entitled to the protections that the Third Geneva Convention provides to prisoners of war. I hereby reaffirm that determination.

This is followed by a restatement of the U.S. government's definition of "cruel, inhuman, and degrading treatment or punishment" [the type of treat-

58. *Supra* note 50, at sec. 6(a)(3).
59. E.O. 13440, Interpretation of the Geneva Conventions Common Article 3 as Applied to a Program of Detention and Interrogation Operated by the Central Intelligence Agency, July 20, 2007, Fed. Reg. Vol. 72, No. 141, 40705–09 (July 24, 2007).

ment prohibited by Common Article 3(1)(c)], once again defining such treatment as the cruel, unusual, and inhumane treatment prohibited by the Fifth, Eighth, and Fourteenth Constitutional Amendments (treatment that "shocks the conscience" of the Court).

The EO text that follows then explicitly confirms the continued existence and use of a second U.S. detainee legal regime—one that, while clearly at odds with the DOD program—unmistakably represents an essential component of the Administration's "war on terrorism."

In Section 3, the President states that the Order interprets the meaning and application of the text of Common Article 3 with respect to "certain" detentions and interrogations, and is to be treated as authoritative as a matter of U.S. law, to include the "… satisfaction of the international obligations of the United States." In view of his authority to render a definitive interpretation of Article 3, as well as the resultant U.S. international obligations under this article, the President then notes that a Program of detention and interrogation approved by the Director of the Central Intelligence Agency will "fully" comply with U.S Article 3 obligations when such a Program meets certain criteria. Among the more relevant of these are the following:

The Program's confinement and interrogation practices cannot include: torture, as defined by the United States;[60] any acts prohibited by Section 2441(d), Title 18 of the United States Code (the MCA amendment of the War Crimes Act listing the "grave breaches of Common Article 3"); any other acts of cruel, inhuman, or degrading treatment or punishment prohibited by the Military Commissions Act and the Detainee Treatment Act (the "shocks the conscience of the court" standard); and "willful and outrageous acts of personal abuse done for the purpose of humiliating or degrading [an] individual in a manner so serious that any reasonable person, considering the circumstances, would deem the acts to be beyond the bounds of human decency, such as sexual or sexually indecent acts undertaken for the purpose of humiliation.…"

This latter provision of prohibited practices has drawn substantial concern, with critics contending that it is so substantially caveated that it intentionally affords the CIA with the flexibility to engage in any number of abusive interrogation techniques, measures prohibited for use by DOD, and almost universally viewed as, if not torture, acts of cruel, inhumane, and degrading treatment.[61]

---

60. For the U.S. definition of "torture" *see supra* note 50, at sec. 3, 10 U.S.C., Section 950v.

61. *See* P.X. Kelley & Robert F. Turner, "War Crimes and the White House: The Dishonor in a Tortured New 'Interpretation' of the Geneva Conventions," WASH. POST, Jul. 26, 2007, at A21.

As to the individuals to whom this CIA Program of detention and interrogation would apply, the President has mandated its use in connection with any alien detainee determined by the Director of the CIA: "to be a member or part of or supporting al Qaeda, the Taliban, or associated organizations, and [who are] likely to be in possession of information that could assist in detecting, mitigating, or preventing terrorist attacks within the United States ... or against its allies or other countries cooperating in the war on terror, or [that] could assist in locating the senior leadership of al Qaeda, the Taliban, or associated forces."[62] Such a determination results, of course, in an alien detainee automatically assuming the status of an "unlawful enemy combatant"—with all of the resulting ramifications of this designation—indefinite detention, "enhanced" interrogation, and potential trial by Military Commission.

In Summary

The United States currently employs not one, but two detainee legal regimes. In an encapsulated manner, EO 13440 clearly confirms and details the existence and framework of a U.S. legal regime applied exclusively to a very broadly defined category of "unlawful enemy combatant" detainees. This regime now functions in parallel to that embodied by the Department of Defense. The U.S. decision to formulate two distinct detainee regimes gives rise to these essential questions. Is this dual detainee system a sustainable U.S. approach toward this issue? And, even more importantly, is such an approach lawful? In arriving at answers, it is useful to briefly review the government's decision making process leading to the establishment of these parallel regimes—and to consider a series of questions evolving from this process.

1. The terrorist attacks of 9/11 were viewed as but the latest in a series of al Qaeda strikes on U.S. property and personnel that cumulatively amounted to an ongoing "armed attack" on the United States.

Questions:
- Can a terrorist act—regardless of the scope of its destructive nature— be viewed and responded to by the State in which the act occurred as an "armed attack"?
- Does an act of terrorism assume the nature of an "armed attack" only if the non-State terrorist organization involved is supported by an identifiable State entity?

---

62. *Supra* note 58, at sec. 3 (b) (ii).

- Absent the involvement/support of an identifiable State entity in an act of terrorism against another State, (i.e., the Taliban government's provision of sanctuary/support for al Qaeda) how might a victim State respond to what it considers an "armed attack" by a terrorist organization?
- That is—what/whom would a victim State target in its use of force response to a terrorist "armed attack"?
- Does the previous question offer an explanation as to why the current U.S. Administration felt it necessary to declare "war" on the phenomenon of "terrorism," writ large?

2. As a result of the al Qaeda attack on the United States, and drawing upon the September 18, 2001 Congressional Authorization for [the] Use of United States Armed Forces (AUMF) to respond to this attack, the President has determined that the United States is at "war" with not only al Qaeda, but with "terrorism," worldwide. In waging this "Global War on Terrorism," the President, in exercising what he perceives as the resulting Constitutional "war making" powers of a Commander-in-Chief, has chosen to frame legal issues associated with this "armed conflict" in the context of the Law of War, vice both the domestic and international law applicable to "terrorism" and "terrorists."

Questions:
- Did the President act in a legitimate exercise of his Constitutional authority in declaring "war" on terrorism—and then acting pursuant to his perceived "war making" powers—even though the congressional AUMF contained no language ostensibly supporting such a declaration?
- Did congressional acquiescence in President Bush's consistent use of his "war making" powers nevertheless serve to legitimate his declaration of "war"?
- Having chosen to frame the U.S. response to 9/11 as an ongoing "war" or "armed conflict" with "terrorism," the Bush Administration attempted to apply the Law of War to legal issues arising in the context of this "war"—to include the matter of framing a legal regime for the individuals seized, detained, interrogated, and brought to trial during this "conflict."
- Does the Law of War readily lend itself to resolving legal issues evolving from a "conflict" of this nature?
- Would the United States have been better served by applying—and seeking to enhance/revise—both the U.S. and international law applicable to terrorism and terrorist acts following 9/11?

3. In issuing his Presidential Order of 13 November, 2001, concerning the
Detention, Treatment, and Trial of Certain Non-Citizens in the War Against
Terrorism, the President defined an "individual subject to this Order" in a manner so exceptionally broad that it has been interpreted to include any terrorist, worldwide, considered a threat to any number of U.S. interests, as well as
any individual who may have "harbored" such a person.

In the purported exercise of both his Constitutional "war making" powers and
treaty interpretation authority, the President, in interpreting the relevant provisions of the Third Geneva Convention, made the determination that neither
al Qaeda, nor Taliban personnel captured during the conflict with Afghanistan,
were entitled to POW status. Moreover, as these individuals had engaged in
hostile acts against the United States during the course of hostilities in Afghanistan,
they were accordingly deemed, "unlawful combatants." By analogy, this reasoning has also been applied to all "international terrorists," as well as those
who may have harbored such terrorists, who, subject to the above noted 13 November Presidential Order, are considered threats to U.S. interests and "captured" on the worldwide "battlefield" of the "Global War on Terrorism."

4. The ability of Military Commissions to try individuals seized during the
course of this "war on terrorism" is fully dependent upon such personnel being
designated as "unlawful combatants." This flows from the fact that specific provisions of the Third Geneva Convention (Articles 84 and 102) require that
POW be tried, for alleged offenses, by the same type of military court, using
the same procedures, as would the military personnel of the detaining State,
that is, by Court-Martial under the Uniform Code of Military Justice.

Questions:
- Is there any support in the Law of War for the broad based definition of
  an "individual subject to trial by Military Commission" adopted by the
  U.S. government for the purpose of bringing individuals seized, worldwide, during the "war on terrorism" to trial before Military Commissions?
- Was the President's designation of both al Qaeda and Taliban captives as
  "unlawful combatants" a lawful exercise of his constitutional authority?
- Is such a Presidential interpretation of the Third Geneva Convention
  binding on other State actors in the international community?

5. A large number of personnel captured in Afghanistan and elsewhere outside the United States, and designated as "unlawful combatants, were transported to the U.S. Navy Base at Guantanamo Bay, Cuba for detainment and
interrogation purposes. As these "unlawful combatant" detainees were said to
not be entitled to the protections of the 1949 Geneva Conventions—and it

was these Conventions that drove the pre-9/11 DOD regulatory and doctrinal guidance applicable to DOD detainees, it was determined that this guidance no longer applied. Dismissive of any additional international law provisions that might arguably have pertained to these Guantanamo detainees, the U.S. government chose to structure a legal regime that differed significantly from that applicable to such personnel, pre-9/11.

Question:
- Was the U.S. government correct in taking the position that, in the absence of the applicability of the Geneva Conventions to the "unlawful combatant" detainees at Guantanamo, no other international law-driven safeguards and protections were available to these individuals?

6. Essential elements of the legal regime established for "unlawful combatant" detainees held at Guantanamo and elsewhere by the United States were driven by both a 7 February 2002 Presidential determination concerning the standard of treatment to be afforded such detainees and DOJ August 2002 and March 2003 opinions dealing with the legality of certain coercive treatment and interrogation techniques proposed for use against these individuals.

Questions:
- Was the standard of detainee treatment set forth in the Presidential Memo of 7 February, 2002, a legitimate exercise of the President's Constitutional authority?
- Was this an exercise of his "war making" authority—his treaty interpretation authority—or both?
- Was the application of this standard of treatment by U.S. personnel lawful—even though it arguably departed from international norms?
- Are U.S. personnel who applied this standard in the treatment and interrogation of "unlawful enemy combatant" detainees held at Guantanamo, or elsewhere, subject to prosecution in either U.S. or non-U.S. judicial forums?

7. Following the public revelation of the abuse of detainees at Abu Ghraib prison in Iraq, attributed, in part, to the prior authorization of a number of coercive treatment and interrogation practices for use at Guantanamo, and the Supreme Court's 2004 issuance of a trilogy of decisions bringing into question the legitimacy of the due process afforded "unlawful combatant" detainees confined in both the United States and at Guantanamo, Congress passed the 2005 Detainee Treatment Act (DTA). This legislation mandated that all detainees held in the custody of DOD be treated and interrogated in strict compliance

with the Army Field Manual dealing with this subject, a Manual which complies with all relevant U.S. international law obligations. Conversely, however, Congress also chose to both legislatively sanction a standard of treatment and interrogation for "unlawful combatant" detainees held by non-DOD U.S. agencies that departed significantly from that of DOD's and bar U.S. federal courts from hearing writs of *habeas corpus* filed by Guantanamo detainees that challenged the basis for their indefinite detention and trial by Military Commission; i.e., that they were, in fact, "unlawful enemy combatants." As a result, the DTA served to legislatively endorse and formally establish dual legal regimes for U.S.-held detainees.

Questions:
- Was the legislative establishment of parallel legal regimes for U.S.-held detainees intentional on the part of Congress?
- Did Congress knowingly sanction the use of "enhanced" interrogation techniques for "unlawful combatant" detainees when, in the DTA, it chose to define "cruel, inhuman, and degrading" treatment as it did?
- Was the Congressional stripping of the jurisdiction of U.S. federal courts to hear *habeas* appeals from Guantanamo detainees, in essence, a Congressional ratification of the President's authority to establish Military Commissions for the trial of these detainees?

8. Following the Supreme Court's decision in *Hamdan v. Rumsfeld*, ruling that the President's establishment of the Military Commission process violated both the U.S. Armed Forces Uniform Code of Military Justice and Common Article 3 of the Geneva Conventions, Congress passed the 2006 Military Commissions Act (MCA). The MCA legislatively reaffirmed a dual legal regime for U.S.-held detainees. Akin to the Presidential Order originally establishing Military Commissions, the MCA's sweeping definition of "unlawful enemy combatant" serves to subject individuals who have never committed a belligerent act against the United States to indefinite confinement, "enhanced" interrogation, and trial by Military Commission. The Act also reaffirms the previous DTA legislative stripping of the jurisdiction of federal courts to entertain *habeas* appeals from detainees designated as "unlawful enemy combatants." And, very importantly, the MCA not only endorses the "shocks the conscience of the court" standard for adjudging the legality of the treatment of "unlawful combatant" detainees, in sanctioning the use of coerced testimony in trials by Military Commission, Congress appears to have specifically authorized the use of coercive measures against such detainees.

The MCA's amendment of the War Crimes Act (WCA) introduced the concept of "Common Article 3 grave breaches," legislatively defined these "grave breaches," and mandated that only these Article 3 offenses were to be punishable under the WCA. The intended purpose of this amendment was to eliminate the possibility of WCA prosecution of non-DOD U.S. agents who engage in the use of "enhanced" interrogation techniques in violation of Article 3(1)(c)—the "humiliating and degrading treatment" of "unlawful combatant" detainees.

Questions:
- The MCA definition of "unlawful enemy combatant" is even more comprehensive than that of an "individual subject to trial by Military Commission." Is this MCA definition of such a "combatant" valid under the existing Law of War?
- Does this definition serve as a basis for the use of U.S. military force to seize such individuals, wherever they might be found—with or without the consent of the State in which they are located?
- Did Congress knowingly intend to authorize, in the MCA, the use of coercive interrogation techniques against non-DOD "unlawful combatant" detainees?
- The DTA and MCA legislative prohibition against federal courts hearing *habeas* writs filed by Guantanamo detainees has been challenged before the Supreme Court in *Boumediene v. Bush*. At issue is the adequacy of the due process afforded these detainees, under the existing CSRT procedures, to challenge their designation as "enemy combatants." What impact would a Court decision granting some form of relief to the detainee litigants have on the government's legal regime established specifically for "unlawful enemy combatant" detainees?
- Is the Congressional legislative concept of "grave breaches of Common Article 3," which interprets and limits the scope of this article, a legitimate exercise of its constitutional authority?
- Is this Congressional action lawful, in terms of international law?

9. The MCA required that the President issue an Executive Order (EO) providing guidance to the CIA concerning detainee treatment and interrogation practices not authorized for use by DOD, but which he deemed compliant with the provisions of Common Article 3, to include 3(1)(c). EO 13440, issued in July, 2007, essentially encapsulates the legal basis for and reaffirms the existence of the second, non-DOD, U.S. detainee legal regime for "unlawful enemy combatant" detainees.

Questions:
- Does the President possess the sole constitutional authority to interpret the 1949 Geneva Conventions?

- Are Presidential interpretations of the Geneva Conventions binding on the international community?
- Does EO 13440 meet the assumed congressional intent that the President issue clear guidance to the CIA concerning Article 3—compliant detainee treatment and interrogation methods?
- Can Congress demand greater clarity from the Executive branch on this matter?
- If Congress chooses not to seek such clarity, would its failure to do so constitute a continued congressional sanctioning of the CIA detainee legal regime now in place?
- Is the EO sufficiently clear to enable an attorney to provide legal advice to CIA personnel concerning interrogation techniques that are—and are not—available for their use?

These are but some of the issues and questions that surround the government's formulation and use of dual detainee legal regimes in waging its "war on terrorism." It is an approach founded on questionable policy decisions—and even more questionable legal determinations. An objective assessment of its viability and legality must result in the conclusion that it is largely counterproductive and in patent violation of U.S. obligations under international law. It will not stand. It is certain to be subjected to future legislative and judicial challenges, as these branches of the government seek to strike a lawful and prudent balance between the nation's security and its commitment to both the domestic and international rule of law.

Chapter 2

Military Commissions as the Forum to Prosecute Acts of Terrorism and Other Violations of the Law of War

Major General John Altenburg[1]

United States v. Hamdan focused public attention on a relatively esoteric area of law—the use of Military Commissions to prosecute acts of war or terrorist acts against the United States. The U.S. government has failed effectively to educate the public, the Congress, and the courts about when and why Military Commissions are the most appropriate forum for prosecuting such offenses—more so than Courts—martial or domestic criminal courts. That failure was exacerbated by flawed policy decisions in the rule-making process for both the pre-*Hamdan* and post-*Hamdan* military commissions. The purpose of this chapter is to discuss the unique role of Military Commissions in wartime criminal proceedings and propose a more durable and appropriate statutory solution.

---

1. Major General John Altenburg (U.S. Army, Retired) is a principal at the international law firm of Greenberg Traurig. General Altenburg served 28 years as a lawyer in the Army, where he represented the Army before Congress, numerous state and local governments, and in court in the United States and Germany. He advised, counseled, and negotiated at all levels within the Army, the Department of Defense, and the Department of Justice, frequently on matters of great interest to Members of Congress and the national media. He served as the Deputy Judge Advocate General for the Department of the Army from 1997 to 2001. He advised senior military and civilian leaders on critical legal and policy issues and directed the day to day operations of approximately 1800 civilian and uniformed attorneys in 70 offices and 3000 National Guard and Army Reserve attorneys in providing comprehensive legal services to commanders, soldiers, and civilians of the Army worldwide. He returned to Greenberg Traurig in November, 2006, from a public service leave of absence as the Appointing Authority for Military Commissions, Office of the Secretary of Defense.

Terrorist acts against the United States before September 11, 2001 were routinely tried in United States District Courts as U.S. Criminal Code violations,
although that was never the only option available. The forum for such offenses
is chosen by the sovereign who pursues prosecution. Thus, the United States
prosecuted the 1993 al Qaeda attack on the World Trade Center and the 1998
East African embassy bombings in the U.S. District Courts as Title 18 Conspiracy violations. Al Qaeda's 1996 "Declaration of War against the Americans
Occupying the Land of the Two Holy Places," and al Qaeda's subsequent actions
to effect that declaration lend considerable support to the United States view
of the September 11, 2001 attacks by al Qaeda as acts of war—*unlawful* acts
of war. The U.S. Government altered its approach in various ways consistent
with the view that the United States was "at war." Responses included the September 18 Joint Congressional Resolution authorizing the President to use military force[2] and subsequent statutory enactments like the Patriot Act; the
demand to the Taliban government in Afghanistan to turn over the war criminals; combat operations in Afghanistan to overthrow the Taliban and pursue
the war criminals; and the November 13, 2001 Presidential Military Order
(PMO) authorizing the use of military commissions to prosecute war crimes.
Absent any effort to educate the public on the basis for using a war court not
used since the 1940s, publication of the PMO produced immediate criticism
that incongruously faulted military commission procedures for failing to comport with domestic criminal justice procedures.

While the Government's military response to al Qaeda's acts of war made
military prosecutions a legitimate policy option, public acceptance of commissions has been less than enthusiastic. Some argue the commissions' lack of
public support influenced the Supreme Court's decisions in *Hamdi, Rasul, and
Hamdan*.[3] The last of those decisions, *Hamdan*, suggests that even the Court
may not have fully understood the established and central role that military
commissions have played throughout our history in the prosecution of war
crimes.

Perhaps no specific policy, practice, or event created this misunderstanding
among laymen, lawyers, and academics, but the combination of secrecy and
exertion of unitary executive power did much to put proponents of military commissions on the defensive. In hindsight, the secrecy surrounding the formulation and piecemeal implementation of military commissions also served to
discourage effective education of both the public and the press regarding the

---

2. Authorization for Use of Military Force, P.L. 107-40.
3. *Hamdi v. Rumsfeld*, 542 U.S. 507 (2004); *Rasul v. Bush*, 124 S.Ct. 2686 (2004); *Hamdan v. Rumsfeld*, 584 U.S. 557 (2006).

history and diversity of the various military tribunals. This chapter will shed much needed light on military commissions in general and those at Guantanamo Bay in particular.

Forums for Administering Military Law

The terms "military law" and "military justice"—much like the terms "commercial law" or "criminal law"—are not specific. They are nebulous subject matter references to vast areas of law that vary greatly according to forum and jurisdiction. While more distinct, the term "military tribunal" remains a gross label for the various proceedings convened by military commanders pursuant to statute, regulation, and custom or practice. Historically, and as a matter of law and regulation, these proceedings have included courts-martial, courts of inquiry, provost courts, and military commissions. Together they comprise the jurisprudential choices available to military commanders from which individual or multiple forums are selected and convened depending on the location, purpose, offense, offender, and circumstances confronted. Each of these tribunals involves senior commanders, called appointing authorities or convening authorities, and Judge Advocates, licensed military attorneys who serve as judges, prosecutors, defense lawyers, and staff attorneys.

This chapter will not conduct a detailed analysis of each type of military tribunal, but it is essential to understand at least the historical and legal context of each to discuss intelligently whether and how military commissions should be employed

Courts-Martial

Courts-martial are statutory creations;[4] their form, jurisdiction, and rules of practice are subject to control by Congress. Court-martial jurisdiction is limited primarily to crimes committed by members of the U.S. armed forces. Courts-martial may also exercise jurisdiction over certain crimes committed by prisoners of war and over persons alleged to have committed war crimes, although this grant of jurisdiction is not restricted to courts-martial alone.[5] Courts-martial have universal venue; they may be convened at any time or

---

4. Beginning with the Articles of War and proceeding through the Uniform Code of Military Justice (UCMJ).

5. Articles 2 and 18, UCMJ.

place, ensuring that the commander convening the court is never deprived of this forum, whether in the United States, overseas, in garrison, in the field, or while conducting humanitarian, peacekeeping, or combat operations.

Congress granted considerable authority to the President in the UCMJ (notably Articles 36 and 134), to (1) prescribe rules of practice and evidence;[6] (2) punish offenses not specifically designated by Congress within limited parameters; (3) dictate required elements of proof for all offenses; and (4) prescribe maximum punishments for all offenses not capital. The Military Rules of Evidence used in courts-martial substantially track the Federal Rules of Evidence used in United States District Courts, and though the pre-trial and post-trial processing requirements are unique to military practice, the procedural rules applicable to conducting trials also substantially track federal criminal practice.

Congress and the President are not the only authorities governing Courts-martial. Courts-martial are also subject to decisions of a congressionally designed appellate system, as well as applicable decisions of the Supreme Court. It is important to recognize that Congress has focused most of its attention in the UCMJ on courts-martial (beginning with the Military Justice Act of 1950) compared to other military tribunals because the court-martial is both the most common military tribunal and the sole tribunal devoted to prosecution of members of our armed forces, all of whom are either U.S. citizens or resident aliens.

Courts of Inquiry

The Court of inquiry is also a statutory creation (UCMJ Article 135 since 1950; Articles of War 115–121 and Articles for the Government of the Navy 21 and 42 before 1950). Courts of Inquiry have been in continuous use since the eighteenth century.[7] Analysts agree that they are not truly courts because they lack the power to determine guilt or to impose sentence.[8] Rather, they are fact-finding bodies, whose proceedings are reviewed and acted upon by the commander who convenes them. That commander (or a service regulation)[9] may

---

6. The Military Rules of Evidence now in force were actually enacted by Congress

7. Article 25, Articles of War (May 31, 1786).

8. W. Winthrop, Military Law and Precedents (2d. Ed., 1920), at 517 (hereinafter "Winthrop"); G. B. Davis, A Treatise on the Military Law of the United States (2d. Ed. 1912), at 220 (hereinafter "Davis").

9. *See, e.g.*, paragraph 10-9d, Army Regulation 27-10, Military Justice, 16 November 2005.

empower a court of inquiry to make recommendations, but courts of inquiry have no independent authority to do so. Courts of inquiry, like courts-martial, can be employed anywhere, at any time, no matter the nature of military operations. They are used to investigate and report on matters criminal and non-criminal. They may compel production of witnesses, and may be open or closed to the public. The best known recent use of a Court of Inquiry investigated the collision between the nuclear submarine USS Greenville and the Japanese fishing vessel Ehime Maru off the coast of Hawaii in February, 2001.

Provost Courts

Provost courts are also statutorily recognized by Congress.[10] (They are essentially regulatory and continue to be available to field commanders for the disposition of offenses committed by civilian internees in occupied territory.[11] This limitation to specific classes of defendants, locations, and conditions distinguishes Provost Courts from the more commonly used courts-martial and courts of inquiry and further explains why little Congressional attention has been paid to Provost Court procedures.

Military Commissions

The fourth UCMJ-recognized tribunal, the military commission, is a wartime and post-war venue available to commanders to prosecute violations of the law of war. "Such power cannot be exercised by courts-martial, which are created by and draw their jurisdiction from enactments of Congress, and martial law or martial rule, as has been seen, is not statutory in character and derives its sanction from the laws of war."[12]

Military commissions predate the U.S. Constitution. Like the other forms of military tribunals they are the progeny of British military law. Because they were created neither by the Constitution nor by Congress, commissions have historically been referred to as the military's "common law war courts,"[13] an

---

10. *See, e.g.*, Articles 21 and 48, UCMJ.

11. Department of the Army Pamphlet 27-9-2, Military Judge's Benchbook for Provost Courts (2004).

12. Davis, at 307.

13. Testimony of General Crowder on S. 3191, to the Senate sub-committee on military affairs, Sen. Rpt. No. 130, p. 40, 64th Cong., 1st Sess., 1916

appellation that does not so much limit commissions' source of authority (military commissions created or authorized by statute would still be military commissions) as it emphasizes the traditional lack of dictated structure critical to both the purpose and utility of military commissions. In short, as a commander's wartime forum a military commission—historically, and today—must, without sacrificing public confidence in the fairness of the process and resulting sentence, satisfy three principle concerns: national security, physical security, and evidentiary and procedural flexibility. Military commissions were repeatedly and routinely convened in the Mexican-American War and Civil War, and judicial review repeatedly recognized the validity of the forum (if not the jurisdiction of each application).[14]

Critics of the President's (and later the MCA's) implementation of military commissions as the forum for terrorist trials has focused precisely on the feature that makes military commissions useful: the rules and procedures of the forum differ from U.S. domestic criminal trial practice procedures. Although different, these procedures are lawful and consistent with international legal standards, even when ill-advised for policy reasons. While it is true that military commissions have, historically and as a matter of custom, substantially employed the procedural and evidentiary rules applicable at the time to courts-martial, that custom has been replaced by the statutory mandate[15] of the MCA to employ other procedures and rules of evidence.

Contrary to *Hamdan's* erroneous application of UCMJ Articles 21 and 36, the UCMJ itself provides ample authority to modify the procedures of military commissions to promote their utility in a tactical and legal environment not contemplated by custom.

Brief History of Military Commissions

Structuring the rules for a particular commission or set of commissions was the responsibility of commanders (including the Commander in Chief) until the enactment of the 2006 Military Commissions Act. For this reason Congress did not previously "authorize" military commissions, but rather "recognized" their validity by specific reference in sections of the Articles of War, and the subsequent Uniform Code of Military Justice.[16] Each of these statutory

---

14. *See, generally,* Milliken, Vallandingham, *Lincoln Conspirators* (2001).
15. The Military Commissions Act of 2006, §§71.
16. "Since our nation's earliest days, such commissions have been constitutionally recognized agencies for meeting many urgent governmental responsibilities related to war.

regimes protects the jurisdiction and authority of military commissions, but does not authorize, define, construct, or restrict military commissions. Notwithstanding its flaws, the majority opinion in *Hamdan* noted the loose and often quoted language of *Quirin* regarding whether Congress "authorized" military commissions. This distinction between authorization and recognition is important. Prior to passage of the Uniform Code of Military Justice (UCMJ) in 1950, the role of both Congress and civil courts in oversight of the military justice system was far more distant than today. As Winthrop observed in 1920:

> Further, the court-martial being no part of the Judiciary of the nation, and no statute having placed it in legal relations therewith, its proceedings are not subject to being directly reviewed by any federal court, either by *certiorari*, writ of error, or otherwise, nor are its judgments or sentences subject to be appealed from to such tribunal.[17]

Articles of War

Dating to Richard II (1385) and the British Articles of War, the U.S. Articles of War (AW) were first enacted by the Continental Congress in 1775 and contained no reference to military commissions or to courts of inquiry. The 1786 AW contained provisions for courts of inquiry (Articles 25–27), but no reference to military commissions. Subsequent versions of the AW followed suit, including the Act of June 22, 1874, in which Section 1342 promulgated the AW, while Section 1343 provided for trial and punishment of certain offenses committed in time of war by either general court-martial or military commission. This language was derived from Acts of similar purpose passed in 1863 and 1867.

The earliest form of what became UCMJ Article 21 appeared in 1920 as AW Article 15. 1920 AW Article 15 explicitly confirmed the jurisdiction of "military commissions, provost courts, or other military tribunals," notwithstanding the AW's establishment of the jurisdiction of courts-martial, particularly general courts-martial, which by 1920 AW Article 12 were empowered "to try any person who by the law of war is subject to trial by military tribunal." The

---

They have been called our common-law war courts. They have taken many forms and borne many names. Neither their procedure nor their jurisdiction has been prescribed by statute. It has been adapted in each instance to the need that called it forth." *Madsen v. Kinsella*, 343 U.S. 341 (referring specifically to military commissions in occupied post-war territory). During the Civil War, Congress did direct that certain offenses and offenders be tried by military commission, but did not specify procedures or evidentiary rules.

17. Winthrop, at 50. *See also* Davis, at 15.

Army's Judge Advocate General explained proposed Article 15 to the Senate in 1916: "It just saves to these war courts the jurisdiction they now have and makes it a concurrent jurisdiction with courts-martial, so that the military commander in the field in time of war will be at liberty to employ either form of court that happens to be convenient. Both classes of courts have the same procedure."[18] Fully supported by the commentary of both Winthrop and Davis, this testimony clarifies (1) the common law origin and nature of military commissions; (2) the jurisdiction of military commissions over war crimes; (3) the concurrence of that jurisdiction with general courts-martial; and (4) the historical commonality—absent any statutory provision to the contrary—of commissions and courts-martial as to procedure and evidence.

The 1917 Espionage Act reiterated Congressional recognition of the existence and jurisdiction of military commissions by providing that no provision of that Act "shall be deemed to limit the jurisdiction of the general courts-martial, military commissions, or naval courts-martial."

The 1930 version of AW Article 15, in force at the time of President Roosevelt's 1942 Military Order directing trial by military commission of the suspected German saboteurs, was identical to 1920 AW Article 15. The Supreme Court's 1942 decision *Ex parte Quirin*[19] confirmed the jurisdiction of Military Commissions as war crimes courts. The Supreme Court in 1942 inferred that the President's action in convening a Military Commission had sufficient Congressional authority by virtue of Congressional approval of AW Article, or that during wartime the President's inherent authority was sufficient even without the Congressional authorization of AW Article.

Acts of 1863[20] and 1867

Both Acts recognized *and* authorized military commissions. The Act of 1863, §30, authorized trial by military commission for certain felonies. 3 of the Reconstruction Act of 1867 specifically authorized commanders of the military districts of confederate states to "organize military commissions or tribunals for that purpose [suppress insurrection, disorder, and violence]."[21] Winthrop summarized the judicial review of notable cases arising from this statute: the

---

18. *See* note 14.

19. 317 U.S. 1 (1942).

20. An amendment to the AW which later became Article 58, AW (1874), but omitted the words "military commission." *See* Winthrop at 833, n. 71.

21. *Id.*

Supreme Court "refused to enjoin the President and Secretary of War respectively from carrying such laws into effect, on the ground that the power and duty conferred and imposed thereby were purely executive and political in their nature."[22]

Pre-WWII Military Commissions

Military tribunals—not courts-martial as we have come to know them—have been employed in various forms throughout the history of our Nation. George Washington used them in the Revolutionary War, as did Andrew Jackson during the War of 1812. During the Mexican American War, General Winfield Scott convened several different tribunals. From at least the time of General Scott, tribunals bearing the name "military commissions" were regularly used to try defendants like Vallandingham, Harris, the Lincoln conspirators, and Captain Henry Wirz.[23] Later, they were again used in the Philippines, following the Spanish American War. Military commissions were not always popular. They were criticized not so much for their frequently summary nature, but because the abdication of existing courts of record raised questions of political motivation, unjust retribution, and fear of military criminal jurisdiction over part or all of a civilian populace. Despite such criticism, they remained an important attribute of the Executive's war powers.

Military Commission Summary

Military commissions have historically been a singular forum, repeatedly recognized by United States statutes, international law, and Supreme Court decisions as an incident of war, arising not from the judicial power of the United States, but firmly within the power and authority of a military commander. This is no mere academic distinction; it is the seminal point from which flowed post-2001 misunderstandings of military commissions. Historical validity aside, the necessity and importance of military commissions in the current conflict has been occluded by (1) the six decades during which military commanders chose not to use them and (2) the unprecedented evolution in criminal procedure and evidence during those same decades. These facts altered the setting in a way that policy makers failed to recognize when drafting the President's Military Order of November 13, 2001.

---

22. Winthrop, at 851.
23. *Id.*

Significant Developments in Evidence and Criminal Procedure, 1943–2001

When the Administration originally set up post-9/11 military commissions, they copied almost verbatim Roosevelt's 1942 military order regarding the Nazi saboteurs. It is inconsequential whether Administration advisors wished to emulate Roosevelt's broad exercise of wartime presidential power while ignoring the reality of legal evolution or that they simply sought to reanimate a long-dormant system that had once served the Nation well. The fact is that neither Congress nor the courts were idle during the six decades between Roosevelt's and Bush's orders, particularly with respect to protecting the rights of criminal defendants. As noted by LaFave, Israel, and King: "Over a stretch of several years in the 1960s, covering the latter half of Chief Justice Warren's tenure, the Court produced what commentators came to describe as the 'criminal justice revolution' of the Warren Court." And while this revolution was based almost entirely on protections arising under the Constitution—a source of rights largely unintended for application to unlawful belligerents—the effect of the revolution on three generations of world citizens was to sharpen and elevate the sense of fairness applied to any criminal trial, particularly one conducted by the U.S. government.

These Supreme Court decisions established rights that three generations now regard as bedrock, but these rights did not evolve until well after the Supreme Court's review of *Quirin* in 1942: the right to warnings preceding custodial interrogations and the exclusion of subsequent statements tainted by the lack of warning or the presence of coercion; the right of a defendant to have exculpatory information and impeachment information for government witnesses; the right to government-provided counsel at all critical stages of criminal proceedings; the right to government-funded experts for indigent defendants; the right to exclusion of evidence obtained by unlawful searches and seizures; the right to exclusion of evidence that flowed from an unlawful confession or illegal search; the right to suppression of evidence obtained from the person of a defendant in a manner that "shocks the conscience."

Statutory Developments in Military Law, 1948–2001

The 2001 PMO carefully emulated the AW-based Roosevelt order published and upheld by the Supreme Court in 1942. To accord such weight to a 59 year old presidential order was, at the least—as lawyers would say—a litigation risk. Why? Because the statutory basis of the Roosevelt order, the 1920 AW, had been revised several times between 1942 and 2001. In 1948 Congress dramatically reformed courts-martial practice and passed the 1948 Articles of War. Two years later, Congress set aside the 1948 AW when it passed the Uniform Code of Military Justice (UCMJ). The 1950 Military Justice Act revolutionized not only the practice and review of courts-martial, but also the extent of congressional oversight of the military justice system. This Act, and the President's Executive Order implementing it (which retained the name "Manual for Courts-Martial"), enhanced substantially the rights of American service members. After enactment of the UCMJ, the rights of military members paralleled, and even exceeded in some respects, the rights of Americans accused of crimes in civilian jurisdictions. The next four decades would see the rights of the military defendant expand even more.

UCMJ Article 31, predating *Miranda v. Arizona* by sixteen years, provided, as it does today, that no service member suspected of an offense—whether in custody or not—could be questioned concerning that offense without first being advised of the right to silence and the potential legal consequences of answering questions or making a statement.

UCMJ Article 32 restricted general courts-martial (courts of felony jurisdiction) to only those charges that had been the subject of a formal hearing at which the accused and his counsel could be present and question the government's witnesses, contest the evidence against him and present witnesses and evidence on his own behalf. Contrast this to the protections afforded by a federal grand jury, which is a secret proceeding where only the prosecution controls all the evidence presented and the potential defendant has no right even to know of the proceeding against him

UCMJ Article 37 prohibited unlawful influence over court-martial proceedings by the command. No small matter, this statutory prohibition and the case law interpreting it (see, ultimately, *Biagase*[24]) was a great step toward establishing the independence of courts-martial as a matter of law.

UCMJ Article 66 strengthened appellate review of court-martial convictions, bringing an unprecedented level of judicial autonomy and a unique appellate function. The judges appointed to the appellate boards, which operated independently of service oversight, were mandated to review the cases before them not just for errors of law, but for sufficiency of fact, as well. In this latter regard, the Board's authority went far beyond the usual appellate review for legal

---

24. *Id.*

sufficiency. The Boards of Review were required to act as appellate-level juries. A conviction could be sustained only if the judges' review of the record of trial convinced them, beyond a reasonable doubt, that every element of each offense had been satisfied by competent evidence. UCMJ Article 67 created a new civilian court to hear appeals from Board of Review decisions. Composed of three civilian judges appointed by the President and confirmed by the Senate to serve a term of fifteen years, the Court of Military Appeals reviewed each appeal for errors of law and acted as the final tier in the review system.

The 1968 Military Justice Act went so far beyond military custom that the court-martial system it created would likely have been unrecognizable to Winthrop and Davis. By creating the position of Military Judge, the Military Justice Act relegated the President of each court-martial, who previously controlled the proceedings, to a role similar to jury foreman. It vested in the Military Judge what had formerly been the power of the President of the Court to rule on questions of law. The Military Judge was given most of the authority of a federal district judge over criminal proceedings: calling the court-martial into session without members present to adjudicate motions, ruling on objections, and controlling the courtroom. Each Military Judge was required to be a judge advocate, appointed by his or her service Judge Advocate General and completely insulated from oversight or control by the convening authority. Further, the Act required that at general courts-martial, both the trial counsel (prosecutor) and defense counsel must be judge advocates. Finally, the Act instituted, as an election to be made by each accused on the record, a right to be tried before Military Judge instead of a court-martial panel in all cases not referred capital.

Procedural and Evidentiary Evolution in Courts-Martial

Critical to any discussion of the evolution of military law since 1942, *O'Callahan v. Parker*[25] significantly limited the subject matter jurisdiction of courts-martial and marked a nadir in Supreme Court regard for courts-martial as a judicial forum. Justice Douglas' opinion highlights the Court's observation of the truncated nature of military proceedings of the day (Sergeant O'Callahan's court-martial took place in 1956) and the extent to which they were viewed to be disciplinary or even summary proceedings. It is no surprise that the Supreme

---

25. 395 U.S. 258 (1969).

Court in *Quirin* did not criticize either the form or adequacy of the commissions convened by Roosevelt's order because they were characteristic of and consistent with the military courts of that era. As the President's advisors in 2001 apparently failed to observe: "that was then; this is now."

Owing largely to reforms in 1968 and 1983, and to the protectionism of the Court of Military Appeals (CMA), the Supreme Court reversed *O'Callahan* in 1987 and in subsequent decisions expressed confidence in the new procedures and evidentiary rules of courts-martial. By 2001 most informed observers were convinced of the legitimacy, if not the primacy, of courts-martial in the fair dispensation of criminal justice. Nonetheless, there are significant differences in the methodology applied by federal district courts and courts-martial in weighing and applying the rights of criminal defendants. For U.S. service members, limited restrictions on Constitutional rights are axiomatic. The rights afforded civilian citizens and residents are necessarily balanced against the military's need for good order and discipline. The result is that simple analysis of the Constitution itself for a description of the rights of service members can be misleading. Before 1970 this balance heavily favored good order and discipline, but during the 1970s CMA rendered a series of decisions affording significantly greater protection to defendants in military proceedings than those afforded to their civilian counterparts. Many of these protections were extended to protect service member defendants from undue action by the chain of command, or more generally, from the coercive nature of a military structure built on discipline and rank. In the decades since, the Court of Military Appeals and its successor, the United States Court of Appeals for the Armed Forces (CAAF), vastly strengthened service member protections in the areas of compulsory self-incrimination, search and seizure, pretrial hearings, guilty plea inquiries, court member challenges, expert witnesses, defense discovery, and ineffective assistance of counsel, just to name a few. One need only look to the strained statutory and regulatory interpretation evident in such decisions as *Wiessen*[26] and *Warner*[27] to see just how far CAAF has gone to avoid any perception of unfairness to the accused. The point of these observations is not to disparage any decision of either CMA or CAAF, but rather to emphasize the dedication of these courts, from 1952 until 2001 (and beyond) to the creation and protection of the rights of American service members accused of crimes. The non-DoD drafters of the MCA were well aware of CAAF's dedication and activist interpretive theory when they rejected this court as the appellate body for mil-

---

26. 56 M.J. 172 (2001).
27. 62 M.J. 114 (2005).

itary commission cases, notwithstanding the fact that, jurisdictionally, CAAF is the court most suited to hear appeals of commission cases.

The year 1980 brought another move toward parity between courts-martial and Article III trials when Congress implemented the Military Rules of Evidence, adapted from the Federal Rules of Evidence. Of particular note is Section III, which codifies military case law in Fourth and Fifth Amendment litigation. For example, MRE 304 prohibits introduction of involuntary statements against the accused and defines as "involuntary" any statement obtained in violation of either the Fifth Amendment, UCMJ Article 31, or that is the product of "coercion, unlawful influence, or unlawful inducement." MRE 311 prohibits introduction of evidence against an accused obtained as a result of an unlawful search. Both these rules place the burden on the prosecution, after objection by the defense, to prove by a preponderance of the evidence that the statement or evidence is admissible.

International Law of War

While the United States experienced its own criminal procedure revolution, international courts were also evolving. Prominent prosecutions in Sierra Leone, Rwanda, the former Yugoslavia, and before the International Criminal Court were conducted under rules specifically designed to promote the legitimacy of the proceedings. Based largely on a civil law concept, the form of these prosecutions is difficult to compare with the "jury" model of courts-martial, military commissions, or Article III prosecutions. Each trial is presided over by a panel of judges (which has its own investigative body). While the judges may consider hearsay or other forms of evidence disfavored in American courts, the verdict of each tribunal must be rendered in the form of a written ruling that discusses which evidence was considered, and if considered, what weight was given to the evidence. In contrast, our courts relegate admissibility decisions to a judge, who may instruct on weight, but the lay jury who decides the ultimate issue is usually prohibited by law from disclosing the reasons for its verdict, including the weight accorded any or all evidence. Despite these differences, the existence of "integrity" rules in these international courts says much about international expectations of criminal courts in general and "war courts" in particular. Rule 95 (ICTY and ICTR) vested in these civil court hybrids the authority of the judges to reject any evidence "obtained by methods which cast substantial doubt on its reliability or if its admission is antithetical to, and would seriously damage, the integrity of the proceedings." This is a "super exclusionary" rule. Its second clause has no direct corollary in American trials, but may be roughly equated to the fundamental fairness requirement of Fifth Amendment cases. In military practice RCM 102(b), MRE 102, and MRE 403 produce similar judicial authority independent of the Fifth Amendment.

Rule 89(d), ICTY provides that a "Chamber may exclude evidence if its probative value is substantially outweighed by the need to ensure a fair trial." Couched in language facially similar to FRE/MRE 403, the trigger is significantly different: "the need to ensure a fair trial" is substantially broader than the "danger of unfair prejudice." Again, the value or result of direct comparison is far less important than the fact that international courts, and international observers, have become increasingly attuned to protecting the integrity of criminal proceedings.

Development of Law Summary

A revolution in the rights afforded to criminal defendants during the investigation, pre-trial procedures, and trial of cases occurred between 1942, when the *Quirin* decision was rendered by the Supreme Court, and 2001, when the Bush Administration attempted to copy those procedures for trials at Guantanamo Bay. The failure to adjust commission procedures to account for 60 years of changes in the law resulted in the Supreme Court's rejection of those procedures when it decided the *Hamdan* case in 2006.

PMO: Military Commissions — Pre-*Hamdan*

U.S. Government attempts to utilize Military Commissions to address the unique problems posed by terrorism trials must necessarily be divided into two categories: those authorized by the PMO prior to the *Hamdan* decision in 2006, and those authorized by the MCA which followed that decision. In both forms military commissions, without losing focus on fair disposition of offenses, attempt to create a unique forum which elevates legitimate national security concerns over legal protections never intended for application to unprivileged belligerents. Just as many questions sharply divide military commission proponents from their detractors, many similar questions sharply divide those same proponents from senior U.S. Government officials. Many present and former uniformed lawyers who worked closely with the system believe that the PMO Military Commissions procedure, as it would have been implemented by the Office of Military Commissions, would have produced full and fair trials. Such trial procedures, as modified by the 2005 Detainee

Treatment Act, would also have met international standards for war crimes
trials. These same lawyers agree that the administration's greatest failure regarding the use of Military Commissions was the failure to address the public
education and public diplomacy aspects of their policy decisions.

The failure to articulate to the public how the Military Commissions complied
with requirements of international law unfamiliar to most citizens allowed critics to define the debate in terms of domestic criminal justice, rather than the
International Law of Armed Conflict. Instead of debating relevant questions
such as how to determine when the unique war against non-state actors would
be terminated definitively or how non-state actor-detainees could be "repatriated"
at war's end, the debate became about the right to an attorney and the right to
speedy trial. The latter rights are non-existent for detainees captured on the battlefield. There might have been a debate to define "battlefield," but instead the
debates all focused on domestic criminal justice issues because the administration failed to engage in public education and public diplomacy.

Because the PMO Military Commissions would have been implemented by
uniformed attorneys committed to modern concepts of justice, they ultimately
would have produced full and fair trials. The PMO should have been drafted differently or at least modified significantly by the President in 2005 when the Office of Military Commissions urged such changes. In addition to the quickly
overlooked views and opinions of military attorneys in November 2001, almost
all in the Office of Military Commissions urged significant modifications from
2004–2006. Had the administration implemented these changes to the PMO,
Hamdan might very well have been decided differently by the Supreme Court.

Hamdan

The OMC-proposed changes were rejected, however, by the Executive branch.
In late June, 2006 a majority of the Supreme Court determined in the *Hamdan* decision that as an equitable matter military commissions as created by
the Bush administration using 1942 jurisprudential standards should not proceed. The court then employed strained logic to implement that decision.

Legal Status of Military Commissions
Post-*Hamdan*

The Supreme Court's decision in *Hamdan* sent the administration back to
step one with the opportunity to re-build a system for prosecuting acts of ter-

rorism from the ground up. Use of domestic criminal law was not a feasible option for cases developed in an international armed conflict. Domestic criminal enterprises, even highly organized ones such as the mafia and drug cartels, have finite economic goals and finite means to achieve them. Terrorist organizations have cosmic goals which they seek to achieve by cataclysmic means. A system of laws and procedures for fighting the former will not be effective against the latter. Consider, for example, the 1993 World Trade Center bombing. The Clinton administration chose to prosecute this al Qaeda attack as a domestic criminal law violation. Among others, Omar Abdel-Rahman was charged pursuant to federal statute with conspiracy to commit murder. The trial, which didn't begin until 1995, took nine months. Discovery rules in federal conspiracy cases require the prosecution to turn over to the defense the names of all known unindicted co-conspirators. Despite objections from the intelligence community, the names of everyone known to be associated with the al Qaeda network, including Osama Bin Laden, were given to Rahman in 1995. We now know that this is how Bin Laden first learned that US intelligence networks were aware of his role in the organization. The U.S. use of domestic criminal law to prosecute WTC 1993 enabled al Qaeda members to obtain significant information about U.S. intelligence capabilities, World Trade Center vulnerabilities, and commercial jetliner capabilities. All of this information was used to plan attacks against the United States. This is one of the best reasons to isolate the GTMO detainees so that they cannot pass on information as Rahman and Ramsi Yousef, the nephew of KSM, did through their U.S. lawyers, who were subsequently convicted.

As many commentators and scholars have observed, the Constitutional concept of "war" has necessarily and predictably evolved, as have interpretations of the Constitution's numerous war powers, primarily vested in the Legislative and Executive branches. This chapter makes no attempt to define either the scope or limitations or of those various powers; however, there seems little debate that (1) the President has independent authority to direct immediate military action in defense of the Nation; (2) Congress and the President, acting together,[28] may speak for the Nation in determining whether a threat constitutes war, criminal enterprise, or both; (3) the President may authorize prosecution of law of war violations; and (4) the Judiciary may play a role in review of those prosecutions. Whatever one makes of the Supreme Court's application of UCMJ Articles 21 and 36 in *Hamdan*, the Supreme Court made clear

---

28. As the conclusion of this chapter is that the most prudent path is for Congress and the President to act together in this regard, the independent authority of the President to designate an allegedly unlawful attack as "war" or "crime" need not be discussed.

that the UCMJ imparts sufficient authority to the President to authorize trial by military commission of certain offenders and offenses. When Congress and the President act together to designate a threat or violent act as one prosecutable as a violation of the law of war, rather than one constituting only a civil crime, that designation should receive the highest measure of deference from the Judiciary.[29] Whether any group or individual *should* be designated "enemy combatant" or "criminal," or both is the ultimate political question to be determined by the sovereign.

Just as important as a matter of international law, each sovereign state bears authority and responsibility for determining whether it is engaged in armed conflict with an individual, group, or entity, and if it is so engaged, to determine the status of captives. If any such captive is determined to be an unprivileged belligerent or unlawful enemy combatant, it is within the authority of the capturing power to determine whether it will prosecute that captive for crimes arising under the law of war, crimes arising under the state's civil system, or both. Again, these are political questions to be determined by the sovereign in accordance with domestic law and law of war provisions.

National Security Concerns

Satisfied by the State Secrets doctrine in civil cases, national security interests are weighed and protected in Article III criminal trials by CIPA and in courts-martial by MRE 505. Courts and courts-martial have balanced the rights of defendants for decades in hundreds of cases using these rules; the practice has been honed and respected. Notwithstanding criticism from those who would tip the scales drastically in favor of secrecy and against the accused, the structure and execution of CIPA/505 procedures has been highly successful. "Graymail" (implied threats by the defense blithely to seek or disclose classified information) remains a concern in trials of terrorists, but that concern must never be permitted to reduce a criminal trial to the evidentiary and procedural level of a detention hearing. In protecting national security interests, it is important to recognize that some cases may simply not be triable. The number of such cases is relatively small and the potential threat to our National values is great. Therefore, the Government should not risk achieving a criminal conviction by employing rules and procedures that reduce a defendant's trial rights in a way that justifies international derision of the legitimacy of the

---

29. *Youngstown Sheet & Tube Company, et. al. v Charles Sawyer, Secretary of Commerce* 343U.S. 579 (1952).

proceedings. Military commissions can and must adhere to the procedures in MRE 505 or CIPA, with minor modifications to account for evolving intelligence methods and sources.

Physical Security

It is possible for a conventional courthouse court to be hardened adequately, both physically and electronically, to protect trial participants and U.S. interests during trial, but such accommodations would be disruptive to the rest of that court's docket, at a minimum. In the wake of dozens of related terrorism or war crimes trials, this could present a palpable danger to the surrounding civilian community. Because neither courts-martial nor military commissions are standing courts, or tied to any particular facility, installation, or even continent, preparation of a facility sufficient to satisfy both national and physical security requirements for trials by military commission need not have the same disruptive effect or danger to the populace.[30] In order to accommodate the government's need to protect itself from disclosure of classified information, protect the identity of covert operatives, and lessen the potentially substantial burden of adhering to constitutional confrontation requirements, significant changes in the physical structure of any existing courtroom would be essential, requiring the facility literally to stand down during reconstruction. Although U.S. courts have accommodated terrorism trials like WTC 1993 in New York and Moussaoui in Northern Virginia those trials were extremely disruptive to other courthouse operations and the surrounding residents and businesses. Use of a permanent structure designed specifically for terrorism trials and situated in a remote location, such as Guantanamo, significantly reduces the risk of escape or attacks both inside and outside the courtroom.

MCA Commissions: An Unnecessarily Targeted Solution

Immediately following *Hamdan*, Congress considered numerous, often conflicting bills to create an appropriate trial forum for accused terrorists. There were frequent public and private negotiations between the Congress and the White House. Perhaps the most prominent proposal was the so-called Mc-

---

30. Military Judges, counsel, and members alike are not unaccustomed to trying even complex cases in tents, conference rooms, or other makeshift facilities.

Cain/Warner/Graham bill. The bill that that became the Military Commissions Act of 2006, however, was quite different. It was drafted within the Executive and introduced only a few days before passing both houses. The Office of Military Commissions (OMC) participated in discussions with DOJ and service representatives during the legislative drafting process, but neither the armed services nor OMC had any meaningful opportunity to analyze or comment on the MCA before it was enacted.

Ironically, OMC's truncated participation opportunity in what was to become the MCA was likely to the result of OMC's zealous participation in earlier meetings with non-DOD attorneys on draft legislation to respond to *Hamdan*. Non-military attorneys seemed surprised to learn that Military Judges, like other Article I judges (tax, claims, bankruptcy, etc.) were truly independent and would themselves determine whether any authority cited to them was controlling, informative, or even worthy of note. The military judiciary's independence seemed to be particularly feared by some in the administration in the areas of jurisdiction, protection of classified information (both in discovery and at trial), and suppression of evidence the admission of which could taint the integrity of the forum. Ultimately this fear of a truly independent judiciary drove non-military attorneys to craft legislation—and later to insist on implementing regulations—that purported to restrict significantly the judges' authority in these critical areas. To date, Military Judges in MCA commissions have exercised independence at both the trial and appellate levels. Military Judges have rejected the MCA/MMC's scheme for irrebuttable presumption of jurisdiction based on a CSRT's administrative determination,[31] excluded evidence they regarded as having been procured through "highly coercive" means,[32] and protected the accused from highly prejudicial evidence with little probative value[33] despite some drafters' efforts in the MCA to thwart such rulings. Many rulings on discovery and admission of evidence are yet to come, but there is every reason to expect that Military Judges will not act as automatons or mere referees, but rather will continue to conduct proceedings that exemplify fairness and integrity. Rather than create a permanent, flexible solution (such as the proposed draft Article 135a), the Administration, acting with a speed apparently born of perceived political necessity rather than national security, proposed a statutory solution to *Hamdan* that covers only the present conflict and pertains only to those enemy combatants detained at Guantanamo Bay. Appearances and substance aside, the future utility of this "quick

---

31. Judges Brownback and Allred in *Khadr* and *Hamdan*, respectively.
32. Judge Allred in *Hamdan*.
33. *Id.*

fix" legislation is limited by its own terms to providing only a potential model for future Congressional action in future conflicts. Congress and the President eschewed the opportunity to avoid future *ex post facto* debates by limiting unnecessarily the scope and applicability of the MCA.

Despite its merits, and owing largely to the origin of its content (a drafting team largely bereft of military trial experience) the MCA—as implemented by the Manual for Military Commissions (MMC)—contains provisions of questionable utility which might undermine the perception of legitimacy of these proceedings. A few examples are highlighted below.

Irrebuttable Presumption of Jurisdiction

The MCA purports to apply an irrebuttable presumption of personal jurisdiction to nearly all Guantanamo detainees.[34] Unique in criminal law and procedure, the rule permits the possibility of trial and conviction of a detainee for a capital offense without any opportunity for the detainee to contest the court's jurisdiction over him. The presumption attaches from a Combatant Status Review Tribunal (CSRT) finding that the detainee is an "unlawful enemy combatant;" however, neither the form nor proceedings of a CSRT is quasi-judicial—never mind judicial—nor does it make any determination of the lawfulness of an enemy combatant. Finally, the detainee's right of appeal from such a finding is limited, at best.

A CSRT is an administrative body composed of officers, who generally are not lawyers, convened to determine whether a detainee should be classified as an enemy combatant (note the absence of "unlawful") and detained. Each detainee may be represented at the CSRT by a line officer, not a lawyer. The detainee sees no evidence against him that is classified. Witnesses requested by the detainee have routinely been denied.

A detainee can appeal only the sufficiency of the detention decision, but that appellate court (the DC Circuit) has no stated authority in the MCA to review the *status* determination of "enemy combatant;" and the DC Circuit lacks any authority, within the rule, to find that a detainee is *not* an enemy combatant. The fact that the protections provided by the CSRT process far exceed those provided by Geneva Convention III Article 5 tribunals reinforces the uninformed decision-making by the U.S. government in the fall of 2001. Ad-

---

34. The Executive ignored advice to conduct Geneva Convention III Article 5 tribunals in Afghanistan. Justice O'Connor's opinion in *Rasul* repudiated the decision not to conduct Article 5 tribunals.

ministration officials in 2001 flatly rejected the advice of military attorneys who advocated the use of Geneva Convention III, Article 5 tribunals. Those decisions which disregard competent military attorney advice continue to haunt the government.[35] The findings of Geneva Convention Article 5 tribunals, had the United States conducted them in Afghanistan as advised, would have been binding under international law but would not have prevented Military Judges from conducting their own fact finding.

Absence of Any Independent Mandate for Full and Fair Proceedings

Unlike the PMO commissions, both the MCA and MMC are devoid of any mandate to the presiding legal officer to ensure "full and fair" proceedings. Suggestions to include such independent authority were opposed by non-DOD attorneys drafting the MCA on the grounds that the statute itself states that its procedures are full and fair, thereby depriving Military Judges of authority to conclude that it is not. The PMO specified "full and fair trial" authority for the Presiding Officer, using language drawn directly from President Roosevelt's order in the Quirin case. That language, broad and nonbinding, satisfied two central concerns of Administration policy leaders in 2001: (1) mimicking the language of the Quirin order, which they believed produced the highest chance of surviving on appeal, and (2) limiting the role of military judges, who did not exist at the time of Quirin, and who some policy leaders feared would "over-judicialize" the process, perhaps introducing a variable of independence or unpredictability. In practice, military judges have not needed to rely on "full and fair" language, because the MCA and the MMC provide them with authority consistent with the Military Justice Act of 1968, sharpening the teeth of a vague near-slogan such as "full and fair."

Protection of Classified Information

MCRE 505 was designed to broaden slightly the time-tested provisions of both CIPA and MRE 505. Much of the rule is critical to protect legitimate na-

---

35. The Executive ignored advice to conduct Geneva Convention III Article 5 tribunals in Afghanistan. Justice O'Connor's opinion in *Rasul* repudiated the decision not to conduct Article 5 tribunals.

tional security interests, but other portions have the potential for government abuse, legal condemnation, and international criticism. Some will character-ize this rule as an attempt by the government to apply the state secrets privi-lege in a criminal context, creating a default win for the government whenever classified information is at issue. Only judicious use can defuse that criticism. The measure was invoked several times in the first several post-MCA com-missions cases, and while the defense often criticized the ex parte nature of the process, most observers had trouble finding grounds on which to criticize 505 as applied; in fact, there was some criticism coming from the other direc-tion, asking whether the successful and regular use of 505 were proof that com-missions cases could and should be tried in federal court.

One area of concern is the limited role for Military Judges written into the MCA and MMC by administration lawyers who feared an independent judi-ciary.[36] As in courts-martial, Military Judges have no express authority to look behind the government's claim of classification. An inopportune use of this provision by the Government will likely evoke criticism that "classification" is being used, not to protect national security, but to prevent embarrassment to the administration (perhaps regarding interrogation techniques) or to conceal possible criminal conduct by U.S. agents. Unlike many other criminal fora, MCRE 505 contains numerous provisions that require the Military Judge to take specified action at the request or insistence of the prosecution, e.g., pro-tective orders, alternatives to discovery of classified information, sources, meth-ods, and activities.

Second, in the name of protecting "sources, methods, or activities," the prosecution may invoke the commissions equivalent of "double secret proba-tion," or at a minimum, Dean Wormer's directive to the defendants that "I'll tell you what's fair, Mister."[37] Provided that the prosecutor can demonstrate to the Military Judge without the defendant's knowledge or presence, that (1) the sources and methods used to get the evidence are classified, and (2) the evi-dence is reliable, the Military Judge *shall* protect from disclosure those sources and methods. This rule appears to prohibit the Military Judge from consider-ing the evidentiary value to the defense of the methods and activities them-selves and requires a reliability determination with no defense input. In a scenario permuted by the rule, the prosecution could offer (*in camera, ex parte*) a statement allegedly made by the accused, while shielding from the defense the identity of the hearer, as well as the exact location, time, and date of the alleged

---

36. *Discussion* to MCRE 505(e)(5(B), MCRE 505(h)(7)(E), and RMC 806(b)(2)(B).
37. *Animal House*, National Lampoon, 1978.

statement (on the grounds that disclosure would "burn" an asset and further detail is "impracticable"). The government could establish reliability (*in camera, ex parte*) by uncontested evidence of factual corroboration. Because the statement would be hearsay, the burden would then shift to the defense to prove that the statement was unreliable, a Herculean task made all the more difficult by the fact that the Military Judge will at that point already have determined that the statement is reliable.

Third, the effect of the "sources, methods, and activities" MMC rules on the testimony of the accused deserves its own category. The rules permit prosecutors to seek suppression of an accused's testimony if they assert that it would be classified. On its face, MCRE 505 could be invoked to prevent the accused from testifying about the very same sources and methods that were used to produce his statements, or those of others used to incriminate him. However, the MMC arms the military judge with the authority to impose significant sanctions on the government if he finds them to be obstructionist or unable to justify its claim of the need for protection of some kind. If the Government continues to object to disclosure of the information following rulings by the military judge, the military judge shall issue any order that the interests of justice require. The judge may issue an order that may include:

i.   striking or precluding all or part of the testimony of a witness;
ii. declaring a mistrial;
iii. finding against the Government on any issue as to which the evidence is relevant and necessary to the defense;
iv. dismissing the charges, with or without prejudice; or
v.   dismissing the charges or specifications or both to which the information relates.

It also is important to remember that the vehicle of 505 is available to the defense as well, enabling it to present or advocate for the consideration of evidence that comes from classified sources. This, in addition to the equal availability of the liberalized hearsay rule, provides opportunities for an imaginative and well prepared defense counsel—critics sometimes forget that the defense has unique access to the most valuable asset in case preparation, the client himself—to exploit the military commissions procedures and structure to the lawful advantage of the defendant.

The MCA prohibits the admission of **statements** obtained by the use of torture, and prohibits certain **statements** obtained through an unspecified level of coercion. The Act is silent regarding how to handle evidence that is discovered by the government through those statements, so-called "derivative evidence."

The MCRE includes no "derivative" exclusionary rules,[38] reasoning that: (A) The defense should not be permitted to question the means by which the United States military and intelligence communities obtained evidence presented at trial, thereby putting the intelligence community on trial;[39] and (B) No such standard is used in courts-martial, civilian courts or international tribunals.[40]

Because there is no express "fair trial" evidentiary rule, no "integrity of the proceedings" rule, and no derivative evidence rules, an argument that RMC 102/801 gives sufficient authority to the MJ to conduct fair trials will only succeed if Military Judges are willing to "read in" fair trial requirements—not as a result of the rules themselves.

Hearsay

Both in what they say and how they operate, the hearsay rules for MCA commissions go beyond evidentiary rules of most nations. Both federal district and courts-martial operate under a presumption that hearsay is inadmissible. Numerous exclusions and exceptions then operate to assure reliability and guarantee satisfaction of the confrontation clause and the reliability of the trial process. As in nearly every area of evidence, the proponent—the party who offers the hearsay—must convince the court, upon objection, that the evidence is admissible.

It is important to note that most international criminal fora (ICTY, ICTR, Sierra Leone, ICC) permit use of hearsay evidence, but there are critical structural differences that should be discussed in any comparison. In those "quasi-civil law" or "hybrid" courts, each court may act as its own investigative body, gathering and assembling evidence. Whether to "admit" such evidence, and the determination of weight, is decided by a panel of judges. These judges,

---

38. *See, e.g.*, MRE 304, 311, and 321. *C.f.* Fourth and Fifth Amendments, U.S. Constitution.

39. Hardly a novel concept for criminal trial attorneys in any U.S. forum.

40. Although this is one of the arguments advanced in support of removing the proposed exclusionary rule, Rule 95 of both the ICTY and ICTR provides that "no evidence shall be admitted if obtained by methods which cast substantial doubt on its reliability or if its admission is antithetical to, and would seriously damage, the integrity of the proceedings." Rule 89(D), ICTY provides that a "Chamber may exclude evidence if its probative value is substantially outweighed by the need to ensure a fair trial. "Similarly, both civilian courts and courts-martial must adhere to Supreme Court interpretations of the Fourth, Fifth, and Sixth Amendments, regardless of evidentiary rule content, thus incorporating basic notions of due process, fair trial, etc.

who are also the triers of fact, issue verdicts in the form of written memoranda of law, which explain the weight given to evidence in reaching their decision. On appeal, all parties know how evidence was used in arriving at the verdict, contrary to American criminal courts, in which the verdict consists of only a few words and is not subject to further inquiry.

There is no such requirement that any trial judge in the United States—including those in military commissions—justify or explain rulings on hearsay, but those trial level decisions are subject to appellate review. More to the point, the judges ordinarily put the proponent of such evidence through rigorous steps to test the evidence or meet a codified hearsay objection before it is admitted. In general, US courts have moved toward liberalizing hearsay testimony while holding a firm line on Sixth Amendment confrontation opportunities. The military commission hearsay rule is identical in most respects to the military rule of evidence (which is nearly identical to the Federal rule). It does, however, broaden the admissibility pipe for hearsay, primarily because the evidence often has been collected in battlefield situations or other circumstances that would make it impossible or extremely difficult to satisfy the conventional authenticity concerns that are a part of hearsay advocacy. Consider examples both of testimony and documentation. A potential witness may have been interviewed or confronted in a battlefield or operational context, often through an interpreter and now several years ago. It would be impossible to lay a foundation for that person's testimony through conventional means—and even the burden of establishing unavailability is considerable and time-consuming (further complicated by factors such as cultural differences—no conventional addresses, little Western-style record keeping, and naming conventions that include but one name in some cultures). Regarding documents, it is quite common for soldiers to have seized evidence in a complex, chaotic and volatile battlefield environment in which it is not reasonable to expect they will obtain receipts or carefully track chain of custody. In any event, they are not trained to do so with the care or rigor of American law enforcement personnel. Not only might it be difficult to establish such a foundation, but in other circumstances the national interest might call for obscuring the possible source of the information (it might not be wise to disclose where we operated or with whom we were working), which provides the opportunity for interplay between the hearsay rule and Rule 5095, addressed elsewhere. The hearsay rule requires the proponent of such evidence to give notice to the opposing party and to describe "the particulars of the evidence (including information on the general circumstances under which the evidence was obtained, the name of the declarant, and, where available, the declarant's address)." (Rule 803(b) (1) (B). That notice must be sent in writing 30 days in advance and the proponent must provide "the opposing party with any materials regarding the time, place, and conditions under which the statement was produced that are in the possession of the proponent of the evidence. Absent such notice, the military judge shall determine whether the proponent has provided the adverse party with a fair opportunity under the totality of the circumstances." (B)(2) Even if the proponent of the evidence meets the evidentiary burden, final authority remains with the independent military judge: "Hearsay evidence otherwise admissible under subsection (b) (1) shall not be admitted if the party opposing the admission of the evidence demonstrates by a preponderance of the evidence that the evidence is unreliable under the totality of the circumstances." Just as either party may advocate for admissibility of such evidence, either party may oppose it, and the judge's ruling is conclusive.

This is hardly a unilateral process for the government's exploiting its rule-writing advantage (in what forum does the government not write the rules) or, more importantly, an avenue for the government's casual exploitation of battlefield turbulence to sneak junk evidence before the trier of fact. Even if the evidence is admitted under these circumstances—and again note the judge's significant authority—that only places it before the panel, which is free to give it whatever weight it chooses. Additionally, though the evidence is admitted into evidence, it does not foreclose the opposing party's efforts to argue to the panel that the evidence is not worthy of weight. In practice, the defense has used this provision several times, and by the nature of the defenses likely to be raised in commissions and the likely unavailability of or difficulty in locating corroborating witnesses, it is likely to be employed by the defense as well as by the government.

A Better Statutory Alternative

If the MCA/MMC is the proverbial bathwater, then military commissions are the baby worth saving. Our common law war courts are not only relevant, but imperative, as the United States seeks a practical forum that focuses on just disposition of offenses, while elevating national security concerns over rights never intended for application to unprivileged belligerents. In adhering to *Hamdan's* requirements, Congress and the President need not have enacted a system of trials that jettisons substantive and procedural rights revered not only by the international community but by our own citizens. We must avoid the over-arching flaws of the MCA/MMC: (1) limited applicability, requiring repeated Congressional enactment; (2) real and apparent evisceration of the military judiciary; and (3) rules formulated to advantage unnecessarily the prosecution and obscure appropriate fact-finding.

The 2001–2009 administration's determination to model Military Commissions in their own fashion, with little reference to modern military law and custom, and the haste in which the MCA was drafted and passed lend credence to criticism that at least the second and third of these flaws are directly attributable, not to the protection of national security, but to the desire to achieve convictions while avoiding embarrassment to the administration. The United States should enact an enduring statutory scheme that results in a practical, rationally based balance between court-martial procedures and legitimate security concerns. A system of justly formed procedural and evidentiary rules would enhance both international and domestic understanding and acceptance of military commissions as an appropriate forum for the trial of terrorists—both state and non-state—who have repeatedly declared war on the United States. Rules cannot be viewed as a mechanism designed to drive convictions; the government must accept that a certain number of acquittals and dismissals may occur, as it is the very nature of a criminal trial that factual uncertainties must be resolved by the jury (or military court members) who determine the weight they will give to any evidence, as well as the ultimate verdict.

Those rules, in the case of a military commission, must account for and appropriately protect national security and the security of trial participants and observers. The end product need not mirror the UCMJ or Article III procedures, just as it need not, in the name of protecting national security, create a forum that rejects fundamental trial rights for the accused. The Military Commissions Office developed drafts of just such a product. They were in the form of a proposed amendment to the UCMJ which would add Article 135a, Military Commissions Procedures. OMC attorneys first drafted it in June 2005, fully one year before the Supreme Court's decision in *Hamdan*. The proposed Article 135a was the product of months of work on another proposed document, the Manual for Military Commissions (MMC). OMC work on the MMC began in late October, 2004, several weeks before the November 8, 2004 District Court decision to stay the Guantanamo Bay proceedings in *Hamdan*.

The numbering of the proposed statute was selected to fit it within the UCMJ just after Article 135, Courts of Inquiry. Similar in format to Article 135, the proposed Article 135a would provide authority to specific senior commanders to convene military commissions. It described the composition of military commissions, the qualifications of counsel and presiding officers, and the duties of counsel and presiding officers. It addressed classified evidence procedures and provided authority to the President to prescribe rules of evidence that authorized hearsay evidence and streamlined other evidence rules. It ensured compliance with U.S. obligations under Article 15 of the Convention Against Torture.

The proposed Article 135a permitted the broadest possible jurisdiction over appropriate statutory offenses and violations of the law of war without creating ex post facto issues. It addressed deliberations procedures and post trial actions and appellate procedures. It provided that both interlocutory appeals and post trial appeals would be to the United States Court of Appeals for the District of Columbia Circuit, not a military service Court of Appeals. Significantly, it identified other existing (since 1950) UCMJ provisions that address military commissions, something that neither the PMO commissions nor the MCA included. Both the 2001 PMO-derived procedures and the 2006 MCA itself ignored UCMJ statutes more than 50 years old that specifically address aspects of military commissions.

Proposed Article 135a did the work not addressed since 1950; it provided a cohesive framework of military commission procedures that anticipated their use well into the future. Unlike the MCA, the proposed Article 135a could be implemented whenever and wherever needed. It would not be limited to the current detainees at Guantanamo Bay.

Testimony by senior uniformed attorneys before the SASC hearings on the statutory response to Hamdan in August 2006 included recommendation of the proposed Article 135a.[41] Administration attorneys never expressed interest in Article 135a or other OMC proposals. If a new administration sees more clearly the long term implications and shortcomings of the MCA, it may turn first to the proposed UCMJ Article 135a as a solution

Conclusion

Trial of those who are accused of acts of terrorism ultimately requires a system of justice which reflects the reality of sophisticated worldwide terrorist networks conducting military operations against American civilians from isolated locations. The civilian criminal justice system is ill-equipped to address the realities of how this enemy will be detected and captured. Military Commissions offer the best framework for conducting these trials. They are a legal, time-honored forum offering the flexibility necessary to adapt to a changing enemy. The Executive branch blundered badly by failing adequately to adapt its procedures to developments in the law that had occurred in the 60 years since the United States last used military commissions. On the other hand, the 2006 MCA is too narrow in its approach. But Military Commissions, in what-

---

41. MG Jack Rives, TJAG, United States Air Force.

ever form they are ultimately convened, will be carried out by military judges, prosecutors, and defense counsel committed to traditional concepts of justice, who will defy any systemic attempt to deny a defendant a full and fair trial.

Chapter 3

Habeas Corpus and the Detention of Enemy Combatants in the Global War on Terror

Honorable James Terry[1]

Introduction

Since the al Qaeda attacks on the World Trade Center and the Pentagon on September 11, 2001, the United States has been engaged in an armed conflict that rivals far more traditional conflicts in its brutality and carnage. Like other enemies we have faced in the past, al Qaeda and its affiliates possess both the ability and the intention to inflict catastrophic harm, if not on this nation, on its citizens. Considering the nature of this adversary, we cannot expect that this conflict will conclude around a negotiating table.

Recognizing this threat and to preclude further attacks on our homeland, U.S. military forces have captured enemy combatants and terrorists on battlefields in Afghanistan, Iraq and Southwest Asia. Patterning its actions on past conflicts, the United States has determined it necessary to detain these combatants until the conclusion of hostilities, if only to preclude their return to the

---

1. James Terry currently serves as Chairman of the Board of Veterans Appeals in the Department of Veterans Affairs. He previously served as Principal Deputy Assistant Secretary and Deputy Assistant Secretary in the Department of State and as Legal Counsel to the Chairman of the Joint Chiefs of Staff. He received his bachelors and masters' degrees from the University of Virginia (1968 and1976), his law degree from Mercer University (1973), and his Master of Laws (1980) and Doctor of Juridical Science Degrees (1980) from The George Washington University. A retired Marine Corps Colonel, he is widely published in the areas of coercion control and national security law.

battlefield. Soon after the September 11, 2001 attacks, the Bush Administration established a detention facility outside United States territory at the U.S. Naval Base at Guantanamo Bay. This would permit effective detention, without the legal requirement to entertain continual court suits by the detainees. While this result was true under the law existing prior to June 12, 2008, the whole equation has now changed.

Prior to this conflict, alien detainees held on foreign soil had been denied access to U.S. federal courts to contest detention (habeas corpus). The lawsuits and legislation arising from the detention of alien combatants at Guantanamo since 2002 have led to refinement in the law regarding detainees and further development of the law of habeas corpus during armed conflict.

Habeas Corpus: The Historical Antecedents

In our nation's history, aliens held by our military forces in foreign territory have not been entitled to the civilian remedy of habeas corpus in the United States Federal Courts, because the courts had no jurisdiction over the land on which they were being held. As the Supreme Court explained over 50 years ago in *Johnson v. Eisentrager*,[2] "[w]e are cited to no instance where a court, in this or any other country where the writ is known, has issued it on behalf of an enemy alien who, at no relevant time and in no stage of his captivity, has been within the territorial jurisdiction. Nothing in the text of the Constitution extends such a right, nor does anything in our statutes."[3] The implementing legislation, 22 U.S.C. 2241, similarly limited access to the courts to those within its jurisdiction.[4]

An underlying concern in granting access to U.S. courts to alien combatants detained abroad during armed conflict, quite apart from the jurisdictional element, relates to the nature of warfare. The witnesses who would be needed to provide personal testimony and rebut the aliens' contentions in a judicial, as opposed to an administrative forum, are engaged in military operations or subject to commitment to combat. Requiring them to leave their units and appear in habeas proceedings would be both disruptive and divisive. The original documents necessary to present the government's position would

---

2. 339 U.S. 763 (1950).

3. *Id.* at 768.

4. The habeas statute states that "Writs of habeas corpus may be granted by the Supreme Court, any justice thereof, the district courts and any circuit judge within their respective jurisdictions." 22 USC 2241(a).

likely not be available until all hostilities are concluded. Identification and transport of foreign witnesses demanded by the detainees for in-person testimony would often prove infeasible, if not logistically impossible. Moreover, there is no authority over such foreign witnesses and their appearance could not be assured.

In fact, the historical common law underpinnings of the legal right to habeas corpus, and its limitations, reflect many of the tenets of the *Eisentrager* case. The history of habeas corpus as the "symbol and guardian of individual liberty"[5] for English, and now American, citizens is well established. What we know now as the 'Great Writ' originated as the "prerogative writ of the Crown,"[6] its original purpose being to bring people *within the jurisdiction* into court, rather than out of imprisonment.[7] By the early 13th century, the use of the writ for this purpose (to bring them to court) was a commonly invoked aspect of English law.[8]

The reformation of the writ to one in which freedom from incarceration was the focus can be traced to the 14th century, when, as an aspect of the earlier Norman conquest,[9] the French conquerors developed a centralized judicial framework over existing local courts. During this period, prisoners began to initiate habeas proceedings to challenge the legality of their detention.[10] The first such use was by members of the privileged class who raised habeas claims in the superior central courts to challenge their convictions in the local inferior courts. The central courts would often grant such writs to assert the primacy of their jurisdiction.[11]

Thus, the rationale behind the grant of these writs more often focused on the jurisdiction of the particular court than concerns over the liberty of the petitioners.[12]

The availability and meaning of habeas corpus expanded in the 15th century. Clarke notes that the writ became a favorite tool of both the judiciary

---

5. *See Peyton v. Rowe*, 391 U.S. 54, 59, 88 S.Ct. 1549, 20 L. Ed. 2d. 426 (1968).

6. The phrase, *habeas corpus*, refers to the common law writ of habeas corpus, or the "Great Writ." *Preiser v. Rodriguez*, 411 U.S. 475, 484–85 and n.2, 93 S.Ct. 1827, 36 L.Ed. 2d. 439 (1973), citing *Ex Parte Bollman*, 8 U.S. (4 Cranch) 75, 95, 2 L.Ed. 554 (1807).

7. *See* Alan Clarke, *Habeas Corpus: The Historical Debate*, 14 N.Y.L. Sch Jl Hum. Rts. 375, 378 (1998); William F. Duker, A Constitutional History of Habeas Corpus 17 (1980).

8. Clarke, *supra* at 378.

9. The Norman Conquest took place in the 11–12th centuries.

10. *Supra* note 8.

11. *Id.*

12. *See discussion* in Gerald L. Newman, *Habeas Corpus, Executive Detention, and the Removal of Aliens*, 98 Colum. L. Rev. 961, 970–71 (1998).

and the Parliament in contesting the Crown's assertion of unfettered power.[13]
By the late 1600s, habeas corpus was "the most usual remedy by which a man
is restored again to his liberty, if he has been against the law deprived of it."[14]
Despite its status, it was not uncommon for the Crown to suspend the right
during periods of insurrection, during conspiracies against the King (1688 and
1696), during the American Revolution, and during other periods in the 18th
century.[15]

In the early American colonies, New Hampshire, Georgia and Massachusetts
adopted provisions in their State constitutions prohibiting suspension of the
right of habeas corpus for their citizens under nearly all circumstances.[16] During debate on the U.S. Constitution, some delegates in Philadelphia sought a
guarantee of habeas corpus in the federal Constitution.[17] The compromise
which emerged forbade the suspension of habeas corpus unless necessary in the
face of "rebellion or invasion."[18] Despite the compromise, habeas corpus remains the only writ at common law referenced in the Constitution. In section
14 of the Judiciary Act of 1789,[19] moreover, the Congress specifically gave authority to the newly created federal courts to issue the writ.

Suspension of the writ had been authorized by the Congress only four times
in the nation's history,[20] that is, prior to Congress' and the Court's consideration
of the Guantanamo detainees. The first occurred during the Civil War when
Congress, after the fact, gave approval to President Lincoln's earlier permission
to his Commanding General of the Army Winfield Scott to suspend the right
between Washington and Philadelphia. This was in response to rioting by southern sympathizers as Union troops moved down the coast.[21] The second occurred
after the Civil War in 1871 when Congress in the Klu Klux Klan Act gave President Grant authority to suspend the writ in nine South Carolina counties where

---

13. Clarke, *supra* note 7 at 380.

14. *Bushell's Case*, Vaughan 135, 136, 124 Eng. Rep. 1006, 1007 (1670).

15. *See* Rex A. Collins, *Habeas Corpus for Convicts—Constitutional Right or Legislative Grace*, 40 CAL L. REV. 335, 339 (1952)

16. Max Rosenn, *The Great Writ—A Reflection of Societal Change*, 44 OHIO ST. L. JL. 337, 338, n. 14 (1983).

17. Erwin Chemerinsky, *Thinking about Habeas Corpus*, 37 CASE W. RES. L. REV. 748, 752 (1987).

18. U.S. Const., art. 1, sec. 9, cl. 2.

19. Act of Sept. 24, 1789, ch. 20, sec. 14, 1 Stat. 73, 81.

20. Duker, *supra* note 7 at 149.

21. Act of Mar. 3, 1863, 12 Stat. 755. *See also* James Terry, THE PRESIDENT'S ARTICLE II AUTHORITY AND THE USE OF MILITARY FORCE, in press, for a discussion of the circumstances underlying Lincoln's decision.

rebellion was raging.[22] The third and fourth authorizations occurred in 1902 and in 1941, respectively. During the insurrection in the Philippines following the Spanish American War, President McKinley sought and obtained Congressional authorization to suspend the writ.[23] Similarly, in 1941, immediately after the Japanese attacked our fleet at Pearl Harbor, President Roosevelt asked the Congress to suspend habeas corpus throughout the Islands and that body authorized the territorial Governor of Hawaii to temporarily do so.[24] Unlike the current circumstance involving the Guantanamo detainees, each of the prior suspensions of the right involved "rebellion or invasion," as required by Article I of the Constitution. *But rebellion or invasion has never been required to preclude habeas jurisdiction if the detainee was held outside U.S. territory.*

In each of the four prior instances cited, Congress was authorizing suspension of habeas corpus over territory in which the United States was sovereign. Conversely, in the 1950 *Eisentrager* decision, where the Supreme Court held that the right of judicial access in habeas cases did not extend beyond the territorial jurisdiction of the United States, the part of Germany where Eisentrager was held and the confinement facility in which he was incarcerated were under the complete control and authority of U.S. forces, but it was not U.S. sovereign territory.[25]

The foreign detention in *Eisentrager* had been informed by the government's experience in two principal cases arising from World War II. In *Ex parte Quirin*,[26] a 1942 Supreme Court decision, a team of German saboteurs were captured in the United States and tried before a military commission, similar to that established for the Guantanamo detainees.[27] The Presidential Proclamation establishing their military tribunal, by its terms, had precluded access to the federal courts.[28] Held in a federal confinement facility in Washington, D.C., the saboteurs nevertheless sought relief through a petition for a writ of habeas corpus in the U.S. District Court. The Supreme Court, in rejecting arguments by the Solicitor General that judicial access through a writ of habeas corpus was precluded by the Presidential Proclamation, stated that "neither the Proclamation nor the fact they are enemy aliens forecloses consideration by the courts of petitioners'

---

22. *See* Duker, *supra* note 7, at 178, n. 190.

23. Act of July 1, 1902, ch. 1369, 32 Stat. 691.

24. *See discussion* in *Duncan v. Kahanamoku*, 327 U.S. 394, 307–08, 66 S.Ct. 606, 90 L.Ed. 688 (1946).

25. *Supra* note 2 at 768. This replicates the situation in Guantanamo.

26. 317 U.S. 1 (1942).

27. *Id.*

28. *Quirin*, 317 U.S. at 20–24.

contention that the Constitution and laws of the United States constitutionally enacted forbid their trial by military commission."[29]

In 1948 in *Ahrens v. Clark*,[30] the Supreme Court addressed the habeas petitions of 120 German nationals held on Ellis Island in New York awaiting deportation to Germany. Filing their petitions in the U.S. District Court for the District of Columbia, the German petitioners named the Attorney General, located in the District, respondent in their suit under the theory that they were under his control.[31] The Supreme Court dismissed. The court held that a district court may only grant a writ of habeas corpus to a prisoner confined within its territorial jurisdiction.[32] The court addressed the 'immediate custodian rule,' addressed more fully below, only in passing. They stated: "Since there is a defect in the jurisdiction of the District Court that remains uncured, we do not reach the question whether the Attorney General is the proper respondent."[33] The Court's reasoning in *Ahrens* concerning the locus of incarceration would be heavily relied upon by Justice Rehnquist in his decision in *Padilla*, discussed below.[34]

In the current Global War on Terror, the detainees held at Guantanamo are under the complete control of U.S. forces but on territory over which the Republic of Cuba is sovereign.[35] Until 2004, the Bush Administration was successful, as reflected in *Al Odah v. United States*,[36] in precluding access to U.S. federal courts on the part of detainees based on our lack of sovereignty over the Guantanamo Naval facility. This changed with the Supreme Court's decisions in the *Enemy Combatant Cases of 2004*[37] and in *Boumediene v. Bush*,[38] decided June 12, 2008.

---

29. *Id.* at 25. The German saboteurs were convicted by the Military Commission and executed.

30. 335 U.S. 188 (1948).

31. *Id.* at 189.

32. *Id.* at 190, 192.

33. Id. at 193.

34. *See Padilla v. Rumsfeld*, 542 U.S. 426 (2004).

35. LEASE OF LANDS FOR COALING AND NAVAL STATIONS, Feb. 23, 1903, U.S.-Cuba, Art.III, T.S. No. 418. The leasehold has no termination date.

36. 355 U.S. App. D.C. 189, 321 F.3d 1134 (D.C. Cir. 2003). The D.C. Circuit affirmed the district court's dismissal of various claims, habeas and non-habeas, holding, with regard to the habeas claims, that "no court in this country has jurisdiction to grant habeas relief, under 28 U.S.C. 2241, to the Guantanamo detainees." 321 F. 3d at 1141. Regarding the non-habeas claims, the court noted that "'the privilege of litigation' does not extend to aliens in military custody who have no presence in 'any territory over which the United States is sovereign." *Id.* at 1144.

37. *Rasul v. Bush*, 542 U.S. 466 (2004); *Padilla v. Rumsfeld*, 542 U.S. 426 (2004); *Hamdi v. Rumsfeld*, 542 U.S. 507. (2004).

38. *Boumediene v. Bush*, 128 S. Ct. 2229 (2008); 2008 WL 2369628 (U.S.); 76 USLW 4391, 76 USLW 4406.

The 2004 Enemy Combatant Cases

The Enemy Combatant Cases decided by the Supreme Court in 2004, *Rasul v. Bush*, *Padilla v. Rumsfeld*, and *Hamdi v. Rumsfeld*,[39] were collectively interpreted by many as strong judicial direction for the administration on its detainee policies. These cases addressed both foreign detention of enemy combatants and their detention within the United States. In ruling against the government in *Rasul v. Bush*,[40] the Supreme Court, per Justice Stevens, reversed the DC Circuit in *Al Odah v. United States*,[41] and held that the federal habeas statute, 22 U.S.C. 2241, extended to alien detainees[42] at Guantanamo. The Court decided "the narrow but important question whether United States courts lack jurisdiction to consider challenges to the legality of detention of foreign nationals captured abroad in connection with hostilities and incarcerated at the Guantanamo Bay Naval Base, Cuba."[43] Although the Guantanamo detainees themselves were held to be beyond the district court's jurisdiction, the Supreme Court determined that the district court's jurisdiction over the detainees' military custodians was sufficient to provide it subject matter jurisdiction over the aliens' habeas corpus claims under section 2241.[44] The Court also found subject matter jurisdiction over the detainees' non-habeas claims (5th Amendment, etc.) because it found that nothing in the federal question statute[45] or the Alien Torts Act[46] excluded aliens outside the United States from bringing these claims in federal court.[47]

In *Padilla v. Rumsfeld*,[48] decided the same day, the Court, per Justice Rehnquist, determined that there was no jurisdiction in a New York District Court to hear the habeas petition of Jose Padilla, a U.S. citizen confined in a Charleston, South Carolina naval brig after having been transferred from New York as an alleged enemy combatant.[49] The Supreme Court found that the

---

39. *Id.*
40. *Id.*
41. 355 U.S. App. D.C. 189 (D.C. Cir. 2003).
42. These are unlawful alien combatants but not technically *enemy aliens* since they do not represent any country with which the United States is at war.
43. *Rasul*, 542 U.S. at 470.
44. *Rasul*, 542 U.S. at 483–84.
45. 28 U.S.C. 1331.
46. 28 U.S.C. 1350.
47. *Rasul*, 542 U.S. at 484–485.
48. *Supra* note 37.
49. *Padilla*, 542 U.S. 441–43, 450–51.

only person who could be named as respondent in the habeas petition was the custodian of the Charleston brig, Commander Marr, as she was the only one of the named respondents who could produce the body.[50] She, however, was not within the jurisdiction of the Southern District of New York. The Court, in dismissing the habeas petition, found that Secretary Rumsfeld, likewise, could not be considered Padilla's custodian or named as respondent of the petition, as he did not qualify as such under the 'immediate custodian rule,' nor was his Pentagon office within the jurisdiction of the District Court in New York.[51]

In *Hamdi v. Rumsfeld*,[52] the third of the *Enemy Combatant Cases*, the Supreme Court provided clear guidance on the protections to be afforded enemy combatants in custody. From the standpoint of jurisdiction, there were no significant issues raised in Hamdi's habeas petition, and the Supreme Court considered the case upon its merits. The petitioner, Hamdi, a U.S. citizen of Saudi origin, was incarcerated in the brig at the U.S. Naval Base in Norfolk as an alleged enemy combatant serving in Afghanistan.[53] The petition was filed in the Eastern District of Virginia, the locus of Secretary Rumsfeld (the Pentagon is in Arlington, Virginia), and the Commanding Officer of the Norfolk brig, satisfying the 'immediate custodian rule.'[54] The case is significant in holding that enemy combatants who are U.S. citizens detained by the U.S. military in the United States in furtherance of the Global War on Terror, are entitled to due process protections, specifically "notice of the factual basis for the classification, and a fair opportunity to rebut the Government's factual assertions …"[55]

The Congressional Response to the Enemy Combatant Cases

The Congress, at Bush Administration urging, responded quickly to the decisions in *Rasul v. Bush* and *Hamdi v. Rumsfeld* with the Detainee Treatment Act

---

50. *Id.*
51. *Id.* at 435. Secretary Rumsfeld's office was in the Eastern District of Virginia at the Pentagon.
52. *Hamdi v. Rumsfeld*, 542 U.S. 507 (2004).
53. *Hamdi*, 542 U.S. at 510.
54. *Hamdi*, 542 U.S. at 525.
55. *Hamdi*, 542 U.S. at 533. Hamdi was later released from confinement and returned to Saudi Arabia, having served three years of incarceration without charge.

(Act) of 2005.[56] This legislation was designed to restore the status quo reflected in *Eisentrager*,[57] at least with respect to Guantanamo detainees. In this Act, the Congress added a subsection (e) to 28 U.S.C. 2241, the habeas statute. This new provision stated that, "[e]xcept as provided in section 1005 of the Detainee Treatment Act, no court, justice, or judge may exercise jurisdiction over

(1) an application for a writ of habeas corpus filed by or on behalf of an alien detained by the Department of Defense at Guantanamo Bay, Cuba; or

(2) any other action against the United States or its agents relating to any aspect of the detention by the Department of Defense of any alien at Guantanamo Bay, Cuba, who

(A) is currently in military custody; or

(B) has been determined by the United States Court of Appeals for the District of Columbia Circuit ... to have been properly detained as an enemy combatant.[58]

The Act further provided in section 1005 for exclusive judicial review of Combatant Status Review Tribunal (CSRT) determinations and Military Commission decisions in the D.C. Circuit.[59] On its face, this legislation appeared to have undone the harm created by *Rasul* and *Hamdi* and restored the delicate balance created years earlier by *Eisentrager*.

In June 2006, however, the Supreme Court, in *Hamdan v. Rumsfeld*,[60] interpreted the Detainee Treatment Act restrictively, finding that the Act only applied prospectively from the date of enactment and did not remove jurisdiction from the federal courts in habeas proceedings pending on that date. The Court pointed to section 1005(h) of the Act which states that subsections (e)(2) and (e)(3) of section 1005 "shall apply with respect to any claim ... that is pending on or after the date of the enactment of this Act," and then compared this with subsection (e)(1). The Court found that no similar provision stated whether subsection (e)(1), the dispositive subsection, applied to pending habeas cases. Finding that Congress "chose not to so provide ... after having been provided with the option," the Court concluded the "[t]he omission [wa]s an integral part of the statutory scheme."[61]

---

56. Pub. L. No. 109-148, 119 Stat 2680 (2005). Signed into law December 30, 2005.
57. *Eisentrager, supra* note 2.
58. Detainee Treatment Act, sec. 1005 (e)(1).
59. Detainee Treatment Act, sec. 1005(e)(2), (e)(3).
60. 126 S. Ct. 2749, 165 L.Ed. 2d. 723 (2006).
61. 126 S. Ct. at 2769.

Frustrated once again, the Congress quickly passed the Military Commissions Act of 2006,[62] which, in section 7, again amended section 2241(e) (habeas statute) to clearly provide that subsection (e)(1) "shall apply to all cases, without exception, pending on or after the date of enactment ..."[63] Both the proponents and opponents of section 7 understood the provision to eliminate habeas jurisdiction over pending detainee cases.[64]

Nevertheless, the detainees in *Hamdan* were undeterred. Despite the fact that anyone who followed the interplay between Congress and the Supreme Court knew full well that the sole purpose of 2006 Military Commissions Act was to overrule *Hamdan,* the detainees claimed otherwise. In *Boumediene v. Bush,*[65] the same detainees urged the D.C. Circuit to find that habeas jurisdiction had not been repealed. Arguing that if Congress had intended to remove jurisdiction in their cases, it should have expressly stated in section 7(b) that habeas cases were included among "all cases, without exception, pending on or after" the Military Commissions Act became law.[66] Otherwise they argued, the Military Commissions Act did not represent an "unambiguous statutory directive []" to repeal habeas corpus jurisdiction.[67]

The D.C. Circuit, however, made clear in their February 20, 2007 decision in *Boumediene,*[68] that the Military Commissions Act applied to the detainees' habeas petitions.[69]

On June 20, 2007, the Court of Appeals for the D.C. Circuit further denied the appellant Boumediene's motion to hold the collected cases in abeyance and

---

62. Pub. L. No. 109-366, 120 Stat. 2600 (2006). The President signed the Military Commissions Act into law on October 17, 2006.

63. Sec. 7, Military Commissions Act, *supra* note 52.

64. *See, e.g.,* 152 Cong. Rec. S.10357 (daily ed. Sept. 28, 2006) (statement of Sen. Leahy) ("The habeas stripping provisions in the bill go far beyond what Congress did in the Detainee Treatment Act.... This new bill strips habeas jurisdiction retroactively, even for pending cases."); *id.* at S10367 (statement of Sen. Graham) ("The only reason we are here is because of the *Hamdan* decision. The *Hamdan* decision did not apply ... the Detainee Treatment Act retroactively, so we have about 200 and some habeas cases left unattended and we are going to attend them now."); *id* at S10403 (statement of Sen. Cornyn) ("[O]nce ... section 7 is effective, Congress will finally accomplish what it sought to do through the Detainee Treatment Act last year. It will finally get the lawyers out of Guantanamo Bay. It will substitute the blizzard of litigation instituted by *Rasul v. Bush* with a narrow DC Circuit-only review of the CSRT hearings.").

65. 476 F.3d 981 (2007).

66. *Id.* at 987.

67. *Id.*

68. *Supra* note 65.

69. *Id.* at 985.

to stay issuance of the mandate.[70] This followed the Supreme Court's April 2, 2007 denial of the appellants' petition for a writ of certiorari.[71] On June 29, 2007, however, the Supreme Court vacated its prior denial and granted the detainees' petition for a writ of certiorari.[72]

Boumediene v. Bush (2008):
A New Chapter in Habeas Proceedings

On June 12, 2008, the Supreme Court reversed course in its approach to the Guantanamo detainees. In a 5–4 decision authored by Justice Kennedy, the Court in *Boumediene v. Bush*[73] reversed the Court of Appeals for the D.C. Circuit and held that aliens detained as enemy combatants at the Naval Station at Guantanamo Bay, Cuba, were entitled to the right of habeas corpus to challenge the legality of their detention.[74] The court further held that the provision of the Military Commissions Act denying federal courts jurisdiction to hear habeas corpus suits that were pending at the time of its enactment constituted an unconstitutional suspension of the writ to these individuals.[75] Further, the Supreme Court found that the Suspension Clause had full effect at the Naval Station at Guantanamo Bay,[76] that the detainees were entitled to prompt habeas corpus hearings,[77] and that they could not be required to exhaust other review procedures prior to filing their habeas petition.[78]

In addressing this complete reversal of precedent by the Court, Chief Justice Roberts, joined by Justices Scalia, Thomas and Alito, decried the decision as ill-founded and labeled the new approach mandated by the Court's majority as "misguided."[79] In examining what the Court did, Chief Justice Roberts stated that

> [h]abeas is most fundamentally a procedural right, a mechanism for contesting the legality of executive detention. The critical thresh-

---

70. *Boumediene v. Bush*, 2007 U.S. App. LEXUS 14883, June 20, 2007.
71. *Boumediene v. Bush*, 127 S. Ct. 1478 (2007).
72. *Boumediene v. Bush*, 2007 U.S. 8757; 75 U.S. L.W. 3707, June 29, 2007.
73. *Boumediene v. Bush*, *supra* note 38.
74. *Id.* at 2234.
75. *Id.* at 2234–35.
76. *Id.* at 2235, 2276.
77. *Id.* at 2237.
78. *Id* at 2275.
79. *Id.* at 2280.

old question in these cases, prior to any inquiry about the writ's scope,
is whether the system the political branches designed protects whatever rights the detainees may possess. If so, there is no need for any
additional process, whether called "habeas" or something else.

Congress entrusted that threshold question in the first instance to
the Court of Appeals for the District of Columbia Circuit, as the Constitution surely allows Congress to do. See Detainee Treatment Act of
2005 (DTA), sec. 1005(e)(2)(A, 119 Stat. 2742. But before the D.C. Circuit has addressed the issue, the Court cashiers the statute, and without answering this critical question itself. The Court does eventually
get around to asking whether review under the DTA is, as the Court
frames it, an "adequate substitute" for habeas, *ante*, at ___, but even
then its opinion fails to determine what rights the detainees possess and
whether the DTA system satisfies them. The majority instead com-
pares the undefined DTA process to an equally undefined habeas
right—one that is to be given shape only in the future by district
courts on a case-by-case basis. This whole approach is misguided.[80]

Similarly, Justice Scalia, joined by Chief Justice Roberts and Justices Thomas
and Alito, vigorously dissented, the dissenters finding the decision to have been
driven by a "notion of judicial supremacy."[81] As succinctly stated by Justice
Scalia:

There is simply no support for the Court's assertion that constitutional rights extend to aliens held outside U.S. sovereign territory, *see
Verdugo-Urquidez*, 494 U.S. ___, at 271, 110 S.Ct. 1056, and *Eisentrager*
could not be clearer that the privilege of habeas corpus does not extend to aliens abroad. By blatantly distorting *Eisentrager*, the Court
avoids the difficulty of explaining why it should be overruled. *See
Planned Parenthood of Southeastern Pa. V. Casey*, 505 U.S. 833, 854–55,
112 S. Ct. 2791, 120 L.Ed. 2d. 674 (1992) (identifying stare *decisis*
factors). The rule that aliens abroad are not constitutionally entitled
to habeas corpus has not proved unworkable in practice; if anything,
it is the Court's "functional" test that does not, (and never will) provide clear guidance for the future. *Eisentrager* forms a coherent whole
with the accepted proposition that aliens abroad have no substantive
rights under our Constitution. Since it was announced, no relevant factual premises have changed. It has engendered considerable reliance

---

80. *Id.* at 2279–80.
81. *Id* at 2302.

on the part of our military. And as the Court acknowledges, text and history do not clearly compel a contrary ruling. It is a sad day for the rule of law when such an important constitutional precedent is discarded without an *apologia*, much less an apology.[82]

Despite these criticisms, the law *has changed* and the writ of habeas corpus is no longer suspended with respect to the alien detainees held at the detention facility at Guantanamo. It is to the Suspension Clause that we now turn.

The Suspension Clause and Its Relationship to the Guantanamo Detainees

Separate from, but related to, the jurisdictional arguments of the detainees in the *Boumediene* case were their claims under the Suspension Clause[83] of the Constitution. The Supreme Court had previously held in 2001 that the Suspension Clause protects the writ of habeas corpus "as it existed in 1789," when the first Judiciary Act created the federal court system and granted jurisdiction to those courts to issue writs of habeas corpus.[84] Before the D.C. Circuit in the *Boumediene*[85] appeal, however, appellants argued that in 1789, the privilege of the writ extended to aliens outside the sovereign's territory.[86]

Unfortunately, in none of the cases cited by appellants in the Circuit Court were the aliens outside the territory of the sovereign.[87] More significantly, the historical antecedents in England upon which U.S. practice is based show that the writ was simply not available in any land not the sovereign territory of the Crown. As Lord Mansfield explained in *Rex v. Cowle*,[88] cited with authority by the D.C. Circuit in *Boumediene*:[89] "To foreign dominions … this Court has no power to send any writ of any kind. We cannot send a habeas corpus to Scot-

---

82. *Id.*

83. The Suspension Clause in Article I, sec. 9, cl. 2, directs that "[t]he Privilege of the Writ of Habeas Corpus shall not be suspended, unless when in Cases of Rebellion or Invasion the public Safety may require it."

84. *See INS v. St. Cyr*, 533 U.S. 289, at 301 (2001).

85. *Supra* note 64 at 988.

86. In *Boumediene*, *supra* note 64, at 988, the appellants cited three cases for this proposition: *Lockington's Case*, Bright. (N.P.) 269 (Pa. 1813); *The Case of Three Spanish Sailors*, 96 Eng. Rep. 775 (C.P. 1779); and *Rex v. Schiever*, 97 Eng. Rep. 551 (K.B. 1759).

87. *See id.*

88. 97 Eng. Rep. (2 Burr.) 587 (K.B. 1759).

89. *Supra* note 64 at 989.

land, or to the electorate; but to Ireland, the Isle of Man, the plantations [American colonies] ... we may." Each territory that Lord Mansfield cited as a jurisdiction to which the writ extended (e.g., Ireland, the Isle of Man and the colonies) was a sovereign territory of the Crown at the time.

Given the clear history of the writ in England prior to the founding of this country, habeas corpus would not have been available to aliens in the United States in 1789 without presence or property within its territory. This is born out by the Supreme Court's 1950 decision in *Johnson v. Eisentrager*,[90] noted earlier, where the Court said: "Nothing in the text of the Constitution extends such a right, nor does anything in our statutes."[91] Similarly, the majority in *Boumediene* in 2007 observed: "We are aware of no case prior to 1789 going the detainees' way, and we are convinced that the writ in 1789 would not have been available to aliens held at an overseas military base leased from a foreign government."[92]

Notwithstanding the obvious logic of these prior cases, the Supreme Court in *Boumediene*,[93] *supra*, adopts a factor analysis approach which allows them to ignore precedent and the history of the writ's application at common law and hold that aliens held abroad at Guantanamo are subject to habeas jurisdiction.[94]

The Way Forward: Implications in Light of the *Boumediene* and *Rasul* Decisions

With the 2008 Supreme Court decision in *Boumediene, supra,* the limitations inherent in the Detainee Treatment Act (Act) of 2005[95] and the Military Commissions Act of 2006,[96] (beyond section 7 which is declared unconstitutional) are magnified and more difficult to overcome. While the extension of habeas corpus in *Boumediene* only addresses detention of enemy combatants at the U. S. Naval Base at Guantanamo, the requirements inherent in the Global

---

90. *Supra* note 2 at 768.

91. *Id.*

92. *Supra* note 64 at 990–91.

93. *Boumediene, supra* note 38.

94. *Id.*

95. *Supra* note 55, Pub. L. No. 109-148, 119 Stat 2680 (2005). Signed into law December 30, 2005.

96. *Supra* note 61, Pub. L. No. 109-366, 120 Stat. 2600 (2006). The President signed the Military Commissions Act into law on October 17, 2006.

War on Terror will likely warrant expansion of habeas corpus limitations through broader Congressional mandates and further amendment of 22 U.S.C. 2241 (habeas statute). It is clear, for example, that challenges to the detention of enemy combatants in Iraq held by the U.S. government will be the next step in the detainee litigation process.

Now that the provisions of the Detainee Treatment Act and the Military Commissions Act have been largely emasculated vis-a-vis the detainees held at Guantanamo as a result of *Boumediene*,[97] at least with respect to the right to detention hearings, these legislative enactments may no longer provide the roadmap to proscribe habeas jurisdiction for enemy combatants held elsewhere in the current conflict. For those enemy combatants held in U.S. custody in Iraq and/or Afghanistan, it is hard to believe that U.S. Courts, now that the distinction of foreign confinement is removed, will not have to face the hard question whether the insurgency in either or both nations currently constitutes a 'rebellion or invasion' against the United States. If it is not deemed to meet that standard, without legislation applicable to the specific incarceration facilities in Baghdad or Kabul, e.g., *Rasul* would appear to dictate these petitioners would have access to any of the U.S. District Courts.

The lack of any restriction on enemy combatants in terms of the forum in which they can challenge their foreign confinement, stands in stark contrast to the jurisdictional limits for domestic confinees, including U.S. citizens, who are limited to the District Court in the jurisdiction of their confinement.[98] Not only does the Court's interpretation of 22 U.S.C 2241 in *Rasul*[99] appear to grant foreign detainees access to any of the 94 federal district courts, as the key to jurisdiction is now the custodian and not the detainee, but it invites forum shopping in the most liberal fora.

A more fundamental problem arises from the impact of bringing the cumbersome machinery of our domestic courts into military affairs.[100] The obvious potentially harmful effect of the recent decisions upon the nation's conduct of war is reflected in the judicial adventurism of *Rasul, Hamdi,* and *Boumediene, supra,* where heretofore authorized actions in furtherance of the war effort are now subject to blatant judicial direction. This new approach by the courts, unless halted, threatens the historic division among the three branches, and will frustrate our military leaders' traditional reliance upon clearly stated prior law.

---

97. *Supra* note 38.

98. *See Padilla,* 542 U.S. at 426.

99. *Rasul,* 542 U.S. at 478–79.

100. *See Rasul,* 542 U.S. at 506. *See also Boumediene,* 128 S.Ct. 2306–07. In his dissent in both cases, Justice Scalia raises this and other concerns.

Chapter 4

U.S. Constitutional Issues in the Struggle Against Terror

Robert F. Turner[1]

Introduction

Some of the most controversial and interesting legal issues in the struggle against international terrorism are constitutional in character.

- May the President authorize the National Security Agency to intercept electronic communications between suspected foreign terrorists abroad and American citizens or permanent resident aliens inside the United States without "probable cause" and a judicial warrant? Does the answer change if Congress enacts legislation prohibiting such conduct without a warrant?

---

1. Robert F. Turner holds both professional and academic doctorates from the University of Virginia School of Law. He co-founded the Center for National Security Law with Professor John Norton Moore in April 1981. During 1994–95, he occupied the Charles H. Stockton Chair of International Law at the U.S. Naval War College. A veteran of two Army tours in Vietnam, he served as a Public Affairs Fellow at Stanford's Hoover Institution on War, Revolution and Peace before spending five years in the mid-1970s as national security adviser to Senator Robert P. Griffin, a member of the Senate Foreign Relations Committee. He has also served in the executive branch as a member of the Senior Executive Service, first in the Pentagon as Special Assistant to the Under Secretary of Defense for Policy, then in the White House as Counsel to the President's Intelligence Oversight Board, and at the State Department as Acting Assistant Secretary for Legislative Affairs. In 1986–87, he was the first president of the congressionally established United States Institute of Peace. A former three-term chairman of the ABA Standing Committee on Law and National Security (and for many years editor of the *ABA National Security Law Report*), Professor Turner is the author or editor of more than a dozen books and monographs, has contributed articles to most of the major U.S. newspapers, and has testified before more than a dozen different congressional committees on issues of international or constitutional law and related topics.

- If the President believes that provisions of a statute enacted by Congress are unconstitutional, may he simply declare in a "signing statement" that the statutory language will not be enforced and ignore them?
- May the President properly refuse to turn over sensitive foreign policy or military documents to Congress or the courts?
- How do we reconcile the powers of the President as "Commander in Chief" with the power of Congress to "declare War?" For example, may Congress properly prohibit the President from deploying forces being held in reserve during a period of congressionally authorized armed conflict (e.g., the various congressional efforts to block the "surge" of new forces to Iraq announced in January 2007)?
- Does the congressional "power of the purse" entitle Congress to place "conditions" on appropriations that have the effect of controlling discretionary authority vested in the President by the Constitution? Obviously, Congress has no obligation to "raise and support Armies" or "provide and maintain a Navy," and without such legislation the "Commander in Chief" has nothing to "command"; but may Congress properly create an Army on the condition that the President appoints an certain individual to be the top general or agrees not to deploy the force to a specified location?

These and many other hotly debated issues of post-9/11 political debates cannot be fully appreciated without an understanding of the separation of constitutional powers among the three branches of government.

Competing Theories

A careful reading of the Constitution reveals that it fails to mention "national security" or "foreign affairs." Indeed, many scholars have marveled at the absence of clear guidance in this important area. In his classic mid-20th century study, *The President: Office and Powers,* Princeton's Professor Edwin S. Corwin wrote: "the Constitution, considered only for its affirmative grants of powers capable of affecting the issue, is an invitation to struggle for the privilege of directing American foreign policy."[2] This chapter will discuss some of the more popular analytical approaches to the separation of constitutional powers related to the war against terrorism, concluding in the end that there is greater clarity in this field than might at first appear to be the case from a reading of the constitutional text.

---

2. Edwin S. Corwin, The President: Office and Powers 171 (4th rev. ed. 1957).

To some non-specialists—including some very able law professors who are not trained in the relatively new field of national security law—the answer to these questions may seem clear. After all, under our Constitution the Congress sets public policy by statute and the President is charged with seeing the laws "faithfully executed."[3] A central tenet of our political system is that America is governed by the "rule of law," and no one, not even the President, is "above the law." By this theory, foreign affairs is no different from domestic policy making, and while the President may have some discretion to act in settings where Congress has remained silent, once Congress sets policy by legislation the President's duty is to enforce the will of Congress, to see the laws "faithfully executed." This is a popular view in Congress, among much of the general public, and even with many respected scholars today.

Another approach is to compare the powers related to foreign affairs expressly vested by the Constitution in Congress and the President to determine which branch was intended by the Framers to be the "senior partner" in foreign affairs. Thus, former Yale University Law School Dean Harold Hongju Koh, in his prize-winning 1990 volume, *The National Security Constitution*, writes:

> One cannot read the Constitution without being struck by its astonishing brevity regarding the allocation of foreign affairs authority among the branches.... [T]he first three articles of the Constitution expressly divided foreign affairs powers among the three branches of government, with Congress, not the president, being granted the dominant role.[4]

Similarly, former Stanford Law School Dean John Hart Ely wrote in *War & Responsibility*:

> Article II grants the president but four powers bearing on foreign relations—the power to receive ambassadors (which is his alone), the powers to appoint ambassadors and make treaties (each of which must be exercised jointly, with the advice and consent of the Senate), and the power to act as commander in chief (which depends on Congress's having authorized a war ...).[5]

If there is one constitutional paradigm that might be described as the "conventional wisdom" in the early twenty-first century, it is probably the idea that

---

3. U.S. Const. Art II, Sec. 3 ("[the president] shall take Care that the Laws be faithfully executed....").

4. Harold Hongju Koh, The National Security Constitution 67, 75 (1990).

5. John Hart Ely, War and Responsibility 139 n.3 (1993).

the powers of government relative to the nation's external relations are "shared" between the Executive, Legislative, and Judicial branches. In a sense, there is merit to this approach—as many important decisions with respect to the external world do require action by both the President and either Congress or the Senate. Thus, the President may not ratify[6] a treaty without the consent of two-thirds of the Senate, he cannot engage in major offensive war without statutory authorization, and no funds may be expended from the treasury without an appropriation made by law.

The problem with the "shared powers" paradigm is that the specific roles of each political branch (Executive and Legislative) are not "shared" or interchangeable. The Senate may not "nominate" an ambassador or secretary of state, the Congress has no role in directing the actual conduct of military operations, and the President may not appropriate money. More importantly, the "shared powers" approach is at odds both with the clearly expressed intentions of the Founding Fathers and more than a century-and-a-half of consistent governmental practice.

Since the days of George Washington, Presidents have routinely claimed special authority to deal with the outside world that is largely unchecked by Congress. While contending that the Constitution gave "Congress a dominant role in the making of foreign policy," even Dean Koh acknowledges that practice from the earliest days of our history was quite contrary to this theory:

> When, in the early years of the republic, foreign sovereigns inevitably began to breach the *cordon sanitaire* that the British Royal navy had imposed between the Old and New Worlds, it quickly became apparent that the Congress was poorly structured to respond. The varied tasks of nation building—recognition of and by foreign states, establishment of diplomatic relations, and conclusion of treaties—all demanded a branch of government that could react quickly and coherently to foreign initiatives. Not only was the office of the president ideally struc-

---

6. Although it is commonly asserted that the Senate "ratifies" treaties, that language is frowned upon by experts because the term "ratify" has a special meaning in treaty law and refers to the final step by which a nation commits itself to an international agreement—typically by an exchange of instruments of ratification between the executive branches of the countries accepting the agreement or by the depositing of a formal notice that a State is becoming a treaty party with the United Nations or some other depository. Properly understood, the Constitution makes Senate "advice and consent" a condition precedent to presidential ratification of a treaty. Two-thirds of a quorum of the Senate present and voting must give their consent before the president may ratify, but even if every senator consents the president is then not in the least obligated to ratify the treaty.

tured for such responsive action, it was filled during those early years by founding presidents of unusual personal force. For that reason, the president's constitutional authorities grew rapidly during this first era.[7]

Dean Koh is certainly right that from the earliest days of the Washington administration American Presidents have exercised a great deal of independent authority over foreign affairs. But I submit he is profoundly mistaken in his assumption that this practice was a pragmatic departure from the original scheme developed in Philadelphia during the summer of 1787 and embodied in the language of our Constitution. To fully understand the constitutional separation of foreign affairs powers, it is necessary to examine the views of the fifty-five men who authored it.

When the Constitution was written it took six weeks to get a message from Europe to the United States by ship, and members of Congress had no staff to help them even draft legislation, much less keep track of what was going on in London or Paris. There were certain "institutional competencies" associated with large deliberative bodies like Congress and the Senate that made it difficult for them to play an effective role in the day-to-day conduct of diplomacy, the collection of foreign intelligence, the conduct of war, and the like. Largely because of this, the preeminent political theorists of the era—men like John Locke, the Baron de Montesquieu, and Sir William Blackstone (collectively often called the "political bibles" of the Constitutional Fathers)—reasoned that control over a nation's external affairs of necessity had to be placed within the "executive" power of government.

John Locke coined the term "federative" power to describe the control of "war, peace, leagues, and alliances"—essentially the "foreign affairs" power—and explained in his influential *Second Treaties on Civil Government* (which Thomas Jefferson once described as "perfect"[8]):

> These two Powers, Executive and Federative, though they be really distinct in themselves, yet one comprehending the Execution of the Municipal Laws of the Society within its self, upon all that are parts of it; the other the management of the security and interest of the publick without, with all those that it may receive benefit or damage from, yet they are always almost united. And though this federative Power in the well or ill management of it be of great moment to the commonwealth, yet it is much less capable to be directed by antecedent, standing, pos-

---

7. Koh, National Security Constitution 77–78.
8. 8 Writings of Thomas Jefferson 29 (Mem. ed. 1903).

itive Laws, than [by] the Executive; and so must necessarily be left to the Prudence and Wisdom of those whose hands it is in, to be managed for the publick [sic] good.... [W]hat is to be done in reference to Foreigners, depending much upon their actions, and the variation of designs and interest, must be left in great part to the Prudence of those who have this Power committed to them, to be managed by the best of their Skill, for the advantage of the Commonwealth.[9]

Montesquieu—whose *Spirit of the Laws* James Madison had studied extensively as a student at Princeton and whom Madison in *Federalist* No. 47 described as "the oracle who is always consulted and cited" on the subject of separation of powers—divided the "executive power" into the power to carry out the laws made by the legislature (the common meaning today) and "the executive [power] in respect to things dependent on the law of nations," by which the executive magistrate "makes peace or war, sends or receives embassies, establishes the public security, and provides against invasion."[10] Blackstone, whose *Commentaries on the Laws of England* were the most popular law books in colonial libraries, also included the control of foreign affairs within his definition of "executive" power.

In the early days of the Constitutional Convention, there was a good deal of opposition voiced to the creation of a strong executive. Indeed, at one point there was very strong support for the proposition that the new nation ought to have a plural executive,[11] and scholars today often quote some very anti-executive statements from Madison's *Notes* and the official *Journal* of the Convention. On Friday, June 1, 1787—the end of the first full week of substantive deliberations at the Convention—Madison provided this summary of a statement by James Wilson:

> He did not consider the Prerogatives of the British Monarch as a proper guide in defining the Executive powers. Some of these prerogatives were of a Legislative nature. Among others that of war & peace &c. The only powers he conceived strictly Executive were those of executing the laws, and appointing officers not (appertaining to and) appointed by the Legislature.[12]

Later that same day, Madison recorded:

---

9. John Locke, Second Treatise on Civil Government § 147.

10. 1 Montesquieu, The Spirit of Laws 151–52 (Charles T. Nugent, trans. 1949).

11. 1 Max Farrand, Records of the Federal Convention of 1787 at 97. Madison's *Notes* are *available at* http://www.yale.edu/lawweb/avalon/debates/601.htm.

12. *Id.* at 65–66.

> Mr. Sherman was for the appointment [of the executive] by the Legislature, and for making him absolutely dependent on that body, as it was the will of that which was to be executed. An independence of the Executive on the supreme Legislative, was in his opinion the very essence of tyranny if there was any such thing.[13]

These are indeed strong statements, but they were atypical and were made in the very early days of the Convention. One of the classic treatises on this topic was originally done as a Ph.D. dissertation at Johns Hopkins University. Dr. Charles Thach explained in *The Creation of the Presidency*:

> The idea, more than once utilized as the basis of the explanation of Article II of the Constitution, that the jealousy of kingship was a controlling force in the Federal Convention, is far, very far, from the truth. The majority of the delegates brought with them no far-reaching distrust of executive power, but rather a sobering consciousness that, if their new plan should succeed, it was necessary for them to put forth their best efforts to secure a strong, albeit safe, national executive.
>
> Madison expressed the general conservative view when he declared on the Convention floor:
>
>> Experience had proved a tendency in our governments to throw all power into the legislative vortex. The Executives of the States are in general little more than cyphers; the legislatures omnipotent. If no effective check be devised for restraining the instability and encroachment of the latter, a revolution of some kind or the other would be inevitable.[14]

Article II, Section 1, of the final Constitution provided: "The executive Power shall be vested in a President of the United States of America." That the Founding Fathers understood "executive power" as that term was used by writers like Montesquieu and Blackstone is absolutely clear from a variety of unambiguous statements recorded for posterity. In the early days of the First Congress, Representative James Madison introduced a bill to establish a Department of Foreign Affairs (later redesignated the Department of State). A dispute arose over where the Constitution had placed the power to remove a cabinet officer, and Madison carried the day with this argument:

> The constitution affirms, that the executive power shall be vested in the President. Are there exceptions to this proposition? Yes, there are.

---

13. *Id.* at 68.

14. Charles Thach, *The Creation of the Presidency 1775–1789* at 52 (1922).

The constitution says, that in appointing to office, the Senate shall be associated with the President, unless in the case of inferior officers, when the law shall otherwise direct. Have we a right to extend this exception? I believe not. If the constitution has invested all executive power in the President, I venture to assert that the Legislature has no right to diminish or modify his executive authority.[15]

That the "executive" power included the general control over foreign affairs in the eyes of the Founding Fathers is also clear. Madison's friend and mentor, Thomas Jefferson, was in Paris when the Constitution was written. But shortly after returning to America to learn he had already been confirmed by the Senate as the nation's first Secretary of Foreign Affairs, Jefferson wrote to President Washington:

The constitution has divided the powers of government into three branches, Legislative, Executive and Judiciary, lodging each with a distinct magistracy. The Legislative it has given completely to the Senate and House of [R]epresentatives: it has declared that 'the Executive powers shall be vested in the President,' submitting only special articles of it to a negative by the Senate; and it has vested the Judiciary power in the courts of justice, with certain exceptions also in favor of the Senate.

The transaction of business with foreign nations is executive altogether; it belongs, then, to the head of that department, *except* as to such portions of it as are specially submitted to the senate. *Exceptions* are to be construed strictly....[16]

Just three days later, Washington noted in his diary that Madison and Chief Justice John Jay agreed with Jefferson that the Senate had "no constitutional right to interfere"[17] in the business of diplomacy save for the exceptions identified by Jefferson. And three years later, Jefferson's chief rival in Washington's cabinet made the same argument embraced earlier by Madison and Jefferson:

The general doctrine then of our constitution is, that the EXECUTIVE POWER of the Nation is vested in the President; subject only to the exceptions and qu[a]lifications which are expressed in the instrument....

It deserves to be remarked, that as the participation of the Senate in the making of Treaties, and the power of the Legislature to declare

---

15. 1 ANNALS OF CONGRESS 481.
16. 16 PAPERS OF THOMAS JEFFERSON 378–79 (1961) (emphasis in original).
17. 4 GEORGE WASHINGTON DIARIES 122 (J. Fitzpatrick, ed. 1925).

war, are exceptions out of the general "Executive Power" vested in the President, they are to be construed strictly—and ought to be extended no further than is essential to their execution.[18]

In his classic 1922 treatise, *The Control of American Foreign Policy*, Professor Quincy Wright explained that "Thus when the constitutional convention gave 'executive power' to the President, the foreign relations power was the essential element in the grant, but they carefully protected this power from abuse by provisions for senatorial or congressional veto."[19] In a similar vein five decades later, Columbia Law School Professor Louis Henkin observed: "The executive power ... was not defined because it was well understood by the Framers raised on Locke, Montesquieu and Blackstone."[20]

Foreign affairs were different from domestic affairs. Professor Wright explained: "In foreign affairs, therefore, the controlling force is the reverse of that in domestic legislation. The initiation and development of details is with the president, checked only by the veto of the Senate or Congress upon completed proposals."[21]

Throughout most of our history, this was the common understanding. During the election of 1800, one of the key issues in Congress was a Republican resolution criticizing President John Adams for having surrendered a British deserter found in the United States under the provisions of an extradition clause in the 1794 Jay Treaty without involving the judiciary. Virginia Federalist John Marshall—later to serve as perhaps the most famous Chief Justice in American history   carried the day even with many Republicans when he reasoned the President was "the sole organ of the nation in its external relations" because "[h]e possesses the whole Executive power."[22] As will be discussed, this language has repeatedly been cited with approval by the Supreme Court.[23]

Early congressional deference to the President in foreign affairs was reflected in the very first appropriation for foreign intercourse. In language repeated for many years thereafter, the statute provided:

> [T]he President shall account specifically for all such expenditures of the said money as in his judgment may be made public, and also for the amount of such expenditures as he may think it advisable not to

---

18. 15 THE PAPERS OF ALEXANDER HAMILTON 38–42 (H. Syrett ed. 1969).
19. QUINCY WRIGHT, THE CONTROL OF AMERICAN FOREIGN RELATIONS 147 (1922).
20. LOUIS HENKIN, FOREIGN AFFAIRS AND THE CONSTITUTION 43 (1972).
21. WRIGHT, THE CONTROL OF AMERICAN FOREIGN RELATIONS 149–50.
22. 1 ANNALS OF CONG. 613 (Gales ed., 1851).
23. *See, e.g., United States v. Curtiss-Wright Export Corp.*, 299 U.S. 304, 319 (1936).

specify, and cause a regular statement and account thereof to be laid before Congress annually...."[24]

Indeed, the consistent practice during the new Nation's first fifteen years was explained in a letter from President Thomas Jefferson to his Secretary of the Treasury, Albert Gallatin:

> The Constitution has made the Executive the organ for managing our intercourse with foreign nations.... The Executive being thus charged with the foreign intercourse, no law has undertaken to prescribe its specific duties.... From the origin of the present government to this day.... it has been the uniform opinion and practice that the whole foreign fund was placed by the Legislature on the footing of a contingent fund, in which they undertake no specifications, but leave the whole to the discretion of the President.[25]

When the Senate first created a Committee on Foreign Relations in 1816, one of its first reports observed: "The President is the constitutional representative of the United States with regard to foreign nations."[26] As recently as 1959, Senate Foreign Relations Committee Chairman J. William Fulbright declared in a lecture at Cornell Law School: "The pre-eminent *responsibility* of the President for the formulation and conduct of American foreign policy is clear and unalterable. He has, as Alexander Hamilton defined it, all powers in international affairs 'which the Constitution does not vest elsewhere in clear terms.' "[27] As will be discussed below, all of this changed a decade later. But first it is useful to consider some of the more important Supreme Court cases in these areas.

Judicial Guidance

Because through most of our history Congress has been deferential to the President on matters of diplomacy, intelligence, and the conduct of war, there has not been a lot of litigation in this area. But cases have made their way to the Supreme Court from time to time, and the Court has traditionally been deferential to presidential power in these areas.

---

24. 1 Stat. 28 (1789).

25. 11 WRITINGS OF THOMAS JEFFERSON 5, 9, 10 (Mem. ed. 1903).

26. 10 ANNALS OF CONG. 613 (1800).

27. J. William Fulbright, *American Foreign Policy in the 20th Century Under an 18th-Century Constitution*, 47 CORNELL L. Q. 1, 3, (1961) (emphasis in original).

Perhaps the most famous Supreme Court cases of all times is *Marbury v. Madison* (1803), in which Chief Justice John Marshall declared:

> By the constitution of the United States, the President is invested with certain important political powers, in the exercise of which he is to use his own discretion, and is accountable only to his country in his political character, and to his own conscience.... [A]nd whatever opinion may be entertained of the manner in which executive discretion may be used, still there exists, and can exist, no power to control that discretion. The subjects are political. They respect the nation, not individual rights, and being entrusted to the executive, the decision of the executive is conclusive.[28]

To illustrate this point, Chief Justice Marshall continued:

> The application of this remark will be perceived by adverting to the act of congress for establishing the department of foreign affairs. This officer, as his duties were prescribed by that act, is to conform precisely to the will of the president. He is the mere organ by whom that will is communicated. The acts of such an officer, as an officer, can never be examinable by the courts.[29]

It is important here to note that Chief Justice Marshall was clearly not saying that foreign policy decisions are "shared" powers, or that the President has authority to act so long as Congress does not direct otherwise. He declared that certain decisions concerning "the nation" and "foreign affairs"—and not involving the rights of individuals—were entrusted *exclusively* to the discretion of the President, and there exists "no power to control that discretion"—no power in the courts, and no power in Congress.

Perhaps the most famous, and certainly the most frequently cited, Supreme Court foreign policy case is *United States v. Curtiss-Wright Export Corporation*, where in 1936 the Court expounded at length about the constitutional separation of powers in the foreign affairs realm:

> Not only, as we have shown, is the federal power over external affairs in origin and essential character different from that over internal affairs, but participation in the exercise of the power is significantly limited. In this vast external realm, with its important, complicated, delicate and manifold problems, the President alone has the power to

---

28. *Marbury v. Madison*, 5 U.S. [1 Cranch] 137, 165–66 (1803) (emphasis added).
29. *Id.* at 166.

speak or listen as a representative of the nation. He makes treaties with the advice and consent of the Senate; but he alone negotiates. *Into the field of negotiation the Senate cannot intrude, and Congress itself is powerless to invade it.* As Marshall said in his great argument of March 7, 1800, in the House of Representatives, "The President is the sole organ of the nation in its external relations, and its sole representative with foreign nations.".…

It is important to bear in mind that we are here dealing not alone with an authority vested in the President by an exertion of legislative power, but with such an authority plus the very delicate, plenary and *exclusive power of the President as the sole organ of the federal government in the field of international relations*—a power which does not require as a basis for its exercise an act of Congress but which, of course, like every other governmental power, must be exercised in subordination to the applicable provisions of the Constitution.[30]

The statements "Congress itself is powerless to invade it" and "plenary and exclusive power of the President as the sole organ of the federal government in the field of international relations" are consistent with Chief Justice Marshall's theory that there exists "no power to control" presidential discretion over foreign affairs beyond the narrowly-construed negatives vested in the Senate and Congress. As we have seen, the idea the presidential authority in this area is exclusive—save, again, for the specific "exceptions" expressly vested elsewhere—was also embraced by Washington, Jefferson, Madison, and Jay in 1790 and by Hamilton three years later.

While *Curtiss-Wright* is not the only case in the foreign affairs area, it is by far the most frequently cited. And it has often been cited for the proposition that the President is "exclusively responsible" for the "conduct of foreign affairs"[31]; and that "This Court also has recognized 'the generally accepted view that foreign policy was the province and responsibility of the Executive."[32]

In 1947, reaffirming a principle that goes back to *Marbury* in 1803, the Supreme Court declared:

[T]he very nature of executive decisions as to foreign policy is political, not judicial. Such decisions are.… of a kind for which the Judiciary has neither aptitude, facilities nor responsibility and have long

---

30. *United States v. Curtiss-Wright Export Corp.*, 299 U.S. 304, 319–20 (1936) (emphasis added).
31. *Johnson v. Eisentrager*, 339 U.S. 763 (1950) (emphasis added).
32. *Haig v. Agee*, 453 U.S. 280, 293–94 (1981).

been held to belong in the domain of political power not subject to judicial intrusion or inquiry....

We conclude that.... the final orders embody presidential discretion as to political matters beyond the competence of the courts to adjudicate.[33]

A Forgotten History and Paradigm Shift During the Vietnam War

Indeed, such statements were the accepted norm until the later years of the Vietnam War. It is almost as if America had a hard-drive meltdown as the nation tore itself asunder over that tragic conflict, and by 1973 neither Congress nor the Executive Branch were referring much to the grant of "executive Power" as a source of presidential authority in this area. Congress began legislating in areas it and the judiciary had traditionally recognized as the constitutional province of the executive.

In 1973, congress enacted the War Powers Resolution over a presidential veto, asserting authority to control military deployments in settings short of "war." The following year, with passage of the Hughes-Ryan Amendment, Congress demanded access to highly-classified intelligence secrets that for more than 180 years had been viewed as the exclusive province of the Executive.

It is worth noting that the Supreme Court has repeatedly given great weight to unbroken historic practice. In *Burrow-Giles Lithographic Co. v. Sarony,* the Court declared in 1884:

> The construction placed upon the constitution by ... [acts passed between 1790 and 1802], by the men who were contemporary with its formation, many of whom were members of the convention which framed it, is of itself entitled to very great weight, and when it is remembered that the rights thus established have not been disputed during a period of nearly a century, it is almost conclusive.[34]

Similarly, in 1981, the Court majority in *Dames & Moore v. Regan*[35] quoted this language from Justice Felix Frankfurter's concurring opinion in *Youngstown*

---

33. *Chicago & Southern Airlines v. Waterman*, 333 U.S. 103, 111, 114 (1948). *See also, United States v. Belmont*, 301 U.S. 324, 328 (1937); *Haig v. Agee*, 453 U.S. 280 ("Matters intimately related to foreign policy and national security are rarely proper subjects for judicial intervention"), 292 (1981); and *Department of the Navy v. Egan*, 484 U.S. 518 (1988).

34. *Burrow-Giles Lithographic Co. v. Sarony*, 111 U.S. 53, 57 (1884).

35. *Dames & Moore v. Regan*, 453 U.S 654, 686 (1981).

Sheet & Tube Co. v. Sawyer (an important case that will be discussed in greater detail below):

> [A] systematic, unbroken, executive practice, long pursued to the knowledge of the Congress and never before questioned, engaged in by Presidents who have also sworn to uphold the Constitution, making as it were such exercise of power part of the structure of our government, may be treated as a gloss on 'executive Power' vested in the President by § 1 of Art. II.[36]

But the historical understanding of "executive power" shared by all three branches had apparently been forgotten by 1973, and soon thereafter, following public hearings in both the House and Senate during which past abuses by agencies of the Intelligence Community were disclosed, both houses established permanent intelligence committees and began demanding more sensitive information. In 1978, Congress enacted the Foreign Intelligence Surveillance Act (FISA), prohibiting the President from engaging in electronic surveillance of even known foreign spies within the United States without a warrant from a newly established federal court.

Many Americans welcomed this greater congressional involvement in foreign affairs, believing that earlier legislators who had failed to supervise such activities had been derelict in their duty. Oblivious to the theory that (subject to certain narrowly-construed negatives vested in Congress and the Senate), the Nation's external relations were confided exclusively in the President, the new congressional activism seemed more than appropriate.

A mythology developed in the later years of the Vietnam War that contributed to support for this new activism and continues to affect the legal debates even today. A detailed discussion of that controversy is beyond the scope of this chapter, but it may be useful to keep a few facts in mind. For example, in 1955, with only a sole dissenting vote, the Senate consented to the ratification of the SEATO Treaty in which the United States agreed that it would "act to meet the common danger in accordance with its constitutional processes" in the event of an armed attack against a "protocol state"—i.e., South Vietnam, Laos, or Cambodia—to the treaty.

For many years there was a heated debate about whether Communist North Vietnam was behind the "National Liberation Front" (or "Viet Cong") effort to overthrow the government of South Vietnam by armed force; but, after the war ended, Hanoi repeatedly bragged about the May 1959 decision of its Com-

---

36. *Youngstown Sheet & Tube Co. v. Sawyer*, 343 U.S. at 610–11 (Frankfurter, J. concurring).

munist party to open the Ho Chi Minh Trail and send troops and supplies south to "liberate" South Vietnam.[37] Those who assert "Vietnam" was a "senseless" or "unnecessary" war need to consider that Communist leaders from Beijing to Havana declared it to be a "test case" that would pave the way for insurgency warfare throughout the Third World. Thus, Chinese Communist Party Central Committee Vice Chairman Lin Biao declared that, if the Americans lost in Vietnam, "[t]he people in other parts of the world will see still more clearly that U.S. imperialism can be defeated, and that what the Vietnamese people can do, they can do too."[38] Simply walking away from Indochina in 1965 might well have led an outbreak of Communist directed, supplied, and funded guerrilla wars across the Third World.

In response to Hanoi's aggression, in August 1964 Congress by a combined vote of 504-to-2 (a 99.6% majority) enacted a statute that authorized the President to "take all necessary steps, including the use of armed force, to assist any member *or protocol state* of the Southeast Asia Collective Defense Treaty requesting assistance in defense of its freedom."[39] That this was intended by Congress to authorized the President if he deemed it necessary to take the nation to "war" is clear from the debate,[40] as is the fact that the statute authorized the defense of Cambodia as well as South Vietnam—both "protocol states" of the SEATO Treaty.

But the conventional wisdom today is that—just as President Truman allegedly dragged the Nation kicking and screaming into the Korean War without involving Congress and against public opinion (and for the record, both claims are false[41])—President Johnson went to war in Indochina without pub-

---

37. *See, e.g., The Legendary Ho Chi Minh Trail,* VIETNAM COURIER (Hanoi), vol. XX, no. 5, May 1984 at 9.

38. LIN PIAO, LONG LIVE THE VICTORY OF PEOPLE'S WAR (Peking: Foreign Languages Press 58 (1965).

39. *Joint Resolution To Promote the Maintenance of International Peace and Security in Southeast Asia* (Gulf of Tonkin Resolution), Pub. L. No. 88-408, 78 Stat. 384 (1964) (emphasis added).

40. *See, e.g.,* the exchange in which Senator John Sherman-Cooper, the Republican floor leader supporting the resolution, asked Senator J. William Fulbright whether by enacting the resolution Congress would "authorize the president to use such force as could lead into war," and the Foreign Relations Committee chairman (who had introduced the resolution) responded: "That is the way I would interpret it." 110 CONG. REC. 18,409 (1964).

41. In fairness, despite subsequent attacks from Republicans, Truman played the Korean conflict by the book. He repeatedly asked to address a joint session of Congress and had the State Department draft an authorization for the use of military force. But he decided not to push the idea when in consultation with congressional leaders he was repeatedly told to stay away from Congress and assured he had the power to send troops into hostilities pursuant to the Constitution and the UN Charter. And as for public support, the initial

lic support or legislative authorization. This is simply not true. Indeed, LBJ's approval rating in the Gallup Polls shot up 58 percent—a jump of 30 full points—in the month surrounding his first serious use of airpower against North Vietnam in August 1964.

Regardless of what actually occurred in Indochina, the angry debate at home produced a new generation of scholars and a substantial portion of the public determined to rein in perceived Executive abuse of power. As in Korea in 1950, the more people heard that their President believed he was "above the law" the more anxious they were to force him back on the constitutional reservation.

The real issue, of course, is not whether the President is "above the law," but rather *which* law the President is to see "faithfully executed" when confronted by a statute that is contrary to the Constitution itself. In the landmark 1803 *Marbury* decision, Chief Justice Marshall wrote for the Court majority: "a legislative act contrary to the constitution is not law:.... an act of the legislature, repugnant to the constitution, is void." Ergo, the President has no duty to see such an act faithfully executed—and, even if a contrary case could be argued, any such duty would be clearly subordinate to the duty in Article II, Section 1, to "preserve, protect and defend the Constitution...."

"Shared Powers," Harold Koh, and the *Youngstown* "Steel-Seizure" Case

In the angry aftermath of the Vietnam War, it was perhaps not surprising that young scholars were attracted to constitutional interpretations that would reduce unchecked Executive power and might in so doing prevent future "Vietnams." Among the more able of these young scholars was a Yale Law School professor named Harold Hongju Koh, who went on to become Dean of Yale Law School.

Although the *Curtiss-Wright* case has been the most often-cited foreign affairs case for more than seventy years, even before Vietnam the idea of largely unchecked Executive power troubles many scholars. Several articles were written over the years noting that Justice George Sutherland, in writing for the *Curtiss-Wright* majority, went beyond the requirements of the case (which involved a setting where Congress and the President were on the same side), and

---

polls showed roughly 80% of the American people favored using force to protect South Korea. *See* Robert F. Turner, *Truman, Korea, and the Constitution: Debunking the "Imperial President" Myth.* 19 HARV. J. L. & PUB. POL. 533 (1996).

thus these statements constituted *obiter dicta* and are not binding on other courts.

While this is technically correct, the *Curtiss-Wright dictum* that the President is the "sole organ" in foreign affairs has been repeatedly ratified by Supreme Court majorities over the past seven decades. In 1990 Professor Koh published a highly-acclaimed volume that attempted to dismiss *Curtiss-Wright* on a different theory: that it had been effectively overturned by the more recent 1952 case of *Youngstown Sheet & Tube Co. v. Sawyer.* Dean Koh's *The National Security Constitution* has had a tremendous impact upon scholarship in this area, and it is important for those seeking to understand this issue to be familiar with his argument.

He does not merely try to dismiss *Curtiss-Wright.* Dean Koh contends that the Founding Fathers gave the bulk of foreign affairs powers to Congress rather than the Executive, but Presidents managed to usurp that authority from the beginning. He writes:

> At the Republic's birth, the Framers deliberately drafted a Constitution of shared powers and balanced institutional participation, fully aware of the risks that arrangement posed to the nation's international well-being. By mandating that separated institutions share powers in foreign as well as domestic affairs, the Framers determined that we must sacrifice some short-term gains for speed, secrecy, and efficiency in favor of the longer-term consensus that derives from reasoned interbranch consultation and participatory decision making. Although in the early years of the Republic, all three branches condoned a de facto transformation of the original National Security Constitution from a scheme of congressional primacy to one of executive primacy, they never rejected the concept of power sharing and institutional participation....[42]

He asserts that *Curtiss-Wright* radically changed the historic paradigm:

> In 1936, *Curtiss-Wright's* dicta boldly asserted the alternative vision of unfettered presidential management. But even as the Cold War raged, the 1947 National Security Act, *Youngstown,* and finally the post-Vietnam era framework statutes (e.g., War Powers Resolution) definitively rejected that vision as America's constitutional model for dealing with the outside world. Vietnam (and Watergate, as well, to the extent that it arose from Vietnam) then taught that even in a nu-

---

42. Harold Hongku Koh, The National Security Constitution 211 (1990).

clear age, America would not conduct globalism at the price of constitutionalism. It is therefore ironic that the *Curtiss-Wright* model should now resurface....[43]

In reality, in the decades following *Youngstown* the Supreme Court continued to rely upon *Curtiss-Wright* as the prevailing foreign affairs paradigm—as is true today. If its status in that role was in any way weakened by *Youngstown*, someone clearly forgot to tell the Supreme Court, which continues to cite *Curtiss-Wright* more than any other case dealing with foreign affairs more than half-a-century after *Youngstown*.[44]

We have seen that there was a broad consensus among key Founders that Congress and the Senate were to be excluded from many decisions in the foreign affairs realm, and the powers they were given in this area were viewed as *exceptions* to the general grant of "executive Power" vested in the President and thus were intended to be construed strictly. In contrast, ignoring this history (which, in fairness, he does not appear to have known), without any effort to document his assertion, Professor Koh simply asserts to his readers: "the first three articles of the Constitution expressly divided foreign affairs powers among the three branches of government, with Congress, not the President, being granted the dominant role."[45] And to be fair, this has almost certainly become the modern conventional wisdom. Elsewhere in *The National Security Constitution*, Professor Koh writes:

> This structural vision of a foreign affairs power shared through balanced institutional participation has inspired the National Security Constitution since the beginning of the Republic, receiving its most cogent expression in Justice Robert Jackson's famous 1952 concurring opinion in *Youngstown*. Yet throughout our constitutional history, what I call the *Youngstown* vision has done battle with a radically different constitutional paradigm. This counter image of *unchecked executive discretion* has claimed virtually the entire field of foreign affairs as falling under the president's inherent authority. Although this image has surfaced from time to time since the early Republic, it did not fully and officially crystallize until Justice George Sutherland's con-

---

43. *Id.* at 211–12.

44. A 2009 WestLaw search reveals that *Curtiss-Wright* has been relied upon in Supreme Court cases in five of the last seven years. *See, e.g., Pasquantino v. United States*, 544 U.S. 349, 369 (2005) ("In our system of government, the Executive is "the sole organ of the federal government in the field of international relations," *United States v. Curtiss-Wright*....").

45. *Id.* at 75.

troversial, oft-cited 1936 opinion for the Court in *United States v. Curtiss-Wright Export Corp.* As construed by proponents of executive power, the *Curtiss-Wright* vision rejects two of *Youngstown's* central tenets, that the National Security Constitution requires congressional concurrence in most decisions on foreign affairs and that the courts must play an important role in examining and constraining executive branch judgments in foreign affairs.[46]

Candidly, one must wonder if Dean Koh has carefully *read* Justice Jackson's *Youngstown* concurrence, or the majority opinion in the case written by Justice Hugo Black. For both went to great lengths to emphasize that they were *not* endeavoring to constrain the powers of the President in dealing with the external world. At issue in *Youngstown* was whether the President's "war powers" (in a conflict Jackson noted had not been approved by Congress[47]) authorized Truman to order the Secretary of the Interior to seize domestic steel mills—the *private property* of American citizens—in order to prevent a labor strike that might affect the availability of steel for the Korean War. (Keep in mind that the Fifth Amendment guarantees that "[n]o person shall ... be deprived of ... property, without due process of law....")

There is no reason to believe that Justice Jackson was in the slightest way hostile to *Curtiss-Wright* as the appropriate *foreign policy* paradigm. On the contrary, just two years before *Youngstown*, Jackson wrote for the Court majority in *Johnson v. Eisentrager*:

> Certainly it is not the function of the Judiciary to entertain private litigation—even by a citizen—which challenges the legality, the wisdom, or the propriety of the Commander-in-Chief in sending our armed forces abroad or to any particular region.... The issue ... involves a challenge to conduct of diplomatic and foreign affairs, for which the President is *exclusively* responsible. *United States v. Curtiss-Wright Corp....*[48]

Consider also this excerpt from Justice Black's majority opinion in *Youngstown*:

> The order cannot properly be sustained as an exercise of the President's military power as Commander-in-Chief of the Armed Forces. The Government attempts to do so by citing a number of cases upholding broad powers in military commanders engaged in day-to-day fight-

---

46. *Id.* at 72.
47. *See supra*, note 40.
48. 339 U.S. 763 (1950) (emphasis added).

ing in a theater of war. Such cases need not concern us here. Even though "theater of war" be an expanding concept, we cannot with faithfulness to our constitutional system hold that the Commander in Chief of the Armed Forces had the ultimate power as such to take possession of *private property* in order to keep labor disputes from stopping production. This is a job for the Nation's lawmakers, not for its military authorities.[49]

Similarly, Justice Jackson in *Youngstown* was very deferential to presidential power with respect to the external world:

[N]o doctrine that the Court could promulgate would seem to be more sinister and alarming than that a President whose conduct of *foreign* affairs is so largely uncontrolled, and often is even unknown, can vastly enlarge his mastery over the *internal* affairs of the country by his own commitment of the Nation's armed forces to some foreign adventure....

That military powers of the Commander in Chief were not to supersede representative government of *internal* affairs seems obvious from the Constitution and from elementary American history.... Such a limitation [the Third Amendment] on the command power, written at a time when the militia rather than a standing army was contemplated as a military weapon of the Republic, underscores the Constitution's policy that Congress, not the Executive, should control utilization of the war power as an instrument of *domestic* policy....

We should not use this occasion to circumscribe, much less to contract, the lawful role of the President as Commander in Chief. I should indulge the widest latitude of interpretation to sustain his *exclusive* function to command the instruments of national force, at least when turned against the *outside* world for the security of our society. But, when it is turned *inward*, not because of rebellion but because of a lawful economic struggle between industry and labor, it should have no such indulgence.... What the power of command may include I do not try to envision, but I think it is not a military prerogative, without support of law, to seize person or property because they are important or even essential for the military or naval establishment.[50]

---

49. 343 U.S. 579, 587 (1952) (emphasis added).
50. *Id.* at 642, 644, 645 (emphasis added).

Even more fundamentally, in *Youngstown* Justice Jackson actually cited *Curtiss-Wright*, but then explained in a footnote: "That case does not solve the present controversy. It recognized internal and external affairs as being in separate categories...."[51] And as both Justice Black and Jackson repeatedly emphasized, *Youngstown* was an "internal affairs" case.

That is also the consensus of scholars like Columbia Law School's Professor Louis Henkin, who in *Foreign Affairs and the Constitution* noted:

> *Youngstown* has not been considered a "foreign affairs case." The President claimed to be acting within "the aggregate of his constitutional powers," but the majority of the Supreme Court did not treat the case as involving the reach of his foreign affairs power, and even the dissenting justices invoked only incidentally that power or the fact that the steel strike threatened important American foreign policy interests.[52]

Consider also the reaction of Justice Rehnquist, joined by Chief Justice Burger and two other members of the Court, in the 1979 dispute over President Carter's constitutional power to terminate the mutual security treaty between the United States and Taiwan. Senator Goldwater had urged the Court to decide the case on *Youngstown*, but Rehnquist wrote:

> The present case differs in several important respects from *Youngstown* ... cited by petitioners as authority both for reaching the merits of this dispute and for reversing the Court of Appeals. In *Youngstown*, private litigants brought a suit contesting the President's authority under his war powers to seize the Nation's steel industry, an action of profound and demonstrable *domestic* impact.... Moreover, as in *Curtiss-Wright*, the effect of this action, as far as we can tell, is "entirely *external* to the United States, and [falls] within the category of *foreign affairs*.[53]

Thus, my own conclusion after four decades of scholarly work in this area is that Professor Koh—and, because his work has been so influential on other scholars, their writings as well—has profoundly misunderstood the significance of the *Youngstown* case; and *Curtiss-Wright* continues to prevail as the seminal decision on the separation of foreign affairs cases. Put simply, the two cases are not in conflict. *Youngstown* controls governmental acts within the United States that in-

---

51. *Id.* at 637 n.2.
52. Henkin, Foreign Affairs and the Constitution 341 n.11.
53. *Goldwater v. Carter* 444 U.S. 996 (1979) (emphasis added).

volve private property seizures and similar primarily domestic or internal matters, while *Curtiss-Wright* addresses government behavior towards the external world.

Obviously, not every case falls into a hermetically sealed category. Indeed, as will be discussed in other chapters of this volume, the Supreme Court has since 9/11 been called upon to address several major cases involving both the President's power during wartime and the rights of individuals detained at Guantanamo Bay and elsewhere as "enemy combatants." The vociferous dissents found in those opinions have demonstrated that honest and able legal scholars can differ on precisely where lines need to be drawn, but it is nevertheless useful to bear in mind this fundamental distinction between domestic and foreign affairs as we examine some of the recent controversies.

Warrantless "Wiretaps" and the Foreign Intelligence Surveillance Act

Prior to the 1970s, there was a broad consensus in all three branches that—to quote John Jay in *Federalist* No. 64—the Constitution had left the "business of intelligence" to be managed exclusively by the President "as prudence may suggest." We have already discussed the early appropriations statutes that expressly permitted the President to conceal the purposes for which such expenditures were made from Congress if he felt they could not safely be made public. During an 1818 floor debate in the House of Representatives, the legendary Henry Clay declared that it would not be "proper" for Congress to inquire into expenditures from the President's foreign affairs account, and this view was embraced by others and challenged by none.

As recently as 1968, when the Congress enacted the first statute regulating "wiretapping," it included language in the bill expressly exempting the independent constitutional authority of the President in this area:

> Nothing contained in this chapter ... shall limit the *constitutional power of the President* to take such measures as he deems necessary to protect the Nation against actual or potential attack or other hostile acts of a foreign power, *to obtain foreign intelligence information* deemed essential to the security of the United States, *or to protect national security information* against foreign intelligence activities.[54]

---

54. 18 USC §2511(3) (1970) (emphasis added).

It should be noted that the courts as well were deferential to presidential power in this area. For example, when the Supreme Court for the first time in the 1967 *Katz* case held that a wiretap was a "seizure" under the Fourth Amendment and thus required a judicial warrant, it includes a footnote in the decisions declaring: "Whether safeguards other than prior authorization by a magistrate would satisfy the Fourth Amendment in a situation involving the national security is a question not presented by this case."[55]

Five years later, the Court in the *Keith* case held that when the target of a national security investigation was an American with no known or suspected ties to a foreign power, a warrant would be required. But, writing for the unanimous Court, Justice Lewis Powell repeatedly emphasized that the case did not involve the collection of *foreign* intelligence information: "Further, the instant case requires no judgment on the scope of the President's surveillance power with respect to the activities of *foreign powers, within or without this country*."[56] Powell found the distinction important enough to reemphasize it near the end of the opinion:

> We emphasize, before concluding this opinion, the scope of our decision. As stated at the outset, this case involves only the *domestic* aspects of national security. We have not addressed and express no opinion as to, the issues which may be involved with respect to *activities of foreign powers or their agents.*[57]

Recognizing that the grounds required for a domestic national security wiretap warrant might differ from those for more traditional criminal warrants, Justice Powell wrote: "Given those potential distinctions between Title III criminal surveillances and those involving the *domestic* security, Congress may wish to consider protective standards for *the latter* which differ from those already prescribed for specified crimes in Title III."[58] However, Congress used this "invitation" that they legislate standards for purely *domestic* national security wiretaps to gain control over the collection of *foreign* intelligence inside U.S. borders—an authority long recognized as the exclusive province of the executive.

When the Foreign Intelligence Surveillance Act (FISA) was pending before the Congress, Carter Administration Attorney General Griffin Bell observed during testified before the House Permanent Select Committee on Intelligence that the bill failed to recognize the President's inherent constitutional power

---

55. *Katz v. United States*, 389 U. S. 347, 358 n. 23 (1967).

56. *United States v. United States District Court*, 407 U.S. 297, 308 (1972) (emphasis added).

57. *Id.* at 321–22 (emphasis added).

58. *Id.* at 322–23 (emphasis added).

to conduct electronic surveillance and emphasized that a statute could not "take away the power of the President under the Constitution." However, he explained, it was not necessary to define the limits of that power, because President Carter, "by offering this legislation, is agreeing to follow the statutory procedure."[59] That was certainly President Carter's prerogative, but he did not have the power to sign away the constitutional discretion of future Presidents.

The saddest part of the ill-informed debate over the "warrantless wiretapping" controversy is that it undermined U.S. security on purely procedural grounds. Clearly, just as congressional and senatorial powers "must be exercised in subordination to the applicable provisions of the Constitution,"[60] the President's inherent power to authorize the collection of foreign intelligence information must be exercised consistent with the Fourth Amendment's prohibition against "unreasonable" searches and seizures. But no serious person has argued that it is "unreasonable" to monitor the communications of our nation's foreign enemies during time of congressionally-authorized war. And presumably it is even more critical to monitor such communications when our enemies are talking with people inside this country. In criminal law, if the government has a warrant permitting it to listen to one side of a telephone conversation we permit it to record all sides — and to use the statements of anyone communicating with the subject of a lawful warrant against them in court without the slightest preexisting probable cause that they were breaking the law. Their constitutional rights essentially become "collateral damage" once the government has obtained a warrant to monitor the communications of another party to the conversation. Yet when the issue becomes protecting the nation from a potentially catastrophic terrorist attack, the critics demand a higher standard than they do for cases involving white-collar criminals.

No member of the Senate or House Judiciary Committees has argued that America should not monitor the communications of al Qaeda members, whether they are located in Afghanistan or in Alabama. No one has said monitoring such communications is "unreasonable" under the Fourth Amendment. The issue, as the critics see it, is whether the President can "ignore the law" by authorizing intercepts outside the framework of FISA.

---

59. Testimony of Attorney General Griffin Bell, FOREIGN INTELLIGENCE ELECTRONIC SURVEILLANCE, HEARINGS BEFORE THE SUBCOMMITTEE ON LEGISLATION OF THE PERMANENT SELECT COMMITTEE ON INTELLIGENCE, HOUSE OF REPRESENTATIVES, January 10, 1978 at 14–15.

60. *United States v. Curtiss-Wright Export Corp.*, 299 U.S. 304, 319–20 (1936), quoted in text, *supra* at note 30.

The real issue here is whether the grant of "executive Power" to the President (or, alternatively, since we are in a period of congressionally-authorized armed conflict, the "commander-in-chief" power given the President in Article II, Section 2) empowers the President to authorize the collection of foreign intelligence information without a judicial warrant or specific statutory authorization. The *Federalist Papers*, Congress in the 1968 wiretap statute, and all four U.S. circuit courts of appeals to have decided the issue say the President has this power vested in him by the Constitution. This was also the unanimous conclusion of the FISA Court of Review. The Supreme Court has twice emphasized that wiretap decisions in related areas did not constrain the President's authority to conduct surveillance of foreign powers or their agents inside the United States. Each of the courts of appeals decisions referred to above was subsequently appealed to the Supreme Court on Fourth Amendment grounds, and each time the Court refused to hear the case. When the issue first arose there were justices who voted to consider the issue, but by 1982 the issue was apparently so well settled that not a single justice voted to grant certiorari in the *Truong* case.[61]

Data-Mining Telephone Records

A related issue arose in May of 2006, when *USA Today* broke the story that several telecommunications companies had voluntarily provided vast amounts of digital data to the government so that the National Security Agency could use sophisticated computer programs to ascertain what telephone numbers were communicating with numbers known or believed to be used regularly by foreign terrorists. The provided data did not include any names, addresses, or content of communications; it was designed to facilitate a long-standing technique of criminal investigation used by the FBI and detectives across the land. By painstakingly identifying associates of known or suspected mobsters or drug dealers, patters can be established that may lead to identifying other possible members of a criminal network. No one is arrested simply for such an association, but once identified the associate can be investigated further and perhaps tied to a criminal enterprise.

Nor is there a Fourth Amendment problem with the government collecting data about what telephones are communicating with other phones. This issue came before the Supreme Court in the 1979 case of *Smith v. Maryland*.[62]

---

61. *Truong Dinh Hung v. United States*, 454 U.S. 1144 (1982).
62. *Smith v. Maryland*, 442 U.S. 735 (1979).

At issue in *Smith* was the use of a "pen register" by the police in cooperation with a local phone company to capture the phone numbers of outgoing calls from the telephone of a man suspected of making threatening and obscene calls to a witness to a crime. The intercepts occurred at the phone company, and there was no intrusion into the home of the suspect. The Supreme Court held the use of the device merely to capture telephone numbers did not constitute a "search" as that term is used in the Fourth Amendment.

Senator Patrick Leahy, the ranking Democrat on the Senate Judiciary Committee, upon learning of the NSA data exploitation program declared: "Are you telling me tens of millions of Americans are involved with al-Qaeda?" Many other privacy and civil liberties groups voiced similar dismay. But it is difficult to distinguish this technology from a variety of other uses of government computers to extract relevant information from large databases.

When police find a fingerprint on a murder weapon at a crime scene, it is standard procedure to have the FBI crime laboratory compare the print with the roughly one billion fingerprints on file in its database—and in theory the computer searches the records of millions of innocent Americans in trying to find a match. Similarly, if a child is snatched while waiting for her school bus, and other children give the police a partial license plate number and vehicle description, they will quickly run the information through the motor vehicle registration database and then likely run the names of partial matches through a police database of known sexual predators. In the process, the computer might briefly scan the files of large numbers of totally innocent people—but who would seriously argue that such a search (whether to identify a killer, a pedophile, or an international terrorist) is "unreasonable" and should be prevented?

Presidential Signing Statements

Although not tied strictly to the war against terror, yet another cause of concern in recent years has been the practice of presidential "signing statements"—essentially a process by which in signing a statute into law the President declares that he will not be bound by one or more sections that he believes to be unconstitutional. An alternative version declares than an ambiguous provision of a statute will be interpreted so as to avoid violating the Constitution.

In August 2006 the American Bar Association House of Delegates approved a resolution declaring that presidential signing statements are "contrary to the rule of law and our constitutional system of separation of powers," and both indignant politicians and editorial writers have denounced the practice in similar terms. The President's constitutional duty, they remind us, is to see the laws enacted by Congress "faithfully executed," not to rewrite them or declare that certain provisions won't be enforced.

Presidential signing statements have been around since the presidency of James Monroe, and the underlying principle dates back at least to the first term of Thomas Jefferson in 1801. Shortly after assuming office, Jefferson announced that he would not enforce the Alien and Sedition Acts because they were unconstitutional, and he ordered all U.S. attorneys with pending cases to cease prosecution.

In 1942, a powerful member of the House Appropriations Committee inserted a rider in an emergency supplemental appropriations bill for World War II providing that no funds could be used to pay the salaries of three named government employees who had been identified as "subversives" by the House Committee on Un-American Activities. Some legislators compared the provision to "star chamber" proceedings and others described it as a "legislative lynching." The Senate repeatedly rejected the conference report on the bill in an effort to get the language dropped. But the money was desperately needed to fight the war, so the Senate ultimately yielded.

While signing the bill into law, President Roosevelt issued a signing statement declaring that the provision in question was unconstitutional and therefore would not bind either the executive or judicial branches. It took four years for a suit challenging the provision to make its way to the Supreme Court, which promptly struck the provision down as an unconstitutional bill of attainder.[63]

The use of signing statements has expanded dramatically since the end of the Vietnam War, and many of them have been attached to statutes that seek to control presidential discretion in foreign affairs or related areas that traditionally have been understood by all three branches to be beyond the reach of legislation. But by far the single most common reason for issuing a signing statement is the attachment by Congress of "legislative vetoes"—providing in a law that Congress or a component thereof (a single chamber, or even a single committee or chairman thereof) can reverse a decision taken by the Executive Branch without going through the constitutionally-mandated process for enacting a new law.

In 1974, acting pursuant to a provision of the Immigration and Nationality Act, the Attorney General suspended the deportation of a foreign exchange student named Jagdish Rai Chada on humanitarian grounds and reported the action to the Congress as required by the statute. As provided in the act, the

---

63. *United States v. Lovett*, 328 U.S. 303 (1946).

House of Representatives then voted to overturn the Attorney General's action and ordered the immediate deportation of the alien. Article I, Section 8 of the Constitution expressly vests in Congress the power to "establish a uniform Rule of Naturalization," so there was no doubt about the power of Congress to legislate in this area. But in the summer of 1983, the Supreme Court held that, to have legal effect, actions by Congress must comply with the formalities set forth in Article I of the Constitution (*e.g.*, be approved by both chambers and be submitted to the President for signature or veto). Efforts by Congress to empower a single branch or committee to overturn executive action, or even to empower both houses to act by concurrent resolution without submitting the resolution to the President for possible veto, were held to be unconstitutional. The *Chada* decision also struck down by implication legislative vetoes in national security legislation like section 5(c) of the 1973 War Powers Resolution.

One might have expected Congress to respond to the Court's ruling by directing its staff to search the statute books to identify legislative vetoes so they could be repealed. Instead, Congress elected to ignore the Supreme Court's ruling—and since the 1983 *Chadha* decision the Congress has enacted no fewer than 500 new legislative vetoes. Presidents have tended to issue signing statements declaring that they will not be bound by these clearly unconstitutional provisions, and to refuse to enforce them in practice.

Signing statements have become more frequent in modern times in part because Congress has attempted to assert control of presidential discretion far more readily since the Vietnam War. Another factor is that President George W. Bush was particularly willing to challenge Congress when he felt it was usurping the powers of his office. Indeed, it would be difficult to argue that Bush did not step over the lines in some situations, issuing statements and claiming discretionary powers that the Constitution clearly vests in the legislature.

For example, when Congress enacted the Detainee Treatment Act of 2005, President Bush declared: "The executive branch shall construe … the Act, relating to detainees, in a manner consistent with the constitutional authority of the President to supervise the unitary executive branch and as Commander in Chief and consistent with the constitutional limitations on the judicial power...."[64] While many modern legislative acts related to war or foreign affairs do arguably conflict with the President's constitutional discretion in this area, one of the clear "exceptions" vested in Congress by Article I, Section 8 is the power "To define and punish … Offences against the Law of Nations...."

---

64. *Available at* http://www.whitehouse.gov/news/releases/2005/12/20051230-8.html.

Not only does the 1987 Convention Against Torture (CAT)—signed by the United States on April 18, 1988, and ratified by President Clinton on October 21, 1994—establish that "torture and other cruel, inhuman, or degrading treatment or punishment" is an offense against the law of nations; but Common Article 3 of the 1949 Geneva Conventions provides that "[p]ersons taking no active part in the hostilities, including members of armed forces who have laid down their arms and those placed hors de combat by sickness, wounds, detention, or any other cause, shall in all circumstances be treated humanely…." One may quarrel about whether water boarding constitutes "torture" in the narrow sense defined by the Senate when it consented to ratification of the CAT (I think it does), but no one can seriously contend that it complies with a duty of "humane treatment."

To say that signing statements were sometimes abused during the administration of George W. Bush is one thing; but the ABA assertion that all such statements are inherently contrary to the "rule of law" is absurd. A fundamental principle of the American legal system is that the President's duty to see the laws "faithfully executed" begins with upholding the Constitution itself (a commitment reaffirmed in his oath of office), and when Congress passes statutes that cannot reasonably be vetoed (e.g., emergency funding for a war, or an omnibus continuing resolution that if not signed immediately would cause the shutdown of government functions), and the Supreme Court has already declared that the process is unconstitutional, to conclude that the President must nevertheless enforce the statute over the Constitution makes no sense at all.

No President has claimed a power to be the final judge of the constitutionality of a statute. Prior to Chief Justice Marshall's decision in *Marbury*, President Jefferson was not alone in believing that each branch was to decide for itself the constitutional limits of its power. (Even after *Marbury*, Jefferson held to that view.) Today, it is well established that the judiciary—ultimately, the Supreme Court—interprets the Constitution. If the people disagree, they have the power to amend the Constitution as provided in Article V. But until the Supreme Court has ruled, the other branches have a duty to "defend" (in the case of the President) or "support" (in the case of legislators) the Constitution. That oath of office creates a duty, in the first instance, to interpret the meaning of the Constitution—subject to correction by the judiciary.

Under Article III of the Constitution, the judiciary may only decide "Cases" or "Controversies" properly brought before it. Five months after *Marbury*, at President Washington's request, Secretary Jefferson wrote the justices to inquire whether they could give advisory opinions about treaty construction and other issues beyond the formal competence of the Court. On August 8, 1803, the justices responded that the giving of any "advisory opinions" was beyond their constitutional power: "[T]he lines of separation drawn by the Constitution between the three departments of the government" prevented it.[65]

Thus, in order to obtain authoritative guidance from the Supreme Court on the relative constitutional powers of Congress and the President, there must be an actual dispute between the two branches. Such a dispute is created when Congress enacts a statute and the President formally instructs the Executive Branch by signing statement not to faithfully execute it. Assuming good faith on the part of both political branches (which, in the case of legislation involving legislative vetoes, is admittedly difficult), both branches will remain true to their understanding of the Constitution until the judiciary can clarify the matter.

In addressing this issue, it is useful to keep in mind the fears expressed by the Founding Fathers about the risks of legislative tyranny. Both political branches were created to be independent, and each has a duty to the Constitution that supersedes other obligations. The great Harvard Law Professor Charles Warren observed in 1930:

> Under our Constitution, each branch of the Government is designed to be a coordinate representative of the will of the people.... Defense by the Executive of his constitutional powers becomes in very truth, therefore, defense of popular rights—defense of power which the people granted him.... In maintaining his rights against a trespassing Congress, the President defends not himself, but popular government; he represents not himself, but the people.[66]

Should "Original Understanding" Really Matter in the Twenty-First Century?

Before leaving our discussion of constitutional issues in the struggle against terror, there is a fundamental issue that probably ought to be mentioned. Even if we can tell what the Founding Fathers had in mind more than two centuries ago, are we—and should we be—bound by that understanding in the modern world?

When the Fourth Amendment was written in 1789, no one envisioned that people would someday have the ability to write or speak to a person thousands of miles away by email or telephone—much less that modern technology

---

65. *Vieth v. Jubelirer*, 541 U.S. 267, 302 (2004) (plurality opinion by Justice Scalia).
66. Charles Warren, *Presidential Declarations of Independence*, 10 B. U. L. REV. 1, 35 (1930).

would permit government agencies to secretly monitor those communications. Perhaps we can decipher the "original understanding" of various parts of our Constitution, but how much will that tell us about what the Framers of our Constitution would have thought about the same issues in the modern world? On the one hand, in the Framer's world it took weeks to get word of developments in Europe that today can be watched on CNN as they unfold. Today, nuclear-tipped missiles can be launched from across the globe that within minutes can instantaneously destroy entire cities. So, on the one hand we have increased threats to individual privacy, and on the other arguably a greater need for speed and dispatch in our dealings with the outside world.

In the early years of our government, legislators had no personal staffs and legislative drafting generally fell to the Executive Branch. Following World War II, staffs grew rapidly, and between 1958 and 1982, the staff of the Senate alone increased from 2500 to 7000 employees.[67] Many committees and individual senators today have staff members with advanced academic degrees and/or extensive professional experience in the military, the Department of State, or the Intelligence Community. Does it make sense to take advantage of this talent by entrusting to the legislature decisions about foreign policy and the conduct of war that once were viewed as exclusively the province of the Executive? Or might creating a shadow Executive Branch on Capitol Hill merely confuse things and undermine the important principle of unity of design?

The goal of this chapter has been to explain the original constitutional scheme of the separation of constitutional powers relating to the struggle against terrorism and to examine current controversies in light of that scheme. Readers should keep in mind that (as other chapters in this volume will clearly demonstrate) this is a field in which experts often differ. Many will argue that, as times and circumstances change, so must the Constitution. Others might argue that, since constitutions are primarily designed to protect the rights of minorities against the excesses of the majority, it is safer to require change by formal amendment than to entrust judges, legislators, or the incumbent President with the authority to decide when modern realities warrant new constitutional interpretations. The present writer falls more in the latter camp, but will gladly leave each reader to consider that issue independently.

---

67. *Available at* http://www.senate.gov/pagelayout/visiting/d_three_sections_with_teasers/hart_senate_building_web_page.htm.

Chapter 5

National Security, Litigation, and the State Secrets Privilege

*Robert M. Chesney**

Legal issues relating to national security frequently implicate the inherent tension between the government's interest in preserving secrecy and the public's interest in knowing as much as possible about the government's conduct and policies. Both interests, of course, are of great weight. The government's capacity to provide security would be hampered considerably, if not crippled, if military, intelligence, and diplomatic activities were entirely exposed to public scrutiny. On the other hand, a representative system of government premised on democratic accountability implies an informed electorate, particularly with respect to government conduct that may be unlawful. Summarizing this tension in1975—at a time of pronounced public skepticism concerning the trustworthiness of government officials in matters of national security—Attorney General Edward Levi observed that "we are met with a conflict of values ... demanding continual reassessment and reflection."[1]

Few topics more directly implicate this tension—and the need for continual reassessment and reflection—than the state secrets privilege. The state

* Charles I. Francis Professor of Law, University of Texas School of Law. For a more detailed exploration of the origins, evolution, and recent application of the state secrets privilege, see Robert M. Chesney, *State Secrets and the Limits of National Security Litigation*, 75 GEO. WASH. L. REV. 1249 (2007), *available at* http://ssrn.com/abstract=946676. And for a contrasting perspective on the origins of the privilege, see William Weaver, *The Origins of the State Secrets Privilege* (manuscript), *available at* http://ssrn.com/abstract=1079364. Portions of this chapter are derived from testimony I provided to the Senate Judiciary Committee on February 13, 2008, as well as a related article forthcoming in the Roger Williams Law Review.

1. Attorney General Edward Levi, Address to the Association of the Bar of the City of New York 13 (Apr. 28, 1975) (transcript available in Gerald R. Ford Presidential Library and Museum, Edward Levi Papers, Speeches and Scrapbooks Collection, Volume I).

secrets privilege functions as an absolute bar to the disclosure during litigation of information that would harm national security if shared publicly. In the years since 9/11, the government has invoked the privilege in connection with lawsuits dealing with subjects ranging from extraordinary rendition, to warrantless surveillance, to the firing of intelligence community employees. In many instances invocation of the privilege has resulted not just in evidentiary limitations, however, but in the outright dismissal of lawsuits. Not surprisingly, the privilege has become the subject of intense controversy as a result.

This chapter begins with a survey of the origins and evolution of the privilege, including discussion of its common law roots, its recognition by the Supreme Court in 1953, and the government's extensive reliance on the privilege beginning in the 1970s. Next, the chapter explores post-9/11 applications of the privilege with a focus on litigation arising out of the war on terrorism. The chapter concludes with a discussion of the post-9/11 movement to limit or at least regulate the privilege, including a survey of potential reforms.

Origins and Development of the Privilege Prior to 9/11

The origins of the state secrets privilege have been the subject of considerable dispute in recent years. In part, this reflects the fact that the privilege did not assume its modern form until the Supreme Court expressly recognized and defined the privilege in 1953. In part it reflects the fact that published opinions discussing the privilege were rare until the 1970s. And in part it reflects current disagreement concerning the extent to which the privilege has constitutional foundations (a possibility that might impact the ability of Congress to legislate reform of the privilege), or instead derives entirely from the common law of evidence and judicial considerations of public policy.

In any event, it is possible to shed at least some light on the origins of the privilege by tracing its development forward from its first appearance in American legal sources in the early 19th century. One cannot accomplish this task solely by reviewing published legal opinions, however. Instead, one should first look to the common law of evidence as expressed in the work of the leading treatise writers of that era. To be sure, the early 19th century treatise writers did not refer expressly to a "state secrets" privilege as such. But they did identify a "public policy" privilege in both American and British law (as with other common law subjects in that era, scholars routinely cited British precedent as relevant for American litigation).

The "public policy" privilege contained the seeds of the modern state se-crets concept. In 1826, for example, Thomas Starkie observed in his widely-circulated treatise that in some contexts the law "excludes particular evidence, not because in its own nature it is suspicious or doubtful, but on grounds of public policy, and because greater mischief and inconvenience would result from the reception than from the exclusion of such evidence."[2] Starkie cited the attorney-client privilege as an example, but he also went on to describe as an additional example circumstances in which disclosure of evidence would be "prejudicial to the community."[3] In such cases, he wrote, the evidence is ex-cluded on "grounds of state policy."[4] Starkie's examples of "state policy" priv-ilege in turn encompassed three scenarios. First, he noted cases in which the identity of informers had been protected from disclosure. Second, he noted cases in which confidential government communications had been shielded. And third, he gave the example of *Rex v. Watson*, an 1817 English decision in which the King's Bench refused to permit a witness to authenticate a map of the Tower of London on the ground "that it might be attended with public mis-chief, to allow an officer of the tower to be examined as to the accuracy of such a plan."[5] Put another way, otherwise-admissible evidence was suppressed in order to avoid a risk of harm to national security that might follow from public disclosure.

Subsequent treatise writers such as Henry Roscoe also would cite English precedents as examples of a "state" privilege of this variety.[6] But actual U.S. precedent was exceedingly scarce in the 1800s. Chief Justice Marshall had touched lightly on the topic during the 1807 treason trial of Aaron Burr when he was faced with the question of whether to compel the Jefferson adminis-tration to disclose an allegedly inculpatory letter that had been sent to the pres-ident from General James Wilkinson.[7] Marshall made clear that he was reluctant to deny production should the document prove necessary to Burr's defense. But he also made a point of observing that the government had made no claim

---

2. THOMAS STARKIE, A PRACTICAL TREATISE ON THE LAW OF EVIDENCE AND DIGEST OF PROOFS IN CIVIL AND CRIMINAL PROCEEDINGS §LXXVI, at 103 (Boston, Wells and Lilly, 1826).

3. *Id.* §LXXX, at 106.

4. *Id.* (notation in margin).

5. *Rex v. Watson*, (1817) 171 Eng. Rep. 591, 604 (K.B.); *see* STARKIE, *supra* note 2, §LXXX, at 106.

6. *See, e.g.,* HENRY ROSCOE, A DIGEST OF THE LAW OF EVIDENCE IN CRIMINAL CASES WITH NOTES AND REFERENCES TO AMERICAN DECISIONS, AND TO THE ENGLISH COMMON LAW AND ECCLESIASTICAL REPORTS 148–49 (George Sharswood ed. P.H. Nickline & T. John-son, 1836).

7. *See United States v. Burr*, 25 F. Cas. 30, 37 (C.C.D. Va. 1807) (No. 14,692).

in this case that production would "endanger the public safety."[8] The statement was no more than dicta, but nonetheless was enough to prompt subsequent treatise writers to cite the *Burr* proceedings as the first American judicial
opinion supporting the existence of a state secrets privilege.

The next significant development bearing on the evolution of the privilege
occurred after the Civil War, with the Supreme Court's 1875 holding in *Totten v. United States.*[9] Enoch Totten, the plaintiff in this civil suit, administered
the estate of a man who claimed to have spied for the Union during the war
pursuant to a personal service agreement he allegedly had struck with President Lincoln himself. According to Totten, the spy had never been paid the
money owed to him according to that contract, and so Totten brought a breach
of contract action in the Court of Claims to recover the wages. That court proceeded to the merits of the dispute, splitting evenly on the question of whether
President Lincoln would have had the authority to bind the government to a
contract in such circumstances. A unanimous Supreme Court held, however,
that the Court of Claims should never have reached that question in the first
place. Justice Field explained:

> [P]ublic policy forbids the maintenance of any suit in a court of jus-
> tice, the trial of which would inevitably lead to the disclosure of mat-
> ters which the law itself regards as confidential, and respecting which
> it will not allow the confidence to be violated.[10]

In today's debates over the state secrets privilege, one of the more sharply
contested questions is whether *Totten* should be understood as an example of
the state secrets privilege. Some argue that the decision instead merely reflects
a stand-alone rule against the justiciability of suits involving espionage contracts, while others contend that the outcome in *Totten* flowed directly from
application of the privilege. In 2005, the Supreme Court addressed this issue
to some extent, in a decision detailed in the next section. At this stage in the
historical survey, however, the important point is that both treatise writers
and courts in the late 19th and early 20th centuries routinely cited *Totten* (as
well as the dicta in *Burr*) as evidence that the privilege did indeed exist in American law. In the 1912 decision *Firth Sterling Steel Co. v. Bethelehem Steel Co.*, for
example, a judge relied on *Totten*—as well as descriptions of the state secrets
privilege in Wigmore's evidence law treatise—to preclude the production of evidence of military secrets (in this case, schematics for armor-piercing projec-

---

8. *Id.*
9. 92 U.S. 105 (1875).
10. *Id.* at 107.

tiles).[11] The court in *Pollen v. Ford Instrument Co., Inc.* reached a similar conclusion, citing *Totten*, in a 1939 opinion that invoked the privilege to suppress documents containing schematics for gunsights used by the Navy.[12]

These developments provided the legal backdrop when the Supreme Court in 1953 considered the status of the privilege in *United States v. Reynolds.* The case arose out of tragic circumstances. A B-29 bomber had crashed in Georgia during a mission to test classified radar equipment, resulting in numerous deaths. The plaintiffs—widows of victims of the crash—sued the United States for negligence under the recently-enacted Federal Tort Claims Act, and eventually issued discovery requests encompassing the Air Force's post-accident investigative report. The government initially refused to disclose the report on the ground that production for litigation might discourage witnesses from cooperating in future post-accident investigations. Subsequently, however, the government argued in the alternative that the document in any event could not be produced because it contained sensitive information relating to the classified equipment on board the plane. The district court did not reject these argument out of hand, but did insist upon an *in camera, ex parte* inspection of the report in order to determine whether it in fact contained such information. The government refused to cooperate, prompting the judge to sanction the government through an order finding for the plaintiff on the merits of the case.[13]

After the Third Circuit affirmed the district court's ruling, the government successfully petitioned for *certiorari.* In its brief to the Supreme Court, the government argued first that separation of powers considerations forbade the judiciary (as well as Congress) from compelling the executive branch to disclose information when in the executive's view the public interest would be best served by keeping it secret. The government placed particular emphasis on a 1942 British decision in *Duncan v. Cammell, Laird, & Co.,* in which the House of Lords had recognized unreviewable authority in a government minister to refuse to produce otherwise-discoverable documents in litigation, on the ground that disclosure would be harmful to the public interest.[14] And as an alternative to this broad constitutional argument, the government cited both *Totten* and the Wigmore treatise for the proposition that in any event "there is a common law privilege for matters concerning military or international affairs," a privilege that precluded even the "judge alone" from reviewing the accident report

---

11. *See Firth Sterling Steel Co. v. Bethlehem Steel Co.*, 199 F. 353, 355 (E.D. Pa. 1912).

12. 26 F. Supp. 583, 585 (E.D.N.Y.).

13. The details of the district court dispute are set forth in the Third Circuit's opinion, *Reynolds v. United States*, 192 F.2d 987, 989–91 (3d Cir. 1951).

14. [1942] A.C. 624, 632–42 (H.L.).

once a government official asserted the need for secrecy.[15] The government argued, in short, that as a constitutional matter executive officials have unreviewable discretion to determine whether documents in their possession should be disclosed, and that in the alternative the common law state secrets privilege produced the same result in this particular case.

The Supreme Court responded in its landmark 1953 decision in *Reynolds*, which manages to elaborate the doctrinal details of the state secrets privilege and yet at the same time sow a degree of uncertainty regarding its practical implementation. As an initial matter, the court expressly declined to address the government's lead argument to the effect that the Constitution vests executive branch officials with unreviewable discretion to withhold documents on public interest grounds. Instead, the court focused its holding on what it described as the "privilege against revealing military secrets, a privilege which is well established in the law of evidence."[16] In support of that latter claim, the court cited *Totten, Firth Sterling, Pollen,* and a handful of other cases, as well as several academic commentaries.[17]

Turning to the operational details of the privilege, the court began by specifying a series of formalities that must be satisfied before the privilege even in theory might attach. First, the privilege may only be invoked by the government, and never by a private litigant. Second, the invocation must be made "by the head of the department which has control over the matter," and third, the department head must have personally considered the issue before invoking the privilege.[18] But what occurs next once a properly-framed invocation of the privilege occurs?

In contrast to the government's argument that a proper invocation of the privilege should be conclusive and not subject to judicial review, the court held that the "court itself must determine whether the circumstances are appropriate for the claim of the privilege."[19] This raised a further question, however. What substantive test should a judge apply when making that determination? The opinion is not entirely clear on this point, but subsequent decisions and commentary seem to agree that under *Reynolds* the privilege attaches if the government's *in camera, ex parte* submissions persuade the judge that public dis-

---

15. Brief for the United States, United States v. Reynolds, No. 21 (S. Ct.), *available at* 1952 WL 82378.

16. 345 U.S. 1, 6–7.

17. *See id.* at 7 & nn. 11 & 13. Notably, the Supreme Court recently held that the *Totten* jurisdictional bar should be understood as a doctrine distinct from the state secrets privilege. *See Tenet v. Doe*, 544 U.S. 1, 9–10 (2005).

18. *Id.* at 7–8.

19. *Id.* at 8.

closure of the contested information would pose a reasonable risk of harm to national security. And where that standard is satisfied, *Reynolds* made clear, the privilege was inviolable no matter the litigant's need for the information in issue.

It is not hard to imagine why a judge might conclude that this standard would be satisfied with respect to the public disclosure of schematics and technical details relating to a classified radar technology. Indeed, such a scenario would closely track earlier privilege cases such as *Firth Sterling* and *Pollen*. But that assumes that such information actually appeared in the post-accident investigative report sought by the plaintiffs in *Reynolds*. As would become clear only decades later when the document became available to the public, this was not in fact the case; the report apparently contained only glancing references to the classified equipment on board the flight, and nothing that plausibly could satisfy even a "reasonable danger" standard for applying the privilege. And yet the Supreme Court in *Reynolds* ultimately held that the privilege did attach to the report, reversing the decision below. How did this come to pass?

The answer lies in the court's approach to a key logistical question associated with invocation of the privilege. Should the judge review the very document that is in issue when determining whether the privilege attaches to it, or should it instead base its review solely upon the briefs and other representations made by the government in the course of invoking the privilege? Addressing this issue, the court pointed out that in determining the applicability of the privilege care must be taken to ensure that it does not expose the very secret sought to be protected. And the court also noted that there could be circumstances in which the nature of the information requested so plainly would warrant protection that it would gain nothing to require the government to engage even in an *in camera, ex parte* production. One can imagine, for example, an interrogatory requesting technical specifications for tank armor for use in connection with a patent infringement suit; the court would have little need to see those specifications in order to conclude that the privilege attaches to them. Building from these premises, the court concluded that judges should not automatically require actual disclosure of protected information in order to resolve privilege disputes. All of which in the abstract appears rather sensible. Somewhat remarkably, however, the court proceeded to conclude that under this standard it was reversible error for the trial judge in this case to have insisted on *in camera, ex parte* review of the post-accident investigative report. When the Secretary of the Air Force filed a formal claim of the privilege as to that document "under circumstances indicating a reasonable possibility that military secrets were involved," the court held, "there was certainly a sufficient showing of privilege" to allow the matter to be resolved without review of the document itself.

This was a poorly-reasoned conclusion. It caused an opinion that otherwise amounted to a victory of sorts for civil litigants—the court did, after all, reject the proposition that judges must accept that the privilege applies once it has been invoked in the correct manner—to instead become viewed as an example of how the privilege can be put to an abusive end.

In any event, *Reynolds* did serve to eliminate any doubt that the state secrets privilege existed in American law, and it did play a role in a handful of published judicial opinions in the decades that followed. We cannot say with any confidence that these few opinions marked the only occasions on which the government invoked the privilege during the 1950s and 1960s, however. Not all judicial opinions are published, and in any event not all invocations of the privilege necessarily will result in a formal ruling discussing whether and why the privilege might apply. The most we can say, perhaps, is that in the aftermath of *Reynolds* the privilege did not generate sustained public attention or controversy.

This began to change in the 1970s, contemporaneous with a range of potentially explanatory factors. The number of occasions for potentially invoking the privilege almost certain increased in the 1970s thanks to a series of public revelations about controversial and potentially unlawful activities by various components of the intelligence community. And government awareness of the existence and utility of the privilege undoubtedly increased in the 1970s as a result of the ultimately inconclusive effort to include a codified version of the state secrets privilege in the Federal Rules of Evidence. In any event, the number of published judicial opinions involving state secrets claims began to increase during this period.

With the apparent increase in frequency of privilege cases came variety in terms of the litigation posture of the cases involved. Most notably, the 1970s saw cases in which the privilege arose not in connection with discovery motions targeting specific documents—as had been true in early cases such as *Reynolds*, *Firth Sterling*, and *Pollen*—but instead in connection with the government's obligation to admit or deny factual allegations at the pleading stage of a lawsuit. The decision of the D.C. Circuit in *Halkin v. Helms* provides perhaps the best example.[20]

Foreshadowing more recent debates, *Halkin* arose out of revelations that various components of the intelligence community—including the NSA—had engaged in warrantless surveillance activities within the United States. Rather than admit to such facts in the course of answering the complaint, the government moved to dismiss the suit on state secret privilege grounds, reasoning that admissions of allegations pertaining to otherwise-protected information would

20. 598 F.2d 1 (D.C. Cir. 1978).

be tantamount to production of a document containing such information. Raising privilege concerns at the pleading stage rather than in connection with particular documents did raise a logistical issue with respect to what if anything the judge would review in camera in the course of determining the privilege's applicability. Ultimately, the district judge resolved that question by reviewing both classified and unclassified affidavits from the Secretary of Defense explaining why the allegations at issue should be deemed privileged. The judge then concluded that the government had established the applicability of the privilege as to most of the alleged activities in issue, barring a single exception: the judge concluded that the NSA's SHAMROCK program, involving surveillance of international telegram traffic, had been the subject of sufficient public disclosures to obviate any claim to continuing secrecy. The D.C. Circuit reversed that aspect of the holding, however, reasoning that whatever else may have been printed in the papers, there had been no public revelation regarding SHAMROCK's particular targets. The case was remanded for dismissal.

Published opinions applying the privilege continued to proliferate in the 1980s and 1990s.[21] Whereas there had been only six published opinions construing the privilege during the period from 1954 through the end of 1972, at least sixty-five such opinions would appear between 1973 and 2001. Of those sixty-five opinions, nearly half (twenty-eight, to be precise) involved an attempt to have some or all of a litigant's claims dismissed, whereas the remainder sought merely to limit discovery without also seeking dispositive relief. Far more often than not, moreover, the government prevailed. Of the twenty-eight dismissal motions, twenty-three were granted. Of the thirty-seven discovery motions, thirty were granted. On the eve of the 9/11 attacks, one could fairly say that the privilege had reached maturity, with results that often were harsh from the perspective of private litigants.

Post-9/11 Applications of the Privilege and the Emerging Controversy

In sharp contrast to the public's relative apathy toward assertions of the privilege prior to 2001, the Bush administration's reliance on the privilege in a series of high-profile cases challenging the legality of covert activity associ-

---

21. As noted above, one must use data on published opinions advisedly. One cannot know how many comparable cases happened not to be published or not to have produced a formal ruling.

ated with counterterrorism operations has generated a significant public back-lash. The privilege has been asserted in this period in other, less-politically-charged contexts, of course, but there is little doubt that it is the use of the privilege in "war on terrorism" cases—and the intersection of that use with a larger critical narrative focused on the administration's alleged misuse of government secrecy—that has fueled public interest in the privilege.

There are two lines of cases that have played an especially important role in the changing atmospherics of the state secrets privilege. One line concerns litigation against the government and private sector entities in connection with allegedly unlawful surveillance activities, including but not limited to warrantless surveillance conducted in the United States by the National Security Agency. The other line concerns so-called "extraordinary renditions," pursuant to which the government seizes noncitizens and transfers them to the custody of other states, allegedly in order to facilitate abusive interrogations. In both contexts plaintiffs allege the existence of highly-classified government counterterrorism programs, and in both contexts they are aided in this claim by a variety of media disclosures and subsequent confirmations by government officials. As a result, each such case presents difficult questions regarding the extent to which the allegedly unlawful conduct at issue even remains secret and thus theoretically eligible for protection via the state secrets privilege. Additionally, in both contexts the government has invoked the privilege at the pleading stage as a ground for dismissal of suits, rather than at the discovery stage as a ground for precluding production of specific documents or items. These suits thus draw attention to the potentially-dispositive impact of privilege invocations.

NSA Surveillance Litigation

In late 2005, an article in the *New York Times* revealed to the public that the National Security Agency for several years had been intercepting communications between overseas targets believed to be linked to al Qaeda and persons within the United States, without first obtaining a warrant pursuant to the Foreign Intelligence Surveillance Act of 1978 ("FISA"). The president and other officials soon thereafter confirmed the existence of a "terrorist surveillance program" ("TSP") along such lines. Critics contended that the program was unlawful as a violation of FISA, the Fourth Amendment, or both. The government responded that the program was a lawful exercise of the president's commander-in-chief function in connection with an ongoing armed conflict, and that the Authorization for Use of Military Force passed by Congress one week after the 9/11 attacks in any event provided controlling statutory authority for such activities. Not surprisingly, litigation ensued against not only the government agencies and officials involved but also a variety of telecommunications companies alleged to have assisted NSA in its TSP activities.

In each of these suits, the government has interposed the state secrets privilege as a ground for dismissal, an argument with which courts continue to grapple at the time of this writing. The bulk of the private-defendant suits, for example, have been concentrated by the United States Judicial Panel on Multi-District Litigation in the United States District Court for the Northern District of California, where *Hepting v. AT&T* now serves as the lead case. In May 2006, the government intervened with a motion to dismiss or, in the alternative, for summary judgment on state secrets grounds. The government contended that the plaintiffs could not establish standing without exposure of state secrets (i.e., information concerning which communications the NSA saw fit to surveil on suspicion of an al Qaeda-linkage), and that the merits of the suit turned on the details of a classified program and thus could not be litigated in any event. The district court conducted an *in camera, ex parte* review of affidavits from the Director of National Intelligence and the Director of the NSA explaining why in the government's view the requisite disclosures posed a reasonable risk of harm to national security. Ultimately, however, the court concluded that the extensive disclosures and confirmations relating to the TSP precluded the argument that the very subject matter of Hepting's suit was secret and warranted immediate dismissal. The plaintiffs instead would be allowed to proceed to discovery, with individual state secrets issues dealt with as they might arise in that context.[22]

The *Hepting* decision at the time of this writing remains on appeal to the Ninth Circuit. In the interim, however, the Ninth Circuit already has ruled in the related case of *al-Haramain Islamic Foundation, Inc. v. Bush*. The plaintiff in that case is an Islamic charity that has been designated by the government as a foreign terrorist organization, and as a result has had its assets frozen. In connection with litigation relating to the assert frieze, the government in 2004 accidentally produced a document to al-Haramain that apparently made clear that al-Haramain had been subject to warrantless surveillance in connection with the TSP. After the TSP became public and the import of the document became clear, al-Haramain filed suit. Thanks to the disclosure, al-Haramain appeared to have strong grounds to assert standing, but the government responded that al-Haramain should not be permitted to rely in any way on the privileged information it accidentally had received. Ultimately the Ninth Circuit agreed, holding in November 2007 that although the TSP itself was no longer a state

---

22. *Hepting v. AT&T*, 439 F. Supp.2d 974 (2007).

secret, the identity of its particular targets was, and that the accidentally-disclosed information could not be used by al-Haramain to establish its standing. As a consequence, the court concluded, dismissal ordinarily would be appropriate. But the court refused to order dismissal nonetheless. Instead, it remanded the case so that the district court could determine whether the state secrets privilege might be overcome in this instance by a provision in FISA stating that judges may consider the legality of covert surveillance activity where an "aggrieved person" alleges a FISA violation.[23]

These decisions, along with still others arising out of TSP activities and other alleged post-9/11 surveillance programs, have proven extremely controversial. From the point of view of administration critics, the effort to invoke the privilege in these cases compounds frustration already felt with respect to the legal and policy merits of the programs at issue. That the privilege is being invoked not simply to prevent disclosure of a document but to prevent litigation altogether exacerbates the matter, fueling the view that the privilege functions to shield the executive branch from accountability in the courts or elsewhere. From the point of view of the administration's supporters, on the other hand, it is hardly shocking that the government would seek to prevent further public disclosure of the means and methods by which the intelligence community seeks to monitor the communications of al Qaeda-linked individuals.

Rendition Litigation

The disparate perceptions surrounding invocation of the privilege in the TSP context are precisely replicated in the controversy over civil suits seeking compensation for persons allegedly subjected to so-called extraordinary rendition: the practice of capturing an individual in one state and transferring him to the custody of another, whether for purposes of incapacitation, intelligence-gathering, or both.[24] In its post-9/11 iteration, the CIA's rendition program has become the focus of intense controversy both domestically and overseas, with critics describing it as a mechanism for outsourcing torture and other forms of abusive treatment.[25] Such criticisms have been particularly fierce

---

23. *Al-Haramain v. Bush*, 507 F.3d 1190 (2007).

24. For a discussion of extraordinary rendition, *see* Statement of Philip Zelikow, Hearing of the Senate Foreign Relations Committee on "Extraordinary Rendition, Extraterritorial Detention, and Treatment of Detainees" July 26, 2007, *available at* http://www.senate.gov/~foreign/testimony/ 2007/ZelikowTestimony070726.pdf.

25. *See, e.g.,* Statement of Tom Malinowski, Hearing of the Senate Foreign Relations Committee on "Extraordinary Rendition, Extraterritorial Detention, and Treatment of De-

in connection with situations in which the government allegedly subjected an innocent individual to rendition.

One such situation involved a German citizen named Khaled el-Masri, resulting in a high-profile civil suit that ultimately foundered in the face of the state secrets privilege. El-Masri alleged that he was seized while on vacation in Macedonia by local officials acting at the behest of or in conjunction with the CIA. After protracted interrogation there, he claims to have been transferred to the custody of CIA agents who stripped, beat, and forcibly sedated him before flying him to a prison in Afghanistan. After several months of incarceration and interrogation there, he finally was flown to Albania and left along the side of a road near a border station.

Less than two years after these events, el-Masri filed suit in the United States District Court for the Eastern District of Virginia, asserting violations of substantive and procedural due process rights protected by the Fifth Amendment, as well as claims under the Alien Tort Statute based on violations of customary international law prohibitions against prolonged arbitrary detention and the use of torture and other forms of abuse. The suit named then-director of central intelligence George Tenet, as well as a number of John Doe defendants and three corporate entities alleged to have served as fronts for the CIA's rendition operations. Before any defendant answered, however, the government intervened to assert the state secrets privilege, and to seek dismissal of the complaint on that ground; according to the motion, dismissal was required without further litigation because the nature of the issues in the case necessarily "would require the CIA to admit or deny the existence of clandestine CIA activity," as well as requiring proof of various details regarding the actual conduct of such operations.[26]

The district court agreed, rejecting el-Masri's argument that public disclosures confirming the existence of a CIA rendition program sufficed to defeat any claim of the privilege in connection with el-Masri's case. According to the court, there is a "critical distinction between a general admission" to that effect and "the admission or denial of the specific facts at issue in this case. A general admission provides no details as to the means and methods employed in these renditions, or the persons, companies or governments involved."[27] The court then concluded that the parties could not even plead in response to the complaint without making admissions of protected information, and that

tainees" July 26, 2007, *available at* http://www.senate.gov/~foreign/testimony/2007/ MalinowskiTestimony070726.pdf.

26. The government's motion is *available at* http://www.calu.org/pdfs/safefree/govt_mot_dismiss.pdf.

27. *El-Masri v. Tenet*, 437 F. Supp.2d 530, 538 (E.D. Va. 2006).

no special procedures would suffice to overcome the suit's focus on such information. Accordingly, the court granted the government's motion to dismiss, and the Fourth Circuit subsequently affirmed.[28]

The Question of Reform

Invocation of the privilege in cases such as *el-Masri* and the NSA suits have fueled growing awareness of the harsh impact of the privilege, and as a result interest in the prospects for reform of the privilege has grown considerably in recent years. Calls for legislative reform have multiplied, including much-publicized reports favoring reform issued by the Constitution Project[29] and the American Bar Association.[30] As of spring 2008, the reform movement has culminated in a bipartisan legislative package put forward by Senators Edward Kennedy (D-MA) and Arlen Specter (R-PA), known as the State Secrets Protection Act ("SSPA").[31]

Perhaps the best way to come to grips with the SSPA is to compare its provisions to current practices relating to the privilege, with an eye towards distinguishing that which is mere codification of the status quo from that which constitutes a substantial change. It helps, moreover, to conduct this comparison in a way that corresponds to the conceptual sequence of questions a judge must resolve when confronted with an invocation of the privilege. This approach demonstrates that a substantial part of the SSPA merely codifies practices that either are required or at least are common under the status quo, and should not be objectionable now. That said, there are a few aspects of the legislation that constitute significant breaks with current practice. Those provisions warrant more careful consideration. In a few instances, there are alternative approaches that might strike a better—and more sustainable—balance among the competing equities.

The Formalities of Invoking the Privilege

The threshold question in any state secrets privilege scenario is whether the privilege has been invoked with the requisite formalities. In theory, such requirements serve to reduce the risk that the privilege will be invoked gratu-

28. *El-Masri v. United States*, 479 F.3d 296 (4th Cir. 2007).
29. The Constitution Project, Reforming the State Secrets Privilege (May 31, 2007).
30. American Bar Association, Revised Report 116A, Report to the House of Delegates (Aug. 2007).
31. *See* S. 2253.

itously. The SSPA does not introduce any significant innovations under this heading, but rather codifies existing practice.

Under the SSPA, "the United States shall provide the court with an affidavit signed by the head of the executive branch agency with responsibility for, and control over, the state secrets involved explaining the factual basis for the claim of privilege."[32] This closely tracks current practice. *Reynolds* requires a "formal claim of privilege, lodged by the head of the department which has control over the matter, after actual personal consideration by that officer."[33] Both the SSPA and current practice, moreover, limit invocation of the privilege to the United States.[34]

The Substantive Test for Application of the Privilege

The substantive scope of the state secrets privilege is a function of three variables: subject matter, magnitude of harm that might follow from public disclosure, and the degree of risk that such harm might be realized. Though there is room for disagreement on this point, the best view is that the SSPA does not depart significantly from the status quo with respect to any of these three variables.

Consider first the question of subject matter. Under the SSPA, information must relate to "national defense or foreign relations" in order to qualify for privilege.[35] The status quo at least arguably encompasses a similar range of topics.[36]

The next question is whether the SSPA tracks the status quo with respect to the magnitude of harm that might follow from public disclosure of the information in question. The SSPA frames the inquiry in terms of "significant harm."[37] There is no comparable terminology in *Reynolds*, nor has any standard terminology on this question of calibration emerged in that case's progeny. Nonetheless, it is difficult to view the "significant harm" standard as a meaningful change from the status quo. *Reynolds* itself admonished that the privilege was "not to be lightly invoked,"[38] implying that *de minimus* harms should not come within its scope.

---

32. *See* SSPA § 4054(b).
33. 345 U.S. at 7–8.
34. Compare SSPA § 4054(a) with *Reynolds*, 345 U.S. at 7.
35. SSPA § 4051.
36. *See* Chesney, *supra* at 1315–32 (specifying nature of information at issue in published state secrets adjudications between 1954 and 2006).
37. SSPA § 4051.
38. 345 U.S. at 7.

The third issue under this heading concerns the probability that disclosure of the information actually will precipitate the feared harm. Under both the status quo and the SSPA, that variable is framed in terms of "reasonable" risk.[39]

Authority to Decide Whether the Privilege Attaches: The Role of the Judge and the Question of Deference

In its brief to the Supreme Court in *Reynolds*, the government had contended that "the power of determination is the Secretary's alone."[40] That is to say, the government argued that courts cannot and should not second guess the determination of the relevant executive branch official that disclosure of the information in question would be harmful. Among other things, the government reasoned that executive officials are far better situated than judges to assess the probable consequences of a disclosure.[41] On the other hand, unchecked authority to assert the privilege naturally would give rise to assert the privilege in circumstances were the substantive standard is not met, whether out of an excess of caution or even as a shield for misfeasance. The Supreme Court ultimately gave greater weight to that offsetting concern, holding in *Reynolds* that "[j]udicial control over the evidence in the case cannot be abdicated to the caprice of executive officers," and insisting that the judge have the final say with respect to whether the privilege attaches.[42]

This principle is no longer seriously contested today in formal terms.[43] But the relative authority of the judge and the executive branch continues to be a matter of controversy today because of the lingering question of how much deference the judge should give to the executive's claim, even if the claim is not strictly binding. In *el-Masri*, for example, the Fourth Circuit concluded that

---

39. SSPA § 4051(emphasis added). *Reynolds* actually is vague with respect to the question of how strong the likelihood of harm from disclosure must be (most of its discussion of risk concerns the distinct question of whether and when judges should personally examine allegedly privileged documents en route to making a decision on the privilege), but courts nonetheless appear to understand *Reynolds* to require a reasonable-risk standard. *See, e.g., El-Masri v. United States,* 479 F.3d 296, 302 (4th Cir. 2007).

40. *See United States v. Reynolds,* No. 21, Petitioner's Brief, at 47, available at 1952 WL 82378.

41. *See id.* (stating that the government's position rests in part "on reasons of policy arising from the fact that the department head alone is truly qualified and in a position to make the determination").

42. 345 U.S. at 9–10.

43. *See, e.g, el-Masri,* 479 F.3d at 305 ("The Executive bears the burden of satisfying a reviewing court that the *Reynolds* reasonable-danger standard is met.").

the "court is obliged to accord the 'utmost deference' to the responsibilities of the executive branch" when determining the harm that might follow from a disclosure.[44] Such deference was owed both "for constitutional reasons" and for "practical ones: the Executive and the intelligence agencies under his control occupy a position superior to that of the courts in evaluating the consequences of a release of sensitive information."[45] Similarly, the Ninth Circuit stated in *al-Haramain* that it "acknowledge[d] the need to defer for the Executive on matters of foreign policy and national security and surely cannot legitimately find ourselves second guessing the Executive in this arena."[46] In light of such statements, some might argue that judges have final authority to determine the applicability of the privilege only in formal terms, while the mechanism of deference shifts that authority back to the executive branch in practical terms.

The SSPA codifies the status quo insofar as it plainly contemplates that the judge shall have ultimate responsibility for determining whether the privilege should attach.[47] In its current form, however, it makes no attempt to regulate the degree of deference, if any, that judges should give to the executive branch's judgment regarding the consequences of a disclosure.

The Mechanics of the Judge's Review: Evidentiary Basis for the Ruling

When Specific Documents Are in Issue

The paradigm state secrets privilege scenario involves an attempt by a private litigant to obtain a particular item during discovery, as occurred with respect to the post-accident investigative report in *Reynolds*. When the government claims privilege in that context, it typically justifies its assertion with an explanatory affidavit from the official asserting the privilege.[48] But should the judge also review the item in question in the course of determining whether the privilege should apply?

The SSPA departs from the status quo to a small extent with respect to this issue. Under the SSPA, judges not only can but *must* review the actual item of

---

44. 479 F.3d at 305 (quoting United States v. Nixon, 418 U.S. 683, 710 (1974)).

45. *Id.*

46. 507 F.3d at 1203.

47. *See* SSPA §4054(e) (describing the judge's role in determining whether the privilege attaches).

48. *See, e.g., al-Haramain*, 507 F.3d at 1202 (referring to "classified and unclassified declarations" filed by the Director of National Intelligence and the Director of the NSA).

evidence.[49] Under the status quo, in contrast, they are expressly admonished by *Reynolds* to be reluctant to require such *in camera* production unless the litigant has shown great need for the document.[50]

The SSPA's requirement of *in camera* disclosure reflects a lesson derived from the original *Reynolds* litigation. Famously, the plaintiffs in *Reynolds* had sought production of an Air Force post-accident investigative report in connection with their tort suit, prompting the government to invoke the state secrets privilege on the ground that the report contained details of classified radar equipment. The Supreme Court concluded such details could not be disclosed publicly, which is a plausible enough conclusion under the substantive test described above. But though it did not follow that the accident report necessarily did contain such details, the court assumed that it did and found the privilege applicable on that basis. Notoriously, it turned out much later that the report had not contained substantial details about the radar. Thus conventional wisdom holds that the privilege ought not to have been invoked on that basis in the first place, something that almost certainly would have been revealed by judicial inspection of the document.[51]

Reynolds thus has come to stand for an important, common-sense proposition: where the privilege is asserted in connection with a document the government seeks to withhold from discovery, the judge should ensure that the item in question actually contains the allegedly-sensitive information said by the government to warrant application of the privilege. It is important to appreciate, however, that this type of mistake does not reflect standard practice under the state secret privilege today. Notwithstanding language in *Reynolds* cautioning judges not to conduct *in camera* inspections unnecessarily, courts today routinely do examine documents personally en route to determining whether the privilege

---

49. *See* SSPA § 4054(d)(1) (requiring the United States to submit for the court's review not only an explanatory affidavit but also all evidence as to which the privilege has been asserted).

50. *See* 345 U.S. at 10–12.

51. *See* LOUIS FISHER, IN THE NAME OF NATIONAL SECURITY: UNCHECKED PRESIDENTIAL POWER AND THE *REYNOLDS* CASE 166–68 (2006). *But see* Statement of Carl Nichols before the Senate Committee on the Judiciary, "Examining the State Secrets Privilege: Protecting National Security While Preserving Accountability," Feb. 13, 2008 (arguing that the report in privilege invocation in *Reynolds* was proper because the report contained technical details relating to the operations of B-29 bombers, separate and apart from details relating to the radar equipemnt); *Herring v. United States*, 2004 WL 2040272, at *5–6, 9 (E.D. Pa. 2004) (holding that the Air Force had not committed fraud in *Reynolds* because the B-29 data justified application of the privilege), *aff'd*, *Herring v. United States*, 424 F.3d 384 (3rd Cir. 2005).

should attach.[52] The change that would be wrought by the SSPA on this issue, accordingly, is simply to remove any question as to whether this should be done.

When Abstract Information Is in Issue

Not every invocation of the privilege arises in connection with requests for production of specific documents or records capable of being inspected. The government also may have occasion to invoke the privilege in connection with discovery requests seeking protected information in the abstract, as with an interrogatory or a deposition question. In such cases there is no specific document or item for the court to review, other than the explanation offered by the government in the form of an affidavit from the official asserting the privilege. In that respect, the SSPA's requirement that such an affidavit be submitted merely codifies the status quo.[53]

When Pleading Would Require Revelation of Privileged Information

A similar scenario arises at the pleading stage when the allegations in a complaint would reveal state secrets if admitted or denied. Here, however, the SSPA introduces a useful innovation that functions to put off the question of whether the privilege properly applies to the information at issue. Under SSPA §4053(c), the government may simply plead the privilege in response to such allegations, rather than admitting or denying them as otherwise required by Federal Rule of Civil Procedure 8(b).[54] The allegation(s) in question presumably then would be deemed denied,[55] without any need for the judge at that stage to consider whether the privilege in fact attaches to the information at issue. Arguably the government could have achieved the same result under the status quo by ob-

---

52. *See, e.g., Al-Haramain Islamic Foundation, Inc. v. Bush*, 507 F.3d 1190, 1203 (2007) ("We reviewed the Sealed Document *in camera* ...").

53. SSPA §4054(b). In that sense, the SSPA's adoption of an affidavit requirement is unexceptionable. But there is a problem with respect to the related requirement that the classified affidavit be accompanied by an unclassified version for public release: one might read that provision to preclude the judge from being able to order the unclassified document to be sealed. As a general proposition, it seems unwise to deprive (or to risk depriving) judges of discretion to seal any particular document in this sensitive context.

54. SSPA §4053(c).

55. The text currently provides that "[n]o adverse inference shall be drawn form a pleading of state secrets in an answer to an item in a complaint." *Id.* This language should be amended to more clearly state that a privilege plea should be treated as a denial for pleading purposes.

jecting on privilege grounds to particular allegations in a complaint, though
it is not clear that the government ever pursued such a course. In any event,
this aspect of the SSPA at a minimum is a useful clarification even if not an outright alteration of what is permitted under current practice.

The Mechanics of the Judge's Review: Ex Parte and in Camera Procedures

When reviewing the government's invocation of the privilege, should the
judge permit the government to submit some or all of its explanation on an *in
camera, ex parte* basis? In current practice, the government routinely submits
classified documents and affidavits on an *ex parte* basis in the course of asserting the privilege. These submissions are reviewed by the court alone; they
are not made available to opposing counsel. As a result, the process of determining whether the privilege attaches is in an important sense non-adversar-
ial. This approach is optimal from the perspective of ensuring against an
improper disclosure of the information, but it is far from optimal from the
perspective of ensuring against inaccurate determinations by the court.

Both values are substantial. The question, therefore, is whether there are
solutions that would sufficiently preserve the government's interest in security
while simultaneously reducing the risk of error by introducing elements of adversariality in the review process. In a major departure from the status quo,
the SSPA seeks to accomplish precisely this.

Ex Parte Proceedings

The SSPA would break with current practice in a significant way by limiting
the ability of the government to justify its invocation of the privilege through
ex parte submissions. First, §4052(a)(1) recognizes that the judge has discretion
as to whether *ex parte* submissions will be allowed at all, subject to the "interests of justice and national security."[56] No doubt most judges in most cases
would exercise this authority wisely.[57] Even if the judge decides to permit *ex*

---

56. SSPA §4052(a)(1). As an alternative to precluding *ex parte* filings, §4052(a)(2) permits the judge to order the government to provide the other litigants with a "redacted, unclassified, or summary substitute" of its *ex parte* submissions. This authority in practice
may turn out to track status quo procedures in which the government typically provides
both a classified affidavit justifying its assertion of the privilege and also an unclassified version that can be made available to opposing parties and to the public.

57. The comparable provision in the Classified Information Procedures Act ("CIPA")
permits but does not on its face require the government to submit its filings *ex parte. See*

parte filings in the first instance, however, §4052(c)(1) appears to ensure that before ruling upon the government's invocation of the privilege the otherwise *ex parte* filings will be subject to at least some degree of adversarial testing:

> A Federal court shall, at the request of the United States, limit participation in hearings conducted under this chapter, or access to motions or affidavits submitted under this chapter, to attorneys with appropriate security clearances, if the court determines that limiting participation in that manner would serve the interests of national security. The court may also appoint a guardian ad litem with the necessary security clearances to represent any party for the purposes of any hearing conducted under this chapter.

There is considerable wisdom in finding a way to inject some degree of adversariality into the currently *ex parte* portion of the privilege adjudication process. The trick, however, is to manage this without undermining the overriding goal of ensuring that there is no disclosure of the assertedly-protected information unless and until the judge determines that it is not in fact protected. Under the SSPA approach, the parties' own attorneys might be given direct access to the government's most sensitive secrets prior to determining whether they are in fact privileged. This goes too far, assuming that there are less intrusive alternatives available that might address the accuracy considerations described above. And, as noted above, §4052(c)(1) actually contains such a middle ground alternative, in the form of a guardian-ad-litem mechanism.

The guardian-ad-litem approach has the virtue of ensuring at least some degree of adversarial testing, while reducing the risk of a leak (to the parties themselves or to the public at large) in comparison to having the party's own attorneys involved. For this reason, other countries are experimenting with precisely this approach in analogous contexts. Canada, for example, recently has adopted a "special advocate" system in which attorneys are appointed for

---

18 U.S.C. App. 3, §4. That said, it appears that no court has ever barred the government from making its application *ex parte. See* David S. Kris & J. Douglas Wilson, National Security Investigations & Prosecutions §24.7 (2007) (observing that "[a]lthough this procedure denies the defendant the ability to make a meaningful challenge to the government's argument, no court in a published opinion has prevented the government from filing its Section 4 application *ex parte* and *in camera*."). This suggests that judges can be trusted not to act rashly, but perhaps also that there is little point in providing an option to bar such filings. CIPA §6 hearings, in contrast, are required to be *in camera* but are not normally *ex parte. See* 18 U.S.C. App. 3, §6(a). Such hearings arise in a distinguishable context, however, insofar as the defendant in that scenario already possesses classified information, information that the government seeks to suppress.

the specific purpose of contesting otherwise *ex parte* information used by the government in connection with removal of non-citizens from the country.[58] The U.K. has a comparable system, originally designed for comparable immigration removals.[59] Unlike the SSPA's guardian mechanism, however, the Canadian system does not allow the court to appoint just any attorney to this sensitive role, but instead require the appointee to be chosen from a pre-determined list of screened and qualified individuals.[60]

In order to strike a more reasonable and sustainable balance between the competing equities at stake in this sensitive context, §4052(c) should be amended to focus attention on the guardian mechanism as a solution to the adversariality problem (that is to say, the more extreme alternative of ordering the government to provide access directly to the parties' attorneys should be removed). At the same time, the guardian mechanism should be amended so as to create a pre-selected list of attorneys eligible for such an appointment. Such a list could be created by the Chief Justice of the United States, for example, and following the Canadian example might also involve substantial training for the potential appointees.[61] This solution concededly is not ideal from the litigants' perspective, of course, but even from that viewpoint it does constitute a substantial improvement over the status quo.[62]

In Camera Proceedings

Beyond the question of whether filings and arguments will take place on an *ex parte* basis is the question of whether and when privilege litigation should take place *in camera*, without public access.[63] Under the status quo, judges typically employ a blend of ordinary and *in camera* procedures when adjudicating an assertion of the privilege.

---

58. *See* Bill C-3, An Act to amend the Immigration and Refugee Protection Act (certificate and special advocate) and to make a consequential amendment to another Act, *available at* http://www2.parl.gc.ca/content/hoc/Bills/392/Government/C-3/C-3_2/C-3_2.PDF.

59. Special Immigration Appeals Act, 1997, c. 68, §6 (Eng.).

60. *See* Bill C-3, §85.

61. *See* Richard Foot, *Lawyers Line Up to Become Special "Terror" Advocates*, Nat. Post, Feb. 17, 2008, available at http://www.nationalpost.com/news/canada/story.html?id=315669.

62. It is worth noting, in that regard, that nothing comparable is available to criminal defendants—whose very liberty is at stake—in the analogous context of §4 proceedings under the Classified Information Procedures Act ("CIPA"), in which *ex parte* review is the rule. *See supra* note 50.

63. An *in camera* procedure is not necessarily *ex parte*, though the two concepts are conflated often.

The impact SSPA § 4052(b)(1) would have on this practice is unclear, but probably will not constitute a significant departure from the status quo. This section establishes a default presumption that hearings concerning the state secrets privilege will be conducted *in camera*, and permits public access only "if the court determines that the hearing relates only to a question of law and does not present a risk of revealing state secrets."

The Mechanics of the Judge's Review: Special Masters

One of the core difficulties associated with judicial review of the state secrets privilege involves the question of expertise. Critics of the status quo argue that judges in practice merely rubber-stamp executive invocations of the privilege because the judges do not feel confident that they can evaluate the executive's claims regarding the impact of disclosure on security or diplomacy, while others draw on the same notions to contend that judges should in fact be extremely if not entirely deferential. And certainly it is true that a federal judge on average will not be as well-situated in terms of experience and fact-gathering resources as the Director of National Intelligence or the Secretary of State to assess such impacts.[64] At the same time, *Reynolds* itself acknowledges that the judge has ultimate responsibility for ensuring the validity and propriety of privilege assertions, lest the privilege become a temptation to abuse.[65]

The tension between these values appears intractable at first blush, but there are mechanisms for ameliorating the problem. Some scholars have pointed out, for example, that judges currently have authority to appoint expert advisers such as special masters under Federal Rule of Civil Procedure 53 and independent experts under Federal Rule of Evidence 706.[66] Section 4052(f) of the SSPA would clarify that such authorities in fact can be used in connection with state secrets litigation, an approach that may prove particularly valuable in cases involving assertion of the privilege with respect to voluminous materials.

---

64. *See, e.g., al-Haramain*, 507 F.3d at 1203 ("we acknowledge the need to defer to the Executive on matters of foreign policy and national security and surely cannot legitimately find ourselves second guessing the Executive in this arena").

65. 345 U.S. at 9–10.

66. *See, e.g.,* Meredith Fuchs & G. Gregg Webb, *Greasing the Wheels of Justice: Independent Experts in National Security Cases*, A.B.A. Nat'l Security L. Rep., Nov. 2006, at 1, 3–5, *available at* http://www.abanet.org/nat-security/nslr/2006/NSL_Report_2006_11.pdf.

Consequences Once the Privilege Attaches: Substitutions

SSPA §4054(f) provides that where the privilege attaches, courts should consider whether it is "possible to craft a non-privileged substitute" that provides "a substantially equivalent opportunity to litigate the claim or defense." Drawing on the model set forth in CIPA §6, the SSPA goes on to specify several options that might be used in that context, including an unclassified summary, a redacted version of a particular item of evidence, and a statement of admitted facts.[67] Where the court believes that such an alternative is available, it may order the United States to produce it in lieu of the protected information.[68] The United States must comply with such an order if the issue arises in a suit to which the United States is a party (or a U.S. official is a party in his or her official capacity), or else "the court shall resolve the disputed issue of fact or law to which the evidence pertains in the non-government party's favor."[69]

It is not clear that any of these provisions depart from what a court might order even in the absence of the SSPA. But in any event, it certainly is advisable to codify the judge's obligation to exhaust options that would permit relevant and otherwise-admissible information to be used without actually compelling disclosure of that which is subject to the protection of the privilege.

Consequences Once the Privilege Attaches: Ending Litigation

The most controversial aspect of current doctrine may well be the sometimes fatal impact it has on litigation once the privilege is found to attach to some item of evidence or information. As discussed earlier in this essay, this phenomenon is not new. The government has moved to dismiss (or in the alternative for summary judgment) in these circumstances with some frequency since the 1950s, and such motions have frequently been granted.[70] But the use of this approach in high-profile post-9/11 cases—particularly those relating to NSA surveillance and to rendition—has proven especially controversial, drawing attention to the fact that application of the state secrets privilege can have harsh consequences for litigants even where the litigants allege unlawful government conduct. Accordingly, one of the most important questions as-

---

67. SSPA §4054(f).

68. *See id.*

69. *See id.* §4054(g). No sanction is provided by the SSPA for scenarios in which the U.S. is merely an intervenor.

70. *See* Chesney, *supra* note 67, at 1306–07, 1315–33.

sociated with the SSPA is whether it would limit the set of circumstances in which application of the privilege proves fatal to a suit.

When Denial of Discovery Precipitates Summary Judgment

Application of the privilege can prove fatal to a suit in more than one way under current doctrine. First, the privilege may function to deprive a litigant of evidence needed in order to create a triable issue of fact and hence survive a summary judgment motion.

Let us assume that a judge has denied a discovery request based on the state secrets privilege. If it so happens that the plaintiff has no other admissible evidence sufficient to raise a triable issue of fact with respect to a necessary element of his or her claim, this discovery ruling necessarily exposes that plaintiff to summary judgment under Rule 56. In that setting, the Rule 56 ruling conceptually is subsequent to the state secrets ruling, rather than being based directly on it. The discovery ruling is no less fatal to the plaintiff's case for that, however, and if the motions happen to be adjudicated simultaneously it might even appear that the court has granted summary judgment "on" state secrets grounds. It does not appear that the SSPA is intended to alter the outcome in this scenario, though it might be wise to clarify that this is so in the text of the legislation.

When the Government Must Choose between Disclosing Protected Information and Presenting a Defense

A second scenario that can be fatal to a claim under current doctrine arises when the government would be obliged to reveal protected information in order to present a defense to a claim. This scenario differs from the first in that the plaintiff may be able to survive summary judgment with the evidence it has assembled. The problem here is not the plaintiff's efforts to acquire evidence, then, but the fact that the government must opt between presenting a defense and maintaining the secrecy of protected information. In that setting, current doctrine provides for dismissal on state secrets grounds.

In some senses, the SSPA codifies this result. Under §4055 a judge may dismiss a claim on privilege grounds upon a determination that litigation in the absence of the privileged information "would substantially impair the ability of a party to pursue a valid defense," and that there is no viable option for creating a non-privileged substitute that would provide a "substantially equivalent opportunity to litigate" the issue.[71] But §4055 also mandates that the judge

---

71. SSPA §4055(1) & (3). For what it is worth, §4055(2) also requires a finding that dismissal of the claim or counterclaim "would not harm national security."

first review "all available evidence, privileged and non-privileged" before determining whether the "valid defense" standard has been met. This suggests that the judge is not merely to assess the *legal* sufficiency of the defense (assuming the truth of the government's version of events, in a style akin to adjudication of a Rule 12(b)(6) motion), but instead is to resolve the actual merits of the defense (including resolution of related factual disputes). If that is the correct interpretation, it would seem to follow that §4055 contemplates a mini-trial on the merits of the defense.

The problem with this approach is that the court may or may not permit the use of *ex parte* and *in camera* procedures in this context, as described above. Denying either protection (but especially the latter) would put the government on the horns of a dilemma, forcing it to choose between waiving a potentially-meritorious defense and revealing privileged information to persons other than the judge even in the face of the judge's conclusion that the information is subject to the privilege. This approach is questionable from a policy perspective insofar as it would force the government to elect between partial or even complete exposure of concededly protected information and the loss of a meritorious defense and hence potential civil liability (including injunctive as well as financial consequences). And for much the same reasons, this approach presumably will precipitate constitutional objections as well. At a minimum, therefore, §4055 should be amended to provide that the judge's assessment of the merits of a defense must take place on an *in camera* basis. Any move away from *ex parte* procedures in this context, moreover, should be limited to the modified guardian-ad-litem mechanism recommended above. Beyond that, it might also be wise to structure the judge's review of the defense at issue in terms of a Rule 12(b)(6)-style legal-sufficiency inquiry rather than as a mini-trial.

When the Very Subject Matter of the Action Implicates State Secrets

One scenario remains. Under current doctrine, "some matters are so pervaded by state secrets as to be incapable of judicial resolution once the privilege has been invoked."[72] The idea here is not that certain discovery should be denied to the plaintiff, nor that the government has a defense it could present if only it were not necessary to preserve certain secrets. Rather, the notion is that some types of claims are not actionable as a matter of law because they in-

---

72. *See el-Masri*, 479 F. 3d at 306.

evitably would require disclosure or confirmation of state secrets in order to be adjudicated. Under this approach, therefore, a suit may be dismissed at the pleading stage even if the plaintiff could have assembled sufficient evidence to create triable issues of fact on all the necessary elements of a claim, and even if the government is not prevented by its secrecy obligation from presenting a defense to that claim. Not surprisingly, this is the most controversial dismissal scenario in current doctrine.

The SSPA overrides the result in this scenario in the narrow sense that it permits suits to survive that under current doctrine would have been dismissed at the very outset. First, as noted above, the SSPA permits the government to avoid affirming or denying sensitive fact allegations by instead citing the privilege in its responsive pleading. Second, § 4053(b) plainly states that "the state secrets privilege shall not constitute grounds for dismissal of a case or claim" unless, as described above, the government has a "valid defense" it would present but for privilege concerns. Taken together, these provisions have the effect of requiring cases in what might be called the "very subject matter" category to go forward at least to the discovery stage.

Ultimately, however, the SSPA will not necessarily spare such suits from dismissal. During the course of discovery, the privilege remains wholly functional as a shield against production of protected documents or information, which may expose the plaintiff to summary judgment in the end. The SSPA expressly authorizes the government to use the privilege as a sword, moreover, enhancing the prospects for dismissal in the "very subject matter" scenario. Specifically, § 4054(a) states that the government not only may use the privilege to resist discovery, but also "for preventing the introduction of evidence at trial."[73] Much turns on the interpretation of this language.

This language appears to allow the government to move to suppress otherwise-admissible evidence in the plaintiff's possession, on state secrets grounds. In that case, a plaintiff who is otherwise able to assemble sufficient evidence to create a triable issue of fact without discovery from the government nonetheless may find himself or herself without critical evidence at trial, necessitating judgment in the government's favor. The only question then would be whether the government must await the plaintiff's case-in-chief in order to exercise this suppression power, setting the stage for judgment as a matter of law pursuant to Rule 50(a), or if it instead could exercise this option prior to trial and thus proceed under Rule 56. The language of § 4054(a) suggests the former, but if the option is to be allowed at all it makes far more sense from an efficiency

---

73. SSPA § 4054(a).

perspective to permit pre-trial resolution. Section 4054(a) accordingly should be amended to say as much.[74]

The important point for now is that the "sword" aspect of §4054(a) at least arguably will produce an end result comparable to that which obtains under the current doctrine's "very subject matter" line of cases. The difference, which is by no means unimportant, is that under the SSPA the litigation process will proceed through the pleading and discovery stages, with the privilege being wielded as a scalpel rather than a bludgeon. Combined with the other procedural elements of the SSPA—including especially the role of special masters, guardians-ad-litem, and the emphasis on finding substitutions when possible—the net effect of this "proceduralization" of the privilege should be to ensure much more careful tailoring of it to the facts and evidence in particular cases. This in turn should reduce the risk of erroneous applications (and thus injustice). Though this benefit will come at the costs of increased litigation expense and complexity, that is a cost that most likely is worth bearing. At the very least, the experiment is worth undertaking.

Conclusion

The SSPA will not entirely please either critics or supporters of the state secrets status quo. By subjecting the privilege to a more rigorous procedural framework, the SSPA may reduce the range of cases in which the privilege is found to apply, and in some respects it may cause marginal increases in the risk that sensitive information will be disclosed (though with the amendments proposed above such risks would be significantly diminished). On the other hand, even under the SSPA the privilege will continue to have a harsh impact on litigants who bring claims that implicate protected information: discovery will still be denied, complaints will still be dismissed, and summary judgment will still be granted. Such tradeoffs are inevitable, however, in crafting legislation designed to reconcile such important public values as national security, access to justice, and democratic accountability. The SSPA has its flaws, to be sure, but subject to the caveats noted above it marks an important step forward in the ongoing evolution of the state secrets privilege.

---

74. The statute also needs to be amended to ensure that the government has an adequate opportunity to use the privilege in this fashion, meaning that some form of notice will have to be given to the government by a party intended to make use of information that may be subject to the privilege. This precise dilemma is addressed in the criminal prosecution context by CIPA §5, which has been upheld against constitutional challenge on many occasions. Presumably a comparable procedure can be added to the SSPA.

Chapter 6

Civil Liberties in the Struggle Against Terror

Elizabeth Rindskopf Parker[1]

Introduction: The Need for a New Domestic Security Paradigm

In some respects, the threats faced by the United States today from weapons of mass destruction in the hands of individual terrorists may be no greater than those in earlier times. Certainly our nation's very existence has been challenged in the past from forces both outside and inside our borders. The Revolutionary and Civil Wars, World Wars I and II, and the Cold War, each brought their own unique threats to our nation's continued existence and way of life. Still, there is something essentially different in today's terrorist threat which is profoundly unsettling to our traditional constitutional balance between national security and individual liberty. The possibility of nuclear weapons in the hands of terrorists is a part of this disturbing new reality. What our responses should be to preserve both our nation and its fundamental commitment to individual rights and liberties here at home has become a matter of critical importance and is the theme of this chapter.[2]

Today's clash between civil liberties and national security, occasioned by this emerging terrorist threat, has a multi-part explanation.

---

1. Dean, University of the Pacific, McGeorge School of Law. This chapter has been immeasurably assisted by the contributions of my two research assistants, Matthew Koski and Yury Kolesnikov, to whom I extend my most profound thanks.

2. While this chapter does not address disturbing developments in the U.S. response to the terrorist threat overseas, many developments not directly germane to our domestic situation, e.g., allegations about the use of torture or denial of habeas corpus rights to noncitizens detained in Guantanamo and elsewhere, create a context which heightens concern for the domestic issues discussed here.

- First, the current terrorist threat is unprecedented in its unpredictability and size. It is thus qualitatively different from past threats because it combines the flexibility of individual actors with a destructive power normally possible only for nation states.
- Next, today's terrorist threat follows a half century of relative freedom from direct citizen experience with existential challenges to our national tranquility. The ability of the terrorists to attack the nation, operating both from inside and outside our borders, has caught both government and the public by surprise. Unprepared for the sudden change in our security environment produced by the 9/11 terrorist attacks, we are struggling to find solutions to balance our needs for both collective security and individual liberty.
- Finally, the terrorist threat has confounded basic definitions and legal structures long relied upon to organize our responses to security threats and to protect our basic constitutional liberties.

Responses to the terrorist threat thus face a profound dilemma. On the one hand, citizens have demanded that the full range of the nation's security capabilities be available to prevent a reoccurrence of attacks like 9/11 or the 2005 London bombings. Accordingly, Congress' immediate response after 9/11 was to place the nation on a "war footing" by passing the Authorization for Use of Military Force (AUMF).[3] Yet, there was seemingly little thought about the potentially broad implications of such an action in the face of this immediate strong public consensus to provide the federal government with all workable means to address the terrorist threat. Even capabilities heretofore confined to the military, acting abroad, were made available when Congress broadened law enforcement investigatory authorities.[4] Nonetheless, there has been a gradual yet increasing recognition that government action must be restrained and organ-

---

3. Pub. L. No. 107-40, 115 Stat. 224 (2001). The AUMF authorized the President to "use all necessary and appropriate force against those nations, organizations, or persons he determines planned, authorized, committed, or aided the terrorist attacks," or "harbored such organizations or persons, in order to prevent any future acts of international terrorism against the United States by such nations, organizations or persons." *Id.*

4. *See* USA PATRIOT Act, Pub. L. No. 107-56, 115 Stat. 272 (2001). Among other things, the Patriot Act altered the restrictions on intelligence gathering within the United States. Section 213 of the Act, for example, authorized the use of "sneak and peek" search warrants, whereby the notice that the government had searched a place, appropriated an item, or placed an individual under surveillance could be delayed almost indefinitely. *Id.* §213. Section 505, broadened the use of National Security Letters by lowering the requirements that had to be shown before one could be issued while at the same time expanding the scope of material that could be sought. *Id.* §505.

ized according to law, if the civil liberties of individual citizens are to be preserved. Our experience since 9/11 shows how these two imperatives, protecting national security and the rights of individual citizens, can often conflict. Yet we are learning that unless we achieve both, the nation we value will not survive.

This tension between liberty and security is not new.[5] Past experience teaches that during wartime, this tension will be greatest, with the balance likely struck in favor of security and at the expense of individual liberties. Yet this balance between security and liberty is dynamic and, almost inevitably, the overreaction caused by wartime emergencies will subside as the crisis reduces.[6] This process of reaction and adjustment is paralleled by an ebb and flow of power among the three branches of government as such crises wax and wane. Initially, the two political branches, the Executive and the Legislative, respond rapidly to protect national security; their concern for protecting individual liberties is at its nadir during such times. Later, as the emergency subsides, the third branch, our court system, steps in and re-evaluates the risks, typically re-adjusting the balance according to more traditional interpretations of our constitutionally guaranteed rights and reigning in the political branches in the process.

Our history has many examples of the effects of such reaction and counter-reaction to the pressures of wartime on civil liberties.[7] Even so, the current "War on Terror" has, in the eyes of some, raised novel questions as to whether this progression will continue.[8] This latest war seems to lack traditional boundaries of space and time: might it be *sui generis*—a new paradigm of warfare—

---

5. For a careful analysis of the United States government's actions in six different "wartime" periods, *see* GEOFFREY R. STONE, PERILOUS TIMES: FREE SPEECH IN WARTIME FROM THE SEDITION ACT OF 1798 TO THE WAR ON TERRORISM (2004).

6. For a description of this reaction and response to national emergencies in Hawaii during World War II, *see* Harry N. Scheiber & Jane L. Scheiber, *Bayonets in Paradise: A Half-Century Retrospect on Martial Law in Hawai'i, 1941–1946*, 19 U. HAW. L. REV. 477 (1997).

7. There are numerous examples throughout history of courts evaluating the propriety of Executive action during wartime. *See, e.g.*, Johnson v. Eisentrager, 339 U.S. 763 (1950) (finding that German nationals convicted by military tribunals for engaging in military activities in China against the United States after Germany surrendered in World War II had no right to habeas corpus); *Ex parte* Quirin, 317 U.S. 1 (1942) (denying habeas corpus relief to alien combatants detained while engaging in espionage in the United States during World War II); *Ex parte* Milligan, 71 U.S. 2 (1866) (condemning the suspension of the writ of habeas corpus and the imposition of martial law during the Civil War).

8. *See, e.g.*, PHILIP B. HEYMANN, TERRORISM, FREEDOM, AND SECURITY: WINNING WITHOUT WAR 19–33 (2003) (noting the implications of defining the dangers from terrorism as a "war").

immune from the traditional ebb and flow of protection for individual liberties in response to the nation's existential threats? If we make unrestricted use of our complete arsenal of national security authorities, from law enforcement to military force, both at home and abroad, and over a long period, what rules and structures will govern them to prevent moving in the direction of a police state? Under such circumstances, will we need new legal mechanisms to help the government protect our security, while also safeguarding individual liberties during wartime? Or are there, in fact, Constitutional limits that will inevitably re-emerge and from which no deviation can long be tolerated, even in a national security emergency, lest the very character of our nation be lost?[9]

These and other questions are now beginning to be asked and gradually answered. More remains to be done, however, and understanding how our Constitutional structure can and should respond to the current War on Terror remains a critically important task for every citizen. This is so notwithstanding the role the U.S. Supreme Court has slowly begun to play in readjusting the balance between collective security and individual liberty in a series of high profile cases that considered the rights of citizens and non-citizens alike.[10] It is to these questions to which this chapter is addressed.

Responses to the Terrorist Threat

Policy Challenges to Greater Use of Law Enforcement and Military Techniques

Adapting our law enforcement and military security structures—both their policies and procedures—to the current terrorist threat, while remaining true to our Constitutional principles, has proved challenging. Our constitutional structures have been resilient thanks to the Supreme Court's historical skill in adapt-

---

9. As Justice Sandra Day O'Connor stated in her plurality opinion in *Hamdi v. Rumsfeld*, "It is during our most challenging and uncertain moments that our Nation's commitment to due process is most severely tested; and it is in those times that we must preserve our commitment at home to the principles for which we fight abroad." 542 U.S. 507, 532 (2004).

10. *See Hamdan v. Rumsfeld*, 548 U.S. 557 (2006) (examining the validity of using military commissions to try alien enemy combatants); *Hamdi v. Rumsfeld*, 542 U.S. 507 (2004) (examining the legality of government's detention of a U.S. citizen as an enemy combatant); *Rasul v. Bush*, 542 U.S. 466 (2004) (examining the detention of alien enemy combatants held at Guantanamo Bay); *Rumsfeld v. Padilla*, 542 U.S. 426 (2004) (examining the detention of a U.S. citizen as an enemy combatant).

ing constitutional principles to a time of rapid technological change. Yet legal and policy adaptations require time, first to build consensus among the political branches of government and the public, and then for review by the courts. And employing national security capabilities in the domestic arena is an area with relatively little judicial precedent to guide our choices.[11] Not surprisingly, consensus has likewise been slow to develop. Often, the Executive Branch has acted impatiently, without waiting for consensus among the political branches and the public.[12]

Traditional Security Policy

At the most fundamental level, ours is a government based on laws which implement an overarching set of Constitutional policies. Thus, *all* security authorities, whether they are law enforcement or military, are also subject to law. Indeed, it is in the need for security where government power over, and in support of, citizens is greatest that our policy choices must be the clearest and subject to unwavering legal controls. As a nation, our custom has been to achieve security by differing means, based on the location and nature of the threat involved. There are practical, Constitutional, and legal reasons for this. Today, however, many long-standing legal controls over our security structures seem counterproductive to protecting us against the terrorist threat.

- Within our borders, the law enforcement system has been chiefly responsible for managing all internal threats, using a variety of activities from

---

11. The principal judicial authority for managing the intersection of domestic civil rights and the government's actions to protect national security remains *Youngstown Sheet & Tube Co. v. Sawyer*, 343 U.S. 579 (1952), the famous 1952 "Steel Seizure Case." There, the Supreme Court rejected President Truman's nationalization of the steel industry during the Korean War because the process failed to satisfy basic notions of due process of law applied to a takings situation where the Executive's actions ran counter to the will of Congress expressed in statute. The concurring opinion of Justice Robert Jackson remains the clearest expression of the President's power as Commander-in-Chief: greatest if pursuant to a statute; less if based on his inherent, but necessarily concurrent, powers; and least when based on inherent powers which contravene Congressional enactments. *Id.* at 635–38.

12. Even as this chapter was being written, the Department of Homeland Security announced its intention to incorporate a complete array of the nation's most advanced spy technology into its surveillance collection techniques, but without Congressional approval as to the legal controls that would govern such a change in the use of traditional military technologies such as radar, satellite imagery, electronic-signal information, and other monitoring capabilities. *See* Spencer S. Hsu, *Administration Set to Use New Spy Program in U.S.*, WASH. POST, Apr. 12, 2008, at A03.

policing to investigation of crimes to prosecution.[13] Historically, laws in this area are based on a policy of *reacting* to events after they occur, rather than *anticipating* and *preventing* them. Traditionally, it is only when criminal conduct has occurred, or is a certainty, that law enforcement is authorized to intervene. Such a policy involves an element of risk: a crime may occur that could have been prevented but for our delay to establish certainty. This unwillingness to interfere at an earlier point, however, is produced by our need to protect individual liberty. In the end, since law enforcement authorities operate largely within the United States and are designed to manage individual risk, this risk is seen as sufficiently limited to be acceptable and necessary to protect individual citizen liberties.

• In contrast, outside our nation's borders, we have used a combination of approaches for protection: foreign policy, military action, and, to a much lesser extent in recent years, the traditional law enforcement responses of investigation and prosecution.[14] Here, because we do not control the territory in which we operate and because the size of the threats faced is significantly greater, possibly even existential, detection and warning are of critical importance. Unlike the individualized threats for which a law enforcement response is designed, the size of these threats and the existential risk they pose to our nation's security causes a shift in the balance between warning and reaction. Our actions become less circumscribed; we are unwilling to assume risk to the nation's very existence.

A central question raised by responses to the 'War on Terror' is how these two principal functional areas of security, law enforcement and military responses, will work together. Both are necessary parts of our security arsenal, but have historically been confined either inside or outside our boarders; they are thus unaccustomed to close cooperation. Today, the movement of individual terrorists makes national borders far less relevant and their access to ex-

---

13. After the Civil War, interest in prohibiting military activity within the nation's borders produced the Posse Comitatus Act, ch. 263, §15, 20 Stat. 145, 152 (1878) (current version at 18 U.S.C. §1385 (2000)), which until recently has banned all military activities inside the U.S.

14. The increased problems of weapons of mass destruction, drug trafficking, and terrorism, all of which are cross-border threats, led Congress to enact criminal statues in the early 1990's for certain conduct abroad. This in turn extended FBI jurisdiction to certain events overseas which possessed a dual character as both national security and law enforcement threats. *See, e.g., United States v. Rezaq*, 899 F. Supp. 697, 700–01 (D.D.C. 1995) (prosecution for the 1985 hijacking of an Egyptian airliner); *United States v. Yunis*, 867 F.2d 617, 618 (D.C. Cir. 1989) (prosecution concerning the 1985 hijacking and destruction of a Jordanian airliner).

istential force makes important the use of the full range of tools in our security arsenal—including military capabilities and technologies, no matter where the threat may arise. Yet our policies and laws have not been designed for this situation. There are other important governmental players as well, many now incorporated in the new Department of Homeland Security. They are neither part of law enforcement nor the military, but they have a role to play in achieving national security. Coordination with them is likewise essential.

It is not surprising that cooperation among the various parts of our security arsenal has been notoriously challenging. Like all large regulated bureaucracies, cooperation is difficult when entities are designed for distinctly different purposes. Their roles and rules are predetermined by the function and values each serves. Typically, if cooperation was not a factor in their original design, it will be challenging to introduce it after the fact.

For example, law enforcement, and its tools of investigation and prosecution, are structured to support the crown jewel of our legal system: an open and fair trial within the United States, before an independent and impartial judge, leading to eventual incarceration or even death, if guilt is established. In contrast, our military capabilities, and the intelligence collection and analysis which support them, do not presume so specific a use, but more generally support our political leadership and the foreign policy choices they make abroad. Military intelligence is often derived from sensitive sources with long term value, but often lacks the probity and clarity demanded of criminal evidence. The rules governing intelligence are typically less restrictive, both because the rights of U.S. citizens are unlikely to be impacted and because it is directed at protecting the nation against the most serious threats to our national security and well-being.

Over time, the natural tendency of these two systems of security—law enforcement at home and military force abroad—to remain distinct has been re-enforced by laws designed to insure citizens' rights. Rules have been deliberately designed to keep our law enforcement and military capabilities apart. We have not wanted our citizens to be subject to the broad and relatively less precise controls necessary for effective military action.[15] Thus, although our

---

15. To see the potential for abuse, one need only look to the Watergate era. The Church Committee reports revealed numerous law violations, such as the opening of first class mail by the CIA and the FBI, monitoring of activities of political dissenters by the Army, acquisition of millions of private telegrams by the NSA, and the creation of a large number of files on American individuals and groups by all of the above agencies. *See* 2 SELECT COMM. TO STUDY GOVERNMENTAL OPERATIONS, FINAL REPORT OF THE SELECT COMMITTEE TO STUDY GOVERNMENTAL OPERATIONS WITH RESPECT TO INTELLIGENCE ACTIVITIES, S. REP. No. 94-755, at 6–7 (1976) [hereinafter CHURCH COMMITTEE]. The reaction to these activ-

law enforcement and military authorities may share a common goal of protecting our nation and its citizens, even when their specific means of doing so are technically identical, e.g., wire tapping, they will be subject to governance structures so fundamentally different that they may appear to conflict. In short, a difference in degree of control can create a fundamental difference in the underlying capability.

This once clear divide between the use of law enforcement and military techniques has become blurred in our response to the AUMF imperative "to use all necessary and appropriate force" to counter the terrorist threat. In the current "War on Terror," this confusion between the differing approaches of the two systems to surveillance, investigation, and detention is particularly noteworthy. The need to alternate between the law enforcement and military approaches to surveillance, investigation, and detention in our domestic responses to the terrorist threat has produced a deeply unsettling situation where legal limits are no longer predictable. Our constitutional rights and guarantees as citizens often seem capricious. And the public trust in the government has been eroded as a result.

When the 9/11 attacks occurred, such policy and legal distinctions were seen as unnecessarily technical and counterproductive. The nation's understandable response was to move away from individual liberty and dramatically in the direction of security. Few questioned the response of Congress to place us on a war-time footing with enactment of the AUMF. Support for ending the separation between law enforcement and intelligence was almost universal. As a nation, we moved rapidly to use all existing techniques that might enhance our security and to design new approaches as well. There was little concern about what these well-intentioned changes might mean to our individual rights and liberties in actual application.

The Executive Branch, with primary responsibility for our security and the prevention of future attacks, took advantage of this opportunity and urged Congress to expand its authority to address the terrorist threat. In response, Congress passed the USA PATRIOT Act which enhanced governmental authority in numerous respects.[16] In addition, detention authorities were cobbled together, combining Material Witness Warrants with military detention authorities, and all were directed at those with apparent Arab or Muslim connections who seemed speculatively threatening to us.[17] Our borders were closed

---

ities produced laws and procedures to insure that using military techniques to spy on Americans could not reoccur.

   16. *See supra* note 4 (describing some of the changes made by the USA PATRIOT Act).

   17. Typically, a material witness warrant is issued to detain a person whose testimony is "material" to a criminal proceeding and when it is "impracticable" to secure such per-

with the increased use of visa and immigration authorities and controls.[18] Surveillance activities were enhanced through both public and secret actions.[19] Furthermore, over the last seven years, disturbing reports from overseas have gradually confirmed the use of intelligence gathering techniques which are questionable at best, torture at worst, and "rendition" practices which have been used in some cases to deliver those suspected of terrorist links to nations whose security practices, particularly the use of torture in investigations, are highly questionable.

Together, these changes in approach, if not in policy, were taken without effective national debate about what each might mean. They created a laissez faire context for government action if security were the rationale and, not surprisingly, there was also little discussion about the need for carefully designed internal operating rules for those government entities who would manage these new authorities. In several cases, notably the Terrorist Surveillance Program and the Total Information Awareness Program discussed below, additional actions were taken, too often in secrecy, by the Executive Branch, well beyond anything approved by Congress. Most importantly, little attention was given to

---

son's presence with a subpoena. 18 U.S.C. § 3144 (2000). After 9/11 attacks, however, the government used such warrants to hold people that it suspected of having ties to al Qaida— even when these suspicions were based on weak facts or rumors. *See* Human Rights Watch, Witness to Abuse: Human Rights Abuses under the Material Witness Law since September 11, at 15–19 (June 2005), http://hrw.org/reports/2005/us0605/us0605.pdf. According to the Human Rights Watch, "[s]ince the attacks of September 11, 2001, at least seventy men living in the United States—all Muslim but one—have been thrust into a Kafkaesque world of indefinite detention without charges, secret evidence, and baseless accusations of terrorist links. They have found themselves not at Guantánamo Bay or Abu Ghraib but in America's own federal prison system, victims of the misuse of the federal material witness law in the U.S. government's fight against terrorism." *Id.* at 1.

18. "In the wake of September 11, the U.S. government arrested, interrogated, detained, and removed from the country thousands of Arab and Muslim noncitizens." Kevin R. Johnson, *Protecting National Security through More Liberal Admission of Immigrants*, 2007 U. CHI. LEGAL F. 157, 169 (2007). Specifically, "[p]rofiling, security checks, and removal campaigns resulted in record levels of deportations, with almost all of the noncitizens having nothing whatsoever to do with terrorism." *Id.* at 173.

19. As noted earlier, one of the major public actions was the passage of the USA PARTIOT Act shortly after the 9/11 attacks. *See supra* note 4 (discussing some of the changes made by the Act). On the non-public side, the NSA's Terrorist Surveillance Program ("TSP") is one example. It allowed the NSA to monitor numerous conversations without the Foreign Intelligence Surveillance Court's oversight. Likewise, Department of Defense programs such as TALON (Threat And Local Observation Notice), which allowed DoD to spy on activities that "may or may not be related to an actual threat" to the DoD, have only recently been made public.

supporting oversight structures for the new authorities thus granted, notwith-standing their obvious potential to impact citizens' rights and liberties.[20]

Lessons Learned: The Need to Rebalance Security Procedures

The passage of time since the 9/11 attacks makes possible some preliminary conclusions about the choices that were made in response to the attacks and what must be done now to restore the balance between security and liberty in our responses to terrorism here at home:

- To avoid destroying the fundamental constitutional values which are the foundation for rules governing both military intelligence and law enforcement, greater balance is needed; the Supreme Court has signaled this in several recent decisions, but it cannot achieve this goal alone.
- In contrast, to insure our domestic security, changes in how we manage our law enforcement and military capabilities, particularly techniques of investigation, intelligence, and detention, must yield to the realities of modern technology and a new generation of national security threats—but careful oversight of such changes will be essential.
- Any resulting permanent change in managing the balance between national security and civil liberties must involve the public through its elected officials and must also be transparent; the consequence of not doing so will be to continue a climate of suspicion and distrust, eroding confidence in our government and the essential public support needed for fighting terrorism effectively.

Practical Challenges and Choices for Improving Domestic Security

Early criticism after 9/11 of governmental actions focused on the failure of coordination between law enforcement and military intelligence. It was widely assumed that a key failure in preventing the attacks was the inability of the CIA and FBI to "connect the dots" and share the precise bits of information which

20. Arguably some oversight structures may actually have been weakened. As one example, the President's Intelligence Oversight Board (PIOB) has been changed to limit its independence by requiring that it work only through the Office of the White House Counsel, thereby removing independent access to the agencies it was designed to monitor. *See* Charlie Savage, *President Weakens Espionage Oversight*, Boston Globe, Mar. 14, 2008, at 1A.

together could have provided a complete picture of the 9/11 terrorists' plot and enabled action to prevent their success. Such a remarkable achievement might have been possible, but was unlikely. Ordinarily, the vast amounts of information collected by the numerous agencies in both the law enforcement and military communities makes precise coordination in the analysis and dissemination of information, followed by effective action, a practical problem of great proportion.[21] This work becomes even more complex, however, when the lack of common technical systems, procedures, and understandings to facilitate communication is considered.

Moreover, not all information relevant to the prevention of a future attack will reside within military or law enforcement agencies. Almost two dozen different domestic agencies have a possible role in collecting the information relevant to future terrorist attacks. This was the reason for creating a new

---

21. As one example, consider the existence of the "wall" between law enforcement and intelligence personnel prior to the passage of the USA PATRIOT Act. *See, e.g.*, David Kris, *The Rise and Fall of the FISA Wall*, 17 STAN. L. & POL'Y REV. 487 (detailing the history of the "wall"). According to Kris,

> Th[e] conceptual dichotomy between law enforcement methods and all other lawful methods of protecting national security gave rise to a "wall" between intelligence and law enforcement elements within the Department of Justice (DOJ). As applied by DOJ, enforced by the courts, and urged by Congress, the FISA wall restricted coordination between DOJ intelligence and law enforcement officials, limiting the flow of information and advice between them. In some cases, the wall came to require parallel law enforcement and intelligence investigations of the same targets, run by separate squads of FBI agents who could not freely consult with one another. It was a regime that prevented the government from connecting the dots.

Id. at 488. As the FISA court noted, when the continued validity of the "wall" was challenged, because of the "wall,"

> FBI criminal investigators and Department prosecutors were not allowed to review all of the raw FISA intercepts or seized materials lest they become de facto partners in the FISA surveillances and searches. Instead, a screening mechanism, or person, usually the chief legal counsel in an FBI field office, or an assistant U.S. attorney not involved in the overlapping criminal investigation, would review all of the raw intercepts and seized materials and pass on only that information which might be relevant evidence.

In re All Matters Submitted to Foreign Intelligence Surveillance Court, 218 F. Supp. 2d 611, 620 (Foreign Intel. Surv. Ct. 2002), *rev'd in part, In re* Sealed Case, 310 F.3d 717 (Foreign Intel. Surv. Ct. Rev. 2002). Not surprisingly, this greatly reduced the effectiveness of communication between the different agencies. *See, e.g., In re* Sealed Case, 310 F.3d at 744 (noting that it has been suggested that the "wall" has contributed, "whether correctly understood or not, to the FBI missing opportunities to anticipate the September 11, 2001 attacks").

Department of Homeland Security (DHS) in 2003. Even now, over five years later, and notwithstanding great efforts, co-ordination among relevant agencies within the DHS is a problem not fully resolved. Organizing these DHS agencies to work well with one another, as well as to coordinate with their law enforcement and military counterparts, where the differences in role and responsibility are still greater, raises substantial practical and policy questions.

Which agency should be responsible for leading the process of collecting, analyzing, and disseminating intelligence about the terrorist threat *inside* the United States? Law enforcement is the lead domestic security agency but its focus is on criminal prosecutions. Until recently, it also lacked analytic capability, and even now it is far less capable in this regard than are the agencies in the "Intelligence Community." Constitutional limits on its collection authorities further restrict its effectiveness.

In contrast, military intelligence has the experience, vast collection capabilities, and analytic capacity to manage intelligence collection, analysis, and dissemination, but its methodologies are poorly suited to operating within the United States, where citizens' rights are implicated and constitutional limitations on government action are correspondingly greater. Homeland Security, on the other hand, is a new entity specifically designed to work in the domestic arena. It exists outside the limitations imposed on law enforcement and, as a non-law enforcement agency, its collection and analytic flexibility might be more acceptable to the public. Still, it lacks both the background and experience that law enforcement and the military enjoy. In addition, concern remains about whether it should even function as a domestic intelligence agency.

No single department or agency is thus ideally suited for the information gathering task created by the terrorist threat. If we do not want to combine all authority in any one agency, the unavoidable answer is that we must learn to manage a group of agencies, each with a different role in responding to terrorism. The practical need to improve our ability to coordinate will remain a fact of life for our government structures for a long time to come. Leadership, money, patience, and hard work will be required, as well as personnel systems which incentivize cooperation. None of this will happen automatically.

Learning from Past Examples of Cooperation

Despite the evident difficulty in coordination among the increasing number of agencies involved in protecting our domestic security, both inside and outside of the law enforcement and intelligence communities, the situation is not hopeless. Examples of successful coordination do exist. Consider, for example, our evolving response to espionage—a crime which, in both peace and wartime, brings law enforcement and intelligence into close cooperation.

For our country, the threat of espionage has existed throughout history: during the American Revolution, the Civil War, in-between the two World Wars, and in the ensuing Cold War. Yet, for many years, a domestic law enforcement prosecution of a spy seemed intractable, incompatible with the guarantees of a fair trial contained in the 5th and 6th Amendments to the U.S. Constitution which rely heavily on openness. To afford an open trial and due process, a jury of one's peers, and the right to confront one's accusers would have meant that the very secrets to be protected would be revealed in such a prosecution. As a result, responses to espionage and its cousin sabotage—both threats to the nation's security from internal individual actors—were typically confined outside the traditional legal system.[22] But in the late 1970s new approaches were designed to prosecute espionage matters involving national security information. Court protective orders, and later the Classified Information Procedures Act,[23] were specifically devised to create ways in which domestic law enforcement and the judicial system could work effectively with intelligence to serve national security ends and preserve the values of an open trial.

Is this experience in the evolution of espionage prosecutions relevant to the so-called "War on Terror"? The terrorist prosecutions of the 1990s suggest this as a possibility; during this period, both investigations and prosecutions were successfully managed, while secret information was also protected.[24] Yet these lessons dissolved abruptly in the face of the 9/11 threats, perhaps because of the belief that a much larger threat was present. Suddenly the U.S. govern-

---

22. *Ex parte* Quirin, 317 U.S. 1 (1942), provides an example. While nominally arising within our federal court system, the case employed processes exceptional to those normally applicable in peace time, denying habeas corpus relief to saboteurs who were alien combatants detained while engaging in espionage in the United States during World War II, and reaching a verdict of death directly in the U.S. Supreme Court.

23. Classified Information Procedures Act, 18 U.S.C. app. 3 §§ 1–16 (2000 & West Supp. 2007). The Act "encourages judges to approve the use of redaction, substitution and other methods meant to reconcile a defendant's rights with the government's obligation to preserve the secrecy of sensitive information." Robert Chesney & Jack Goldsmith, *Terrorism and the Convergence of Criminal and Military Detention Models*, 60 STAN. L. REV. 1079, 1098 (2008).

24. *See, e.g., United States v. Yousef*, 327 F.3d 56, 78–82 (2d Cir. 2003) (prosecutions concerning the 1993 World Trade Center bombing and the 1994 "Bojinka" Plot that involved a foiled attempt to blow up twelve airliners over the Pacific); *United States v. Rahman*, 189 F.3d 88, 103–11 (2d Cir. 1999) (prosecution for attempted 1993 bombings of New York landmarks); *United States v. Salameh*, 152 F.3d 88 (2d Cir. 1998) (prosecutions for the 1993 World Trade Center bombing).

ment changed its earlier approach to the terrorist threat, backing away from its past willingness to use traditional prosecutions in response and, instead, reached out to novel and untested legal approaches which risked abridging the civil liberties of both aliens and citizens alike. The motivation appears to have been a fear that our domestic court processes would not be able to manage the prosecution of terrorists. Rather than employ the court processes which existed, whether in the domestic or military systems of justice, we sought new and novel approaches. In fact, the Executive Branch appears in a number of instances to have gone to considerable lengths to avoid judicial review of many of its actions.[25] Gradually, case by case, these moves away from our traditional approach to law enforcement have been documented by the press and challenged in litigation. Now, a series of Supreme Court decisions is beginning to reject these unprecedented approaches, causing the pendulum to begin to swing back and gradually restoring the *status quo* relationship between public safety and civil liberties.[26] The conclusion appears to be emerging that our courts

---

25. A perfect example of such efforts to avoid judicial review is the case of Jose Padilla, an American citizen, who was detained as an enemy combatant. When his detention was set to be reviewed for the second time by the U.S. Supreme Court, the administration abruptly transferred him. *See* Dan Eggen, *Padilla is Indicted on Terrorism Charges; No Mention Made of "Dirty Bomb" Plot*, WASH. POST, Nov. 23, 2005, at A01; Eric Lichtblau, *Threats and Responses: The Padilla Case; In Legal Shift, U.S. Charges Detainee in Terrorism Case*, N.Y. TIMES, Nov. 23, 2005, at A1. This strategy effectively mooted the Supreme Court's review of the administration's detention methods. *See Padilla v. Hanft*, 547 U.S. 1062 (2006) (mem.).

Additional examples include civil lawsuits against the telecommunication companies which cooperated with the government's secret Terrorist Surveillance Program after 9/11. To prevent disclosure of the details about the TSP, the government intervened in those lawsuits and sought dismissal based on the state secrets defense. *See, e.g., Terkel v. AT&T Corp.*, 441 F. Supp. 2d 899, 900–01 (N.D. Ill. 2006); *Hepting v. AT&T Corp.*, 439 F. Supp. 2d 974, 979 (N.D. Cal. 2006). The government likewise asserted the state secrets defense in the civil litigation against the National Security Agency, which was responsible for operation of the TSP. *See ACLU v. NSA*, 438 F. Supp. 2d 754, 758–59 (E.D. Mich. 2006), *rev'd*, 493 F.3d 644 (6th Cir. 2007).

Finally, the government also relied on state secrets defense when intervening in litigation arising out of its "extraordinary rendition" program. *See, e.g., Mohamed v. Jeppesen Dataplan, Inc.*, 539 F. Supp. 2d 1128, 1130–32 (N.D. Cal. 2008) (noting that the government sought to intervene into and dismiss upon state secrets grounds lawsuits brought by foreign nationals against a California-based company that provided aviation, logistical, and travel services to the CIA, which were used to transfer persons unlawfully seized from one country to another).

26. *See Hamdan v. Rumsfeld*, 548 U.S. 557 (2006) (holding that no congressional act authorized military commissions instituted to try enemy combatants held at Guantanamo Bay, that those commissions' procedures violated the Uniform Code of Military Justice, and

can, in fact, manage the challenging issues and procedures required for successful prosecutions against the terrorist threat.[27]

Will our response to the current War on Terror take advantage of what we have learned earlier in contexts where national security issues and domestic law enforcement responses were managed successfully? If so, there is hope that the historical pattern of overreaction followed by self-correction will occur in the present terrorist threat. Such adjustments require time, however. And our ability to rebalance our approach is likely to depend on our ability to avoid further cataclysmic events such as 9/11 before we have fully learned the practical realities of managing trials involving the threat of terrorism. Ironically, success in avoiding further terrorist attacks requires not that we protect intelligence by secret trial proceedings, but rather that we use intelligence *affirmatively* to identify, prevent, and limit such future attacks.

Proactive Use of Domestic Intelligence to Protect Security and Liberty

The relationship between intelligence and domestic law enforcement is complex. It is easy to confuse the value of intelligence by treating it as simply another type of evidence after the fact, useful principally in achieving successful individual criminal prosecutions. Intelligence can have this use, but in this context, tensions between the two capabilities, as discussed above, are often greatest, while the contribution of intelligence information to our security is likely to be modest, often duplicative of evidence obtained through law enforcement investigations. Intelligence can play a far more important role in supporting our law enforcement system if it serves its most valuable function

---

that those commissions did not comport with the Geneva Conventions); *Hamdi v. Rumsfeld*, 542 U.S. 507, 533 (2004) (holding that "a citizen-detainee seeking to challenge his classification as an enemy combatant must receive notice of the factual basis for his classification, and a fair opportunity to rebut the Government's factual assertions before a neutral decisionmaker"); *Rasul v. Bush*, 542 U.S. 466, 484 (2004) (holding that the federal habeas statute "confers on the District Court jurisdiction to hear petitioners' habeas corpus challenges to the legality of their detention at the Guantanamo Bay Naval Base").

27. In this regard, consider three recent terrorist prosecutions of Richard Reid, Zacarias Moussaoui, and Jose Padilla—all of them conducted in federal district courts. *See* Thanassis Cambanis, *Sentenced to Life, Reid Denounces US 'You Will Be Judged By Allah,' He Shouts*, BOSTON GLOBE, Jan. 31, 2003, at A1; Adam Liptak, *A New Model of Terror Trial*, N.Y. TIMES, Aug. 18, 2007, at A1; United States District Court for Eastern District of Virginia, *United States v. Zacarias Moussaoui*, *available at* http://www.vaed.uscourts.gov/notablecases/moussaoui/.

to *warn* and *prevent* the 9/11 type of attacks that will inevitably destabilize the balance between liberty and security, as well as the operation of our domestic law enforcement system. To achieve this goal, however, a different approach to intelligence collection, analysis, dissemination, and use within our borders is required.

When used to warn and prevent, intelligence can easily conflict with traditional interpretations of constitutionally guaranteed rights and liberties, particularly those of free speech, assembly, and privacy contained in the First and Fourth Amendments to the U.S. Constitution. This poses policy and practical problems. It becomes necessary to look again at the exact ways in which our intelligence tools are authorized and controlled to see what practical accommodations can be made in their implementation so that using intelligence domestically will not undercut our most important constitutional values.

In all of this there is a conundrum. The "tools" of law enforcement are equally important to intelligence. Informants, physical searches of places and persons, and data interception and collection—all are examples of such shared techniques. As we have seen, the rules governing their use will differ, depending on whether the purpose is one of foreign or military intelligence abroad or information relevant to a law enforcement prosecution at home. What does this mean if intelligence is instead used domestically, not for law enforcement prosecution, but only for purposes of warning and prevention? The questions raised are significant as the following consideration of the limits of the First and Fourth Amendments reveals.

Practical Application and Evolving Constitutional Standards

The Fourth Amendment at Home and Abroad

As we have seen, the agencies in the Intelligence Community commonly use the same methods for information collection as do their law enforcement counterparts. While constitutional guarantees and limitations apply to both forms of information collection, the details of their application differ depending on whether a law enforcement or military and foreign intelligence purpose is involved. The result is identical techniques subject to differing constitutional requirements. This difference is the result of judicial decisions which have responded to the need to harmonize constitutional principles with evolving technology. The history of the Fourth Amendment as applied to wire taps, an intrusive but important form of shared collection (called "signals intelligence" by the Intelligence Community), provides one example of how Constitutional interpretations have been adapted to changing practical realities and differing uses.

The Fourth Amendment protects "the right of the people" to be free from both "unreasonable searches and seizures" by the government, as well as from government warrants that are not issued upon oath and affirmation with probable cause and particularity of focus. Intrusive technical collection by a wiretap, however, was not always considered subject to Fourth Amendment regulations. This changed in 1967 with the case of *Katz v. U.S.*[28] As a result, today, Fourth Amendment protections cover both the physical entry into a home as well as technical collection of information such as wire taps.[29] But requiring a warrant in such situations would create a problem if applied to foreign intelligence collection. Particularized warrants (e.g., name, phone number, and precise criminal activity) can often be an insurmountable hurdle abroad where the intelligence goal is to learn generally what may happen in the future, rather than specifically to investigate what has happened in the past. Moreover, even if possible to obtain, gathering such particularized information overseas may be difficult and dangerous. Must such foreign intelligence collection also satisfy all requirements applicable to law enforcement's intrusive collection techniques at home? And what will the Constitution require if national security collection for purposes of warning and threat prevention occurs at home? Such questions raise profound issues that must be considered.

- Do the Fourth Amendment's two protections, the first against unreasonable searches and seizures, and the second against general warrants, operate independently of one another or must they always be combined?
- Should collection standards abroad and at home differ, and if so—why?
- How significant is the difference in information collection goals? Does it matter if collection focuses on gathering information about possible threats against the nation's security, rather than more individualized law enforcement threats?

---

28. 389 US 347 (1967).

29. *Katz* held that the Fourth Amendment protection against "unreasonable searches and seizures" extends to grounds of constitutionally protected individual rights of privacy and does not depend on "the presence or absence of a physical intrusion." *Id.* at 353. It is thus a citizen's reasonable expectation of privacy which, without prior approval by a neutral judge or magistrate, is violated, when the government listens to and records a telephone conversation.

- What significance is there if collection techniques are unlikely to involve the privacy rights of citizens, whether because it occurs overseas or because individual identity cannot be determined?
- If warning, not prosecution, is the collection goal, will the same entities and legal authorities govern collection both abroad and at home?
- What new structures and laws do we need to address such problems and the way in which our security functions work in a time of terrorist threat?

Some of these questions have begun to be answered by the courts and Congress, but more work remains.

Beginning with the *Katz* case in 1967, the Supreme Court for the first time applied the warrant requirement to "technical collection," and also reaffirmed the principle that, subject to a few specifically established and narrowly defined exceptions, a warrantless domestic search is *per se* unreasonable.[30] One of these exceptions was for "national security," raising the possibility that some collection techniques usually subject to Fourth Amendment restrictions might nonetheless be exempt when done for national security purposes, even if conducted at home.[31] The decision made no mention of collection overseas. This has led to the view that, for intelligence collection abroad, only the first clause (preventing unreasonable searches and seizures) is relevant, even though for most domestic law enforcement, both clauses will apply.

But what of national security collection at home? The language in *Katz* could be read to support the argument that such collection was part of the President's inherent powers as Commander-in-Chief pursuant to Article II, Section 2 of the Constitution. This power authorizes the President to protect the nation, even without Congressional legislation. Even so, many commentators argued that, as to intrusive domestic surveillance, this theory was effectively foreclosed when Congress passed the Foreign Intelligence Surveillance Act ("FISA")[32] in 1978. FISA created a warrant procedure for national security collection activities conducted domestically and its language limited action which the President might take outside its strictures. Yet the language of FISA was technical, authorizing collection only against foreign intelligence targets specifically defined as foreign powers and their agents,[33] or against U.S. persons, if they were

---

30. *Id.* at 357.

31. Specifically, the Supreme Court left open the possibility of a lesser standard when questions of "national security" were involved. *Id.* at 358 n.23.

32. Foreign Intelligence Surveillance Act of 1978, Pub. L. No. 95-511, 92 Stat. 1783 (codified as amended at 50 U.S.C.A. §§ 1801–1811 (West 2003 & Supp. 2007)).

33. These are terms of art, specifically defined by FISA. *See* 50 U.S.C. § 1801(a)-(b) (2000 & Supp. V 2005).

acting on behalf of a foreign power *and* if their activities could, or did, violate criminal law.[34] Nevertheless, some argued that, despite this technical language, collection was still possible even if these precise requirements could not be met, as long as the President exercised his Commander-in-Chief powers to protect against existential threats such as those of 9/11.[35] Thus, great importance was attached to the fact that Congress had placed the nation on a war time footing by passing the AUMF. This was seen by some as a signal of Congress' agreement that the President could use his Commander-in-Chief powers in exactly such a way, notwithstanding FISA's language. This was the argument on which the Bush Justice Department relied later when it authorized its "Terrorist Surveillance Program" (TSP) described below.[36]

Such issues became the focus of intense public debate when the secret Terrorist Surveillance Program operated by the National Security Agency was revealed by the press in 2005.[37] Although the full scope of its operations still remains secret today, the TSP appeared initially to have been designed to use electronic surveillance technology domestically, but *outside* the legal parameters of the Foreign Intelligence Surveillance Act. Explained as a response to changing technology, it has been described as a system to gather large amounts of data transiting the United States from overseas in order to identify and exploit possible terrorist communications.[38]

---

34. "U.S. person" is defined as either a U.S. citizen, a permanent resident alien, a corporation that is incorporated in the U.S., or an association that is substantially composed of U.S. citizens or permanent resident aliens. *Id.* § 1801(i). The stricter standard with respect to U.S. persons is needed because this is the area where, absent such guidelines, the line can easily be blurred between domestic security surveillance, which the Supreme Court stated requires a higher compliance with the Fourth Amendment, and foreign security surveillance, which arguably does not require as high of compliance.

35. Language supporting this point appeared in a decision by the appeals court created by FISA. *See In re* Sealed Case, 310 F.3d 717, 742 (Foreign Intel. Surv. Ct. Rev. 2002) ("We take for granted that the President does have [inherent] authority [to conduct warrantless searches to obtain foreign intelligence information] and, assuming that is so, FISA could not encroach on the President's constitutional power.").

36. *See* DEPARTMENT OF JUSTICE, WHITE PAPER ON THE LEGAL AUTHORITIES SUPPORTING THE ACTIVITIES OF THE NATIONAL SECURITY AGENCY DESCRIBED BY THE PRESIDENT (January 19, 2006) at 2, *available at* http://www.usdoj.gov/opa/whitepaperonnsa legalauthorities.pdf.

37. *See* James Risen & Eric Lichtblau, *Bush Lets U.S. Spy on Callers without Courts*, N.Y. TIMES, Dec. 16, 2005, at A1.

38. *See* Dan Eggen, *NSA Spying Part of Broader Effort*, WASH. POST, Aug. 1, 2007, at A01; David Johnston & Neil A. Lewis, *Defending Spy Program, Administration Cites Law*, N.Y.

While details of the TSP remain secret, some of the legal debate surrounding it has begun to emerge. In early 2007, at least one judge on the FISA Court (a court composed of lifetime federal judges under Article III of the Constitution and created by the FISA statute to hear in secret matters related to FISA warrant requests) issued an order authorizing the surveillance contemplated under the TSP.[39] This action allowed the TSP to continue its collection activities with the legal approval of the FISA court. Some months later, a second FISC judge significantly curtailed this authority, prompting a series of efforts by the administration to introduce legislation to cover the "legal gaps" created in the TSP domestic intelligence collection program.[40]

The back and forth of this legal struggle over the TSP between Executive, Judicial, and Legislative Branches suggests that, in the end, the changes needed to support or expand FISA's continued effectiveness may be more technical concerns, rather than issues of broad constitutional policy. Yet, "getting this right" is essential to the nation's security. Gathering and assessing large amounts of technical data entering the United States from abroad is critical to designing new approaches to warning about, and preventing, the terrorist threat. This is not a new idea.[41] Indeed, the reasons behind the Terrorist Surveillance Program may well be appropriate and necessary. What is profoundly disturbing to many, however, is the manner used to implement the new TSP approach.

Secrecy and uncertain regard for Constitutional and legal limitations characterize the TSP and may prove counterproductive—even dangerous, if public confidence is eroded and rational resolution of these technical issues within a constitutional framework becomes impossible for the political branches of government. At the very least, the secrecy in which the TSP program was created and implemented complicates attaining the legal and policy consensus needed for enhanced collection of domestic intelligence for warning and prevention purposes.

TIMES, Dec. 23, 2005, at A20; Eric Lichtblau & James Risen, *Spy Agency Minded Vast Data Trove, Officials Report*, N.Y. TIMES, Dec. 24, 2005, at A1.

39. These orders are still secrets. Recent ACLU litigation to have them declassified was unsuccessful. *See In re* Motion for Release of Court Records, 526 F. Supp. 2d 484 (Foreign Intel. Surv. Ct. 2007).

40. The efforts by the administration resulted in the passing of Protect America Act on August 5, 2007. *See* Pub. L. No. 110-55, 121 Stat. 552 (2007). The Act contained a sunset provision, pursuant to which the amendments made would cease to have effect after 180 days. *Id.* §6(c). On February 17, 2008, the Act expired without being renewed.

41. *See* HEYMANN, *supra* note 8, at 61–84 (discussing the importance of intelligence gathering in fighting terrorism and concluding that "[t]o prevent a terrorist event (and any immediate substitute for it) intelligence must identify a critical number of the group involved and do that secretly so that they can be found and incapacitated").

These problems, and the loss of national consensus produced by the TSP, are the more disappointing because they seem so unnecessary. Collaboration among the Executive, Legislative, and Judicial branches should have been possible. In the past, both Congress and the courts resourcefully addressed the tensions of changing technology and new collection demands when those collided with traditional Constitutional and legal interpretations. Immediately after 9/11, Congress responded to Executive Branch requests by amending both FISA and other legal provisions with the USA PATRIOT Act.[42] The changes made by the TSP might have been achieved by working with Congress, but there was no attempt to do so. Had that occurred, the courts, too, might have concurred. In fact, in the dynamic and evolving area of electronic signals collection, court decisions have been far from static, instead playing an important role in the three branch dialogue moving the nation toward solutions.

Nonetheless, the Executive Branch has continued the TSP program, and added additional intrusive domestic collection programs, but all without approval by Congress or the FISA Court.[43] Possible court review of such actions remains, but for many features of such secret surveillance programs, court jurisdiction will be difficult to establish and opportunities for court review will develop slowly.

Thus the question remains: what outcome is likely if the Supreme Court were to review the TSP? Only speculation is possible and even this has become increasingly difficult as the personalities on the U.S. Supreme Court change. Still, the apparent techniques of the TSP appear well suited to achieve the warning and detection functions of intelligence in the domestic arena and may actually be necessary to our future safety. Citizens' constitutional protections cannot be ignored, however, and new approaches have been suggested that may offer hope both for protecting the nation and the individual liberties of citizens.

Testimony reflects that the TSP's operational design included one approach to protecting American citizens' privacy. That approach used the "minimization" procedures to limit or exclude specific references to the identity of U.S. persons in collected information unless specific review and approval on grounds of necessity could be obtained.[44] Minimization features could limit the negative

---

42. For changes to FISA by the Patriot Act, see §§ 206–07, 214–15, 218, 225, 504, and 1003 of the Act. Pub. L. No. 107-56, 115 Stat. 272 (2001).

43. *See supra* note 12 (describing Department of Homeland Security's intention to incorporate a complete array of the nation's most advanced spy technology into its surveillance collection techniques).

44. Minimization procedures, as defined by FISA, refer to "specific procedures, which shall be adopted by the Attorney General, that are reasonably designed in light of the purpose and technique of the particular surveillance, to minimize the acquisition and reten-

impacts of domestic intelligence gathering on the privacy of individual U.S. persons. Properly structured, and with the benefit of independent oversight, such minimization procedures offer one approach to balancing the security and liberty issues raised by the TSP. Hopefully, the secret development and implementation of TSP, and its resulting erosion of a long history of co-operation on FISA between the three branches, has not created lasting harm that will prevent such future creative approaches to balancing security and liberty as we confront the novel and existential threats of terrorists with nuclear arms.

In the last analysis, Congress and the Executive Branch must agree on an appropriate approach that the Judicial Branch can then endorse after review. Failing this, public distrust and dissention about the TSP and other related programs will continue. The loss of public confidence weakens our ability to adopt the domestic security structures we need. The fundamental lesson to be learned is that changes in domestic intelligence collection are constitutionally, legally, and practically possible, *as long as* the three branches of government co-operate and the public is informed.

The First Amendment at Home and Abroad

Turning to the First Amendment, similar concerns arise. The First Amendment provides that Congress shall pass no laws abridging the freedom of speech, press, or the right of the people to assemble, among other things. However, differences arise when its application abroad and at home are compared. At home, First Amendment protections are vitally important when the government seeks to investigate groups or individuals on general suspicion or as the result of group activity. While such collection activity is essential for effective intelligence gathering, it can also place citizens' First Amendment rights at risk and quickly undermine a free society. Too often in our history unfounded suspicions based on free association have led to intrusive forms of unwarranted domestic information collection in the name of national security.[45] The uproar

---

tion, and prohibit the dissemination, of nonpublicly available information concerning unconsenting United States persons consistent with the need of the United States to obtain, produce, and disseminate foreign intelligence information." 50 U.S.C. § 1801(h)(1) (2000). Minimization procedures typically allow for exceptions when the retention or dissemination of information is required to preserve evidence of a crime that "has been, is being, or is about to be committed" or when required to prevent death or serious bodily harm to any person. *See id.* § 1801(h)(3)-(4).

　　45. As the Supreme Court noted, "national security cases ... often reflect a convergence of First and Fourth Amendment values not present in cases of 'ordinary' crime. Though the investigative duty of the executive may be stronger in such cases, so also is there greater

that results when such government activity is revealed inevitably leads to responses that limit such broad government collection tactics with laws that impose precise approval and review requirements. In contrast, because foreign
intelligence has largely been an activity conducted abroad, not impacting the
rights of citizens at home or used for criminal prosecution, it has avoided a
collision with the Constitutional guarantees central to the American way of
life as long as U.S. persons are not involved. Overseas intelligence agencies like
the Central Intelligence Agency and the Defense Intelligence Agency have thus
been able to collect the human intelligence (as a form of intelligence called
"humint") they need, as long as they are operating overseas and do not focus
on U.S. persons.

With the terrorist threat arising both inside and outside our borders, however, there is a need to take advantage of these traditional intelligence collection techniques in both arenas—foreign and domestic. Certainly, no one wants
to see the creation of a police state, with government access to all features of
the average citizen's life. Moreover, the lessons drawn from the abuses of Nazi
Germany, the Soviet Union, and countless other nations, not to mention our
own misguided efforts like the Cointel Program,[46] demonstrate that real abuse
can occur when a government's need for national security information is not
carefully bounded.

How then do we manage the logical concern that effective warning and prevention will only be possible if information of suspicious activity can be gathered *before* an attack is imminent? The balance between freedom and risk would
seem appropriate to adjust where the threat is not from a single criminal act,
but instead from an attack of existential proportions against the entire nation.
Is there a middle ground? What should be the limits on intelligence collection
authorities when they operate *within* the United States for the purpose of warn-

---

jeopardy to constitutionally protected speech." *United States v. U.S. District Court (Keith)*,
407 U.S. 297, 313 (1972).

46. The term COINTELPRO refers to Counter Intelligence Programs run by the FBI
that were generally illegal and focused on repressing political dissent. Natsu Tailor Saitu,
*Whose Liberty? Whose Security? The USA PATRIOT Act in the Context of COINTERLPRO
and the Unlawful Repression of Political Dissent*, 81 Or. L. Rev. 1051, 1079 (2002). The tactics used included surveillance and infiltration of politically active groups, dissemination of
false information about those groups, creation of intra- and inter-group conflicts, abuse of
the criminal justice system, and collaboration in assaults and assassinations. *Id.* at 1081–88.
As the Church Committee has noted, "[m]any of the techniques used [by the FBI in its
COINTELPRO operations] would be intolerable in a democratic society even if all of the
targets had been involved in violent activity, but COINTELPRO went far beyond that." 3
Church Committee, *supra* note 15, at 3.

ing and prevention *beyond* mere prosecution for which law enforcement authorities have been created? Is a different standard of Constitutional protection appropriate when collection of information is of a general nature, showing broad patterns of activity, but not revealing individual identities or intended for use in criminal prosecutions?

These questions were raised by the introduction of a data mining and analysis project called Total Information Awareness (TIA), which was announced in 2003 and was more thoroughly analyzed in 2004 press reports.[47] TIA has been described as an effort to explore practical solutions to collecting information to allow computer analysis of broad patterns of public activity to identify possible terrorist initiatives. However, instead of identifying specific individuals, it was suggested that individuals would only be identified when sufficient information could be provided to satisfy the particularity demanded by traditional warrant requirements. While this approach certainly had promise, it was implemented clumsily, once again provoking a level of distrust and public outcry so intense that it was ultimately abandoned as a public program.

The story of the TIA project represents yet another lost opportunity to develop new approaches to gathering, analyzing, and using information to warn against and prevent future terrorist attacks, while exploring practical solutions for protecting basic constitutional values. This raises squarely the question of what the constitutional limits are when the government collects domestic information, even where there is no expectation of privacy or where individual identities are not readily available. Does it matter that the information thus gathered will not impact the rights of individual citizens because no prosecution is intended and citizens are not individually identifiable? Are there structures which might be designed to protect citizens' constitutional rights by carefully controlling such a data mining project like the TIA? Its demise removes one opportunity to explore and answer these questions.

Other examples of problematic governmental efforts to achieve our dual goals of security and liberty in the post 9/11 period are less novel in design but, once again, clumsy in application. For example, in the "No Fly List" program of the Transportation Security Administration, governmental officials inadvertently included the names of some anti-war protesters, as well as key Democrats. These actions raised questions as to what response would be appro-

---

47. The TIA program was described by numerous press accounts. *See, e.g.*, Adam Clymer, *Threats and Responses: Electronic Surveillance; Congress Agrees to Bar Pentagon From Terror Watch of Americans*, N.Y. TIMES, Feb. 12, 2003, at A1; Siobhan Gorman, *Adm. Poindexter's Total Awareness*, NAT'L J., May 8, 2004, at 1430; Heather MacDonald, *The 'Privacy' Jihad*, WALL ST. J., Apr. 1, 2004, at A14.

priate to restore citizen confidence when well-motivated government employees mistakenly collect personal information as part of an effort to warn and protect against further terrorist attacks.

Similar problems have arisen in the Administration's management of National Security Letters (the "NSLs"),[48] an extraordinary search procedure by which the FBI compels disclosure of certain private records without prior judicial approval. Prior to 9/11, several statutes authorized the FBI use of NSLs, which together provided a significant collection capability.[49] The USA PATRIOT Act made significant changes to these FBI collection powers. First, it allowed full credit reports to be obtained on individuals in investigations about international terrorism. Second, it relaxed the standards for such collection, so that the FBI no longer needs to determine the target to be a foreign power or an agent thereof, but may request information if it is simply "relevant to"[50] or "sought for"[51] an investigation about international terrorism or espionage.[52] Third,

---

48. For a comprehensive review of the National Security Letters' history and practice, *see* OFFICE OF THE INSPECTOR GENERAL, A REVIEW OF THE FEDERAL BUREAU OF INVESTIGATION'S USE OF NATIONAL SECURITY LETTERS (Unclassified), Special Report (March 2007), *available at* http://www.usdoj.gov/oig/special/s0703b/final.pdf [hereinafter NSL REVIEW 2007].

49. First, the Right to Financial Privacy Act authorized the FBI to obtain financial records in foreign counterintelligence cases, including information from open and closed checking and savings accounts, safe deposit box records, credit unions, investment companies, operators of credit card systems, real estate companies, and other entities. 12 U.S.C. § 3414(a)(5)(A) (2000). Second, the Electronic Communications Privacy Act authorized the FBI to obtain historical information on telephone calls made and received from a specified number (including cell phones and prepaid phone cards), e-mails, screen names, and billing records and method of payment. 18 U.S.C § 2709(b)(1)(B) (2000). Third, the Fair Credit Reporting Act allowed the FBI to obtain limited information about an individual's credit history, including all financial institutions where he or she had an account, current and former addresses, and current and former places of employment. 15 U.S.C. § 1681u (2000). Finally, the amendment to National Security Act in 1994 allowed for NSLs to be issued in connection with the investigations of governmental employees. 50 U.S.C. § 436(a)(1) (2000).

50. *See, e.g.*, Pub. L. No. 107-56, § 505(a)(2)-(3), 115 Stat. 272 (2001) (codified as 18 U.S.C. § 2709(b)(1)-(2) (2000 & West Supp. 2007)).

51. *See, e.g., id.* § 505(b) (codified as 12 U.S.C. § 3414(a)(5)(A) (2000 & West Supp. 2007)); *id.* § 505(c) (codified as 15 U.S.C. § 1681u(a)-(c) (2000 & West Supp. 2007)).

52. This standard is not demanding—the information must make the fact "more or less probable." Electronic Communication from General Counsel, Nat'l Sec. Law Policy and Training Unit, to All Divisions of Federal Bureau of Investigation (June 1, 2007) at 5 [hereinafter FBI electronic communication]. Thus, a NSL is permitted if the information sought would either support or weaken the facts being investigated. *Id.* at 5–6.

there is no longer a need for the targeted individual to be a subject in the underlying investigation. Finally, the number and status of authorizing officials for these letters has also been relaxed. Before the Act's passage, judicial approval was not required, but NSLs could only be approved by a limited number (10) of FBI headquarters officials. The USA PATRIOT Act expanded significantly the number of individuals authorized to approve such NSLs.[53]

Predictably, this expanded authority soon became problematic. A 2007 report of the Office of the Inspector General (OIG) identified inaccuracies and abuses, with the potential to harm civil liberties, in the following three areas processes: an FBI database in the Office of General Counsel was inaccurate, or incomplete, as to the number of NSLs issued;[54] there was delayed entry of information into the central database, with resulting inaccurate reporting to Congress;[55] and there were errors in uploading NSL information into the database, which distorted the actual numbers involved.[56]

The OIG also found examples of improper or illegal use of NSLs in cases where the original authorization for a target had lapsed. There were also requests for unauthorized information (e.g., school admission applications, emergency contact information, and campus organization information). Finally, some billing records and e-mail subscriber information was incorrect and, in some cases, providers furnished more data than the FBI actually requested, but that data was never purged, as required.

Such violations raise serious civil liberties concerns that innocent persons' records may be collected and analyzed without knowledge or accountability. In the end, however, the OIG found that generally the FBI received only information that it would have been able to request had it properly followed applicable guidelines, statutes, and internal policies. Moreover, the OIG concluded that in no case was there any indication that any of this misuse of NSLs constituted criminal misconduct.

Even more serious issues arose in yet another category—"exigent letters." Normally, the FBI provides the telephone company with either a grand jury subpoena, or an NSL request, *before* the information is released. To avoid

---

53. *See, e.g.*, Pub. L. No. 107-56, §§505(a)(1), (a)(2)(A), (a)(3)(A), (b)(1), (c)(1)(A), (c)(2)(A), (c)(3)(A), 115 Stat. 272 (2001).

54. The OIG discovered approximately 17 percent more NSLs in the case files they examined than were recorded in the database. NSL REVIEW 2007, *supra* note 48, at 32.

55. The OIG determined that "from 2003 through 2005 almost 4,600 NSL requests were not reported to Congress as a result of these delays." *Id.* at 33. The FBI discovered this in March 2006 and promptly notified the Attorney General and Congress.

56. The OIG discovered that this affected approximately 8,850 NSL requests, or 6 percent of NSL requests issued by the FBI during that period. *Id.* at 34.

weeks-long delay in gaining the needed information after such requests are made, "exigent letters" can be used to save time. Applicable statutes allow such an approach in an emergency and when a subpoena has been sought. However, the OIG discovered that on numerous occasions letters were provided when there was neither a subpoena nor the intent to obtain one. More problematic, such requests were typically signed by unauthorized persons,[57] and often FBI personnel were later uncertain whether the required NSLs or subpoena had ever been obtained.[58]

Overall, however, the OIG concluded that the fault was likely due to a lack of communication among FBI internal elements, rather than a deliberate attempt to circumvent the requirements of the statutes and applicable guidelines. Furthermore, the FBI has taken a number of affirmative steps since then in the right direction.[59] These efforts were acknowledged in the OIG's subsequent report.[60] In addition, the FBI created an Office of Integrity and Com-

---

57. The OIG was provided with copies of 739 such exigent letters, which together requested information on approximately 3,000 different telephone numbers between March 11, 2003, and December 16, 2005. *Id.* at 89–90.

58. The FBI attempted to defend its practice by relying on the Electronic Communications Privacy Act's "voluntary disclosure authority" for acquiring non-content information. *See* 18 U.S.C. §2702(c)(4) (West Supp. 2007). However, the OIG found that these exigent letters did not ask for "voluntary" disclosure. On the contrary, they "requested" that the information be provided and represented that a formal subpoena will be served "as expeditiously as possible." NSL REVIEW 2007, *supra* note 48, at 96. Furthermore, this justification was not relied upon by the issuing personnel at the time when the exigent letters were issued. *Id.* at 96–97.

59. The FBI attempted to address most of these issues in June 2007 by sending out an Electronic Communication to all divisions. *See* FBI electronic communication, *supra* note 52. This advice noted, among other things, that (1) all NSLs must be reviewed by attorneys for legal sufficiency, (2) the accompanying cover letters must state in sufficient detail that the information sought is relevant to the investigation, (3) a separate determination of non-disclosure is required in each specific case, (4) specific regulations must be adhered to in cases of overproduction by the companies, and (5) there is now a prohibition on the use of "exigent letters." *Id.* at 7, 11–12, 16–19. It also noted that the applicable law is that "there must be sufficient detail within the four corners of the EC so that a reasonable person without independent knowledge of the investigation can fairly judge whether the underlying investigation was adequately predicated and whether the information sought is relevant." *Id.* at 11.

60. In 2008, the OIG noted that the FBI has made "significant progress" in implementing the recommendations of the 2007 survey and that it has "devoted significant energy, time, and resources toward ensuring that its field managers and agents understand the seriousness of the FBI's shortcomings in its use of NSLs and their responsibility for correcting these deficiencies." OFFICE OF THE INSPECTOR GENERAL, A REVIEW OF THE FBI'S USE OF NATIONAL SECURITY LETTERS: ASSESSMENT OF CORRECTIVE ACTIONS AND EXAMINA-

pliance, whose mission is "to develop, implement, and oversee a program that ensures … processes and procedures in place that promote FBI compliance with both the letter and spirit of all applicable laws, regulations, and policies."[61] Despite the subsequent measures, however, these stories show how easily problems can arise when government agencies rush head-long to develop security capacity without clear policy guidance, training, and supervision.

There are other programs and techniques which raise concerns about privacy and civil liberties when used by the government. Watchlists, data mining, and roving wiretaps are only a few examples. They show both how new technology can help to protect this county from the next terrorist attack, and also how, in the wrong hands, such collected data can be misused.[62]

As a nation whose citizens have historically distrusted government power, all such data collection within the United States raises serious concerns. There

---

TION OF NSL USAGE IN 2006 (Unclassified), Special Report (March 2008) at 15, *available at* http://www.usdoj.gov/oig/special/s0803b/final.pdf.

61. Press Release, Federal Bureau of Investigation, Justice Department and FBI Unveil Measures to Enhance National Security Oversight (July 13, 2007), *available at* http://www.fbi.gov/pressrel/pressrel07/oversight071307.htm. In fact, such measures, while a staple in private corporations, have never before been utilized by federal agencies and should prove to be a valuable contribution to the balance between national security and civil liberties.

62. A 2007 audit by the DoJ of the FBI's consolidated watchlist revealed that it contained a total of 724,442 records. OFFICE OF THE INSPECTOR GENERAL, FOLLOW-UP AUDIT OF THE TERRORIST SCREENING CENTER (Redacted), Audit Report 07-41 (September 2007) at 7, *available at* http://www.usdoj.gov/oig/reports/FBI/a0741/final.pdf [hereinafter TSC AUDIT]. However, since multiple records exist to account for the use of aliases and alternate identities, as well as because of mistaken and duplicate entries, this figure is likely much larger than the actual number of suspected or known terrorists on the watchlist. *Id.* at 7 n.27, 20–24. Consequences from mistaken identification can be dire—including detention of innocent travelers and even rendition of some of them to countries that practice torture. *See, e.g.,* COMMISSION OF INQUIRY INTO THE ACTIONS OF CANADIAN OFFICIALS IN RELATION TO MAHER ARAR, REPORT OF THE EVENTS RELATING TO MAHER ARAR: ANALYSIS AND RECOMMENDATIONS (Redacted), (September 2007) at 16–36, *available at* http://epe.lac-bac.gc.ca/100/206/301/pco-bcp/commissions/maher_arar/07-09-13/www.ararcommission.ca/eng/AR_English.pdf (describing how Maher Arar, a Canadian and Syrian citizen, was detained in New York because of erroneous watchlist data provided to the U.S. and was then flown and rendered to Syria, where he was tortured). Problems still exist despite the efforts made to improve the program and to provide for means of redress. *See* TSC AUDIT, *supra,* at 45–60 (reviewing the redress procedures of the Terrorist Screening Center and concluding that, although a number of positive steps have been taken, unnecessary delays still exist); *see also* Scott Shane, *Canadian to Remain on U.S. Terrorist Watch List,* N.Y. TIMES, Jan. 23, 2007, at A11 (noting that, despite subsequent clearance of any wrongdoing, U.S. nevertheless decided to keep Mr. Arar's name on the watchlist).

is fear that the government will misuse such information. This, in turn, can lead to unsubstantiated accusations and, eventually, will erode First Amendment rights when unchecked governmental power begins to chill free speech and limit debate.[63] Inevitably, citizens' trust in government and their willingness to co-operate in fighting terrorism declines. Those engaged in intelligence collection are also placed at risk when standards that support their judgments about collection activities are unclear. Public criticism, even if not an outright challenge to the legality of their actions, will diminish their enthusiasm and lead to excessive caution. Overall, there is a need for open processes which reassure the public that individual constitutional rights are being protected even as information collection, analysis, and dissemination are enhanced. Once again, minimization procedures offer one such approach with great potential.

Minimization procedures operate as safeguards which regulate the acquisition, retention, and dissemination of information about U.S. persons. These procedures necessarily vary according to the type of surveillance used, but as a rule, will limit the initial intake of information about U.S. persons. Roving wiretaps, data mining, and blanket warrants for electronic surveillance will make sorting through the information at the initial stage difficult, but rigorous safeguards, applied at the retention and dissemination stages, can serve as effective complements. Additional safeguards can also be developed in the form of criminal or civil penalties for *intentional* violations of the relevant statutory authorities involved in the various collection systems and their minimization features.

---

63. More than thirty years ago, just before Congress enacted FISA, the Senate Committee on the Judiciary noted that:

> Also formidable—although incalculable—is the "chilling effect" which warrantless electronic surveillance may have on the constitutional rights of those who were not targets of the surveillance, but who perceived themselves, whether reasonably or unreasonably, as potential targets. Our Bill of Rights is concerned not only with direct infringements on constitutional rights, but also with government activities which effectively inhibit the exercise of these rights. The exercise of political freedom depends in large measure on citizens' understanding that they will be able to be publicly active and dissent from official policy, within lawful limits, without having to sacrifice the expectation of privacy that they rightfully hold. Arbitrary or uncontrolled use of warrantless electronic surveillance can violate that understanding and impair that public confidence so necessary to an uninhibited political life.

S. Rep. No. 95-604, pt. 1, at 8 (1977). These concerns are equally valid today. A person who would otherwise protest against the war in Iraq, or discuss the current conditions in Guantanamo Bay, would be more hesitant if he believed that the government might be recording his statements and if he was not sure what will happen to him as a result of his views.

Conclusion: Oversight, Future Roles, and Responsibilities

Improving the use of the warning and detection capabilities of intelligence in the "War on Terror" requires thoughtful reexamination of current legal and practical limitations, with regard to the intelligence activities involved. Unfortunately, such analysis has been the exception, not the rule, since the 9/11 attacks. Now, with the new Obama Administration, we have the opportunity to consider again the fundamental questions necessary to design a more effective domestic security system. It will be important to consider whether, how, and by whom various types of intelligence information will be gathered domestically and abroad, and what impact such actions will have on traditional interpretations of Constitutional and legal limitations, as well as on public sensitivities.

As the TSP and the TIA programs demonstrate, the Bush Administration's "ask forgiveness, not permission" approach to new program development with the use of intelligence was not helpful in designing new policies. In fact, the hostile reaction when both programs were revealed severely undermined our ability to fully explore such approaches in the future. In the end, our government today is less able to collect and analyze data relevant to the terrorist threat than is the private sector because reactions out of fear blinded us to how legal structures might have been developed to empower the government's access to information while also insuring citizens' rights.

It follows that an important lesson from the government's handling of intelligence collection in response to 9/11 is the need for effective oversight, not limited to one specific agency, but encompassing *all* branches of the government. To be sure, each department or agency should have its own *internal* oversight structure—a combination of training, supervisory review, automated controls, and audits. For such oversight to be maximally meaningful and objective, however, participation by *outside* entities will be necessary as well.

Lastly, there must be meaningful and bipartisan oversight of all domestic intelligence collection activities by Congress. In the future—unlike the past—procedures must be followed and civil liberties safeguarded. Efforts should be taken so that some level of disclosure is made to Congress as a whole rather than to select members, albeit protecting intelligence sources and methods. Only when, in this way, the three branches of our government exercise concurrent responsibility for intelligence surveillance can the American people be certain that their nation will be simultaneously protected and the rights of its citizens safeguarded.

Chapter 7

Hate Propaganda and National Security[1]

Robert M. O'Neil[2]

Could the United States government (or that of any state) restrict or suppress hateful messages in the interest of national security? Before the terrorist attacks on the World Trade Center and the Pentagon, any such notion would have seemed perverse, even bizarre. The ready response would have been that such a proposal was unnecessary, unwise and almost certainly unconstitutional. Since September 11, however, many thoughtful Americans seem willing at least to entertain such a prospect in the interest of national security. Even seasoned First Amendment scholars would respond with far less certainty. The relevant factors have become substantially more complex in the struggle against terror. Revisiting such issues in the twenty-first century is the focus of this chapter.

Anyone who regards such a prospect as wholly implausible in the post-September 11 environment might ponder some recent and ominous developments:

- In the fall of 2007, the U.S. Commission on International Religious Freedom urged the State Department to close a private school in Northern Virginia, supported by the Saudi government, unless school officials could demonstrate that they were not teaching "a type of religious in-

---

1. The phrase "hate propaganda" is not a legal term of art. It denotes any of various hateful messages, communications, in traditional or electronic form, that preach hate against racial, religious, national or ethnic groups and/or invite attacks upon or against such groups to a degree that might evoke serious public disorder or civic unrest.

2. Robert M. O'Neil became founding director of The Thomas Jefferson Center for the Protection of Free Expression in August, 1990, after serving five years as president of the University of Virginia. He continues as a member of the University's law faculty, teaching such courses as First Amendment and the Arts, Speech and Press, Church and State, and Free Speech in Cyberspace.

tolerance potentially dangerous to the United States." Although the Commission cited no hard evidence of such teachings, even a cursory appraisal of instructional materials used by comparable schools in Saudi Arabia had aroused the agency's concern. Two resulting reviews of the texts slated for study in the U.S. school provided tangible evidence that alarmed at least one Commission member, with special concern derived from "denunciations of specific religious groups as evil or enemies" as well as "blatant anti-Semitism, blaming the Jews for even divisions within Islam."[3]

- The House of Representatives by a nearly unanimous vote in late October, 2007, approved the Violent Radicalization and Homegrown Terrorism Prevention Act. Although this bill would not by its own force criminalize any terrorist activities that were not already unlawful, civil liberties groups and other critics expressed alarm that a new commission would be established and charged to identify ideologies that might be considered to be catalysts to terrorism. One of the bipartisan sponsors' premises was that the United States increasingly faces threats from domestic terrorist sources—specifically, in the words of lead sponsor Rep. Jane Harman, that the Internet provides Americans with "access to broad and constant streams of terrorist-related propaganda" leading to the "violent radicalization" noted in the bill's title.[4]

- Representative Harman's stated concern about use of the Internet to disseminate dangerous views has been widely shared, and underlies several quite specific proposals for restraints on hate propaganda. Several reputable legal scholars have recently proposed measures that would curb the dissemination of such material, both to protect vulnerable groups and to enhance national security interests. Professor Alexander Tsesis, for example, has urged that "laws should be enacted against any [such potentially harmful] Internet hate propaganda ..."[5] A recent and thoughtful student comment proposed the shaping of "new tools for winning

---

3. Strauss, "Critics of Saudi Academy Say Textbooks Promote Intolerance," *Washington Post*, Jan. 10, 2008, p. B2. Freedom House and its Center for Religious Freedom had for some time been concerned about such materials, *see* Saudi Arabia's Curriculum of Intolerance, *available at* http://www.freedomhouse.org/uploads/special_report/48.pdf.

4. Shaffer and Robinson, "Here Come the Thought Police," *Baltimore Sun*, Nov. 19, 2007, P. 13A. The American Civil Liberties Union charged, with reference to this bill, that "Internet censorship was spurred on under the false illusion of making us safer from terrorist." ACLU Blog, http://blog.aclu.org/index.php?/archives/381 The Year in First Amendment Rights, Jan. 4, 2008.

5. Tsesis, "Prohibiting Incitement on the Internet," 7 *Va.J.L. & Tech.* 5, (2002).

the war against Cyber Jihad," given the reality that "more than guns, bombs or missiles, the Internet is the most important tool for terrorist groups today."[6]

· Lest U.S. observers find such suggestions remote as well as uncongenial, we should recognize that our neighbors to the north have taken substantial and concrete steps in precisely that direction. Canadian lawmakers, agencies and courts (though in other respects such as obscenity and pornography more protective of civil liberties than are we in the United States) have long embraced the silencing of extreme hate propaganda. In the spring of 2006, for example, the Canadian Human Rights Tribunal ruled that racist messages posted on two blatantly white-supremacist websites contravened federal hate laws, and for that reason the sites were ordered to be shut down.[7] That action followed at least a half dozen earlier cases in which racist and hate-disseminating sites had been silenced, and reflects Canadian Supreme Court jurisprudence that establishes a legal view of such material markedly less tolerant than the view that prevails south of the border.[8]

· Quite apart from the unique context of the Internet, there have been serious proposals to restrict the dissemination of hateful material through more traditional media. One scholar recently suggested an analogy between the call for genocide cited in the Rwandan Media Trial and the degree to which the Al-Jezeera network on occasion broadcasts material that may serve to incite violence and encourage terrorism, even though the network could not fairly be charged with deliberately seeking such results. Though despairing of any restraint based on current international law, this author warns that "only when the international community takes serious steps toward adopting an incitement to terrorism standard" will there be an effective antidote."[9] Others have noted the potential impact of Hezbollah's al-Manar Television network as "the com-

6. Davis, "Ending the Cyber Jihad: Combating Terrorist Exploitation of the Internet with the Rule of Law and Improved Tools for Cyber Governance," 15 *Comm. Law Conspectus* 119, 174, 199 (2006).

7. Richard Blackwell, "Web Messages Hate, Tribunal Rules," *Toronto Globe & Mail*, March 11, 2006, sec. C.

8. *E.g., R. v. Keegstra*, [1990] 3 S.C.R. 697, [1991] 2 W.W.R. 1; *see* generally Bailey, "Private Regulation and Public Policy: Toward Effective Restriction of Internet Hate Propaganda," 49 *McGill L.J.* 59 (2004).

9. Davis, "Note: Incitement to Terrorism in Media Coverage: Solutions to Al-Jazeera After the Rwandan Media Trial," 38 *Geo. Wash. L. Rev.* 749, 778 (2006).

munications arm of one of the world's most dangerous terrorist organizations," which "foster[s] a culture of terrorism and incite[s] violent attacks."[10]

- Two recent and fascinating lawsuits may illustrate the potential path by which litigation might serve to constrain such disturbing material. When the principal daily newspaper in Tucson published a letter proposing that, "whenever there is an assassination or another atrocity [in Afghanistan or Iraq] we should proceed to the closest mosque and execute five of the first Muslims we encounter," a group of understandably indignant Islamic readers brought suit for intentional infliction of emotional distress. The trial court declined to dismiss the suit, but the Arizona Supreme Court eventually ruled that the First Amendment precluded any such relief, despite the abhorrent and deeply disturbing nature of the letter. Since it contained neither "fighting words" nor a "true threat," the letter's content fell "far short of unprotected incitement," at least on the publisher's part.[11] That ruling left open, however, the intriguing question whether a suit against the letter's author (who could never be served and thus escaped potential liability) might have fared differently.

- The other case posed an analogous issue in a markedly different way. An Islamic subscriber to America Online became so deeply offended by anti-Muslim statements he encountered in AOL chat rooms that he filed suit in federal district court against the giant Internet service provider. Appearing pro se, he claimed not only a breach of his contract with the Internet Service Provider, but also a violation of federal laws that guaranteed non-discriminatory treatment in places of public accommodation—a duty that arguably applied even to AOL. The district judge eventually dismissed the suit on all counts, noting that servers and ISPs are protected from any liability for third-party postings by section 230 of the Communications Decency Act of 1996, and that such an electronic entity did not fall within any statutory definition of "place of public accommodation." Along the way, however, the court recognized that a Muslim subscriber had "understandably complained about ... offensive, obnoxious, and indecent statements" he encountered in the chat rooms he visited.[12]

---

10. Foundation for Defense of Democracies, "Shutting Down Terrorist Media," Press Release, Sept. 13, 2007.

11. *Citizen Publishing Co. v. Miller*, 210 Ariz. 513, 115 P.3d 107 (2005).

12. *Noah v. AOL Time Warner*, 261 F. Supp. 2d 532, 535 (E.D. Va. 2003), aff'd, 2004 U.S. App. LEXIS 5495 (4th Cir. 2004).

- Finally among recent developments that might give one pause before dismissing as wholly implausible the notion that government might suppress hate propaganda, there has been a spate of federal prosecutions for aiding and abetting terrorism or for conspiracy to achieve particular terrorism goals. In each of several notable cases, the charges and the evidence fell well short of specific or concrete acts. The essence of each prosecution was that the alleged conspirators had met persistently to discuss (usually in considerable detail) and seemed to possess the requisite intent to achieve such a result. Moreover, in the case of the Lackawanna Six, a group of U.S. citizens of Yemeni ancestry residing in Western New York, the essence of the charged conspiracy was that the defendants had gone to Afghanistan for training as al-Qaeda operatives, had received weapons training there and come under the influence of al-Qaeda leaders, returning eventually to Lackawanna as part of a "sleeper cell," allegedly awaiting an order to attack targets in the U.S. As one account noted, "this was the first major case in which the defendants were not being prosecuted for a crime committed, but effectively for what they might have done," adding that "the prosecution never even offered evidence that the men ever planned to do anything."[13]

The most recent such case, charging the "Liberty City Seven" in South Florida with planning to blow up Chicago's Sears Tower, also involved an alleged plot or conspiracy totally lacking evidence of any overt acts.[14] Such a prosecutorial posture strongly implies a belief that merely plotting and discussing a subversive goal (the achievement of which would clearly be unlawful) may now warrant legal intervention before concrete steps or acts ever occur, or even clear proof that such acts were imminent. So a range of recent criminal cases, none of which has resulted in an appeal (or even a reviewable conviction) strongly implies the possibility of punishment based upon speech alone without concrete acts. Once again, it would be quite naïve to dismiss out of hand the possibility that hateful propaganda and other deeply unsettling messages might be suppressed in the interests of national security. The stage is now clearly set for a deeper inquiry.

---

13. Khaleel Mohammed, "Six of a Kind," *San Diego Union-Tribune*, Sept. 16, 2007, p. E-5.

14. Kirk Semple, "U.S. Falters in Terror Case Against 7 in Miami," *N.Y. Times*, Dec. 14, 2007.

Reflections and Recollections:
We Have Been There Before

Such pressures and forces are hardly new in the United States; antecedents long predate the September 11 terrorist attacks. Most notable among earlier advocates of restricting hate propaganda was David Riesman, who had become a distinguished legal scholar and law teacher long before he achieved eminence as a sociologist. Riesman's three most pertinent articles, published in the *Columbia Law Review* at the height of World War II, bore the arresting title "Democracy and Defamation: Control of Group Libel." The central thesis of these articles was that lessons the world had learned from Nazi Germany during the previous decade not only justified but compelled protective measures in the U.S, aimed at comparable propaganda and mass communications. Specifically, Riesman argued that specific legal safeguards were vital to protect not only vulnerable groups, but the larger fabric of a democratic society as a whole from the ravages of fascism. His premise was that vulnerable groups (religious, racial, national and ethnic) needed and deserved stronger protection than U.S. safeguards ensured if they were to flourish in a democratic society. Noting that the law of defamation had been used by the Nazis for their own protection and benefit, Riesman insisted that "there is no inherent reason why it cannot be used as a weapon for democracy."[15]

Professor Riesman candidly recognized a deep potential conflict between his proposal for enhanced legal protection against group libel and the constitutional stature of free expression under the First Amendment. But he responded with two distinct lines of argument. On one hand, he cautioned that free speech protected only "fair comment" and not the full range of messages that would be targeted by group libel laws; indeed, to the extent such a concern was valid, it could presumably be accommodated by recognizing a defense of truth to any group libel prosecution. But Riesman's response went further, insisting that the exigencies of the World War II world warranted a refinement of First Amendment freedoms that should tolerate such sanctions. "In this state of affairs," Riesman argued with reference to recent events in Western Europe, "it is no longer tenable to continue a negative policy of protection from the state; such a policy, in concrete situations, plays directly into the hands of the groups whom supporters of democracy need most to fear."[16]

---

15. Riesman, "Democracy and Defamation: Control of Group Libel," 42 *Colum. L. Rev.* 727 (1942).

16. *Id.*

Riesman had articulated, as legal historian Evan Schulz recently observed, "a bold advocacy of group libel." His position, Schulz continued, clearly implied "the American government had a duty to protect its constituent groups to uphold democracy. If that meant reconceptualizing American society to diminish the role of the individual and instead to grant primacy to social groups, so be it. With that social change done, any legal problems would take care of themselves."[17]

Indeed, the constitutional landscape during World War II would seem to warrant such a casual assumption about the expendability of free expression concerns. In the very year that Riesman wrote his portentous articles, a unanimous Supreme Court not only sustained a conviction for "fighting words" but added, almost gratuitously, its view that "the prevention and punishment ... of certain well-defined and narrowly limited classes of speech ... have never been thought to raise any Constitutional problems." Among those exempted categories of expression were not only the volatile and provocative epithets involved in the actual case, but also "the lewd and obscene, the profane, the libelous, and the insulting or 'fighting' words ..." since "it has been well observed that such utterances are no essential part of any exposition of ideas, and are of such slight social value as a step to truth that any benefit that may be derived from them is clearly outweighed by the social interest in order and morality."[18] Though later judgments would substantially limit the scope of this sweeping language, eventually leaving obscenity as virtually the only one of those disfavored categories still unprotected, the key point is that while Riesman was making the case for protecting democracy through such measures as group libel laws, one could hardly fault his analysis as insensitive or hostile to prevailing notions of free expression.

Many states did in fact heed Riesman's warning and adopted the course he urged. Although group libel laws were already on the books in some parts of the country, their scope expanded in the immediate post-war period. The *Columbia Law Review*, which had served as Riesman's medium, returned to the fray five years later by offering a model group libel or Statutory Prohibition of Group Defamation Law. Yet the proposed model proved to be less helpful than its caption seemed to imply; Evan Schulz notes that it harbored three nearly fatal flaws: allowing demonstrated truth as a defense (though not permitting merely a good faith belief in veracity); it required a plaintiff or prosecutor to post bond; and the only relief it would support was either a mandated retraction or an injunction against future defamatory statements.

---

17. Schulz, "Group Rights American Jews, and the Failure of Group Libel Law," 66 *Brooklyn L. Rev.* 71, 125–27 (2000).

18. *Chaplinsky v. New Hampshire*, 315 U.S. 568 (1942).

These issues would return to the Supreme Court a decade after Riesman's views first appeared, in the case of *Beauharnais v. Illinois*.[19] In its initial appraisal of group libel laws, a bare majority of the Justices sustained against First Amendment challenge a rather typical statute designed to protect vulnerable racial and religious groups from "contempt, derision, or obloquy" on the basis of "race, color, creed or religion." or offense. Justice Frankfurter, writing for himself and four colleagues, took judicial notice of racial tensions in the Chicago-area community where the case arose and the charges had been filed against the purveyor of incendiary leaflets. The majority gave explicit deference to the Illinois legislature in gauging the need for such a remedy as the group libel law provided against such threats to order and security, as well as the dignity and security of the vulnerable groups targeted by hate propaganda. Given such ominous conditions, and the legislative judgment about an appropriate governmental response, the *Beauharnais* majority found no need to base the hate-mongers' convictions on a finding of clear and present danger (which conceivably might have been but, given the posture of the case, had never been established).[20]

One other Chicago-based judgment provides a useful counterpoint to *Beauharnais*. A speaker named Terminiello had been convicted for arousing a highly receptive audience (and goading angry opponents) by venting racist views that the Supreme Court characterized as "following, with fidelity that was more than coincidental, the pattern of European fascist leaders." The conviction was reversed on the almost technical ground that the jury had been told that it might convict if it found that the speaker's rhetoric "stirs the public to anger, invites dispute, brings about a condition of unrest, or creates a disturbance."[21] Such a standard, declared the majority, was simply incompatible with the First Amendment, since "a function of free speech under our system of government is to invite dispute" so that "it may indeed best serve that high purpose when it induces a condition of unrest, creates dissatisfaction with conditions as they are, or even stirs people to anger." That view was in fact wholly consistent with several high Court rulings during the late 1930s, which had vindicated the free-speech claims of radical labor organizers and others whose volatile rhetoric unsettled public order and stability, but was found to be First Amendment protected.

---

19. 343 U.S. 988 (1952).

20. For a thoughtful review of *Beauharnais*, including its potential contribution to contemporary discussions about hate propaganda and national security, *see* Knechtle, "When to Regulate Hate Speech," 110 *Penn. St. L. Rev.* 539, 555–58 (2006).

21. *Terminiello v. Chicago*, 337 U.S. 1 (1949).

The case is perhaps best remembered, however, for the final sentence in Justice Robert Jackson's long and impassioned dissent. Having recently returned from serving as chief prosecutor at the Nuremberg War Crimes Tribunal, Jackson brought to the case a starkly different view of the potential risk posed by inflammatory propagandists like Terminiello. He began by chiding his colleagues for being out of touch with reality, noting that the trial court in which Terminiello had been tried "was not indulging in theory [but] ... was dealing with a riot and a speech that provoked a hostile mob and incited a friendly one, and threatened violence between the two." Thus, he warned in his characteristically elegant coda: "The choice is not between order and liberty. It is between liberty with order and anarchy without either. There is danger that, if the Court does not temper its doctrinaire logic with a little practical wisdom, it will convert the constitutional Bill of Rights into a suicide pact."[22]

That portentous conclusion was preceded by extensive excerpts from Terminiello's harangue, graphic evidence of the volatile reaction of both supporters and antagonists, but most especially by poignant references to lessons that Justice Jackson had gleaned from his Nuremberg assignment. At one point, he even quoted Nazi propaganda czar Josef Goebbels to the effect that "when democracy granted democratic methods for us in the times of opposition, this [the Nazi seizure of power] was bound to happen in a democratic system." For Jackson, the lessons of World War II and its antecedents were not only inescapable, but compelled a conclusion that was profoundly at variance with the views of his more speech-tolerant colleagues. While disclaiming any design broadly to suppress speech in the interests of security or order, Jackson left no doubt of his belief that the majority was naïve and misguided in its belief that provocative or incendiary rhetoric short of incitement or fighting words must be tolerated. It was that belief that led to the famous "suicide pact" language as the concluding caution.

Justice Jackson was soon to restate his warning on an even larger stage, and one that more directly anticipates the focus of this chapter. When in 1951 the Supreme Court majority sustained the Smith Act convictions of a group of alleged conspirators active in the post–World War II Communist Party, deference to speech suppression now commanded a clear majority, with only Justices Black and Douglas dissenting.[23] Central to the majority's acceptance of broad Congressional power to proscribe such advocacy was the doctrine of "clear and present danger," which all other Justices assumed to furnish the appropriate

---

22. *Id.* at 37.
23. *Dennis v. United States*, 341 U.S. 494 (1951).

constitutional template, even as they diverged sharply in its interpretation and application to the facts of the case.

Justice Jackson alone doubted the efficacy of such a standard, insisting it should be applied only to threats of a far different order where "the issue is the criminality of a hot-headed speech on a street corner, or circulation of a few incendiary pamphlets, or parading by some zealots behind a red flag," but had no bearing upon situations like the one then before the Court—"a well organized, nation-wide conspiracy" that seeks the violent overthrow of the government itself. Adherence to "clear and present danger" under conditions such as those that faced the nation in the early Cold War period would, Jackson warned, mean that "the Government can move [against Communist conspirators] only after imminent action is manifest, when it would, of course, be too late."

The Constitutional Framework Changes: Brandenburg and Hess

As the law governing contentious advocacy was to evolve in the decades following the Communist conspiracy rulings, the Jackson view would claim steadily fewer adherents. When the Justices eventually revisited the constitutional status of contentious advocacy, a unanimous Court headed by conservative Chief Justice Warren Burger would announce strikingly different guidelines.[24] The case concerned a racist agitator who had aroused a gathering of Ku Klux Klan members on a southwest Ohio farm, and was charged with unlawful advocacy of "the duty, necessary or propriety of crime, sabotage or violence or unlawful methods of terrorism ..." Earnest Brandenburg, the accused speaker, persistently warned his partisans that if government "continues to suppress the white, Caucasian race," "some revengeance [sic]" might become inevitable. The Ohio courts affirmed the conviction, rejecting Brandenburg's First Amendment claims on the basis of what seemed well settled Supreme Court jurisprudence.

The reversal of Brandenburg's conviction was striking far more for the principles it declared than for the result, though it did mark the first time since the late 1930s that the Justices had extended such protection to radical agitators. Henceforth, declared the Court, advocacy of unlawful action could be punished only if "such advocacy is directed to inciting or producing imminent law-

---

24. *Brandenburg v. Ohio*, 395 U.S. 444 (1969).

less action and is likely to produce such action." On that basis the Ohio statute failed a First Amendment test which seemed markedly more protective than the standard applied to the post-World War II advocacy and conspiracy cases.

A successor case would soon reinforce *Brandenburg*'s protection for political expression. A radical Indiana University student leader named Hess was arrested for "disorderly conduct" while exhorting an anti-Vietnam War rally on a Bloomington street corner. So clear to the Supreme Court seemed the invalidity of his conviction that a brief per curiam opinion would suffice as the medium of reversal.[25] Three essential elements of a constitutionally valid charge were missing in the Hess case. First was the absence of the requisite proof that "Hess' statement was … directed to any person or group of persons" since he had been addressing a rather amorphous crowd that ebbed and flowed through a busy intersection. Lacking such evidence, concluded the *Hess* Court, "it cannot be said that he was advocating, in the normal sense, any action." The second flaw was the failure of the prosecution to prove a specific intent on the speaker's part—an element that could fairly have been implied from the *Brandenburg* ruling but had not been made explicit in the earlier case.

Finally and perhaps most compelling to the *Hess* majority was the absence of proof (or even "rational inference from the import of the language") that "his words were intended to produce, and likely to produce, *imminent* disorder," without which proof "those words cannot be punished by the State on the ground that they had 'a tendency to lead to violence.'"[26] The basis for this rather startling statement lay in the circumstances of the case. Hess had invited his audience to consider taking control of one of Bloomington's main thoroughfares, after police had told the demonstrators to clear that street. But at the critical moment, witnesses agreed that Hess had said either "we'll take the fucking street later" or "we'll take the fucking street again."

Whichever version prevailed, it was now clear that *Brandenburg*'s requirement of "imminence" could not be met if the speaker used (as Hess clearly did) language that stopped short of urging immediate lawless action, even if the relevant words did not expressly counsel delay or postponement. Indeed, the highly symbolic italicization of "imminent" in so brief an opinion reflects the certainty with which the *Hess* majority had now embraced that element of *Brandenburg*. If the illegality a speaker urged could be deferred or postponed, then an incitement charge could not stand—a cautionary view that seemed strikingly reminiscent of Justice Brandeis' caution four decades earlier that "if

---

25. *Hess v. Indiana*, 414 U.S. 105 (1973).
26. *Id.*

there be time to expose through discussion the falsehood and fallacies, to avert the evil by the processes of education, the remedy to be applied is more speech, not enforced silence."[27]

What is most remarkable about the *Brandenburg-Hess* doctrine has been its durability. Even the *Hess* dissenters differed with their majority colleagues only on technical and factual issues, making no attempt to undermine or even qualify the basic mandate of *Brandenburg*. Skeptics, of course, might caution that the ensuing decades have never forced the Court to revisit (or reassess dangerous advocacy under) conditions remotely comparable to the international Communist conspiracy; the relevant cases, including *Brandenburg* and *Hess*, have really involved Justice Jackson's "street corner hotheads" more than subversive groups plotting the violent overthrow of the United States. Thus, in a more than superficial sense, the question that is central to the issues on which we focus here has not yet been presented—though such an encounter seems increasingly inevitable in the post-September 11 efforts to detect and regulate terrorist activity.

Along the way, three closely related First Amendment issues (verbal threats, hate speech and cross burning) have received the high Court's attention, and their resolution offers at least modest guidance. Each judgment merits brief consideration to complete the constitutional context within which current questions must be appraised. The First Amendment status of threats remains surprisingly elusive, chiefly because it has received so little of the Supreme Court's attention. In the one pertinent case, the Justices said essentially two things that are not readily reconcilable. On one hand, "true threats" (a term this case did not attempt to define) lie beyond the protection of free expression, while on the other hand what appeared to have been a clear challenge to the life of a sitting president did not meet that standard. Specifically, addressing a draft-resistance rally near the White House during the height of the Vietnam War, a young man declared, "If they ever make me carry a rifle the first man I want to get in my sights is L.B.J."[28]

While upholding the validity of the federal statute that criminalizes threats on the president's life, the majority insisted that such "political hyperbole" could not constitute a "true threat" of the type that a valid statutory ban might properly reach; "the language of the political arena, like the language used in labor disputes, is often vituperative, abusive and inexact"—and, accordingly, for the most part merits First Amendment protection.[29] Given such elliptical guidance, the lower federal courts have understandably adopted vastly variant

---

27. *Whitney v. California*, 274 U.S. 357, (1927) (Brandeis, J., concurring).
28. *Watts v. United States*, 394 U.S. 705, (1969).
29. *Id.*

views of what constitutes the "true threat" that may be punished consistent with free expression. Thus the threat doctrine, though potentially promising, turns out to contribute little to the current inquiry.

Similarly disappointing for our purposes has been the high Court's disposition of the "hate speech" issue. Without erasing the long shadow of the *Beauharnais* case, the Justices in 1992 struck down hate speech bans as violative of First Amendment freedoms—albeit on two utterly irreconcilable grounds.[30] A bare majority ruled that government may not disfavor expression which reflects a particular viewpoint, even in the course of regulating less than fully protected speech (in this case, fighting words.) Thus a municipal ban on words or symbols that might evoke anger or resentment "on the basis of race, color, creed, religion or gender" ran afoul of the newly defined constitutional mandate of content-neutrality. The concurring Justices would have reached the same conclusion, albeit by more familiar grounds such as vagueness and overbreadth, finding the "selectivity" doctrine to be "disheartening" or "illogical" or worse. Just as clarity seemed to emerge in the hate-speech area, a unanimous Court held barely a year later that states could impose harsher penalties on hate-motivated non-speech crimes—even though the only likely source of evidence of such bias was a defendant's racist, sexist or homophobic speech. In the later case, the Justices insisted that penalty enhancement for bias-driven crimes targeted conduct, and not expression, and thus posed no problems under the hate-speech doctrine.

Whatever hope one might have harbored for clarity of guidance as the Court considered bans on cross-burning proved similarly elusive. In 2003 the Justices reviewed a Virginia law which the state's highest court had struck down on free speech grounds in reversing the conviction of a Klansman named Barry Black. One of those grounds commanded a majority and brought a narrow affirmance in one of three combined cases, since the statute inferred evidence of the requisite "intent to intimidate" from the simple act of burning a cross, regardless of other factors or conditions. But the core of the case concerned the validity of targeting a particular (albeit hateful) symbol—a focus that even casual readers of the hate-speech ruling might have believed could not survive close First Amendment scrutiny. For Justice O'Connor and a majority of her colleagues, however, cross-burning was different, even to a constitutional degree: Since intimidation (notably, the still imprecisely defined "true threats") can claim no First Amendment protection, and since "the history of cross burning in this country shows that cross burning is often intimidating," states might single out for sanctions this one especially abhorrent form of symbolic expression.

---

30. *R.A.V. v. St. Paul*, 505 U.S. 377 (1992).

In reaching this curious conclusion the majority was helped by a major qualification in the 1992 hate-speech case: While government may not randomly disfavor an uncongenial viewpoint in regulating expression, selectivity might be permissible either as a means of redressing "secondary effects" that would not implicate content or viewpoint, or "when the basis for the content discrimination consists entirely of the very reason the entire class of speech at issue is proscribable." The majority was also comforted by assuming that a ban on cross-burning could be read as viewpoint-neutral, and on that basis escaped the fatal flaw of the hate-speech regulations. The dissenters, in stark contrast, found the cross-burning prohibition indistinguishable from the hate-speech ban for First Amendment purposes, and would have invalidated it for that reason as well as on the narrower inference-of-intent rationale.

Many critical issues were left unanswered by the *Black* decision. The critical paradox could be phrased in several different ways—what, for example, so clearly differentiated cross-burning from other hateful messages as uniquely to warrant criminal sanctions? Could the *Black* doctrine possibly extend to other expression that is unmistakably designed (and quite likely) to intimidate—for example, marching through a heavily Jewish community such as Skokie, Illinois, displaying a Nazi swastika and other insignia?[31] Or if burning crosses with an intent to intimidate was truly unique, what broader principles emerged from that judgment to guide adjudication of similar questions elsewhere? And what remained, after the *Black* ruling, of the hate-speech doctrine itself, to which the Court had given such seemingly consistent adherence until it took on cross-burning? These and other questions emerged quickly in the aftermath of the cross-burning case, and continue to trouble and divide legal scholars. While the current analysis we pursue here does not demand answers to such questions, recognition of the quandary that *Black* created for constitutional scholars is surely appropriate.

How Different Is the Post-September 11 Environment?

We come now to the central issue of this chapter: To what extent might national security imperatives since September 11, 2001, cause any relaxation of

---

31. Such hateful symbolic expression had been held to be First Amendment protected in *Collin v. Smith*, 578 F.2d 1197 (7th Cir.), cert. denied, 439 U.S. 916 (1978).

the constitutional standards that protect contentious political expression, including hate propaganda? The short answer—that the *Brandenburg-Hess* formula still governs all such cases—may turn out to be accurate, although such a simplistic summary response seems naïve, and surely overlooks the vastly different climate created by the terrorist attacks. It is true that no court has rendered a post-9/11 judgment on a speech issue that in any way undermines or qualifies the *Brandenburg-Hess* doctrine.

On the other hand, several portentous criminal prosecutions that might well have yielded such a judgment became moot when the defendants pleaded guilty to lesser charges and thus not only avoided a protected trial, but also waived a host of First Amendment claims that would have otherwise have been ripe for assertion on appeal. Thus, rather than insisting that the law governing post-September 11 speech remains intact and unaltered, it would be far safer (and more accurate) to note simply that no court has yet been called upon to address that issue in the radically different current national security climate.

Before anticipating how that issue might well arise, and how it should be resolved, we should recognize several important qualifications. For one, as Professor Stephen Shiffrin has observed, there is even some doubt whether *Brandenburg* unambiguously adopted an "incitement" standard. Since the *Brandenburg* opinion rather casually used alternative language in the formulation of its template, "incitement is not necessary to divorce the speech from first amendment protection ... [I]t is enough that the speech is directed to producing imminent lawless action and is likely to produce such action."[32] One might respond, however, that what *Brandenburg* left ambiguous seems to have been clarified by the far stricter and more precise standards that were soon added by the *Hess* decision—after which it would be more difficult to claim that anything less than "incitement" would warrant sanctions against contentious political speech. That is also the assumption on which most courts have proceeded in the ensuing nearly four decades, insisting not only on imminence (and directedness) but also on advocacy that is much stronger than merely hortatory, but rises to the level of actual incitement.

On a related point, Professor Shiffrin seems correct—that *Brandenburg* and *Hess* provide protection that is limited to the political realm. He inquires provocatively: "How different would it be if the factual context were to involve advocacy of murder in a non-socio-political context?"[33] Not only would the

---

32. Shiffrin, "Defamatory Non-Media Speech and First Amendment Methodology," 25 *U.C.L.A. L. Rev.* 915, 947 (1978).

33. *Id* at 950.

First Amendment analysis be radically different in such a case, but advocacy of that sort might well be charged as "solicitation" or under some other criminal law rubric (e.g., "conspiracy," "accessory," etc.) that would deprive the speaker of any First Amendment protection whatever. At the very least, a non-political call to commit homicide would properly be analyzed under very different principles.

Beyond such an easy exception, however, the distinction may be more elusive than Professor Shiffrin suggests. When the Supreme Court ruled in *Cohen v. California*[34] that the public use of taboo or vulgar words may not be criminalized, it left tantalizingly open the question whether such protection was limited to the use of such language to convey a political message (such as the actual speaker's "Fuck the Draft") or whether an offensive but non-political utterance enjoy comparable immunity. Scholars have divided on that issue ever since—some insisting that a political context and purpose are indispensable for such protection, while others insist with equal conviction that the ruling is far broader and protects any use of such offending words. The opinion contains language potentially supporting both views—sometimes suggesting that vulgarity and profanity are per se exempt from sanctions, while elsewhere seeming to stress the risks of "suppressing ideas in the process" of demanding decorum in public utterance. Given such ambiguity, we should approach with caution Professor Shiffrin's "political speech only" notion, even in the incitement context. Though such high-order expression is surely entitled to optimal protection, we cannot preclude the possible reach of *Brandenburg-Hess* to speech that neither advances a political viewpoint nor urges homicide.

A third distinction may be worth noting, and comes closer to the issue that is now before us. Professor Harry Kalven creatively observed that *Brandenburg-Hess* protections apply with certainty only to *individual* speech, so that expression or political activity by controversial *organizations* might well receive a lesser degree of First Amendment solicitude: "Is it possible, he wondered two decades ago, "that [*Brandenburg*] has preserved the group/individual distinction [developed in Communist Party regulation cases] ... and the *Brandenburg* incitement-to-immediate-action standard would apply [only] to the individual speaker?"[35] Applying such a distinction (though never tested through litigation, much less Supreme Court analysis), publications or postings by groups or organizations might be restricted under a standard less protective

---

34. 403 U.S. 15 (1971).
35. Kalven, *A Worthy Tradition* 234 (1988).

than *Brandenburg-Hess* would seem to demand of any sanctions imposed on individual speakers.

With all deference to Professor Kalven and his impeccable insight on free speech issues, however, such a distinction seems suspect. For one, it omits any mention of freedom of association as a concomitant rationale for protecting the expression of controversial groups or organizations. A 1974 Supreme Court case, not noted by Professor Kalven, strongly implied that *Brandenburg* should guide review of a state's ballot-access oath required of all registered political parties. The flaw in Indiana's law, wrote Justice Brennan, was the state's posture that it denied access to the ballot "not because the [Communist] Party urges others to 'do something now or in the future, [but] merely to believe in something.'"[36] Nor were earlier rulings any more prophetic on this issue; the *Beauharnais* decision, although sustaining against a racist organization's First Amendment challenge a state "group libel" law, so far antedated *Brandenburg* as to be unhelpful on the "group/individual" issue. Later cases are no more indicative since this issue has simply not returned to the courts. Moreover, the few most closely analogous rulings—striking down, for example, campus speech codes that apply alike to groups and individuals[37]—seem to imply no difference in the recognition of collective and individual free-speech claims in such a setting. Thus, we should be prepared to treat individual and group challenges to speech curbs essentially alike for *Brandenburg-Hess* purposes.

Finally, and almost too obvious to require separate mention, was the context within which the *Brandenburg-Hess* standard emerged. The defendants in both cases were classically the sorts of "street-corner hotheads" or "flag-waving zealots" that Justice Jackson envisioned in his *Dennis* concurrence. Although *Hess* arose at the height of protest over the Vietnam War, the context could not fairly be compared to that of the early Cold War years. And surely the Klan rally that Brandenburg was arrested for arousing on a southwest Ohio farm could hardly be viewed as analogous to the context of the *Dennis* decision. Yet neither of the later cases suggested any such limitation, although one would have expected such a distinction had it seemed appropriate. Even the *Hess* dissenters disputed facts, not legal doctrine.

The tortured course of the "clear and present danger" doctrine both complicated and illuminated this process. In the last of its pre-war speech-protective rulings, the Supreme Court majority insisted upon the most rigorous application of that well settled Holmesian standard; Justice Frankfurter and

---

36. *Communist Party of Indiana v. Whitcomb*, 414 U.S. 441 (1974).
37. *E.g., Doe v. University of Michigan*, 721 F. Supp. 852 (E.D. Mich. 1989).

his fellow dissenters decried what they deemed inadequate concern about national security needs in the face of almost certain U.S. immersion in another World War.[38] When that war ended, the status of the "clear and present danger" doctrine remained in doubt for some time, until the Communist Conspiracy (*Dennis*) case reached the courts. Curiously, Justice Jackson was the only member of the *Dennis* Court who deemed the "clear and present danger" test wholly inapposite to the threat posed by an international Communist conspiracy; to his dissenting colleagues that doctrine (as the majority now construed it) was seriously under-protective of political advocacy, though still supplied the appropriate standard. (Indeed, Justice Douglas was at pains in his dissent to hypothesize conditions that he felt might pose just such a danger—hungry and unemployed protestors during the depths of the Depression, for example—thereby sharing the majority's view that the familiar constitutional test survived the war and its aftermath.

It was in *Brandenburg* that the wheels were to come off "clear and present danger," and by a curious process that has only recently come to light. The writing of an opinion for a unanimous Court was first assigned to Justice Fortas, who in his initial draft expressly invoked clear and present danger. But before the ruling could be announced, Justice Fortas was forced to resign from the Court. The case was then reassigned to Justice Brennan, who drafted a per curiam opinion that contained no mention of "clear and present danger," without explaining such a major omission.[39] For that matter, the *Brandenburg* per curiam invoked *Dennis* not—as one would have expected—to administer last rites before its effective overruling. Rather, *Dennis* was cited as the very source of the "incitement" doctrine which the Court was about to put in its place.

A *Brandenburg* footnote did explain in passing that the Smith Act (on which the *Dennis* charges were based) had been sustained only by inferring an "incitement" standard that was clearly nowhere to be found in that statute, but was now declared to have been a sine qua non of its continuing validity.[40] Thus unfolded the seamless process—characteristic of Justice Brennan's jurisprudence—by which one doctrine yielded to a far from compatible successor as though the two shared a common source and could comfortably coexist. Any objective reader would conclude that little of the substance of *Dennis* survived *Brandenburg* and *Hess*, despite the Court's continuing assurance to the contrary and despite the absence of anything resembling a decent burial.

---

38. *Bridges v. California*, 314 U.S. 252 (1941).

39. *See* Schwartz, "Holmes Versus Hand: Clear and Present Danger or Advocacy of Unlawful Action?" 1995 *Sup. Ct. Rev.* 237.

40. 395 U.S. 444 (1969).

Always the maverick and sometimes the spoiler, Justice Douglas alone refused to let the issue vanish so quietly. Noting that even Justice Holmes had begun to question "clear and present danger" after his conservative colleagues invoked it to sustain protestor convictions, Douglas now expressed his own "doubt if the 'clear and present danger' test is congenial to the First Amendment in time of a declared war," adding that "I am certain it is not reconcilable with the First Amendment in days of peace." It seemed to have survived this long only because (in his view) the *Dennis* Court had distorted it "beyond recognition." Now, in *Brandenburg* (clearly a peacetime case), wrote Douglas, "I see no place in the regime of the First Amendment for any 'clear and present danger' test whether strict and tight as some would make it or free-wheeling as the Court in *Dennis* rephrased it."[41]

Thus, as we approach the inescapable post-September 11 quandary, it might be well to define as precisely as possible the constitutional standard that would otherwise govern contentious advocacy, including hate propaganda. "Clear and present danger," once the dominant desideratum, has been quietly bypassed or treated as an historical anachronism, even by courts professing to reaffirm its centrality. As recently as 1941, and surely in the late 1930s, that test proved (at least in the hands of a sympathetic Court) potentially quite speech-protective. Yet this doctrine has been effectively replaced by "incitement to imminent lawless action," to which elements of directedness or targeting, specific intent and imminence (as well as likely impact) have been added. Such a succession or displacement may have been the inevitable outcome of the "distortion" that Justice Douglas rightly blamed on the *Dennis* Court, though his own dissent in that case left him at least slightly culpable in the doctrine's demise. Though none of the "clear and present danger" decisions has ever been overruled—even by implication—it should be clear that in the twenty-first century new rules apply.

The qualifications to "incitement" under *Brandenburg-Hess* are now familiar. Obviously this doctrine embraces only expression that would otherwise enjoy full First Amendment protection—unavailable to such obvious outliers as verbal solicitation, conspiracy, fraud, bribery or extortion, including "true threats," and uncertainly available to categories of partially protected speech like obscenity, advertising, fighting words and the like where such issues would seem highly improbable. But within the core expressive sector, absent proof of each of the requisite elements—direct incitement, targeted to a person or group, urging imminent lawless action, reflecting a specific intent, and likely

41. *Id.*

to have the presumed effect—even the most contentious and unsettling political advocacy would seem to claim First Amendment protection.

One final piece fits awkwardly into this constitutional puzzle. Potentially dilutive decisions—dealing, most notably, with fighting words and with group libel—have never been overruled and thus must be deemed to remain within the legal framework that governs adjudication of such issues. The fighting words case (*Chaplinsky*) poses few problems; not only has it been narrowly construed and applied only to face-to-face insults and epithets almost certain to provoke immediate physical retaliation, but in a world of increasingly electronic communications that separate speaker and listener, fighting words situations occur with diminishing frequency. The group libel case (*Beauharnais*) survives uneasily, and thus creates a residual potential for speech-restrictive laws that might punish advocacy short of incitement. Yet despite the absence of actual overruling, and even occasional passing references in Supreme Court opinions, the precedential force of *Beauharnais* seems tenuous at best.

Moreover, a central premise of that decision was the complete absence at the time of any First Amendment protection for defamation, a gap which left "group libel" subject to extensive regulation. The decision in *New York Times v. Sullivan*,[42] however, radically changed the landscape and profoundly altered that premise; virtually any defamatory statements that might be targeted by a group libel law would today enjoy substantial protection, since they typically address "matters of public concern" even if they do not implicate public officials or public figures. Thus the technical survival of *Beauharnais* turns out to be less troublesome than might initially appear—though proponents of hate speech laws and codes never tire of reminding their opponents that such a ruling remains on the books.

How Might "Hate Propaganda" Be Regulated?

Those who entertain or endorse the prospect of curbing "hate propaganda" usually cite two distinct types of governmental interests that might possibly warrant such sanctions—protecting the dignity and reputation of vulnerable groups from verbal assault or offense, and protecting public order and stability from violence.[43] The former can be rather readily dismissed on grounds we have already canvassed; the latter requires far deeper analysis.

---

42. *New York Times v. Sullivan*, 376 U.S. 255 (1964).
43. *See* Knechtle, *supra* note 20, at 542–46.

Looking initially at the "dignity" interest, it should be clear that under the First Amendment, government may not suppress or restrict expression in order to spare vulnerable groups from offense, obloquy or indignity. However laudable such a purpose may seem, and however responsive to it are the laws of many other nations, our current free-speech jurisprudence simply does not accept such a rationale for restricting otherwise protected speech. We insist that members of vulnerable groups risk exposure to slurs, insults, and demeaning remarks—even in the most hateful and venal forms—as a price for ensuring the free flow of ideas and information. Though many critics argue with conviction that such a price is excessive, and that our uniquely tolerant policy gives open season to hate-mongers, our courts have been quite consistent in rejecting such a rationale for regulating expression. Thus every college or university speech code that has been challenged in court has been invalidated on one of more First Amendment grounds; though no judge has categorically foreclosed the drafting of a constitutionally viable code, the failure of any of the myriad attempts to protect human dignity in ways that comport with free expression strongly suggests the futility of such a mission.[44] Thus we can put aside the first of the proffered regulatory interests, and focus instead on the other.

The relationship between hate propaganda and the potential for violence, civic unrest and even the instability of government, presents a far different dimension. Such concerns have emerged with renewed intensity in the post-September 11 period. The nexus between such hateful messages and security are of course hardly new, as even a cursory reading of David Riesman's articles of over a half century ago should quickly remind us. Moreover, we can hardly overlook steadily growing concern about such links in other parts of the world—most especially the tragic effects posed for the Tutsi community of Rwanda by a spate of hate messages broadcast by Radio-Television Libre des Mille Collines (RTLM). Nearly a decade after the massive genocide that was apparently inspired in major part by these broadcasts, the International Tribunal for Rwanda sentenced several RTLM officials after finding them guilty of various offenses, including incitement to commit genocide.[45]

Much closer to home, we are regularly reminded that our neighbor to the north takes a far less tolerant view of such hateful messages. The Human Rights Tribunal of Canada has on several occasions imposed sanctions on the operators of racist Internet websites (and has shut down a half dozen such sites), typi-

---

44. *See* O'Neil, *Free Speech in the College Community*, 1–26 (1997).
45. *See* Davis, *supra* note 6 at 765–72.

cally for posting jokes about killing blacks, Jews, Sikhs and Muslims—all in clear violation of Canada's rather stringent hate speech laws.[46] While the Canadian view of hate propaganda (mirrored by the public policies of Germany and other European nations) reflects in substantial part a commitment to protect human dignity, concern for public safety and order are never far below the surface.

Finally, recalling the variety of recent incidents we reviewed at the start of this chapter, we should recognize that our remarkably tolerant views on hate propaganda and similar messages are being sorely tested in the far more security-conscious climate of the post 9/11 period. Thus we come squarely to the central issue: Suppose in the aftermath of a heightened terrorist threat to domestic security, measures were proposed (or actually adopted) that would penalize purveyors of extreme hate propaganda for posting or broadcasting such material? Had such sanctions been proposed before September, 2001, the response would have been unambiguous: Without proof of direct incitement to imminent lawless action that meets the stringent *Brandenburg-Hess* standard, even the most hateful or provocative messages may not be suppressed. The precise form of the sanction would be irrelevant—whether criminal prosecution, administrative order, collateral penalty, denial of government benefits, or any other adverse consequence. The critical issue concerns the applicable constitutional standards.

We hardly need be reminded that—even without another terrorist attack on U.S. soil—life will never be the same after September 11. In the event of an actual declared war, of course, conditions might be radically different; in the very case that spawned the clear and present danger test, Justice Holmes observed: "When a nation is at war many things that might be said in time of peace are such a hindrance to its effort that their utterance will not be endured so long as men fight...."[47] But the critical test would occur under conditions such as those we have experienced in the post-9/11 period—a nation not officially at war, but on substantially higher national security alert than it was before the attack on the World Trade Center and the Pentagon.

In such times as these, any court asked to rule on charges against contentious or hateful advocacy would presumably begin with a powerful presumption in favor of continued adherence to the *Brandenburg-Hess* doctrine. Such a commitment would thus establish a transcendent constitutional framework—valid for tense as well as relaxed times—within which to appraise what may be the most perplexing conflict between free expression and national security. Let us,

---

46. Blackwell, "Web Messages Hate, Tribunal Rules," *Toronto Globe & Mail*, March 11, 2006, section C.

47. *Schenck v. United States*, 249 U.S. 47, (1919).

then, consider how each of the essential elements of the established First Amendment standard might apply under such conditions.

We might profitably begin our analysis with the requirement that (according to *Hess*) alleged incitement must be "*directed to a ... person or group*" and not simply uttered to the world at large. Accordingly, it seems very doubtful that sanctions could ever constitutionally be imposed on the operator of a hate propaganda website or electronic bulletin board for the simple reason that such messages are seldom "directed" or "targeted" save in special situations where they are either e-mailed to named addressees or are posted within an electronic environment so secure and of such limited access that a putative audience could readily be defined and circumscribed. Accordingly, thoughtful suggestions that certain especially virulent or provocative hate sites on the Internet might be subject to administrative or criminal sanctions[48] seem to disregard this basic premise of the controlling constitutional doctrine. Only where adequate evidence of "directedness" exists should such a proposal receive even serious consideration. Most electronic communications, however hateful and however provocative may be their content, simply would not satisfy this requirement. This conclusion presumably draws added force from *Brandenburg*'s requirement that provocative advocacy must constitute "direct" incitement before it can be punished—although the Supreme Court has offered no guidance on the significance of that element in the formula.

Suppose, however, the charged messages are sufficiently "directed" to qualify—for example, person-to-person or person-to-defined-group communications in electronic or specifically targeted in traditional media. A court would then need to apply the remaining elements of the constitutional equation. Proving the requisite intent to incite would probably not be difficult in such a case; indeed the very process by which the speaker or sender had targeted or directed such provocative messages would typically supply the needed proof of an intent to incite.

Far harder would be assessing the *probability* that such messages would have the desired effect upon their intended audience—an element required by both *Brandenburg*'s and *Hess*'s stress upon "likely to incite or produce such action." The application of this criterion is not hypothetical or conjectural; the Rwandan genocide experience in fact offers a useful illustration. When the prospect of imposing major sanctions against the RTLM first surfaced, both the United States and France responded that the suspect messages were ambiguous, and their likely impact was thus difficult if not impossible to assess. The Canadian ambassador was even less persuaded of the need to in-

---

48. *See, e.g.,* Tsesis,"Prohibiting Incitement on the Internet," 7 *Va. J.L. & Tech.* 5 (2002).

tervene, noting that "there were so many genuinely silly things being said on the station, so many obvious lies, that it was hard to take it seriously." Eventually, when mass genocide became a tragic reality, and the catalytic role of RTLM could no longer be doubted or disregarded, the major Western powers backed the International Criminal Tribunal's call for sanctions.[49] Although of course the Western diplomats were not invoking the *Brandenburg-Hess* desiderata, their initial uncertainty about the appropriateness of sanctions reflected a parallel concern—that intervention should occur only if the suspect messages were intended to incite, and if a violent response was highly probable if not inevitable.

This analysis leaves for last the hardest question: what does the *"imminence"* requirement add to the calculus in a time of grave national security concerns? Vital though this element obviously is to judging the status of contentious advocacy, we lack any useful guidance. The *Hess* Court did italicize that term twice in its brief per curiam opinion, once to add specific emphasis in quoting the critical language from *Brandenburg* (where none of the key terms were thus highlighted) and again in its own refinement of the earlier standard. Moreover, the *Hess* majority deemed fatal to the state's case the clear import of the facts—that the speaker's appeal "amounted to nothing more than advocacy of illegal action at some indefinite future time" and could even "be taken as counsel for present moderation." Such cautionary language would strongly imply a reaffirmation of Justice Brandeis' insistence that government must stand aside "if there be time to expose through discussion the falsehood and fallacies ..."

So stringent a test seems to impose a standard of immediacy that may be met only by showing a gap in time between message and likely response so brief as to preclude any less drastic form of government intervention. If, therefore, heightened national security conditions provide any rationale for flexibility, it must be with regard to the interpretation of "imminent." Thus, for example, a court might be persuaded that an especially provocative and dangerous message—assuming it met the other desiderata in terms of directedness, intent and probable effect—need not demand a momentary response from a targeted and susceptible audience in order to be treated as "direct incitement." Here, in other words, might be the one situation in which recognition of the difference between a "street corner hothead" and an international movement would be acceptable and even consistent with the *Brandenburg-Hess* rationale. At least this facet of the test invites closer study as unavoidable tests of government power over provocative speech reach the courts.

---

49. *See* Knechtle, *supra* at 54.

It is still far too early to offer definitive answers to this most difficult of all post-9/ll constitutional challenges. Clearly those who argue for a suspension of well settled (albeit peacetime-based) principles of free expression disregard the durability of the *Brandenburg-Hess* standard as well as its inherent logic. The notion that a government bound by the First Amendment is free to prosecute those who post hateful and provocative messages is not only extremely dangerous, but is fundamentally discordant with deeply rooted principles of free expression. Granting that the Bill of Rights is not, as Justice Jackson cautioned nearly six decades ago, "a suicide pact," even the most turbulent and anxious of times should not warrant departure from principles that have served and guided this nation well through many earlier perils.

Finally, whatever the legal answer, we should also seek guidance from public policy. Even if the First Amendment imposed no limits on the power of government to punish hate propaganda in the interests of national security, would such sanctions be consistent with basic principles of democracy? Several factors counsel caution in this volatile area. For one, the mere creation of such sanctions may create false hopes on the part of vulnerable groups—hopes that vilification and its effects may diminish, when experience shows that the likeliest result of such measures is to drive the hate-mongers underground and intensify rather than moderate the animus that drives such messages. There are other quite practical concerns: The facts are often ambiguous and subject to varying interpretations, as the shifting international reactions to the Rwandan broadcasts made starkly clear. Even where there may be no doubt or dispute about the facts, predicting probable consequences is always a perilous process; one day a hateful message may galvanize an angry crowd to extreme violence; the next day, or in the next community, the actual response may differ dramatically. Even more ominous is the prospect that a sanction created one day for "good" reason—to protect the weak and vulnerable—may in less sensitive hands furnish a weapon of oppression that will be used in precisely the opposite manner. (Ironically, for example, there is evidence that the very minority groups whose interests were the object of solicitude have been more often victims than beneficiaries of campus speech codes adopted in the 1990s.)

Most troubling of all is the central premise of any such regulation of expression—that it is proper or even permissible for government to anoint certain views or messages while disfavoring or banning others. As former Harvard President Derek Bok asked rhetorically in his trenchant critique of campus speech codes: "Whom will we trust to censor communications and decide which ones are 'too offensive' or 'too inflammatory' or too devoid of intellectual content?" Quite clearly we in the United States pay a sometimes heavy price for our nearly unique insistence on tolerating hateful messages. We should not be surprised that most kindred Western nations draw the line quite differently, and give higher priority to human dignity and national security. Yet we are also wise to note that our First Amendment is by far the oldest and most durable guarantee of free expression to be found anywhere in the world. So perhaps our tolerance of vile and hateful messages is one of the things we seem to be doing right.

Chapter 8

Civil Litigation Against Terrorism: Neglected Promise

*John Norton Moore**

> *"For as in absolute governments the king is law, so in free countries the law ought to be king; and there ought to be no other."*
> Thomas Paine,
> *Common Sense* (1776)

> *"It is essential to the idea of a law, that it be attended with a sanction...."*
> Alexander Hamilton,
> *The Federalist* no. 11 (1787)

---

* John Norton Moore is the Walter L. Brown Professor of Law at the University of Virginia and Director of the Center for National Security Law. He formerly served as Counselor on International Law to the Department of State, United States Ambassador to the United Nations Conference on the Law of the Sea, Chairman of the National Security Council Task Force on the Law of the Sea and Deputy Special Representative of the President for the Law of the Sea, and the founding Chairman of the Board of Directors of the United States Institute of Peace. He is a four term Chairman of the American Bar Association Standing Committee on National Security Law and is co-counsel in the case of *Acree v. Republic of Iraq*, 271 F.Supp.2d 179 (D.C. Dist. Col. 2003), 370 F.3d 41 (D.C. Cir. 2004), *cert. denied*, 125 S.Ct. 1928 (2005), (*see also* the motion for relief under Fed. R. Civ. P. 60(b)(6) 2005), discussed in this chapter. As the Counselor on International Law to the Department of State he drafted the United States Convention against the Spread of Terrorism in the aftermath of the Munich Olympics massacre and was one of the draftsmen of the original Foreign Sovereign Immunities Act. The author would like to thank Allan Gerson and Steven R. Perles for their comments on a draft of this chapter. Both attorneys have been pioneers in the use of civil litigation against terror states.

Introduction

In an age in which "the rule of law" has become a universal slogan, as well as a core component in United States and democratic nation foreign policy, one might think that civil suits against terror states would be an established part of the war on terror. But sadly this is not the reality; in large part because the movement in international law away from the complete sovereign immunity of "the King can do no wrong" has been glacially slow, and because, in the United States "old thinking" in the Executive legal offices has all too often vigorously opposed such civil suits.[1] Change, however, is coming and coming fast, thanks primarily to the practicing bar and to more forward thinking from the Congress.

This chapter urges that civil litigation against terrorism, including against states complicit in supporting terrorism, may be one of the most important tools available for democratic nations in the fight against terror. In doing so, it offers the model of a Protocol to the United Nations Conventions on terrorism as a next step in moving forward to energize this important tool. But first this chapter will explore the glacial movement away from "The King Can Do No Wrong," a slowly eroding principal of "sovereign immunity" which has dominated international law and the thinking of foreign offices, and in doing so it will discuss the important new "Lautenberg Amendment" signed into law in the 2008 Defense Authorization Act. The chapter will then make the case as to why civil litigation is a uniquely capable and important tool in the fight against terror, discuss why traditional arguments against use of civil litigation are flawed, and finally provide a case study of a recent extraordinary effort by the Executive branch to prevent state accountability, as an illustration of the extreme nature of Executive branch "old thinking" in this area.[2]

---

1. As one example of State Department opposition to civil judgments even against terror states, approximately 90 days after President Bush declared Iran one of the nations in the "axis of evil" the Perles Law Firm attached Iranian real estate assets in California in support of a flagship judgment in *Flatow v. Islamic Republic of Iran,* 999 F. Supp. 1 (D.D.C. 1998) against Iran's knowing support of terror only to have the State Department intervene to quash the attachment.

2. *See also* on this general subject John Norton Moore (ed.), CIVIL LITIGATION AGAINST TERRORISM (2004); A. GERSON AND J. ADLER, THE PRICE OF TERROR (2001); "Civil Suits Against Terrorists, Terrorist Organizations, and States That Sponsor Terrorism," in J.N. Moore and R.F. Turner, eds., NATIONAL SECURITY LAW 484–490 (2nd Ed. 2005); and the Panel on "Civil Litigation in the War on Terror," (December 1, 2006) at the American Bar Association/Center for National Security Law 2006 Annual Conference on National Security Law, Washington, D.C. (including "Introductory Comments" by the author). While this chapter will focus on civil litigation against terror states, and their leaders, there is also

The thesis of this chapter is not simply to unleash unrestrained use of the courts in the fight against terror. There are important principles at stake in ensuring that causes of action are those rooted in broad general agreement about core principles of international law, that foreign states are treated fairly in the civil justice system, and that attachment or execution will not be directed at assets entitled to diplomatic or counselor immunity, military assets, or assets of foreign central banks. Rather the thesis of this chapter is that the use of the civil justice system, as with other dimensions of the rule of law, has a crucial place in the fight against terror.[3] Indeed, as a Nation we are shockingly behind the curve in moving forward with well-structured efforts to empower the use of the civil justice system against terror states. Astoundingly, at a time in which we are supporting international and national law holding individuals, including heads of state, criminally responsible for acts of terrorism, and in which we have long since permitted suit against our own government for terror acts, the Executive is still too frequently shielding terror states from civil liability.

We know today that real world application of the criminal justice system is largely only for a few low-level "terror mules" we have apprehended. This does little to deter the regime elites of terror states, and the state machinery itself of such states, from their support for terror. In contrast, large civil judgments

---

portant opportunity in the use of civil litigation against non-state actors, financers and abettors, including the use of RICO Act treble damage civil actions against non-state actors involved in terrorism or its knowing support. *See generally* letter of February 12, 2007 from Michael C. Rakower to John Norton Moore (on file at the Center for National Security Law, University of Virginia). "In light of our conversation several weeks ago, I have looked into public and private efforts to use RICO Act as a tool against terrorist networks. Using RICO against terrorism is consistent with its main purpose—to stop organized crime—and can be quite effective, because RICO provides for treble damages to the injured party." *Id.* at 1. Michael C. Rakower practices law in New York. For an excellent overview discussion of the potential for civil litigation against terrorism in U.S. courts *see* Beth Van Schaack, Finding the Tort of Terrorism in International Law (unpublished manuscript from a University of Texas School of Law symposium). "Civil suits involving claims of international terrorism have the potential to play a part in a comprehensive anti-terrorism strategy. In particular, harnessing the motivation and resources of private attorneys general can enhance the government's ability to bring targeted criminal suits and promote the rule of law in the face of acts of terrorism." *Id.* at 47.

3. Secretary of Defense Robert M. Gates recently acknowledged the difficulty the United States is having in seeking to deter illegal actions of Iran. In that context he noted: "We need to figure out a way to develop some leverage ..." Karen, DeYoung, "GATES: U.S. Should Engage Iran with Incentives, Pressure," WASHINGTON POST May 15, 2008, at A4, Cols 5–6. The author would note that the use of civil litigation against acts of terror—with its resulting large judgments against terror states, is an important source of additional leverage.

against terror states and their leaders who have ordered these acts of terror; judgments then reciprocally enforced in democratic nations around the world, have great potential to deter state sponsored terrorism. The democracies of the world are financial and economic superpowers. Terror states, and their leaders, need to trade with them, use their banking systems, and otherwise financially interact with them in crucially important ways. Further, the democracies are the leaders in the rule of law, and in application of their civil justice systems. Terror, as a form of asymmetric warfare in response to the conventional military superiority of the democracies, may be a self-perceived comparative advantage of non-democratic terror states. But the use of the rule of law in the courts of the democracies, combined with their financial and economic power, is one of their comparative advantages in fighting back. Law and lawyers are today so pervasive in the democracies that surely turning law loose on terror states, rather than simply on tobacco companies and corporate targets, will be greeted by broad public support and understanding.[4]

A Summary History of Sovereign Immunity in International and United States Foreign Relations Law

Toward "[a] government of laws, and not of men."
A phrase popularized in the United States by
John Adams and incorporated in the
Constitution of Massachusetts

A core meaning of the rule of law is the use of law as a check on power. Not surprisingly, monarchs and authoritarian leaders did not embrace the rule of law, just as this principle is rejected by terror states today. Thus the rise of the nation state following the Peace of Westphalia, which in its manifestation in most

---

4. For an interesting analogy urging more effective international cooperation in the use of civil litigation as a core mechanism to deter bribery of governments, *see* Paul D. Carrington, "Law and Transnational Corruption: The Need for Lincoln's Law Abroad" in Law and Contemporary Problems 109 (2007). *See also* as to the promise of financial leverage in stopping terror behavior Rachel L. Loeffler, "Bank Shots: How the Financial System Can Isolate Rogues" in Foreign Affairs (March/April 2009) at 101. "The two most recent chapters in this unfolding story—Iran and North Korea—suggest that using global finance to shape the behavior of international actors can be remarkably powerful." *Id.* at 101.

states was non-democratic, was accompanied by a strong principal of sovereign immunity or, popularly "the King can do no wrong."[5]

The traditional view, widely accepted in international law and the foreign policy of the United States up until the mid 20th Century, was absolute immunity of the state from the jurisdiction of national courts. In the United States this view was reflected in the classic 1812 case of *The Schooner Exchange*.[6] No less a voice than that of Chief Justice John Marshall spoke in that case of the "perfect equality and absolute independence of sovereigns."[7] While a few states begin to question this as a principal of international law even prior to World War II, and democracies were adopting reforms permitting civil actions against their own states, as with the Federal Tort Claims Act in the United States, the absolute theory of immunity has been tenacious.

The first seismic crack in absolute immunity occurred in the United States in 1952 and was revealed in an obscure letter. Thus, the United States moved to the "restrictive theory" of sovereign immunity as set out in a letter from the Acting Legal Adviser of the Department of State, Jack B. Tate, written to the Acting Attorney General, and subsequently called "The Tate Letter." The Tate Letter adopted the view, as the official view of the United States, that where nations are acting as private parties (actions *de jure gestionis* rather than *de jure imperii*), as in commercial transactions, they would no longer be immune from suit in the courts.[8] Difficulty in *ex parte* Executive determinations of this standard, and later in Executive efforts at adjudication on this issue, led John R. Stevenson, as Legal Adviser to the Department of State, to turn this issue over to the courts under a statutory mandate concerning the scope and application of sovereign immunity and actions against foreign nations in U.S. courts. As Counselor on International Law to the State Department I worked on the

---

5. *See generally* on the history of sovereign immunity I RESTATEMENT OF THE LAW THIRD OF THE FOREIGN RELATIONS LAW OF THE UNITED STATES 390–454 (1987).

6. The Schooner Exchange, 11 U.S. (7 Cranch) 116 (1812). While this case is usually cited for "absolute immunity," it has been pointed out that the Court waived its jurisdiction simply as a matter of "grace and comity" so that there was really nothing "absolute" about the granting of immunity. Moreover, some other decisions did not grant immunity for state actions in violation of international law. *See, e.g.,* Jordan Paust, "Federal Jurisdiction Over Extraterritorial Acts of Terrorism and Nonimmunity for Foreign Violators of International Law Under the FISA and the Act of State Doctrine," 23 VIRGINIA JOURNAL OF INT'L LAW 191 (1983), and "Notes and Questions" in PAUST, VAN DYKE & MALONE, INTERNATIONAL LAW AND LITIGATION IN THE U.S. 679–82 (2nd ed. 2005).

7. *Id.* at 137.

8. Given that a mere commercial breach of contract is subject to civil liability, surely it makes no sense to shield intentional acts of terror from such liability.

procedural provisions in this legislative package and cleared the package, with minor changes, through the interagency process before formal Executive Branch submission to the Congress. Subsequently, this statutory mandate, turning the issue over to the courts, was enacted into law in 1976 as the Foreign Sovereign Immunities Act (FSIA).[9] Today this law still provides the exclusive basis for suits against foreign nations in United States courts.

Contrary to popular, and sometimes even judicial, opinion the FSIA is not solely jurisdictional, but made a series of important substantive changes in the law, including providing a detailed structure for service of process and altering the provisions for attachment and execution against the assets of foreign states.[10] With respect to the scope of immunity, the FSIA eliminated immunity in most commercial transactions, claims in tort for injury to persons or property in the United States, and certain claims concerning property. As FSIA, itself an initiative of the State Department reflects, for over a quarter century a

---

9. 90 Stat. 2891, 28 U.S.C. §§ 1330, 1332(a)(2)(3)(4), 1391(f), 1441(d), 1602–11.

10. It was understood by all who worked on the FSIA that it would be rooted in causes of action from underlying state law, as well as any other bases for federal statutory or common law causes of action. This is reflected in decisions in countless cases in the federal courts, is set out by the United States Supreme Court in the case of *First Nat'l City Bank v. Banco Para el Comercio Exterior de Cuba*, 462 U.S. 611, at 622 n.11 (1983), and remains the official view of the United States, despite the surprising action of the D.C. Circuit Court of Appeals in *Acree v. Republic of Iraq*, 370 F.3d 41 (2004), with no briefing or hearing, to dismiss the District Court decision in *Acree* as having no cause of action; a lower court decision in reality rooted in multiple bases for cause of action, including underlying state law of assault, battery and intentional infliction of emotional distress, the international/foreign relations law of the United States against torture, and at least *respondeat* superior from the FSIA statutory provisions themselves. For the official United States view that state law provides a basis for cause of action in FSIA cases *see* Brief for Amicus Curiae the United States of America in Support of Plaintiffs-Appellees in *Kilburn v. Socialist People's Libyan Arab Jamahiriya*, No. 03-7117, at 11, 13 (May 14, 2004) (stating under the FSIA "the foreign state ordinarily may be held liable according to state or local foreign laws that apply to private individuals generally," and urging that "[t]he Court ... should allow the plaintiffs here an opportunity to show in the district court whether state or local foreign law would provide them a cause of action...."). *See also Cicippio-Puleo v. Islamic Republic of Iran*, 353 F.3d 1024 (2004), and the discussion of this Court of Appeals decision defying the intent of the Congress subsequently in this chapter. The Congress subsequently declared in the 2008 Defense Authorization Act that the holding in *Cicippio-Puleo* was *never* the law. For a discussion questioning whether "having lost the legislative battle [against 1605(a)(7) actions], should the government now play an active role in discouraging this kind of litigation because of possible negative impacts on U.S. interests? [and asking] Does the FISA make any provision for such intervention?" *see* "Suing Terrorists and Their Sponsors," Chapter 23 in S. DYCUS, W. BANKS, P. RAVEN-HANSEN, COUNTERTERRORISM LAW (2007) at 753. *See also* the further question of the *Cicippio-Puleo* decision *id.* at 752.

broad range of actions against foreign states have been permissible in our courts.

Though the FSIA had greatly narrowed where "the King can do no wrong" it was narrowly interpreted by the courts as not permitting actions for civil damages against states or their instrumentalities where the tort against Americans took place abroad, even if the tort was a terror attack. In this setting, a second seismic shift occurred in limiting absolute immunity, also led by the United States. Thus, in response to the bombing of Pan Am Flight 103 "Maid of the Seas" over Scotland, and in the aftermath of the terror shock from the bombing of the Murrah Federal Building in Oklahoma City, Congress passed amendments to the FSIA adding a new section 1605(a)(7) permitting such suits against actions abroad by states on the State Department terror list at the time the act occurred. These amendments were enacted as part of the Anti-Terrorism and Effective Death Penalty Act of 1996. They were vigorously fought by the Executive.

The new § 1605(a)(7) of the FSIA ushered in substantial litigation against terror states for actions against Americans abroad, despite a pattern of strained and narrow reading of the amendments by the D.C. Circuit, showing that the D.C. Circuit Court of Appeals was sympathetic to the "old-thinking" arguments of the Executive branch and in setting after setting effectively supporting the old rule of "the King can do no wrong." The 1996 amendments themselves were very narrowly tailored. They applied only against states which were designated by the State Department as terror states at the time the act occurred. They applied only after offering the defendant state "a reasonable opportunity to arbitrate the claim in accordance with accepted international rules of arbitration." They applied to permit suit only in a narrow category of cases "for personal injury or death that was caused by an act of torture, extrajudicial killing, aircraft sabotage, hostage taking, or the provision of material support or resources for such an act." They permitted suit only if the claimant or the victim was a national of the United States. Trial in the federal system could only be by a trial judge, not a jury. And even in these circumstances were the state not to show up the Judge had to specifically find the facts and the law, precisely as would be required for suit against the United States Government.

Five months after enactment of this important tool in the fight against terror Congress passed the "Flatow Amendment" clarifying damages available in such actions, and clarifying the scope of the federal statutory cause of action against foreign states in actions brought under 1605(a)(7). In its report on the original version of the state-sponsored terrorism amendment, the House Judiciary Committee stated that the purpose of the amendment was "to allow U.S. citizens who have been subjected to the terrorist actions enumerated in the exception "to maintain a federal cause of action for damages against the foreign government involved."[11]

The latest act in this continuing struggle between the Congress and the Executive, with the Congress determined to permit suit in United States courts against terror states in circumstances such as those permitted under the 1996 FSIA Amendments is the enactment of the "Lautenberg Amendment" as part of the 2008 Defense Authorization Act.[12] This comprehensive updating of § 1605(a)(7) clarifies some of the ambiguities introduced into the previous law by the courts, including clarifying that the statute of limitations to this provision applies for all actions filed before April 24, 2006 or "10 years after the date on which the cause of action arose;"[13] establishing that in addition to being available for United States nationals, actions under this section are also available for members of the armed forces of the United States, and certain employees or contractors of the United States Government; and ending the abuse of terror states delaying accountability by continually subjecting the denial of their motion for sovereign immunity to interlocutory review. It also clarifies that the law provides a statutory federal cause of action against the state itself, an important clarification made necessary by the extraordinary decision of the Court of Appeals for the D.C. Circuit in *Cicippio-Puleo v. Islamic Republic of Iran*, 353 F.3d 1024 (D.C. Cir. 2004), which simply ignored that the language in the Flatow Amendment was the same language used to create a federal statutory cause of action against the United States itself[14] and that the Report of the

---

11. H.R. Rep. No. 103-702, at 2 (1994). *See also* further acknowledging this conclusion Dissenting Views, at 12.

12. *See* § 1083 of the National Defense Authorization Act for Fiscal Year 2008, Pub. L. No. 110-181, § 1083 (2008). Senator Frank Lautenberg, working with Senator Arlen Specter, was the principal sponsor of this update to the FSIA anti-terror provisions as initially embodied in § 1605(a)(7) of the 1996 Anti-Terrorism and Effective Death Penalty Act.

13. *See also Simon v. Republic of Iraq*, 529 F.3d 1187 (D.C. Cir. 2008) which reaffirmed the original liberal meaning of the statute of limitations in the 1996 Amendments to the FSIA even without relying on the 2008 Defense Authorization Act. This decision may signal a welcome new openness toward civil litigation against terror states by the Court of Appeals for the District of Columbia Circuit.

14. The language is "An official, employee, or agent of a foreign state designated as a state sponsor of terrorism ... while acting within the scope of his or her office, employment, or agency *shall be liable* to a United States national ... for personal injury or death caused by acts of that official, employee, or agent...." It is a preposterous interpretation of this language, which at minimum would create *respondeat superior* liability, to hold in the context of its enactment and the background of the language itself as creating a statutory federal cause of action against the U.S. Government, that it only creates a cause of action against the individual and not the terror state, of which the individual in question is by definition an "of-

House Judiciary Committee specifically stated that the language was intended to create "a federal cause of action for damages against the foreign government involved."[15] Most importantly, the new "Lautenberg Amendment" to the 2008 Defense Authorization Act substantially strengthens the provisions for attachment and execution against the assets of terror states in support of judgments under this section. This includes permitting in these anti-terror actions against designated terror states more effective application against state agencies and instrumentalities free from a former presumption that such agencies or instrumentalities should be treated as entities juridically separate from their parent state.[16] At this writing, the Executive, the Congress, and affected American litigants are engaged in negotiations to resolve Libyan liability.

---

ficial, employee or agent," as was the decision of the Court of Appeals of the D.C. Circuit in *Cicippio-Puleo v. Islamic Republic of Iran*, 353 F.3d 1024 (D.C. Cir. 2004). One can only charitably suggest that the presentation by counsel to the court in this case, which overlooked the clear House Judiciary Committee Report language, may have been a factor in this decision seemingly reaching to undermine the effectiveness of this anti-terror provision. One also wonders whether the D.C. Circuit may have wrongly believed, because of the pervasive State Department "old thinking" in opposition to 1605(a)(7) actions, that in seeking to interpret all "ambiguities" in opposition to effective actions under this section that the court was putting itself on the side of an effective U.S. foreign policy, rather than in reality undermining the obvious purpose of the Congress and inhibiting what is likely one of the strongest tools available to the Nation in its struggle against terror states."

15. *See* H.R. Rep. No. 103-702, at 2 (1994), *see also* to the same effect Dissenting Views, at 12.

16. This problem in attachment or execution against the assets of agencies or instrumentalities of the state was known as the *Bancec* doctrine. For an excellent post "Lautenberg Amendments" review of the struggle under United States law to permit meaningful civil actions against terror states, including this problem, *see* Steven R. Perles, "The Evolution of Current Trends in Anti-Terrorism Civil Litigation" (Speech delivered before the District of Columbia Bar Association, March 2008). *See also* for an important historical review of the struggle in U.S. law to permit suits against terror states, by one of the pioneers in this field, Allan Gerson, "Privatizing Justice: The Role of Individual Civil Claims in the Fight Against Terrorism," (Remarks at Hebrew University Law Faculty, Jerusalem, May 15, 2007); Allan Gerson, "Accountability Versus Immunity-Civil Suits vs. States and Aiders and Abbettors of Terrorism," (Remarks before the International Bar Association, April 10–11, 2008, Barcelona, Spain). Professor Gerson emphasizes the domestic effect of the truck bombing of "the Alfred F. Murrah federal building in Oklahoma City, killing 168 Americans," in the subsequent passage of the 1996 Anti-Terrorism and Effective Death Penalty Act, which brought in the FSIA anti-terror 1605(a)(7) actions. Alan Gerson, 2007 remarks *supra* at 8–9. Gerson also notes as an example of the extreme State Department "old thinking" in defense of immunity even against terror states the following: "In the summer of 1992, as the case *Smith v. Libya* convened in the U.S. District Court in Washington, Judge Stanley Sporkin presiding, the backdoors of the court room suddenly swung open as a pha-

It should be noted that because the "tolling" provision in the statue of limitations ran out on April 24, 2006, for the future only terrorist acts of terror states, committed during the period the state was on the State Department list of terror states and then filled within 10 years of the date on which the cause of action arose, will be able to be heard under this section unless they had been previously filed in the courts. This should remove much of the concern about actions brought under stale fact circumstances. This was true both under the original 1605(a)(7) and under the comprehensive updating of the Act pursuant to the Lautenberg Amendment.

Not surprisingly, in response to the Lautenberg Amendment, which would effectively hold Libya, among other terror states, liable for its acts of terrorism, Libya hired high-profile American lobbyists in an effort to win exemption from the law.[17] Further, indicating that the State Department continues its enthusiastic commitment to "old thinking" in this area, on March 18, 2008, the George W. Bush Administration sent a letter to Speaker Nancy Pelosi seeking a waiver of the entire Lautenberg Amendment with respect to Libya and other states that have been removed from the U.S. list of terror states. The letter, sent from Secretaries Condoleezza Rice, Robert Gates, Carlos M. Gutierrez, and Samuel W. Bodman, says in part:

> When states, at our urging, take the necessary steps for this change in status under U.S. law, the United States has a strong interest in developing commercial and security relationships with them to provide a continuing incentive to stand with us against the threats of global terrorism. Indeed, in some cases offering them such relationships en-

---

lanx of U.S. Justice Department Attorneys appeared. "This is good," I said to my client, Bruce Smith, sitting alongside me, as I recognized my associates from the time I served with the Justice Department's Civil Division. Smith pulled at my arm and said, "Look, Allan, they are going over to sit at Libya's table, not ours." This was during the height of the war of words and deeds against Libya. Yet the U.S. government chose to cast its lot not with the American families victimized by terrorism but with Libya. Clearly, upholding the principle of non-accountability—sovereign immunity—was deemed more important than allowing indicted perpetrators of terrorism to be held accountable to its victims." Allan Gerson 2008 remarks *supra* at 4.

17. *See* Eric Lipton, "Libya Seeks Exemption for Its Debt to Victims," NEW YORK TIMES (April 22, 2008). The *New York Times* noted that: "If Libya loses a half dozen court cases still pending, $3 billion to $6 billion could be at stake, according to lawyers' estimates … [and] Libya has hired White & Case, the New York-based law firm that has successfully defended a long list of international clients in often touchy cases. Its goal is to try to negotiate a settlement to all the outstanding cases at once, which might reduce the payments to a total of $1 billion or less."

courages states to end their support for terrorism. In its current form, Section 1083 still operates to hamper severely this vital foreign policy and national security goal ...

Section 1083 applies both to current state sponsors of terrorism and states such as Libya, which is no longer designated a state sponsor after having met the conditions necessary ... It subjects them without distinction to a new set of potential lawsuits retroactively, significantly greater potential liability over longer periods, and interference with their assets both before and after judgments. Besides signaling that states that meet our counterterrorism concerns will not reap benefits in their relationship with the U.S., Section 1083 also discourages states whose terrorism designation has been rescinded from investing in the United States, and seriously disadvantages U.S. companies engaging in business ventures with these states. Decreased economic engagement, in turn, will make it more, rather than less, difficult for American claimants to receive compensation for claims they have brought in U.S. courts ...

The case of Libya illustrates the gravity of this problem. Despite the passage of Section 1083, Libya continues participating actively in the U.S. legal system to resolve pending claims and has been exploring possible settlement of many of these cases, which would have the advantage of sparing claimants the burden of many years of litigation and uncertain recovery at the end of the process. However, implementation of Section 1083 will seriously hamper this effort by creating doubts for Libya and other countries about the utility of cooperating with the U.S. legal system. In addition, the attachment provisions of Section 1083 will appear to such countries as a new form of economic sanctions, and will also have a chilling effect on potentially billions of dollars of investments by U.S. companies in Libya's oil sector, investments affecting U.S. energy security, and on substantial anticipated U.S. construction projects with Libya.[18]

The effect of any such waiver, of course, would be to give a free ride to terror states for terrorist acts committed against Americans while they were on the State Department terror list.

Just as human rights violators have pushed back against human rights norms by a take-over of the United Nations Human Rights Commission, so too have governments unfriendly to the rule of law sought to hold back—and even roll

---

18. 102 AMERICAN JOURNAL OF INTERNATIONAL LAW 642 (2008).

back—the progressive elimination of "the king can do no wrong." Thus, in 2004 the United Nations General Assembly passed a resolution supporting a new draft Convention on Jurisdictional Immunities of States and Their Property.[19] This new draft Convention would ensure sovereign immunity for state-sponsored acts of terrorism and would otherwise dramatically narrow the potential for civil suits against states. Most recently, on December 23, 2008, Germany instituted proceedings against Italy before the International Court of Justice for allegedly failing to respect Germany's sovereign immunity growing out of international humanitarian law violations by Germany in World War II.[20] These recent developments show that progressive development of the rule of law against state-sponsored terrorism and other illegal actions by states is at serious risk unless the United States Executive Branch drops its "old thinking" and the United States assumes its rightful role as champion of the rule of law.[21]

But there are also more positive signs in acceptance of civil litigation as an important tool against terrorism. Thus, on June 2, 2009, the Canadian Minister of Public Safety, the Honorable Peter Van Loan, announced tabling of legislation "to allow victims of terrorism to sue perpetrators of terrorism and their supporters."[22] The new law would lift state immunity for states identified by the Government of Canada as supporters of terrorism, would create a new cause of action in Canadian courts, and would facilitate effective recovery through assistance of the Ministers of Foreign Affairs and Finance. The official Canadian press release reads: "The Government of Canada is determined to take decisive steps to protect Canadians from the threat of terrorism. By tabling this legislation, the Government of Canada is sending a clear message

---

19. *See* General Assembly Res 59/38 "United Nations Convention on Jurisdictional Immunities of States and Their Property," UNGA A/Res/59/38 (16 December 2004).

20. *See* "Germany institutes proceedings against Italy for failing to respect its jurisdictional immunity as a sovereign State," ICJ Press Release No. 2008/44 (23 December 2008).

21. Iraq, in its brief in *Republic of Iraq v. Beaty*, and *Republic of Iraq v. Simon* (NOS. 07-1090 & 08-539) (March 2009), as a *certiorari* Petitioner before the Supreme Court, also seeks to turn the clock back to pre-FISA days in which claims concerning torture and taking of "human shields" were pursued "through State-to-State negotiations, rather than subjecting each nation to coercive lawsuits in the courts of the other." *Id.* at 56. Not only does this repudiate the legislative structure of the FISA and any meaningful rule of law, but it also would return to the failed accountability of the past with its fictional redress. Sadly, the "old thinking" Department of Sate Legal Claims Office supported Iraq in its effort to set aside the FISA.

22. *See* "Minister of Public Safety announces legislation to allow victims of terrorism to sue perpetrators and supporters of terrorism," from the Public Safety Canada website, www.publicsafety.gc.ca (02 June 2009).

that perpetrators of terrorism and their supporters will be held accountable for their actions."[23] Orchids to you, Canada!

The Potential for Civil Litigation as a Core Weapon in the War on Terror

"I call on all who love freedom to stand with us now.
Together we shall achieve victory."
Gen. Dwight David Eisenhower
D-Day Broadcast June 6, 1944

Terror is a form of asymmetric warfare used against the United States and other democratic nations by nations and groups which cannot hope to match our regular military capabilities. Bombings, kidnappings, torture and attacks against the civilian and business interests of the democracies, as well as against the infrastructure of international commerce such as civil aviation, all of which are implemented so as to be concealed in their origin, are modalities employed by totalitarian and authoritarian states and groups who hope by these modalities to avoid response.[24] Moreover, because full scale military response is so politically and economically costly, in addition to the inevitable loss of life, it takes an extremely high threshold of attack before the democracies will respond with the use of military force. Further, the built-in deniability of the terror state or group that it is implicated in the terror attack adds a high political barrier against military response, with the democratic nation population generally opposed to war and skeptical about claims largely known, even if then, to their intelligence services. Yet another limitation with respect to full scale military response is that such a response inevitably hits not only the terror state regime elite, but also many innocent civilians (and even military) not involved in the decision to wage an aggressive campaign of terrorism in support of their objectives. Increasingly we are learning that deterrence should be focused on the regime elites ordering aggression, democide and terrorism,

---

23. *See* "Justice for Victims of Terrorism Act," Public Safety Canada Press Release No. 2009/06/02 (02 June 2009).

24. For an excellent analysis of Iran's sophisticated use of non-state politico/military armed groups in its support for terror, *see* Keith A. Petty, "Veiled Impunity: Iran's Use of Non-State Armed Groups," 36 DENVER JOURNAL OF INTERNATIONAL LAW AND POLICY 191 (2008).

rather than the state as a whole.[25] Invasions, or even air strikes, are blunt instruments in this respect. Of course, if the attacks are serious enough, these military actions may sometimes be a necessary mode of response, as Israel has found in response to the continuing terror attacks directed against it.

Economic sanctions have much the same problem. They are a blunt instrument whose costs are generally externalized on the population by the regime elite responsible for the campaign of terror, they also shoot the democracies in the foot in that the existing trade to be interrupted was in being precisely because it was win/win for both parties. In addition, they must be agreed by all of the principal trading partners unless they are to be hollow actions simply displacing the profitable trading of the democracies themselves as other states fill the vacuum they have left. For these reasons it is frequently difficult to put together an effective campaign of economic sanctions. Again, this is not to argue against such sanctions in extreme cases, as, for example, in the effort to prevent Iran from obtaining nuclear weapons.

Criminal sanctions may apply to regime elites responsible, as well as those implementing the acts of terror, but they too have significant limitations. First, unlike the clear criminalization of waging aggressive war and committing grave breaches of the laws of war as were declared criminal under the original Nuremburg standard, it is less clear that regime elites ordering terrorism may always be covered. More importantly, it is extremely rare to catch any of the high-level elite ordering these actions in a setting permitting criminal trials. Rather, the usual subjects of anti-terror criminal actions are the low level terror "mules" carrying out the bombings or kidnappings. Because such sanctions at least theoretically include regime elites we should seek to enhance the effectiveness of this strand in the war on terror, particularly as it applies to regime elites ordering acts of terror. But this strand at present offers only limited deterrence.

And, of course, neither military action, nor economic sanctions, nor criminal trials compensate the victims of terror, who surely also deserve our attention. One of the more remarkable elements in the persistence of the absolute theory of immunity against knowing actions of terror states has been to ignore the legal rights to compensation of those injured by these actions. It is an ordinary and usual application of the rule of law that those harmed by the intentional wrongful acts of others should receive compensation from the wrong-doers. This not only deters future wrongful acts but seeks to provide at least some justice for the innocent injured party. Their injury and resultant plight in terror cases is frequently horrific. To ignore compensation for them is itself

---

25. *See generally* JOHN NORTON MOORE, SOLVING THE WAR PUZZLE (2004).

inconsistent with the rule of law.[26] Moreover, even if it were necessary to take their rights against those who injured them for compelling foreign policy purposes, elemental fairness, as well as the Fifth Amendment to the United States Constitution, would require the payment of compensation for the taking of the claim against the foreign state for this public purpose.[27] Sadly, all too frequently the Executive seems to have little concern for such compensation in its zeal to support the absolute theory of immunity.

In contrast to these conventional responses to terrorism, focused civil actions directed against the purveyors of terror, including setting aside the old thinking "the King can do no wrong," and holding the state and the regime-elites accountable, offer substantial advantages which have been largely overlooked. First, they provide focus on the regime-elites and their individual assets hidden around the world, as well as on the state itself which is controlled by these totalitarian leaders. As such, they place deterrence more squarely and precisely on those responsible than all approaches but the criminal approach. And unlike the criminal approach they provide abundant opportunity to be carried out against the regime-elites and their assets. For totalitarian leaders and states typically do interact economically with the democracies. Thus, they frequently store their assets in bank accounts abroad (sometimes out of fear that they might

---

26. It should also be noted in this connection that change of government, within the United States or in any other nation in the world, does not alter the debts and liabilities of the nation itself. This is the official position of the United States and is settled international law. Any other position would throw financial markets into turmoil and inhibit assistance to developing countries. Moreover, with respect even to an "innocent" new government why should the new government be favored over the innocent *and injured* victims of state action?

27. The Fifth Amendment to the Constitution of the United States provides that "[n]or shall private property be taken for public use without just compensation." In his concurring opinion in *Dames & Moore v. Reagan*, 453 U.S. 654, 690 (1981), Justice Lewis Powell summarized the Supreme Court's view on the taking of judicially cognizable claims against foreign nations for public policy reasons as a setting in which the parties may file a "taking" claim in the Court of Federal Claims. Thus, he writes: "The Court holds that parties whose valid claims are not adjudicated or not fully paid may bring a 'taking' claim against the United States in the Court of Claims, the jurisdiction of which this Court acknowledges. The Government must pay just compensation when it furthers the Nation's foreign policy goals by using as 'bargaining chips' claims lawfully held by a relatively few persons and subject to the jurisdiction of our courts. The extraordinary powers of the President and Congress upon which our decision rests cannot, in the circumstances of this case, displace the Just Compensation Clause of the Constitution." *See also* the famous "*French Spoliation*" case, *Gray v. U.S.*, 21 Ct. Cl. 340, 392–93 (1886) ("the citizen whose property is thus sacrificed for the safety and welfare of his country ... has a right to compensation.").

have to leave the country quickly or simply to hide their assets), and their state enterprises must engage in activities in other nations, making them vulnerable to large judgments. Further, fair trials provide the evidence and build the record of their complicity prior to any sanction, and the resulting judgments both deter and provide compensation for the victims of terror. Nor is there anything new or remarkable about applying the civil justice system against assault, battery and intentional infliction of emotional distress, standard torts in the legal systems of the democracies. The remarkable fact is that we have given immunity to those who carry out such acts rather than applying the quite ordinary rule of law to their actions. Importantly also, large civil judgments effectively enforced against terror states directly reduce their ability to support terror. This may be particularly true in drying up their ability to support terror abroad by pressuring their dollar, yen and euro denominated assets. Finally, normal application of the rule of law against terror states through fair trials in our courts is likely to receive broad general support from the populations of democratic nations, unlike the likely far greater difficulty in sustaining support for military actions and even economic sanctions. In addition, such civil judgments are likely to generate less opposition from third states, which, at least if such judgments are limited to proven settings of actions in violation of United Nations terror conventions, should have broad international support.

We also have good reason to believe that large civil judgments can make a difference in the struggle for peace and human rights. Within the United States a pattern of determined civil actions brought by the Southern Poverty Law Center largely put the Ku Klux Klan out of business as a purveyor of terror in America. We also saw how effective the seizure of a small sum of bank assets was in dealing with the rogue actions of North Korea. In the case of Iran, it was so aware of the potential for large civil judgments against it when it had earlier illegally seized United States Embassy personnel that it insisted in the Algiers Accord, which obtained their release, that it be protected against civil suits from its illegal seizure. Surely the recent decision of Judge Royce Lamberth holding Iran liable for more than $2.6 billion in its complicity in the 1983 Marine Barracks bombing in Beirut Lebanon which killed 241 American servicemen will be noticed by Iran.[28] This is precisely the kind of large, but fair, judgment which can dramatically turn the tide against knowing involvement of states in the terror business.

Of particular importance in this connection, not only do the democracies have huge military superiority against the terror states, but they also have huge

---

28. *See Peterson v. The Islamic Republic of Iran*, 2003 WL 21251867 (D.D.C. May 30, 2003).

financial superiority. It is the banks and financial markets of America, Japan and the European Union which dominate global finance. A concerted effort at direct financial pressure, through cooperative enforcement of judgments against terror states, can have a devastating impact on the purveyors of terror. Indeed, we already have in place such cooperation against non-governmental terror groups such as Al-Qaida. Why should such cooperation not be extended to the reciprocal enforcement of large anti-terror judgments against terror states? Looking specifically at Iran as a purveyor of terror in the world today, Iran cannot in the slightest compete with democratic nation control of global financial markets and resources.[29]

The Fallacy of Traditional Objections

"Equal and exact justice to all men,
of whatever state or persuasion...."
Thomas Jefferson,
First Inaugural Address, March 4, 1801

There are a variety of traditional objections to application of the civil justice system to terror states. The principal such objections are that America or American officials would become vulnerable to lawsuits in the courts of terror states, that such trials against foreign governments would not be fair to them, that such actions would interfere with foreign relations, and that there is no agreement about terrorism; that is "one man's terrorist is another man's freedom fighter." While these objections sound plausible, in reality they are greatly exaggerated and do a disservice to the rule of law.

First, let us examine more closely the objection that America or American officials would become vulnerable to lawsuits in the courts of terror states. To begin, why is this objection not also applicable to virtually any response against terror states, including military action, economic sanctions and even crimi-

---

29. For an analysis which supports more vigorous use of civil litigation against terrorists and terror states but, unlike this chapter, would assign only a peripheral role to its importance in the war on terror, *see* H. Hume & G.D. Todd, "How Private Lawsuits for Civil Damages Can Help Combat International Terror," The Federalist Society National Security White Papers (2007). The authors write: "Over the past two decades, this country has become a world leader in providing a judicial forum for private rights of action against foreign terror groups and the regimes that support them." *Id.* at 3. And they conclude, consistent with the core message of this chapter, that: "the Executive should ... adopt a principled approach that will encourage the robust development of these private actions." *Id.* at 9.

nal trials? When another nation commits to a pattern of terror attacks against us we are, by no action of our own, in a deadly serious struggle with them. Unless we are to do nothing, which surely should be unacceptable, it is to be expected that the aggressor will fight using whatever tools they have decided will be most effective. But in this case they have already decided to attack us with suicide bombers, kidnappings, torture and terror. The prospect of their bringing civil actions in their courts harbors little additional concern over their actions already seeking directly to kidnap or kill us. In addition, the resulting setting is one in which Americans likely have long since pulled back from residence and business in the terror state, and thus likely we have only limited asset exposure. But in sharp contrast the terror state cannot as readily cut its financial ties with the dominant economic superpowers. Moreover, unless America is itself engaging in terror such trials will simply be sham trials and will be internationally understood as such. Surely, if we believe in the rule of law, including the civil justice system as a core component of the rule of law, the age-old reality that totalitarian nations may simply use the law to do their bidding should not cause us to abandon the rule of law. This first concern does suggest, however, that we should be careful to limit such actions to those broadly understood internationally as constituting terrorism and which will only be effectuated with due process of law.

In connection with this first objection we should remember that it is no longer new to subject foreign states to suits in domestic courts. That, after all, was the very purpose of the Foreign Sovereign Immunities Act when enacted in 1976. Further, the FSIA, carrying out that purpose, has now been copied by many nations around the world. No longer is it generally accepted as a principal of international law that "the King can do no wrong." Thus the real question becomes why should terrorist actions, by states we know to be committed to carrying out a pattern of such actions, and which are in violation of widely accepted international conventions against torture, bombing and terror, be exempted from the rule of law? Moreover, with respect to criminal actions it is now accepted by every nation in the world, in the 1949 Geneva Conventions, that there is a universal obligation to seek out and criminally try before your national courts those who engage in "grave breaches" of the Geneva Conventions, including the torture of POWs or the intentional killing of non-combatants in settings covered by the Conventions.[30] Again, if we accept universal criminal liability before national courts of every nation in the world for sim-

---

30. *See,* for example, Article 129 of the 1949 Third Geneva Convention (the POW Convention) which provides in clause 2: "Each High Contracting Party shall be under the obligation to search for persons alleged to have committed, or to have ordered to be committed,

ilar actions why should we not encourage civil liability in national courts in such settings?

With respect to the second objection, actions against foreign states, even terror states, should be carried out only with due process of law. Such actions do have foreign policy consequences and should be carefully cabined to provide fairness. Such fairness is in part also an answer to any effort by the terror states to respond with sham trials. Fortunately, the 1605(a)(7) actions, as supported by the Congress, have been established with scrupulous fairness for the foreign nations. That is the model we should follow, and encourage others to follow.

Principles of fairness in these cases include the following, as mandated in the current law of 1605(a)(7) actions against terror states. First, these actions are limited to those states on the State Department terror list—a dubious achievement of the terror state reflecting a serious commitment to terror.[31] Second, these actions are limited to a small category of actions, each of which is labeled as internationally illegal by a widely adhered United Nations or other international convention, including "torture, extrajudicial killing, aircraft sabotage ... [and] hostage taking."[32] Third, they can be brought only after an elaborate procedure for service of process designed to produce full notice of the action and its nature, and even to translate this into the language of the country in question.[33] Fourth, they can be brought only by nationals of the United States or members of its armed forces or contractors in order to avoid the use of United States courts as a litigating repository for all acts of terror against anyone.[34] Fifth, before any such action can be filed in Federal District Court the foreign state must first be offered "a reasonable opportunity to arbitrate the claim in accordance with accepted international rules of arbitration."[35] Jury trial is not available against the foreign state in Federal District Court and such trials will be held only before a federal district judge, thus avoiding the emotionalism which might be expected in such cases from a jury. And finally, "[n]o

---

such grave breaches, and shall bring such persons, regardless of their nationality, before its own courts."

31. 28 U.S.C. §1605(a)(7) of the Foreign Sovereign Immunities Act, *supra* note 9.

32. Section 1605(a)(7), *supra* note 9.

33. Section 1608, *supra* note 9. This language requirement is taken sufficiently seriously as to even generate debate about whether a translation into Latin in an action against the Vatican is a sufficiently good translation into Latin as to provide fair notice, when obviously Latin has not really been "spoken" in the Vatican for years and the translated English was easily understood!

34. Section 1605(a)(7), *supra* note 9, as modified by the new 28 U.S.C. §1605A(c) of the "Lautenberg Amendment" to the 2008 Defense Authorization Act.

35. Section 1605(a)(7)(B), *supra* note 9.

judgment by default shall be entered by a court of the United States or of a State against a foreign state, a political subdivision thereof, or an agency or instrumentality of a foreign state, unless the claimant establishes his claim or right to relief by evidence satisfactory to the court."[36] This last provision ensures that there can be no default judgment absent a written finding as to the facts and the law by a federal district judge. It also ensures that actions in our national courts against foreign states will provide no less in fairness guarantees than those brought against the United States itself.

Foreign governments today have access to a range of top law firms throughout the United States, and, indeed, throughout the world. They have the resources to hire the best attorneys and barristers in the world. Increasingly, in these cases the foreign governments are seeking and obtaining top counsel. Certainly if the terror states have every option to fairly litigate in our courts on terms no less favorable than that accorded to our own government one should not feel that they have been treated unfairly.

The third principal objection to the use of civil judgments against terror states is that such judgments would interfere with our foreign relations. But this objection fails to notice that it was the State Department itself, in the original FSIA, which determined that it was in the interest of our foreign relations to remove the State Department from the business of passing on exceptions to immunity. Thus, FSIA has for over a quarter century permitted the judiciary to make these determinations of immunity under a statutory framework. The only question is whether we should remove immunity from the actions of foreign states who knowingly engage in efforts to kill, torture, kidnap, bomb, or otherwise engage in terror acts against Americans, rather than simply those who break contracts with Americans or run over them in Washington D.C. with an embassy vehicle. Moreover, under current law such anti-terror actions can only be brought following a determination by the Department of State placing the state in question on its list of terror states. It is not easy to get on that list. And if a state is on that list the United States quite obviously has a strong, indeed overwhelmingly strong, national interest in deterring further terror from that state. Surely a practice of the United States will strongly effectuate that national interest which makes it clear that if a state already on the State Department terror list commits any of these terror acts against Americans there will be no second guessing or possibility of pressuring the State Department to excuse the actions, but rather that the state will be held accountable in a fair trial with the potential for a large adverse judgment. Indeed, the implica-

---

36. Section 1608(e), *supra* note 9.

tion of saying that these actions may interfere with our foreign policy simply means that the State Department should be free to give them a pass for their killing or torturing of Americans, even following the clear warning to the responsible state of being placed on the terror list. That does not sound like an effective way to enhance deterrence against terrorism. Nor does it sound like a way to clearly establish that some state actions, terrorism as well as torture and genocide, are not acceptable. Simply put, some actions directed against our citizens and against world peace are so serious that we should insist on full application of the rule of law. No state has a justifiable expectation that it will be held immune for such acts.[37] Further, is not the very purpose of the State Department terror list to deter systematic state terror by attaching consequences to being placed on the list? Civil liability as one such consequence will strengthen the deterrent effect of the list itself. Will the United States get push-back from a vigorous policy of holding terror states accountable? Of course; the more effective the accountability the more strident the likely push-back. But will that be any less true of other actions to effectively seek to deter terror? Should we perhaps be more worried about the actions we take to deter terror which produce no or only little push-back?

It should also be noted, with respect to this "interference with foreign relations objection," that recognized governments can always *bring* suit in national courts. But if civil actions in national courts are an anathema to foreign relations why do we permit states to sue in our courts? Is it not hypocritical to freely permit states to sue while the state, in turn, is immune from such suits? A spectacular example of this occurred in recent civil litigation concerning Iraq when Prime Minister Nouri Kamel al-Maliki persuaded George W. Bush to veto the 2008 Defense Authorization Act to prevent applicability of U.S. law to Iraq in long-standing cases against Iraq in U.S. courts. But after seeking to erase the cases against it in U.S. courts, in June 2008, Iraq then filed an action in the Southern District of New York against 93 corporations seeking approximately $2 billion in damages under U.S. treble damage laws.[38] As with Iraq

---

37. In a famous dissent in the sovereign immunity case of *Hugo Princz v. Federal Republic of Germany,* 26 F.3d 1166, 1179–83 (D.C. Cir. 1994), Judge Patricia Wald wrote: "the operative question, then, is whether the executive branch would have recommended immunity for perpetrators of the Holocaust. The intuitive answer is no. In the mid-1940s, Germany could not, even in its wildest dreams, have expected the executive branch of the United States ... to suggest immunity for its enslavement and confinement (in three concentration camps) of an American during the Holocaust.... [and] Germany could not have helped but realize that it might one day be held accountable for its heinous acts by another state."

38. *Republic of Iraq v. ABB AG,* Civ. Act. No. 5951 (S.D.N.Y. compl. Filed June 27, 2008).

in this case, states would, of course, like to be able to sue without, in turn, being subject to suit. But does such an arrangement promote compliance with law? Does it provide the elemental fairness essential to the rule of law?

There is an easy answer to the final objection; despite the truth in this objection that there is not complete agreement internationally as to what is "terrorism." The easy answer is that such civil actions in the national courts of states can easily be limited to those actions broadly accepted as internationally illegal. For this purpose the core of anti-terror actions might be rooted in substantive violations of the United Nations Conventions against terrorism to which the state is a party and for which the specified act has already been internationally agreed through the applicable convention to be a crime. Other possibilities include the widely accepted Convention against Torture and the Genocide Convention.[39] There is no reason that states which support acts of terror broadly accepted internationally as illegal terror, and thereby even made criminal by an overwhelming consensus of the international community, should be exempt from civil suits for their intentional acts of terror or their knowing material support for such acts.

One interesting paradox, as noted above, is that nations have broadly accepted principles of international law generating personal criminal responsibility for violating certain conflict management norms. For example, the 1949 Geneva Conventions, including the POW Convention, which are universally in force, create an obligation on every nation in the world to search out and try before their national courts those held accountable for grave breaches of the Conventions. Yet, as the case study below illustrates, at least the United States has been far slower to embrace civil liability for the same actions, even though the POW Convention declares that no state may "absolve" a torturing state of "any liability" for the torture of POWs, a designated "grave breach" of the Convention. And this is despite the fact that it is quite simple for nations to protect their government officials from substantial civil judgments with which they disagree, simply by adopting laws which reimburse civil damages for authorized governmental action, or which, before their own courts, simply transform certain actions against governmental officials into actions against the state itself as the United States has done.[40] In sharp contrast, this obviously cannot be

---

39. Yet another parallel in a setting of broad international consensus would be the commission of "grave breaches" of the laws of war as specified in the 1949 Geneva Conventions. At minimum actions by terror states in torturing prisoners of war should be actionable in national courts, particularly since Article 131 of the POW Convention contemplates as one of the core deterrent mechanisms against such torture that no state party to the Convention may "absolve" a torturing state of "any liability" for the torture of POWs.

40. *See* the Westfall Act, 28 U.S.C. § 2679 (1988).

done for personal criminal liability, yet which we already have accepted as a basis for national action in enforcing many basic provisions of the law of war, including "grave breaches" of the 1949 Geneva Conventions.[41]

There is also a purely *legal* objection to civil litigation against terrorist actions of terror states. It is argued that such actions go beyond permissible limits of non-immunity under international law.[42] Never mind that the sovereign's support for terrorism in question is in blatant violation of international law. And never mind that even heads of state have personal criminal liability for such actions. This argument still stubbornly asserts that it is illegal to sue the sovereign in domestic courts for terror actions. No doubt many foreign offices, eager to retain maximum immunity, support this view. But leadership for the rule of law must start somewhere. And thoroughly bad law, were this assertion correct, begs for change.

In any event, under the foreign relations law of the United States, national law will trump international law if the legislative intent is clear. Moreover, surely a widely adhered protocol to the United Nations anti-terror conventions, as suggested here, would be a powerful tool for change and clearly not a violation of international law. But even applying ordinary principles of international law, national judicial actions against actions widely understood as illegal terror acts constitute a classic setting for lawful non-forceful reprisal which would thus make the actions lawful whatever the immunity rule. For such actions are announced to be in response to the prior illegal terror attacks, are quintessentially proportional, submit to third party dispute settlement (even initially offering international arbitration), and end when the terror attacks end. They thus meet all of the requirements for lawful reprisal, a core enforcement mechanism in international law.[43] Most importantly, if we are se-

---

41. The current disconnect within the democracies as to application of criminal standards against government officials, illustrated by actions in Belgian, German and Spanish national courts, for example, suggests that this is an area in which the United States should take the lead in working out a comprehensive treaty to more effectively resolve the full range of associated issues concerning these criminal proceedings in national courts without losing the proper core of criminal accountability for grave breaches of the laws of war. The parallel here, of course, is also to the range of issues associated with the International Criminal Court and the challenge of an effective United States policy toward that Court.

42. *See, e.g.,* Ronald J. Bettauer, "The Foreign Sovereign Immunities Act's Anti-Terrorism Exception and International Law," presented at the 22nd Sokol Colloquium on Human Rights Litigation in U.S. Court, University of Virginia School of Law (April 2, 2009).

43. *See, e.g.,* J.N. Moore, "Enhancing Compliance with International Law: A Neglected Remedy," 4 VIRGINIA JOURNAL OF INTERNATIONAL LAW 881 (1999); Damrosch, Henkin, Pugh, Schachter & Smit (eds.), INTERNATIONAL LAW: CASES AND MATERIALS (4th ed. 2001),

riously to seek to enforce international law against terrorism it is a travesty to
seek to invoke international law for its protection.

A Case Study in "Old Thinking"

"These are the times that try men's souls."
Thomas Paine, *The American Crisis,*
no. 1, December 23, 1776

The following case study is offered by the author as one of too many examples illustrating the extent to which the Executive branch mind-set in support of
"sovereign immunity," and in opposition to civil litigation against terror states,
has meant that the Executive has vigorously fought against accountability for
terror in court and in the Congress. It remains a national tragedy that the United
States has not instead provided international leadership to move the world toward more effective application of the rule of law, in the form of effective use of
the civil justice system against terror states engaged in killing and terrorizing our
nationals and our allies. This sad, indeed shocking, case study is one in which I
have a detailed knowledge, having served as one of the co-counsel in the case.

A Brief History of the Case

On April 4, 2002, seventeen American Gulf War POWs who had been brutally tortured by Saddam Hussein and Iraq during the 1991 Gulf War, and
thirty seven of their family members, filed an historic suit in federal district court
in the District of Columbia to hold their torturers accountable. The suit was
brought under the 1996 amendments to the Foreign Sovereign Immunities Act
(FSIA) which for the first time, as mandated by Congress, permitted suit against
certain states which torture Americans abroad. At the time there was $1.7 bil-
lion in blocked Iraqi assets in the United States that Congress subsequently
earmarked as available to pay judgments of Americans against Iraq. Acting at
the request of the district court the Department of State served process on Iraq
and the principal witness for the American POWs was the then top law of war
expert in the United States Army JAG Corps. The very day the complaint was
filed it was couriered to the Vice President, the Deputy Secretary of Defense,
and the Legal Advisers of the State and Defense Departments. Further, an informal "heads up" was given to the Executive Branch before the case was filed

---

at 714; and 2 RESTATEMENT OF THE LAW THIRD OF THE FOREIGN RELATIONS LAW OF THE
UNITED STATES (1987), at 380.

and no objection was forthcoming. Counsel in the case were Monroe Leigh, a former Legal Adviser to the Department of State and partner in the law firm of Steptoe & Johnson (his law firm has continued representation after Monroe's death), and John Norton Moore, a former United States Ambassador and Counselor on International Law to the Department of State. As required by the 1996 FSIA amendments, the case was brought only after Saddam Hussein and Iraq refused to submit the claim to international arbitration. Liability of Saddam Hussein and Iraq was then determined after a full review of the law and the facts by a federal judge, precisely as the law provides for claims brought against the United States itself.

The American POWs who brought this historic case were tortured through brutal beatings, starvation, electric shock, whipping, burning, mock executions, threatened dismemberment, threats to their families, subjection to bombing, breaking of bones and eardrums, and horrifying genital inspections aimed at discrimination against Jews. For spouses and other family members in the United States, Iraq's refusal to permit notification of capture, its public statements about using POWs as human shields, and its coerced propaganda tapes of beaten POWs produced severe mental anguish. The Plaintiff for whom this case takes its name, Marine Colonel Cliff Acree, endured a perfect hell of torture requiring him to endure one painful operation after another on his return because of his courageous refusal to criticize President George H.W. Bush to his Iraqi captors. The horrifying specifics for each of the POWs and their family members are set out in detail in the opinion of the district court in *Acree v. Republic of Iraq*[44] which the Administration then assiduously sought to erase.

Despite a plea to the President on a bi-partisan basis from twenty distinguished former high level national security officials of the United States that funds from the blocked Iraqi assets be set aside to pay any judgment obtained by the POWs in their historic suit, as had been mandated by Congress, the Administration seized $1.7 billion in blocked Iraqi assets from the 1991 Gulf War, first setting aside $110 million to pay a judgment of Americans held hostage by Iraq during that war while ignoring the claims of tortured American POWs from that War. In their plea to the President these distinguished Americans, including Thomas H. Moorer, a former Chairman of the Joint Chiefs of Staff, John Lehman, a former Secretary of the Navy, Ambassador Max Kampelman, a former U.S. SALT and CSCE negotiator, Ambassador Richard Schifter, a former Assistant Secretary of State for Human Rights, Governor Bill Richardson, a former United States Ambassador to the United Na-

---

44. 271 F.Supp.2d 179 (D.C. Dist. Col. 2003).

tions, Anthony Lake, a former Assistant to the President for National Security Affairs, and Jerome J. Shestack, a former President of the American Bar Association, said that the case brought by the POWs against Iraq is "truly one of the first serious efforts to add deterrence against the torture of American POWs [and] we believe that this is an historic opportunity that should not be lost." Their letter to the President, like other pleas to the Administration on behalf of the POWs, was never answered.

Though the funds to pay the POWs judgment had already been seized, after the POWs won a substantial judgment against Saddam Hussein and Iraq, the Administration still went into court asking the court to kill the historic judgment and arguing that the money—which was by then no longer available—was needed for "the reconstruction of Iraq." The district court dismissed this post-judgment effort by the Administration to set aside the judgment as both untimely and legally incorrect. But on appeal the court of appeals for the DC Circuit set aside the judgment, asserting in a dramatic departure from pre-existing FSIA law, failing to provide any meaningful opportunity for a hearing, and ignoring clear language in the 1996 Congressional amendments and their legislative history, that the POWs had no "cause of action" against Iraq, an argument not even made by the Administration. Despite pleas from members of Congress, the National League of Families of POWs and MIAs, and former high level military urging the Supreme Court to then take the case, the Administration argued to the Court that it should not hear the case in view of the President's action in opposition and the wartime need for funds "for the reconstruction of Iraq." The case then went back before the district court at the request of the POWs under the residual legal and equitable powers of that court embodied in Federal Rule of Civil Procedure 60(b)(6)[45] and a subsequent re-filing of the original action.

A History of Vigorous George W. Bush Administration Opposition in This Case Study of "Old Thinking"

The national revulsion against the Abu Ghraib scandal, and the resulting overwhelming congressional rejection of torture, demonstrate that the people of America are committed to reasserting our traditional national leadership against torture and inhumane treatment. Yet the George W. Bush Administration continued to seek to set aside an historic federal district court judg-

---

45. *See* Motion for Relief Under Fed. R. Civ. P. 60(b)(6) in Civil Action No. 02-632 (RWR) (June 3, 2005).

ment holding Saddam Hussein and Iraq accountable for their brutal torture of American POWs during the 1991 Gulf War and to absolve them of their judicially determined liability. And, in doing so, it even walked away from our Geneva Convention obligation never to "absolve" a torturing state of "any liability" for the torture of POWs. One possible reason would seem to be the climate of hostility toward the use of civil suits against foreign states emanating from legal offices in the State Department and the White House.

Thus, the Bush Administration ignored the suggestion for a negotiated compromise as made by the federal judge who decided the case, it ignored repeated entreaties from the POWs that the Government talk to them about settlement—including detailed appeals directly to the Attorney General and the White House, it failed to respond to a bipartisan plea made to the President on behalf of the POWs from twenty distinguished American former high-level national security officials, including a former Chairman of the Joint Chiefs, and it even failed to comply with three unanimous Senate resolutions supporting the legal rights of these tortured American POWs against Iraq. Only after a strong congressional response did the administration make even the slightest effort to support the claims of these American heroes against Iraq, a traditional obligation of our Government on behalf of its citizens. Further, the Administration has ignored the cost to the Congress of undermining the credibility of congressional resolutions when its actions contradict two unanimous House and Senate resolutions passed during the 1991 Gulf War designed to protect our American POWs by putting Iraq on notice that it would be held accountable if they were mistreated in violation of the POW Convention.

Not surprisingly the Administration has also not been willing to candidly share with the American people its decision to set aside our Geneva Convention obligation and side with the torturers of American POWs. Its only public statement to date on the matter, made in response to a question at a White House Press Briefing on November 6, 2003, and then repeated by Scott McClellan the President's Press Secretary four more times in declining meaningful comment, has been the overly clever mantra "there is simply no amount of money that can truly compensate these brave men and women for the suffering that they went through at the hands of Saddam Hussein's brutal regime."

A particularly astounding chapter in this saga is that the President vetoed the 2008 Defense Authorization Bill to prevent restoration of the rule of law in United States courts holding Iraq accountable for its torture of American POWs and enabling the POWs to reinstate their judgment against Iraq; a veto made apparently at the request of Iraq. It is difficult to believe that an American president would follow entreaties from Iraq to set aside the rule of law in United States courts holding that country accountable for the torture of American

POWs while Americans are dying to bring the rule of law to Iraq. Further, this action violates the treaty obligation binding on both nations never to "absolve" a torturing state of "any liability" for the torture of POWs. To obscure the real nature of its veto, the Bush Administration's veto message, and subsequent statement of justification for its waiver of the rule of law as it applies to Iraq, never mentioned that a target of the Administration's actions were American POWs tortured by Iraq.

It is today common knowledge that funds for the reconstruction of Iraq are in large measure still available from many sources. Indeed, in vetoing the 2008 Defense Authorization Bill, which included provisions restoring the original intent of the Congress for the POWs, Iraq and the Administration conceded that there may be as much as $20 billion in Iraqi funds now in U.S. banks. But, more importantly, were this a problem it could be solved by payment through issuance of long term Iraqi bonds backed by Iraq's huge oil reserves, a mechanism used by the Administration and Iraq to settle billions in pre-war commercial debts of Iraq owed to foreign corporations. The Administration, however, as of this writing has refused to enter into negotiations about holding Iraq accountable and instead remains committed to an approach to kill this historic legal precedent that those who torture POWs will be held accountable. Indeed, Attorney General Gonzales refused to meet with the POWs about resolving the case and did not see fit even to answer the POWs' letter requesting a meeting, despite testimony during his confirmation hearing indicating openness to such a meeting. And, directly revealing the hypocrisy of the argument that settlement of the POWs' debt of honor is not possible because the funds are needed for the reconstruction of Iraq, the Administration is encouraging settlement of pre-war Iraqi commercial debts owed to foreign corporations such as Japan's Mitsubishi Group and Korea's Hyundai. The debts of these foreign corporations are being settled through the issuance of long term Republic of Iraq bonds, which are even now trading on world markets. Indeed, memoranda obtained from the Treasury Department through FOIA showed that the Administration had been assisting the Iraqis in working through New York banks to securitize and settle $20 to $30 billion in these pre-war commercial debts of Iraq owed to foreign corporations. For the Administration, Japanese and Korean corporations come ahead of tortured American POWs![46]

Most recently, in response to a Congressional request in the 2008 Defense Authorization Act that the President resolve these claims, and those of the

---

46. *See* Business Week (Online edition 7:00 p.m. ET Jan. 12, 2006); & "Bonds and Bombs," Barron's (March 20, 2006), at 53.

"human shield" claimants against Iraq, the Justice Department hosted an interagency meeting on April 22, 2008, to vet valid judicially active claims against Iraq. At that meeting representatives of the POWs and the "human shield" victims pointed out that the Administration was assisting resolution of billions in foreign private commercial claims of Iraq while opposing resolution of these claims of injured Americans. The representatives also suggested illustrative settlement amounts deeply discounting their judgments and noted that, collectively, they amounted to less than 1% interest for one year on the $50 billion Iraq held in U.S. banks. Sadly, rather than espouse these claims and take the opportunity of this extraordinary compromise offer as a unique opportunity for settlement, the Administration informed the claimants that, while it recognized their claims and felt that Iraq was obligated to pay, it could do nothing to assist them.

A new round of legislative consideration of solutions has begun, starting with a hearing before the House Judiciary Committee on June 17, 2008. At this hearing members of Congress seemed determined to defend the Congressional word and to ensure that Iraq's obligations would be paid.[47] The latest round in this saga was preparation within the House Judiciary Committee of the Justice for Victims of Torture and Terrorism Bill. Despite vigorous lobbying in opposition from the George W. Bush Administration the Justice for Victims Bill passed the House of Representatives in September of 2008 without dissenting voice. The Bill would have resolved the POW and "human shield" cases by requiring Iraq to pay a compromise amount which would have waived all punitive damages against Iraq as well as approximately two-thirds of compensatory damages. The Bush White House stopped the legislation through an anonymous "hold" in the Senate after the Bill was cleared through the Democratic majority of the Senate.

The Huge Cost the George W. Bush Administration Was Willing to Pay to Oppose Civil Litigation against Terror

Clearly, despite the vigorous Congressional response against torture and inhumane treatment, the Bush Administration was committed to setting aside this Nation's treaty obligation as set out in the Third Geneva Convention (the POW Convention) that no nation can "absolve" a torturing state of "any liability" for the torture of POWs, apparently in part at least out if its stubborn

---

47. *See* Hearing on "Victims of State-Sponsored Terrorism" (House Judiciary Committee June 17, 2008). (The author was one of the principal witnesses testifying at this hearing).

opposition to civil suits against terror. Yet as Senators George Allen and Susan
Collins wrote in 2004 to Attorney General John Ashcroft in support of protecting the POWs' judgment: "[t]he protection of American POWs is a vital
national security interest and the goal of rebuilding Iraq should not be viewed
as inconsistent with the goal of protecting future American POWs from torture and abuse. We can and should meet both of these important goals." Costs
for the Nation and the rule of law, all to be set aside in pursuit of "the King can
do no wrong" principal in this example include:

- Is it consistent with our national commitment against torture for the Administration to set aside the solemn treaty obligation of the United States
  in Article 131 of the POW Convention never to "absolve" a torturing state
  of "any liability" for the torture of POWs? And is setting aside this core enforcement mechanism under the Convention consistent with the President's
  post-Abu Ghraib pledge to the Nation that the Administration will adhere
  in full to our Geneva Convention obligations? The POW Convention is not
  an obscure legal technicality. It is in force not only for the United States
  and Iraq, but for 192 other nations as well. There is no more widely adhered treaty in the world today; in fact every nation in the world is a party.
  And this Convention, with its important Article 131 enforcement mechanism, is of utmost importance for the future protection of American POWs;
- What effect will it have on future treatment of American POWs that the
  Administration has intervened in federal court on the side of their torturers to absolve them of liability—particularly when combined with
  Abu Ghraib? What effect will this siding with the torturers of American
  service personnel have on the morale of American servicemen and women
  and future enlistment rates? Is siding with the torturers of American
  POWs consistent with the duty to protect that our Commander-in-Chief
  owes to all American service personnel?
- How can the United States credibly take the lead in promoting the rule
  of law and ending torture if the Administration is willing to ignore a
  treaty obligation as elemental as holding those who torture American
  POWs accountable for their torture?
- Is it right to ask American Gulf War heroes, brutally tortured by Iraq, to
  personally pay for the reconstruction of Iraq, surely a public purpose
  and national responsibility?
- Is it right for the Administration to continue to make payments for Kuwait
  and Saudi infrastructure damage from the 1991 Gulf War while refusing
  to pay the claims of tortured American POWs from that War? Is it right
  for the Administration to have agreed to pay $110 million to American

civilian hostages held by Iraq during the War while simultaneously turning its back on the claims of American POWs tortured in core violation
of one of the clearest prohibitions in law?

- Is it right for the Administration to have participated in settling $20–30
billion in foreign commercial claims against Iraq while turning its back
on the claims of tortured U.S. POWs who obtained a judgment in U.S.
courts?

- Is settlement of this matter not preferable to continued litigation in which
our own Government shockingly perseveres on the side of torturers of American POWs?

- As we seek to build a democratic rule of law nation in Iraq is it right that
we urge Iraq to set aside their non-absolvable treaty obligation of liability for the torture of POWs? Would not the American people welcome Iraqi
agreement to honor their treaty liability to tortured American servicemen as a concrete sign that the new Government is committed to the
rule of law? Would this not be an important action signaling that the
new Government of Iraq stands in sharp contrast with the Hussein regime?
Would not a compromise settlement of this "debt of honor" owed to the
United States offer a powerful argument for the United States and Iraq
to use in seeking to reduce the sovereign debts owed by Iraq to Saudi
Arabia and certain Gulf States? and

- What is the effect on the credibility of the United States, and of unanimous resolutions of the Congress of the United States, of putting Iraq on
notice that it would be held accountable for the torture of American
POWs, if the Administration then seeks to absolve that accountability?

In short, for the United States this matter is one of national credibility of our
word and our treaty obligations, a return to effective national leadership against
torture, leadership in the rule of law—including leadership in encouraging a
rule of law culture in the new Iraq, deterrence against future torture of American POWs, supporting troop morale and enlistment rates, and elemental fairness to national heroes who have given so much for their country.

Clearly the issue is not, as the Bush Administration repeatedly asserted in
court and in its veto message, about money for "the reconstruction of Iraq."
Rather, for thoughtful Americans, it is about this great Nation's commitment to
the rule of law, leadership against torture of POWs, and keeping faith with those
among us who go in harms way. It is also, most certainly, about national honor.

Sadly this case study illustrates the lengths to which "old thinking" against
the use of the civil justice system has been entrenched in the Executive branch,
and to some extent perhaps even in the Judiciary. It is to be hoped that the

Lautenberg Amendment in the 2008 Defense Authorization Act may, in time, usher in a more flexible attitude within the Executive and the Courts.

Empowering the Rule of Law in the Fight for the Fourth Freedom[48]

"the best test of truth is the power of the thought
to get itself accepted in the competition of the market"
Oliver Wendell Holmes, Jr.,
Abrams v. United States, 250 U.S. 616, 630 (1919)

The revolution in empowering civil litigation as a crucial tool in the fight against terror has already begun. It began in earnest with the passage by Congress of the 1996 Amendments to the Foreign Sovereign Immunities Act which permitted the bringing of 1605(a)(7) actions in United States courts. Congress has reaffirmed and strengthened its leadership in this regard in the recent "Lautenberg Amendments" to the 2008 Defense Authorization Act despite continuing opposition from the Executive and past sniping from the Court of Appeals for the District of Columbia Circuit. Whatever the continuation of short-term "old thinking" in the Executive in opposition to such civil suits, the application of the rule of law against terror states is here to stay and will likely only get stronger. As Stephen R. Perles, who has been one of the principal innovators in this area of the law, summarizes the current U.S. national law permitting suits against terror states:

> There has been a dramatic evolution in anti-terrorism civil litigation since the filing of the first successful case for the state sponsorship of terrorism against US citizens in 1996. We have seen the field of anti-terrorism litigation grow from a handful of cases against states like Iran to a flood of cases against states and recently a diversification into cases against foundations and financial institutions charged with aiding and abetting acts of terrorism. On January 28, 2008 Congress modernized the Foreign Sovereign Immunities Act's ("FSIA") terror-

---

48. The "Fourth Freedom" is "freedom from fear ... anywhere in the world," as set forth in Franklin Delano Roosevelt's famous four freedoms Message to Congress on January 6, 1941, eleven months before Pearl Harbor and America's entry into World War II. I have coined, and prefer as a title, "The Fight for the Fourth Freedom: the Freedom from Fear" as an alternative to the Bush Administration's "War on Terror," as taken from this classic human rights statement by President Roosevelt.

ism exception with the passage of the National Defense Authorization Act for Fiscal Year 2008....

Today, U.S. victims of international terrorism have a robust legal right against the terrorists that attack them, their state sponsors, and private individuals or organizations that knowingly support or facilitate terrorism. Despite inconsistent and conflicting signs of support or hostility from the Executive Branch and law enforcement and investigatory officials, the field of anti-terrorism litigation has stabilized and continues to evolve as our understanding of international terrorism increases.[49]

It is strongly in the interest of the United States in the struggle against terror not only for the Executive to support the present 1605(a)(7) actions as created by the Congress, but also to encourage every other democratic nation in the world to adopt a parallel structure in their own FSIA equivalent law. Thus, the United States Executive should take the lead in encouraging these actions as a core tool in the struggle against terror. In addition to not seeking to inhibit these actions while they are in court, but rather assisting them with Executive support where appropriate, the Executive should also take the lead internationally in promoting a protocol on civil liability to the United Nations anti-terrorism conventions.[50] Since these Conventions are now broadly in force for

---

49. Steven R. Perles, *supra* note 16 at 1.

50. This concept of a protocol on civil liability to supplement the principal United Nations terrorism conventions was first suggested by me in John Norton Moore (ed.), CIVIL LITIGATION AGAINST TERRORISM (2004), at 9–10. The relevant United Nations Conventions for the purposes of this protocol are: the Convention on the Prevention and Punishment of Crimes Against Internationally Protected Persons, Including Diplomatic Agents, G.A. Res. 3166, Annex, 1035 U.N.T.S. 167 (Dec. 14, 1973); the International Convention Against the Taking of Hostages, G.A. Res. 34/146, 34 U.N. GAOR Supp. (No. 39), U.N. Doc. A/39/819 (Dec. 17, 1979); the International Convention for the Suppression of Terrorist Bombings, G.A. Res. 52/164, U.N. Doc. A/Res/52/164 (Dec. 15, 1997); the International Convention for the Suppression of the Financing of Terrorism, G.A. Res. 54/109, U.N. Doc. A/Res/54/109 (Dec. 9, 1999); the International Convention for the Suppression of Acts of Nuclear Terrorism. G.A. Res. 59/290, U.N. Doc. A/Res/59/290 (April 13, 2005); the Convention on Offences and Certain Other Acts Committed on Board Aircraft, 1969 U.N.T.S. 220–241 (September 14, 1963); the Convention for the Suppression of Unlawful Seizure of Aircraft, 1973 U.N.T.S. 106–111 (Dec. 16, 1970); the Convention for the Suppression of Unlawful Acts Against the Safety of Civil Aviation, 1975 U.N.T.S. 178–184 (Sept. 23, 1971); the Convention on the Physical Protection of Nuclear Material, 1987 U.N.T.S. 125–132 (March 3, 1980); the Protocol on the Suppression of Unlawful Acts of Violence at Airports Serving International Civil Aviation, 1990 U.N.T.S. 474–478 (Feb. 24, 1988); the Convention for the Suppression of Unlawful Acts Against the Safety of Maritime Navigation, 1992 U.N.T.S. 222–234 (March 10, 1988); the Protocol for the Suppression of Un-

most nations of the world it is a simple matter to support a protocol to these
Conventions which would apply civil liability in national courts where the
Conventions have already authorized criminal liability in national courts. Such
a protocol could also put in place a mechanism for reciprocal enforcement of
such civil judgments which would greatly multiply the effectiveness of this tool
against terror. Since this concept of a supplemental protocol to the terrorism
conventions was first suggested in 2004, the 2005 Protocol to the Convention
for the Suppression of Unlawful Acts Against the Safety of Maritime Navigation with respect to weapons of mass destruction adds in its Article 5 a provision that "liability [under the Convention with respect to a legal entity located
in the state parties' territory or organized under its laws] may be criminal, civil,
or administrative. And it also adds that "[s]uch liability is incurred without
prejudice to the criminal liability of individuals having committed the offences."
As such, the concept of civil liability has now already been accepted for at least
one of the United Nations terrorism conventions.[51]

Set forth below as an annex to this chapter is a first draft of such a convention. As a process for moving forward with this draft the Executive might convene a group of expert attorneys experienced with 1605(a)(7) actions to review
the draft, clear any resulting draft through the U.S. interagency process, and
then begin discussions with nations around the world with a strong interest
in the fight against terror. After the Convention has been revised as necessary
to generate strong democratic nation support, particularly among major financial powers, then it should be introduced jointly by a broad coalition within
the United Nations for adoption at an early time.[52]

---

lawful Acts Against the Safety of Fixed Platforms Located on the Continental Shelf, 1992 U.N.T.S.
304–310 (March 10, 1988); and the Convention on the Marking of Plastic Explosives for
the Purpose of Detection, ICAO Doc. 9571 A.40/12A.

51. See generally on the 2005 Protocol N. Klein, "The Right of Visit and the 2005 Protocol on the Suppression of Unlawful Acts Against the Safety of Maritime Navigation," 35
DENVER JOURNAL OF INTERNATIONAL LAW AND POLICY 287 (2007).

52. One possible forum for exploring consensus on this draft might be the Community
of Democracies, an organization created in response to a past initiative from the author
jointly with Ambassador Mark Palmer which is now coordinating actions of the democracies in seeking to promote the rule of law internationally. See "Note: Origin of the Community of Democracies," J.N. Moore, G.B. Roberts, R.F. Turner, eds., NATIONAL SECURITY
LAW DOCUMENTS 742–44 (2nd ed., 2006).

Annex: A Draft Protocol to the United Nations Anti-Terrorism Conventions

MULTILATERAL

Protocol to the United Nations Conventions on Terrorism to Enhance Compliance Through Application of Civil Damages

The States Parties to this Protocol,

Having in mind the purposes and principles of the Charter of the United Nations concerning the maintenance of international peace and the promotion of friendly relations and co-operation among States,

Considering that acts of terrorism in violation of the United Nations Conventions on Terrorism are a core threat to international peace and security,

Determined to enhance compliance with these Conventions,

Conscious that these Conventions affirm criminal liability for the offenses within their purview;

Conscious that the civil justice system is an important component of the rule of law and in important ways supplements criminal liability,

Conscious that damage awards can provide both deterrence against terrorism and justice for victims of terrorism, and

Convinced that there is an urgent need to enhance compliance with these Conventions against terrorism,

Have agreed as follows:

Article 1. States Parties to this Protocol undertake to provide actions for civil damages under their national law for offenses set forth as criminal within any of the United Nations Conventions on Terrorism to which they are a Party.

Article 2. For purposes of this Protocol the United Nations Conventions on Terrorism include the Convention on the Prevention and Punishment of Crimes Against Internationally Protected Persons, Including Diplomatic Agents, of 14 December 1973; the International Convention Against the Taking of Hostages, of 17 December 1979; the International Convention for the Suppression of Terrorist Bombings, of 15 December 1997; the International Convention for the Suppression of the Financing of Terrorism, of 9 December 1999; the International Convention for the Suppression of Acts of Nuclear Terrorism, of 13 April 2005; the Convention on Offences and Certain Other Acts Committed on Board Aircraft, of 14 September 1963; the Convention for the Suppression of Unlawful Seizure of Aircraft, of 16 December 1970; the Convention for the Suppression of Unlawful Acts Against the Safety of Civil Aviation, of 23 September 1971; the Convention on the Physical Protection of Nuclear Material, of 3 March 1980; the Protocol on the Suppression of Unlawful Acts of Violence at Airports Serving International Civil Aviation, of 24 February 1988; the Convention for the Suppression of Unlawful Acts Against the Safety of Maritime Navigation, of 10 March 1988; the Protocol for the Suppression of Unlawful Acts Against the Safety of Fixed Platforms Located on the Continental Shelf, of 10 March 1988; and the Convention on the Marking of Plastic Explosives for the Purpose of Detection, of 1 March 1991.

Article 3. The action for civil damages for criminal offenses designated as such under any of the United Nations Conventions on Terrorism, as set out in Article 2, shall be applicable against persons, organizations, states, political subdivisions of states, and agencies or instrumentalities of states, as provided in this Protocol.

Article 4. Actions against persons shall be for offenses as set out in the applicable United Nations Convention on Terrorism. Actions against organizations, states, political subdivisions of states, and agencies or instrumentalities of states shall be for intentional participation in offenses, or knowing assistance or material support to any such offense, if such participation, assistance or support is engaged in by an official, employee, or agent of such entity while acting within the scope of his or her office, employment, or agency, and results in personal injury or death.

Article 5. The obligation to provide civil actions under this Protocol applies only to settings in which the claimant or the victim is a national of the providing state.

Article 6. Any such civil action against a foreign state shall, as an alternative, first afford the foreign state a reasonable opportunity to arbitrate the claim in accordance with accepted international rules of arbitration.

Article 7. In any such action against a foreign state the foreign state shall be liable in the same manner and to the same extent as a private individual under like circumstances. The defenses of act of state and sovereign immunity shall not be available. Nor shall failure to appear serve as a defense.

Article 8. Any such action shall accord defendants due process of law and a fair trial, and in the event of a state defendant, or any designated subdivision of a state or agency or instrumentality of a state, a trial shall follow the same procedure as a trial in a civil action against the Government of the providing state itself.

Article 9. Damages in such cases shall be monetary damages only, which may include economic damages, solatium, and pain and suffering. Such monetary damages may also include punitive damages, provided that national law of the State Party normally permits punitive damages in such circumstances, and provided further that no punitive damages may be awarded in an amount greater than compensatory damages.

Article 10. The providing state may optionally provide that actions under this Protocol for acts committed subsequent to entry into force of this Protocol shall have no statute of limitation.

Article 11. States Parties to this Protocol undertake to honor in their national legal systems judgments rendered by other States Parties under actions established consistent with this Protocol provided;

- A judge of the honoring State Party reviews the foreign judgment and determines that the judgment was fair and consistent with due process of law;
- No State Party is required to honor damage awards, such as those for punitive damages, which are inconsistent with its own national law; and
- No attachment or execution shall be permitted against facilities protected by diplomatic or counselor immunity, military assets, or assets held by national central banks.

Article 12. States Parties may make reservations to this Protocol for the purpose of ensuring compliance with their national law, including principles of their civil justice system and/or their Constitution.

Article 13. States Parties may, at the time of signature, ratification or accession, announce that they will follow the principles of this Protocol with respect to designated Regional Conventions on Terrorism, as between themselves and other States Parties to such Regional Conventions who undertake reciprocally to accept the obligations of this Protocol with respect to the designated Regional Conventions.

Article 14. This Protocol shall be opened for signature by all States who are Party to any of the United Nations Conventions on Terrorism, until 31 December, 2014, at United Nations Headquarters in New York.

Article 15. This Protocol is subject to ratification by any State which is Party to any of the United Nations Conventions on Terrorism. The instruments of ratification shall be deposited with the Secretary-General of the United Nations.

Article 16. This Protocol shall remain open for accession by any State Party to any of the United Nations Conventions on Terrorism. The instruments of accession shall be deposited with the Secretary-General of the United Nations.

Article 17. 1. This Protocol shall enter into force on the thirtieth day following the date of deposit of the twenty-second instrument of ratification or accession with the Secretary-General of the United Nations.

2. For each State ratifying or acceding to the Protocol after the deposit of the twenty-second instrument of ratification or accession, the Protocol shall enter into force on the thirtieth day after deposit by such State of its instrument of ratification or accession.

Article 18. 1. Any State Party may denounce this Protocol by written notification to the Secretary-General of the United Nations.

2. Denunciation may take effect at any time, as specified by the denouncing State, following the date on which notification is received by the Secretary-General of the United Nations.

Article 19. The Secretary-General of the United Nations shall inform all States, *inter alia:*

(a) of signatures to this Protocol, of the deposit of instruments of ratification or accession in accordance with Articles 14, 15 and 16 and of notifications made under Article 18;

(b) of the date on which this Protocol will enter into force in accordance with Article 17.

Article 20. The original of this Protocol, of which the Chinese, English, French, Russian and Spanish texts are equally authentic, shall be deposited with the Secretary-General of the United Nations, who shall send certified copies thereof to all States.

IN WITNESS THEREOF, the undersigned, being duly authorized thereto by their respective Governments, have signed this Convention, opened for signature at New York on ___ December 2010.

Chapter 9

U.S. Intelligence and the War on Terror

Frederick P. Hitz[1]

This chapter will analyze the capability of the U.S. Intelligence Community to successfully wage the war on terror that President George W. Bush declared shortly after the al Qaeda attacks on New York and Washington on September 11, 2001. To do that cogently and coherently, however, a short review of the legislative history of the Central Intelligence Agency (CIA) and the precursors of some of the 15 other Intelligence Community (IC) agencies might be helpful.

The idea that U.S. intelligence has a statutory history is itself anomalous in speaking of the world's second oldest profession. Intelligence gathering has long been justified among states as the prerogative of the ruler, intended largely for the purpose of self-defense. The principle function of intelligence is to collect, analyze and disseminate to appropriate parties in one government, secret information stolen from other governments. Its very operating principle is clandestine and illegal and would thus not normally be considered fitting for

---

1. Frederick P. Hitz is a Senior Fellow at the Center for National Security Law. Since 1998 he has been lecturing at the Woodrow Wilson School of Princeton University and at the University of Virginia School of Law. A graduate of Harvard Law School, he entered the Career Training Program at the CIA and served in the clandestine service in Africa. In 1974, he returned to law practice but re-entered government service in congressional liaison capacities with the State, Defense, and Energy departments before resuming his career at the CIA in 1978 as Legislative Counsel to the Director of Central Intelligence. Hitz was responsible for managing the Agency's response to the Intelligence Charters legislation that came out of the Church Committee hearings in 1976. In 1980, he became Deputy Director for Europe in the Directorate of Operations. Hitz was appointed the first statutory Inspector General of CIA by President George H.W. Bush. He served in that capacity from 1990–1998 when he retired. Among the many investigations he led at the CIA was the Aldrich Ames betrayal. He has written extensively about espionage and intelligence issues.

open legislative consideration and enactment, but in the U.S. context, it is and was. I shall start with enactment of the National Security Act of 1947 that created the first civilian intelligence agency in U.S. history, although it had been preceded by creation of Army and Navy intelligence organizations in the 19th century, and the wartime Office of Strategic Services (OSS) during World War II, primarily to collect military intelligence in time of war.

CIA was established after much debate in 1947 primarily to provide warning of a future "Pearl Harbor," but also to counter the Soviets' western push in Europe that signaled the start of a Cold War that was to last forty-six years. It was in the context of "containing" Soviet expansion that the 1947 Act creating CIA also gave it the power to perform "such other foreign policy acts as the U.S. National Security Council might direct" that the Agency derived its authority to mount "covert action" to impede Soviet advances. "Covert action" is political action: funding pro-western elections, propaganda, regime change, subversion, where "the hand of the United States is intended NOT to show." In other words, it is any kind of political action by the United States to further U.S foreign policy or national security goals, mounted clandestinely. It is distinguished from what is normally called espionage, or the traditional foreign intelligence-gathering mission, intended to provide presidents with other nations' secrets.

An additional comment is in order on the distinction between classic espionage and covert action. U.S. intelligence would doubtless not be expected to play the important role President G.W. Bush intended for it to play in the war on terror if it did not have this covert action authority. Covert action is the operational arm of U.S. intelligence that is supposed to enable it to pre-empt or prevent future 9/11 attacks. It will allow the IC to work with allied governments to infiltrate terrorist cells and to secretly interdict a terrorist act, not just report on its planning or its aftermath.

Although revisionists have begun to question some of the covert action "successes" of CIA during the Cold War, such as the placement of the Shah on the throne of Iran in 1953 and the removal of President Arbenz in Guatemala in 1953, in the context of the times, these actions appeared to thwart Soviet expansion into areas where they were not welcome to American policymakers. It must also be noted that there were many other unsuccessful covert actions such as the Bay of Pigs fiasco that undermined U.S. foreign policy goals, as well as our international reputation, so this will always be a controversial foreign policy tool. However, it might come in extremely handy in the context of anti-terrorist operations, if we still have the capacity to mount them covertly and successfully.

The next important statute impacting CIA was the National Security Act of 1949 that transferred more fully to the Director of Central Intelligence the authorities he would need to accomplish his clandestine mission. It gave him authority to hire and fire CIA employees outside the constraints of the U.S. civil service system. It also authorized him to procure materiel in support of the intelligence mission without following cumbersome bureaucratic regulation, principally so he could do so clandestinely. This so-called Section 8 authority permitted the DCI to purchase stinger missiles (and donkeys to transport them) over the Hindu Kush to support the mujahedin in Afghanistan as they sought to drive out the Soviet occupiers in the 1980s.

So flexible were the DCI's procurement authorities that it permitted Allen Dulles to argue that CIA ought to be in charge of the overhead reconnaissance program and thus the U-2 project in the 1950s. This enabled CIA to contract with Kelly Johnson at Lockheed's famous "skunkworks" to build the plane without the interference and oversight of hundreds of government bureaucrats. The effort was successful enough that it became the operating model for the National Reconnaissance Office (NRO), created in 1960, until the DCI's authorities were turned over to the new Director of National Intelligence (DNI) upon passage of the Intelligence Reform and Terrorism Prevention Act of 2005.

From 1950, when DCI Walter Bedell Smith corralled the CIA's covert action organization operating ostensibly under the State Department and brought it directly under his authority, and resurrected the estimative function of U.S. intelligence that had been abandoned in 1945 with the demise of OSS, the IC perked along as the Cold War heightened, learning as it went along. The Board of National Estimate re-established by Bedell Smith was intended to look down the road and advise the president of future national security problems he would be faced with. Covert action budgets doubled and tripled in the 1950s, as the United States sought to limit the spread of Soviet influence all over the world.

Critical to successful intelligence gathering against the Soviets at this time was the capture of wireless radio signals from the Soviet Union and Bloc countries. In the United States this was principally the mission of the Army and Navy signals intelligence agencies that had done such a spectacular job during World War II, allied with the UK and Commonwealth signals intelligence agencies in Australia, Canada and New Zealand. In 1951, President Truman decided to amalgamate all U.S. signals intelligence authority in one secret central agency, the National Security Agency (NSA), to be located at Fort Meade, Maryland. It would be an agency reporting to the Secretary of Defense, but it would have a tie to the DCI through the IC. *Sigint*, as it was abbreviated in the bureaucracy, would play an enormous role in the effort to contain the Soviets during the Cold War and will be equally critical in the war against terror. It is no longer just radio signals that the NSA is seeking to recover but electronic emissions of all kinds, from cell phones to the Internet. It is a daunting task, but one luckily that can still count on the wartime alliance of *sigint* partners in the United Kingdom among others.

The first nearly three decades of the IC's existence was largely unhampered by legislative oversight. Annual intelligence budgets were approved by a handful of senior congressional leaders in the House and Senate after cursory hearings in secret. Americans did not know and did not seem to want to know much about espionage and covert action. They took their leaders' word for the fact that spying against the Soviets was necessary and that the Soviets were doing it to us, so the work of the IC was almost exclusively an Executive Branch function until *New York Times* reporter Seymour Hersh broke the story of "the family jewels," in December 1974. The Hersh articles flowed from an inquiry mounted by DCI James Schlesinger in which he invited all officers of CIA to step forward if they knew of any instance in which the CIA had acted beyond U.S. Constitutional bounds in its operations. This became a major turning point in IC and CIA history. Since the turbulent 60s, Americans had been growing more skeptical about their government, caused primarily by the trauma of the Vietnam War. Presidents' words were no longer taken at face value. If it were true that the CIA and FBI were surveilling ordinary Americans; reading their mail bound for the USSR and elsewhere in the Bloc; infiltrating anti-Vietnam War protests in the United States; and plotting to kill political leaders overseas, as the *New York Times* asserted, then it was time for a day of reckoning. It occurred as a consequence of hearings held in 1975 by House and Senate investigative committees—the results of which were the establishment of permanent oversight committees in both chambers and a statute passed in 1980 requiring that the DCI keep the committees "fully and currently" informed about all U.S. intelligence operations, including covert actions. Prior to the 1980 legislative change, the Congress in 1974 had passed an amendment to the foreign assistance legislation of that year requiring that the president specifically "find" that all future covert actions are in the national security interest of the United States before they are undertaken and report these findings to the appropriate committees of Congress. So much for rogue operations by CIA where the president is allegedly not in the know. The Ford administration was able to forestall further restrictions on future IC activity by drafting its own charter for intelligence activities in an executive order that has been continued to the present day with minor revisions by follow-on executive orders promulgated by President Ford's immediate successors, Carter and Reagan. For example, it is in the Ford Executive Order, continued by Carter and Reagan, that the prohibition against political assassinations, directly or by surrogates, is contained.

Thus, by the end of the Reagan administration, the IC was beginning to take its present form, as far as overseas operations were concerned. The Iran-

Contra scandal provoked legislation in the early 90s to make CIA the default agency for the mounting of covert action (CA) operations. The president could select an agency other than CIA for CA but it would have to notify the Congress specifically. Furthermore, any CA proposed would have to be congruent with stated U.S. foreign policy goals and not bargaining with terrorists as Iran-Contra had been, when President Reagan had promised never to do so.

CIA was still top dog in the IC, although subject to greater congressional scrutiny. NSA and NRO were free-standing defense intelligence agencies, providing critical foreign intelligence information when they could access it. The Department of Defense (DOD) was on the way to creating a Defense *humint* service to compete in the military theater with CIA. The FBI had domestic intelligence responsibilities, largely of a defensive or counter-intelligence nature, but inexorably it was being pulled overseas as the foreign terrorist threat to Americans and U.S. interests abroad increased.

Then in 1991, the Soviet Union self-destructed and the Cold War came to an abrupt end. The principal mission of the IC for the preceding 45 years, collecting intelligence on the Soviet Union and its allies, halted. Experienced intelligence officers resigned in droves, having won their war. By the end of the decade of the 90s, CIA would be operating with 50% fewer case officers in the clandestine service than at the start.

The U.S. government took a painfully long time to re-direct the IC to the principal post-Cold War targets of tracking the spread of weapons of mass destruction, and the rise of international terrorism, with the result that more officials resigned in frustration (or boredom) from the IC than had been anticipated. For example, it was not until 1996 that the Clinton White House promulgated Presidential Decision Directive (PDD) 35 that enumerated up-to-date targets for the IC. This document remains classified. PDD 35 was combined with an IC budget cut-back, misguidedly designed to present the American people with a "peace dividend" on intelligence gathering to parallel the draw-down in defense expenditure during the 90s, leaving the IC with fewer resources to devote to tracking Islamist fundamentalists like Osama Bin Laden who began to attack overseas U.S. assets with increasing boldness.

In 1993, shortly after the attack on the Alfred Murrah Government Building in Oklahoma City, a Yemeni terrorist associated with al Qaeda named Ramzi Yousef led an attack on the World Trade Center (WTC) in New York City. He and his confederates rented a U-Haul truck; filled it with store-bought explosives they had fashioned into a bomb; and parked it in the garage under WTC tower 2 where it exploded, injuring 40 persons and causing millions of dollars in damage. The sanctuary had been broken. The United States had been attacked by foreign terrorists at one of its iconic buildings in New York, and if it had not been for the amateurish nature of the attack, cataclysmic damage might have been done. In retrospect, these two events ought to have been more of a wake-up call of America's increasing vulnerability to domestic terrorist attack, and the need to strengthen homeland defenses.

Several high profile studies of threats to the American homeland followed the attacks; one written by former U.S. Senators Gary Hart and Warren Rudman was particularly alarming; and there were others, from former State Department Counterterrorist chief, Ambassador L. Paul Bremer (later George W. Bush's viceroy in Iraq), and former Governor James Gilmore of Virginia. But they prompted no immediate response from President Clinton or the Congress. The perpetrators of both attacks were apprehended. Ramzi Yousef was "snatched" and rendered from Pakistan by the CIA and FBI working in concert with Pakistani authorities. They were tried and convicted in U.S. courts and sentenced to life imprisonment without parole. That convinced the president, and the American people for the time being, that terrorist attacks against U.S. targets were really like every other law enforcement problem that could be adjudicated in U.S. courts, as long as the United States could obtain jurisdiction over the terrorists by grabbing them with the help of allies like Pakistan.

It was during this period that the United States was offered access to al Qaeda leader Osama bin Laden by the government of Sudan, but refused to take custody of him despite his reputation for planning acts of terrorism against the United States, because the authorities did not have enough evidence to indict him and bring him to trial in America.

In 1998, in attacks that occurred within hours of one another, al Qaeda operatives successfully destroyed the U.S. Embassies in Nairobi, Kenya and Dar-es-Salaam, Tanzania killing hundreds and injuring thousands. Bombs had been placed in trucks that were driven into the two embassy compounds and detonated. The bombings demonstrated the increasing competence of al Qaeda to destroy Western targets, but provoked only a feeble response from the United States, consisting of two cruise missile attacks: the first on a dusty compound in Southern Afghanistan where Osama was believed to be holding a meeting; and the second, a pill factory in Sudan, believed to be owned by Osama. Neither was successful in achieving its goal, and apparently only further convinced the al Qaeda leadership that the United States had no stomach for putting boots on the ground to oppose al Qaeda's efforts in the Middle East.

The year of the millennium was supposed to be a time of testing for western technology in the form of terrorist attacks and computer failures, but thanks to several foiled plots, 2000 arrived with few disruptions. In the spring of 2000, however, an auxiliary motor launch laden with explosives struck the prow of the USS *Cole* in Aden, Yemen and ripped a 40-foot hole in it, killing twenty U.S. sailors. Despite the outcry in the United States, President Clinton ordered no response. Thus as the U.S. presidential year unfolded, the world and the United States in particular, were facing a growing international terrorist threat mounted by Islamist fundamentalists determined to strike the "far enemy" and believing that the United States had lost the will to strike back.

The George W. Bush administration had other priorities as it assumed power in 2001 and had no time to listen to the IC's concerns that al Qaeda was preparing to mount a big strike against the United States either overseas or domestically. Increasingly, as the circuits blinked red, DCI George Tenet pressed his operatives to come up with hard information on where and when the terrorists might strike. Then came the attacks in New York and Washington D.C on September 11 (9/11).

Post-mortems would later show that the IC had collected relevant bits and pieces of information prior to 9/11: two al Qaeda persons had traveled to the United States after an al Qaeda meeting in Malaysia in the spring of 2001, but CIA failed to timely pass this information to the U.S. Immigration Service and the FBI, so they could be put on a watch-list. They were later to become two of the 19 hijackers of U.S commercial aircraft on 9/11. An FBI agent in the southwestern United States had reported, prior to the attacks, that an unusual number of Arabs had been enrolled in airline flight schools in that region, but nobody in FBI headquarters picked up on the tip. 9/11 was a colossal intelligence failure by any reckoning, but it was also a government-wide failure of understanding that the United States could be so vulnerable to the hijacking of commercial airliners that would then be used as suicide weapons to destroy major U.S. buildings with massive loss of life. To be sure, the FBI and CIA had not shared information in a way that might have prevented the 9/11 attacks, but as at Pearl Harbor some 60 years earlier, there was not much intelligence information to share prior to the event. CIA had no penetrations of al Qaeda and likewise no sources of allied governments in a position to pass on hard information about al Qaeda's plans. There had not been a successful hijacking of U.S. aircraft in the preceding twenty-five years in U.S. airspace, so American pilots were still acting on the old assumption that the hijackers wanted to live and might be talked into diverting the flight to an alternate location. In short, there were precious few dots of information to connect when the country was caught so completely unaware and unprepared.

Nonetheless, 9/11 became a watershed event for the Intelligence Community, as it did for the rest of the U.S. government. Although the president opposed its creation, the congress appointed a 9/11 Commission of bipartisan notables who examined the events of and prior to 9/11 in minute detail. When the Commission filed its report in the summer of 2004, it excoriated the IC for failing to have human sources in the Middle East; for failing to speak the languages of the region; and for not knowing more about the tenets of fundamentalist Islam and its potential to attack the United States. It deplored the lack of imagination at CIA in failing to forecast the probability of airline hijackings given all the information it had collected about Khalid Sheikh Mohammad and the "Bojinka" plot of several years previously. The Commission report criticized the lack of information sharing among the IC's 15 agencies, but especially the CIA and the FBI, and concluded that what the IC really needed was "an attending physician in charge of U.S. intelligence" responsible for supervising and controlling the work of the 15 specialized components of the IC who were running around ordering tests but were not accountable overall for the final product. This became the basis for the 9/11 Commission's primary recommendation that the IC henceforth be governed by a Director of National Intelligence (DNI) reporting directly to the president, who was not also the chief executive officer of CIA.

The 9/11 Commission made other recommendations as well, such as the creation of a National Counterterrorist Center (NCTC), modeled on the CIA's successful Terrorist Threat Integration Center (TTIC) that sought to collect and analyze terrorist information from all over the world, using analysts from all the U.S. government agencies engaged in intelligence collection and law enforcement worldwide. The Commission noted that the 9/11 attacks hit the major organizational gap in U.S. coverage of terrorist events, i.e. it was a domestic attack mounted by foreign terrorists. With the rigid separation of foreign intelligence from domestic law enforcement that dated from the creation of CIA in 1947, as a practical matter, the United States had been configured to resist a domestic attack from domestic terrorists or a foreign attack from foreign terrorists, but not the 9/11 assault which involved Saudi, Egyptian and other foreigners plotting in Hamburg and Spain to commit terrorist attacks in New York and Washington. The U.S. government was not set up to deal with this threat and it was now time to get ready.

Finally, the 9/11 Commission wanted the U.S. Congress to get its anti- and counter-terrorist jurisdictions sorted out as well. As far as intelligence was concerned, it recommended that both authorization and appropriation functions be discharged by one intelligence oversight committee in each body, to maximize the expertise and minimize the possibility of political horseplay, calculated leaks and special pleading from interfering with the important business of combating terrorism. At this writing, reforms in the legislative oversight process have not been enacted by the Congress, but the House is experimenting with one oversize intelligence committee headed by Rush Holt (D, N.J.) comprised of authorizers and senior appropriators that worked successfully on this year's intelligence authorization and appropriations bills. That's a start.

It is still too early to judge how the DNI will work out, or even the NCTC for that matter. Created by the Intelligence Reform and Terrorism Protection Act of 2004, in the midst of the presidential election campaign, and pushed mightily by the so-called 9/11 families (those families who had lost relatives in the World Trade Center and Pentagon bombings), it was not fully debated or considered before being passed and rushed to the president's desk for signature. Early indications are that the DNI and his office may just be an additional layer of bureaucracy over the IC, not adding much value, but cherry-picking functions from the 15 other line intelligence agencies. It is also unclear how much sway the DNI has over the principal so-called Defense intelligence agencies: NSA, DIA NRO, and NGIA.

As far as the NCTC goes, unless the foreign intelligence components learn how to well and truly work with and share intelligence information with the law enforcement agencies(read CIA and FBI primarily), the "reform" will not have achieved much. As noted earlier, the 9/11 attacks proved that the distinction between international and domestic intelligence gathering, analysis and dissemination on terrorist questions is artificial and outdated.

The 9/11 Commission was concerned whether the FBI was up to its new responsibilities in the domestic intelligence field surrounding anti- and counterterrorism. It worried, as have other critics such as federal judge Richard Posner, that the FBI is invested too deeply in traditional law enforcement: investigating, arresting and trying criminals. The Commission flirted with recommending the creation of an American MI-5, the British domestic intelligence agency, but reportedly backed off when it heard the testimony of FBI Director Robert Mueller who apparently argued convincingly that the leopard could change its spots.

That brings us to the black box that is the Department of Homeland Security (DHS). The biggest U.S. government department created since DOD in 1947, it is a conglomerate's conglomerate. Its responsibilities run from the Federal Emergency Management Agency (FEMA) to the U.S. Coast Guard; from the Immigration and Naturalization Service to the new Transportation Security Administration. It will take years for the department to find its sea legs, if ever, which presents real problems for meeting the challenge of domestic terrorism. DHS has no intelligence gathering assets of its own, but depends on CIA and the FBI primarily for its intelligence feedstock, out of which it is supposed to analyze the threats to the homeland. As far as the threat of domestic terrorism is concerned, DHS's major role is to interface with first responders all over the U. S.—the local police, firefighters, public health services and hospitals who will have to actually contend with the casualties of a domestic terrorist attack. It is a formidable collection of responsibilities employing an army of employees, many of whom have little knowledge or familiarity with the tasks of their brethren in the department, thus creating a monster to administer by a single cabinet officer. Once again, it is too early to tell how the DHS experiment will work out. The Bush administration was never in favor of it until the end, when public and political opinion became insistent that it was important to create something to provide homeland security, even if was the wrong thing. Thankfully, we have yet to be tested in 9/11 terms and perhaps that is because DHS has been doing its job, but if one judges from the reaction of the nation's major cities like New York, they are mounting their own efforts at homeland defense.

I have skipped over passage of the USA PATRIOT ACT in the days that immediately followed 9/11. It caused a hue and cry among civil libertarians after its contents became fully known, so speedy was its passage in the six weeks after 9/11. Actually, a good many of the provisions contained in the Patriot Act had been awaiting consideration in the House and Senate—awaiting a traumatic national event that would provide the impetus for passage—so it was not completely unfamiliar to many lawmakers. For example, the provision in the bill making a warrant for surveillance run to the individual whose conversations the government wants to capture, rather than merely to the instrument through which he intends to communicate, makes great sense in a time of throw-away cell phones. Likewise, the amendment of Rule 6 (e) of the Federal Rules of Criminal Procedure to permit access to grand jury testimony in a terrorist case, without specific court permission, by the intelligence and law enforcement agencies that have an interest in the proceeding makes sense, if the use to which this knowledge is put is restricted to intelligence or terrorist matters, as the act specifies. I do not believe the provisions in the act permitting the U.S. Treasury to follow terrorist money transfers through the international banking system should be controversial either, particularly if the U.S. government preserves a paper trail that indicates the propriety of the inquiry, for law enforcement purposes.

The problem appears to arise when the Attorney General or the FBI are perceived to have too much latitude in the inquiries they can mount under the act, and the perceived lack of accountability for the inquiry if it is too broadly based. The "administrative letters" that the FBI is now permitted to issue without a judge's signature to obtain from an individual or corporation records that might indicate involvement in funding terrorist activity are controversial, as are the AG's power to close immigration hearings or extend the time of detention of a terrorist suspect. These powers are presently being challenged in U.S. courts.

There is also a significant re-write of the Foreign Intelligence Surveillance Act (FISA) contained in the Patriot Act that broadens the subject area jurisdiction of FISA from intelligence surveillance to include terrorism. The

U.S. Government may now seek a FISA warrant against suspected terrorists operating in the United States on the same basis that it seeks warrants against suspected foreign spies, i.e. *ex parte*, before the Foreign Intelligence Surveillance Act Court (FISC) meeting in secret, with no advice to the subject of the surveillance unless the suspect later becomes subject to federal prosecution.

There was some discussion prior to passage of the revisions that the standard for involvement in terrorist preparations might be a mere excuse for seeking surveillance of an individual whom the government might really be pursuing for other crimes, where a 4th Amendment warrant would otherwise be required. After much debate as to whether to gain information about terrorist preparations should be "the" purpose for the proposed surveillance or merely "a" purpose, the lawmakers agreed that terrorism had to be "a significant purpose" of the proposed surveillance. It is too early to tell how the FISA amendments are working, but it is clear that they have led to a big uptick in applications for warrants.

FISA, in fact, has become the subject of additional revision, this time to encompass the warrantless activity of NSA since 9/11, in capturing conversations from overseas al Qaeda suspects that either transit the United States because of the current technical routing of worldwide communications traffic or because they might be intended for al Qaeda operatives in the United States. The Bush administration directed the NSA to perform these intercepts without seeking either congressional approval or approval under FISA, on the theory that such a tasking was within the constitutional power of the president as commander-in-chief. A temporary settlement of the dispute between the Democrat-controlled Congress and the Bush Administration on the legality of the intercepts was achieved through February, 2008, by pulling the FISC in to review NSA's intercepts for propriety. What has become clear after the debate has cooled is that FISA, as approved in 1978, is outdated in the manner in which it relates to current communications technology and the needs of the IC to combat domestic terrorism. Nobody wants to cut off NSA's access to these calls if they contain useful counter-terrorist information, so a way must be found to do it constitutionally. The FISC may provide the best forum to bring that about.

Thus far we have been concentrating on the IC's efforts to collect intelligence information on terrorists and terrorism aimed at the United States. This was the priority that President G.W. Bush impressed upon the Community in order to pre-empt or prevent another 9/11 attack. Of equal importance, however, is how the IC goes about analyzing and disseminating the intelligence it does collect. For that, we have as the cautionary tale the fiasco over the existence of weapons of mass destruction (WMD) in the run-up to the war against Saddam's Iraq in March, 2003.

The irony is that most intelligence services of countries with knowledge of Iraq in 2002–3 would have argued that Saddam *had* retained a store of biological and chemical weapons that had been unaccounted for after the UN weapons inspectors had been driven from Iraq in 1998. They would point to the fact that Iraq had possessed chem.-bio ordinance in 1991, at the end of the Gulf War, and indeed had used it against Iraqi Shia at that time in the Basra region. There was no proof that he had disposed of or accounted for it, and it was counter-intuitive to think that he would destroy his stock out of respect for UN Resolutions, when he had given the weapons inspectors such a hard time in their efforts to track WMD from the beginning. Nuclear weapons would not have been an issue since it was pretty clear that Saddam had not yet been successful in his nuclear weapons program efforts. The intelligence services of the United States, Israel, the UK, Germany, Russia, and France would likely have been together in these views with the primary difference being that all but the United Kingdom and the United States were willing to wait until Hans Blix had concluded his efforts on behalf of the UN before they would act on these views.

No, the primary sticking point with the IC's analysis of the Iraqi WMD question was the certainty it assumed on the matter, based on evidence that was fragmentary, dated, and unreliable. The key document at issue was the National Intelligence Estimate of October 2002, requested by the Senate intelligence committee, and prepared hurriedly by the IC in six weeks. Post-mortem critiques performed by both the Senate committee, and the Silberman-Robb commission appointed by President Bush, flayed the IC for its shoddy craftsmanship in preparing this document. The United States had no controlled unilateral sources in Iraq after 1991, and lost its cooperating UN weapons inspectors in 1998, yet it was judgmentally positive, without any qualifications, in its conclusion that Saddam still possessed WMD in late 2002, although Chief UN Inspector Blix had not yet turned up a trace. Indeed, the NIE contained no description of the basis for the emphatic judgment that there were still WMD hidden or unaccounted for in Iraq. The post-mortems indicted the IC for groupthink, a lack of imagination, a failure to test the unorthodox hypothesis that Saddam might have destroyed his WMD to get out from under UN sanctions, and a failure to advise the NIE's readers of the skimpy and dated nature of its sources.

Adding to this disappointing performance, the IC supported Secretary of State Colin Powell when he testified in February, 2003 before the United Nations in New York to state the case for war in Iraq. Many of the overconfident judgments contained in the October 2002 NIE were repeated, but two additional claims were made that had to be disowned later. In the first instance, Secretary Powell stated that the United States possessed evidence that Iraq had developed mobile laboratories to work on and spread chem./bio weapons, advancing the supposed eyewitness report of a German agent, deliciously code-named Curveball, whom the IC had never met and who turned out to be a fabricator.

The second issue that Secretary Powell testified on erroneously to the UN was the use to which specific aluminum tubes imported by the Iraqis were to be put. Based on the opinion of a CIA analyst with experience in the nuclear industry, the IC had concluded that the tubes were destined for use in the nuclear fuel enrichment process, thus evidencing that Saddam was still working towards a nuclear weapon. In point of fact, U.S Energy Department analysts who had also examined the tubes dissented, saying they believed that the tubes were more likely replacement tubes for rocket motors on some ancient, outdated Iraqi missiles. In the event, the Energy Department analysts were right.

The outcome of these several instances of poor analytical tradecraft added to the pressure on the Intelligence Community and the new DNI to go back to basics in re-tooling the performance of the analytical side of the IC. An example of this recalibration of standards was the decision of the Community in November 2007 to recall its 2005 NIE on Iran, in which the IC had stated that Iran was actively in pursuit of a nuclear weapon. In a later pronouncement on the subject, the Community declared that Iran in 2003 had decided to terminate its effort to build a nuclear bomb, and it was still reasonably confident in 2007 that that remained the case. The IC was meticulous in describing the sources (obviously without identifying particulars) that caused them to reverse their earlier position.

As revealed in a rash of hostile comment after the IC's new position was announced, however, the new NIE appeared to be playing down the fact that Iran continued to improve its capacity to refine uranium fuel that could eventually be converted to bomb-making in a short period of time. Iran has 3000 centrifuges up and running, processing uranium at the present time.

What then must we conclude about the capability of the Intelligence Community to be effective in the war against terror?

First, it must be acknowledged that there is no shortage of financial resources. The budget of the DNI and the 16 IC components for FY 2008 was appropriated at approximately $60 billion dollars—a number declassified this year for the first time since the early George Tenet years. Yet it remains unclear whether the president's goals to increase the number of CIA case officers by 50% and the number of hard language speakers who will serve overseas by a similar percentage were met. More importantly, it is unclear whether the new national clandestine service (the name given to CIA's Directorate of Operations and the military's Defense *Humint* Service) can meet the extraordinary demands being placed upon it in the war against terror and still discharge its responsibilities in China, North Korea, Africa and Latin America as well. The CIA was the principal U.S. vehicle for *humint* collection during the Cold War and after passage of the Intelligence Reform and Anti-terrorism Act of 2004, it is a shadow of its former self. The heart of the intelligence analytical function has migrated to the DNI to support his efforts to advise the president, as have many of CIA's former responsibilities in science and technology and overhead reconnaissance.

At the same time as its world has shrunk, the tasks that CIA is expected to perform have grown immeasurably more difficult. The United States will not be meeting new sources of intelligence on terrorist cells at embassy cocktail parties. Non-official cover (NOC) will be necessary to insert case officers in difficult locations in the Middle East and elsewhere. Many of these NOC assignments will be in dangerous places where families cannot safely be stationed. As noted above, foreign language competence and cultural knowledge, so disastrously absent from the U.S. presence in Afghanistan and Iraq, will be critical tools of the trade if the United States is to be successful. Finally, it will be difficult being an American in most of these prospective spy locations. Unlike at the time of the Cold War, when the United States was the only realistic counterweight to Soviet domination, we are not the good guys anymore. It will likely not be this way indefinitely, but at the end of the Bush presidency, the United States was profoundly resented in many parts of the world. If spy recruitments occur in large measure for personal and ideological reasons, American NOC officers will have a lot of ground to make up.

Sadly, there are also clear signs that the clandestine service is unable to recruit, and perhaps more importantly, retain, the best and the brightest of today's qualified candidates. The Valerie Plame outing in 2004 did not help. If the United States is unable to promise every officer who signs up for under-cover work that, at the very least, their identities will be protected by their fellow U.S. Government employees, it is unrealistic to assume that we shall be successful in recruiting the ones we want. Further, I would argue that the current controversy over torture and extraordinary rendition is taking a toll on both current CIA employees and those who are contemplating signing up. Nobody wants to be part of an outfit that commits human rights violations, or permits others to do so, when it is unclear that this is the necessary way to extract intelligence from a suspected terrorist. To make matters worse, one certainly does not want to be pilloried for following what one believes is a lawful order, only to discover that the chain of command has changed its mind and it is not lawful any more; and you are subject to punishment for what you did believing it to be lawful.

In summary, these are difficult if not impossible times for U.S. intelligence and the IC. The good news is that the United States will get through them because we have to. There is no substitute for the role of the national clandestine service working with the FBI and law enforcement, and DHS, to confront the terrorist threat we face both domestically and internationally, at the present time and for the foreseeable future. Whether it is a "Marshall Plan" for learning needed exotic languages and to study foreign cultures; or an extra stipend to bring in qualified NOCs, there must be sufficient presidential and congressional leadership to bring this about or the consequences will be unacceptable to most Americans. It is clear that technology will also play a big role. We face some technological barriers to accessing all the signals we would like to read in the terrorist world; and an extraordinarily difficult job keeping up with the open signals we can read but do not get to in a timely fashion because of the proliferation of new sources.

Chapter 10

A New Recipe for Renditions and Extraditions

A. John Radsan[1]

From the beginning of history, human beings have crossed boundaries and borders. Some have done so by their own choice, seeking better pastures, clearer waters, and more opportunities. Some have done so against their will, being sold into slavery or fleeing political persecution, pogroms, or civil wars. In modern times, national governments play a significant role in these crossings. To achieve their ends, law enforcement agencies and intelligence services are often involved in a sort of human trafficking.

The paradox is that kidnapping, by the government or by private parties, is itself a crime, but sometimes humans must be trafficked so that they may be prosecuted. Since criminals do not always stay put, American prosecutors must often search for suspects and convicts in other jurisdictions. A woman who killed her husband in Santa Barbara may flee to Oaxaca. A man connected to the bombing of the World Trade Center may be living in Hamburg. Rather than hunt down these suspects and convicts by a personal posse, complete with horses, ten gallon hats, and shotguns, American prosecutors use mutual legal assistance agreements (MLATs) and extradition treaties between countries to bring the sought after people back into American jurisdiction. MLATs and extradition treaties are modern weapons in an American arsenal.

---

1. John Radsan, the Founder and Director of the National Security Forum, is a Professor at the William Mitchell College of Law and holds a J.D. from Harvard Law School. A leading authority on national security issues, Radsan has a unique combination of professional experience in both law enforcement and intelligence activities. His research and writing pursue an appropriate balance between individual liberty and public safety. He has served as a federal prosecutor and as assistant general counsel at the CIA, in addition to his work as a corporate lawyer and consultant. Professor Radsan has also advised officials from other countries, including Russia, Kazakhstan, Uzbekistan, Turkmenistan, and Ukraine.

Sometimes when MLATs and extradition procedures are ineffective, American officials rely on nontraditional means to pursue their missions. Mexican bounty hunters may find the suspect in their country and, without involving the Mexican government, dump him on the other side of the Rio Grande. Sometimes, when prosecution is not the primary purpose of the transfer, agencies other than the Justice Department may become involved. The Central Intelligence Agency (CIA), for one, may transfer a suspect to a foreign intelligence service that uses different methods to extract information from him. Some tactics, not condoned/permitted by American law, are commonplace in other jurisdictions.

Since 9/11, the number of transfers between the United States and other jurisdictions increased. Moreover, the purpose of many transfers shifted from law enforcement to intelligence gathering. Under the George W. Bush administration, prosecuting terrorists after the fact was not as vital as disrupting their plots before they could crash other planes into commercial towers and government buildings. Compared to the era before 9/11, it became less likely that a suspect would be transferred, by extradition or otherwise, back to the United States to face criminal charges. It became more likely that a prisoner would be transferred, with the assistance of American personnel and American equipment, from one foreign jurisdiction to another. Irregular rendition, instead of the regular rendition known as extradition, made the headlines.

So far, the topic of irregular rendition has stirred more extreme emotion than dispassionate analysis. Since the topic has made news and since Hollywood has produced the movie "Rendition," calling on Reese Witherspoon from the less than profound movies, *Legally Blonde* and *Legally Blonde II*, sensation often substitutes for cognition. This chapter, less sensational than the Hollywood screen, reviews the history of America's rendition program, assesses the references that affect rendition's legality, analyzes the pros and cons of rendition, and proposes a solution for bringing rendition within the rule of law in a safe and efficient manner.

Rendition in American History

Before 9/11, as the 9/11 Commission made clear, the United States did, from time to time, rely on irregular rendition to bring criminal suspects back to this country for trial.[2] In that sense, the irregularities occurred on the front

---

2. 9/11 Commission Report, 109th Cong., Report by the 9/11 Commission, at 141–42 (2004).

end of the process when custody was obtained by something other than ex-tradition.[3] Irregular means were necessary because the countries in which the suspects found themselves were unsafe, dysfunctional, or unwilling to coop-erate fully with formal requests from the American government. Two cases of "returning" suspects for prosecution stand out from the pre-9/11 period.

One case concerns Fawaz Yunis, a Lebanese citizen connected to airplane hijackings in the mid-1980s in the Middle East. For the Americans, request-ing Yunis's extradition from Lebanon did not make sense because that coun-try did not have a stable government and those who did exercise some control there were unfriendly toward the United States. Instead of extradition, the CIA and the FBI settled on an undercover operation to lure Yunis into international waters. There, as the United States Justice Department had opined, he could be snatched consistent with American law and then brought back to the United States on the basis of a "sealed" (or secret) arrest warrant in a federal case. Yunis, it turned out, became one of America's first modern cases of irregular rendition.

American officials, with the help of an undercover informant from Lebanon, convinced Yunis to travel from Cyprus into the Mediterranean. According to the scheme, Yunis believed he was going out to sea to be greeted by a prospec-tive partner on a large drug deal, a high-roller with his own yacht. While at sea, and outside any country's jurisdiction, Yunis was greeted by undercover FBI agents—part of the high-roller's supposed entourage—some of whom wore nothing other than bikinis. Everything looked fine to Yunis until the FBI agents refused to talk about any drug deal with him. Instead, the agents sprung their trap on the unsuspecting terrorist, roughing him up during an arrest.

The FBI moved Yunis from the yacht to a small Navy ship which, over a several day journey, transported him to an American aircraft carrier. To avoid implicating any other countries in Yunis's snatch, the flight from the aircraft carrier continued non-stop until it reached Andrews Air Force Base. Upon landing, Yunis was taken before an American judge. The court, despite its con-cerns about the rough methods of Yunis's capture, allowed the American pros-ecutors to bring their case. In due course, Yunis was convicted and sentenced in federal district court in Washington, D.C.

Another case concerns Humberto Alvarez-Machain, a Mexican physician. American investigators suspected that he had played a role in the torture and murder of Enrique Camarena Salazar, a Drug Enforcement Administration

---

3. The "back end" of the process, as I define it, concerns whether and where the suspect is transferred after the United States takes custody.

agent who had disappeared while serving for the United States Embassy in Mexico. Alvarez-Machain, it seemed, had used his medical skills not to treat Camarena's pain for recovery but to prolong his life so that his Mexican captors could continue to torture him. The DEA, frustrated that the Mexicans were dragging their feet on American requests to extract information for Alvarez-Machain's extradition, decided to take control of Alvarez-Machain by irregular means. In 1990, Mexican private parties, spurred on by an American reward and guided by the DEA, captured the "doctor of death" in Mexico and dumped him into American territory where he was taken by American officials.

Although Alvarez-Machain was not captured in compliance with the U.S.-Mexican extradition treaty, the United States Supreme Court decided that the criminal case against him could continue.[4] Taking control of him by rough and irregular means did not divest jurisdiction since the Court did not view extradition as the exclusive means of bringing him to trial. As a result, Alvarez-Machain faced the criminal charges against him. The irony of his case is that he eventually was acquitted in federal court because much of the evidence against him was inadmissible in court. The abduction, after many twists and turns, was for naught.

For Yunis and Alvarez-Machain, the back end of the process—a trial in federal district court—was regular. Indeed, President Clinton, years before President George W. Bush took office, issued National Decision Directive 39 which formalized some of what was going on in practice. It stated: "When terrorists wanted for violation of U.S. law are at large overseas ... return of suspects by force may be effected without the cooperation of the host government." For such purposes, Yunis fell more clearly into the core definition of "terrorist" than did Alvarez-Machain. In any event, what was irregular about the pre-9/11 cases was the front end: their coming into American custody by violent snatches instead of a calm judicial process.[5]

Then, 9/11 generated a radical shift in United States policy. After 9/11, irregularities occurred on both the front ends and the back ends of various captures. Suspects were snatched from the streets and transferred, not to courts but to secret American sites or to countries that were secretly allied with United States efforts against terrorism. At the back end, the prisoners were not greeted by judges or defense counsel. Instead, the only company they found, for weeks, months, and years, was the interrogators in the room with them.

---

4. *United States. v. Alvarez-Machain*, 504 U.S. 655, 657 (1992).
5. Even so, Michael Scheuer, the former head of the bin Laden unit at the CIA, claims that the pre-9/11 program involved some transfers to Egypt from third countries.

Rising from the rubble at ground zero was an American policy that emphasized prevention over prosecution. Convicting people after they hatched their terrorist plots seemed less desirable than disrupting and neutralizing them before they could repeat 9/11 or, through weapons of mass destruction, do something worse. Whether the American public acknowledged it or not, putting a few hundred suspects in a sort of preventive detention seemed to be the cost we were willing to accept—or to impose—to ensure security and a sense of well-being.

The United States Government, in the broadest terms, has acknowledged a rendition program as a part of its counterterrorism policies since 9/11. Sometimes, through a revolving door, the suspect will go to foreign hands—and back to American hands. One mystery is the level of suspicion, if any, that makes someone subject to rendition in the first place. That mystery, like many others in the struggle against terror, should trouble us all.

Not all is black on irregular rendition, however. Estimates about the scope of the American rendition program put the number of prisoners in the hundreds. Yet what little the public does know about irregular rendition is due more to the work of investigative journalists, including Stephen Grey,[6] Jane Mayer,[7] and Dana Priest,[8] than the result of anything the White House has revealed on the record. The rest of the government has been mum.

In a related context, although journalists speculated and reported for several years that the CIA was a running a secret detention and interrogation program, it was not until September 6, 2006, during the lobbying that followed the *Hamdan* decision about the procedures for military commissions at Guantanamo, that the president confirmed that high-level al Qaeda suspects had been held in black sites. To this day, neither the president nor any of his advisers has confirmed where those sites were located. The White House, keeping the public guessing, neither confirms nor denies speculation about past sites in Thailand, Poland, Romania, and various other places.

---

6. STEPHEN GREY, GHOST PLANE: THE TRUE STORY OF THE CIA TORTURE PROGRAM, (St. Martin's Press 2006) (exposing the government's controversial detention and interrogation program; Grey was one of the first journalists to investigate the CIA's rendition program).

7. Jane Mayer, *Outsourcing Torture*, THE NEW YORKER, Feb. 14, 2005 at 106 (discussing the "secret history" of America's "extraordinary rendition" program).

8. Dana Priest & Barton Gellman, *U.S. Decries Abuse but Defends Interrogations*, WASH. POST, Dec. 26, 2002 at A1 (discussing the "stress and duress" tactics used on terrorism suspects in overseas facilities).

The Legality of Rendition

Many bodies of law, one piled on the other, affect American counterterrorism. In other words, all of American counterterrorism does not fall neatly within the laws of armed conflict (also known as international humanitarian law) or within any other body of law. Where a particular law of war or practice falls depends very much on the facts and circumstances. For instance, a Predator strike in Afghanistan on an al Qaeda leader differs from the detention of a mid-level operative in Iraq. As to rendition, my sense[9] is that more of the snatches since 9/11 occurred in streets and alleys in Pakistan and elsewhere than on traditional battlefields in Afghanistan and Iraq. Just so, rendition often takes place somewhere between war and peace. For this reason, based on a sort of *lex specialis*, my analysis of rendition's legality revolves around sources that are more specific about rendition than the Geneva Conventions, that is, around sources that do not depend on armed conflict.[10]

Even if American courts avoid cases of irregular rendition through standing, the state secrets privilege, the political question doctrine, and other techniques, the American executive branch must still take care to carry out its program against terrorists consistent with the rule of law. Americans remain true to *Marbury v. Madison's* notion that ours is a "government of laws, and not of men." Therefore, an analysis of rendition's legality reaches several levels: the laws of foreign jurisdictions, American law, and international law.

Depending on the circumstances, American involvement in an irregular rendition could have one or two steps. In some renditions, American officials are not involved in the initial snatch or the taking of the suspect into custody; the suspect comes into American hands, outside United States territory, courtesy of a bounty hunter or some service (law enforcement, military, or intelligence) in another country. The Pakistani intelligence service, for example, may hand an al Qaeda member over to the CIA in Karachi. Here, despite the possibilities of accessory or conspiracy liability for the snatch under Pakistani law, American officials stay clear. Yet the suspect's transfer to a third jurisdiction, say, to Egypt, might invoke that country's law, American law, and international law.

In other cases, the CIA may handle both the snatch and the transfer from that country to a third country. This two-step process is what may have hap-

---

9. This is based on the public record.

10. Common Article 3, which calls for the humane treatment of prisoners, is just one example of a provision from the laws of armed conflict that may be relevant. Common Article 3, however, does not contain any specific provisions on the transfer of prisoners.

pened to Abu Omar, a radical Muslim cleric of Egyptian origin who had political refugee status in Italy. Suspected of ties to al Qaeda, Abu Omar was
swept by men in black from the streets of Milan in 2003. He claims that, after
he was thrown into a van and put on a plane, the CIA transferred him to Egypt
where he was tortured. If so, foreign laws were involved. What is most murky
about this rendition is whether any Italian officials participated in the operation or whether they received advanced notice.

Foreign Laws

It would be dangerous for the CIA to snatch an Italian resident without no-
tifying the Italian government. The political danger is that the Italians would
not react well to an invasion of their sovereignty. For one thing, the Italians may
lessen their support for American activities in Afghanistan, Iraq, and on many
other fronts against terrorism. Failure to provide the Italians with notice also
creates an operational danger. By providing advanced notice, the CIA officers
might eliminate or minimize the chances that an Italian police officer on the
Milan street, concerned that a kidnapping was taking place, would try to stop
the operation through force. Moreover, if the Americans do not have permission for the snatch, they would be subject to prosecution in Italy for kidnapping or related charges.

In a twist of fate, an Italian magistrate did indict over a dozen CIA officers
for their alleged role in Abu Omar's snatch. This indictment, perhaps for public consumption in Italy, should not be shocking in the United States, though.
CIA officers are accustomed to breaking the laws of other countries. On a daily
basis, they encourage citizens from foreign countries to commit espionage and
to subject themselves to great risks. Nonetheless, CIA officers, advised by CIA
lawyers, tend not to take unnecessary risks; they do not expose themselves to
the laws of foreign countries unless there is a strong countervailing interest.
All in all, in the Abu Omar operation it was in the CIA's interest to notify its
Italian allies.

To reassure the CIA, the Bush administration made clear that CIA officers
will not be transferred back to Italy, by regular or irregular means, to face the
criminal charges related to Abu Omar. Extradition and rendition, it seems, are
more often practiced on suspected terrorists than on American officials.

American Law

American law on rendition is quite complicated. Possible references include
the Constitution, statutes, regulations, and the self-executed and congres-

sionally adopted portions of international treaties. Because irregular rendition relates to non-U.S. citizens transferred between two foreign jurisdictions, some commentators have argued that the Constitution does not provide any protections.[11] The suspects are, by this argument, outside the American rule of law. Many other commentators, encouraged by the Supreme Court's decision that gave Guantanamo detainees access to American courts,[12] argue that the suspected terrorists are entitled to due process. Even if those subjected to rendition receive some protections, it is not clear how much process they are due.

The Convention Against Torture

The United States has ratified the Convention against Torture (CAT)[13] and the International Covenant on Civil and Political Rights (ICCPR).[14] In general, both these treaties aim to eliminate the torture or inhumane treatment of prisoners. The CAT, however, is more specific on the practice of rendition. Article 3 of the CAT states that a prisoner should not be transferred if there are "substantial grounds" for believing he will be tortured in the receiving country. American law, according to the Senate's understanding of the CAT, interprets substantial grounds to mean "more likely than not." As a matter of policy, this is the standard the Bush administration used on renditions from Guantanamo and perhaps on renditions from points farther outside United States jurisdiction.[15] Although the Bush administration kept the courts from assessing the likelihood of torture upon transfer, the administration did claim, primarily through the State Department's legal adviser, to have assessed the risks of torture in a realistic manner and to have taken measures to lower those risks. It expected the public to take these claims on faith.

The CAT is key. Not only is the CAT a possible source of law on renditions, it serves as a simple proxy for other possible sources such as due process and customary international law. Even if other sources do apply, their protections are unlikely to go much farther than the CAT's.

---

11. *See, e.g.*, John Yoo, *Transferring Terrorists*, 79 Notre Dame L. Rev. 1183, 1184 (2004).

12. *Rasul v. Bush*, 542 U.S. 466, 484 (2004).

13. Convention Against Torture and Other Cruel, Inhuman or Degrading Treatment or Punishment, *adopted* Dec. 10, 1984, 1465 U.N.T.S. 85 (*entered into force* June 26, 1987).

14. The International Covenant on Civil and Political Rights, Mar. 23 1976, 999 U.N.T.S. 171. The ICCPR does not factor very much into my analysis since I accept the Bush administration's statement that it "does not impose a non-refoulement obligation."

15. As a matter of law, the Bush administration seems to have relied on John Yoo's argument, based on a parallel to the Refugee Convention, that the CAT is limited to transfers from United States territory to other countries.

After the CAT was ratified, Congress revised the federal code to conform American law to the international convention. Congress passed a torture statute[16] and then enacted legislation[17] that required the "relevant agencies" to put regulations in place "not to expel, extradite, or otherwise effect the involuntary return of any person to a country in which there are substantial grounds for believing the person would be in danger of being subjected to torture, regardless of whether the person is physically present in the United States." Accordingly, the CAT affects extraditions, immigration removals, and irregular renditions. United States regulations, in basic terms, track the language of the CAT to preclude people from being sent to places where they will be tortured. The Justice Department, the Department of Homeland Security, and the State Department, all complying with the congressional act, enacted regulations that applied the CAT standard. By such compliance, it seemed that the United States, once upon a time, was ready to lead the world in bringing government behavior up to the level of decency and humanity.

The CIA, however, is notably silent about any regulations like those at Justice, Homeland Security, and State. Perhaps the CIA does not consider itself a relevant agency. Indeed, the CIA treats the existence or non-existence of a regulation regarding transfers of people as classified information. This classified treatment increases the difficulty of determining whether and how the CIA follows the CAT. As a result, the public experiences a substantial gap in knowledge about American counterterrorism policies, especially when it perceives the CIA as the main practitioner of America's program of irregular rendition.

The State Department's former legal adviser, John Bellinger, much like the lawyers who work for the CIA, was crafty in protecting the CIA from significant scrutiny on irregular rendition. Although Mr. Bellinger has said that the United States complies with the CAT on transfers from Guantanamo, he was careful to carve out the CIA from this compliance on other possible transfers. Further, when Mr. Bellinger appeared before the International Committee of Jurists which oversees compliance with the CAT, he excluded the CIA from his report. So, when it comes to the CIA, everybody is left guessing.

Applying the "More Likely Than Not" Standard

To determine whether the person about to be transferred faces a risk of torture, the executive branch is committed to examining the totality of the cir-

---

16. 18 U.S.C. § 2340A (2004).

17. Foreign Affairs Reform and Reconstructing Act, Pub. L. No. 105-277, div. G, 112 Stat. 2681–761 (codified in scattered sections of 8, 22, and 42 U.S.C.).

cumstances. The CAT refers to the risk of mistreatment in the receiving country as "substantial grounds." As the CAT notes: "For purposes of determining whether there are such grounds, the competent authorities shall take into account all relevant considerations including, where applicable, the existence in the State concerned of a consistent pattern of gross, flagrant, or mass violations of human rights." Under the CAT, the inquiry is not whether there is some risk of torture; there always is. The objective inquiry, perhaps not capable of mathematical precision, is whether it is more likely than not that torture will occur. If yes, transfer may not occur; if no, transfer may.

At least two sets of variables affect the calculation of whether it is more likely than not that a person will be tortured upon transfer: first, conditions in the receiving country and second, facts about the person to be transferred. To assess the human rights record of the receiving country, the executive branch—and a special court, as proposed below—should refer to the State Department's reports on human rights practices, to reports from reputable human rights organizations, and to books and articles available in the public record about various countries. This public record can be supplemented by classified analyses from the State Department, the Directorate of National Intelligence, and the CIA.

Regarding the individual factors, the executive branch should determine what experiences, if any, the person about to be rendered has had with the receiving country. The executive branch should hear from that person, recognizing that he has an interest in maximizing the perceptions about the risk of torture. Was he persecuted there? Have members of his family been mistreated? Is he from a religious or ethnic group that is not in favor? These questions should be answered with diligence and honesty.

If the executive is committed to getting at the truth on a particular rendition, it can draw on classified sources. The executive branch should hear from all parts of the government, recognizing that some of them have an interest in downplaying the risk of torture. As a supplement, the CIA may use clandestine means to gather information about the receiving country's leaders. As examples, the CIA can request information from the receiving country's intelligence service or from other intelligence services that gather information about the receiving country. The French intelligence services, as a result of their colonial experiences in Africa, may know more about conditions in Algeria than the American services. Sometimes all one has to do is ask friends.

As a result of a careful weighing of such factors on rendition, some countries will emerge as clean candidates. Others will be too dirty for further analysis. Still others will present close calls.

Assurances of Proper Treatment

To reach toward legality on irregular renditions, the executive branch can use two basic techniques: assurances of proper treatment from the receiving country and monitoring of the person's situation after he has been transferred. Those two techniques are most important on close calls, say, in a rendition to Bulgaria. They are less important on calls at the extremes. Assurances are probably not necessary in a rendition to Finland, a country with one of the world's best human rights records. Conversely, assurances are probably not enough in a rendition to Syria, a country with one of the world's worst human rights records.

Assurances can take many forms. They can be oral or in writing. They can be general, stating that the receiving country will comply with the CAT. Or they can be specific, listing tactics such as water-boarding, bombarding with music, and sleep deprivation which both the sending and receiving countries may agree are disallowed. The assurances can come from the head of state, addressed to the American president. Or they can come from a cabinet minister, whether in law enforcement, the foreign ministry, the intelligence services, or some combination of these agencies. If symmetry is necessary for the protocol, an assurance from the law enforcement side should be addressed to the Attorney General, one from the foreign ministry to the Secretary of State, and one from the intelligence services to the Director of National Intelligence (or to his subordinate, the Director of the CIA). Moreover, a high-level assurance can be combined with a low-level assurance, for instance, from the head of the detention facility in which the rendered suspect will be held.

The human rights community does not put much faith in assurances. It doubts that the actual practice of obtaining assurances is sincere. It has called them shams and empty promises, among other names. In its view, assurances are worthless pieces of paper that distract from the winks and nods that occur between the intelligence services on the two sides of a rendition. But to the extent these assurances are in fact sincere, they do make a difference in irregular rendition—at which point the gap between the views of the human rights community and mine would be narrowed.

Post-Transfer Monitoring

Post-transfer monitoring offers more possibilities. Yet the Bush administration, relying mainly on assurances, gave less attention to monitoring the prisoner's situation after transfer to a foreign country. Before a transfer, the executive branch could make the transfer contingent on some sort of monitoring of the prisoner's situation.[18] This monitoring could take place through technology, whether photographs, videotapes, or interrogation logs. Additionally, this monitoring could include outside visits. The more frequent the visits and the less notice required in advance of a visit, the better. Third-party visits from the International Committee of the Red Cross and similar organizations mean more than visits by American diplomats and intelligence officers because third-parties are more neutral and less likely to have a bias in showing, after the fact, that the irregular rendition had been done in accordance with the CAT.

Going further, in a sort of secret spot-checking, the CIA could use other means to confirm that the prisoner is being properly treated in the foreign country. These checks could be reported back to the president and to the secret court, as discussed below, in my proposal for more oversight.

Again, so much depends on the sincerity of the executive branch on irregular rendition. From now on, the United States should do much more to show that it is complying with the CAT when carrying out irregular renditions that serve the nation's counterterrorism policies.

Due Process

A person who is about to be transferred by rendition, somebody who is not a United States citizen or a resident alien, may dispute the notion that the CAT provides a cap on his due process rights. He might claim that the Fifth Amendment entitles him to additional protections. How one responds to that claim depends on whether the Fifth Amendment is viewed more as a restraint on government conduct or as an entitlement for members of our community. The restraint argument, it seems, would be less influenced by the citizenship of the person about to be transferred and more on making sure that the executive branch behaves properly and reasonably.

Not many would dispute that the person about to be transferred, regardless of citizenship, has a substantive interest that is being affected. His liberty has been restrained by the snatch, and will continue to be restrained in the custody of the receiving country. In addition, if the receiving country is Egypt, Morocco, or Syria, a mistake on a rendition decision, be it innocent or illicit, would result in high chances of physical and psychological mistreatment upon transfer. For these reasons, the interests at play in an irregular rendition are as high as, if not higher than, the termination of welfare payments[19] or disability payments,[20] interests at the heart of two leading cases on due process. Through evo-

---

18. How such a condition would be enforced is another matter.
19. *Goldberg v. Kelly*, 397 U.S. 254 (1970).

lution from these cases, rendition may be able to establish a jurisprudence of due process in the age of terror.

For irregular rendition, the debate under the Fifth Amendment of the United States Constitution could be more about procedures than the substance of rights. As to procedures, there are a multitude of questions. Is the prisoner entitled to a hearing before the transfer? If so, how extensive should the hearing be? Should he be represented by counsel? If he is indigent, should the government pay for counsel? If the hearing is delayed until after the transfer, what recourse will there be if the United States later accepts that the transfer was improper? As one response, the United States could set aside money in an American account for the person's damages. More important to the abused prisoner, in verified cases of abuse, the United States must use its power of persuasion to convince the receiving country to transfer the prisoner back to the United States or to another country which has a better human rights record.

Customary International Law

Customary international law[21] may also affect the legality of rendition. Whenever possible, American officials should practice rendition in compliance with international law, including the CAT and the ICCPR. Yet, for two reasons, my discussion of customary international law concerning irregular rendition is not so elaborate. First, customary international law on rendition is less precise than the relevant American statutes and regulations. Second, it has been the position of the Justice Department's Office of Legal Counsel, whether under Democrats or Republicans, that the president may act contrary to international law if necessary to execute the Constitution and other American laws.

Thus, my perspective on irregular rendition differs from that of the human rights community. The human right community starts high from customary international law, working down through treaties, conventions, statutes, and regulations. I tend to start low, working up through regulations, statutes, conventions, and treaties. In reality, my analysis corresponds with how American policymakers, aided by their lawyers, approach the problem of irregular rendition. While American policymakers often mention the "more likely than not" standard which stems from the CAT, they spend less time discussing customary international law.

---

20. *Mathews v. Eldridge*, 424 U.S. 319 (1976).

21. By this, I mean the common practices of nation-states which are in line with prevailing opinions of law.

The Policymaker's Pros and
Cons of Rendition

Government lawyers are asked to assess rendition's legality when policymakers are dissatisfied with extradition as the sole method for transferring suspected terrorists. Policy drives the law. American policymakers are not going to admit, even if it were true, that the purpose of rendition is to extract information from suspects through abusive interrogations. Such candor is not an attribute of politicians. Thus, the Bush administration was adamant in denying that the purpose of irregular rendition is, to borrow Jane Mayer's term, an "outsourcing" of torture. On the other hand, American policymakers have not been very specific about any legitimate reasons for rendition.

Unless a decision has been made to prosecute a suspected terrorist here, American policymakers will hesitate to bring him into American territory. Even with non-U.S. citizens, the deeper the suspect gets into United States territory, the stronger his argument for due process. The stronger the case for due process, the less room there is for CIA interrogators to conduct aggressive interrogations. Therefore, if the decision has been made that an aggressive interrogation is necessary, the suspect will probably stay outside the United States.

Outside United States territory, a follow-up decision is whether an interrogation will be conducted by Americans, by foreign officials, or by some combination of forces. Strictly speaking, a rendition occurs only when the United States transfers the suspect to another jurisdiction. In other words, a rendition will not have occurred if the United States, with permission from another country, maintains full control over the suspect—whether in an acknowledged site or in a "black" site.

The Case for Irregular/Extraordinary Rendition

Despite the reticence of American politicians, there is a case for rendition. American policymakers may say, in private, that they use irregular rendition because they do not have sufficient space in American facilities. That argument is not so convincing, however, given the size of the facilities at Guantanamo and the number of people Americans have detained in Iraq. It also does not explain why the transfer must occur in an abbreviated process.

A related argument is that it is safer for the custodians if a transfer occurs. Soon after 9/11, American forces detained hundreds of people in Afghanistan as a result of strikes on al Qaeda and Taliban strongholds. Because of the ongoing attacks from al Qaeda and the Taliban and because of inadequate facilities in that war-torn country, it made sense to transfer some prisoners to other countries.

Later, in the struggle against terror, the CIA is reported to have played a role in some high-level captures in Pakistan, taking Abu Zubaydah in March 2002 and Khaled Sheikh Mohammed in March 2003. If the Pakistanis cooperated on these captures, the Pakistani leader, Pervez Musharraf, probably did not want to deal with the repercussions of holding senior members of al Qaeda within his country. They were too hot to handle. If Musharraf did not want them, the choice for Americans was to take control of them or to transfer them to some country that did want them.

Other countries may have a stronger interest than the United States in taking control of a suspected terrorist. He may be a citizen of that country. He may be wanted on criminal charges. He may be sought for questioning by the foreign intelligence service. For such reasons, rather than move foreign intelligence officers as well as their files and witnesses, it may be more practical to transfer the suspected terrorist to the interested country. Further, the foreign country probably has plenty of people who speak the suspected terrorist's native language, obviating the need for interpreters to help the Americans and adding to the effectiveness of the interrogation.

Finally, by giving foreign officials a suspected terrorist they would like to question, it will be easier for the CIA, down the line, to convince that country to give the United States control of a suspect the CIA would like to question. In the free market between intelligence services, people can be traded just like pieces of information.

The Case Against Irregular/Extraordinary Rendition

There is a strong case against extraordinary rendition. One should be cautious—especially about practices that take place in the shadows—about a concentration of too much power in one branch of government. Indeed, for some American Founders, such a concentration was the definition of tyranny.[22]

Soon after 9/11, the White House asked for quick and broad changes to the laws that applied to American counterterrorism. Within a few days, Congress passed an Authorization for Use of Military Force that empowered the president to "use all necessary and appropriate force" against those responsible for

---

22. "The accumulation of all powers, legislative, executive, and judiciary, in the same hands ... may justly be pronounced the very definition of tyranny." The Federalist No. 47, at 301 (James Madison) (Clinton Rossiter ed., 1961).

the 9/11 attacks.[23] The Patriot Act[24] was also passed, adding to executive power and breaking down walls between the law enforcement and intelligence sectors of the American government. These powers were not enough, though, for a power-hungry president and a vice-president who wanted to settle old scores with Congress. Hooked on the high of a unitary executive, President Bush and Vice President Cheney both kept going back to their own branch for a quick fix.

In 2004, when the Supreme Court was hearing *Hamdi v. Rumsfeld*[25] on whether a United States citizen could be designated an enemy combatant and *Rasul v. Bush* on whether the Guantanamo detainees deserved access to American courts, the then-Deputy Solicitor General, Paul Clement, kept pushing extreme arguments for the executive. Clement's argument was that Hamdi could be designated an enemy combatant on the president's say-so and that the Guantanamo detainees did not deserve American justice. "Trust us," Clement seemed to say, "You are in good hands with this government." Between the time of the oral argument and the Supreme Court's decisions in the two cases, the photographs and other evidence of abuse at Abu Ghraib leaked out for the world to see. After that, Clement was in a spot.

After Abu Ghraib, except for those who were most indifferent to signals from the courts, from Congress, and from international opinion, it became much more difficult to defend complete deference to the president in waging his self-described War on Terrorism. It became time to retreat back to the center, a process that continues to this day with intermediate stops at the McCain Amendment in 2005,[26] the *Hamdan v. Rumsfeld*[27] decision in 2006, and the Military Commissions Act of 2006.[28] Although some politicians have now adopted the policy of radical centrism, the country has still not found a sustainable middle ground on detention, interrogation, rendition, and on many other practices in the long-term of American counterterrorism. Radical skepticism, of the Humean and other varieties, still permeates the national mood.

---

23. Authorization for the Use of Military Force, Pub. L. No. 107-40, 115 Stat. 224 (2004).

24. Uniting and Strengthening America by Providing Appropriate Tools Required to Intercept and Obstruct Terrorism (USA PATRIOT Act) Act of 2001, Pub. L. No. 107-56, 115 Stat. 272.

25. 542 U.S. 507 (2004).

26. Detainee Treatment Act of 2005, Pub. L. No. 109-148, 119 Stat. 2680, §§ 1001–1006 (2005).

27. 126 S. Ct. 2749 (2006).

28. Military Commissions Act of 2006, Pub. L. No. 109-366, 120 Stat. 2600 (2006).

A defender of executive power might try to limit the mistakes since 9/11 to the Pentagon. Guantanamo and Abu Ghraib, after all, have been Department of Defense facilities. The defender might argue that the CIA is nimble, agile, and special, not prone to the bungling of the military. That argument, though, would be based more on fantasy than fact. As highlighted in a recent book,[29] the CIA is more like the Department of Education than the images of omnipotence projected in popular spy novels. The CIA makes mistakes—many of them. But the cloak of secrecy over CIA activities, in conflict with American values of transparency and democracy, prevents the public from knowing the full truth about the dark side of American foreign policy. That cloak even prohibits former CIA officials, like this one, from telling too much of what goes on in the sausage factory. Not subject to much challenge, the CIA still says, by a tired bit of marketing, that its triumphs are always hidden, its failures always trumpeted. That is more self-justification than self-awareness.

All fantasies aside, the United States government does not operate with the precision of a neurosurgeon. It has made mistakes on irregular renditions. Two mistakes stand out: the cases of Khaled el-Masri and Maher Arar.[30] Both men filed lawsuits against the United States, but the executive's assertion of the state secrets privilege in Masri's case and jurisdictional challenges in Arar's case have prevented them from reaching the merits.

Masri, a German citizen of Lebanese origin, was having heated disagreements with his wife in Germany. To unwind and to take some distance from his domestic problems, he traveled to the Balkans. At the end of 2003, he garnered the attention of the Macedonian security services since his name matched that of a person they had connected to al Qaeda plots. Masri told them they had the wrong guy, but, while in Macedonian control, he did not receive a judicial hearing to contest his innocence. Moreover, the Macedonian officials did not pay much attention to his denials of any connection to terrorism because they figured he was applying standard al Qaeda training to keep them guessing with disinformation.

The Macedonians, to curry favor with their American friends, handed their prize over to the CIA. The CIA, in turn, is said to have put Masri, stripped and sedated, on a plane for Afghanistan—although it is still not clear who took control of him upon arrival, Americans or Afghanis. Masri claims he received rough treatment in an Afghan prison facility. His captors may have con-

---

29. Tim Weiner, Legacy of Ashes: The History of the CIA (Doubleday 2007).

30. My narrative about these cases draws only from the public record, taking both Masri's and Arar's allegations to be true.

fused him with somebody else with a similar name. They had a good Masri, it turned out, not a bad one.

In the end, Masri was dumped in Albania from where he made his way back home to Germany. Although American officials have not apologized to him or acknowledged their mistake, the German leader, Angela Merkel, made clear that her American allies had done something wrong.[31] As a result, criminal charges were filed in Germany against those CIA officers accused of participating in Masri's rendition and interrogation, and a European commission heightened its investigation into alleged CIA abuses. Following his civil case against the United States,[32] Masri has been in the news for several years. Overall, the Masri case is one black eye for the CIA.

The second black eye for America's program of irregular rendition comes from Maher Arar, a dual citizen of Syria and Canada. In 2002, Arar arrived from Switzerland at New York's Kennedy airport. Hoping to connect on a flight to Canada, he was making his way back home for a business meeting. At the checkpoint, Arar presented his passport to the immigration officer. Unfortunately for Arar, when the INS officer entered Arar's name into the system, the result was an indication that he was a "lookout ... of a known terrorist organization." For thirteen days, Arar was detained and interrogated within the United States. Although Arar did receive the attention of an INS regional director, he was not allowed to challenge his detention before a judge. The Justice Department, intoxicated in the same way as the Pentagon and the CIA, exercised its own discretion.

When Arar learned that he was headed for Syria, he pleaded with his American captors, certain that he would be tortured there. But the Americans ignored or discounted his fears. At the end of Arar's interrogation in the United States, he was sent back not to Canada, but to Jordan, where he was met and transported by car to Syria.

Arar's treatment in the "Palestine branch" of a Syrian prison was harsh; he alleges that the only times he was released from a cramped cell were to be tortured by merciless Syrian interrogators. Having received tips from the Amer-

---

31. Glenn Kessler, *Rice to Admit German's Abduction Was Error*, WASH. POST., Dec. 7, 2005, at A18.

32. The Supreme Court declined to accept his case. *El-Masri v. U.S.*, No. 06-1613, 2007 WL 1646914, at *1 (U.S. Oct. 9, 2007). Therefore, the Fourth Circuit's ruling stands, affirming the district court's dismissal of the civil suit because of the executive's assertion of the state secrets privilege. *El-Masri v. U.S.*, 479 F.3d 296, 313 (holding that "[I]n view of these considerations we recognize the gravity of our conclusion that el-Masri must be denied a judicial forum for his complaint, and reiterate our past observation that dismissal on state secrets grounds is appropriate").

icans and the Canadians, the Syrians clearly suspected that Arar was connected to al Qaeda or other terrorist groups. The source of this suspicion may have been faulty information from the Canadians, guilt by association for his contacts in Ottawa. (In a step back from Syria, this faulty information may have served as the basis of the alert in the computer system of American immigration authorities.)

In Syria, as horrible as his conditions were, Arar was not completely cut off from his home. The consul from the Canadian embassy in Damascus was allowed to visit Arar several times in prison. Months into Arar's captivity, and despite his fears of retaliation from the Syrian interrogators, he eventually told the Canadian consul that he was innocent and was being tortured. Next, perhaps in response to pressure from the Canadian government, the Syrians, without any convincing evidence other than coerced confessions from Arar, released him to Canada.

After Arar's release, an official Canadian Commission of Inquiry, separate from the Canadian executive branch, pursued a thorough investigation into the Arar case. This inquiry led to an official admission of fault, an apology to Arar, and a huge payment from the Canadian government. As far as the Canadians were concerned, Arar was a case of mistaken identity. But the Americans, not learning from their neighbors, are not so contrite. In search of justice, Arar still pursues a civil case against the United States. His last stop was the full panel for the Second Circuit Court of Appeals, in December 2008. For now, Arar—and Masri—show that more mistakes than apologies have flowed from America's rendition program.

A Middle Ground

Just because the CIA has made some mistakes does not mean all its operations should be shut down. To be effective on rendition and other activities, the CIA must be able to protect secrets. Human sources will not commit espionage, risking their lives to provide the CIA with valuable information, unless the CIA protects them. Foreign intelligence services will not share information with American intelligence agencies unless the United States continues to show that it can protect sources and methods. If the CIA were to capture Osama bin Laden, for example, it would be good tradecraft not to let the world know. The CIA could use bin Laden, having him communicate with operatives through email, phone calls, and couriers, to draw in more of the al Qaeda network. In this way, one nasty fish would serve as bait to catch more nasty fish.

A foreign intelligence service might only agree to accept a suspected terrorist or to transfer a suspected terrorist if the United States keeps the cooperation a secret. Because foreign officials fear reaction by their own populations, many countries are willing to cooperate on American intelligence activities only if that cooperation is kept secret. For these and many other reasons, there is no doubt that the CIA must be allowed a degree of secrecy to get the job done.

The question for American democracy is not whether to have secrecy. The question is how much. Measuring the proper balance between secrecy and democracy is done, alas, more on hunches than on empirical data. The relative weight that American citizens place on liberty and security depends on differences in their values, on the points at which they are willing to trade one value for another. In short, a precise regression analysis is not possible for determining the proper balance between liberty and security.

One hunch, supported by many in the human rights community, is that the Bush administration conducted its counterterrorism policies with too much secrecy. American counterterrorism could thus benefit from some transparency. The American public, preferring light to darkness, would provide greater support if it could see the wisdom to executive discretion. The ripples of confidence would spread to American allies and the rest of the world.

The Masri and Arar cases, as noted, are blows to American prestige. The American public might expect mistakes to be made when thousands of people are rounded up on conventional battlefields in Afghanistan or Iraq. Yet, the CIA, separate from the military, has created the impression that its operations are much more streamlined, much less prone to error. The CIA, cheered on by Hollywood adaptations of Tom Clancy and Robert Ludlum novels, has bought into the myth of its own invincibility. So an American public that sees magic on the big screen does not expect mistakes in the field of rendition, a fact especially true for a program whose scope is limited to about one hundred suspects. Hiding behind a veil of secrecy on one or two cases of mistaken identity is unacceptable.

Rather than try to hide all mistakes, the United States should be more open about them to prevent their repetition. As a part of this improvement, the CIA should encourage the American public to be more realistic. Mistakes, no doubt, will be made. The task is to do everything within reason to prevent those mistakes while keeping the nation safe. The challenge is to do so with less than total secrecy.

Letting Go of Criminal Justice

Another downside to irregular rendition is that it creates an exception to the criminal justice system, the preferred model for putting people into cages. Rendition, so the critics say, eats away at America's rule of law. In the criminal justice system, suspects are taken with promptness to the nearest available magistrate. They are informed of the charges against them and are represented by counsel. Before a defendant is convicted, federal prosecutors must convince a grand jury and then a petit jury of the defendant's guilt. At trial, the burden of proof is beyond a reasonable doubt. During the trial, a judge, defense lawyer, the media, and the public observe the proceedings to ensure that they are fair.

Irregular rendition, by contrast, excludes the judges and the suspects' lawyers. Full process is traded for an abbreviated process, and the level of suspicion against the suspected terrorist is not clearly delineated. Suspects can be snatched on hunches rather than on proof.

Rendition, of course, is not the only exception to the criminal justice system. People are confined during quarantines and through civil commitment for mental illness. Such confinement can be based on something other than proof beyond a reasonable doubt. When the risks and dangers are acute in the struggle against terror, prevention of bad acts may take precedence over punishment for those acts. That is the new American reality.

Just because some exceptions to the criminal justice system have been made does not mean that an exception must be made for renditions. Analogies only go so far. Yet, the possibilities of quarantines and civil commitments under American law are useful reminders to those who claim criminal justice is the only model for detention.

Even the criminal justice system recognizes situations when a dangerous person will not be given any process. Note that FBI agents will be in the right if they shoot a fleeing felon who is armed, dangerous, and combative, showing no signs of surrender without a fight. Indeed, FBI agents are trained to react to such emergencies.

Extradition as a Solution

So how can the process for transferring suspected terrorists be improved? Purists in the debate are inclined toward banning irregular rendition. They oppose snatches on the front-end, and they only accept prosecution as the purpose for the back-end. In their view, people should not be transferred against their will for intelligence gathering—only for law enforcement.

The purists distrust any process that does not include courts and foreign ministries. For them, formal arrest and extradition are the necessary components of transferring people between jurisdictions. As a matter of policy or as a strict interpretation of American law, they might require that all transfers be conducted either by knowing, intelligent, and voluntary consent, or by extradition.

An advantage of extradition is its accepted status under international law. Countries, not people, enter into extradition treaties and carry them out. These treaties can be bilateral or multi-lateral, and usually provide for transfers only for law enforcement purposes. One country asks another country to take control of a person in its jurisdiction and then to transfer the person back to the requesting country. Spain, for example, asked the United Kingdom to transfer Augusto Pinochet, the former Chilean leader, to face charges for killing Spanish citizens in Chile during a dark reign of bringing order to his country.

Under most extradition treaties, the requesting country provides a detailed and credible summary of the criminal case against the person it would like transferred. In Pinochet's case, this was handled by the Spanish magistrate, Baltasar Garzon. The requested country, to be sure, will not just put the person on a plane for transfer. The courts and the foreign ministry in the requested country will review the request. The person who is the subject of the request, aided by legal counsel, will be able to challenge the request for extradition, and, even if the charges are credible, he may be able to convince the requested country that he faces a significant risk of torture or mistreatment if he is extradited.[33]

Under extradition, even if the charges are credible and even if there is no risk of torture or mistreatment, the requested country usually retains some political discretion not to go through with an extradition. Many countries have carve-outs that do not require them to extradite to jurisdictions that use the death penalty. These carve-outs, of course, complicate some American requests to other countries for extradition. In addition, many countries refuse to extradite if the crime which is the basis of the extradition is deemed "political" or does not exist in the requested country. These carve-outs sometimes cause complications when the basis of an American request is a violation of the Foreign Corrupt Practices Act, a bribery statute that rarely has a counterpart in foreign criminal codes.

In contrast to irregular rendition, extradition has many disadvantages for American policymakers. Extradition does not address the trading of information and people that goes on between intelligence services. Instead, extradition, with the assistance of the courts and the foreign ministries, is a match-making between justice departments. Extradition is slow and burdensome. Not all countries have extradition treaties, and even those that do have not been so responsive to requests for assistance from the United States. In this sense, the Alvarez-Machain and Yunis scenarios have been revisited. It

---

33. The vast majority of countries in the world has ratified the CAT.

would be one thing if al Qaeda operatives were all concentrated in Canada. It is another thing when al Qaeda is scattered around the globe in countries such as Afghanistan, Iran, Libya, Pakistan, Saudi Arabia, Syria, and Sudan. Extradition, at best, is a partial solution.

A Statutory Solution

Another solution is necessary. For that solution, I no longer trust the executive, on its own, to do the right thing regarding rendition. So John Yoo is left to one side. Nor do I expect Article III courts to take care of all our problems in the age of terror. So Amnesty International is left to another side. My solution lies somewhere in the middle.

Having served in the Justice Department and the CIA, I appreciate the need for decisiveness. If the president always hesitates, crimes go unsolved, lives are lost, and the nation is threatened. Now that weapons of mass destruction are not limited to the arsenals of governments and are capable of being used by lone lunatics, the need for decisiveness is pronounced.

No law is higher for Americans than the Constitution. In our system, as Abraham Lincoln reminded the American public during the pain of the Civil War, protecting the nation against internal and external dangers is the president's highest duty. "Are all the laws, but one," he asked, "to go unexecuted, and the government itself to go to pieces, lest that one be violated?"[34] In other words, sometimes the laws are bent to serve the nation. If the nation does not survive, its Constitution would be meaningless.

The president has many powers. He (or she)[35] is vested with the executive power, serves as our commander in chief, and appoints our ambassadors. The president provides the nation's sole voice in diplomacy, and is given great leeway in deciding what information is secret or classified. Clearly, some secrecy is required for the president to carry out diplomatic, military, and intelligence functions. Rendition falls within the scope of these powers and functions.

In constructing the nation's policy on irregular rendition, the president rests on more solid ground if he combines his powers with those of the other elected branch. If President George W. Bush had toned down his politics, he could have placed himself more firmly in the first category of Justice Jackson's famous concurrence from the Steel Seizure Case. "When the President acts pur-

---

34. Abraham Lincoln, Speech to Special Session of Congress (July 4, 1861), *reprinted in* 4 THE COLLECTED WORKS OF ABRAHAM LINCOLN 430 (Roy P. Basler ed., 1953).

35. Read this to mean the possibility of President Hillary Clinton.

suant to an express or implied authorization of Congress, his authority is at its maximum, for it includes all that he possesses in his own right plus all that Congress can delegate." That is the position of good government.

George W. Bush is correct that the conflict with international terrorism is real, a conflict that will span generations. For this reason, he should have done more to motivate the American people and other parts of their government for the long haul. Two presidential terms of irregular renditions, based mainly on executive prerogative, is too long. The time has come to deepen the support through moderation.

Learning from the errors in the Masri and Arar cases, our president should seek congressional authorization for the practice of irregular rendition. This authorization would put to rest any arguments that the president may only use extradition to exchange suspected terrorists with other countries. The president should propose a statute by which a special court, along the lines of the FISA court, is created to review irregular renditions.

If the president is concerned that he is whittling away presidential powers by asking for Congress's support, he should include a statement that the request for authority does not mean the president lacked such authority on independent grounds. Rather than push the argument about a unitary executive to the point of absurdity, a responsible president can set clear markers to protect the constitutional balance.

The special court, respecting presidential prerogative, would not rule on the reasons for a transfer. Rather, it would protect the integrity of the process. Involving the court should reassure the American public and the rest of the world that the president sincerely abides by CAT standards when practicing irregular rendition. The proceedings in this court would be secret, and an ombudsman with a security clearance would appear on behalf of the person about to be transferred. Thus, the court could keep track of the number of renditions and of the identities of those being rendered. Just as important, the presence of the ombudsman would improve the analysis of whether it is more likely than not that the person will be tortured in the receiving country.

Those who oppose a congressional role in irregular rendition will compare the tactic of transferring and receiving suspected terrorists to decisions on the battlefield, to the movement and placement of tanks, destroyers, and bombers. Although the comparison is not farfetched, it is not enough to prevent Congress from regulating some aspects of irregular rendition. The urgency of battlefield decisions differs from the urgency of rendition decisions. Certainly, in a ticking time-bomb scenario, government officials will seek to gather information from the suspect in the quickest manner. That situation, however, is not identical to the process of transferring someone from one jurisdiction to another.

A transfer, whether by car, train, or plane, allows for and requires time. Elsewhere, the battlefield calls for quick decisions on whether to shoot, shell, or bomb. The question on the battlefield, in less than Shakespearean terms, is to kill or not to kill. If Congress tried to interfere in those decisions, it would be putting Americans in danger. The questions in rendition, by contrast, are to transfer or not to transfer, to detain or not to detain. The context is different. The conventional battlefield, to be clear, sometimes involves decisions about transfer and detention; often troops must decide whether enemy combatants are surrendering. There, killing is the primary activity, and surrender only becomes a possibility when the enemy combatant makes clear that he is no longer interested in killing.

Irregular rendition should not be conducted according to the full process of the criminal justice system. More flexibility is needed for a necessary tool of counterterrorism. Even so, rendition should not be a free for all. More care should be applied in transferring live bodies from place to place.

A middle course, on rendition and on many other things, is possible. Ours is the recipe of radical centrism, the best recipe for serving both safety and liberty.

Chapter 11

Homeland Security, Information Policy, and the Transatlantic Alliance

Stewart A. Baker* & Nathan Alexander Sales**

It's June 14, 2003, at Chicago's O'Hare International Airport. The U.S.-led war to topple Saddam Hussein's Ba'athist regime in Iraq was launched a little less than three months ago. Resurgent fears of terrorism have kept some passengers from the skies, but O'Hare is still operating at a fairly brisk pace.

A Jordanian man named Ra'ed al-Banna is among the throng of passengers who have just arrived on KLM flight 611 from Amsterdam. After waiting in line, al-Banna presents his passport to U.S. Customs and Border Protection officers. The CBP officers consult the computerized targeting system used to screen passengers who seek to enter the United States. The information about al-Banna—drawn from his airline reservations and past travel—triggers a closer look. The officers examine al-Banna's documents, and they begin asking him questions.

Something doesn't add up. Al-Banna has a legitimate Jordanian passport; he holds a valid visa that allows him to work in the United States; and he had visited the United States before for a lengthy stay. But the officers aren't satisfied that he's being completely truthful with his answers, so they decide to re-

---

* Distinguished Visiting Fellow, Center for Strategic and International Studies; Partner, Steptoe & Johnson LLP.

** Assistant Professor of Law, George Mason University School of Law. Messrs. Baker and Sales previously served at the U.S. Department of Homeland Security as Assistant Secretary for Policy and Deputy Assistant Secretary for Policy Development, respectively. The opinions expressed in this chapter are those of the authors alone, and do not reflect the views of current or former employers or clients. The authors are grateful to Jeremy Rabkin, Neomi Rao, Paul Rosenzweig, and Mike Scardaville for their helpful and insightful comments. Special thanks to Mark Bass for excellent research assistance.

fuse him admission. Al-Banna's fingerprints are taken, and he is put on a plane back to Jordan.

So far it sounds like a fairly routine day at the border. And it was, until events in Iraq nearly two years later gave it a new, and sinister, significance.

On February 28, 2005, at about 8:30 in the morning, several hundred police recruits were lined up outside a clinic in Hilla, a city in the south of Iraq. With no warning, a car drove into the crowd and detonated a massive bomb; 132 people were killed, and about as many were wounded. At the time, it was the deadliest suicide bombing Iraq had seen.

The driver was Ra'ed al-Banna. We know that because when authorities found the steering wheel of his car, his forearm was still chained to it.[1]

No one knows why al-Banna wanted to be in the United States in 2003, or what he would have done if he had gotten in. But we do know what kept him out—the government's ability to quickly marshal the data that first triggered a closer look, and that the CBP officer later used to question al-Banna closely and to conclude that his answers weren't satisfactory. At the center of that system was airline reservation data, known as Passenger Name Records, or "PNR."

In the years since 9/11, a consensus has emerged among American policymakers that a crucial way of preventing future attacks is to ensure that counterterrorism officials have access to new sources of information. A perceived need for better, more accurate, and more comprehensive data has animated virtually every major post-9/11 legislative innovation, from the USA PATRIOT Act of 2001 to the 9/11 Recommendations Implementation Act of 2007.

While this approach commands fairly broad support in the United States, it is not without its detractors—especially among America's traditional allies in Europe. Citing European data privacy norms, some European Union policymakers have tried to restrict the ability of the United States to gather, use, and share data for counterterrorism purposes. It is important not to overstate the magnitude of these transatlantic frictions; Washington and Brussels remain close friends and important strategic partners. Yet neither should the significance of this recent and growing trend be missed. Rather than acknowledging the right of the United States as a sovereign to pursue its own policy objectives, some in Europe have sought to export the Continent's data privacy laws to this country.

This chapter will consider the reasons for, implications of, and possible solutions to this growing rift between Washington and Brussels. Before we can turn to that, it's necessary to have a better understanding of how the govern-

---

1. Charlotte Buchen, *The Man Turned Away*, PBS, Oct. 10, 2006, *available at* http://www.pbs.org/wgbh/pages/frontline/enemywithin/reality/al-banna.html.

ment uses data at the border and its legal basis for doing so. Part I discusses the United States's use of various types of information in its efforts to detect and incapacitate terrorist operatives, especially the Department of Homeland Security's use of airline passenger reservation data. In Part II, we survey the legal authorities under which these activities are carried out. Part III examines the response of European policymakers to American efforts to gather and analyze passenger data and related information. In Part IV, we examine possible explanations for Europe's new enthusiasm for projecting its data privacy values globally, and consider solutions that will preserve both individual privacy and national autonomy.

I. PNR and Homeland Security

Information policy is a central front in the war on terrorism. First, the big picture. Since 9/11, Congress has enacted a number of measures designed to improve the flow of data to and within the government. For example, section 203 of the USA PATRIOT Act of 2001 authorizes the sharing of information acquired during grand jury proceedings and through electronic surveillance.[2] Section 218 of the same legislation tore down the "wall" that prevented intelligence officers from cooperating with agencies pursuing traditional criminal investigations.[3] Likewise, section 202 of the Homeland Security Act of 2002 granted the Secretary of Homeland Security access to "all" information in the government's possession that he deems relevant to terrorist threats against the United States.[4] And the Intelligence Reform and Terrorism Prevention Act of 2004 comprehensively restructured the U.S. Intelligence Community, including the creation of an "Information Sharing Environment" intended to facilitate the sharing of data among federal, state, and local players.[5]

Why has Congress devoted so much effort to reforming national security information policies? Because information—especially about the tiny handful of terrorist suspects trying to hide in a flood of travelers—allows a targeted response to the challenge of terrorism. Without good data, the United States is

---

2. Uniting and Strengthening America by Providing Appropriate Tools Required to Intercept and Obstruct Terrorism Act of 2001, §203, Pub. L. No. 107-56, 115 Stat. 272, 279 (2001).

3. *Id.* §218, 115 Stat. at 291; *see also In re*: Sealed Case, 310 F.3d 717 (FISCR 2002).

4. Homeland Security Act of 2002, §202, Pub. L. No. 107-296, 116 Stat. 2135, 2149-50 (2002).

5. Intelligence Reform and Terrorism Prevention Act of 2004, §1016, Pub. L. No. 108-458, 118 Stat. 3638, 3664–70 (2004).

stuck playing defense. And that's an expensive proposition. A dollar spent hardening a target against terrorist attack—say a nuclear power plant—will make that particular facility marginally more secure. But it does nothing to protect the nearby oil pipeline or skyscraper. By contrast, spending that same dollar to upgrade data collection and analysis capabilities better enables the government to detect and disrupt any number of terrorist plots.[6] In other words, Congress reasonably concluded that investments in intelligence reform would produce greater returns (measured in overall security against terrorist attacks) than investments in the security of individual potential targets.

One of the most crucial types of information available to counterterrorism officials is airline passenger reservation data. Consider what a terrorist must do to successfully bring off an attack. He must be trained; he must receive funding; he must meet with his handlers to receive direction; he must enter the country he means to strike; and he must case his intended targets. Each of those steps typically involves travel. That's why the 9/11 Commission emphasized that, for terrorists, the ability to travel is "as important as weapons."[7] And it called on the government to deploy "[i]nformation systems able to … detect potential terrorist indicators … at consulates, at primary border inspection lines, in immigration services offices, and in intelligence and enforcement units."[8]

Al Qaeda is dependent upon travel, and each time an operative boards a plane or crosses an international border, we have an opportunity to detect and capture him. Doing so requires that officials have access to information about airline passengers. In the trade, this data is known as "PNR," or Passenger Name Records. PNR consists of basic personal information that travelers provide to airlines or travel agents in the course of booking airline reservations. PNR is hardly a dossier of passengers' most intimate secrets. It typically includes pedestrian data such as name, passport number, frequent flyer number, address, telephone number, and so on. Airlines that fly to and from the United States are required by law to provide DHS this information (more on this requirement below). DHS then uses a computerized system—the Auto-

---

6. *Cf.* RICHARD A. POSNER, UNCERTAIN SHIELD: THE U.S. INTELLIGENCE SYSTEM IN THE THROES OF REFORM 209 (2006) (arguing that "[i]ntelligence is cheap relative to defensive measures such as hardening potential targets, sealing the nation's borders, and inspecting cargoes," but cautioning that "[i]ts cheapness is seductive, fostering the illusion that intelligence can be perfected at modest cost").

7. NAT'L COMM'N ON TERRORIST ATTACKS UPON THE U.S., THE 9/11 COMMISSION REPORT 384 (2004).

8. *Id.* at 385.

mated Targeting System, or "ATS"—to analyze the data to help determine which of the 87 million passengers who enter the United States by air each year should be subject to a little extra scrutiny.[9]

The information contained in PNR may be fairly simple, but it is a powerful analytical tool. At the most basic level, collecting PNR and passenger manifest data enables officials to check travelers' names against watchlists of known or suspected terrorists.[10] (It also enables the government to resolve potential false positives more expeditiously. Suppose one "U. Abdulmutallab"—a name that we'll further suppose appears on the no fly list—is traveling from London to JFK. If the only thing officials know about the passenger is his name, he likely is going to be pulled aside at Heathrow and asked a number of questions to establish his true identity. Making more information available to the government allows that process of identity resolution to take place behind the scenes, and more quickly. If officials have not just U. Abdulmutallab's name, but also his date of birth, his passport number, his fingerprints, and so on, it becomes possible to know immediately whether this is a man to worry about, or whether he's an innocent with the misfortune of sharing a name with an international terrorist. PNR thus is more than just a useful counterterrorism tool. It also has the potential to produce meaningful customer service benefits for individual travelers.)

More sophisticated analytics are possible as well. By using simple forms of link analysis, PNR makes it possible to discover hidden connections between known terrorists and their unknown associates. If a traveler has used the same phone number or mailing address as Khalid Shaikh Mohammed, mastermind of the September 11 plot, he probably merits a closer look than a typical airline passenger.

Let's dwell on that point for a moment. According to a Markle Foundation report, if counterterrorism investigators had been able before 9/11 to apply rudimentary link analysis techniques to airline reservation data and related information, they could have uncovered the ties among all 19 of the hijackers.

Start with two men who helped fly American Airlines flight 77 into the Pentagon: Nawaf Al-Hazmi and Khalid Al-Midhar. Their names appeared on a U.S. watchlist, because they previously had been spotted at a terrorist meeting in Malaysia. So they would have been flagged when they bought their tickets. Tugging on that thread would have revealed three other hijackers who used the same addresses as the first two: Salem Al-Hazmi, Marwan Al-Shehhi, and

---

9. *See* U.S. Customs and Border Protection, Automated Targeting System, System of Records, 72 Fed. Reg. 43,650, 43,651 (Aug. 6, 2007).

10. *See id.*

Mohamed Atta, the plot's operational ringleader. Officials would have discovered another hijacker (Majed Moqed) who used the same frequent-flyer number as Al-Midhar. Five other hijackers used the same phone numbers as Mohamed Atta: Fayez Ahmed, Mohand Alshehri, Wail Alshehri, Waleed Alshehri, and Abdulaziz Alomari. That's eleven of 19. Officials could have found a twelfth hijacker in an INS watch list for expired visas (Ahmed Alghamdi), and the remaining seven could have been flagged through him by matching other basic information.[11]

PNR is good for more than Monday morning quarterbacking; it has produced a number of tangible successes. For instance, in 2006, at Minneapolis-St. Paul airport, DHS officials used PNR data and other information to flag a high-risk traveler for additional scrutiny before he arrived. Once the passenger was referred to secondary inspection, it was discovered that he had a manual on how to make Improvised Explosive Devices, or "IEDs"—the kind of bombs terrorists use to kill and maim American forces in Iraq and Afghanistan. Inspecting the traveler's computer, officers also found video clips of IEDs being used to kill soldiers and destroy vehicles, as well as a video on martyrdom. The passenger later pled guilty to visa fraud.[12]

II. PNR and the Law of Data Privacy

The legal authorities—constitutional, statutory, and international—under which the United States collects and uses these sorts of information are fairly straightforward. Let's start with the Constitution. The Fourth Amendment's prohibition on unreasonable searches and seizures generally requires the government to obtain a search warrant before gaining access to facilities or information in which the holder has a "reasonable expectation of privacy."[13] Over the course of several decades, the Supreme Court has held that a person generally has no such reasonable expectation in data he voluntarily turns over to a third party in the ordinary course of business.

For example, the government need not obtain a search warrant before installing a pen register or trap and trace device—which collect data about the

---

11. Protecting America's Freedom in the Information Age: A Report of the Markle Foundation Task Force 28 (2002). One of the authors was a member of that task force.

12. See Remarks of Stewart Baker, Assistant Sec'y for Policy, Dep't of Homeland Security, at the Ctr. for Strategic and Int'l Studies (Dec. 19, 2006), http://www.dhs.gov/xnews/speeches/sp_1166557969765.shtm.

13. Katz v. United States, 389 U.S. 347, 360 (1967) (Harlan, J., concurring).

numbers dialed or received by a particular telephone, but not the content of the conversations themselves—because the caller necessarily reveals that information to the phone company when he places a call.[14] Nor is a warrant needed when the government asks a bank to turn over a customer's financial records. Because a "depositor takes the risk, in revealing his affairs to another, that the information will be conveyed by that person to the Government," a depositor has no "legitimate 'expectation of privacy' in … information voluntarily conveyed to the banks and exposed to their employees in the ordinary course of business."[15]

The "third party doctrine," as it is known, has come in for its fair share of criticism. Maybe more than its fair share. Orin Kerr has dubbed it "the *Lochner* of search and seizure law."[16] The leading criminal law treatise pronounces it "dead wrong,"[17] and other scholars aren't much more temperate in their denunciations.[18] More recently, Professor Kerr has mounted a defense of the doctrine, arguing that it is sound because it ensures technological neutrality. Under the third party doctrine, the same amount of privacy protection is available regardless of whether a criminal personally ventures into public spaces to commit his crimes, or remains in the private sphere by commissioning a third party to assist the criminal enterprise.[19]

Whatever the strengths or weaknesses of the third party doctrine, PNR is a fairly straightforward application of it. As is true with phone numbers and financial information, travelers provide basic personal data to airlines or travel agents in the ordinary course of booking a reservation—the name they wish

---

14. *See* Smith v. Maryland, 442 U.S. 735, 744 (1979) ("When he used his phone, petitioner voluntarily conveyed numerical information to the telephone company and 'exposed' that information to its equipment in the ordinary course of business. In so doing, petitioner assumed the risk that the company would reveal to police the numbers he dialed.").

15. United States v. Miller, 425 U.S. 435, 442, 443 (1976); *see also id.* at 443 ("[T]he Fourth Amendment does not prohibit the obtaining of information revealed to a third party and conveyed by him to Government authorities, even if the information is revealed on the assumption that it will be used only for a limited purpose and the confidence placed in the third party will not be betrayed.").

16. Orin S. Kerr, *The Case for the Third-Party Doctrine*, 107 MICH. L. REV. 561, 563 (2009) (citing Lochner v. New York, 198 U.S. 45 (1905)).

17. 1 WAYNE R. LaFAVE, SEARCH AND SEIZURE: A TREATISE ON THE FOURTH AMENDMENT § 2.7 (4th ed. 2004).

18. *See, e.g.*, Clark D. Cunningham, *A Linguistic Analysis of the Meanings of "Search" in the Fourth Amendment: A Search For Common Sense*, 73 IOWA L. REV. 541, 580 (1988) (indicating that the Supreme Court's third party decisions "top the chart of the most-criticized Fourth Amendment cases").

19. *See* Kerr, *supra* note 16, at 564-65.

to appear on the ticket, the method of payment, a phone number at which they can be contacted in the event there is a schedule change, and so on. Again, like phone numbers and financial data, providing this information to an airline doesn't simply help facilitate the transaction. The transaction wouldn't be possible without it. DHS's use of PNR thus fits pretty comfortably within established constitutional norms concerning government access to data voluntarily conveyed to third parties.

Even those who reject the Supreme Court's gloss on the Fourth Amendment—that a person *never* has a reasonable expectation of privacy in data turned over to third parties, no matter how sensitive it is or how narrowly he intends it to be distributed, because he assumes the risk it will find its way into the government's hands—can conclude that PNR works no undue harm to travelers' privacy interests. A narrower principle is available here. A depositor typically shares data with his bank in the expectation that the bank, as his agent, will protect it from further disclosures to outside entities. By contrast, a passenger may well benefit if airlines or travel agents provide his PNR data to the government. Doing so can lead to a better customer service experience at the border. In the absence of PNR, U.S. Customs and Border Protection officials would need to ask arriving passengers several dozen questions at the passport control booth, backing the lines up to the tarmac in the process. Providing that information electronically in advance of arrival allows the vast majority of passengers to enter the country quickly as the government focuses its scarce resources on the travelers most likely to pose a threat. Passengers don't merely "assume the risk" that airlines will share their reservation data with the government. Typically it is in their interest that airlines do so.

The statutory framework surrounding PNR is equally straightforward. Less than two months after the September 11 terrorist attacks, Congress enacted the Aviation and Transportation Security Act of 2001. Section 115 of that legislation directs all air carriers that fly to the United States to provide the government with a passenger and crew manifest (including each passenger and crew member's full name, their dates of birth, their passport numbers, and "[s]uch other information" as is deemed "reasonably necessary to ensure aviation safety") as well as "passenger name record information."[20]

International law likewise recognizes the legitimacy of American efforts to collect reservation data. The 1944 Chicago Convention on International Civil Aviation acknowledges that every nation has "complete and exclusive sover-

20. 49 U.S.C. §44909(c)(2), (3).

eignty" over its airspace.[21] As a corollary, Article 11 of the agreement expressly directs airlines to comply with a country's laws "relating to the admission to or departure from its territory of aircraft engaged in international air navigation."[22] A similar obligation attaches to individual passengers. Article 13 requires passengers—and those who act on their behalf, such as airlines—to comply with a country's laws governing "the admission to or departure from its territory," including "regulations relating to entry, clearance, immigration, passports, customs, and quarantine."[23]

As we've seen, one of the laws "relating to ... admission ... or departure" with which U.S.-bound airlines must comply is the obligation that they share PNR and other passenger information. The United States then uses that data for the various purposes spelled out in the Convention—e.g., deciding whether a particular traveler should be allowed to enter the country, assessing his immigration status, checking the authenticity of his passport, and so on. Indeed, the Convention expressly requires airlines to collect and turn over basic information about the passengers they carry. When it was signed in 1944, data-collection and data-processing capabilities were still in their infancy. Yet the Convention still obliges "[e]very aircraft" that flies internationally to carry "a list of [passengers'] names and places of embarkation and destination,"[24] and to make that list available to authorities upon arrival.[25] That's an embryonic form of PNR.

Not only is collection and analysis of PNR data legally permissible under the Chicago Convention, the agreement actually encourages it as sound public policy. States have an obligation under the Convention "to prevent unnecessary delays" to passengers, "especially in the administration of the laws relating to immigration, quarantine, customs, and clearance."[26] PNR helps accomplish exactly that. Advance transmission of reservation data enables the United States to begin screening passengers while their flights are still in the air, or even before they depart. That means officials are able to wave the vast majority of arriving passengers through immigration and customs with very little additional face-to-face scrutiny. PNR lets officers speed these bona fide travelers along while focusing their attention on the small number of passengers who present special risks.

---

21. Chicago Convention on International Civil Aviation art.1, Dec. 7, 1944, 61 Stat. 1180, 15 U.N.T.S. 295.
22. *Id.* art. 11.
23. *Id.* art. 13.
24. *Id.* art. 29.
25. *Id.* art. 16.
26. *Id.* art. 22.

III. The EU Strikes Back

Europe's approach to data privacy is different from that of the United States. While U.S. courts generally hold that sharing data with a third party vitiates one's expectation of privacy, EU law provides that government access to information typically must be on the basis of the data subject's "consent." The EU's Charter of Fundamental Rights sweepingly proclaims that "[e]veryone has the right to the protection of personal data concerning him or her." It further provides that "[s]uch data must be processed fairly for specified purposes and on the basis of the consent of the person concerned or some other legitimate basis laid down by law."[27] To European eyes, the American approach to data privacy must look incomplete, if not downright primitive.

To say that Europe's privacy values are "different" than America's is not to say that they are somehow "better" or "more protective." Americans and Europeans simply have different understandings of what is meant by privacy, to say nothing of different views on how to go about protecting it. As one scholar has observed:

> [W]e will not do justice to our transatlantic conflicts if we begin by declaring that American privacy law has "failed" while European privacy law has "succeeded." That is hogwash. What we must acknowledge, instead, is that there are, on the two sides of the Atlantic, two different cultures of privacy, which are home to different intuitive sensibilities, and which have produced two significantly different laws of privacy.[28]

In a nutshell, European privacy law aims primarily at protecting human dignity against the depredations of mass media, while the American law of privacy is generally preoccupied with preserving individual liberty against government encroachments.[29] Perhaps equally divisive, Americans and Europeans have different legal styles even when they seek to protect the same basic interest. European privacy law soars with generalities; American privacy law is relentlessly particular.

As a result, American privacy law looks partial and niggling from a European standpoint. But from America's vantage point, European privacy law often looks long on talk and short on results. Take wiretapping. In the United

---

27. Charter of Fundamental Rights of the European Union art. 8(1), (2), Dec. 7, 2000 O.J. (C 364) 10.

28. James Q. Whitman, *The Two Western Cultures of Privacy: Dignity versus Liberty*, 113 YALE L.J. 1151, 1160 (2004).

29. *See id.* at 1219.

States, protections against electronic surveillance are more a matter of procedure than grand theory. Police cannot tap a suspect's phone unless they obtain a "superwarrant"[30]—in addition to establishing probable cause, they must also exhaust other means of obtaining the information and take steps to minimize the interception of innocent conversations.[31] In Europe, the procedures are looser, with predictable results. French and German phones are tapped ten to 30 times more frequently than their American counterparts, and the rates in Italy and the Netherlands are an order of magnitude greater still—between 130 and 150 times the American rate.[32]

Preventive detention presents similar differences. Criminal suspects in the United States typically are brought before a judge for arraignment—the formal filing of charges—within 48 hours of being arrested.[33] Yet the European Convention of Human Rights acknowledges the power of member states to subject a person to preventive detention "when it is reasonably considered necessary to prevent his committing an offense."[34] In France, it's even possible to be kept in preventive detention after completing one's sentence, if authorities consider the person dangerous or a likely recidivist.[35]

Nor are the differences limited to criminal procedure. Most European countries require their citizens to carry an official identity card and to display it on demand. Americans have never accepted such a requirement, and most would consider it a violation of their privacy. Some European nations even have the authority to veto the names parents have picked for their newborns, and the European Court of Human Rights has held that such veto power does not violate personal privacy.[36] That sort of government interference would be anathema to Americans, whose Constitution protects the privacy-based right to direct the upbringing of one's children.[37]

---

30. Orin S. Kerr, *Internet Surveillance Law After the USA PATRIOT ACT: The Big Brother That Isn't*, 97 Nw. U. L. Rev. 607, 620 (2003).

31. *See* 18 U.S.C. §2518(3)(c), (5).

32. *See* Whitman, *supra* note 28, at 1159 & n.40.

33. *Cf.* County of Riverside v. McLaughlin, 500 U.S. 44, 55-58 (1991).

34. Convention for the Protection of Human Rights and Fundamental Freedoms, Dec. 10, 1948, art. 5(1)(c), Europ. T.S. No. 5.

35. Press Release, Amnesty International, *France: Amnesty International's Concerns on "Preventive Detention" Bill* (Feb. 8, 2008), http://www.amnestyusa.org/document.php?lang=e&id=ENGEUR210022008.

36. *See* Whitman, *supra* note28, at 1216–17 & n.327 (citing Guillot v. France, App. No. 22500/93 (Eur. Ct. H.R. Oct. 24, 1006)).

37. *See, e.g.*, Pierce v. Society of Sisters, 268 U.S. 510, 534–35 (1925); Meyer v. Nebraska, 262 U.S. 390, 399 (1923).

What's noteworthy is not just that America and Europe understand personal privacy in different terms, or pursue that mutual goal through different means. These sorts of disagreements are inevitable, even among countries that spring from a common political culture. What's noteworthy is the newfound willingness of some in Europe to assume that values differing from European values, and even procedures differing from European procedures, are presumptively inadequate.

In May 2004, the Department of Homeland Security signed an agreement with representatives of the European Union governing the transmission of PNR for flights originating in Europe. A principal impetus for the agreement was the fear of some European airlines that complying with their obligation under U.S. law to provide PNR would run afoul of European data privacy law. The airlines thus faced a Hobson's choice: Either provide PNR and risk liability in Europe, or refuse to provide PNR and risk liability in the United States. The 2004 agreement was designed to alleviate those concerns.

Though well intentioned, the agreement sharply limited DHS's ability to collect, use, and share PNR data. Under its terms, DHS was only allowed to use European PNR in certain kinds of investigations—namely, cases involving "terrorism" or "serious crimes … that are transnational in nature."[38] That meant PNR was off the table in domestic criminal cases—even serious ones, such as investigations of kidnapping and child exploitation. DHS further was barred from collecting certain types of passenger data, such as frequent flyer numbers.[39] (Recall that comparing passengers' frequent flyer numbers before 9/11 would have enabled investigators to identify Majed Moqed, one of the hijackers on American flight 77.[40]) The agreement also called on representatives of the EU to engage in periodic "adequacy" audits of DHS's use of PNR[41]—i.e., to assess whether the United States was satisfying European data privacy standards.

Most significant of all were the restrictions on DHS's ability to share information. Not only was DHS barred from routinely sharing European PNR with outside entities like the FBI or state and local law enforcement; it was even barred from doing so within DHS. U.S. Customs and Border Protection—the DHS component with immediate custody of PNR data—was allowed to use

---

38. Undertakings of the Department of Homeland Security Bureau of Customs and Border Protection Regarding the Handling of Passenger Name Record Data, 69 Fed. Reg. 41,543, 41,543 (July 9, 2004) ["2004 PNR Agreement"].

39. *Id.* at 41,547.

40. *See supra* note 11 and accompanying text.

41. 2004 PNR Agreement, 69 Fed. Reg. at 41,547.

it, but other DHS entities could only gain access on a case-by-case basis.[42] In effect, the European Union had rebuilt the "wall" between intelligence and law enforcement, a wall that Congress quite consciously tore down after September 11.

The EU also sought to insert European privacy norms into the United States' relationships with other countries. In the run-up to the 2007 Cricket World Cup, DHS entered into a data sharing arrangement with a number of the Caribbean countries set to host the games. These nations agreed to share passenger information with DHS, and DHS in turn would analyze it to determine whether any high-risk persons were traveling to those countries.[43] When the EU learned of the arrangement, it threatened to impose trade sanctions on the participating Caribbean nations. The Caribbean countries thus found themselves caught in the crossfire of a policy dispute between Brussels and Washington, much like the European airlines whose liability fears initially spawned the 2004 PNR agreement.

The 2004 agreement wasn't just inconsistent with American law and policy; it was in tension with international law. The Chicago Convention repeatedly stresses the importance of equal treatment: Aircraft, crew, and passengers may not be subjected to special burdens—or extended special benefits—based on their country of origin. Thus the Convention requires states to apply their laws "to the aircraft of all contracting States without distinction as to nationality."[44] It obliges nations to make available airport facilities, such as radio services, "under uniform conditions to the aircraft of all the other contracting States."[45] And it allows states to bar planes from carrying hazardous cargo, but only if "no distinction is made in this respect between its national aircraft ... and the aircraft of the other States."[46] In short, the Chicago Convention aims at uniformity. Yet the EU was seeking to carve out special rules for European PNR. Brussels effectively was arguing that, notwithstanding the fact that Australian and Japanese—and American—carriers had to comply with U.S. law, European airlines should receive special treatment.

The European Parliament wasn't fond of the 2004 agreement either, though for different reasons. In a lawsuit before the European Court of Justice (ECJ),

---

42. *Id.* at 41,545.

43. *See* U.S. Dep't of Homeland Security, Office of Inspector General, Management of Dep't of Homeland Security Int'l Activities and Interests 39 (June 24, 2008), http://www.dhs.gov/xoig/assets/mgmtrpts/OIG_08-71_Jun08.pdf.

44. Chicago Convention on International Civil Aviation art.11, Dec. 7, 1944, 61 Stat. 1180, 15 U.N.T.S. 295.

45. *Id.* art. 15.

46. *Id.* art. 35.

the parliamentarians claimed both that the agreement's terms were inconsistent with EU privacy law, and that the EU lacked legal authority to enter into it. On May 30, 2006, the ECJ handed down its decision.[47] The court sidestepped the Parliament's privacy-based claims, and struck down the agreement as beyond the EU's powers.

A little background is needed to make sense of that ruling. Originally, the European Union was created for economic reasons—to harmonize and reduce trade barriers and create a free-trade area. Matters relating to trade and travel (known as "First Pillar" issues) are ones where the sovereign member states ceded substantial powers to the new central government in Brussels. At the same time, the member states retained most of their traditional powers in matters of foreign policy and national defense ("Second Pillar" issues), as well as law enforcement and internal security ("Third Pillar" issues). At the risk of oversimplifying, it might be helpful to think of the architecture of Europe's legal system as resembling nineteenth century American federalism. Brussels is the seat of a strong but limited central government that wields a defined set of powers, while the residual powers not granted to Brussels are retained by the separate member states.

As the court pointed out, the EU adopted the PNR agreement under its First Pillar powers—the ones governing trade, travel, and other economic issues related to the common market. But even though air carriers collect PNR data for commercial purposes, the U.S. law requiring transfer of the data and the agreement limiting the U.S. government's use of that data were not directed at trade regulation. The purpose of the law was to assist in detecting potential terrorists and criminals. According to the court, the agreement "concerns not data processing necessary for a supply of services, but data processing regarded as necessary for safeguarding public security and for law-enforcement purposes."[48] As a result, the EU had no power under its First Pillar authorities to sign the agreement. If the EU wanted a PNR agreement, it would have to enter it under the Third Pillar. Again, at the risk of oversimplifying, it's as if the United States Supreme Court held that Congress lacked power under section 5 of the Fourteenth Amendment to ban private commercial establishments from engaging in racial discrimination,[49] but reasoned that it could enact the same prohibition under the Commerce Clause.[50]

47. See Joined Cases C-317/04 & C-318/04, European Parliament v. Council of the European Union & Commission of the European Communities, 2006 E.C.R. I-4721.
48. Id. ¶ 57.
49. See The Civil Rights Cases, 109 U.S. 3 (1883).
50. See Heart of Atlanta Motel v. United States, 379 U.S. 241 (1964).

The denouement came in 2007. After signing an interim agreement in October 2006,[51] DHS and the European Union reached a final agreement in July of the following year. The 2007 edition departs from its 2004 predecessor in a number of important respects. The new agreement retains the original use limitation — "terrorism" and "serious crimes ... which are transnational in nature" — but it now emphasizes that PNR can be used for any other purpose if "otherwise required by law."[52] The 2007 agreement reduces the number of data elements from 35 to 19, mainly by combining the old elements into new categories, but it also makes clear that certain types of information that previously were off limits can now be collected, including frequent flyer data.[53]

In the 2007 agreement, the EU once again deems that DHS ensures an "adequate" level of data protection.[54] But this time important reciprocity provisions have been added, which clarify that the EU is no longer sitting in judgment of American policy choices. Instead of a one-way "adequacy" audit, the agreement contemplates that DHS and EU representatives will jointly participate in assessments "with a view to mutually assuring the effective operation and privacy protection of their systems."[55] The agreement also states that neither DHS nor the EU will ask the other to implement data protection measures that are more stringent than the ones it is willing to adopt itself.[56] And the EU pledged that, as a "[c]oncomitant[]" of its conclusion that DHS's data practices are "adequate," it "will not interfere with relationships between the United States and third countries for the exchange of passenger information on data protection grounds."[57] That clause will help ensure that other countries don't get caught in any future transatlantic crossfire.

The information sharing terms represent the most significant departure from the 2004 agreement. The signatory of the agreement is DHS as a whole, not a subsidiary DHS component. That means PNR information can be shared

51. *See* Interim Agreement Between the European Union and the United States Regarding the Transfer of Passenger Name Record Data, 72 Fed. Reg. 348 (Jan. 4, 2007).

52. Letter from Michael Chertoff, Secretary, U.S. Dep't of Homeland Security, to Luis Amado, President, Council of the European Union at 1 (July 26, 2007) ["Chertoff letter"], http://www.dhs.gov/xlibrary/assets/pnr-2007agreement-usltrtoeu.pdf.

53. *See id.* at 2.

54. Agreement Between the United States of America and the European Union on the Processing and Transfer of Passenger Name Record (PNR) Data by Air Carriers to the United States Department of Homeland Security (DHS) ¶6, July 26, 2007, http://www.dhs.gov/xlibrary/assets/pnr-2007agreement-usversion.pdf.

55. *Id.* ¶4.

56. *Id.* ¶5.

57. *Id.* ¶6.

within DHS without restriction—provided, of course, that it is used for purposes of combating terrorism or serious transnational crimes. Likewise, the 2007 agreement expressly contemplates that DHS may share PNR with "other domestic government authorities."[58] The new agreement thus implements Congress's instructions to eliminate barriers to effective information sharing.

The PNR story has a happy ending—Washington and Brussels signed an agreement with which both sides were satisfied—but the trend it represents is still troubling. DHS's passenger screening system was deployed at the direction of Congress and in reliance upon on a series of Supreme Court rulings; in effect, all three branches of the federal government participated in the decision. The EU could have acknowledged that, while American law policy did not comport with its own preferences, the United States nevertheless was entitled as a sovereign to choose differently. It did not. Instead, Brussels claimed the right to sit in judgment of American data privacy practices.

The European Union's tactics throughout the PNR episode posed fundamental challenges to basic principles of multilateralism and international law. The EU never explained why its internal commercial data protection law should be read in a fashion so at odds with the multilateral Chicago Convention. It never justified its assumption that no law governing data used in criminal investigations could be adequate unless it was nearly identical to European law. Nor did the EU clarify why European data-privacy rules should trump American data-disclosure requirements. It would have been hard-pressed to do so. The Restatement (Third) of Foreign Relations Law actually reflects the opposite principle: legal requirements "by the state in whose territory the act is to be carried out ordinarily prevail over orders of other states."[59] When a private party is subject to conflicting laws of two nations, it generally must comply with the laws of the country where the conduct in question occurs, not the country of which it is a national. Under the Restatement, U.S. laws directing airlines to turn over PNR were entitled to priority.[60] Finally, and most troubling for large multinational enterprises, the European Union seemed almost en-

---

58. Chertoff letter, *supra* note 52, at 1–2.

59. RESTATEMENT (THIRD) OF THE FOREIGN RELATIONS LAW OF THE UNITED STATES §441 cmt. b (1987).

60. The relevant "act" referred to in the Restatement is the act of entering the United States. This is actually a compound act, comprising a number of antecedent steps that must be taken before one can set foot on American soil. Those steps include purchasing a ticket, boarding the plane, and—especially important here—the transmission of PNR to U.S. officials. Because the antecedent steps are part of the compound act of entering the United States—i.e., because they are intelligible only in relation to the act at which they ultimately aim—the Restatement provides that American law prevails.

thusiastic about threatening airlines with sanctions as a way of attacking American policies and practices with which it disagreed. For obvious reasons, putting private actors in a position of having to violate the laws of one sovereign in order to heed the laws of another is dubious practice under international law. One of the key goals of the Restatement is "to protect persons caught between conflicting demands."[61]

Regrettably, threats against private firms are a growth industry on the Continent. The European Union seems to have concluded that the tactic should be applied to new fields, including financial records. After 9/11, the U.S. Treasury Department served subpoenas on the Belgium-based Society for Worldwide Interbank Financial Telecommunication, or SWIFT, a financial data exchange that monitors banking transactions across the globe. Treasury wanted access to bank records that could be used to identify and locate al Qaeda financiers, and SWIFT complied with the subpoenas.[62] After EU officials called for a criminal investigation, Belgian authorities declared that the consortium had violated European data protection law;823;841;842;843;823;841;842;843:

> SWIFT should have, as of the beginning, been aware of and should have taken into account the fact that, in addition to the application of U.S. law, the fundamental rules of European law on data protection had to be complied with, in particular the proportionality principle, the limitation of the retention of data for the period required by processing requirements, the transparency principle, the requirement of an independent control and the existence — prior to any transfer outside the European Union — of standards ensuring an adequate level of protection in the country of destination.[63]

What is significant about these requirements is that SWIFT could not meet any of them. In essence, the authorities were saying that, before complying with U.S. law, SWIFT had an obligation to ensure that the U.S. government met European procedural and substantive legal standards. Since no private actor has the leverage to demand such assurances, particularly after receiving a subpoena, such a requirement dooms the actor to simply deciding which law to violate.

---

61. *Id.* §441 cmt. a.

62. *See* Eric Lichtblau & James Risen, *Bank Data Sifted in Secret by U.S. to Block Terror*, N.Y. Times, June 23, 2006, at A1.

63. Commission for the Protection of Privacy, Control and Recommendation Procedure Initiated with Respect to the Company SWIFT (Dec. 9, 2008) (Belgium), http://www.privacycommission.be/en/static/pdf/cbpl-documents/a10268302-v1-0-151208_translation_recommswift_fina.pdf.

The United States responded to the EU's tactics by suggesting that threats against private firms should be out of bounds in transatlantic privacy disputes. Reasoning that U.S. and European criminal data protection standards were not far apart in practice, the United States proposed that a "High Level Contact Group" try to reconcile U.S. and European norms with a view to declaring them broadly consistent so that private companies could continue to obey the investigative demands of both jurisdictions without fear of liability. This effort is ongoing. As expected, broad agreement has been reached on criminal data protection principles, but thus far the European Union has been reluctant to adopt a straightforward assurance that private companies will not be put in a position of uncertainty about their data protection liability when they comply with subpoenas and other investigative requirements. This assurance is precisely what private firms receive when a jurisdiction is declared "adequate" under European data protection law, and the talks have been stalled by the High Level Contact Group's failure to provide an equivalent assurance even after reaching broad agreement on data protection standards. Nonetheless, progress continues to be made, and an agreement that provides assurances to multinational companies (and criminal investigators) seems within reach at this writing.

IV. Explanations, Implications, and Solutions

What accounts for Brussels's apparent determination to export its data privacy values throughout the globe, and its insistence that other countries adhere to European norms? Why would Europe sacrifice its traditional commitment to multilateralism and international law in order to restrict terrorism investigations in other countries? A number of possible explanations come to mind, some more creditable than others.

Part of it is good faith substantive disagreement about the meaning of privacy and how best to preserve it. To Continental eyes, the American approach to data privacy looks narrow and lacking in broad protective principles. Indeed, the EU may not even recognize its actions as intrusive, seeing them rather as beneficent efforts to nudge their American cousins toward right thinking. Another explanation is the occasionally stated desire of some European policymakers that the EU serve as a counterweight to the American "hyperpower." By binding the United States in a web of international obligations, as the Lilliputians bound Gulliver, the EU is able to project its own power.[64]

---

64. *See, e.g.*, Robert Kagan, *Power and Weakness*, POLICY REV. (June & July 2002).

Neither of those observations is especially original. A third, and less noticed, possible reason for Brussels's privacy evangelism has to do with the distribution of powers within Europe. Recall that the EU's central government has broad authority when it comes to trade, travel, and other First Pillar economic powers, but the individual member states remain sovereign over issues such as national defense and internal security. It is not surprising that Brussels would want to accumulate new powers traditionally held by the member states, especially the national security powers that have assumed even greater importance in the post-9/11 era.

The question is how to do so. A shrewd way for Brussels to expand its power is to take familiar and uncontroversial First Pillar rules that originally were crafted for commercial purposes and relocate them into new law enforcement and counterterrorism contexts. The central government gains new authorities, since it is transplanting broad authorities into realms where its power is nominally more limited, and it does so in a way that is less likely than a naked power grab to attract the attention of the member states that stand to lose from the arrangement. That may be what happened in 2004, when the EU sought to apply commercial data privacy norms to what was at root a law enforcement and counterterrorism matter. The ECJ later struck down the 2004 PNR agreement as *ultra vires*, but by then a political consensus had congealed in Brussels that negotiations on PNR were necessary and that only the EU could conduct them.

In general, transatlantic conflict has proven a reliable way for Brussels to expand its authority. Sometimes the EU accumulates new powers, not by *sotto voce* transplantation of established First Pillar rules, but by persuading its member states to grant it an express mandate to negotiate on their behalf with a foreign interlocutor. Because member states have "a duty of loyal cooperation" with the European Union, they may not undercut Brussels's negotiators by adopting rules inconsistent from those being negotiated for the EU as a whole. But this apparently straightforward principle means that, simply by opening negotiations with the United States, Brussels gains a veto over new areas of member state action.

Once an agreement is reached, the expansion of authority becomes even more explicit. Under EU law, if a foreign country signs an agreement with Brussels concerning a Second or Third Pillar matter, and the EU's member states approve the agreement, then Brussels will have new legal authority over the member states' practices as long as it couches its role in terms of enforcing the agreement. This is *Missouri v. Holland*[65] on steroids. In that case, Jus-

---

65. 252 U.S. 416 (1920).

tice Oliver Wendell Holmes held that Congress had power to regulate lands used by migratory birds as necessary and proper to a treaty with Canada, even though it lacked power to adopt the same requirements under the Commerce Clause. In effect, Congress can acquire new legislative powers simply by ratifying a treaty. The EU's powers would make Justice Holmes envious: Brussels can bootstrap its way into new authorities not only by ratifying a treaty, but by entering a less formal international agreement.

The result is not surprising. Bureaucratic entrepreneurs in Brussels who want to maximize their authority find that transatlantic conflict, transatlantic negotiations, and transatlantic agreements all contribute to that cause. In short, a European Union that hopes to accumulate new powers will want to find new international disagreements and enter into new international agreements. (The dynamic we have described—the creation of conflict and its resolution as a way to expand turf—will change if and when the proposed European constitution is ratified. If member states decide to grant broad new powers to Brussels, the EU won't have the same need to create and resolve disputes in order to gain jurisdiction, because the new constitution will have accomplished that already. Voters in France and the Netherlands rejected the constitution in 2005; those referenda effectively killed it, since all 27 EU members must ratify an agreement for it to go into effect. More recently, the so-called "Lisbon treaty" has resurrected most of the constitution's substantive features. Irish voters said no to Lisbon in 2008 but subsequently endorsed the treaty in October 2009.[66])

American policymakers should be aware of this dynamic when they consider entering into international negotiations or agreements with the European Union and the European Commission. Simply launching such negotiations may tilt the balance of authority between individual member states and Brussels. For that reason, policymakers should always ask themselves whether agreements with individual member states would be preferable, and whether an EU-wide agreement will create incentives to provoke conflicts in the future. We expect that amicable agreements on topics of mutual U.S.-EU interest will raise these concerns only rarely, if ever. But the United States should be especially wary of signing agreements when the issue is one on which Washington and Brussels have widely divergent policy preferences, or incident to a prolonged or contentious dispute with the EU. In those circumstances, the United States may be better served by working with individual countries.

---

66. *See* Eric Pfanner & Sarah Lyall, *Ireland Backs Treaty to Streamline E.U.*, N.Y. TIMES, Oct. 4, 2009, at A6.

That bridge has been crossed, of course, in the context of data protection and antiterrorism measures. The U.S. and EU have already negotiated several arrangements in this field. What remains is to clean up the mess left by the talks. The U.S. and EU should revitalize the High Level Contact Group and develop a shared framework of principles by which future transatlantic disputes over criminal data protection will be resolved. Agreement is within reach on at least the broad principles of how to protect privacy while implementing effective antiterrorism measures. The two jurisdictions should also acknowledge that this broad agreement revolves around a few principles that should inform future international data protection arrangements.[67]

- *Modesty*: It is inevitable that the United States and its allies in Europe will adopt different solutions to commonly recognized problems. It is also inevitable that they will disagree on what amounts to a problem at all. When such disputes arise, both Washington and Brussels should show a measure of restraint. Each should acknowledge that it does not have a monopoly on sound policy ideas, and that its partner is entitled to chart a different course than the one it prefers. Nowhere is modesty more necessary than in disputes related to privacy policy. America and Europe take different roads to the protection of individual rights, and in some cases they may understand privacy differently, but neither side should forcibly convert the other to its own way of thinking.

- *Reciprocity*: Neither the United States nor the European Union should demand that the other take actions that it is not prepared to take on its own. This is of course an elementary principle of international relations, but it bears reemphasizing. The reciprocity principle makes sense from the standpoint of fairness. It also is valuable to the extent it can help prevent conflict among allies. Reciprocity can discourage either partner from proposing arrangements that are likely to prove so controversial as to disrupt the relationship. (Care must be taken, however, to ensure that legitimate reciprocity concerns do not blossom into restraints on creativity and innovation.)

- *Private business*: Private firms whose activities are intertwined with national security operations—airlines, banks, and others—should not be

---

67. These principles echo the recommendations of a task force chaired by the Center for Strategic and International Studies and The Heritage Foundation. *See* HOMELAND SECURITY 3.0: BUILDING A NATIONAL ENTERPRISE TO KEEP AMERICA SAFE, FREE, AND PROSPEROUS 12-13 (Sept. 18, 2008). One of the authors was a member of that task force.

used as pawns in disputes between Washington and Brussels. When the U.S. and EU disagree about how a particular controversy should be resolved, private businesses may well find themselves subject to conflicting legal requirements. The two partners should agree that they will not threaten to impose civil liability or other penalties on companies as a way of strengthening their respective hands in intergovernmental negotiations.

- *Third countries*: A similar principle should apply to relationships with third countries. Washington often will seek to enter into arrangements with independent nations that Brussels finds objectionable, and vice versa. The U.S. and EU should commit to not interfering in each other's independent relationships with third countries—for example, by threatening to retaliate against nations that agree to undertake cooperative initiatives with the other.

* * *

Even the best of friends sometimes have disagreements. The United States and the nations of Europe remain strategic partners on virtually every major issue of the day, from trade and commerce to foreign affairs—and, crucially, in the struggle against global terrorism. Yet, at the margins, the two sides inevitably will have different policy preferences, and those divergent priorities just as inevitably will produce transatlantic conflict. When disputes arise, as they did with PNR, each partner must be free to chart its own course. The United States should not demand that the Continent adopt American priorities as its own. And the same goes for Europe. Washington is well within its rights to insist that Brussels not interfere with measures the United States believes are needed to protect against terrorist attacks.

Chapter 12

The Relations between Military and Civilian Authorities within the United States

Kurt Johnson,[1] Kevin Cieply,[2] & Jeanne Meyer[3]

"The supremacy of the civil over the military authority I deem [one of] the essential principles of our Government, and consequently [one of] those which ought to shape its administration."

Thomas Jefferson, 1st Inaugural, 1801

Introduction

More than eight years after terrorists attacked the World Trade Center and the Pentagon, resulting in the loss of thousands of innocent lives, the neces-

---

1. Associate Director, Center for Homeland Security, National Institute of Science, Space and Security Centers, University of Colorado at Colorado Springs. Senior Legal Advisor for North American Aerospace Defense Command (NORAD) and U.S. Northern Command, 2005–2008. Retired Captain, Judge Advocate, with over twenty-three years active service in the U.S. Navy. LL.M., 1993, University of Virginia School of Law; J.D., 1985, University of Wisconsin Law School; B.A., 1979, University of Wisconsin.

2. Associate Professor, Atlanta's John Marshall Law School. Retired Colonel, Judge Advocate, with over twenty-two years combined active service in the Regular Army and Wyoming Army National Guard. Senior Military College Fellow, Fletcher School of Law and Diplomacy, Tufts University, 2007; LL.M., 1997, The Judge Advocate General's Legal Ctr. & Sch.; J.D., 1993, University of Notre Dame; B.S., 1985, Northern Kentucky University.

3. Legal Advisor for Standing Joint Force Headquarters North, U.S. Northern Command. Lieutenant Colonel in the U.S. Air Force with over fourteen years of active service. M.A (Air Warfare), 2001, American Military University; LL.M., 2000, The Judge Advocate General's Legal Ctr. & Sch.; J.D., 1992, Duke University School of Law; B.A., 1988, Duke University.

sity of a military combatant command located in the heart of the United States
and its relationship to federal, state, and local civilian authorities, remain the
subject of considerable debate. Military *air* defense of the United States against
nation-state military attack dates back to the beginning of the Cold War era—
the North American Aerospace Defense Command (NORAD) celebrated its
50th anniversary on May 12, 2008. The terrorist attacks of September 11, 2001,
however, led directly to the establishment, for the first time in U.S. history, of
a geographic combatant command—U.S. Northern Command (NORTH-
COM)[4]—dedicated to defense of the United States across all domains and
against both traditional nation-state and transnational terrorist attack. NORTH-
COM is designed to provide military defense and support to civil authorities
across all homeland domains: air, land, and sea. As such, it is testing the outer
limits of relations between military and civilian authorities in the United States
in ways never contemplated before September 11, 2001.

Did the September 11 attacks change everything? Lawyers know, perhaps
better than any other profession, that several very important things remained
unchanged in the wake of the attacks. The United States Constitution and its
fundamental principles governing the relationship between military and civilian authorities and between federal and state governments, remain wholly unchanged. Numerous federal statutes on the same subjects remain unchanged.
And literally hundreds of federal executive branch policies and implementing
instructions on these subjects remain in their pre-September 11 form.

NORTHCOM operates day to day in this relatively unchanged legal environment. Through a robust exercise program and real world contingency operations (such as responses to Hurricane Katrina in 2005 and the California
wildfires in 2007 and 2008), military and civilian officials in the United States
are feeling their way through the proper relationships between the active duty
military; the National Guard of the various States; and federal, state and local

---

4. Six combatant commands have geographic area responsibilities:
• United States Africa Command—USAFRICOM
• United States Central Command—USCENTCOM
• United States European Command—USEUCOM
• United States Pacific Command—USPACOM
• United States Northern Command—NORTHCOM
• United States Southern Command—USSOUTHCOM
Four combatant commanders have worldwide functional responsibilities:
• United States Joint Forces Command—USJFCOM
• United States Special Operations Command—USSOCOM
• United States Strategic Command—USSTRATCOM
• United States Transportation Command—USTRANSCOM

civilian authorities. This chapter is designed to survey and discuss the key legal issues associated with developing those relationships and building the most effective system to deliver on a shared promise to defend and protect the American people and provide timely and effective assistance in a disaster. While that effort has come a long way in a relatively short period of time, Robert Frost would likely agree that "[we] have promises to keep, and miles to go before [we] sleep."[5]

Open Borders, New Threats and the NORTHCOM and NORAD Missions

The United States of America is the world's fourth largest nation with 3.5 million square miles of land and 88,000 miles of tidal shoreline. Each year, 11.2 million trucks and 2.2 million railcars cross into the United States from the 7,500-mile land and air border shared with Canada and Mexico. More than 7,500 foreign-flag ships make 51,000 calls annually to U.S. ports. The country routinely admits millions of visitors from around the world. The freedom America enjoys, employs in its commerce, and extends to non-U.S. citizens presents national defense challenges. Ruthless and resourceful enemies seek to threaten the nation with new technologies, dangerous weapons, and nontraditional tactics that exploit our freedoms.

Emerging threats include chemical, biological, radiological, nuclear and high-yield explosive (CBRNE) weapons, ballistic and cruise missiles, and electronic and cyber warfare. As the nation witnessed on September 11, 2001, America's enemies have the resolve and means to commit acts of terrorism against innocent civilians and commercial interests within our country. The historical insularity of the United States has given way to an era of new vulnerabilities and enemies may strike the United States in new and unsuspected ways.

NORTHCOM

As authorized by President George W. Bush on April 17, 2002, the Department of Defense (DoD) announced the establishment of NORTHCOM to con-

---

5. "The woods are lovely, dark and deep, But I have promises to keep, And miles to go before I sleep, And miles to go before I sleep." Robert Frost, "Stopping By a Woods on a Snowy Evening." *Available at* http://www.poetryfoundation.org/archive/poem.html?id=17-1621.

solidate, under a single unified command, those existing Homeland Defense and Civil Support missions that were previously executed by other military organizations. This provides unity of command, which is critical to mission accomplishment. NORTHCOM provides command and control of DoD Homeland Defense efforts and coordinates defense support of civil authorities. Although it has few permanently assigned forces, the command is assigned forces whenever necessary to execute missions as ordered by the President and Secretary of Defense.

NORTHCOM's area of responsibility includes air, land, and sea approaches; and it encompasses the continental United States, Alaska, Canada, Mexico and the surrounding water out to approximately 500 nautical miles. It also includes the Gulf of Mexico and the Straits of Florida. The defense of Hawaii and our territories and possessions in the Pacific is the responsibility of U.S. Pacific Command. The defense of Puerto Rico and the U.S. Virgin Islands is the responsibility of U.S. Southern Command. The commander of NORTHCOM is responsible for theater security cooperation with Canada and Mexico.

NORAD

The commander of NORTHCOM also commands NORAD. NORAD is a bi-national United States and Canadian organization charged with the missions of aerospace warning and aerospace control for North America. Aerospace warning includes the monitoring of man-made objects in space, and the detection, validation, and warning of attack against North America whether by aircraft, missiles, or space vehicles, through mutual support arrangements with other commands. Aerospace control includes ensuring air sovereignty and air defense of the airspace of Canada and the United States. The May 2006 NORAD Agreement renewal added a maritime warning mission, which entails a shared awareness and understanding of the activities conducted in U.S. and Canadian maritime approaches, maritime areas, and inland waterways.

To accomplish these critically important missions, NORAD continually adjusts its structure to meet the demands of a changing world. The commander is appointed by, and is responsible to, both the U.S. president and the Canadian prime minister. The commander maintains his headquarters at Peterson Air Force Base, Colorado. The NORAD-NORTHCOM Command Center serves as a central collection and coordination facility for a worldwide system of sensors designed to provide the commander and the leadership of Canada and the United States with an accurate picture of any aerospace threat.

To accomplish the aerospace warning mission, the commander of NORAD provides an integrated tactical warning and attack assessment to the governments of Canada and the United States. To accomplish the aerospace control mission, NORAD uses a network of satellites, ground-based radar, airborne radar, and fighters to detect, intercept and, if necessary, engage any air-breathing threat to North America. The command is currently developing a concept for implementing the new maritime warning mission.

Finding the Right Balance: National Security and Protection of Civil Liberties

Civilian Control of the Military

To perhaps the same extent that the September 11th attacks inaugurated an unprecedented inward focus of national security efforts by the United States, they also generated a concomitant concern for protection of traditional civil liberties. The establishment of NORTHCOM in the wake of the attacks prodded a legitimate debate about how best to provide security against further attack to the American people while simultaneously guarding their way of life and cherished freedoms. "The establishment of a military command with the responsibility for conducting operations within the United States has caused concern about the implications for our individual liberties. Some have questioned whether this decision is a precursor to an overly intrusive role by the military in our domestic affairs. A renewed commitment to the principles that have minimized military involvement in certain domestic matters has also been urged."[6]

The core principle—civilian control of the military by the President and the Congress—is firmly rooted in the United States Constitution. "The President shall be commander in chief of the Army and Navy of the United States, and of the militia of the several states, when called into the actual service of the United States ..."[7] "The Congress shall have power ... To declare war, grant letters of marque and reprisal, and make rules concerning captures on land and water; To raise and support armies, but no appropriation of money to that use shall be for a longer term than two years; To provide and maintain a navy; To make rules for the government and regulation of the land and naval forces; To provide for calling forth the militia to execute the laws of the union, suppress insurrections and repel invasions; To provide for organizing, arming, and disciplining, the militia, and for governing such part of them as may

---

6. *Balancing National Security and Civil Liberties, Focus on Law Studies,* Spring 2007, Volume XXII, Number 2, American Bar Association Division for Public Education, p. 7.

7. U.S. Constitution, Art II, Sec 2.

be employed in the service of the United States, reserving to the states respectively, the appointment of the officers, and the authority of training the militia according to the discipline prescribed by Congress ...".[8] As with every other U.S. combatant command, NORTHCOM operates at all times under civilian control—answering to the Secretary of Defense and the President when performing its Homeland Defense mission, and to a lead civilian federal agency when performing its Civil Support mission.

Coordination with the States

The words of the Tenth Amendment to the U.S. Constitution have special meaning to NORTHCOM in performance of its missions in the homeland. "The powers not delegated to the United States by the Constitution, nor prohibited by it to the States, are reserved to the States respectively, or to the people."[9]

One of the powers reserved to the states, and key to any discussion of the relationship between military and civilian authorities in the United States, is the "police power." As stated by the United States Supreme Court, "[i]t cannot be denied that the power of the state to protect the lives, health and property of its citizens and to preserve good order and the public morals, 'the power to govern men and things within the limits of its dominion,' is a power originally and always belonging to the states, not surrendered by them to the general [federal] government, nor directly restrained by the constitution of the United States, and essentially exclusive."[10] In its simplest form, the "police power" is the inherent authority of state and local governments to respond to disasters and emergencies, protect their citizens, and enforce laws. Hence, NORTHCOM's Civil Support mission and the entire framework to provide federal assistance to a state in the wake of a disaster or emergency are premised upon a request from the governor of a state.

Improved Interagency Coordination: A Necessity

As the United States strives to improve its means to combat terrorism, perhaps the greatest area for improvement in relations between military and civilian authorities lies in the coordination between various government agencies, particularly at the federal level, commonly referred to as "interagency coordination." Homeland Defense and homeland security pose challenges which exceed the capacity and authority of any one agency or level of government and

---

8. U.S. Constitution, Art I, Sec 8.
9. U.S. Constitution, amend. X.
10. U.S. v. Knight Co., 156 U.S. 1, 11 (1895).

call for a truly integrated approach bringing together the resources of all elements of government. Key to success for North America is a proactive engagement between military and civilian partners across all levels of government and with international partners.

The 1986 Goldwater-Nichols Department of Defense Reorganization Act mandated a dramatic change in Department of Defense structure to enable more effective and efficient military operations. In similar fashion, many have called for a "Goldwater-Nichols reform for the entire federal government" to improve interagency coordination and response to crises. At the forefront of this effort is the NORAD and NORTHCOM Interagency Coordination Directorate.

Since inception, NORAD and NORTHCOM have sought to accomplish unity of effort with their interagency and international partners to establish a collaborative environment that can achieve common objectives in the Homeland Defense and Civil Support arenas. Successful execution of the Commands' missions to anticipate threats, defend, protect, and secure the United States and its interests requires agility in integrating military efforts with those of civilian partners in a unified strategy. Supporting and enabling other agencies, working toward common objectives, and building the capacity of our partners are indispensable elements in this effort.

Agencies Represented

The NORAD and NORTHCOM Interagency Coordination Directorate and the Commander's Joint Interagency Coordination Group (JIACG) established in 2003 integrate and synchronize activities of multiple civilian, state, federal, and private sector organizations for Homeland Defense and Civil Support missions. The JIACG focus is to improve collaboration between NORAD and NORTHCOM and national-level agency and private sector planning efforts, including: developing and implementing private sector engagement strategy; providing an interagency context in the Commander's decision-making process; providing interagency perspective to the military staff and military perspective to external agencies; anticipating requests for Civil Support assistance from the primary agency (usually a civil agency); improving collaboration between NORAD and NORTHCOM and national-level agency planning efforts; synchronizing interagency coordination efforts at the regional and state levels; developing NORAD and NORTHCOM international interagency engagement programs; and promoting interagency innovations and initiatives that lead to mutually beneficial concepts and technologies.

The NORAD and NORTHCOM JIACG includes approximately 60 full-time professionals representing 40 agencies resident or locally available at NORAD and NORTHCOM Headquarters, to include Department of Homeland Security (DHS), Federal Emergency Management Agency (FEMA), Transportation Security Administration (TSA), Customs and Border Protection, United States Coast Guard, Federal Bureau of Investigation, United States Army Corps of Engineers, United States Geological Survey, Department of State, Central Intelligence Agency, and Department of Health and Human Services. Five Federal Aviation Administration (FAA) representatives are also imbedded within NORAD/Cheyenne Mountain Operations Center to ensure responsive aerial threat coordination between NORAD, NORTHCOM, the TSA, and the FAA. The National Aeronautics and Space Administration representative is located locally with Headquarters, Air Force Space Command, which occupies the building adjacent to NORAD and NORTHCOM Headquarters.

Coordination of Homeland Defense and Civil Support Activities

The DoD and NORTHCOM have developed robust and collaborative relationships with the interagency community and the private sector to enable mutual support of Homeland Defense and Civil Support missions to achieve unity of effort prior to, and during, a crisis. As a result of these relationships, NORAD and NORTHCOM have taken and are taking several significant steps to improve preparedness for responding to a wide range of threats. These steps include: developing relationships with the private sector (business, non-profit, non-governmental, faith-based, academia) to promote mutual understanding and unity of effort; placing resident liaison officers at DHS and FEMA Headquarters (additionally, DHS appointed a senior advisor at NORAD and NORTH-COM Headquarters to help synchronize activities and represent DHS Headquarters); hosting conferences, workshops, and video teleconferences with interagency partners, such as weekly video teleconferences between NORAD and NORTHCOM, FEMA and other federal agency planners during hurricane season for mutual understanding, coordination, and unity of effort; working with the DHS Incident Management Planning Team (IMPT) to synchronize DoD and DHS planning activities, including DoD support roles for the Homeland Security Council's National Planning Scenarios; exchanging watch center staff between FEMA's National Response Coordination Center, the National Operations Center, FEMA Operations Center and the NORAD and NORTH-COM Command Center; assigning regional Defense Coordinating Officers (DCOs) supported by Defense Coordinating Elements (DCE) in FEMA's Regions to ensure military coordination of planning at the regional level; co-sponsoring with FEMA the annual Federal Coordinating Officer (FCO)—

Defense Coordinating Officer (DCO) Conference designed to maintain and enhance civilian-military interaction and support of planning and disaster response activities within FEMA Regional Offices; collaborating with DHS and FEMA to develop all-hazard Pre-Scripted Mission Assignments (PSMAs) that facilitate understanding and execution of DOD support capabilities to civil authorities; participating in DoS and DHS led interagency efforts to develop an International Assistance System (IAS) Concept of Operations which establishes, within the National Response Framework, policies and procedures to manage international resources during response operations; teaming with TSA to host an annual Interagency Transportation Security Conference; collaborating with interagency partners for response to a pandemic influenza (to include state, National Guard, and private sector) to ensure an effective and coordinated federal response; in concert with the National Exercise Program, including interagency, private sector, and senior U.S. Government leadership in exercise development and execution to ensure effective representation, training, and evaluation of a coordinated federal response to Homeland Defense and Civil Support scenarios; identifying and supporting technology and concepts initiatives across the federal, state, and local government as well as private sector levels to build partner capacity and enhance the nation's Homeland Defense capabilities; and teaming with interagency partners to fully support state National Guard initiatives, including providing robust communications capabilities, ensuring weapons of mass destruction and CBRNE response capabilities, and engaging with the National Emergency Managers Association and Emergency Management Assistance Compact (EMAC) for mutual support in planning and operations.

NORAD and NORTHCOM also promote interagency relationships with Canada and Mexico to enhance security and promote effective cross-border response efforts. This includes steadily improving relationships between FEMA, U.S. Geological Survey, Environmental Protection Agency, U.S. Army Corps of Engineers, Department of State, U.S. Agency for International Development, Office of Foreign Disaster Assistance, Mexico's Protection Civil, and Public Safety Canada to enable civil-military cooperation during disaster planning and response. The NORAD and NORTHCOM international interagency strategy of engagement includes building on previous efforts to leverage the interagency community to promote cross-border cooperation at the federal, regional, and state levels by enhancing interagency emergency preparedness and response. The ultimate goal is to build on existing authorities and use existing venues and events to collaborate with state partners on each side of the international border to increase collaboration and ensure success.

Looking Forward

Given the nature of operations in the homeland, all Homeland Defense and Civil Support planning efforts should be "coalition plans" and be truly inter-agency and intergovernmental, to include all mission partners and all co-re-sponders, from concept development through plan completion. There is virtually no instance in the homeland in which military authorities would conduct op-erations independently, even in a truly catastrophic situation. Invariably, state, local, private sector, and multi-national partners will respond, and those ef-forts must be well-coordinated with military efforts.

Military authorities should partner with civilian agencies to facilitate "whole of government" Homeland Defense and consequence management responses that fully account for the mission partners that will already be present in an incident area. Areas for improvement include integration of plans and pro-cedures, information sharing and development of a common operating pic-ture, integrated logistics and commodities distribution system (including private sector), and increased evacuation and medical support capacity at all levels. In addition, disaster preparedness exercises need to stress all stake-holders. Currently most multi-echeloned exercises do not provide a scenario that is robust enough over a long enough period of time to stress the systems of all stakeholders, nor do all departments and agencies participate with sen-ior leaders and staff.

The remainder of this chapter will survey the key legal issues impacting re-lationships between military and civilian authorities in the United States in two major areas: Homeland Defense and Department of Defense support of civilian authorities, primarily in the areas of law enforcement and consequence management following a significant manmade or natural disaster.

Military/Civilian Relationships: Homeland Defense

"It is 'obvious and unarguable' that no government interest is more com-pelling than the security of the Nation."[11]

---

11. Hamdan v. Rumsfeld, 126 S. Ct. 2749, 2849 (2006), (Thomas dissent) (*quoting* Haig v. Agee, 453 U.S. 280, 307 (1981) (*quoting* Aptheker v. Secretary of State, 378 U.S. 500, 509 (1964).

Providing for a common defense of the states was one of the reasons the Framers established one nation.[12] Today, the vernacular for a "common defense" is "Homeland Defense." The duty of a common defense belongs to the *federal* government. More specifically, it is the duty of the President. And the President, through the Secretary of Defense, has given the Homeland Defense mission to NORTHCOM.[13]

As a matter of law, this nation is in an armed conflict with al Qaeda and its affiliates.[14] As an integral part of U.S. strategy is to take the conflict to the enemy, so too does the enemy intend to bring the conflict back to America's homeland. Given al Qaeda's explicit intent to kill Americans, civilians, and military alike, Homeland Defense is NORTHCOM's number one mission.

Homeland Defense involves identifying, dissuading, and denying the enemy's ability to successfully attack the homeland.[15] If the enemy successfully initiates or carries out an attack, Homeland Defense also stands for repelling and defeating the enemy.[16] The primary operational challenge with Homeland Defense is, of course, ensuring mission success. Terrorism brings its own unique challenges in that area, not the least of which are legal challenges. The most difficult legal challenge that terrorism presents concerning Homeland Defense is whether any particular situation actually calls for, and thus permits, a Homeland Defense response.

NORTHCOM operates in the homeland in two related but distinct roles. In addition to performing a Defense mission, NORTHCOM also performs a Civil Support mission. The differences between the two roles are fairly significant. Homeland Defense exercises the President's War Powers. In a Homeland Defense mission, the Department of Defense, through NORTHCOM, acts as the President's arm to wage war. This power is a highly effective means to defeat a wartime enemy, but at the same time, exercising this power within the homeland raises serious questions regarding civil liberties in an open society.

Civil Support, on the other hand, is not a war mission; it is the mission NORTHCOM carries out to provide support to other federal agencies and

---

12. *See* U.S. Constitution Preamble, *infra* note 60.

13. PACOM has the responsibility for defense of Hawaii, as well as the territories and possessions in the Pacific.

14. Hamdan v. Rumsfeld, 126 S. Ct. 2749, 2796 (2006). In the course of its holding, the Supreme Court found that Common Article 3 applied to the conflict with al Qaeda. *Id.* Common Article 3 begins with the following words: "In the case of armed conflict...." Geneva Convention, Relative to Treatment of Prisoners of War, August 12, 1949, entered into 21 Oct, 1950, 75 U.N.T.S. 135.

15. *See Joint Chiefs of Staff, Joint Pub,* 3-26, Homeland Security, chapter III, p. 1 (2 Aug. 2005) [hereinafter Joint Pub. 3-26].

16. *Id.*

states in situations such as hurricanes, floods, and support to law enforcement. Civil Support circumscribes the scope of the military's mission and use of force; it is fashioned primarily for consequence management and assistance to law enforcement rather than for war.

Until 9/11, identifying the line between Homeland Defense and Civil Support was fairly easy. The hybrid nature of terrorism, however, has complicated matters; it has made it difficult to ascertain whether any given situation calls for a Homeland Defense response, and if so, to what extent, or, on the other hand, whether the situation is much more appropriately addressed as a Civil Support mission. The difficulty centers on a trade-off between maintaining security versus maintaining the characteristics of a free society. Striking the right balance between security and freedom is what lies at the heart of any legal analysis concerning the foundational decision whether to employ the military in a Homeland Defense response.

In the end, it is the President who must make the call between a Homeland Defense or Civil Support mission. In general, the President relies on his Constitutional Article II authorities to define a Homeland Defense response. Reliance on these authorities is relatively clear-cut when dealing with a "traditional" Homeland Defense action, as discussed below. In responding to a terrorist, or "non-traditional" threat, however, the President's authorities are less clear. For situations involving al Qaeda and its affiliates, the President is able to exercise more expansive discretion that will receive great deference from the courts. When it comes to terrorist organizations and individuals not associated with al Qaeda, however, the President does not possess the same degree of authority. In other words, not all Homeland Defense actions are created equal.

The President's Constitutional Authority and Duty to Secure the Nation

"I will guard it with my life, sir."[17]

A nation's duty to protect its citizens is as Secretary Rice has stated "the first and oldest duty of any government...."[18] The U.S. Constitution places this duty plainly in the hands of the federal government. It is the U.S. Congress that

---

17. William Travis, in the motion picture *Alamo*, played by the actor Patrick Wilson. *Available at* http://www.imdb.com/title/tt0318974/quotes.

18. Secretary Rice Statement, U.S. Sec'y of State, Remarks Upon Her Departure for Europe (December 5, 2005). *Available at* http://www.state.gov/secretary/rm/2005/57602.htm.

must: "provide for the common Defence and general Welfare of the United States; declare War; raise and support Armies; make Rules for the Government and Regulation of the land and naval Forces; provide for calling forth the Militia; provide for organizing, arming and disciplining the Militia; and, make all Laws which shall be necessary and proper for carrying into Execution the foregoing Powers...." Moreover, Article IV, Section 4 states: "The United States ... shall protect each [State] ... against Invasion."

While the Tenth Amendment requires that all powers not specifically delegated to the federal government must remain reserved to the states, it is clear from the Constitution that the duty to provide for a common defense, i.e. Homeland Defense, and the duty to protect the States from *invasion* are explicitly delegated to the federal government.

If the federal government fails in that duty, states retain a limited right to engage in war—to conduct Homeland Defense—if "actually invaded, or in such imminent Danger as will not admit of delay."[19] In addition, the Second Amendment states that: "A well regulated Militia, being necessary to the security of a free State, the right of the people to keep and bear Arms, shall not be infringed." Taken together, states maintain a Homeland Defense role to the extent it is necessary to defend the state and does not impede upon the federal government's duty to defend the nation as a whole.

Within the federal government, it is the President who has the responsibility for Homeland Defense. Article II of the Constitution makes the President the "Commander in Chief" of the military, vests the President with the "executive power," and places a duty on the President to "take Care that the Laws be faithfully executed." The triangulation of these three clauses unequivocally places the Constitutional duty of securing the country on the President and, commensurate with that duty, gives the President the authority and powers necessary to secure the nation. At a minimum, these powers include employing military forces under a declaration of war, under specific statutory authority, and under a national emergency from an attack on the nation or its armed forces.[20] During the 1787 Philadelphia Convention, the Framers specifically addressed the President's authority to repel sudden attacks. While debating whether Congress should have the power to "make" or "declare" War, the

---

19. U.S. Const. Art. IV, Sec. 4.

20. *See* War Powers Resolution, 50 U.S.C. §§ 1541–1548. *See also* The Prize Cases, wherein the Supreme Court stated "[i]f a war be made by invasion of a foreign nation, the President is not only authorized but bound to resist force by force. He does not initiate the war, but is bound to accept the challenge without waiting for any special legislative authority." 67 U.S. 635, 668 (1862).

Framers settled on the power to "declare War," leaving to the President, as James Madison explained, the power to "repel sudden attacks."[21] Arguably, the President's powers extend even further. For instance, combining the Commander in Chief clause with the President's foreign relations authorities, presidents have deployed military forces into hostilities over 300 times, only eleven of which were preceded by a declaration of war by Congress.[22]

The President has the authority to delegate Homeland Defense missions to the states. Congress has set forth, in statute, the manner in which the President may do so. Under Title 32, Chapter 9 of the United States Code, the President, through the Secretary of Defense, may determine that it is "necessary and appropriate" for the National Guard of a state to perform a "homeland defense activity."[23] In addition, the President may authorize, again through the Secretary of Defense, the National Guard to support federal operational missions.[24] Under both authorities, the governor of the state must agree to the use of the National Guard in this fashion and, in fact, the National Guard remains under the control of the governor.

Regardless whether Homeland Defense is actually performed by federal forces under NORTHCOM, or delegated down from the President to state National Guard forces operating under the control of governors, it remains a federal mission. The legal challenge lies not with whether Homeland Defense is a federal mission, but rather whether the situation justifies a Homeland Defense response as opposed to a law enforcement response, where civilian authorities and states maintain primacy with the federal military acting in a Civil Support status.

Traditional Homeland Defense Missions

In October 1962, at the brink of thermonuclear war, President Kennedy ordered U-2 flights and a naval quarantine of Cuba, while readying the nation for possible war. The Soviets had secretly placed Medium Range Ballistic Mis-

---

21. *See* Phillip R. Trimble, *International Law: United States Foreign Relations Law* 198 (2002).

22. Richard F. Grimmett, *Instances of Use of United States Armed Forces Abroad, 1798–2007*, CRS Report for Congress, Jan. 14, 2008. The eleven declarations of war addressed only five distinct conflicts. Nonetheless, the President has only employed forces approximately twenty times without some form of Congressional approval. *See* Phillip R. Trimble, *International Law: United States Foreign Relations Law* 215 (2002).

23. 32 U.S.C. §§ 901–908.

24. 32 U.S.C. § 502(f).

siles on Cuba, capable of delivering a nuclear payload on Washington D.C. The Soviets were also preparing to ship Intermediate Range Ballistic Missiles to Cuba, and intended to make Cuba a submarine base for Submarine-Launched Ballistic Missiles.[25] President Kennedy's quarantine, U2 flights, display of national resolve, and willingness to further use military power caused the Soviets to back down, diverting World War III and removing communist nuclear weapons from the Western Hemisphere.

Similarly, on December 7, 1941, when the Japanese attacked Pearl Harbor, the U.S. military attempted to repel the attack with anti-aircraft fire and with the few military aircraft fighters that were able to take-off from their airfield.

Both the Cuban missile crisis and Pearl Harbor fit the traditional paradigm of Homeland Defense: a threat from a foreign nation, DoD as the lead response agency, military members in uniform, force on force, and application of the laws of armed conflict—all to protect national sovereignty.

This traditional paradigm of Homeland Defense retains validity today. While the Cold War is over, the potential threat from foreign nation-states continues to exist, requiring vigilance in the area of Homeland Defense. For example, in September 2006, NORTHCOM assets tracked the flight of a Taepo Dong 2 missile fired by North Korea's leader Kim Jong-Il;[26] and in 2008, Russian TU-95 Bear heavy bombers have probed North America's Air Defense Identification Zone (ADIZ), near Alaska, on 18 occasions, causing NORAD to scramble F-15 Strike Eagles and F-22 Raptors in response, to assess the intent of the Russian bombers.[27]

In each of these situations, the duty to defend the homeland was clear, and the reaction of the United States involved a military response, or at least the threat of a military response. A law enforcement response was not used, and if it had been attempted, it would have failed. For good reason, there was no debate at Pearl Harbor between DoD and the FBI concerning who should be the lead federal agency in response to the attack. The Japanese attacked and the U.S. military attempted to repel the attack; it was war, not a crime. It was that simple.

---

25. Graham Allison and Philip Zelikow, *Essence of Decision: Explaining the Cuban Missile Crisis* 99 (2nd Ed. 1999).

26. Norimitsu Onishi and David E. Sanger, "Missiles Fired by North Korea; Tests Protested," *N.Y. Times* (Jul 5, 2006). *Available at* http://www.nytimes.com/2006/07/05/world/asia/05missile.html?fta=y.

27. Rowan Scarborough, "Russian Flights Smack of Cold War," *Wash. Times* (Jun. 26, 2008). *Available at* http://www.washtimes.com/news/2008/jun/26/russian-flights-smack-of-cold-war/.

Terrorism: Mutating the Paradigm

Under the emergence of a substantial terrorist threat, the traditional paradigm of Homeland Defense faces challenges. Terrorism pushes and pulls the traditional paradigm to a point that it begins to lose its contours, its identity. Specifically, terrorism does not follow the time-honored markers that separate war from crime. Terrorism, rather, falls in the seam between the two.

To treat terrorism exclusively as war ignores the clandestine, fragmented, decentralized, transnational, and potentially omnipresent nature of the terrorist threat. That is, there generally is no state to attack, no clear battle lines, no uniforms, no particularized description of the enemy, no easy way to clearly differentiate the enemy from civilians, and no method to determine the end of the conflict or to know, with certainty, when it is deescalating. Perhaps most importantly, treating terrorism exclusively as war ignores the fact that its *modus operandi* is committing spectacular and heinous acts that do not fall into any permissible law of war category—other than to qualify as a war crime.

Conversely, treating terrorism simply as a crime misses the point that it is not motivated by forces typically associated with crime. Terrorism is politically, ideologically, and religiously based. It is primarily, although not exclusively, foreign directed. The crime paradigm also woefully underestimates the potential lethality of terrorism. The salient example is al Qaeda's determination to obtain weapons of mass destruction and intentionally target civilians, with the ultimate objective to achieve the eventual destruction of our society, regardless of the time it takes.

Al Qaeda Network (AQN) and Authorization for Use of Military Force (AUMF)

While the *de facto* situation of terrorism is one of ambiguity, the *de jure* situation is clear: the United States and al Qaeda are in an armed conflict, or as some would say, an undeclared (imperfect or unconventional) war.[28] On February 23, 1998, Osama Bin Laden issued what he considered to be a *"fatwa,"*

---

28. Imperfect war is a means to express the existence of war without a declaration of war, of which only Congress may carry out. *See* Phillip R. Trimble, *International Law: United States Foreign Relations Law* 198 (2002). *See also U.S. v. Hamdi*, 542 U.S. 547, 520 (2004) (wherein the Supreme Court refers to the conflict as an "unconventional war"). For a discussion on Congress' authority to authorize, and its responsibility to set limits on, the use of force in undeclared wars, *see* Michael J. Glennon, "A Conveniently Unlawful War," *Policy Review*, No. 150, Aug. & Sep 2008.

stating in part: "The ruling to kill the Americans and their allies, civilians and military, is an individual duty for every Muslim who can do it in any country...."[29] Al Qaeda carried forward on this threat on 9/11.

Three days later, Congress passed the Authorization for Use of Military Force (AUMF) by joint resolution with a Senate vote of 98–0 and a House vote of 420–1.[30] The President signed the AUMF into law on September 18, 2001. The AUMF explicitly authorizes the President to:

> use all necessary and appropriate force against those nations, organizations, or persons he determines planned, authorized, committed, or aided the terrorist attacks that occurred on September 11, 2001, or harbored such organizations or persons, in order to prevent any future acts of international terrorism against the United States by such nations, organizations or persons.[31]

The language goes on to specifically state that the AUMF "is intended to constitute specific statutory authorization within the meaning of section 5(b) of the War Powers Resolution."[32] Meaning that, with the AUMF, Congress is providing the President specific authority to introduce military troops into hostilities in addition to any other Constitutional authority the President may independently possess. In *Hamdan v. Rumsfeld*,[33] the Supreme Court stated that it assumed "that the AUMF activated the President's war powers...."[34]

From its title to its closing, written in the parlance of armed conflict, the AUMF provides broad and sweeping authority for the President. While the AUMF is explicitly limited to those who "planned, authorized, committed, or aided" the 9/11 attacks, i.e. al Qaeda, it is the President who determines the scope of this category. In addition, there is no limit on where the President can invoke this authority or for how long. Nothing prohibits the President from using this authority within the borders of the United States. Moreover, there is no time limit associated with the President's use of force under the AUMF. While the War Powers Resolution typically serves as a marker Congress may point to and argue for a limit to the duration of military operations, the AUMF serves as a

---

29. Rohan Gunaratna, *Inside Al Qaeda: Global Network of Terror*, 61, Berkley Publishing Group, 2003.

30. Richard F. Grimmett, *Authorization for Use of Military Force in Response to the 9/11 Attacks (P.L. 107-40) Legislative History*, CRS Report for Congress, at CRS-3, Jan. 16, 2007.

31. 107 P.L. 40 § 2(a) (2001).

32. *Id.* at § 2(b)(1).

33. Hamdan v. Rumsfeld, 126 S. Ct. 2749, 2775 (2006).

34. *Id.*

Congressional "specific authorization," and thus negates the 60 day limit found in Section 5(b) of the War Powers Resolution. Lastly, the AUMF specifically authorizes the President to use "all necessary and appropriate force," without qualification, to "prevent any further acts of international terrorism against the United States...." It is an expansive grant of power giving the President wide latitude against al Qaeda specifically, but also, in a practical sense, against *any* terrorists who fall under the al Qaeda Network (AQN).

Al Qaeda continues to cultivate a global network. Although significantly weakened by the loss of its ability to operate openly in Afghanistan, as a direct result of U.S. and coalition forces defeating the Taliban and critical elements of al Qaeda, it has reverted to fracturing, dispersing, decentralizing, and developing loose connections throughout the world. The breadth and gravity of the AQN threat, coupled with the broad language of the AUMF, enables the President to reasonably cast a net over a large group of terrorists under the authority of the AUMF.

When the President uses his war powers to cast that net in a way consistent with the explicit will of Congress, the President is at the zenith of his powers. In the concurring opinion of Justice Jackson in the Supreme Court case of *Youngstown Sheet & Tube v. Sawyer*,[35] Justice Jackson established a tripartite framework that is now widely accepted as the standard for analyzing executive authority. Specifically, Justice Jackson explained the first category of authority with the following words: "[w]hen the President acts pursuant to an express or implied authorization of Congress, his authority is at its maximum, for it includes all that he possesses in his own right plus all that Congress can delegate. In these circumstances ... may he be said ... to personify the federal sovereignty ... supported by the strongest of presumptions and the widest latitude of judicial interpretation...."[36]

Under the AUMF, combined with the President's Article II authorities, the President's authority to employ the military in a Homeland Defense role against al Qaeda and associated elements is one in which the President enjoys significant discretion and which will likely receive substantial judicial deference.

Other Terrorists and National Emergencies

For those terrorists groups that are *clearly* not affiliated with AQN, the AUMF does not apply. In Justice Jackson's tripartite analytical model, the President's authority against these terrorists would fall into either the second or third category.

---

35. Youngstown Sheet & Tube Co. v. Sawyer, 343 U.S. 579, 635 (1952) (Jackson, J., concurring opinion).

36. *Id.* at 635–37.

The second category is what Justice Jackson described as a "zone of twilight," where the President and Congress share power or, at the very least, where the distribution of power is uncertain. In that case, "congressional inertia, indifference or quiescence may sometimes, at least as a practical matter, enable, if not invite, measures on independent presidential responsibility."[37] The third category occurs when "the President takes measures incompatible with the expressed or implied will of Congress," placing the President's power "at its lowest ebb, for then he can rely only upon his own constitutional powers minus any constitutional powers of Congress over the matter."[38]

The President, therefore, continues to possess authority to take military action against terrorists not affiliated with al Qaeda, even though they do not fall under the AUMF. In doing so the President must rely solely on his Article II authorities. In cases where there is no "expressed or implied" statute prohibiting the contemplated action, the President is invited to exercise his Article II authorities at his discretion.

Part of the President's Article II authorities includes the authority to defend the nation from attack and employ the military when there is a "national emergency created by attack."[39] Immediately after 9/11, the President declared a national emergency and has continued that declaration every year since.[40] To the extent that the President invokes military forces in a Homeland Defense role to defend the nation and to address concerns with the national emergency, his authority sits in Justice Jackson's second category, and likely will withstand even close judicial scrutiny. The more Homeland Defense actions move away from those two areas and closer to confronting specific statutes addressing individual's rights, the lower the President's authority becomes.

To a large extent, the President has already made tough choices on how the nation will address terrorism inside the homeland. National Security Presidential Directive 5 (HSPD-5)[41] designates the Department of Homeland Security (thorough FEMA) as the lead federal agency for consequence management and support to law enforcement. Moreover, HSPD-5 and Presidential Decision Directive 39 (PDD-39),[42] designate the Department of Justice (thorough the FBI)

---

37. *Id.* at 637.

38. *Id.*

39. War Powers Resolution, 50 U.S.C. § 1541(c).

40. The President has done so most recently with a statement signed on September 21, 2009. *See* 74 Fed. Reg. No. 182, FR Doc. E9-23055 (Sept. 21, 2009).

41. U.S. Dep't of Homeland Security, Presidential Dir. HSPD-5, Management of Domestic Incidents (Feb. 28, 2003).

42. Presidential Decision Directive 39: U.S. Policy on Counterterrorism (Jun. 21, 1995).

as the lead federal agency for counter-terrorism in the homeland. These documents place the military in a presumptive Civil Support role. The President retains the authority, however, under the President's War Powers, to designate an appropriate mission as Homeland Defense.[43]

Implementing Homeland Defense

The answers to three questions help determine when a Homeland Defense mission, within the homeland,[44] is appropriate: (1) *Necessity*. Is the threat so grave that it necessitates a military response? (2) *Al Qaeda*. Is the threat from al Qaeda or one of its affiliates? (3) *Domain*. What domain will the operation primarily use? Will it be in one of the domains most amenable for a Homeland Defense response—the air and sea domains—or will it primarily reside in the domain least likely to call for a Homeland Defense response—the land domain?[45]

Necessity: Survival is a powerful force in nature.[46] Unsurprisingly, nations have consistently exerted the right of survival, and indeed, nations have a duty to protect their children, citizens, and inhabitants, as well as the nation's own political sovereignty. President Abraham Lincoln addressed the duty to secure the nation's political survival by promulgating the Lieber Code in the Civil War, which states: "To save the country is paramount to all other consideration."[47] The United Nations recognized the concept of state survival as an in-

---

43. HSPD-5 explicitly makes the point that "[n]othing in this directive impairs or otherwise affects the authority of the Secretary of Defense over the Department of Defense, including the chain of command for military forces from the President as Commander in Chief, to the Secretary of Defense, to the commander of military forces, or military command and control procedures." HSPD-5, *supra* note 41, at para. (9).

44. A fourth question of whether the operation will be within or outside the homeland is also relevant, but beyond the scope of this chapter. This chapter's particular focus is on those operations within the homeland.

45. These three broad categories of domains can be parsed further into five categories by making space and cyber separate domains. For the purposes of this chapter, both generally fall within the air domain.

46. Survival is the underlying force that occupies the first two levels of primacy in Maslow's Hierarchy of needs. History exhibits its affect. Indeed, it is the ever persistent drive to secure survival that was responsible for the creations ranging from the moat and castle, Wall of China and gunpowder, to the nuclear bomb, intercontinental ballistic missile, and the predator.

47. Lieber Code, Article 5, *reprinted in* Dietrich Schindler and Jiri Toman, eds., *The Laws Of Armed Conflicts: A Collection of Conventions, Resolutions and Other Documents*, 4 (1981).

herent right when it crafted its Charter by making an exception under Article 51 to the general prohibition of force by stating that "[n]othing in the present Charter shall impair the inherent right of ... self-defense if an armed attack occurs against a Member of the United Nations...."[48] The International Court of Justice (ICJ) explicitly recognized this right by refusing to outlaw the threat of the use of nuclear weapons in stating: "[t]he court cannot lose sight of the fundamental right of every state to survival...."[49]

When survival of the citizenry or political sovereignty of the nation is truly at stake, the President has the daunting responsibility to protect both, making it much more likely that the President will invoke Homeland Defense response. Yet not every terrorist situation places survival in the balance. In fact, based on the continuing policies reflected in HSPD-5 and PDD-39, the past and current administrations presumably haved decided that most do not. The rub of this matter, however, is that, other than in hindsight, it is difficult to mark the line that demarcates a survival situation from one that falls short of threatening true survival. Due to that difficulty, it is an area wherein the President maintains great discretion. With that discretion comes the concept of prudence, which may very well dictate that the President err on the side of invoking Homeland Defense too early rather than too late. The potential cost of failing to invoke Homeland Defense when it is necessary is no less than the complete destruction of the nation.

Al Qaeda: Intimately related to necessity, given their stated intentions to obtain weapons of mass destruction and to destroy this nation, is the question of whether the threat involves al Qaeda—our particular present enemy.[50] When the situation involves al Qaeda, the President has broad authority to invoke his war powers and employ a Homeland Defense response. The President's Article II authorities, coupled with the AUMF, place the President's powers at their maximum. Threat from terrorists unaffiliated with AQN would not include authority from the AUMF. But a Homeland Defense response may still be appropriate—it would simply be more dependent on the factual circumstances and exact nature of the threat.

Domain: The domain of the operation—air, sea, or land—is a very important consideration. State sovereignty over air and sea domains is not nearly as entrenched or jealously guarded by the states as sovereignty over their land.

---

48. U.N. Charter of the United Nations, Article 51.

49. *Legality of the Threat or Use of Nuclear Weapons, Advisory Opinion*, 1996 I.C.J. Rep. para. 96. (July 8, 1996).

50. If Congress expands the Authorization of Use of Military Force (AUMF) to include additional groups, this analysis would also apply to those groups.

The federal government "has exclusive sovereignty of airspace of the United States."[51] That is to say that states exercise very little control over navigable airspace above their lands.[52] Likewise, states possess limited authority over the seas. States and the federal government share concurrent jurisdiction out to 3 miles, and then the sea turns into exclusive federal jurisdiction from 3 miles out to 12 miles (with the exceptions of Texas and Florida that have concurrent jurisdiction out to 9 miles).[53] The states' 3 mile concurrent jurisdiction is further limited by federal supremacy, specifically reflected in the following statutory language: "The United States retains all its navigational servitude and rights in powers or regulation and control … of navigable waters for the constitutional purposes of … national defense.…"[54]

The limited nature of the state interest in both the air and sea make these domains more susceptible to a Homeland Defense response, if for no other reason than the pure aspect that it is primarily the federal government that is monitoring and controlling both venues. The leap from one lead federal agency to another, i.e. to DoD, in practice tends to be a shorter one when states are not involved.

This is particularly true with the United States Coast Guard. The Coast Guard serves under the Department of Homeland Security and "is the lead federal agency for maritime security operations for Homeland Security in the US maritime domain."[55] At the same time, it remains a branch of the armed forces and the President has the authority to order the Coast Guard into the service of the Navy.[56] The process is not an onerous one; if the Coast Guard is needed for a Homeland Defense mission, the President can simply issue an executive order placing the Coast Guard under the Navy's control.

The ease in shifting from a law enforcement mission into a Homeland Defense mission similarly exists in the air domain. For instance, NORAD conducts aerospace warning, twenty-four hours a day, 365 days a year, working hand-in-hand with the Federal Aviation Administration (FAA) and NAV Canada (Canada's equivalent to the FAA). The former commander of NORAD and NORTHCOM, General Ralph E. Eberhart, explained the seamless integration

---

51. 49 U.S.C. §4013.

52. *Id.*

53. 43 U.S.C. §1312. For the Texas exception, *see U.S. v. Louisiana*, 363 U.S. 1 (1959). For the Florida exception, *see U.S. v. Florida*, 363 U.S. 121 (1960). The exceptions pertain only to domestic issues and are not meant to address a state's authority to invoke its jurisdiction vis-à-vis foreign nations. *See Louisiana*, 363 U.S. at 35.

54. 43 U.S.C. §1314.

55. Joint Pub. 3-26, at II-4, *supra* note 15.

56. 14 U.S.C. §1.

of military forces in the air domain with the following testimony to the 9/11 Commission:

> "In the aftermath of the 9/11 attacks, NORAD partnered with the FAA to enhance our ability to monitor air traffic within the interior of the country.... Furthermore, we have worked with ... Canada's equivalent, NAV CANADA, to improve connectivity and streamline notification processes ... We have established a system of conference calls to facilitate the sharing of information between the White House, DoD, FAA, U.S. Customs Service and law enforcement agencies.... The President and Secretary of Defense have approved rules of engagement to deal with hostile acts within domestic airspace.... They define what we can and cannot do in responding to a situation."[57]

General Eberhart's testimony highlights the federal exclusivity of the Air Domain and tight nexus between federal civilian agencies and the military. In addition, General Eberhart's testimony implicitly makes another point— the ability to respond with a civilian law enforcement response varies with the domain.

In the air and sea, DoD's capabilities dwarf those of the state and federal law enforcement agencies. While the civilian law enforcement agencies have assets for operations in both the air and sea domains, their ability to project force in the air pales to that which the U.S. Air Force can bring to any potential threat. Likewise, the civilian law enforcement agencies simply cannot match the same degree of parity with DoD in the sea, as they can on land.

Capability alone, however, does not necessarily mean that DoD should operate in a Homeland Defense mode. DoD could, and does, operate in a Civil Support role in both the air and sea domains in support of other federal agencies. The fact that DoD operates in those two domains in a much more exclusive fashion, however, inevitably leads to environments dominated by DoD's tactics, techniques and procedures, setting the scene for a much more seamless transition into the Homeland Defense mode.

Perhaps the most important difference between the domains is the fact that on land, the use of Homeland Defense measures is much more likely to negatively affect the liberties and freedoms of the public. By definition, DoD in-

---

57. General Ralph E. Eberhart, USAF, Cdr NORAD, testimony before the National Commission on Terrorist Attacks Upon the United States, 17 June 2004. *Available at* http://govinfo.library.unt.edu/911/hearings/hearing12/eberhart_statement.pdf.

volvement in the land domain entails the use of soldiers—an extremely visible presence to the American public. In addition, Homeland Defense measures in the land domain would involve far more interaction between the military and citizens, with the greater potential for restrictions on individual liberties. For these reasons, most land domain operations will involve the federal military in a Civil Support role.[58] The most likely exception to this would be a quick reaction type force protecting critical infrastructure, where commanders are able to limit the mission and interaction with the public. Another option when a homeland defense type of response is appropriate is for the President to consider asking whether the governors are willing to use their national guard in a state status.[59] It will only be the most severe circumstances that are likely to push the President to invoke a pure Homeland Defense response in the land domain.

If one compared the domains as far as likelihood that the military would operate in a Homeland Defense role, the order would be as follows: air domain, followed closely by the sea domain and then, dead last—the land domain. It will only be the gravest situations approaching a threat to national survival, as addressed above, that will find the military on land in its Homeland Defense mode.

Conclusion

While terrorism brings new legal challenges to Homeland Defense, the issues presented nonetheless have roots that go back to the Philadelphia Convention in 1787, as exemplified in the text of the Constitution.

Few documents exhibit the care of draftsmanship that the United States Constitution manifests. While the Preamble is, in legal terms, precatory in nature, it nonetheless speaks volumes to the purpose of the document and the intent of the Framers as they laid the foundation and built the structure of our government. The Preamble of the Constitution states as follows:

> We the People of the United States, in Order to form a more perfect Union, establish Justice, insure domestic Tranquility, provide for the common defence, promote the general Welfare, and secure the Bless-

---

58. *See* note 61 *infra* and accompanying text.
59. This could be done under either 32 U.S.C. §§ 901–908 or 32 U.S.C. § 502f. *See supra* notes 23 and 24.

ings of Liberty to ourselves and our Posterity, do ordain and establish this Constitution for the United States of America.[60]

The Framers obviously realized the value and necessity of the states to centralize the function of defense in securing the new nation, and thus explicitly stated that one of objectives of the Constitution was to "provide for the common defence." Indeed, the import and success of a common defense has only increased in time, bearing out the insight that the Framers possessed. The Framers did not, however, set forth in the Preamble "how" the nation should provide for a common defense. Clearly, the military brings a level of force and skill unparalleled by any other entity concerning the ability to provide for the "common defense." Yet a common defense is only one of the seven foundational footings the Constitution rests upon—perfect Union, Justice, Tranquility, general Welfare, Liberty and Posterity appear to hold equal value. And thus, when balancing the need for security on one side against that of preserving the liberties and freedoms of this nation on the other, a Homeland Defense approach risks placing a heavy thumb on only one side of that scale.

For instance, it may be that the most effective way to eliminate the threat of terrorism would be to take a war model and apply it, in a persistent manner, to all terrorist threats and events in the homeland. This would free the military to act more decisively, such as permitting the use of deadly force upon distinction—that is, upon identifying individuals as combatants, regardless of their immediately preceding conduct. But to do so would eviscerate six out of seven pillars of the Constitution anchored in the Preamble, it would play into the hands of the terrorists, and it would give way to their ultimate objectives—the end of America's free society.

Balancing security against civil liberties in a post-9/11 environment is the most difficult contemporary issue facing the Executive Branch as it plans for, and executes, national security. The crux of the problem is a tension between ensuring that enough is being done to prevent a potentially devastating terrorist attack, while at the same time, keeping a free and open society. Terrorists know this and torque that tension by persistently attempting to exploit the seams created by this nation's fidelity to individual freedoms and aversion to military rule. In an attempt to strike the right balance, past and current Presidents have set the military in a default position of Civil Support for consequence management and counterterrorism within the United States. They have also placed Homeland Defense as NORTHCOM's number one priority.

---

60. U.S. Constitution, Preamble.

NORTHCOM stands alert and ready to respond in its Homeland Defense role when called upon by the President.

Military/Civilian Relationships:
Military Support of Civilian Authorities

"It is probable ... that not knowing how to use the military as a civil weapon, [the civil authority] will do too much or too little with it."
Thomas Jefferson to William Carmichael, 1789

As discussed in the previous section, the military may be called upon to defend the United States and its citizens from terrorists and a terrorist attack. In this Homeland Defense role, the military acts in a way we are most familiar with—as a lead entity, applying combat power directly against an enemy. Other instruments of national power and agencies at all levels of government may act in a support role to DoD's military mission.

Equally likely, however, is a scenario where the military will act domestically in a support role to another state or federal agency, commonly referred to as Civil Support (CS) missions. Civil Support is defined by DoD as "DOD support to US civil authorities for domestic emergencies, and for designated law enforcement and other activities."[61] Two examples of CS missions are the military aid provided during Hurricane Katrina and the military's support to counter-drug law enforcement efforts on the Southwest border. In contrast to a Homeland Defense mission, in this role DoD does not act independently, but rather only at the request of, and in support of, another agency. Frequently, the lead federal agency is in support of a State, which maintains, under the Tenth Amendment, police powers and powers to ensure the general welfare of its citizens. In the context of a terrorist threat, the two most likely domestic support roles for the military are provision of consequence management support in the aftermath of a terrorist attack and/or support to civilian law enforcement agencies (LEA) as they work to prevent and deter a terrorist attack or respond to an attack.

Consequence Management: Most people are familiar with military forces, both Active Duty and National Guard,[62] responding to natural disasters such as

---

61. Joint Publication 3-28, *Civil Support,* (14 Sept 2007), Glossary.

62. Every state has a National Guard, who operates under the command and control of the State governor. The Guard is often used by a state governor to respond to a natural disaster within a state, such as a flood. Guard units can also be placed under the command and control of the President to perform federal missions, such as combat tours in Iraq.

floods, hurricanes, and wildfires. What is unknown to many is that the system used to provide for such military support is a national system, designed to provide a comprehensive all-hazards approach to domestic incidents. The use of the military is simply one component of that response framework.

In the wake of the terrorist attacks on 9/11, Congress passed the Homeland Security Act of 2002.[63] The Act established the Department of Homeland Security (DHS), consolidating numerous personnel and agencies with consequence management missions and assets, such as the Federal Emergency Management Agency (FEMA), the Coast Guard, and the Secret Service, into one Department. DHS missions include prevention of terrorist attacks within the United States and consequence management for terrorist attacks that occur in the United States. In addition to creating DHS, the Homeland Security Act directed the development of a national response plan[64] and incident management system[65] that would integrate all levels of government to prepare for, respond to, and recover from domestic events regardless of their cause or complexity. The President carried out this statutory mandate through Homeland Security Presidential Directive 5 (HSPD-5).[66] HSPD-5 maintains the construct whereby the Attorney General is the lead official for conducting criminal investigations of terrorist acts or threats, while the Secretary of Homeland Security is the primary federal official for domestic incident management and response.

Although a national framework exists for a consequence management response, the first response to any incident is at the state and local level. Resources and capabilities at the lowest level are utilized first. In the case of a terrorist attack, local resources likely will be overwhelmed, and the governor will respond with state resources. As mentioned above, one of the governor's primary resources is the state's National Guard. The governor may use all the resources and capabilities of his National Guard to respond to a terrorist attack, to include consequence management resources, planning capabilities, equipment, personnel, and provision of security. The state's National Guard is the military force best positioned and prepared to respond to the aftermath of a terrorist attack, as it trains and plans for such missions as part of its overall responsibility as the militia of the state.

Depending on the severity of the attack and its consequences, however, state resources, including the National Guard, may be insufficient. One of the first

63. Pub. L. No. 107-296 (2002).
64. National Response Framework, Department of Homeland Security (January 2008).
65. National Incident Management System.
66. HSPD-5, *supra* note 41.

resources available to a state governor is the use of the Emergency Management Assistance Compact (EMAC). EMAC is a congressionally ratified organization that provides form and structure to interstate mutual aid.

Through EMAC, a disaster-impacted state can request and receive assistance from other member states, to include their National Guard forces, quickly and efficiently. If EMAC resources are unable to provide the full spectrum of response required, utilizing the national framework for incident management and support, a state or federal agency may request the assistance of the Department of Defense to aid in response to a terrorist incident.[67] The primary mission of the military, however, is to fight and win the nation's wars. Providing support in response to a domestic incident is a secondary mission, and one purposely restricted by laws and regulations. In general, DoD federal response assistance cannot be provided until three criteria exist: (1) civilian resources are overwhelmed or insufficient; (2) appropriate civilian authorities request assistance; and (3) the Secretary of Defense authorizes and orders the provision of support.[68]

While there are various categories and types of support DoD is authorized to provide civilian agencies, in the case of a terrorist attack, the most likely request will be for consequence management support. Much of this support may look very similar to that provided in response to a natural disaster—provision of medical care and supplies, evacuation support, search and rescue, and transportation of food, water, and supplies to an affected area.

Perhaps more relevant to a terrorist attack, however, is DoD's unique capability to provide consequence management response to a chemical, biological, radiological, nuclear, or high-yield explosive (CBRNE) event. While more and more local, state,[69] and federal agencies now possess some level of capability to respond to a CBRNE event, DoD has several unique capabilities and resources to assist in a CBRNE response that likely will be requested almost immediately.

The primary DoD resource for a CBRNE response is Joint Task Force Civil Support (JTF-CS), located in Virginia. JTF-CS is a deployable command and control headquarters for DoD units and personnel executing consequence man-

---

67. Robert T. Stafford Disaster Relief and Emergency Assistance Act, 42 U.S.C. § 1521, *et seq.*, as amended.

68. Immediate response authority.

69. The National Guard maintains a CBRNE Enhanced Response Force (CERF) capability. Currently there are 12 validated CERFs. The CERFs provide immediate response capability to the governor in the event of a CBRNE incident. If the incident occurs in the state in which the CERF is located, they respond to the incident directly. If it is outside the state of the closest CERF, the CERF is activated via the EMAC process discussed above.

agement operations in response to CBRNE incidents. The mission of JTF-CS is responsive—the unit does not focus on the cause of the incident but rather on a response to limit the effects of the incident. The National Guard maintains 55 Weapons of Mass Destruction Civil Support Teams (WMD-CSTs), enough for one in each state, territory, and the District of Columbia. The WMD-CSTs are also responsive units, designed to rapidly deploy members to assist local first responders. The intent of the WMD-CSTs specifically is to complement civilian first responders. Unlike elements of JTF-CS, the WMD-CSTs operate as state assets, under the control of the governor. If they are called to active duty, the WMD-CSTs normally will be placed under the operational control of JTF-CS.

Support to Law Enforcement: The preceding discussion of support provided to civilian agencies in the event of a terrorist attack focused exclusively on consequence management, provided post-attack. Does DoD have any role in the prevention of terrorist attacks? The vast resources, capabilities, and manpower resident in the Department of Defense lead many to the conclusion that DoD is the ideal agency to prevent terrorist attacks in the homeland. As discussed in a previous section, however, it is extremely difficult in the domestic environment to distinguish between a criminal and a terrorist, and decide which weapon to employ to counter the threat—law enforcement or military power. On the surface, the intuitive answer is to use all resources available, including the active duty military. The decision whether DoD assets engage in a Homeland Defense mission against an identified enemy is one held by the President, and is a decision that will vary depending on the necessity of the situation, the threat, and the primary domain where the operation will be conducted. But this does not answer the question of how, if at all, to use the military to *assist* in prevention of a terrorist attack as a Civil Support mission.

The primary law enforcement responsibility for prevention of a terrorist attack rests with the Attorney General, who acts through the Federal Bureau of Investigation. DoD is authorized, in limited circumstances, to provide support to law enforcement agencies in their efforts to prevent terrorist attacks. The power to assist, however, is strictly controlled by law and regulation. From the drafting of the Constitution through our history, our leaders have evidenced a reluctance to allow the federal military the ability to engage in law enforcement activities in the United States. In fact, active duty military personnel[70] are

---

70. The Posse Comitatus Act does not apply to the National Guard forces unless they are in an Active Duty (Title 10) status.

specifically prohibited by the Posse Comitatus Act from "execut[ing] the laws."[71] Court cases, regulations, and DoD policy have defined "executing the laws" to prohibit the military from providing direct, active assistance to law enforcement agencies (LEA), such as a search, seizure, arrest, apprehension, or use of military personnel for surveillance.[72]

Although active duty DoD personnel cannot provide "direct" assistance to civilian LEA,[73] they are authorized to provide various other types of support to civilian LEA, several of which are particularly relevant when working to prevent terrorist attacks and/or apprehend those responsible for an attack. In particular, DoD personnel can share intelligence information with civilian LEA, provide training and advice, loan or lease equipment to civilian LEA, and, at times, provide personnel to operate and maintain equipment.

Since 1981 the military has had the authority under 10 U.S.C. §371 to share information collected during military operations with law enforcement agencies.[74] After the attacks on September 11, 2001, Congress emphasized the importance of information sharing among all domestic entities as a key element in providing for the national security.[75] While the military cannot plan missions for the primary purpose of aiding civilian LEA in gathering information, the

---

71. 18 U.S.C. §1385.

72. United States v. Yunis, 924 F.2d 1086 (D.C. Cir. 1991); United States v. Kahn, 35 F.3d 426 (9th Cir. 1994); DoD Directive 5525.5, DoD Cooperation with Civilian Law Enforcement Officials (15 Jan 1986).

73. Interestingly, there is one area in consequence management and support to law enforcement merge: in 10 U.S.C. §382, Congress authorizes DoD, at the request of the Attorney General, to provide support to the Department of Justice in enforcing section 175 or section 2332e of Title 18 (during an emergency situation involving chemical or biological weapons of mass destruction. Under some circumstances, section 382 allows for direct military participation in civilian law enforcement activities, normally a violation of the Posse Comitatus Act.

74. Sec. 371. Use of information collected during military operations.

(a) The Secretary of Defense may, in accordance with other applicable law, provide to Federal, State, or local civilian law enforcement officials any information collected during the normal course of military training or operations that may be relevant to a violation of any Federal or State law within the jurisdiction of such officials.

(b) The needs of civilian law enforcement officials for information shall, to the maximum extent practicable, be taken into account in the planning and execution of military training or operations.

(c) The Secretary of Defense shall ensure, to the extent consistent with national security, that intelligence information held by the Department of Defense and relevant to drug interdiction or other civilian law enforcement matters is provided promptly to appropriate civilian law enforcement officials.

75. Homeland Security Act of 2002, §891(c).

needs of civilian LEA must be taken into account when planning military operations. If, for example, an Army sensor platform is planning a training mission in South Texas, the unit can consider a request by local LEA to place the sensors in a certain border crossing area during their training. Such a request may be based on the LEA's belief that criminal or terrorist elements are using that area to cross illegally into the United States. If the Army asset gathers information during their training, such as feedback that individuals are crossing the border, they can immediately share that information with local LEA.

The DoD also has the authority to provide certain types of training to LEA. 10 U.S.C. §373 allows DoD personnel to train LEA personnel on the operation and maintenance of equipment, as well as provide expert advice. The DoD policy addressing support to LEA allows the military to provide training that is not large scale or elaborate, and encompasses only basic military skills.[76] For example, an Army Military Police unit could provide a local sheriff's department training in areas such as basic marksmanship, mission planning, patrolling, and survival skills.[77] In addition to the obvious benefit of assisting in the maintenance of the skills of local LEA, training opportunities with LEA also allow for the formation of collaborative relationships between DoD personnel and LEA personnel. Such relationships are invaluable when both entities are called upon to work together in response to a local crisis. As with many other authorized types of DoD support, the assistance is provided on a reimbursable basis.

Not surprisingly, the military possess assets and equipment that most local and state LEA do not. Some equipment, such as firing range training equipment, is relatively easy to loan or lease to local LEA. More often, however, LEA request "high-end" equipment from DoD, such as aerial reconnaissance assets. The military possesses manned and unmanned aircraft that can provide real-time video that would be extremely useful to LEA attempting to track or capture terrorists. However, recall that the Posse Comitatus Act, in conjunction with the restrictions on collection of intelligence against US persons, severely restricts the support that DoD can provide LEA in the area of surveillance. The most likely approach to a LEA request for assistance in this situation might occur as follows: in the wake of a terrorist attack, the FBI requests DoD unmanned aerial assets to survey a specific area where the FBI believes a terrorist suspect is hiding. While DoD would not be able to provide support for this specific request, if DoD had assets airborne in the same area to fulfill an ap-

---

76. DoDD 5525.5.
77. DEPSECDEF memo.

proved request for assessment of the incident area and damage, it could turn over to the FBI any incidentally captured imagery of personnel in the area acting suspiciously.

In supporting such a request, however, DoD must be aware not only of Posse Comitatus restrictions, but also intelligence oversight rules and restrictions concerning the use of certain information. In general, DoD assets and personnel that are dedicated to the "intelligence" mission are restricted to collecting, analyzing, and disseminating information on foreign powers ("foreign intelligence (FI)") and information to protect against intelligence activities and espionage conducted by foreign powers against us ("counterintelligence (CI)"). When DoD intelligence components are conducting these two missions, intelligence oversight rules apply to them. These rules govern the collection, retention, and dissemination of information concerning U.S. persons. Basic Constitutional and privacy rights prevent collecting information about the domestic activities of U.S. persons. In general, in order to legally acquire information on U.S. persons, such action must be necessary to further one of the two missions of intelligence components, FI or CI. In a domestic terrorist event, unless specific information exists that the individual involved is not a U.S. person, DoD intelligence components could not acquire information on the individual as it would not fit into their FI or CI mission. In other words, DoD is not able to provide intelligence on U.S. persons to support LEA to either prevent or respond to a terrorist attack, as DoD intelligence components generally are prohibited from acquiring such information initially.

This does not mean that DoD intelligence components cannot assist LEA. DoD intelligence components can, with specific authorization from the Secretary of Defense, conduct non-intelligence activities such as the incident assessment mission discussed above. The unmanned aerial vehicle used to conduct the post-attack incident assessment could be an intelligence component asset, as long as the Secretary of Defense approved the use of that component for the specific mission discussed. Not only can DoD share incidental law enforcement information with the local LEA (such as the location of a suspicious individual meeting the description of the terrorist), but, for example, can also share the images showing the extent of the post-attack damage with civilian authorities in order to plan rescue or recovery missions.

In addition to the restrictions placed on DoD intelligence components, there are restrictions on information that DoD non-intelligence components can acquire and use. These restrictions focus on information about activities of persons and organizations not affiliated with DoD. Normally this type of information is used to support DoD itself, and not in support of other agencies. For example, if DoD is sending personnel into the post-attack area, clearly the commander should have situational awareness of any potential dangers or threats to his personnel. If information exists that terrorists are still in the area and intend to cause further harm, this information can be utilized and disseminated by the Military Police for use by the military forces.

Broadly speaking, although DoD has significant intelligence and information gathering resources, those resources are intended to be used against foreign enemies, not our own citizens. Complicated issues arise when dealing with the new phenomenon of "homegrown terrorists," who are defined as U.S. citizens, but aligned with a foreign threat against the U.S. The restrictions on the intelligence components of DoD are well-grounded in the Constitutional protections of our citizens; adjusting that balance to address issues such as homegrown terrorists requires significant debate and likely Congressional intervention.

Food for Thought

Clearly the lines between Homeland Defense missions and Civil Support missions are complex and often blurred. A seemingly simple (and realistic) example highlights the difficulties faced by decision-makers in this area:

> *A packed Boston subway "T" train on the Red Line explodes at Harvard Square, killing hundreds and injuring hundreds more. Less than thirty minutes later, across the country near Phoenix, Arizona, a single-engine crop-dusting aircraft meanders its way from the cotton fields and drops in low over Arizona State University, releasing a deadly concocted spray laced with weaponized anthrax into a packed Sun Devil Stadium. Meanwhile, a 10-kilo-ton nuclear blast goes off at the corner of 16th Street and Wynkoop in Denver, Colorado. The National Center for Counter-terrorism reports to the President that the attacks are being orchestrated by an al Qaeda cell operating out of France and Germany, through a sleeper cell in Detroit, Michigan. The sleeper cell is a mix of American citizens and aliens of Middle Eastern descent. Early indications are that this is only phase one in a planned four-phase attack.*

Should the President treat this as a Homeland Defense mission? If so, what aspects? Why? Which aspects, if any, should be treated as a Civil Support mission? Would a Civil Support response be limited by the Posse Comitatus Act? If not, why not?

Chapter 13

Jus ad Bellum in the Struggle Against Terror

*Walter Gary Sharp, Sr.**

Introduction

Sovereignty—no other principle more clearly defines the essence of international law, the customary relationship between states, and the right of states to take action or use force outside their territories against state and non-state sponsored terrorism. It once recognized that states, not individuals, played the exclusive role in international discourse and the use of force. Historically, states have dominated the international power base. For centuries, international law allowed sovereign states to wage war for any reason they considered just, constrained only by the law of war, but otherwise provided individuals no rights or standing. International law allowed states to treat, or mistreat, their own citizens in any way they desired with impunity. Individuals and non-governmental organizations had no standing, equity, or power under interna-

---

* Walter Gary Sharp, Sr. is the Senior Associate Deputy General Counsel for Intelligence, U.S. Department of Defense, and an Adjunct Professor of Law, Georgetown University Law Center, where he currently teaches a counterterrorism law course entitled "The Law of 24." Author of four books and numerous articles on issues relating to national and global security, he holds an S.J.D. from the University of Virginia School of Law; an LL.M. in Military Law from The Judge Advocate General's Legal Center and School; an LL.M. in International and Comparative Law from Georgetown University Law Center; a J.D. from Texas Tech School of Law; and a B.S. in Aerospace Engineering from the United States Naval Academy. Dr. Sharp is a retired Marine judge advocate who previously served as Associate Deputy General Counsel for International Affairs, U.S. Department of Defense, and Deputy Legal Counsel to the Chairman of the Joint Chiefs of Staff. Opinions, conclusions, and recommendations expressed or implied herein are solely those of the author and do not necessarily represent the views of the U.S. Department of Defense or any governmental agency or civilian institution.

tional law, and practically had very little influence or military power. Historically, sovereignty and international law governed the actions of states during peacetime and war, and of their armed forces during war, but domestic law otherwise governed the actions of individuals.

States gave up their sovereign right to wage aggressive war when they adopted the Charter of the United Nations [UN Charter] in 1945; i.e., the UN Charter now prohibits the aggressive use of force by states and embodies contemporary *jus ad bellum*—the law of conflict management that governs the threat and use of force between states. International law has also evolved to recognize the rights of the individual. States are now more willing to address human rights violations within other states, and have recognized a growing right of humanitarian intervention. States have also grown more economically and politically interdependent, and threats to their national security are now global and multidimensional. States now participate in international organizations, trade arrangements, mutual legal assistance treaties, defense alliances, collective security arrangements, and arms control agreements to manage their interdependence and threats to their national security. States have also empowered the UN Security Council with the legal authority to impose mandatory sanctions or to authorize the use of force to maintain and restore international peace and security. Sovereignty and international law have evolved from states having exclusive rights to having reciprocal rights that respect the territorial integrity and political independence of other states as well as recognize individual human rights. Through the end of the 20th century, sovereignty and international law continued to govern the actions of states during peacetime and war, contemporary *jus ad bellum* governed the predominant if not exclusive role of states in the use of force, the law of war governed the conduct of the armed forces of states during armed conflict, and despite that some international tribunals sanctioned individuals for crimes against humanity and war crimes, domestic law continued to principally govern the actions of individuals. Moreover, states have now broadly recognized that a modern liberal democracy—like that of the United States—is an inherently peaceful form of government that respects sovereignty and international law, does not engage in the aggressive use of force, protects individual human rights and civil liberties, and fosters global economic growth and political freedoms.

The world witnessed, however, an unparalleled advent of international terrorism on September 11, 2001 that radically altered the international power base. On that day, a network of individuals, i.e., non-state actors, demonstrated the ability to cause devastating destruction and mass murder on a horrific scale that was previously thought to be the exclusive domain of states. The capacity of individuals to engage in evil acts of mass terrorism is now painfully apparent. Technology now permits individuals with few resources to easily communicate and travel worldwide, to penetrate and destroy corporate and government information systems via the Internet from anywhere in the world, to coordinate simultaneous terrorist attacks over large distances, and to create chemical and biological weapons of mass destruction. Terrorists have now demonstrated the capability to cause destruction and commit murder on a horrific scale across international borders, and some believe this insidious capability of individuals challenges traditional applications of sovereignty, international law, contemporary *jus ad bellum*, the law of war, and domestic law. War, however, is defined under modern international law as an armed conflict or hostilities between two or more governments or states,[1] and prior to September 11, 2001, individuals and networks of individuals who engaged in the destruction of property and murder were considered criminals and were prosecuted under domestic law. After September 11, 2001, however, the world is admittedly a very different place with extraordinary challenges facing international peace and security, but the application of basic principles of sovereignty, international law, contemporary *jus ad bellum*, the law of war, and domestic law have not fundamentally changed.

This chapter describes how contemporary *jus ad bellum* continues to serve as an effective legal regime to govern the right of states to take action or use force outside their territories in their struggle to prevent, deter, detect, and defeat international terrorism in a post-September 11, 2001 world. States have never given up and always retain their sovereign and inherent right of self-defense, regardless whether they are threatened by states or non-state actors; however, states have agreed that their international behavior and right to use force will be regulated by international law. The parties to the UN Charter have agreed, for example, "to accept and carry out the decisions of the Security Council."[2] When international peace and security is threatened, the Security Council may require Member States to apply measures against another state such as the "complete or partial interruption of economic relations and of rail, sea, air, postal, telegraphic, radio, and other means of communication, and the sev-

---

1. *See, e.g.,* MYRES S. MCDOUGAL & FLORENTINO P. FELICIANO, LAW AND MINIMUM WORLD PUBLIC ORDER: THE LEGAL REGULATION OF INTERNATIONAL COERCION 97–98 (1961). In contrast to this modern definition, consider the following definition of war based upon the law prior to 1948:

> War is the exerting of violence by one state or politically organized body against another. In other words, it is the implementation of a political policy by means of violence.

United States v. Wilhelm von Leeb, et al. (*The High Command Case*), XI TWC 485 (1948).
2. UN CHARTER art. 25.

erance of diplomatic relations."[3] Similarly, Member States have agreed that their obligations under the UN Charter prevail over their obligations under any other international agreement,[4] and any treaty that is inconsistent with its states party's obligations under the UN Charter is void *ab initio*.[5] Moreover, Member States have agreed to refrain from the threat or use of force against the territorial integrity or political independence of any state.[6]

Contemporary *jus ad bellum*, however, cannot be analyzed as a legal discipline in a vacuum. In viewing the international community's struggle against terrorism through the lens of game theory as a competition in which the success of one depends on the choices of others, contemporary *jus ad bellum* is a strategic complement to sovereignty, international law, the law of war, and domestic law. These five legal disciplines are mutually reinforcing and supporting. To best understand how contemporary *jus ad bellum* governs the conduct of states in their struggle against terrorism, it must be understood within the spectrum of the entirety of state activities against terrorism. Thus, after an introduction to contemporary *jus ad bellum*, this chapter will provide an overview of the international framework for state action against terrorism by describing the interrelationships between sovereignty, international law, contemporary *jus ad bellum*, the law of war, and domestic law that applies to state action against terrorism. The next two sections will discuss the application of contemporary *jus ad bellum* to the use of force against state and non-state sponsors of terrorism. The final section concludes that contemporary *jus ad bellum* continues to serve as an effective legal regime to govern the right of states to take action or use force outside their territories in their struggle to prevent, deter, detect, and defeat international terrorism in a post-September 11, 2001 world.

Contemporary *Jus ad Bellum*

War has been embraced as a legitimate form of violence throughout human history,[7] and until the late 19th century, war was judged by many as just or

---

3. UN CHARTER art. 41. The term "Member States" is used throughout the UN Charter to refer to states that are members of the United Nations.

4. UN CHARTER art. 103.

5. THE CHARTER OF THE UNITED NATIONS: A COMMENTARY 1122 (Bruno Simma ed., 1994).

6. UN CHARTER art. 2, para. 4.

7. McDOUGAL & FELICIANO, *supra* note 1, at 44; EUGENE V. ROSTOW, TOWARD MANAGED PEACE 41 (1993).

unjust on a moral plane.[8] Others believed that war was beyond law and morality, and that in time of war the law is silent.[9] In practice, efforts to control war by permitting only just war offered no war-preventing effects because either side could argue its use of force was just.[10] Nevertheless, efforts over the last 2,000 years have reduced and controlled international violence.[11] The morality of war was judged first with reference to why states fought, and second with reference to the means that states adopted to fight the war.[12] Medieval writers described these judgments as *jus ad bellum*, an analysis of whether a war is just or unjust, and *jus in bello* (the law of war), an analysis of whether how a war is fought is just or unjust.[13] Conflicts were evaluated on both planes; i.e., a just war of self-defense could be fought unjustly and an unjust war of aggression could be fought justly.[14]

A state's right to resort to war is now defined by contemporary *jus ad bellum* on a legal plane, and war can no longer be justified within the international community as morally just and thus permissible. The decline of seeking a moral justification for war and the reliance upon a legal basis for the resort to the use of force began with the Hague Peace Conferences of 1899 and 1907 that created juristic restrictions on the efforts of a state's right to resort to war.[15] Article 1 of the Hague Convention III of 1907 on the *Opening of Hostilities*, for example, required parties to provide a prior and unambiguous warning before resorting to war—however, this was simply a formalization of a state's right to resort to war.[16] In contrast, Article 1 of the Hague Convention II of 1907 on the *Limitation of the Employment of Force for the Recovery of Contract Debts* prohibited the recourse to war for the recovery of a contractual debt.[17]

From 1913 to 1916, the United States entered into nineteen bilateral treaties that required the parties to refer their disputes to a conciliation commission and not to begin hostilities prior to that commission's report.[18] Similarly, after World War I, parties of the Covenant of the League of Nations were prohib-

---

8. Michael Walzer, Just and Unjust Wars 3 (1977).

9. *Id.*

10. The Charter of the United Nations: A Commentary, *supra* note 5, at 109.

11. *See* National Security Law 29 (John Norton Moore & R.F. Turner, eds., 2d ed. 2005).

12. Walzer, *supra* note 8, at 21.

13. *Id.*

14. *Id.*

15. The Charter of the United Nations: A Commentary, *supra* note 5, at 109.

16. *Id.*

17. *Id.*

18. *Id.* at 109–10.

ited from resorting to war until after they submitted a dispute to judicial settlement, arbitration, or to the Council of the League of Nations.[19] Parties were
also required to then wait for a three-month "cooling-off period" after an arbitral award or Council's report, and were prohibited from resorting to war
against states complying with the an arbitral award or Council's report.[20] Article 2 of the Geneva Protocol of 1924 on the *Pacific Settlement of International
Disputes* obligated states "in no case to resort to war," except in the case of self-
defense or collective enforcement measures, but this protocol never became
binding law.[21] A number of European states also generally prohibited any attack, invasion, or war in Article 2 of the Locarno Treaty of 1925, but that treaty
also had exceptions and lost its binding force in 1935.[22]

The Kellogg-Briand Pact of 1928 was the decisive turning point in the development of juristic restrictions on the resort to war.[23] Almost all states existing
in 1928 became a party to this Pact that prohibited war except in the case of self-
defense.[24] The nations that did not join this Pact were a number of Latin American states, but they signed the Saavedra-Lamas Treaty of 1933 that contained
an identical prohibition on the resort to war as contained in the Kellogg-Briand
Pact.[25] The provisions of the Kellogg-Briand Pact quickly became customary international law and remain valid today; however, it was not linked to a system
of sanctions and did not prohibit the use of force, just the resort to war.[26]

The UN Charter was signed in 1945 "to save succeeding generations from
the scourge of war" and "to maintain international peace and security."[27] The
UN Charter now codifies contemporary *jus ad bellum* in Articles 2(4), 39, and
51.[28] Indeed, contemporary *jus ad bellum* is now a concept of *jus contra bellum*,
i.e., the law against the aggressive use of force.[29] The UN Charter clearly out-

---

19. *Id.* at 110.
20. *Id.*
21. *Id.*
22. *Id.*
23. *Id.*
24. *Id.*
25. *Id.*
26. *Id.* at 110–11. Although the provisions of the Kellogg-Briand Pact that prohibit war
except in self-defense remain valid as customary international law, they are now reflected
in the UN Charter as contemporary *jus ad bellum* and the Kellogg-Briand Pact is seldom referenced.
27. UN CHARTER pmbl. & art. 1.
28. THE CHARTER OF THE UNITED NATIONS: A COMMENTARY, *supra* note 5, at 111.
29. LOTHAR KOTZSCH, THE CONCEPT OF WAR IN CONTEMPORARY HISTORY AND IN-
TERNATIONAL LAW 83, 269–96 (1956). An "aggressive use of force" is a use of force in the
first instance that is inconsistent with the UN Charter, and must be distinguished from of-

laws the aggressive use of force while recognizing a state's inherent right of individual and collective self-defense in Article 51 and the Security Council's obligation under Article 39 to maintain or restore international peace and security. If a state threatens or uses force against another state within the meaning of Article 2(4), it is unlawful unless it is an exercise of that state's inherent right of self-defense or unless it is authorized by the Security Council under its coercive Chapter VII authority.

Articles 2(4), 39, and 51 must be read together to determine the scope of the UN Charter's prohibition on the aggressive use of force, the obligation and authority of the Security Council to enforce this prohibition, and the inherent right of all states to use force in self-defense.[30] Articles 2(4) and 51 provide:

> *Article 2.* The Organization and its Members, in pursuit of the Purposes stated in Article 1, shall act in accordance with the following Principles: ...
>
> (4) All Members shall refrain in their international relations from the threat or use of force against the territorial integrity or political independence of any state, or in any other manner inconsistent with the Purposes of the United Nations....
>
> *Article 51.* Nothing in the present Charter shall impair the inherent right of individual or collective self-defence if an armed attack occurs against a Member of the United Nations, until the Security Council has taken the measures necessary to maintain international peace and security. Measures taken by Members in the exercise of this right of self-defense shall be immediately reported to the Security Council and shall not in any way affect the authority and responsibility of the Security Council under the present Charter to take at any time such action as it deems necessary in order to maintain or restore international peace and security.[31]

Also, as an exercise of the international community's inherent right of collective self-defense, Article 39 of the Charter imposes an obligation on the Security Council to maintain international peace and security:

---

fensive military operations that are conducted in self-defense or pursuant to Chapter VII authority of the UN Charter.

30. WALTER GARY SHARP, SR., JUS PACIARII: EMERGENT LEGAL PARADIGMS FOR UN PEACE OPERATIONS IN THE 21ST CENTURY 280 (1999).

31. UN CHARTER arts. 2, para. 4 & 51.

Article 39. The Security Council shall determine the existence of any threat to the peace, breach of the peace, or act of aggression and shall make recommendations, or decide what measures shall be taken in accordance with Articles 41 [measures not involving the use of armed force] and 42 [measures involving the use of armed force, as may be necessary], to maintain or restore international peace and security.[32]

Articles 2(4) and 51 now reflect customary international law and are binding on all states,[33] and decisions taken by the Security Council under Article 39 are binding on all Member States as a matter of treaty obligation.[34]

Despite the watershed importance of the UN Charter in prohibiting the aggressive use of force, there have been significant challenges in interpreting these Charter provisions. Interpretations, for example, in determining what is a "threat or use of force," what is the "territorial integrity or political independence" of a state, what is an "armed attack," and how contemporary *jus ad bellum* applies to state activities in cyberspace are some of the principal issues.[35] It is important to note, however, in interpreting contemporary *jus ad bellum*, that Article 2(4) provides that Member States "shall refrain in their international relations from the threat or use of force against … *any state* [emphasis added]." Furthermore, Article 51 provides that nothing in the UN Charter "shall impair the inherent right of individual or collective self-defense if an *armed attack* [emphasis added] occurs.…" This textual analysis reflects that the right of a state to threaten or use force outside its territory is limited only with respect to how that threat or use of force impacts the territorial integrity or political independence of another state, or is in some manner inconsistent with the purposes of the United Nations. In contrast, Article 51's recognition of a state's inherent right of self-defense is not limited to an armed attack by a state. Accordingly, a state has an inherent right of self-defense against all armed attacks, regardless whether they are state or non-state sponsored. Sim-

---

32. UN CHARTER art. 39.

33. THE CHARTER OF THE UNITED NATIONS: A COMMENTARY, *supra* note 5, at 126–27, 666–67.

34. UN CHARTER art. 25; THE CHARTER OF THE UNITED NATIONS: A COMMENTARY, *supra* note 5, at 407–18.

35. For a sample of the detailed discussions available of the challenges of interpreting contemporary *jus ad bellum, see generally,* NATIONAL SECURITY LAW, *supra* note 11, at 69–210; THE CHARTER OF THE UNITED NATIONS: A COMMENTARY, *supra* note 5, at 106–28, 605–16, 661–78; IAN BROWNLIE, INTERNATIONAL LAW AND THE USE OF FORCE BY STATES 251–305, 338–423 (1963); WALTER GARY SHARP, SR., CYBERSPACE AND THE USE OF FORCE 27 (1999); and, SHARP, JUS PACIARII, *supra* note 30.

ilarly, the Security Council has the responsibility and the authority under Article 39 to make recommendations or decide what measures shall be taken to maintain or restore international peace and security when *any* threat to the peace, breach of the peace, or act of aggression exists.

No international convention interprets or defines the thresholds of Articles 2(4), 39, and 51. Thus, an analysis of interdependent, subjective, and sometimes politically volatile interpretations of state practice is required to determine what acts of state-sponsored terrorism constitute an unlawful use of force under international law or what acts of state-sponsored terrorism invoke a state's right of self-defense. Inherently, this analysis usually results in conclusions of law that fail to maintain any international consensus or provide any concrete precedent. For example, in response to the murder of seven Americans in two Libyan-sponsored bombings in Rome and Vienna in December of 1985 and the terrorist bombing of a West German discotheque in April of 1986, the United States justified the lawfulness of its April 1986 air strikes against terrorist training camps and military targets in Libya as an exercise of its right of self-defense as recognized by Article 51 of the Charter.[36] The air strikes were widely denounced, however, by the international community primarily because of the concern that it would perpetuate the cycle of violence.[37] A Security Council resolution condemning the U.S. action was vetoed by Great Britain, France, and the United States, but the UN General Assembly adopted a resolution condemning the air strikes by a vote of 79 to 28, with 33 abstentions.[38]

Nevertheless, an analysis of state practice is very useful in predicting when the "threat or use of force" and "territorial integrity or political independence" thresholds of Article 2(4) have been crossed and what is an "armed attack" within the meaning of Article 51. Figure 1 (overleaf) is a graphical illustration of contemporary *jus ad bellum* depicted along the spectrum of interstate relations that provides a useful framework for what is and is not considered a threat or use of force under international law and the corresponding right of states to respond and use force in self-defense. The top of the figure reminds us that policy decisions by states establish state practice that develops customary international law, which will in turn affect future policy decisions and state practice—a möbius strip of state activity that continues to develop and refine customary international law. The row labeled "activity" juxtaposes examples of what is and is not considered a threat or use of force, drawn from state prac-

---

36. *See* Gregory Francis Intoccia, *American Bombing of Libya: An International Legal Analysis*, 19 CASE W. RES. J. INT'L L. 179, 182–85, 191–92, 200–13 (1987).

37. *See id.* at 186–89.

38. *See id.* at 189.

Figure 1. The UN Charter *Jus ad Bellum* Framework and Use of Force Analysis

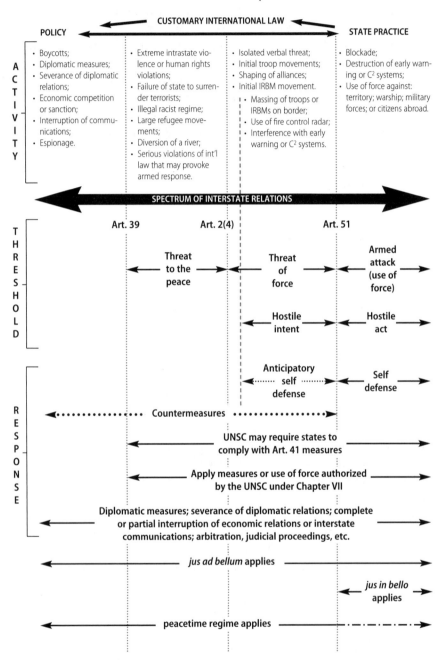

tice and Security Council decisions, along side the corresponding thresholds of Articles 39, 2(4), and 51 found in the row labeled "threshold." These activities represent the spectrum of activities that are examples of interstate relations, and are comprised—from left to right—of state activities that fall short of the use of force threshold to those that constitute an armed attack. These two normative sets are then juxtaposed against the row labeled "response" that identifies when a state may engage in interstate activities that are not considered a use of force; engage in measures authorized by the Security Council under Articles 41 and 42; or respond to a first row activity in anticipatory self-defense and self-defense.[39] Finally, the bottom of the figure reminds us that contemporary *jus ad bellum* applies throughout the spectrum of interstate relations; that *jus in bello* applies only during war or armed conflict; and that the peacetime regime applies throughout the spectrum of interstate relations except to the extent it is inconsistent with a state of hostilities.

Customary international law requires that all uses of force for either individual or collective self-defense be necessary and proportional, and it prohibits the use of force for retaliatory or punitive actions.[40] For example, the requirement of necessity for a state to use armed force in self-defense could clearly be met when a pattern of state-sponsored terrorism is established.[41] In contrast, if a single act of state-sponsored terrorism occurs, and it is evident from the circumstances that it is indeed an isolated act, then the principle of necessity would not justify the use of force in the absence of a continuing threat.[42] For example, in justifying the lawfulness of its April 1986 air strikes against military targets in Libya as an exercise of its right of self-defense, the United States emphasized Libya's policy on exporting terrorism and "compelling evidence of Libyan involvement in other planned attacks."[43]

---

39. Although not discussed in this chapter, the military concepts of "hostile intent" and "hostile act" are also represented in this figure as thresholds that trigger anticipatory self-defense and self-defense, respectively. These two military concepts are defined in Chairman of the Joint Chiefs of Staff Instruction (CJCSI) 3121.01B, *Standing Rules of Engagement/Standing Rules for the Use of Force for US Forces*, June 13, 2005, Encl. A, paras. 3e–3f. Unclassified portions of this CJCSI are discussed and *reprinted in* U.S. Army Judge Advocate General's Legal Center and School, Operational Law Handbook 83–116 (John Rawcliffe ed., 2007), *available at* http://stinet.dtic.mil/cgi-bin/GetTRDoc?AD=ADA 469294&Location=U2&doc=GetTRDoc.pdf.

40. *See* John Norton Moore, Crisis in the Gulf: Enforcing the Rule of Law 156–157 (1992); The Charter of the United Nations: A Commentary, *supra* note 5, at 677.

41. *See* Intoccia, *supra* note 36, at 200–12.

42. *See id.*

43. *See id.* at 191.

In addition to the international law requirement that a use of force in self-defense be a necessary and proportional response, international law similarly requires that a state's use of force during the attack on a military objective be proportional in intensity and magnitude to what is reasonably necessary to promptly secure the permissible objectives of self-defense.[44] The principle of proportionality does not unreasonably limit the use of force that can be used between combatants. Nor does it limit the use of force to destroy a military objective to the strength or firepower of that objective. Proportionality is a limitation on the use of force against a military objective only to the extent that such a use of force may cause unnecessary collateral destruction of civilian property or unnecessary human suffering of civilians.[45] The principle of proportionality is a balancing of the need to attack a military objective with the collateral damage and human suffering that will be caused to civilian property and civilians by the attack.[46] Proportionality categorically imposes *no* limitations on the use of force between combatants in the absence of any potential effect on civilians or civilian property.[47]

---

44. *See* Moore, *supra* note 40, at 158.

45. While civilian property and civilians may not be the *object* of an attack as such, states may use force against civilian objects and activities that support or sustain an enemy state's warfighting capability during armed conflict and are therefore military objectives as defined in art. 52, para. 2, of the 1977 Additional Protocol I to the four Geneva Conventions of Aug. 12, 1949. States may use force during armed conflict, for example, against economic targets such as enemy lines of communication, rail yards, bridges, rolling stock, barges, industrial installations producing warfighting products, and power generation plants. *See* U.S. Dep't of the Navy, NWP 1-14M, The Commander's Handbook on the Law of Naval Operations, para. 8.2 (July 2007) [hereinafter Commander's Handbook], *available at* http://www.nwc.navy.mil/cnws/ild/documents/1-14M_(Jul_2007)_(NWP).pdf. In today's modern society, much of a state's civilian infrastructure—such as telecommunications, Internet services, and power generation—is used for military purposes, and is thus subject to lawful attack during armed conflict. *See* U.S. Dep't of Def., Conduct of the Persian Gulf War: Final Report to Congress Pursuant to Title V of the Persian Gulf Conflict Supplemental Authorization and Personnel Benefits Act of 1991, Pub. L. No. 102-25, app. O at 613 (Apr. 1992) [hereinafter Conduct of the Persian Gulf War: Final Report].

46. It is not unlawful to cause *incidental* injury to civilians, or collateral damage to civilian property, during an attack on a legitimate military objective. The balancing of proportionality does require, however, that such incidental injury or collateral damage not be excessive in light of the military advantage anticipated by the attack. *See* Commander's Handbook, *supra* note 45, para. 8.2.

47. Indeed, one of the four strategic concepts of the national military strategy of the United States is to use decisive force to overwhelm an adversary. *See* Chairman of the Joint Chiefs of Staff, National Military Strategy of the United States of America 3 (1997). Moreover, in December 1990, U.S. Secretary of Defense Dick Cheney threat-

The International Legal Framework for State Action Against Terrorism

Sovereignty, international law, contemporary *jus ad bellum*, the law of war, and domestic law work together in a post-September 11, 2001 world to form a legal framework—a comprehensive body of law—that governs state action to prevent, deter, detect, and defeat international terrorism. This section will first highlight the basic principles of these five legal disciplines, and will then explain how they work together to form a framework for state action against terrorism.

Sovereignty is the touchstone of contemporary international relations. It is the exclusive right of a state to exercise absolute authority and control within its territory and jurisdiction. All states are absolutely independent sovereigns, and the "reciprocal independence of states is one of the most universally respected principles of international law."[48] Principles of sovereignty are embedded, for example, in Article 2(4) of the UN Charter that provides all Member States "shall refrain in their international relations from the threat or use of force against the territorial integrity or political independence of any state." Sovereignty also governs the right of states to take action or use force within the territories of other states.

International law regulates the interaction of states over a wide range of issues that includes statehood; recognition of states and governments; state responsibility; diplomatic and consular protection and immunity; the use of force by states; trade and investment; treaties; status of international organizations; treatment of nationals; immunity of states; jurisdictional conflicts; and, control of the sea, airspace, space, and celestial bodies.[49] Sovereignty, however, dictates that states can only be bound by those rules of international law to which they have agreed through written agreement or state practice.[50] Article 38 of the Statute of the International Court of Justice captures the sources of modern international law.[51] Paragraph 1 of Article 38 provides that the Court shall apply international law reflected in:

---

ened Saddam Hussein that the U.S. response to an Iraqi use of weapons of mass destruction would be "absolutely overwhelming and ... devastating." CONDUCT OF THE PERSIAN GULF WAR: FINAL REPORT, *supra* note 45, app. Q at 641.

48. JOSEPH MODESTE SWEENEY ET AL., THE INTERNATIONAL LEGAL SYSTEM 288–89 (2d ed. 1981).

49. *Id.* at xxiii–xxx.

50. THE CHARTER OF THE UNITED NATIONS: A COMMENTARY, *supra* note 5, at 80, 83.

51. SWEENEY ET AL., *supra* note 48, at 2.

a. international conventions, whether general or particular, establishing rules expressly recognized by the contesting states;
b. international custom, as evidence of a general practice accepted as law;
c. the general principles of law recognized by civilized nations; and
d. subject to the provisions of Article 59, judicial decisions and the teachings of the most highly qualified publicists of the various nations, as subsidiary means for the determination of rules of law.[52]

Article 59, referred to in Article 38(1)(d), provides that the decision of the International Court of Justice has "no binding force except between the parties and in respect of that particular case."[53] Resolutions and declarations of international organizations such as the United Nations are not international law, but if they "are meant to be declaratory of international law, are adopted with the support of all members, and are observed by the practice of states," then they can be considered "evidence of customary international law on a particular subject matter."[54]

Contemporary *jus ad bellum* and the law of war are a part of international law. As discussed in the previous section of this chapter, contemporary *jus ad bellum* is that body of international law embodied in the UN Charter that governs the threat or use of force between states and recognizes a state's inherent right of self-defense. The law of war, which will be discussed in detail in the next chapter of this book, is that body of international law that regulates the conduct of armed hostilities between states.

Domestic law, in the context of this chapter, refers to the laws and legal system of a state that govern its activities to counter state and non-state sponsored terrorism. Domestic law can be influenced, shaped, or constrained by international law. For example, the U.S. Torture Statute[55] implements the Convention Against Torture and Other Cruel, Inhuman, or Degrading Treatment or Punishment.[56] Similarly, the domestic law of one state may be supported by that of another state. For example, the United States has more than sixty bilateral Mutual Legal Assistance Treaties that facilitate cooperation in criminal matters.[57] Although most all states have condemned terrorism, states have not

---

52. STATUTE OF THE INTERNATIONAL COURT OF JUSTICE art. 38, para. 1.
53. STATUTE OF THE INTERNATIONAL COURT OF JUSTICE art. 59.
54. SWEENEY ET AL., *supra* note 48, at 2–3.
55. 18 U.S.C. 2340–2340B (2008).
56. Convention Against Torture and Other Cruel, Inhuman or Degrading Treatment or Punishment, Dec. 10, 1984, 1465 U.N.T.S. 85.
57. *See* Bureau of Consular Affairs, U.S. Dep't of State, Mutual Legal Assistance and Other Agreements, *available at* http://travel.state.gov/law/info/judicial/judicial_690.html.

criminalized terrorism as a matter of international law and it is highly unlikely that terrorists will be brought before an international court for prosecution. Domestic law, therefore, remains as a matter of current practice the sole mechanism for the prosecution of terrorists.

In their struggle against state and non-state sponsors of terrorism, states may use all elements of national power—diplomacy, intelligence, military, economic, financial, information, and legal—to prevent, deter, detect, and defeat terrorism, but these state actions are governed by sovereignty, international law, contemporary *jus ad bellum*, the law of war, and domestic law. During peacetime and armed conflict, for example, states may leverage all elements of national power independently or collectively within the framework of international and domestic law to:

- engage in *diplomacy* to influence the counterterrorism policy of other nations and to undermine or deter support for terrorism;
- collect *intelligence* to prevent future acts of terrorism and to prosecute those responsible for acts of terrorism;
- deploy *military* forces domestically and globally in support of civilian law enforcement organizations or to engage in the use of armed force to counter state and non-state sponsored terrorism;
- use *economic* assistance, economic sanctions, and trade policy to shape international counterterrorism activity and to diminish the underlying economic and political conditions that encourage people to support terrorism;
- deny terrorists access to and the use of *financial* resources and networks that support their terrorist activities;
- engage in the strategic and coordinated use of *information* to win the war of ideas by communicating national intent and views; and
- strengthen and utilize international and domestic laws and *legal* systems to prohibit, prevent, deter, and prosecute acts of terrorism.

As a matter of sovereignty, states have the exclusive right to engage in any or all of these elements of national power within their own respective territory and jurisdiction. Similarly, states have the right to engage in any or all of these elements of national power against non-state actors within the territory or jurisdiction of other states when those states consent to those activities. For example, states may use their military forces in the territory of other states in support of civilian law enforcement organizations when those states consent to the presence and activities of foreign military forces on their territory. The exercise of elements of national power within the territory of other states without their consent, cooperation, acknowledgement, or acquiescence, however, implicates issues of sovereignty and may implicate issues of contemporary *jus ad bellum* and the law of war. These nonconsensual state activities will be addressed in the later section of this chapter that discusses the use of force against non-state sponsors of terrorism. The exercise of any element of national power that does not rise to the level of a threat or use of force under Article 2(4), a threat to international peace and security under Article 39, or an armed attack under Article 51 is not governed by either contemporary *jus ad bellum* or the law of war.

Although states may use all elements of national power in their struggle against state and non-state sponsors of terrorism, the basic character of their response and their international legal authority to respond is actor-dependent, i.e., the response to a state-sponsored act of terrorism is one of a national security character and the response to a non-state sponsored act of terrorism is generally one of a law enforcement character. If a state has committed or supported an act of international terrorism, then the victim state may, depending upon the severity of the terrorist attack and other circumstances, respond with a diplomatic protest, seek Security Council condemnation or authority to use force, or use necessary and proportionate armed force in self-defense. In contrast, if a non-state actor has committed an act of terrorism against a state, then the law enforcement organizations of the victim state have the right to apprehend and prosecute the terrorist. States may, of course, use their armed forces in support of a law enforcement response, consistent with their domestic and international law. If, however, a victim state cannot determine factually who is responsible for an act of terrorism and thus cannot shape either a national security or law enforcement response, the law provides no authority to respond indiscriminately.

States may also seek Security Council authority to use armed force or other coercive measures in response to an act of terrorism, regardless whether that act of terrorism is state or non-state sponsored, although it must still be determined whether the act of terrorism is state or non-state sponsored. Every act of international terrorism is, per se, a threat to international peace and security within the meaning of Article 39.[58] Accordingly, the Security Council has the coercive authority to require all Member States to impose coercive sanctions or authorize them to use armed force in response to any act of international terrorism.[59] Moreover, since the Article 39 threshold extends considerably below the thresholds of Articles 2(4) and 51,[60] the Security Council has the

---

58. The Charter of the United Nations: A Commentary, *supra* note 5, at 119.

59. Decisions taken by the Security Council under Article 39 are binding on all Member States. *Id.* at 407–18; *see also* UN Charter art. 25.

60. The Charter of the United Nations: A Commentary, *supra* note 5, at 119.

power to authorize states to use armed force under circumstances where states do not independently have the right to use armed force in self-defense. For example, threats to international peace and security within the meaning of Article 39 even include the failure of a state to surrender terrorists in accordance with an order of the Security Council.[61]

In practice, however, the identity of the actor and a determination of state-sponsorship can be very difficult to establish. The next two sections of this chapter will address in greater detail the inherent right of states to use force in self-defense in response to state and non-state sponsored acts of terrorism.

The Use of Force Against State Sponsors of Terrorism

A state can sponsor an act of terrorism by ordering or directing the action of its regular armed forces, intelligence agents, or citizens; armed bands; irregulars; mercenaries; or private groups.[62] Similarly, state sponsorship may also be established if a state aids and abets an act of terrorism by encouraging, inducing, inciting, or soliciting a terrorist act against another state; assists in the planning or otherwise facilitates the commission of a terrorist act; or, knowingly receives, harbors, or assists in the escape of a non-state terrorist. Libya in the mid-1980s, for example, is a flagrant example of state-sponsored terrorism. In 1984, Colonel Qadhafi made frequent public statements announcing Libya's right to export terrorism, and it was estimated that Libya spent an estimated one hundred million dollars annually operating over a dozen camps where about 1,000 terrorists were trained in guerrilla warfare, explosives, and arms for use in sabotage.[63] State-sponsored terrorism committed against the citizens, property, or territory of another state is a violation of contemporary *jus ad bellum* that invokes the victim state's inherent right of self-defense. Individuals, however, involved in state-sponsored terrorism may also be subject to law enforcement action and prosecuted under the domestic law of the victim state. Accordingly, state activities against state sponsors of terrorism are governed by sovereignty, international law, contemporary *jus ad bellum*, the law of war, and domestic law, and may

---

61. *Id.* at 113, 611–12.

62. *Id.* at 674.

63. *See* Intoccia, *supra* note 36, at 177, 180–82.

involve the independent and collective use of armed force as well as law enforcement efforts.

As depicted in Figure 1, states have a number of response options when they are the victim of a terrorist attack sponsored by another state. Victim states may publicly denounce the terrorist act; sever diplomatic relations with the terrorist state and expel its diplomats; terminate trade or impose economic sanctions; or, seek civil redress in the International Court of Justice. They may also seek the public denouncement by the United Nations or other regional organizations; request the Security Council to impose mandatory sanctions on the terrorist state; or, request the Security Council to authorize the use of force against the terrorist state. However, even without Security Council authority, a state which has been the victim of a state-sponsored terrorist attack has the inherent right under international law to use necessary and proportional armed force to defend itself.

States also have an obligation under the UN Charter and international law to act peacefully and in good faith, to prevent their territories from being used to the harm of other states, and not to secretly sponsor or harbor non-state actors who engage in international terrorism. Thus, when a state fails to act in good faith to prevent its territory from being used in support of terrorism and refuses to cooperate with a state that has been the victim of international terrorism, the issue arises as to when its lack of cooperation constitutes state sponsorship. For example, the inability of a state that attempted in good faith to locate a terrorist in its territory does not constitute state-sponsorship. In contrast, if the location of a terrorist or a terrorist base camp is known and the territorial state refuses to cooperate with a victim state's law enforcement authorities, then the law enforcement response is completely ineffective in defending the victim state's citizens and interests abroad. Such refusal could be considered state-sponsorship, thus invoking a victim state's inherent right of self-defense. However, even if such refusal is not considered state sponsorship, the simple and powerful guidepost is that a state never loses its inherent right to use necessary and proportional armed force in self-defense, and may do so in the territory of another state to prevent future acts of terrorism when that territorial state refuses to take action or cooperate with the victim state.

Two examples that demonstrate how a state's refusal or unwillingness to cooperate in good faith may constitute sponsorship of a terrorist act is Afghanistan and Sudan's failure to cease their cooperation with the known terrorist Osama Bin Laden. These examples also demonstrate how sovereignty, international law, contemporary *jus ad bellum*, the law of war, and domestic law work together to form the basis for a U.S. response to acts of terrorism. On August 7, 1998, twin truck bombs struck the U.S. Embassies in Kenya and Tanzania, killing more than 200 people, including twelve Americans.[64] President Clinton announced that the United States had "convincing information" that Osama Bin Laden was behind the embassy bombings and "compelling evidence" that Bin Laden was planning further attacks on Americans.[65] Bin Laden had also been linked to a number of other major international terrorist incidents such as the 1995 and 1996 bombings of U.S. military facilities in Saudi Arabia and plots to kill Egyptian President Hosni Mubarak and Pope John Paul II.[66] He also supplied troops to fight U.S. forces in 1993 in Somalia,[67] and had publicly threatened to strike more American targets.[68]

Investigations, bolstered by the confessions of defectors from Bin Laden's terrorist network, determined that he had an extensive terrorist training complex in Afghanistan and ties to a pharmaceutical plant in Sudan determined to produce precursors for nerve agents.[69] Soil samples established the presence at this Sudanese plant of a synthetic chemical that has no use except in making nerve gas.[70] "Highly reliable evidence" also established that Bin Laden poured millions of dollars into Sudan and had reached an agreement with the Sudanese government enabling him to produce chemical weapons in Sudan with government assistance.[71] The United States made repeated efforts to convince the Sudanese government and the Taliban regime of Afghanistan to cease their cooperation with Bin Laden.[72] Afghanistan insisted that Bin Laden had clean hands and that he had no terrorist training camps in Afghanistan.[73] It also stated it could never hand Bin Laden over to the United States.[74] Similarly, Sudan denied any connection with Bin Laden and insisted the pharmaceutical plant produced medicines.[75] In response to the unwillingness of Afghanistan and Sudan to cooperate, President Clinton ordered cruise missile attacks on Au-

---

64. Vernon Loeb, *U.S. Wasn't Sure Plant Had Nerve Gas Role*, WASH. POST, Aug. 21, 1999, at A1.

65. Russell Watson & John Barry, *Our Target Was Terror*, NEWSWEEK, Aug. 31, 1998, at 24.

66. *See* Sam Skolnik, *The Law Behind the Bombs: Experts Debate Legality of U.S. Airstrikes Against Terrorists*, LEGAL TIMES, Aug. 24, 1998, at 8–9.

67. *See* Watson & Barry, *supra* note 65, at 24.

68. *See* Skolnik, *supra* note 66, at 8.

69. Watson & Barry, *supra* note 65, at 24.

70. *See* Loeb, *supra* note 64.

71. *See id.* at A2.

72. *See* Frederic L. Kirgis, *Cruise Missile Strikes in Afghanistan and Sudan* (FLASH INSIGHT), AM. SOC'Y INT'L L. (Aug. 1998).

73. Watson & Barry, *supra* note 65, at 24.

74. *See id.* at 26.

75. *See id.*

gust 20, 1998 against the training facilities in Afghanistan and the pharmaceutical plant in Sudan.[76] The U.S. Federal Bureau of Investigation put Bin Laden on its Ten Most Wanted list, and the U.S. Department of State offered a five million dollar reward for information leading to his capture.[77] Bin Laden and twenty other co-defendants were also indicted by the United States for plotting the 1998 bombings of the U.S. Embassies in Kenya and Tanzania.[78] Four of these embassy bombers received life without parole.[79]

The United States justified the lawfulness of its August 1998 missile strikes in Afghanistan and Sudan as an exercise of its inherent right of self-defense in response to an attack and a continuing threat of attack.[80] It had been established that Bin Laden was responsible for the attacks on two of its embassies and the murder of twelve Americans, and he publicly threatened future attacks against Americans. Despite the evidence and the urging of the United States, Afghanistan provided Bin Laden a safe haven, and Sudan refused to terminate its support of Bin Laden.

When a state supports terrorism or interferes with the ability of a victim state to defend itself through law enforcement channels, then the victim state has the right under international law to defend itself with the use of armed force. The Security Council could have also authorized coercive measures to include the use of armed force against the terrorist infrastructures of Bin Laden in response to his terrorist acts because they constitute threats to international peace and security.[81] It was very unlikely, however, that the Security Council would have authorized armed force to root out Bin Laden or have taken any other effective action to prevent him from engaging in future terrorist acts.[82]

---

76. *See id.*

77. Barbara Slavin, *U.S. Must Deal with a New Facet of Terrorism*, USA TODAY, Aug. 4, 1999, at 7A.

78. Bill Nichols, *U.S. Builds Bombing Case as Bin Laden Still at Large*, USA TODAY, Aug. 4, 1999, at 7A; United States of America v. Usama Bin Laden *et al.*, U.S. District Court, Southern District of New York, Indictment (S(9) 98 Cr. 1023 (LBS)), *available at* http://cns.miis.edu/pubs/reports/pdfs/binladen/indict.pdf.

79. Phil Hirschkorn, *Four Embassy Bombers Get Life*, CNN.COM, Oct. 21, 2001, *available at* http://edition.cnn.com/2001/LAW/10/19/embassy.bombings/.

80. *See* Skolnik, *supra* note 66, at 9.

81. *See* Daniel Pickard, *When Does Crime Become a Threat to International Peace and Security?*, 12 FLA. J. INT'L L. 1, 14–19 (1998).

82. *See* Michael J. Glennon, *The New Interventionism: The Search for a Just International Law*, FOREIGN AFF. 2–3 (May–June 1999) ("When American embassies were bombed in Kenya and Tanzania last August, world attention focused entirely on the propriety of American air strikes against perpetrators allegedly ensconced in Afghanistan and Sudan; the idea that the United Nations might actually do something to combat such bombings was never even raised, so conditioned had observers become to expect it to do nothing.").

Accordingly, in the current illustration, the United States relied upon its inherent right of self-defense. The U.S. attack on Bin Laden's terrorist infrastructure within Afghanistan and Sudan was a necessary and proportional exercise of its inherent right of self-defense.

The Use of Force Against Non-State Sponsors of Terrorism

Non-state sponsors of terrorism are criminals who commit heinous crimes such as murder under domestic law.[83] These acts of terrorism, however, are rarely a criminal violation of international law. Accordingly, state activities against non-state sponsors of terrorism are generally limited by international and domestic law to independent and collective law enforcement efforts, even though a victim state may use its military forces against non-state actors in self-defense and under its law enforcement authorities in its efforts against terrorism. Since they govern the behavior and the use of force between states, sovereignty and contemporary *jus ad bellum* do not apply directly to state activities against non-state sponsors of terrorism. Similarly, as a matter of international law, the law of war does not apply directly to state activities against non-state sponsors of terrorism when a victim state's armed forces are acting under its law enforcement authorities; however, the law of war does apply directly to the actions of a victim state's armed forces against non-state sponsors of terrorism when the victim state is acting in self-defense or are acting against non-state sponsors of terrorism who are within an area of hostilities between states. Since war is defined under modern international law as an armed conflict or hostilities between two or more governments or states,[84] states do not engage in armed conflict with non-state actors even though states may use their armed forces in their efforts against terrorism; thus, contemporary *jus ad bellum* does not apply directly to activities directed toward non-state actors.

Terrorists, however, do not operate in a territorial vacuum. Unless they are found on a flagless vessel on the high seas or within territory not owned by any

---

83. The United States defines terrorism as the "premeditated, politically motivated violence perpetrated against noncombatant targets by sub-national groups or clandestine agents," usually intended to influence an audience, and international terrorism as "terrorism involving citizens or the territory of more than one country." 22 U.S.C. § 2656f(d) (2008). Defined as such, international terrorism is a criminal act committed by non-state actors, and the appropriate response of a victim state to defend against such terrorism is law enforcement.

84. *See, e.g.,* McDougal & Feliciano, *supra* note 1, at 97–98.

state, sovereignty and contemporary *jus ad bellum* apply indirectly to a state's activities against non-state sponsors of terrorism because these non-state actors are within the territory of another state. As discussed, states have the right to respond with any or all elements of national power against non-state actors within the territory or jurisdiction of another state when that state consents to those activities. For example, a victim state may use its military forces in the territory of another state in support of civilian law enforcement organizations when that state consents to the presence and activities of foreign military forces on its territory.

In contrast, sovereignty prohibits and contemporary *jus ad bellum* may prohibit state activities against terrorists that occur in the territory of a nonbelligerent state without that state's consent. Since sovereignty provides that states have the exclusive right to engage in governmental activities within its own territory, a victim state must—as a matter of sovereignty—have consent of the territorial state to engage in activities against non-state sponsors of terrorism within that territorial state. Nonconsensual state activities against non-state sponsors of terrorism in the territory of a nonbelligerent state without that state's consent are a violation of that territorial state's sovereignty. A violation of sovereignty, however, is not ipso facto a violation of contemporary *jus ad bellum*, and if not, does not invoke a territorial state's right of self-defense. To be a violation of contemporary *jus ad bellum*, a state activity must violate the prohibitions of Article 2(4) of the UN Charter in the absence of Article 39 authority to do so or in the absence of the right of self-defense. For example, a victim state of terrorism physically or electronically enters the territory of a nonbelligerent state without the consent of that state to secretly: arrest a terrorist; seize evidence; conduct surveillance; or otherwise deny, degrade, disrupt, or destroy a terrorist's ability to engage in terrorist propaganda, recruitment, fund raising, training, or command and control activities. In doing so, the victim state may break down an apartment door; commit trespass; seize or destroy equipment, weapons, or electronic files; or otherwise destroy terrorist property within the territorial state. The victim state has violated the sovereignty of the territorial state, and agents of the victim state could be prosecuted for violating the domestic law of the territorial state; however, the victim state did not threaten or use force against the territorial integrity or political independence of the territorial state, and did not therefore violate contemporary *jus ad bellum*, i.e., the victim state did not engage in a use of force within the meaning of contemporary *jus ad bellum*.

States must rely upon one another to effectively combat international terrorism committed by non-state actors. While the international community began a concerted effort to control international terrorism in the late 1920s, it has never been able to agree on a definition of international terrorism.[85] Consequently, the international community has taken a piecemeal approach and addressed the problem of international terrorism by identifying particular criminal acts inherently terrorist in nature to be prevented and punished by domestic law.[86] The result has been the adoption of a number of global treaties, regional conventions, and bilateral agreements which are relevant to the suppression of international terrorism, and corresponding domestic laws which implement those arrangements.[87]

The basic function of all of these international arrangements is to establish a framework for cooperation among states to prevent and suppress international terrorism by requiring state parties to cooperate in the prevention and investigation of terrorist acts, to criminalize terrorist acts, to assist other states in the prosecution of terrorists, and to either prosecute or extradite terrorists found in their territory.[88] The goal is to ensure that the accused terrorist is apprehended and prosecuted, but even when all states cooperate in good faith, it can be very difficult to obtain the necessary evidence to convict an international terrorist, and the effectiveness of these arrangements as deterrents is questionable.[89]

The U.S. Congress has taken an increasingly active role in criminalizing international terrorism[90] based upon four internationally recognized principles of extraterritorial jurisdiction.[91] Indeed, the jurisdiction that the United States claims over international terrorism is the most far-reaching of any of its extraterritorial statutes.[92] Regardless of where the act occurs, for example, terrorists who kidnap, assault, or murder an American citizen are subject to U.S. criminal prosecution.[93] Similarly, terrorists who assist in the making of any biological agent, toxin, or delivery system for such agents or toxins anywhere in the world are subject to U.S. criminal prosecution if the intended victim is an American citizen.[94] The United States also criminalizes terrorist acts that dam-

---

85. *See* NATIONAL SECURITY LAW DOCUMENTS 446–47 (John Norton Moore *et al.* eds., 1990).

86. *See id.* at 447, 455.

87. *See id.* at 455. At pages 455–62, this text provides a detailed discussion of these global, regional, and bilateral arrangements as well as proposed conventions. For a collection of documents relevant to the suppression of international terrorism, *see id.* at 293–322.

88. *See* NATIONAL SECURITY LAW, *supra* note 11, at 456–59.

89. *Id.* at 456–57.

90. *See* Howard M. Shapiro, *Terrorism in a Democratic Society*, 1 J. NAT'L SEC. L. 95, 96 (1997).

91. *See* James S. Reynolds, *Expansion of Territorial Jurisdiction: A Response to the Rise in Terrorism*, 1 J. NAT'L SEC. L. 105, 106 (1997).

92. *See id.* at 107.

93. *See* Shapiro, *supra* note 90, at 96.

age aircraft or injure airline passengers of any nationality, regardless of where the incident occurs.[95]

Nevertheless, despite the practical difficulties of multi-jurisdictional efforts to investigate, identify, capture, and prosecute international terrorists,[96] when states cooperate in good faith the appropriate lawful response to non-state sponsored international terrorism is domestic law enforcement. Such a law enforcement response permits a state to rely upon its military and intelligence capabilities to discharge its law enforcement responsibilities, but it must do so consistent with the international law obligations that define the character of a law enforcement response.

Conclusion

States have never given up and always retain their sovereign and inherent right of self-defense, regardless whether they are threatened or attacked by states or non-state actors. Moreover, international law does not require timidity in the face of senseless murder by states or non-state actors. The role of the armed forces of a state against state and non-state sponsors of terrorism can be as aggressive and robust as the national leaders of a state determine is lawful and appropriate to counter the threat. In addition to its right of self-defense, a state may seek Security Council authority to use armed force or other coercive measures in response to an act of terrorism, regardless whether that act of terrorism is state or non-state sponsored. A state's authority, however, to use any of its elements of national power to prevent, deter, detect, and defeat state and non-state sponsored terrorism is governed by sovereignty, international law, contemporary *jus ad bellum*, the law of war, and domestic law. For example, when states act in self-defense or pursuant to Security Council authority, contemporary *jus ad bellum* requires that any use of force must be necessary and proportional. It also prohibits the use of force for purely retaliatory or punitive actions.

States have the right to engage in any or all elements of national power within their own respective territory, and in the territory of another state with that territorial state's consent. The exercise of any element of national power in the territory of a nonbelligerent state without that state's consent is a violation of the territorial state's sovereignty. The basic character of a state's re-

---

94. *See id.* at 97.
95. *See id.* at 96.
96. *See* Reynolds, *supra* note 91, at 108.

sponse and its international legal authority to respond to acts of terrorism is actor-dependent. The response to a state-sponsored act of terrorism is one of a national security character. In contrast, the response to a non-state sponsored act of terrorism is one of a law enforcement character. If, however, a victim state cannot determine factually who is responsible for an act of terrorism and thus cannot shape either a national security or law enforcement response, the law provides no authority to respond indiscriminately.

International terrorism committed by state actors—*however minimal*—is a violation of contemporary *jus ad bellum* that invokes the victim state's inherent right of self-defense. Individuals involved in state-sponsored terrorism may also be prosecuted under the domestic law of the victim state. A state may also be considered a state sponsor of terrorism when it fails to act in good faith to prevent its territory from being used in support of terrorism and refuses to cooperate with a state that has been the victim of international terrorism.

International terrorism committed by non-state actors—*however horrific*—is a criminal act and the only appropriate lawful response of a victim state is a law enforcement response, even though a victim state may use its military forces in self-defense and under its law enforcement authorities in its efforts against terrorism. While contemporary *jus ad bellum* only applies directly to the threat or use of force between states, sovereignty prohibits and contemporary *jus ad bellum* may prohibit state activities against non-state terrorists that occur in the territory of a nonbelligerent state without that state's consent. A violation of sovereignty, however, is not tantamount to a violation of contemporary *jus ad bellum* and does not invoke a territorial state's right of self-defense. To be a violation of contemporary *jus ad bellum*, a state activity against a non-state actor in the territory of a nonbelligerent state without that state's consent must violate the prohibitions of Article 2(4) of the UN Charter through the threat or use of force against the territorial integrity or political independence of the territorial state, and must do so in the absence of Article 39 authority or the right of self-defense.

The legal authorities established by sovereignty, international law, contemporary *jus ad bellum*, the law of war, and domestic law continue to serve as an effective legal regime to protect and govern the right of states to take action or use force outside their territories in their struggle to prevent, deter, detect, and defeat international terrorism in a post-September 11, 2001 world. The legal analysis of the application of this legal regime remains rather straightforward. From a legal perspective, *all* acts of international terrorism are either state sponsored and thus a use of force governed by contemporary *jus ad bellum* and the law of war, or are non-state sponsored and thus a crime addressed by national and peacetime treaty law. From a factual perspective, however, attri-

bution may be very difficult to determine, and deciding when the refusal or unwillingness of a state to cooperate in the suppression or prevention of an acknowledged non-state-sponsored terrorist activity that originates in its sovereign
territory constitutes state-sponsorship of a use of force is a very difficult factual and policy determination. Nevertheless, once a factual determination has
been made whether an act of terrorism was state or non-state sponsored, the
legal analysis of the application of contemporary *jus ad bellum* is straightforward. Contemporary *jus ad bellum* prohibits state sponsored acts of terrorism
and recognizes a victim state's inherent right of self-defense. Contemporary
jus ad bellum also recognizes a victim state's inherent right of self-defense in
response to non-state acts of terrorism, but sovereignty prohibits and contemporary *jus ad bellum* may prohibit state activities against non-state terrorists that occur in the territory of a nonbelligerent state without that state's
consent.

Chapter 14

Jus in Bello in the Struggle Against Terror

W. Hays Parks[1]

The U.S. military response to the September 11, 2001, al Qa'eda hijacking of four U.S. commercial airliners and subsequent attacks on the World Trade Center and the Pentagon triggered application of the law of war. That the military response was against a private organization rather than the military forces of another nation raised questions as to the character of its application. This chapter responds to those questions.

Jus in bello, commonly known as the law of war, is a body of international law intended in the main to regulate battlefield conduct to protect the inno-

---

1. W. Hays Parks entered federal service as a commissioned officer in the Marine Corps. His initial service was as a reconnaissance officer. He served in the Republic of Viet Nam (1968–1969) as an infantry officer and senior prosecuting attorney for the First Marine Division. Subsequent assignments included service as a congressional liaison officer for the Secretary of the Navy. Mr. Parks is Senior Associate Deputy General Counsel (International Affairs) in the Office of the General Counsel, Department of Defense. Previously he was the Special Assistant to The Judge Advocate General of the Army for Law of War Matters from July 1979 to August 2003. He was a legal adviser for the 1986 air strike against terrorist-related targets in Libya, and had primary responsibility for the investigation of Iraqi war crimes during its 1990–1991 occupation of Kuwait. He has served as a United States representative for law of war negotiations in New York, Geneva, The Hague and Vienna. Mr. Parks occupied the Charles H. Stockton Chair of International Law at the Naval War College in 1984–1985. In 1987 he served as a staff member on the Presidential Commission established to examine alleged security breaches in the U.S. Embassy in Moscow. In 1989 he prepared the U.S. Government's legal opinion defining assassination. He has testified as an expert witness in cases against terrorists in the United States and Canada. A retired colonel in the Marine Corps Reserve, he earned Navy-Marine Corps, Canadian and British Parachutist wings, U.S. Army Master Parachutist wings, and 82nd Airborne Centurion wings during his military career.

cent civilian, the civilian population, combatants rendered *hors de combat*, and their military caregivers.[2]

Former Nuremberg prosecutor Telford Taylor observed that one may be a pessimist or an optimist regarding the law of war. One may observe libraries, museums, churches, hospitals, and homes destroyed and civilian lives lost incidental to combat operations, and conclude the law of war is a failure. Alternatively, one may realize that but for the law of war, all libraries, museums, churches, hospitals, and homes might have been destroyed and, but for the law of war, the ancient practice of enslaving or putting to death all captured combatants and innocent civilians would have continued. Context is important. The United States has federal and state laws prohibiting murder, rape, breaking and entering, and robbery. That crimes occur in violation of the law does not lead to the conclusion that the law is a failure. This is particularly important in a society built upon and dedicated to the rule of law.

Origins of the Law of War

The history of the law of war is extensive and beyond the practical limitations of this chapter.[3] Two law of war principles are critical to addressing the trans-national terrorism threat.

Although the origins of the modern law of war can be traced to classical Greek and Roman times, the Middle Ages provided its greatest development prior to the mid-nineteenth century. Today's law of war began as an amalgamation of the *jus militaire*, recognized military practice contained in rules of

---

2. *Law of war* is defined as "that part of international law that regulates the conduct of armed hostilities. It often is termed the *law of armed conflict*. The law of war encompasses all international law for the conduct of hostilities binding on the United States or its individual citizens, including treaties and international agreements to which the United States is a party, and applicable customary international law." Department of Defense Directive 2311.01E (May 9, 2006), Subject: DoD Law of War Program. *Law of war* and *law of armed conflict* are synonymous. "International humanitarian law" is an alternative and less accurate term for *law of war* used within the academic community and some governments. As its name indicates, "international humanitarian law" includes human rights law, some of which is not applicable in armed conflict. Accordingly, this chapter employs the traditional term *law of war*.

3. A leading treatment of this history is Sir Michael Howard, George J. Andreopoulos, and Mark E. Shulman, eds., *The Laws of War: Constraints on Warfare in the Western World* (1994).

chivalry, and canon law known as the Just War Tradition.⁴ Both *jus militaire* and
the Just War Tradition included a requirement for "public war," that is, war
authorized by *right* (competent) *authority*. In the *jus militaire*, "public war"
was the "antithesis of perfidy and cowardly assassinations, actions repugnant
to the conception of chivalry and the membership of the various knightly orders in which knights belonged."⁵ Individuals engaging in unauthorized acts of
war were acting outside "faith and the law of nations." They were regarded as
"marauders and freebooters," treated as war criminals if captured, and usually
summarily executed.⁶

Paralleling *right authority* was the principle of discrimination/non-com-
batant (civilian) immunity. In the conduct of military operations, commanders were obligated to exercise reasonable care to protect innocent civilians from
the harmful effects of combat operations. It also obligated combatants to distinguish themselves from the civilian population, and obligated civilians not
to engage in combatant acts. *Right authority* complemented *discrimination* by
denying lawful combatant and prisoner of war status to private civilians who
engaged in unauthorized acts of violence against enemy military forces

Through the near century and a half of development of the modern law of
war, governments have retained exclusive authority to wage war for practical,
political and humanitarian reasons. First is the responsibility of a government
to protect its citizens. Second, a desire for stability in international relations necessitates a prohibition of unilateral acts by a civilian or civilians that may lead
to war between nations.⁷ Third, the prohibition on civilians engaging in com-

---

4. The Just War Tradition is an historic articulation of *when (jus ad bellum)* it is justifiable for a State to resort to arms, and *what (jus in bello)* use of force is legally permissible;
see James Turner Johnson, *Just War and the Restraint of War* (1981). Discussion of *jus ad bellum* is contained in Walter Gary Sharp's *"Jus ad Bellum* in the Struggle against Terror" that
precedes the present chapter.

5. G.I.A.D. Draper, "The Status of Combatants and the Question of Guerrilla Warfare,"
The British Yearbook of International Law," (1971), at 173, 176. *See also* Maurice H. Keen,
The Laws of War in the Late Middle Ages (1965), at 13–15, 69 *et seq.*

6. Keen, *supra* n. 5, at 50.

7. The classic example is the assassination of Archduke Franz Ferdinand, heir to the
Austrian throne, by the Slav Garrilo Princip, in Sarajevo on June 28, 1914, generally regarded as the spark that ignited World War I. This principle is made clear in the U.S. Constitution, which vests in the President of the United States the authority to act as Commander
in Chief of U.S. armed forces (Article II, §2) and to the U.S. Congress the authority to raise
armies and navies and to declare war (Article I, §8). 18 U.S. Code §960 (Neutrality Act)
makes it a criminal offense for a person within the United States to begin, set on foot, provide for or prepare "a means for or … [furnishing] the money for, or … [taking] part in,
any military or naval expedition or enterprise to be carried out … against the territory or

batant acts serves to implement and enforce the law of war principle of *discrimination*.[8] The private citizen who engages in battle is not entitled to the combatant's privilege, discussed *infra*, and forfeits his or her protection as a civilian from direct attack for such time as he or she takes a direct part in hostilities. If captured, he or she is not entitled to prisoner of war status and may be prosecuted for his or her actions. In applying the law of war against the transnational terrorist threat, an appreciation of the development of the principle of *competent authority* is essential.[9]

The Combatant's Privilege

Combatants are members of the established armed forces of a government who have a legal right to participate directly in hostilities. Combatants enjoy "combatant immunity" under international law, protecting them from prosecution for death or injury to persons or damage or destruction of property resulting from combatant acts that otherwise comply with the law of war in an armed conflict [10] A combatant:

- Has the right to carry out lawful attacks on enemy military personnel and military objectives.
- Is at risk of attack by enemy military forces at any time, wherever located, regardless of the duties or activities in which he or she is engaged.
- Bears no criminal responsibility (a) for killing or injuring (i) enemy military personnel or (ii) civilians taking a direct part in hostilities, or (b) for causing damage or destruction to property incidental to lawful military operations, provided his or her acts, including the means employed to commit those acts, have been in compliance with the law of war.
- If captured:
  - Is entitled to prisoner of war status.

---

dominion of any foreign ... state ... with whom the United States is at peace." *See, e.g., United States v. Stephen E. Black and Joe D. Hawkins*, 685 F. 2nd 132 (5th Cir., 1982), a case in which U.S. citizens were convicted of violation of the Neutrality Act.

8. Charles Cheney Hyde, *International Law Chiefly as Interpreted and Applied by the United States* (1951), at 1692, 1797; Hersch Lauterpacht, ed., *Oppenheim's International Law*, Vol. 2, *Disputes, War and Neutrality* (Seventh edition, 1952), at 203–205.

9. Other issues include the legal regime for detention and prosecution of captured terrorists and utilization of military commissions for their prosecution. These are addressed in chapters by David E. Graham and Major General John Altenburg in this book.

10. *See* U.S. v. Lindh, 212 F. Supp. 2d 541, 552–58 (E.D. Va. 2002).

- May be detained indefinitely until cessation of active hostilities.
- Is entitled to humane treatment.
- May be tried for violations of the law of war.
- May only be punished for violations of the law of war as a result of a fair and regular trial.

Entitlement to the Combatant's Privilege

The primary emphasis of the law of war historically has been and remains the regulation of international armed conflict between uniformed conventional forces of opposing belligerent governments. The reasons are several, not the least of which is that governments train their military for the greatest and most common threat, usually an invasion by enemy conventional forces, and a military trained for conventional battle prefers that an enemy play to its "strong suit." Throughout history, however, many have chosen not to play to an opposing force's strong suit, preferring to wage guerrilla operations, particularly when conventional force operations were not possible.

Guerrilla operations occurred in the French and Indian War (1754–1763) and the U.S. Revolutionary War (1763–1783). They came to the fore as partisans resisted Napoleon's invasions of Spain (1807–1809) and Russia (1812–1813). Counterinsurgency operations against partisans opposing French occupation were brutal. Summary execution was a certainty.[11]

Guerrillas, Partisans, Terrorists and Unprivileged Belligerents

The adage "One man's terrorist is another man's freedom fighter" is a political argument. Distinctions exist in the law of war between guerrillas, insurgents, partisans, and terrorists.

Guerrilla operations feature small, highly mobile units operating behind enemy lines. These operations may be carried out by regular military forces,

---

11. Draper, *supra* n. 5, at 178. The modern law of war began its development a half century after the Napoleonic Wars. The first multilateral law of war treaty was the Declaration respecting Maritime Law, signed by seven nations in Paris on April 16, 1856, and eventually accepted by a total of fifty-two nations. The first law of war treaty related to land warfare was the Geneva Convention for the Amelioration of the Condition of the Wounded in Armies in the Field, signed in Geneva on August 22, 1864.

usually special operations forces, operating in uniform or non-standard uniform,[12] and/or by partisans in uniform or civilian clothing. Historically the focus of guerrilla operations has been on attack of enemy military objectives, including lines of communication and military units and personnel. In modern terms, guerrilla operations are a lawful means of warfare. Based upon State practice in the twentieth century, partisans carrying out guerrilla operations against an invader or occupying power have gained prisoner of war status provided they operate with government authority and meet specific criteria to distinguish themselves from the civilian population.

In development of the law of war, governments have not been as sympathetic to the insurgent. The insurgent challenges the status quo within a nation. Moreover, a common practice of insurgents has been reliance upon terror, including assassination of elected and other public figures, and attack of civilian objects.[13] Terrorism is a means of warfare expressly prohibited by the law of war.[14]

---

12. The history and legal analysis of non-standard uniform wear by special operations forces operating in enemy-held territory and/or in support of indigenous partisan resistance movements is the subject of Parks, "Special Forces' Wear of Non-Standard Uniforms," *Chicago Journal of International Law* 4, 2 (Fall 2003), at 493.

13. Assassination figures for the National Liberation Front (Viet Cong) in the Republic of Viet Nam are representative:

Year	Kidnappings	Assassinations
1960–1961	6,213	6,130
1962	9,000	1,700
1963	7,200	2,000
1964	1,500	500
1965	1,700	300
Total	25,613	10,630

The list is an amalgamation of figures contained in Douglas Pike, *Viet Cong* (1966), at 102; and Pike's subsequent *The Viet Cong Strategy of Terror* (1970, republished in Guenter Lewy, *America in Vietnam* (1978), Appendix II, p. 82. For explanation of Viet Cong assassination programs, see Pike, *Viet Cong*, at 248–249; and Lewy, *id.*, at 272–279.

14. Article 51, ¶2, 1977 Additional Protocol I, states: "The civilian population as such, as well as individual civilians, shall not be the object of attack. Acts or threats of violence the primary purpose of which is to spread terror among the civilian population are prohibited." As will be noted *infra*, in 1987 the United States decided against ratification of the 1977 Additional Protocol I. However, Article 51, ¶2, was not a basis for the decision against ratification.

The American Civil War and the Lieber Code: Beginning of Law of War Codification

Codification of the modern law of war and these distinctions originated in the midst of the U.S. Civil War (1861–1865). Dr. Francis Lieber, a Columbia College law professor, offered to draft a document for the Union Army delineating in practical terms existing law of war rules. President Lincoln accepted Lieber's offer. Signed by President Lincoln on April 24, 1863, as U.S. General Orders No. 100, Lieber's *Instructions for the Government of Armies of the United States in the Field* became the primary source for treaty law developed over the next century.

Of direct relevance to the present discussion is a less-known product requested of Professor Lieber. On August 6, 1862, Henry Wager Halleck, General-in-Chief of the Union Armies, wrote to Lieber seeking his advice and assistance in addressing the issue of private citizens engaging in unauthorized acts of war and Union law of war obligations toward captured Confederate guerrillas. General Halleck viewed partisans and guerrillas as synonymous. Professor Lieber made a distinction between the two in his essay reply, "Guerrilla Parties Considered with Reference to the Laws and Usages of War." Lieber argued that partisans enjoy a formal association with a government and its military forces (and entitlement to prisoner of war status), while the latter were:

> self-constituted sets of armed men in times of war, who form no integrant part of an organized army, do not stand on the regular payroll of the army, or are not paid at all, take up arms and lay then down at intervals, and carry on petty war (guerrilla) chiefly by raids, extortion, destruction, and massacre, and who do not encumber themselves with many prisoners, and will therefore give no quarter.[15]

While Lieber does not identify opposing forces that might have been illustrative of each category, the Virginia cavalry unit commanded by Confederate Colonel John S. Mosby,[16] is regarded as meeting Lieber's category of *partisans,*

---

15. Denial of quarter includes refusal to accept an offer to surrender and summary execution upon capture.

16. Mosby's unit operated under a commission issued by the Governor of Virginia. State commissions were a practice common for Union and Confederate forces. Receipt and retention of a governor's commission was dependent upon a unit carrying out its operations in uniform under a commander responsible for its actions, and compliance with the law of war. Jeffry D. Wert, *Mosby's Rangers* (1990), at 62–63, 69–71, 76, 77–78, 124, 151, 157.

and therefore lawful combatants, while William C. Quantrill's private group of raiders in Missouri[17] were *guerrillas* (as he used the term in his analysis), and, as such, unprivileged belligerents not entitled to the combatant's privilege of prisoner of war status.[18]

Lieber maintained this distinction in General Orders No. 100. Article 57 states "So long as a man is armed by a sovereign government and takes the soldier's oath of fidelity, he is a belligerent; his killing, wounding, or other warlike acts are not individual crimes or offenses...," while acknowledging in Article 59 that "A prisoner of war remains answerable for his crimes committed against the captor's army or people...." Article 81 of General Orders No. 100 states:

> Partisans are soldiers armed and wearing the uniform of their army, but belonging to a corps which acts detached from the main body for the purpose of making inroads into the territory occupied by the enemy. If captured, they are entitled to all the privileges of the prisoner of war.

In contrast, Article 82 declares:

> Men, or squads of men, who commit hostilities, whether by fighting, or inroads for destruction or plunder, or by raids of any kind, without commission, without being part and portion of the organized hostile army, and without sharing continuously in the war, but who do so with intermitting returns to their homes and avocations, or with the occasional assumption of the semblance of peaceful pursuits, divesting themselves of the character or appearance of soldiers—such men, or squads of men, are not public enemies, and, therefore, if captured, are not entitled to the privileges of prisoners of war, but shall be treated summarily as highway robbers or pirates.

Nor was Professor Lieber sympathetic to individual civilians or groups of civilians offering armed resistance to enemy occupation, Article 85 providing:

---

17. Michael Fellman, *Inside War: The Guerrilla Conflict in Missouri during the Civil War* (1989).

18. *See* Richard Shelley Hartigan, *Lieber's Code and the Law of War* (1983), at 2–16, 31–44, 56, 60. A traditional term is *unprivileged belligerent*, meaning a private individual not entitled to the combatant's privilege. Other commonly-used terms are *unprivileged combatant* and *unprivileged belligerent*. In this regard see the comments of U.S. Federal District Court Judge William Young in convicting "tennis shoe bomber" Richard Reed, contained in footnote 48.

> War rebels are persons within an occupied territory who rise in arms against the occupying or conquering army, or against authorities established by the same. If captured, they may suffer death, whether they rise singly, in small or large bands, and whether called upon to do so by their own, but expelled, government or not. They are not prisoners of war; nor are they if discovered and secured before their conspiracy has matured to an actual rising or armed violence.

While Lieber's work aided the Union leadership, the unprivileged belligerent issue had not been resolved internationally. It was resurrected in the Franco-Prussian War (1870–1871), when French Army deserters or private citizens (*franc-tireurs*), acting without government authority, engaged in a mix of battle and looting.[19] In further codification of the law of war, the Institute of International Law on September 9, 1880, adopted what is commonly referred to as the Oxford Manual on the Laws of War on Land. Article 1 stated "The state of war does not admit of violence, save between the armed forces of the belligerent States. Persons not forming part of a belligerent armed force should abstain from such acts." Article 2 specifies those who are armed forces of a State. Professor Lieber's rationale for determination of lawful combatancy had European endorsement.

The Hague Peace Conferences of 1899 and 1907: Formal Codification

Franc-tireur actions in the Franco-Prussian War and the debate over military operations by Boer farmers dressed in civilian clothing in the Anglo-Boer War (1899–1902) brought the issue to international attention at the First International Peace Conference, held in The Hague in 1899.

Hague Convention II with Respect to the Laws and Customs of War on Land was among the treaties adopted by the 1899 Hague Peace Conference. Article 3 of its Annexed Regulations Respecting the Laws and Customs of War on Land

---

19. James Maloney Spaight, *War Rights on Land* (1911), at 41–45; Sir Michael Howard, *The Franco-Prussian War* (1989), at 245, 249–256, 374–375, 377–381, 407, 409, 412. The Prussian practice departed from the categorical language of Article 85 of the Lieber Code, considering captured *franc-tireurs* as lawful combatants if they could produce proof of operating with authority from the French Government. Lacking that, they were regarded as unlawful combatants and shot. L. Oppenheim, *International Law* Vol. 2 (7th ed., 1952, Hersh Lauterpacht, ed.,), at 256.

states: "The armed forces of the belligerent parties may consist of combatants and non-combatants."[20] In case of capture by the enemy both have a right to be treated as prisoners of war.

Following Professor Lieber's lead, recognition as armed forces was provided not only to the regular forces of a belligerent but also to other forces in Article 1:

> The laws, rights, and duties of war apply not only to armies, but also to militia and volunteer corps fulfilling the following conditions:
>   1. To be commanded by a person responsible for his subordinates;
>   2. To have a fixed distinctive emblem recognizable at a distance;
>   3. To carry arms openly; and
>   4. To conduct their operations in accordance with the laws and customs of war.
> In countries where militia or volunteer corps constitute the army, or form a part of it, they are included under the denomination "army."

Entitlement to lawful combatant and prisoner of war status for organizations other than the regular forces of a nation was provisional. It was dependent upon these forces acting under government authority and complying strictly with the four conditions listed. Failure of compliance resulted in denial of the combatant's privilege. Individuals acting unilaterally outside an organization were unprivileged belligerents.

Development of railroads in the late nineteenth century facilitated rapid deployment of military forces, prompting fear by smaller nations such as Belgium, France and The Netherlands of threats posed by stronger powers such as Prussia. Article 2 of the Annex to the 1899 Hague II provided conditional combatant status to what is referred to as a *levee en masse*, as follows:

> The inhabitants of a territory which has not been occupied, who, on the enemy's approach, spontaneously take up arms to resist the invading troops without having time to organize themselves in accordance with Article 1, shall be regarded as belligerents, if they respect the laws and customs of war.

Levee en masse was limited and conditional. It authorized private citizens of a territory about to be or being invaded to resist the invasion provided their ac-

---

20. As used in Article 3, "non-combatants" refers to military medical personnel and chaplains rather than civilians.

tions were in accordance with the law of war, including the prohibition against perfidy.[21] It did not entitle them to prisoner of war status. Repeating Article 85 of the Lieber Code, once the invading force had occupied the territory defended by the *levee en masse, levee en masse* recognition ended.[22]

The Martens Clause

The participating nations appreciated that Hague Convention II was a first effort at international codification of the law of war for ground forces. Of particular importance to the topic of this chapter is language contained in the main treaty:

> It has not … been possible to agree forthwith on provisions embracing all the circumstances which occur in practice. On the other hand, it could not be intended by the High Contracting Parties that the cases not provided for should, for want of a written provision, be left to the arbitrary judgment of the military commanders. Until a more complete code of the laws of war is issued, the High Contracting Parties think it right to declare that in cases not included in the Regulations adopted by them, populations and belligerents remain under the protection and empire of the principles of international law, as they result from the usages established between civilized nations, from the laws of humanity, and the requirements of public conscience.

This provision, referred to as the Martens Clause,[23] was the result of a debate over the status of private citizens who took up arms following enemy occupation. Delegations representing major European military powers argued that such individuals should be treated as unprivileged belligerents subject to summary execution if captured. Smaller European nations argued that they should be regarded as lawful combatants as each citizen has a duty to his nation to resist enemy presence. The argument essentially was one for *levee en masse* *"plus,"* a continuous resistance to enemy occupation. In the end, private citi-

---

21. Article 23(b) of the Annex to the 1899 Hague II prohibits killing or wounding "treacherously individuals belonging to the hostile nation or army."

22. Article 42 of the Annex to the 1899 Hague II states "Territory is considered occupied when it is actually under the authority of the hostile army."

23. Named for its sponsor, Russian delegate Fyodor Fyodorovich Martens (1845–1909).

zens who took up arms in resistance to enemy occupation remained unprivileged belligerents.[24] This prompted incorporation of the Martens Clause.[25]

These provisions were repeated verbatim or without substantive change in Hague Convention IV Respecting the Laws and Customs of War on Land adopted by the Second International Peace Conference in The Hague on October 18, 1907.[26]

A humanitarian basis existed for the decision taken by delegations to the two Hague Peace Conferences. As one international lawyer commented:

> The separation of armies and peaceful inhabitants into two distinct classes is perhaps the greatest triumph of International Law. Its effect in mitigating the evils of war has been incalculable.... But if populations have a war right as against armies, armies have a strict right against them. They must not meddle with fighting. The citizen must be a citizen and not a soldier.[27]

The law of war principle of *discrimination* prohibits military forces from engaging in direct attack of innocent enemy civilians and the enemy civilian population in general. In addition to obligating military forces to distinguish themselves physically and in appearance from the civilian population, the principle of *distinction* obligates civilians to refrain from engaging in combatant-like acts, as such actions may place the general civilian population at risk. That said, the Martens Clause acknowledged the existence of unspecified standards of protection and treatment for unprivileged belligerents upon capture.

World War I: In addition to the bloody and costly conventional trench warfare operations of World War I in France, Belgium, at Gallipoli, and in the

---

24. The debate was limited to a form of extended *levee en masse* following enemy occupation. A private citizen who took up arms against his or her own government or against another government with which his or her nation was at peace remained an unprivileged belligerent.

25. Frits Kalshoven, *Constraints on the Waging of War* (1987), p. 14. Professor Kalshoven notes that "This phrase, although formulated especially with a view to the thorny problem of armed resistance in occupied territory, has acquired a significance far exceeding that particular problem." Continuing, he says "It implies no more and no less than that, no matter what States may fail to agree upon, the conduct of war will always be governed by existing principles of international law." Professor Kalshoven's argument has not been without criticism, in all likelihood the result of overly-enthusiastic extensions by some of the original and limited purpose for the Martens Clause.

26. Article 2 providing lawful combatant status to members of a *levee en masse* was amended to require that its members carry their arms openly in addition to respecting the laws and customs of war.

27. Spaight, *supra* note 19, at 37.

Middle East, the British Government supported unconventional operations such as those waged by T.E. Lawrence (Lawrence of Arabia) and others, training, equipping and leading organized indigenous forces against enemy conventional forces and attacking military objectives such as enemy lines of communication.[28] Lawrence's operations replicated the practice of Confederate Colonel John S. Mosby in operating behind enemy lines, regarded as lawful by Professor Lieber in his 1862 memorandum. The unconventional operations of Lawrence and others did not resurrect the 1899 Hague Peace Conference *franc tireur* issue. The Diplomatic Conference that adopted the Geneva Convention Relative to the Treatment of Prisoners of War on July 27, 1929, approved no new criteria for prisoner of war entitlement, incorporating by reference Articles 1 through 3 of the 1907 Hague Convention IV.

World War II: The invasion of major portions of Europe by Germany and its allies, and of Asia by Japan, brought organized resistance against Axis occupation on a scale previously unseen. The resistance movement within the Soviet Union was massive.[29] The British Special Operations Executive (SOE) and U.S. Office of Strategic Services (OSS) provided organization, training, equipment and other support to indigenous resistance movements in twenty nations under Axis control.[30] Resistance to occupation argued for in 1899 by smaller nations, all victims of German occupation in World War II, became reality. The World War II resistance experience prompted revisitation of the 1899 debate and a major change in entitlement to combatant and prisoner of war status at the 1949 Geneva Diplomatic Conference.

1949 Geneva Diplomatic Conference: The 1949 Geneva Diplomatic Conference met in 1949, completing (from drafts) and adopting four conventions in less than four months:

- Geneva Convention (I) for the Amelioration of the Condition of the Wounded and Sick in Armed Forces in the Field of August 12, 1949;
- Geneva Convention (II) for the Amelioration of the Condition of Wounded, Sick and Shipwrecked Members of Armed Forces at Sea;

---

28. *See* James Barr, *Setting the Desert on Fire: T.E. Lawrence and Britain's Secret War in Arabia, 1916–1918* (2006).

29. *See* Earl F. Ziemke and Magna E. Bauer, *Moscow to Stalingrad: Decision in the East* (Rev. ed., 1985), at 199–219, 252–254, 330, 434–435.

30. Representative histories are Henri Michel, *The Shadow War: European Resistance, 1939–1945* (Richard Barry, tr., 1972); David Stafford, *Britain and European Resistance, 1940–1945* (1980); W.J.M. Mackenzie, *The Secret History of SOE: The Special Operations Executive, 1940–1945* (1948, 2000); and Frank Mills, Robert Mills, and John W. Brunner, *OSS Special Operations in China* (2002).

- Geneva Convention (III) relative to the Treatment of Prisoners of War; and
- Geneva Convention (IV) relative to the Protection of Civilian Persons in Time of War.

The Geneva Conventions are express and exclusive in providing protection. Thus the first two conventions address *military* wounded, sick and shipwrecked. Legal obligations with respect to protection of civilian sick or wounded are not included. Similarly, Article 4 of the prisoner of war convention is quite specific in identifying individuals entitled to prisoner of war status, while the civilians convention is equally specific in identifying the circumstances in which civilians in enemy hands were entitled to protection. The prisoner of war and civilians conventions did not provide all-encompassing, seamless entitlement to protection, but were quite specific in their respective coverage.

With respect to private civilians engaged in combat actions, the prisoner of war convention is directly relevant to the topic at hand.

The criteria for prisoner of war entitlement were reconsidered in light of the World War II experience with State-sponsored organized resistance movements. Paragraph 1 of Article 4A of the prisoner of war convention reconfirms entitlement to prisoner of war status for members of the regular armed forces and militias or volunteer corps of a government.[31] Paragraph 2 amended the criteria for combatant and prisoner of war status for groups not falling within paragraph 1:

> Members of other militias and members of other volunteer corps, *including those of organized resistance movements, belonging to a party to the conflict* and operating in or outside their own territory, even if this territory is occupied, provided that such militias or volunteer corps, including such organized resistance movements, fulfil the following conditions:
>
> (a) that of being commanded by a person responsible for his subordinates;
> (b) that of having a fixed distinctive sign recognizable at a distance;
> (c) that of carrying arms openly;
> (d) that of conducting their operations in accordance with the laws and customs of war.

A common mistake by lay persons and some international lawyers is to recite the four criteria in (a) through (d) of Article 4A, paragraph 2, as the criteria for any armed group to be entitled to combatant and prisoner of war

---

31. In the United States, this includes activated reserve and National Guard forces.

status. Extension of combatant and prisoner of war status in Article 4A(2) is much narrower. Reading Article 4A(2) in its entirety, there are seven criteria, all of which must be met:

> First, there must be an international armed conflict, that is, a conflict between two or more nations.[32]
>
> Second, the individual who falls into enemy hands after engagement in partisan activities must be a member of an organization, that is, he or she cannot be acting unilaterally.
>
> Third, as the italicized text indicates, the organization to which the individual belongs must be operating under the authority of a government, that is, it must have *right authority*.
>
> Finally, the organization must meet each and every one of the criteria listed in (a) through (d).

This change entitled members of an organized resistance movement operating under the authority of a government to prisoner of war status. The requirement for partisan movements to "conduct their operations in accordance with the laws and customs of war" provided lawful combatant status as well.

Article 2 of the Annex to the 1907 Hague Convention IV entitled members of a *levee en masse* to combatant status provided they carried their arms openly and respected the law of war. Article 4A(6) of the 1949 Geneva prisoner of war convention provided prisoner of war status to inhabitants who rise up to resist enemy invasion in cases where they lacked time on organize themselves in a manner consistent with Article 4A(1) or (2), and provided the are commanded by a person responsible for his subordinates and displaying a distinctive sign. Lacking the distinctive sign, they must display their arms openly in order to qualify for prisoner of war status when captured. *Levee en masse* remains applicable only to territory not under enemy occupation. Thereafter, such individuals are entitled to prisoner of war status only if they meet the six criteria in Article 4A(2).[33]

---

32. Article 2 common to the four 1949 Geneva Conventions states in part: "[T]he present Convention shall apply to all cases of declared war or any other armed conflict which may arise between two or more of the High Contracting Parties, even if the state of war is not recognized by one of them." "High Contracting Parties" means nations who are States Parties to the Geneva Conventions. "High Contracting Parties" distinguished between nations who had ratified or acceded to the Geneva Conventions and those who were not yet party to and bound by the Geneva Conventions. As all 194 nations are now parties to the 1949 Geneva Conventions, the 1949 Geneva Conventions are universal.

33. Having resolved the issue that prompted the original Martens Clause in the 1907 Hague IV, the Martens Clause was relegated to the article common to the four 1949 Geneva

This change in entitlement reflected the experience of World War II resistance movements while codifying a distinction first made by Francis Lieber during the American Civil War. Equally important, delegates to the 1949 Geneva Diplomatic Conference declined to provide lawful combatant or prisoner of war status to private citizens acting without government authority.

The Geneva Convention (IV) relative to the Protection of Civilian Persons in Time of War by its title and the language of common article 2 applies only in an international armed conflict between the military forces of two or more nations. The Geneva civilians' convention filled a gap (that is, protection for civilians in enemy hands, including in enemy occupied territory). Article 5, paragraph 3, provides limited protection to a civilian "suspected of or engaged in activities hostile to the state" in an international armed conflict as it is defined in Article 2. Private citizens engaging in combatant-like actions other than in occupied territory or enemy territory do not receive protection under the Geneva civilians convention. This excludes transnational terrorists from protection under that treaty.

The four 1949 Geneva Conventions were not intended to provide a seamless "safety net" of protection for all persons, in particular private individuals or organizations who conduct armed attacks without government authority. The negotiating record for the 1949 Geneva Conventions is clear that the conventions were not intended to provide protection to unprivileged belligerents. In the course of the 1949 diplomatic conference, the delegate representing the International Committee of the Red Cross (ICRC) stated that "although the two conventions might appear to cover all categories concerned, irregular belligerents were not actually protected."[34] Similarly, the representative of the United Kingdom stated "the whole conception of the ... [Geneva civilians' convention] was the protection of civilian victims of war, and not the protection of illegitimate bearers of arms."

Common Article 3: The 1949 diplomatic conference met in a time of withdrawal from colonialism, often through armed insurrection. A separate conflict arose within British-administered Palestine territory for a Jewish state.[35]

Conventions dealing with denunciation of (withdrawal from) the Geneva Conventions by a State Party; *see, e.g.,* Article 142, ¶4, Geneva prisoner of war convention.

34. Vol. IIA, *Final Report of the Diplomatic Conference of Geneva of 1949*, at 622. Other delegations offered similar comments.

35. A representative history of the period, describing postwar events in Asia, is Christopher Bayly and Tim Harper, *Forgotten Wars Freedom and Revolution in Southeast Asia* (2006). The conflict in Palestine is described in David A. Charters, *The British Army and Jewish Insurgency in Palestine, 1945–1947* (1989).

This environment prompted consideration by the diplomatic conference of law of war standards for conflicts internal to one nation. The reluctance by many governments to provide legal recognition or status to private citizens and groups engaged in armed insurrection against lawful authority limited development to a single article with general humanitarian protections.[36] Described as a "convention within a convention," Article 3 common to the four 1949 Geneva Conventions expressly applies only to "an armed conflict not of an international character in the territory of one of the High Contracting Parties." It contains no threshold for its application, that is, the point at which violence against government authority amounts to something more than internal disturbances, tensions, riots, or isolated and sporadic acts of violence, leaving that determination to the government being challenged. Its humane treatment provisions are a distillation of the basic protections provided for in the four 1949 conventions. Common Article 3 does not provide entitlement to lawful combatant or prisoner of war status for captured insurgents.[37] It acknowledges that an impartial organization such as the ICRC, expressly mentioned, may offer its services, but does not obligate either side in the conflict to accept them. Despite more than 100 internal conflicts since its adoption, Common Article 3 has experienced little actual application. [38]

---

36. Professor Kalshoven comments, "In the case of a purely internal conflict ... [t]he authorities in power are the legitimate Government, and their acts are in defense of legitimacy; their opponents are insurgents, whose acts will be punishable as rebellion, treason or the like under the municipal law in force. This legal inequality will only disappear to the extent that the insurgents succeed in obtaining from the legitimate Government their recognition as a Government or a belligerent Party—a rare occurrence which moreover can only be expected once the insurgents have achieved something like equality in fact." *The Law of Warfare* (1973), at 13.

37. The final paragraph of common article 3 states: "The application of the preceding provisions shall not affect the legal status of the Parties to the conflict." Jean S. Pictet, editor of the ICRC's four-volume *Commentary* on the 1949 Geneva Conventions, states unequivocally: "This clause is essential. Without it neither Article 3, nor any other Article in its place, would ever have been adopted....." *Commentary on the Geneva Convention for the Amelioration of the Condition of the Wounded and Sick in Armed Forces in the Field* (1952), at 60.

38. For example, the insurgency against the British colonial government in Malaya began in 1948 and continued until 1960. It involved substantial numbers of police and military forces, cost the lives of 2,376 civilians, 4,886 police and special constables, 717 military personnel, and 6,677 insurgents; Anthony Short, *The Communist Insurrection in Malaya, 1948–1960* (1975), at 507–508. Great Britain referred (and continues to refer) to the 1948–1960 war in Malaya as "The Emergency" based upon the State of Emergency declared on June 18, 1948. It lasted until July 31, 1960. The United Kingdom declined to ratify the

In the development of the law of war from the mid-nineteenth century through the four 1949 Geneva Conventions, combatant status and prisoner of war protection was extended to members of a *levee en masse* and to organized resistance movements operating in enemy occupied territory under the authority of a government provided each met rigid conditions for distinguishing themselves from the civilian population and carrying out their operations in accordance with the law of war. In keeping with the centuries-old standards that originated in *jus militaire* and the Just War Tradition, governments steadfastly have refused to provide legitimacy to or legal recognition for private armed individuals or groups acting without government authority and responsibility. The historic condemnation of such groups remained through their exclusion from combatant or prisoner of war status.

Emergence of Transnational Terrorism

Historians are taught there are two words not to be used: *first* and *never*, as in "This is the *first* time this has ever happened," or "This has *never* happened before," as inevitably another historian can be expected to note the error and publicly excoriate the writer for his or her failure to research history.

Media, pundits, politicians, and others ignored this rule in reaction to the terrorist attacks of September 11, 2001, despite the fact that transnational terrorism existed for more than five decades at the time of the al Qa'eda attacks on New York and Washington. Modern transportation and communications (the Internet and mobile telephones) and opening of borders may have facilitated organization, financing and execution of transnational terrorism, but it is hardly new.

Terrorist attacks into Israel from neighboring Arab nations began with Israel's independence in 1948, increasing through the 1950s. Egyptian President Gamel Abdul Nasser supported the *fedayeen* ("freedom fighters"), providing training camps and funding through the Egyptian Army for attacks into Israel from Egypt and Jordan (the latter with Jordan's consent). In 1964 an Arab Summit Conference in Cairo agreed to establish a Palestinian movement to be known

---

1949 Geneva Conventions until September 23, 1957, after granting Malaya (now Malaysia) independence on August 31, 1957. A 1996 study states there were 126 internal conflicts between 1945 and 1995; K. J. Holsti, *The State, War, and the State of War* (1996), at 6. Only two governments—Columbia (by court decision) and El Salvador—have acknowledged application of Common Article 3 to conflicts within their territory.

as the Palestine Liberation Organization (PLO), generously funding it. The PLO was founded the following year with a covenant calling for a Palestinian state and the destruction of Israel.

An Arab Summit Conference convened in Khartoum following Israel's defeat of the combined forces of Egypt, Syria, and Jordan in the June 1967 six-day war. On September 1, 1967, the conference established Arab policy toward Israel: no recognition of Israel, no negotiations with Israel, and no peace with Israel. A policy was adopted of attack of Israel through other means, including international diplomacy and sponsorship of transnational terrorism.

In addition to attacks against Israel from Egypt and Jordan, the PLO's Fatah headed by Yasser Arafat, George Habash's ultra-radical Popular Front for the Liberation of Palestine (PFLP), and other Palestinian terrorist groups such as Black September began transnational terrorist attacks in July 1968 with the hijacking of an El Al airliner to Algeria. This attack was followed by hijacking and bombing of foreign flag aircraft, attack of Israeli and foreign embassies, and assassination or attempted assassination of Israeli and foreign officials around the world.[39] Sponsored by the Soviet Union, financed by Libya, with both providing training, Palestinian and other terrorist operations of the 1970s through the 1980s were truly transnational.[40]

Transnational terrorism reached a peak (but far from its last) when, on September 5, 1972, eight Black September terrorists entered the Olympic Village in Munich and took hostage eleven members and coaches of the Israeli Olympic team. The crisis played out on television worldwide. It ended tragically at

---

39. Neil C. Livingstone, *The War Against Terrorism* (1982), at 19–20; and Edgar O'Ballance, *Arab Guerrilla Power, 1967–1972* (1973), at 18–19. Yasir Arafat's Al Fatah was the largest component of the umbrella organization known as the PLO. Black September was established expressly to conduct terrorist operations. Black September's first mission was the assassination of Wasfi Tell, Jordan's Prime Minister, in Cairo's Sheraton Hotel on November 28, 1971; Christopher Dobson, *Black September* (1974), at 9. On March 1, 1973, Black September members seized the U.S. Embassy in Khartoum, taking hostage departing U.S. Ambassador George Curtis Moore, incoming Cleo Allen Noel, Jr., Belgian chargé d'affairs Guy Eid, and other foreign diplomats. Moore, Noel and Eid were murdered the following day. David A. Korn, *Assassination in Khartoum* (1993).

40. State-sponsored transnational terrorism was detailed in Claire Sterling's bestseller *The Terror Network* (1981). In addition to supporting the PLO and other Palestinian terrorist organizations, Libya's Muammar Qaddafi provided funding, weapons, and training to the Japanese Red Army, the German Baader-Meinhof Gang, the Italian Red Brigades, Nicaragua's Sandanistas, the Moro National Liberation Front in the Philippines, the Polisario guerrillas fighting Morocco in the former Spanish Sahara, Dhofari rebels in Oman, and the Provisional wing of the Irish Republican Army (PIRA). Livingstone, *id.*, at 17–18.

Fürstenfeldbrück airfield twenty hours later with the death of the hostages and all but one of the terrorists.[41] Four years later Habash masterminded the hijacking to Uganda by PFLP and German Baader-Meinhof Gang members of Air France flight 139, where the passengers and aircrew were held hostage with the connivance of Ugandan dictator Idi Amin. Eventually this terrorist operation was defeated through a daring raid into Entebbe by Israel's General Intelligence and Reconnaissance Unit 269, which successfully rescued 103 passengers and crew. The PLFP, Baader-Meinhoff Gang and Ugandan government engaged in a major trans-national terrorism operation a quarter century before the September 11, 2001, al Qa'eda attack.

The Munich Olympic terrorist attack and German law enforcement failure to respond successfully prompted governments to establish special counterterrorist units to address the transnational terrorist threat.[42] There were several reasons for their establishment. Not the least of these was the nature of the threat—heavily armed, well-trained terrorist forces equipped with weapons that often exceeded those of law enforcement authorities; the necessity for well-trained forces, military or civilian, to engage in time-sensitive, high-threat, high-risk missions where the lives of innocent hostages were at risk; and a capability for a timely response to such situations domestically or internationally. Deployment of these counterterrorist forces came quickly in succeeding years. For example, On February 3, 1976, the French *Groupment D'Intervention De La Gendarmerie Nationale* successfully rescued thirty French children whose school bus had been hijacked in Djibouti by four members of the terrorist group Front for the Liberation of the Coast of Somalia. On April 13, 1977, the Royal Netherlands Marines Close Combat Unit rescued fifty-five civilians taken hostage by nine South Moluccan terrorists. Similarly, with British Special Air Service (SAS) assistance, Germany's *Grenzchutzgruppe 9* engaged in a successful hostage rescue mission in Mogadishu on October 17, 1977, following the hijacking six days earlier of Lufthansa flight LH181 from Palma to Frankfurt by four PFLP terrorists.

---

41. Simon Reeve, *One Day in September* (2000); and Michael Bar-Zohar and Eitan Haber, *Massacre in Munich* (2002), at 124–130.

42. For example, three days after the Munich Olympics massacre, Germany ordered the establishment of a special operations paramilitary unit, *Grenzchutzgruppe 9* (Federal Border Guard Group 9 Special, or GSG 9). France implemented existing plans in 1973 to establish *Groupment D'Intervention De La Gendarmerie Nationale* (GIGN); while the Royal Netherlands Marines designated a unit for hostage rescue and other counterterrorist missions. The U.S. Army created an interim counterterrorist capability until a Special Forces special mission unit was formally activated in 1977. The British Special Air Service earlier developed a counterterrorist capability as a part of British operations against the PIRA in Northern Ireland.

It was in this environment that the next effort to develop the law of war took place.

1974–1977 Diplomatic Conference

Following two years of experts' meetings hosted by the International Committee of the Red Cross (ICRC), in 1974 the Government of Switzerland convened a diplomatic conference of States Parties to the 1949 Geneva Conventions for the purpose of updating the law of war codified in The Hague in 1907, certain provisions in the 1949 Geneva Conventions (such as protection for medical aircraft), and an ambitious plan to produce a treaty for internal conflicts that was to be a mirror image of the law of war for international armed conflicts. Protocol I Additional to the 1949 Geneva Conventions addressed international armed conflicts, while regulation of internal armed conflicts was the subject of Protocol II.

The diplomatic conference floundered from the outset. As Professor Keith Suter reported, "The Western delegations attended the session expecting to find an international law gathering and so tried to discuss the session's business, especially in regard to wars of national liberation, in legal terms. The other delegations saw it more as a political gathering with legal [humanitarian] considerations taking second place."[43] The Group of 77 nations demanded combatant status for private groups fighting in specific conflicts, while the ICRC proposed a relaxation of the criteria for combatant and prisoner of war status from that contained in Article 4A(2) of the 1949 Geneva prisoner of war convention in order to placate Arab governments, essentially trading off customary international law protections for the civilian population and innocent civilians for accommodation of private armed groups with a well-established history of terrorism. This highly-contentious approach was the main point of debate through the 1974 sessions, coming very close to causing collapse of the conference.

Western nation governments opposed the politicization of the law of war through the providing of combatant status to specific so-called "national liberation movements," particularly those that relied on terrorism as their primary if not exclusive means of warfare. Western governments also resisted relaxation of the Article 4A(2) criteria for prisoner of war status, as the standards proposed would place innocent civilians at greater risk in an insurgency

---

43. Keith Suter, *An International Law of Guerrilla Warfare: The Global Politics of Law-Making* (1984), at 128.

environment. The ICRC argued that an individual insurgent should not be
denied prisoner of war status because other insurgents violated the law of war;
the prospect of combatant and prisoner of war status would be an incentive for
law of war compliance. Given the ICRC's failure to execute its self-described
role as the "guardian of the Geneva Conventions" on behalf of U.S. prisoners
of war in North Vietnamese hands during the nine years in which they were
held captive (1964–1973), and the terrorist threat environment preceding the
diplomatic conference, the ICRC's argument contained equal parts of *chutz-
pah* and naiveté.[44]

Facing the threat of a walk out by members of the Group of 77 and the collapse of the conference, Western nation delegations agreed to provisions germane to the topic at hand. In defining the scope of international armed conflicts,
Additional Protocol I reaffirmed Article 2 common to the four 1949 Geneva Conventions before adding the following in Article 1, paragraph 4:

> The situations referred to in the preceding paragraph [reaffirming Ar-
> ticle 2 common to the 1949 Geneva Conventions] include armed con-
> flicts in which peoples are fighting against colonial domination and alien
> occupation and against racist regimes in the exercise of their right of
> self-determination, as enshrined in the Charter of the United Nations
> and the Declaration on Principles of International Law concerning
> Friendly Relations and Cooperation among States in accordance with
> the Charter of the United Nations.

The terms "colonial domination," "alien occupation," and "racist regimes" were
thinly-veiled diplomatic language to provide special recognition and lawful
combatant status to specific private armed groups. "Colonial domination" referred to fighting in Angola (Angola National Liberation Front) and Mozambique (Mozambique Liberation Front) prior to Portugal's decolonialization of
each in 1974; "alien occupation" referred to the PLO/PFLP's fight against Israel;
while "racist regimes" referred to Rhodesia (Zimbabwe African National Union)
and South Africa (African National Conference).

---

44. In addition to al Qa'eda attacks over the last two decades, the ICRC argument has
been disproved on many subsequent occasions. For example, in a plan masterminded by PFLP
Abu Abbas, in October 1985 four Palestinian terrorists hijacked the Italian cruise liner *Achille
Lauro*. In the process a 69-year-old wheel-chair bound American, Leon Klinghoffer, was
murdered and his body thrown overboard. Abu Abbas eventually fled to Baghdad, where
he lived under the protection of Saddam Husain until captured by U.S. military forces on
April 14, 2003. He died of a heart attack on March 9, 2004, while in U.S. custody.

Events since 1977 have diminished the potential for application of Article 1, paragraph 4. The primary target of the term "colonial domination," Portugal, withdrew from its colonies in Angola and Mozambique during the diplomatic conference. The governments of Rhodesia (now Zimbabwe) and South Africa have changed; the national liberation movements of 1974 are now the governments. Fighting continues between Israel and the PLO and its successors, such as Hamas and Hezbollah. Israel declined to ratify Additional Protocol I and therefore is not bound by it. As will be noted, the United States declined to ratify Additional Protocol I. Even were the United States a party to Additional Protocol I, Article 1, paragraph 4, has no application in current military operations against the transnational threat posed by al Qa'eda. Historically, legally and practically al Qa'eda operations do not fall within the scope of Article 1, paragraph 4.[45]

The language contained in Article 43, paragraph 1, of Additional Protocol I amended the law of war with respect to entitlement to combatant and prisoner of war status, as follows:

> The armed forces of a Party to the conflict consist of all organized armed forces, groups and units which are under a command responsible to that Party for the conduct of its subordinates, even if that Party is represented by a government *or an authority not recognized by an adverse Party*. Such armed forces shall be subject to an internal disciplinary system which, *inter alia*, shall enforce compliance with the rules of international law applicable in armed conflict [emphasis supplied].

Relaxation of the standards continued in Article 44, paragraph 3:

> In order to promote the protection of the civilian population from the effects of hostilities, combatants are obliged to distinguish themselves from the civilian population while they are engaged in an attack or in a military operation preparatory to an attack. Recognizing, however, that there are situations in armed conflicts where, owing to the nature of the hostilities an armed combatant cannot so distinguish himself, he shall retain his status as a combatant, provided that, in such situations, he carries his arms openly:

---

45. At the time of its ratification of Additional Protocol I (January 28, 1998), the United Kingdom declared "It is the understanding of the United Kingdom that the term 'armed conflict' of itself and in the context denotes a situation of a kind which is not constituted by the commission of ordinary crimes including acts of terrorism whether concerted or in isolation."

(a) during each military engagement; and

(b) during such time as he is visible to the adversary while he is engaged in a military deployment preceding the launching of an attack in which he is to participate. Acts which comply with the requirements of this paragraph shall not be considered as perfidious within the meaning of Article 37, paragraph 1(c).[46]

Continuing, Article 44, paragraph 4 provides:

A combatant who falls into the power of an adverse Party while failing to meet the requirements set forth in the second sentence of paragraph 3 shall forfeit his right to be a prisoner of war, but he shall, nevertheless, be given protections equivalent in all respects to those accorded to prisoners of war by the Third Convention [1949 prisoner of war convention] and by this Protocol. This protection includes protections equivalent to those accorded to prisoners of war by the Third Convention in the case where such a person is tried and punished for any offenses he has committed.

The contrast between Article 4A(2) of the 1949 Geneva prisoner of war convention and Article 43, paragraph 1, and Article 44, paragraphs 3 and 4, of the 1977 Additional Protocol I, is as shown in Table 1.

The distinction between the customary law language of Article 4A(2) and the new language of Additional Protocol I with respect to carrying arms openly was viewed by many governments as particularly troubling, particularly with respect to providing continued protection for civilians not taking a direct part in hostilities. At the time of its signature of Additional Protocol I on December 12, 1977, the United States declared that "deployment" in Article 44, paragraph 3, Additional Protocol I, meant "any movement towards a place from which an attack is to be launched." With its substantial experience in counterinsur-

---

46. Article 37, paragraph 1 defines *perfidy* as follows:

It is prohibited to kill, injure or capture an adversary by resort to perfidy. Acts inviting the confidence of an adversary to lead him to believe that he is entitled to, or is obliged to accord, protection under the rules of international law applicable in armed conflict, with intent to betray that confidence, shall constitute perfidy.

In a translation error, the English text of article 37(1)(b), API, incorrectly states the definition of *perfidy* as "the feigning of civilian, non-combatant status." In contrast, the French text prohibits "*le statut de civil ou de non-combatant*," that is, the French text construes the comma in the English text as prohibiting "the feigning of civilian _or_ non-combatant status" [emphasis supplied], which is consistent with the historical treaty distinction between civilians and non-combatant military personnel.

Table 1.

Article 4A(2), GPW	Additional Protocol I
Organization	No organization; undefined "authority"
Government (competent) authority	No government (competent) authority
Commanded by a person (a member of the armed forces of a State Party) responsible for the conduct of his or her subordinates	Under a command responsible to that Party (not necessarily a State Party) responsible for the conduct of its subordinates (Article 43, ¶1).
Having a fixed distinctive sign recognizable at a distance	Obligated to distinguish themselves from the civilian population while they are engaged in an attack or in a military operation preparatory to an attack (Article 44, ¶3).
	Member of private group who fails to comply with provision above forfeits his right to be a prisoner of war, but must be given protections equivalent to those of a prisoner of war (Article 44, ¶4).
Carry arms openly	Carry arms openly only (a) during each military engagement, and (b) during such time as he is visible to the adversary while he is engaged in a military deployment preceding the launching of an attack in which he is to participate (Article 44, ¶3).
Conduct their operations in accordance with the law of war	Organization must have internal disciplinary system to enforce law of war compliance. Individual retains lawful combatant status, even if organization to which he or she swears allegiance does not in and of itself comply with the law of war (Articles 43, ¶1, and 44, ¶2).

gency operations in Viet Nam between 1960 and 1973, its concern with the new language was both pragmatic and humanitarian. Governments who saw fit to ratify the Additional Protocol I did so in many cases with statements of understanding qualifying the acceptance of its relaxed standards and vague language, particularly with regard to application of Article 44 and the requirement for carrying arms openly.[47]

---

47. Statements of understanding to this effect were tendered on ratification by Australia, Belgium, Canada, France, Germany, Italy, the Netherlands, New Zealand, Republic of Korea, and Spain. A representative statement is that of Italy, as follows: "The situation described in the second sentence of paragraph 3 of Article 44 can exist only in occupied ter-

While Additional Protocol I contains useful advances in the law of war, the highly-political language of Article 1, paragraph 4, and the changes in qualification for combatant and prisoner of war status in Articles 43 and 44 were determined to be unacceptable to the United States. On January 28, 1987, President Ronald Reagan informed the United States Senate that for policy, military and humanitarian purposes, Additional Protocol I would not be submitted for Senate advice and consent to ratification.[48]

As previously noted, Additional Protocol II governing non-international armed conflicts was to be a mirror image of Additional Protocol I. In the con-

---

ritory. The word 'deployment' in paragraph 3 (b) means any movement towards a place from which an attack is to be launched."

At the time of its ratification the United Kingdom declared with respect to Article 44, ¶ 3, that "the situation in the second sentence of paragraph 3 can only exist in occupied territory or in armed conflicts covered by paragraph 4 of Article 1," limiting application of the broader language of Article 44, ¶ 3.

48. *Message of the President of the United States Transmitting the Protocol II Additional to the Geneva Conventions of August 12, 1949, and Relating to the Protection of Victims of Non-international Armed Conflicts, Concluded at Geneva on June 10, 1977, 100th Congress, 1st Session* (1987); also contained at 26 ILM 561. However, the United States has agreed that certain of its provisions constitute a codification of customary international law; see U.S. Department of State, *Cumulative Digest of United States Practice in International Law 1981–1988* 3434–3435 (1993). As the title of the document indicates, President Reagan's message transmitted Additional Protocol II to the Senate for its advice and consent to ratification. An ICRC representative persuaded Senator Claiborne Pell (D-RI) to block its consideration. Upon his retirement in 1997, the hold on Senate consideration of Additional Protocol II was assumed by another Senator. In 2007 the author was informed by an ICRC representative that the ICRC no longer opposes U.S. ratification of Additional Protocol II.

At the time of its ratification of the Convention on Certain Conventional Weapons (March 24, 1995), the United States tendered its reservation to Article 7(4)(b) of that treaty, which obligates States Parties to the treaty to accept the obligations contained in the 1977 Additional Protocol I. The U.S. reservation states: "The United States declares, with reference to the scope of application defined in article 1 of the Convention, that the United States will apply the provisions of the Convention, Protocol I, and Protocol II to all armed conflicts referred to in articles 2 and 3 common to the Geneva Conventions for the Protection of War Victims of August 12, 1949." This expressly rejected Article 1, paragraph 4, Article 43, paragraph 1, and Article 44, paragraph 3, of the 1977 Additional Protocol I.

Certain Additional Protocol I provisions have been accepted by the United States. For example, the definition of *military objective* contained in Article 52, paragraph 2, of Additional Protocol I was repeated without objection of the United States in Article 2, paragraph 6, Protocol II (Amended Mines Protocol), and Article 3, ¶ 3, Protocol III (Incendiary Weapons), of the 1980 Convention on Certain Conventional Weapons. The United States ratified the Amended Mines Protocol. The United States ratified the Incendiary Weapons Protocol on January 21, 2009.

cluding days of the diplomatic conference, the Group of 77 proceeded to reduce Additional Protocol II to less than one-fifth of its original text, with a
very high threshold for its application:

> This Protocol which develops and supplements Article 3 common to
> the Geneva Conventions of 12 August 1949 without modifying its ex-
> isting conditions of application, shall apply to all armed conflicts which
> are not covered by Article 1 of ... [Additional Protocol I] ... which
> take place in the territory of a High Contracting Party between its
> armed forces and dissident armed forces or other organized groups
> which, under responsible command, exercise such control over a part
> of its territory as to enable them to carry out sustained and concerted
> military operations and to implement this Protocol.[49]

Having achieved its political goal of obtaining political recognition for specific independent private armed groups, proponents of the radical Additional
Protocol I revisions ensured that private armed groups seeking to challenge
their regimes would not qualify for entitlement to lawful combatant status
under Additional Protocol I, while establishing a high threshold for Additional
Protocol II application. Even with its high threshold, Additional Protocol II
continues the practice of Common Article 3 of the 1949 Geneva Conventions
in declining to provide lawful combatant or prisoner of war status for private
citizens engaged in armed violence against their own government.

The language in Article 1, paragraph 4, narrowly extended entitlement to
combatant status for political rather than humanitarian purposes. It was not
intended to nor did it not close the gap in protection between the 1949 Geneva
Conventions for prisoners of war (III) and civilians (IV).

Concerns expressed by some that the language in Articles 1, paragraph 4,
43, paragraph 1, and 44, paragraph 3, would benefit all terrorist groups have
not proved to be the case. In the thirty years since adoption of Additional Protocol I, individuals charged with terrorist acts have been unsuccessful in their
efforts to avail themselves of Additional Protocol I provisions in asserting entitlement to combatant status.[50]

---

49. Article 1, ¶1, 1977 Additional Protocol II.

50. For example, *see Public Prosecutor v. Folkerts*, The Netherlands, District Court of
Utrecht (December 20, 1977), as reported in *International Law Reports*, Vol. 74 (1987), pp.
695–698. The accused, a member of the terrorist Red Army Faction, was convicted of the
murder of one police officer and the wounding of another. The court denied his argument
that his acts were justifiable on the basis that the Red Army Faction was at war not only
with the government of the Federal Republic of Germany, but with "any State in the world

In the aftermath of the September 11, 2001, terrorist attacks, use of the term *unlawful combatant* with respect to captured al Qa'eda was challenged by the ICRC. In response, Sir Adam Roberts, Montague Burton Professor of International Relations, Oxford University, and a respected authority on the law of war, replied:

> The debate about the status of the detainees has sometimes been muddled. On the key question of whether there can be a category of detainee not qualifying for POW status, a press officer of the International Committee of the Red Cross (ICRC) has been quoted as saying that the concept of an "unlawful combatant" does not exist under international law. This is simply wrong. True, it is impossible to find the term "unlawful combatant" in any treaty. But the concept of "unlawful combatant," or something very like it, is implicit in the definitions of lawful combatants that appear in the key treaties.[51]

This view is shared by other leading international law scholars.[52]

---

in which ... a class war is going on," to include the United States and The Netherlands. Denying his argument, the court declared that:

> It is totally unacceptable in democratic countries such as ... [the Federal Republic of Germany and The Netherlands], and also the United States, for individuals who disagree with their country's policy, for that reason to resort to acts of violence such as those which took place here. Such acts attack the most fundamental principles of the constitutional State.

See also U.S. v. Fawaz Yunis, 924 F. 2nd 1986 (D.C. Cir, 1991); *U.S. v. Lindh*, 212 F. Supp. 2d 541, 552–58 (E.D. Va. 2002); *U.S. v. Richard Reid*, 214 F.Supp.2d 84 (D. Mass, 2002). Al Qa'eda member Reid, the "tennis-shoe bomber" who attempted to destroy in flight American Airlines Flight 63 from Paris to Miami on December 22, 2001, was sentenced by Judge William Young to life in prison plus four twenty-year terms plus thirty additional years, to be served consecutively, and a $2,000,000 fine. Reid claimed that he was a "soldier," to which Judge Young responded:

> You are not an enemy combatant. You are a terrorist. You are not a soldier in any war. You are a terrorist. To give you that reference, to call you a soldier gives you far too much stature. Whether it is the officers of a government who do it or your attorney who does it, or that happens to be your view, you are a terrorist.

Available at http://www.cnn.com/2003/LAW/01/30/shoebomber.sentencing

51. *The Washington Post*, February 3, 2002.

52. *See, e.g.*, Robert K. Goldman and Brian D. Tittemore, "Unprivileged Combatants and the Hostilities in Afghanistan: Their Status and Rights under International Humanitarian and Human Rights Law," *available at* http://www.asil.org/taskforce/goldman.pdf, and Jiri Toman,"The Status of al Qa'eda/Taliban Detainees under the Geneva Conventions," 32 *Israeli Yearbook on Human Rights* 271 (2002), at 304.

Terrorism as an Act of War

In considering the necessity for military operations against the transnational terrorist threat, and application of the law of war, appreciation for the history and breadth of that threat is important.

The history of al Qa'eda terrorist attacks is extensive and geographically expansive.[53] A partial list of al Qa'eda trained, financed, directed or supported terrorist attacks is long and geographically widespread, as is the list of victims:

- World Trade Center, February 26, 1993 (6 deaths)
- Hotel Aden, Aden, December 29, 1992 (3 deaths)[54]
- Mogadishu, October 3, 1993 (18 U.S. deaths)
- Riyadh, November 13, 1995 (5 deaths)
- Khobar Towers, Saudi Arabia, June 25, 1996 (19 deaths)
- US Embassies, Kenya and Tanzania, Aug 7, 1998 (301 deaths)
- USS *Cole*, Yemen, October 12, 1999 (17 deaths)
- The foiled "Millennium Plot" attack on Los Angeles International Airport, planned to occur on December 31, 1999
- World Trade Center and Pentagon, September 11, 2001 (2,915 deaths)
- Foiled attempted destruction of American Airlines flight 63 (Richard Reid), December 22, 2001
- El Ghriba Synagogue, Erriadh, Tunisia, April 11, 2002 (21 deaths).
- Bali, October 12, 2002 (202 deaths)
- Jakarta, Indonesia, August 5, 2003 (12 deaths)
- Casablanca, Morocco, May 16, 2003 (43 deaths)

---

53. The pronouncement of media, pundits and some politicians that the September 11, 2001, al Qa'eda attacks on New York and Washington ushered in a new era of Islamic extremism neglects history. The U.S. Embassy in Tehran, Iran, was seized by members of the Ayatollah Khomeini's Iranian Revolutionary Guard on November 4, 1979, holding hostage fifty-two U.S. diplomats and staff for 444 days. On November 20, 1979, heavily-armed radical Islamists seized the Grand Mosque in Mecca, holding it and thousands of worshipers hostage for two weeks until the terrorists were defeated in a pitched battle by Saudi military forces trained and equipped by members of the French counterterrorist force *Groupment D'Intervention De La Gendarmerie Nationale.* Almost simultaneously the U.S. Embassy in Islamabad, Pakistan, was attacked and destroyed by a similar radical group, killing one U.S. Marine in the process. The seizure of Mecca has been identified as the birth of Al Qa'eda; *see* Yaroslav Trofimovm *The Siege of Mecca* (2007), at 7.

54. The attack was directed against 100 U.S. military personnel billeted at the hotel, all of whom had checked out the previous day.

- Istanbul, Turkey, November 15 and 20, 2003 (50 deaths)
- Madrid railroad bombings, March 11, 2004 (191 deaths)
- U.S. Embassy, Damascus, Syria, April 27, 2004 (1 death)
- Radisson Hotel, Amman, Jordan, November 9, 2005 (57 killed)
- Presidential Palace and nearby police station, Algiers (carried out by al Qa'eda Organization in the Islamic Maghreb), April 11, 2007 (33 deaths)
- United Nations compound, Algiers, December 11, 2007 (17 deaths)
- San'a, Yemen, United States Embassy, March 22, 2008, by al Qa'eda militant Hamza al-Dayan (1 death in mortar attack on embassy that missed, striking school in downtown Sawan district; 13 students injured, three seriously)

Had the al Qa'eda attacks been executed by the military forces of a government, there is no doubt that they would have been regarded as acts of war justifying a military response in self defense, as codified in Article 51 of the Charter of the United Nations. That these attacks were executed by private individuals makes them no less "acts of war," a fact acknowledged by President George W. Bush in a joint session to the Congress on September 11, 2001 [55]

In response to the September 11, 2001, al Qa'eda attacks, President George W. Bush declared a "Global War on Terrorism."[56] Metaphorical presidential "declarations of war" are common. In 1964, in his first State of the Union message, President Lyndon B. Johnson declared war on poverty. In 1971, President Richard M. Nixon declared war on illegal drugs and drug abuse. On September 11, 2001, as the al Qa'eda attacks in New York and Washington were unfolding, President George W. Bush was in St. Petersburg, Florida, calling on the Congress to join him in a "war on illiteracy." Apparently missing the metaphorical nature of President Bush's declaration of a Global War on Ter-

---

55. President George W. Bush, Address to a Joint Session of Congress and the American People (September 20, 2001), *available at* http://www.whitehouse.gov/news/releases/2001/09/20010920-8.html.

56. President Bush was not the first to link al Qa'eda operations to *war*. In explaining his decision to order his cruise missile attack against the al Qa'eda training camp at Zawhar Kili, Afghanistan, on August 20, 1998, President William Jefferson Clinton stated that Osama bin Laden had launched "a terrorist war" against the United States. Steve Coll, *Ghost Wars* (2004), at 412. President Clinton's decision was supported by a legal conclusion by the Office of Legal Counsel, Department of Justice that the United States was in an armed conflict with al Qa'eda. National Commission on Terrorist Attacks upon the U.S., *The 9/11 Commission Report* (2004), at 132, 485, n. 123.

rorism, many international lawyers were prompted to ask the question, "Where's the war?," as the threat did not fit treaty definitions.[57]

What is "war"? There is no internationally-accepted definition of "war." Article 2 common to the four 1949 Geneva Conventions, Article 1 of the 1977 Additional Protocol I, and Article 1, paragraph 1 of the 1977 Additional Protocol II, do not define *war* but establish a threshold for treaty applicability. Article 3 common to the 1949 Geneva Conventions contains no threshold. Article 2 common to the four 1949 Geneva conventions establishes the scope of application of each as:

> all cases of declared war or of any other armed conflict which may arise between two or more of the High Contracting Parties, even if the state of war is not recognized by one of them ... [and] to all cases of partial or total occupation of the territory of a High Contracting Party, even if the said occupation meets with no armed resistance.

This definition is narrower than that contained in the post-World War II war crimes trial of *United States v. Wilhelm von Leeb, et al. ("The High Command Case")*: "War is the exerting of violence by one state *or politically organized body* against another. In other words, it is the implementation of a political policy by means of violence."[58] Similarly, the ICTY determined that "an armed conflict exists whenever there is resort to armed force between States or protracted violence between governmental authorities and organized groups or between groups within a State."[59]

In contrast, a representative of the International Committee of the Red Cross took a more limited view of the threat posed by al Qa'eda and the necessity for a military response:

> The counter-terrorist effort is being carried out by a variety of means, including law enforcement, intelligence gathering, police and judicial

---

57. The traditional view was expressed by Professor George Schwarzenberger three decades before the September 11, 2001, attacks: "The existence of *individual* terrorists does not create an armed conflict, internal or international," in "Terrorists, Hijackers, Guerrillas and Mercenaries," *Current Legal Problems* (1971), at 258 [emphasis provided], a situation clearly distinguishable from the transnational terrorist threat faced today.

58. *United States v. Wilhelm von Leeb, et al.,* XI *Trials of War Criminals* before the Nuernberg Military Tribunals under Control Council Law (1948), at 485 [emphasis supplied]. *See also The Brig Amy Warwick*, 2 Black. 635 (1863), the U.S. Supreme Court stated "War has been well defined to be, 'That state in which a nation prosecutes its right by force'" (p. 666), quoting Vattel, *Droit des Gens* (1758), Bk. III, chapter 1.

59. *Prosecutor v. Duško Tadić, Opinion and Judgment* (May 7, 1997).

cooperation, extradition, financial investigations, the freezing of assets, diplomatic demarches and criminal sanctions. "Terrorism" is a phenomenon. Both practically and as a matter of law, war cannot be waged against a phenomenon.[60]

Such skepticism about whether or not a war existed and the necessity for a military response contrasted with the formal international response. The day following the terrorist attacks on the World Trade Center and the Pentagon, the United Nations Security Council passed Resolution 1368.[61] It denounced the attack and reconfirmed "the inherent right of individual or collective self defense" under Article 51 of the Charter of the United Nations. For the first time in its history, the North Atlantic Treaty Organization issued a statement adopted unanimously that "if it is determined that this attack was directed from abroad against the United States, it shall be regarded as an action covered by Article 5 of the Washington Treaty, which states that an armed attack against one or more of the Allies in Europe or North America shall be considered an attack against them all."[62] The United States Congress reacted similarly with a joint resolution authorizing "the use of United States Armed Forces against those responsible for the recent attacks launched against the United States."[63] Subsequent decisions by the United States Supreme Court "confirmed as a matter of law that the war against the al Qa'eda terrorist network and the Taliban militia was indeed a war … authorized by Congress."[64]

In response to UN and NATO actions, more than forty nations have provided military forces for operations against al Qa'eda and the Taliban in Afghanistan.[65]

---

60. Jelena Pejić, "Terrorist Acts and Groups: A Role for International Law?" *British Yearbook of International Law* 75 (2004), at 71, 87–88.

61. S.C. Res. 1368, U.N. Doc. S/RES/1368 (September 12, 2001).

62. Press Release, North Atlantic Treaty Organization, Statement by the North Atlantic Council (September 12, 2001), *available at* http://www.nato.int/docu/pr/2001/p01-124e.htm.

63. Authorization for Use of Military Force, Pub. L. No. 107-40, 115 Stat. 224 (September 18, 2001).

64. John Yoo, *War by Other Means: An Insider's Account of the War on Terror* (2006), at 177, citing *Rasul v. Bush*, 542 U.S. 466 (2004) and *Hamdi v. Rumsfeld*, 542 U.S. 507 (2004). The issue of war in the context of operations against al Qa'eda is discussed in some detail in Robert F. Turner, "Book Review: An Insider's Look at the War on Terrorism," *Cornell Law Review* 93 (2008), at 471, 480–482.

65. Albania, Azerbaijan, Australia, Austria, Belgium, Bulgaria, Canada, Croatia, Czech Republic, Denmark, Egypt, Estonia, Finland, France, Germany, Greece, Hungary, Iceland, Ireland, Italy, Jordan, Korea, Latvia, Lithuania, Macedonia, Netherlands, New Zealand, Norway, Poland, Romania, Slovakia, Slovenia, Spain, Sweden, Switzerland, Turkey, UAE, United Kingdom, United States.

These included battles against well-trained, large-unit forces armed with heavy, crew-served weapons and rocket-propelled grenade launchers, vastly exceeding the capability of any law enforcement agency to respond to much less defeat it.[66]

The highly-experienced counterinsurgency author General Sir Frank Kitson defined *insurgency* as a "rising in active revolt against the constitutional authority of a country," while the aim of *subversion* as "the overthrow and destruction of constitutional authority."[67] Within that context, terrorism is a means of warfare frequently employed by the insurgents, while in the British construct military aid to the civil power is an often necessary and entirely appropriate response to the insurgency. The current transnational terrorist threat is not an "active revolt against the constitutional authority of a country" but, as evidenced by the number of nations in which attacks have occurred and the list of nations whose military forces have joined in the fight against the transnational threat—in Afghanistan and elsewhere—far broader. While disagreeing with the term "Global War on Terrorism," Professor and ICTY Judge Antonio Cassese adds an appreciation of this context:

> Admittedly, the use of the term "war" has a huge psychological impact on public opinion. It is intended to emphasize both that the attack is so serious that it can be equated in its evil effects with a state aggression, and also that the necessary response exacts reliance on all resources and energies, as if in a state of war.[68]

The narrower scope of application of the 1949 Geneva Conventions, the broader yet carefully-tailored scope of the 1977 Additional Protocol I, and the high threshold for application of the 1977 Additional Protocol II manifests a continued desire by governments to decline to recognize violence by private armed groups as triggering entitlement to combatant and prisoner of war status for members of such groups. This history is critical to understanding challenges in applying the law of war in military operations against terrorists.

---

66. *See*, for example, Sean Naylor, *Not a Good Day to Die* (0005), describing the Coalition battle against al Qa'eda in Operation ANACONDA in March 2002.

67. *Low Intensity Operations* (1971).

68. "Terrorism is also Disrupting Some Crucial Legal Categories of International Law," *Eur. K. Intl. L.* 12 (2001), at 993.

Law of War Application in the Fight
Against Transnational Terror

The practice of confusing application of the law of war with thresholds contained in law of war treaties is common. In the 1990s, as the United States and other nations engaged in United Nations peacekeeping operations in Somalia, Haiti, and the Balkans, lawyers in some NATO nations argued that the law of war did not apply, as the military operations did not meet the threshold contained in Article 2 common to the 1949 Geneva Conventions; there was no on-going fighting. Subsequent battles by peacekeeping forces in Somalia in 1993 and the Balkans in 1999 proved otherwise.

This position was inconsistent with State practice. In the late 1990s, following the signing of the Dayton Accords on December 14, 1995, and acting under the authority of UN Security Council Resolution 1088, special forces from NATO nations engaged in missions to locate and capture Persons Indicted for War Crimes (PFWIC) in support of the International Criminal Tribunal for the former Yugoslavia (ICTY). Twenty-three individuals indicted by the ICTY were captured and turned over to the ICTY; two others died during missions to capture them. The missions were planned and executed in accordance with the law of war.[69]

The position taken by the United States differed from its NATO partners. The Department of Defense (DoD) law of war program directive states that it is the policy of the DoD to comply with the law of war "during all armed conflicts, however such conflicts are characterized, and with the principles and spirit of the law of war during all other operations."[70] Pragmatic and legal reasons support this view. First, the precise location of particular military operations on the conflict spectrum may not always be readily apparent, particularly from the differing vantage points of a national capital and the military commander and his troops on the ground. This was the case during Operation URGENT FURY, the U.S. military rescue operation into Grenada in 1983, and

---

69. Members of the British 22 Special Air Service (SAS) executed similar missions to capture Nazi war criminals suspected of carrying out Hitler's Commando Order (murdering captured SOE and SAS personnel) following Germany's formal surrender on May 7, 1945, similarly acting within the law of war. Anthony Kemp, *The Secret Hunters* (1986).

70. Department of Defense Directive 5100.77 (December 9, 1998), Subject: DoD Law of War Program, ¶ 5.3.1. The current directive, Department of Defense Directive 2311.01E (May 9, 2006), Subject: DoD Law of War Program, states "It is DoD policy that Members of the DoD Components comply with the law of war during all armed conflicts, however such conflicts are characterized, and in all other military operations" (¶ 4.1).

Operation JUST CAUSE, the U.S. military operation into Panama to apprehend Panamanian Dictator Manuel Noriega in December 1989. It is better that military forces proceed based upon their law of war training than act as if a gap existed in law of war application. It is an example of the adage "Train as you would fight, and fight as you have trained." As military doctrine is written consistent with the law of war, it is a case of applying the law of war unless and until told otherwise. For example, Army and Marine Corps military police units are trained to and have sound doctrine for establishing and running a prisoner of war camp. As happened in U.S. operations in Viet Nam, Somalia, Haiti, and the Balkans, individuals captured and detained might not meet the criteria for prisoner of war status but were provided prisoner of war *protections*, including private visits with ICRC representatives. The U.S. experience has proved it easy to treat captured and detained individuals as prisoners of war and simply change the sign on the facility from "prisoner of war camp" to "detainee facility" while running the facility as if it were a prisoner of war camp. DoD policy is consistent with the intent of the Martens Clause.[71] The fact that unprivileged belligerents are not entitled to the combatant's privilege or prisoner of war status does not mean that the law of war does not apply in military operations against the transnational terrorist threat.

The response to the threat posed by trans-national terrorism has required and continues to require a broad approach, to include:

- *Diplomacy*: In cooperation with other governments and through international organizations, institute measures to defeat terrorism.
- *Intelligence*: threat identification, assessment, and location, including multinational intelligence coordination and information sharing.
- *Financial*: identify, analyze and track terrorist funding sources and assets, and enact international and domestic laws to defeat terrorist funding.
- *Law enforcement*: Investigate, apprehend and prosecute threats identified within domestic jurisdiction.

---

71. The Martens Clause was reconfirmed in Article 1, paragraph 2, of the 1977 Additional Protocol I:

> In cases not covered by this Protocol or by other international agreements, civilians and combatants remain under the protection and authority of the principles of international law derived from established custom, from the principles of humanity and dictates of public conscience.

Three participants in the 1974–1977 Diplomatic Conference state reaffirmation of the Martens Clause was without controversy. Michael Bothe, Karl Josef Partsch, and Waldemar A. Solf, *New Rules for Victims of Armed Conflicts* (1982), at 38.

- *Military*: Pursue, capture or kill threats that exceed law enforcement capabilities, or operate or are staged where law enforcement does not exist.[72]
- *Rule of law:* The history of counterinsurgency and counter-terrorism reveals over and over that insurgents and terrorists resort to terrorist attacks in part to induce an over-reaction by a government; and that more often than not, governments and their law enforcement and military forces succumb to the bait. The same history provides clearly that at no time is the rule of law more important than when responding to threats of terrorism. It is not a case of abandoning the rule of law in the face of terrorist action, but of a government embracing it and demanding adherence to the law—domestic and international, including the law of war, in every aspect of its operations and conduct.

These areas of endeavor are complementary rather than mutually exclusive. In applying military force, the lengthy history of the law of war with respect to unprivileged belligerents is a case of seeing a glass as half full or half empty. Nations have declined to provide combatant or prisoner of war status to unprivileged belligerents. The United States' emphasis on rule of law makes it imperative that it accepts a leadership role in applying the law of war in military operations against the transnational terror threat and identifying law of war protections it should provide captured unprivileged belligerents.

A key element in countering terrorism is understanding terrorism. A terrorist act is intended to shock and extend influence beyond its immediate victims. It is intended to put fear in the hearts of the innocent, to suggest that its own government cannot protect them. A terrorist attack often is used by terrorists to induce an over-reaction by the targeted government.

At such time the rule of law assumes priority. Notwithstanding denial of combatant and prisoner of war status to terrorists, a government must demand strict adherence to the law of war in military operations where its domestic laws are not applicable.

---

72. Coalition operations against al Qa'eda in Afghanistan beginning in late 2001 are one example. Military operations against al Qa'eda in southern Somalia in early 2008 are another example, as are anti-piracy operations by U.S. Navy forces off Somalia during 2007.

Military and Law Enforcement Responses to the Transnational Terrorist Threat

The transnational terrorist threat requires law enforcement and military responses. A strictly law enforcement response to terrorist threats has not existed for some time. Military force was applied in the more-than-one hundred internal conflicts of the post-World War II era—an era an experienced veteran described as one in which a "legal fiction of war" existed.[73] Applying the law of war to such conflicts was the rationale behind promulgation of Article 3 common to the four 1949 Geneva Conventions, even where governments declined to acknowledge the existence of a common article 3 conflict. The United Kingdom employed its military as aid to the civil power to assist law enforcement authorities in its conflicts in Malaya (1948–1960)[74] and Kenya (1952–1960), and in its long-running war against the PIRA, including the killing of three PIRA terrorists on a mission to plant and detonate a car bomb in Gibraltar in February 1988.[75] France employed more than 300,000 military personnel in its war against the National Liberation Front and National Liberation Army in Algeria (1965–1962), operating hand-in-glove with law enforcement authorities. Similar military-law enforcement counterterrorist planning and coordination took place in the United States as early as the 1980s.[76]

In the mid-1980s, at the urging of the Reagan Administration, Congress enacted long-arm jurisdiction over terrorists who commit acts of violence against United States citizens outside the United States.[77] The first successful prosecution occurred in 1987 following a joint federal law enforcement/military operation resulting in the capture in international waters off Beirut of Fawaz Yunis for a 1985 hijacking of a Royal Jordanian Airlines aircraft. Yunis was re-

---

73. Raymond (Turk) Westerling, *Challenge to Terror* (1952), at 110.

74. For a history of the law enforcement role in Malaya and its relationship to military operations, see Brian Stewart, *Smashing Terrorism in the Malayan Emergency* (2004); and Short, *supra* n. 38, at 277–284.

75. *See* McCann and Others v. The United Kingdom (European Court of Human Rights, No. 34575/04, September 27, 1995, Series A, no. 324).

76. For example, this author participated in coordination and planning meetings between federal law enforcement and military authorities in 1983 in anticipation of possible major terrorist attacks in 1984 against four national events within the United States: the New Orleans World's Fair, the Los Angeles Olympics, and the Democrat and Republican Party National Conventions.

77. 18 U.S. Code §§ 1203, 1203(b)(1)(A–C).

turned to the United States by military aircraft for prosecution.[78] Applications of military force against terrorists preceded the effort that began following the September 11, 2001, attacks on New York and Washington. In 1916, the U.S. Army conducted operations in Mexico to capture or kill Mexican bandit Pancho Villa following his terrorist attack on Columbus, New Mexico, on March 9, 1916.[79] On April 15, 1986, U.S. Navy and Air Force aircraft attacked terrorist-related targets in Libya in response to Libyan terrorist operations.[80] Al Qa'eda's bombing of the U.S. Embassies in Kenya and Tanzania prompted a cruise missile attack against an al Qa'eda training camp at Zawhar Kili, Afghanistan, on August 20, 1998.[81] Each mission was planned and executed in accordance with the law of war obligations of the United States.

Given the Martens Clause and Department of Defense policy that U.S. military forces "will apply the law of war" leads to the question: In the struggle against transnational terrorism, what law?

Sources for International Law and the Law of War

In domestic law practice, lawyers reply upon the Constitution of the United States, state constitutions, state and federal statutes and court decisions, and local laws. International law relies upon treaties and agreements. As recognized in the Martens Clause and frequent codification of the law of war through the twentieth century, law of war treaties have not codified all existing law. State practice remains an important resource in determining the law of war and its application.[82]

---

78. United States v. Fawaz Yunis, 924 F. 2nd 1986 (1991).

79. Eileen Welsome, *The General and the Jaguar* (2006).

80. See this author's "Crossing the Line," U.S. Naval Institute *Proceedings* (November 1986), and "Lessons from the 1986 Libya Airstrike," *New England Law Review* 36, 4 (Summer 2002).

81. Richard Miniter, *Losing Bin Laden* (2003), at 182–183.

82. This point is acknowledged by Sir Adam Roberts, former Montague Burton Professor of International Relations at Oxford University and fellow of Balliol College:

The laws of war are strange not only in their subject matter, which to many people seems a contradiction in terms, but also in their methodology. There is little tradition of disciplined and reasoned assessment of how the laws of war have operated in practice. Lawyers, academics, and diplomats have often been better at interpreting the precise legal meaning of existing accords, or at devising new law, than they have been at asserting the performance of existing accords or at gener-

In identifying the customary law of war as it existed in 1863, Francis Lieber wrote in Article 15 of General Orders No. 100 that:

> Military necessity admits of all direct destruction of life or limb of *armed* enemies, and of other persons whose destruction is incidentally *unavoidable* in the armed contests of war; it allows of the capturing of every armed enemy, and every enemy of importance to the hostile government, or of peculiar danger to the captor.... [emphasis in original]

Dr. Lieber stated the obvious: combatants are subject to being killed or captured, as previously noted in the combatant's privilege. The lawful killing of enemy combatants is well established in the practice of nations through the centuries. Dr. Lieber's language was not limited to members of the military, but all armed threats, whether lawful or unprivileged belligerents.

Law of war treaties subsequent to the Lieber Code are either opaque or devoid of this basic law of war right. Articles 22 and 23 of the Annex to the 1907 Hague Convention IV indirectly refer to killing combatants by listing actions that may not be employed against combatants, while the 1929 and 1949 Geneva Conventions discuss only protections afforded combatants rendered *hors de combat* by wounds, sickness, or capture, that is, combatants who no longer pose a threat. Articles 43 and 44 of the 1977 Additional Protocol I define individuals who are combatants, but make no mention of a combatant's risk of being captured or killed, or his or her legal authority to capture or kill enemy combatants.

Hence it is important to appreciate what law of war treaties do not say, and to determine the law of war from what is commonly known as State practice — a lawyer's term for the history of warfare. The killing of enemy combatants in war is longstanding State practice and a law of war right acknowledged by Dr. Lieber but left unsaid in law of war treaties because of their "humanitarian" focus. As was the case with the narrower scope of a definition of *war* contained in the Geneva Conventions and Additional Protocol I, an understanding of State practice is essential to determine the law.

In applying the law of war to transnational terrorism, there are a number of issues:

---

alization about the circumstances in which they can or cannot work. In short, the study of law needs to be integrated with the study of history; if not, it is inadequate.

"Land Warfare: From Hague to Nuremberg," in Sir Michael Howard *et al.*, *supra* n. 3, at 117.

Weapons: The military response to the transnational terrorist threat prompted some to assume incorrectly that as terrorists were not protected by the law of war, then in a short time the U.S. armed services would began supplying its forces with weapons or ammunition prohibited by the law of war to use against terrorists.

A preambular provision to the 1980 Convention on Certain Conventional Weapons reaffirms the Martens Clause, declaring:

> *Confirming their* [the High Contracting Parties] *determination* that in cases not covered by this Convention and its annexed Protocols or by other international agreements, the civilian population and the combatants shall at all times remain under the protection and authority of the principles of international law derived from established custom, from the principles of humanity and from the dictates of public conscience.[83]

Law of war treaties prohibiting or regulating specific conventional weapons prior to the 1980 Convention on Certain Conventional Weapons were limited. The 1899 Hague Declaration (IV) Concerning Expanding Bullets prohibits parties to it from "use of bullets which expand or flatten easily in the human body, such as bullets with a hard envelope which does not entirely cover the core or is pierced with incisions." This treaty applies only to States Party to it in an armed conflict between them.

The United States is not a party to this treaty, but has stated that it will adhere to its terms in its military operations in international armed conflicts to the extent that its application is consistent with the object and purpose of Article 23(e) of the Annex to the 1907 Hague IV, discussed *infra*.[84]

Article 22 of the Annex to the 1899 Hague Convention (II), declares that "The right of belligerents to adopt means of injuring the enemy is not unlimited." Continuing, Article 23(e) expressly prohibits the employment of "arms, pro-

---

83. *Supra* n. 47. The United States became a State Party on March 24, 1995, to the treaty and its protocols I (prohibiting weapons employing non-detectable fragments designed for wounding purposes) and II (regulating use of landmines, booby traps and other devices), with reservations; and to its Amended Protocol II on May 24, 1999, with reservations and understandings.

84. The ICRC conclusion in rule 77 of its 2005 *Customary International Humanitarian Law* that the prohibition contained in the 1899 Hague Declaration is customary law is not supported by State practice or legal scholars. *See* Parks, "Conventional Weapons and Weapons Reviews," *Yearbook of International Humanitarian Law* VIII (2005), 55, at 88–90. A critical analysis of the ICRC's *Customary International Humanitarian Law* is contained in the joint letter of the William J. Haynes II, General Counsel, Department of Defense, and John B. Bellinger III, Legal Adviser, Department of State, to ICRC President Jakob Kellenberger (November 11, 2006), *International Legal Materials*, 46 ILM 514 (2007).

jectiles, or material of a nature to cause superfluous injury." These provisions were re-adopted in the Annex to the 1907 Hague IV, with Article 23(e) amended to prohibit "arms, projectiles, or material calculated to cause unnecessary suffering," the revised language ("calculated to cause") emphasizing that weapon legality is based upon design intent rather than effect.

In 1974 the U.S. Department of Defense adopted a program for the legal review of all new military weapons and munitions to ensure their consistency with the international legal obligations of the United States, including the law of war. The program has been highly successful. Subsequently, the 1977 Additional Protocol I adopted a requirement for States Parties to develop similar programs within their governments.[85] That obligation has seen limited success, with less than five per cent of the 167 States Parties to Additional Protocol I meeting this obligation.[86]

A common example is hollow point small arms ammunition such as is prohibited by the 1899 Hague Declaration. In a 1985 legal review, U.S. military counterterrorist units were authorized to employ hollow point ammunition when determined appropriate to the mission. At the time emphasis was on hostage rescue missions within confined spaces such as an aircraft, where bullet over-penetration of a targeted terrorist might place hostages and friendly force personnel at risk of injury or death.[87]

Following deployment of U.S. military forces to Afghanistan in 2001, an erroneous assumption was made by some soldiers at the "rumor level" that as U.S. military forces were engaged in operations against al Qa'eda, all units were counterterrorist forces, and therefore entitled to be issued and use hollow point ammunition. Informal inquiries were received by the author from some commands.

The issue arose in part due to a lack of confidence expressed by some soldiers in the 5.56x45mm M855 ammunition used in the M16 rifle and M4 carbine, a problem that existed more as a result of inadequate marksmanship training for conventional forces personnel and internal ballistics factors than M855 terminal ballistics performance.[88] From a wound ballistic standpoint,

---

85. Article 36, 1977 Additional Protocol I.

86. The history of law of war regulation of military weapons and the U.S. weapons review program is contained in Parks, *supra* n. 84.

87. Office of The Judge Advocate General of the Army, Memorandum of Law (September 23, 1985), Subject: Use of Expanding Ammunition by U.S. Military Forces in Counterterrorist Incidents.

88. *See,* for example, Major Glenn Dean and Major David LaFontaine, "Small Caliber Lethality: 5.56mm Performance in Close Quarter Battle," *Infantry* (September–October 2006), at 26–28.

hollow point ammunition is not a panacea guaranteeing improved terminal ballistics vis-à-vis the M855. Hollow point ammunition is issued on a restricted basis to highly-trained military units with an express counterterrorist mission. All forces engaged in missions against al Qa'eda are not counter-terrorist units. For logistical and wound ballistics reasons, the military effort against a transnational terrorist threat was not a basis for issuance of hollow point ammunition to other military units.

Weapons or ammunition prohibited by the law of war for use against terrorists otherwise has not been an issue. Weapons are developed and acquired for their military purpose and value. As was the case with the M855 projectile for the M16 and M4, it is not a matter of legality but of military efficiency. The U.S. military does not acquire and stock "more efficient but illegal" weapons or munitions (that is, weapons or munitions prohibited by the law of war) for the rainy day when it might use such weapons against non-traditional threats not protected by the law of war. The question incorrectly assumes more efficient but illegal weapons and ammunition exist. They do not.

Targeting: As noted in listing the combatant's privilege, combatants may be attacked at all times. This risk exists wherever they are located and regardless of the activity in which they are engaged, whether it is actual fighting, transporting other combatants or supplies, typing reports, sending messages, playing cards, eating or sleeping, or advancing or retreating. There are classic examples from history:

- The April 18, 1943, interception and downing of the aircraft carrying Admiral Isoroku Yamamoto, architect of the 1941 Japanese attack on Pearl Harbor by U.S. Army Air Corps aircraft in the Solomon Islands, deep behind Japanese lines.
- The October 30, 1951, U.S. Navy air attack on a North Korean Army compound east of Kapsan, North Korea, killing 509 senior North Korean and Chinese military and Communist party officials meeting there.
- Military snipers historically have engaged individual enemy combatants with precision fire that is the epitome of the law of war principle of *discrimination*.

The risk of attack contained in the combatant's privilege has as its parallel the fact that military personnel are distinguishable from innocent civilians because the former wear uniforms for that purpose.

An unprivileged belligerent is not entitled to combatant or prisoner of war status, but shares the risk of a lawful combatant with respect to being attacked. There are, however, several distinctions related to targeting an unprivileged belligerent.

Direct Participation in Hostilities: An individual member of a transnational terrorist organization is a civilian. As noted in the history of denial of protection for unprivileged belligerents, two prerequisites for a civilian to be entitled to prisoner of war status is that he or she be distinguishable from innocent civilians by carrying his or her arms openly and displaying an identifiable device. As is the case in counterinsurgency operations, fighting transnational terrorist threats requires a high degree of discrimination in target identification and engagement in order to protect innocent civilians.

Terrorists may be distinguishable by some, but not all, activities in which they engage. No law of war treaty offered amplification of the principle of *distinction* until the 1977 Additional Protocols I and II. Common Article 3 to the 1949 Geneva Conventions provided limited post-capture protection to "persons taking no active part in hostilities" without definition of "active." It did not address engagement with deadly force. As Common Article 3's original purpose was protection of persons engaged in an internal conflict exclusively within the territory of one State, rules for use of deadly force were based upon the challenged nation's law. With the counterinsurgency experience of the post-World War II era through the 1960s, delegations to the 1974–1977 adopted in Article 51, paragraph 3 of Additional Protocol I the following:

> Civilians shall enjoy the protection afforded by this Section [General protection against the effects hostilities], unless and for such time as they take a direct part in hostilities.

Similarly, Article 4, paragraph 1, Additional Protocol II, states:

> All persons who do not take a direct part or who have ceased to take part in hostilities ... are entitled to respect for their person.... [89]

When adopted, delegations had in mind the traditional view of the "farmer by day, guerrilla by night." As the United States military learned in fighting the Viet Cong in the U.S. war in Viet Nam (1960–1973), the "farmer by day, guerrilla by night" view is overly simplistic. It also incorrectly suggested to some that a guerrilla could be attacked only when he or she was actually pulling a trigger or detonating a booby trap. This provided little assistance to the individual soldier as to protection of innocent civilians while identifying and engaging

---

89. Although the United States is not a party to Additional Protocols I or II, the "direct participation in hostilities" formula has found acceptance in practice.

legitimate threats, or to commanders endeavoring to engage the larger insurgent infrastructure.

Commentaries on the phrase "direct part in hostilities" were limited in description and definition. Accordingly, in 2003 the T.M.C. Asser Institute and ICRC hosted what became an annual meeting of law of war experts in an effort to define the phrase beyond the initial conclusion that the answer was situational.[90] Final conclusions were not by consensus nor necessarily the view of a majority. Nonetheless, several points have emerged from the discussion:

- Other than engagement in an armed attack, the point at which an individual may be regarded as taking a direct part in hostilities may be relative to an activity (for example, planning, supplying, financing) or proximity to an actual attack.
- The insurgent's or terrorist's "revolving door" in which an insurgent can move effortlessly from insurgent to innocent civilian and back to insurgent may become a door open at all times when an individual's actions are so frequent that his or her activities have "tilted" to the point that he or she is taking a direct part in hostilities and therefore has lost his or her protection from direct attack.[91]

Use of Force/Capture or Kill: The phrase "direct participation in hostilities" applies only to targeting civilians taking a direct part in hostilities. It is not a legal standard for application of force against members of the military, who may be targeted with lethal force at any time. That said, there may be situations or occasions when it is preferable to capture rather than kill an enemy. Combat patrols to capture an enemy soldier for intelligence-collection purposes—"snatch" missions—have existed from time immemorial. So, too, have missions to capture or kill high-value combatants rather than kill them outright. For example, in September 1942, a British military unit entered Persia to capture or kill General Fazlollah Zahidi, commanding Persian forces in the Isfahan area, believing he was a covert German collaborator. Similarly, on April 26, 1944, two British officers entered Crete with the mission to capture or kill

---

90. The author was a participant in this project.

91. A December 2006 decision by the Supreme Court of Israel considered the Israeli Government practice of "targeted killing." *Public Committee against Torture in Israel et al. v. The Government of Israel et al.,* The Supreme Court Sitting as the High Court of Justice, HCJ 769/02 (December 13, 2006). The term and practice are unique to threats posed to Israel within its pre-1967 borders and its administered territories. The court's decision revealed a mix of law of war and human rights law of limited value outside the unique environment Israel faces.

Major General Karl Kriepe, Commander, 22nd Panzer Division. In each case the targeted soldier was captured. But had either individual resisted capture or had capture not been a viable option, each combatant's death would have been lawful.

Military operations in Iraq and elsewhere provide examples. On July 22, 2003, U.S. forces located Saddam Hussein's sons Uday and Qusay in Mosul. An initial effort to capture each was met with heavy fire from their AK-47s, prompting the capturing forces to back off for what became a major battle. Both succumbed in the battle. Five months later, on December 13, 2003, U.S. forces received information that a high-value target had been located in Adwar. Discovering a concealed underground hide site beneath a two-room hut on a sheep farm, the capturing force had lawful options of placing soldiers at risk by entering the hide site or dropping explosives into it. The unit was successful in persuading former Iraqi dictator Saddam Hussein to surrender. Similarly, on June 7, 2006, U.S. forces established the location of Abu Musab al-Zarqawi, the Jordanian leader of al Qa'eda in Iraq. Rather than place friendly forces at risk in an effort to capture him, an airstrike using precision-guided munitions was employed, killing Zarqawi. In each case, the choice of capturing or killing was situational and within the on-scene commander's discretion.[92]

As was the case with Uday and Qusay Hussein, the capture-or-kill option may not always be within the capturing force's control, even where capture is preferable. On October 3, 1993, acting under UN Security Council Resolution 837, U.S. military forces embarked on an operation to capture Somali warlord Mohammed Farrah Aidid. Emphasis was on capture. As a result of intervening factors, the mission evolved into an eighteen-hour battle in which Aidid eluded capture. Eighteen U.S. soldiers and an estimated 800 Somali fighters were killed.[93]

In such operations, whether against uniformed, lawful combatants in a conventional war or in engaging transnational terrorists or other civilians taking a direct part in hostilities, State practice is clear: Attack of a combatant with lethal force is lawful. There is no law of war obligation to attempt to capture or "shoot to wound" in employing lethal force against a lawful target.

---

92. For similar capture-or-kill successes against al Qa'eda in Iraq, *see* media briefing by Major General Kevin J. Bergner, US Army, May 16, 2008, *available at* http://www.defense link.mil/utility/printitem.aspx?print=http://www.defenselink.mil/news/newsarticle.aspx-?id=49591.

93. Mark Bowden, *Blackhawk Down* (1999).

Sovereignty Considerations

In application of the law of war in the battle against transnational terrorism, law of war rights apply in application of force. If the individual has or individuals have been identified as terrorists, they are lawful targets and may be attacked. Operations since 2001 reveal an additional issue or rationale: attack where sovereignty issues exist. Such an operation may be executed unilaterally as a right of self defense under Article 51 of the Charter of the United Nations or with the consent of the nation in which elements of a transnational threat exist.

For example, on November 5, 2002, a Predator unmanned aircraft launched Hellfire air-to-ground precision-guided missiles to kill al Qa'eda terrorist leader Qa'eda Salim Sinan al-Harethi and other al Qa'eda members in Yemen.[94] Abu Laith al-Libi, described as the *nom de guerre* of the former leader of the Libyan Islamic Fighting Group, a senior al Qa'eda and Taliban field commander, and right-hand man to al Qa'eda leader Dr. Ayman al-Zawahiri, was killed in northwestern Pakistan by what was described by the media as a Predator attack. [95] Similarly, on May 2, 2008, it was reported that Aden Hashi Ayro, the military commander of the Shabab, an Islamist militia linked to al Qa'eda, was killed the previous day in Dusa Marreb, Somalia, by a Tomahawk cruise missile attack launched from a U.S. Navy ship.[96]

Targeting is an international law and law of war issue. The sovereignty of nations must be respected. However, respect for sovereignty is subject to the responsibility of sovereignty. The 1907 Hague Convention V Respecting the Rights and Duties of Neutral Powers and Persons in Case of War on Land obligates a government to prevent use of its territory for attacks or other military operations against another nation with which it is at peace. Failing this duty may result in attacks on its territory by the military of a nation attacked from its territory. This was a basis for the 1986 U.S. airstrike against terrorist-related targets in Libya, for Coalition operations that began in Afghanistan following the September 11, 2001, terrorist attacks on New York and Washington, the 2002 attack in Yemen, 2007 attacks on al Qa'eda terrorists assembling and

---

94. Norman G. Printer, Jr., "The Use of Force against Non-State Actors under International Law: An Analysis of the U.S. Predator Strike in Yemen," *UCLA Journal of International Law and Foreign Affairs* 8,2 (Fall/Winter 2003), at 331.

95. Craig Whitlock and Karen DeYoung, "Al-Qaeda Figure Killed in Pakistan," *Washington Post* (February 1, 2008), at 1.

96. Eric Schmitt and Jeffrey Gettleman, "Qaeda Leader Reported Killed in Somalia," *New York Times*, May 2, 2008, *available at* http://www.nytimes.com/2008/05/02/world/africa/02somalia.html?_r=1&sq=may%2002%202008&st=nyt&oref=slogin&scp=16&pagewanted=all.

training in Somalia, and U.S. attacks on al Qa'eda and Taliban bases in Pakistan. Diplomatic actions to enable execution of each attack were a factor, but beyond the scope of this chapter.[97]

Assassination: Two prohibitions on assassination exist. The domestic prohibition is contained in Executive Order 12333, written during the Administration of President Gerald R. Ford and updated by subsequent administrations. Executive Order 12333 applies to operations by the Central Intelligence Agency. It does not apply to military operations in war.[98] In 1989, The Judge Advocate General of the Army published a memorandum of law defining *assassination* in law of war terms. Article 23, paragraph (b) of the Annex to the 1907 Hague Convention IV prohibits killing or wounding "treacherously individuals belonging to the hostile nation or army." This prohibits *perfidy*, an historic law of war term defined in the 1977 Additional Protocol I as killing, injuring, or capturing an adversary "by resort to ... inviting the confidence of an adversary to lead him to believe that he is entitled to, or is obliged to accord, protection under the rules of international law applicable in armed conflict, with intent to betray that confidence...."[99] Although the United States is not a party to Additional Protocol I, it is bound by the prohibition contained in the 1907 Hague IV to the extent it may apply in operations against transnational terrorism and unprivileged belligerents.

Protection of Civilians from Effects of Military Operations: The law of war right to capture or kill combatants (lawful or unlawful) runs parallel to law of war obligations to protect innocent civilians from injury and avoidance of damage of civilian objects incidental to attack of terrorists.

Beginning with the Just War principle of *discrimination*, protection of the civilian population and individual civilians from the effects of military operations is a key component in the law of war. Every civilian casualty incidental to lawful military actions is regrettable, but is not necessarily a violation of the

---

97. The 1907 Hague Convention V and the inherent right of self defense codified in Article 51 of the Charter of the United Nations formed a part of the basis for operations by Columbia military forces into Ecuador on March 1, 2008, to attack a major base of the *Fuerzas Armadas Revolucionarios de Colombia* (FARC), a major criminal and terrorist organization operating primarily in Columbia but with activities in Ecuador, Panama, and Venezuala. The military operation succeeded in killing Raúl Reyes, purportedly FARC's second-in-command, sixteen other FARC terrorists, and the capture of materials implicating Venezuelan President Hugo Chávez as a FARC supporter and financier.

98. Elizabeth Rinskoff Parker and Timothy E. Naccarato, "Targeting Saddam and Sons: U.S. Policy Against Assassination," IDF L. R. 1 (2003), at 39.

99. Article 37, ¶ 1, 1977 Additional Protocol I. The prohibition does not exist in Additional Protocol II.

law of war. As acknowledged in Article 15 of the Lieber Code, the law of war
"admits of direct destruction of life or limb of armed enemies, and all other
persons whose destruction is incidentally *unavoidable*...."

Good-faith avoidance of collateral civilian casualties and damage to civilian
objects is a law of war obligation that applies across the conflict spectrum. In
counterterrorist operations, precautions in military operations in order to protect civilians are imperative. As in an insurgency, terrorists tend to conceal
themselves within the civilian population, seeking concealment and anonymity
through bribery, sometimes sympathy, and in other circumstances, fear. Intelligence gathering to locate and engage terrorists is highly reliant on assistance from members of the civilian population who are not in sympathy with
the terrorists. Civilian casualties incidental to military operations, while not necessarily illegal, tend to alienate the civilian population and eliminate a key
source of intelligence. Law of war obligations to protect the civilian population
and individual civilians not taking a direct part in hostilities are a key component in the struggle against terror, but often challenged by terrorist practices not only of concealing themselves within the civilian population but taking
innocent civilians hostage for use as human shields in violation of the law of
war. Military forces engaged against transnational terrorist threats must exercise feasible precautions in planning and executing their operations, that is,
taking into consideration such measures that are practicable or practically feasible, taking into account all circumstances at the time, including those relevant to the success of those military operations. Counterterrorist forces
implement their law of war obligations through sound intelligence, effective rules
of engagement to which individual soldiers are well trained, and discreet application of force. Military commanders planning, deciding upon or executing attacks necessarily have to reach decisions on the basis of their assessment
of the information from all sources which is reasonably available to them at
the relevant time.

Exploitation of Captured Unprivileged Belligerents: That captured unprivileged belligerents are not entitled to lawful combatant and prisoner of war status provides a lawful basis in which their voluntary use may be exploited that
is not available with regard to enemy prisoners of war. Article 7 common to the
1949 Geneva Conventions[100] does not permit protected persons such as prisoners of war to renounce the protective rights provided in those conventions.
No similar right is contained in Common Article 3 or the 1977 Additional Protocols I and II. It is not a universal right, but is a right strictly limited to per-

---

100. Article 8 in the Geneva civilians convention.

sons meeting one of the protected person categories contained in the 1949 Geneva Conventions. As explained in this chapter, unprivileged belligerents are not protected persons as that term is defined in the 1949 Geneva Conventions.

Penetration of insurgent or terrorist groups by outsiders for intelligence-gathering purposes is virtually impossible. A successful practice in counterinsurgency operations has been to utilize captured unprivileged belligerents to broadcast propaganda messages to forces to which he or she previously pledged allegiance to encourage their surrender. Unprivileged belligerents also have been encouraged to "change sides," that is, to return to their former units as a double agent to provide information to government authorities, or to operate directly against their former unit as what has been characterized as a "pseudo-gang."[101] As unprivileged belligerents do not benefit from the prohibition on renunciation to which a prisoner of war is entitled, this is a legitimate tool in fighting terrorism.

Wearing of Uniforms: As noted in this chapter, *distinction* is a fundamental law of war principle, requiring combatants to distinguish themselves from the civilian population. International armed conflicts historically have been waged in the main by uniformed military forces engaging their uniformed opponents.

The requirement for military personnel to wear a uniform during conduct of their operations is not rigid in an international armed conflict. [102] It is less rigid in non-international armed conflict. Common article 3 to the 1949 Geneva Conventions and the 1977 Additional Protocol II are silent on the subject. While conventional military forces traditionally have continued to carry out their operations in uniform, certain missions of special operations forces have necessitated dress in non-standard uniforms or other indigenous attire. Governments—both in State practice and treaty codification—prudently have weighed the principle of *distinction* against non-reciprocal actions by terrorists, the military necessity for defeating them, and risks, if any, to innocent civilians.

Detention: The era in which captured unprivileged belligerents faced summary execution is past. Following World War II, Germans were tried, convicted, and in some cases executed for their execution without trial of captured

---

101. *See* Frank Kitson, *Gangs and Countergangs* (1960), and *Bunch of Five* (1977), at 33–41, 290, for discussion of successful use of "pseudo-gangs" in the Kenya Emergency.

102. As noted in footnote 94, the 1977 Additional Protocol I prohibits *perfidy* only. Article 29, Annex to the 1907 Hague IV, places a soldier at risk of punishment for spying under the domestic law of the captor if caught while executing his mission. If he or she returns safely to friendly lines or units and subsequently is captured in uniform, there is no law of war basis for punishment for the previous mission.

members of the British Special Operations Executive, individuals who were lawful combatants caught while wearing civilian clothing and, in other cases, uniforms.[103]

A lack of entitlement to combatant and prisoner of war status does not mean a lack of entitlement to law of war protection. Prior to September 11, 2001, there was consensus that terrorists or others not entitled to prisoner of war status would receive "humane treatment." Operations since September 11, 2001, have necessitated hanging flesh on what previously was a bare skeleton. It does not require new law of war rules; it requires identifying protections that should be regarded as constituting humane treatment. The challenge in part has been to provide humane treatment but not necessarily all protections provided prisoners of war lest unprivileged belligerents be unduly rewarded for their actions; denial of all protections afforded lawful combatants historically has been a disincentive for private citizens to engage in unauthorized combatant acts. The law of war provides rights and responsibilities. Unprivileged belligerents may be detained until the "cessation of active hostilities," as is the case with prisoners of war.[104] Unprivileged belligerents may be provided but are not legally entitled to access to a canteen in which they may purchase sundries, particularly when they are provided *gratis*, nor to an "advance of pay" in Swiss francs as

---

103. *See*, for example, *Trial of Wolfgang Zeiss, et al. (The Natzweiler Trial)*, War Crimes Trials V (Anthony W. Webb, ed., 1949), involving the execution without trial of four female members of the British Special Operations Executive at Natzweiler Concentration Camp on July 6, 1944. The accused were tried and convicted in 1946.

104. Article 118, 1949 Geneva prisoner of war convention. On October 9, 2003, ICRC official Christophe Girod engaged in an uncharacteristic public attack of the United States for its detention of unprivileged belligerents, asserting they had a legal right to know the duration of their detention. Neil A. Lewis, "Red Cross Criticizes Indefinite Detention In Guantanamo Bay," *New York Times*, October 10, 2003, p. 1. Such a "right" would provide unprivileged belligerents greater protection than the Geneva Conventions provide lawful combatants held as prisoners of war, essentially rewarding unprivileged belligerents for their illegal actions. No treaty obligation exists for either lawful or unprivileged belligerents to know the duration of their captivity, information the captor seldom knows until the cessation of active hostilities. Neither Commonwealth prisoners of war captured by the Japanese with the fall of Singapore on February 15, 1942, U.S. military forces who surrendered to the Japanese in the Philippines on April 9, 1942, U.S. military personnel captured by the North Vietnamese between 1964 and 1972, nor Moroccan military forces in the hands of Polisario guerrillas in former Spanish (western) Sahara, knew their term of captivity. In the latter conflict, captured Moroccan soldiers were held as long as twenty years before being released on August 18, 2005; Associated Press, "Long-Held Moroccans Freed," *The Washington Post*, August 19, 2006, at A18. The U.S. Supreme Court confirmed the right to detain unlawful enemy combatants for the duration of the conflict in *Rasul v. U.S.*, 542 U.S. 266 (2004), *Hamdi v. Rumsfeld*, 542 U.S. 507 (2004), and *Hamdan v. Rumsfeld*, 126 S. Ct. 2749 (2006).

prisoners of war are entitled to receive for purchase of sundries. Nor are unprivileged belligerents entitled to musical instruments, particularly where their behavior is such to suggest they would use them to make weapons to be used against their guards. "Humane treatment" means that unprivileged belligerents benefit from the prohibition on torture and if prosecuted for their actions are entitled to a fair trial with appropriate procedural safeguards. This topic is discussed fully by David Graham in his chapter.

The Role of the International Committee of the Red Cross: The International Committee of the Red Cross has a long and distinguished history as an adviser to governments with regard to the Geneva Conventions for protection of war victims. Its potential role is recognized in Article 9 common to the four 1949 Geneva Conventions, permitting it to perform its humanitarian duties subject to the consent of the Parties to a conflict.[105] While the ICRC receives similar recognition in Article 3 common to the four 1949 Geneva Conventions, the 1977 Additional Protocol II is silent on the subject.

The ICRC role is advisory. Decisions as to interpretation of treaty provisions remain the responsibility of governments.

---

105. Article 10 in the 1949 Geneva civilians' convention.

Chapter 15

Legal Issues of Outsourcing Military Functions in Wartime

M.E. "Spike" Bowman[1]

The end of the Cold War was more than a political event—the attenuation of "mutually assured destruction" tensions also served as a catalyst for a dramatic shift in thinking about future conflict. The most obvious change was the fact that, after decades of planning for a massed forces land battle in Europe, it was suddenly no longer necessary to maintain the logistical tail that had been necessary to support that sort of conflict. Accordingly, three logical thought processes followed. First, significant logistics support could be pushed to the private sector and employed only as needed. Second, it became clear that smaller, more agile forces would be required for the most likely conflicts of the future. In turn that meant decision-making would be pushed down; it meant that new ways of fighting had to be employed—from weapons to communications. Third, and most importantly, it meant that, in the newly anticipated conflict arenas, stabilization would be as important as winning the fight. However, that which was unanticipated became as important as the shift in military planning. The unanticipated included the fact that much of the privatization growth would be

---

1. Mr. Bowman is a specialist in national security law and policy. Most recently he served as Deputy, National Counterintelligence Executive. He has been a Senior Research Fellow at the National Defense University and, upon retiring from the Navy had served for more than a decade in the Senior Executive Service of the FBI as Senior Counsel, National Security Law and as Director, Intelligence Issues Group, setting up the National Security Branch of the Bureau. As a naval officer he served as the Chief of Litigation, as a diplomat at the U.S. Embassy, Rome, and as Head of International Law at the Naval War College. He has been an integral player in the prosecution of a large number of espionage and terrorism cases from 1983 to the present. Captain Bowman is a member of the ABA Standing Committee on Law and National Security, is Chairman of the Board of the Association for Intelligence Officers and is a Distinguished Fellow, Center for National Security Law, University of Virginia.

*in services, rather than the products for which our system for contracting with
private industry had been developed. The unanticipated also included an explosion of private, armed security guards who looked and acted like military
personnel, but did not have any recognized status in a conflict arena. Furthermore, the unanticipated included both operation and maintenance of high-tech
weapons systems by private contractors, some of which were operated with lethal
effect. Finally, the unanticipated included uncounted millions that were paid
for security rather than the reconstruction and stabilization efforts for which
they were intended. What we are learning now is that the legal and regulatory
issues that arise from privatization are proliferating, most of which are yet to
be addressed.*

September 11, 2001 was a catalyst that has defined the way people all over
the world now live, communicate and travel. The events of that day were so
catastrophic that it is sometimes difficult to comprehend that they were only
the most poignant in a series of catalysts that generated a world of persistent,
transnational threats. When viewed broadly, the few decades following World
War II bear witness to a world that has become significantly unstable for non-
traditional reasons. If we step back and look at the social order from a distance we can observe a continuum of change, sometimes very subtle, that
stretches from the waning days of that War to the present. Change is, of course,
a constant but this relatively short span of time contained a veritable explosion of change that shaped contemporary existence in ways that differ significantly from the evolution of prior centuries.

It is unnecessary to belabor the changes, but useful to keep some of the
major events in mind. To that end, four catalysts significantly framed a world
vastly different from the pre-War social order. First was the dissolution of empires following the War; as early as 1946 seventy-two nations had come to exist
in the world—nearly double the number the existed between the wars. Second was the incredible technological revolution, spurred by that War, which
accelerates with each waking day. That "revolution" has made out lives more
comfortable and more efficient, but it has also provided criminals and terrorists with tools to threaten our security. Third was the rise of a new and greatly
enlarged [and enfranchised] middle class created by new markets, enhanced technologies and expanded global trade. One of American's elder statesmen, Zbig-
niew Brzezinski, describes the phenomenon this way: "The world is much
more restless. It's stirring. It has aspirations which are not easily satisfied."[2]

---

2. David Ignatius, "Wise Advice: Listen and Engage," *The Washington Post*, June 24,
2007.

Fourth, not precisely catalytic in itself, but with enormous future consequence, was the continued commitment in the United Nations Charter to the Westphalian order of statehood which demands respect for territorial sovereignty. In a world still largely reliant on national efforts to remediate threats to security, it is hard to overemphasize the difficulty of dealing with transnational threats of terrorism, organized crime, cyber-attack, weapons proliferation and even environmental change, none of which respect borders. Moreover, the number of sovereign nations [and inviolate borders] has risen to 192 (not including Taiwan) and is likely still climbing.

The United Nations is a noble experiment, but despite the attempt to create a stable universal governance structure, we continue to witness extensive violent conflict which, in turn, fuels corruption, organized crime and terrorist insurgency. Not even the implosion of the Soviet Union, which ended the last significant threat of a world war brought peace and stability. The much anticipated "peace dividend" was an illusion that gave way to myriad transnational dangers that threaten both personal and national security every day.

Why this is so in a world so full of promise is not obvious. In part this is due to the fact that many small but significant changes seeped into our daily life subtly, without fanfare. Then too, countering threats in this era has been different than was the norm in years gone by. For the first time in modern history, the primary threats to peace and security stem not from state actors but from warlords, organized criminals, thugs of many stripes and terrorists. Henry Kissinger frames the situation well when he states that "The international system is in a period of change like we haven't seen for several hundred years.... [Americans have to realize that] we're in for a long period of adjustment."[3] Former National Security Advisor General Brent Scowcroft adds that "the traditional measures of strength don't really apply so much.... It's a world where most of the big problems spill over national boundaries ..."[4]

It is an irony that a system of governance designed for security is itself a hindrance to countering transnational threats. Nevertheless, today a 17th century formula for sovereignty is being assailed by 21st Century threats, and attempts to counter these threats are, themselves, generating significant, unanticipated problems. One series of problems, very much unanticipated, stems from transnational threats related to decisions of an earlier era to outsource many military needs. When it became evident that we would not likely be fighting the great European-centered land war we had prepared for from

3. *Id.*
4. *Id.*

the end of World War II, both the anticipated size of military forces, as well as the needs of military preparedness changed virtually overnight.

The resultant modifications to perceived needs are readily evident, beginning with the size of the force. Today, the U.S. military is little more than 60% of its 1995 levels, the Soviet collapse meant the demise of the gargantuan Red Army and British forces are at their smallest numbers since the Napoleonic wars. Without the need to maintain logistical strength to fight a land war with the Soviets, it made sense to downsize, eliminate the draft and depend on private industry to supply logistical strength on an "as needed" basis. The result is that in most of the developed nations private industry has absorbed much of the downsized manpower that once donned uniforms and now supplies many military requirements for a price. Meanwhile, continually improving technology has driven additional civilian technical expertise into the force make-up. Both maintenance and even some operations of mission-critical technology are beyond the capabilities of forces that are kept lean to be fighting forces rather than to be logistical forces.

However, even given the intent to privatize military logistics, the unprecedented scale of outsourcing and privatization has been overshadowed by the exigencies of post-9/11 threats. From the moment the U.S. troop buildup began in advance of the invasion of Iraq, the Pentagon realized that private contractors would be an integral part of the operations. Those future needs were not overlooked by private industry. Well in advance of the invasion of Iraq, Halliburton was prepping for massive operations in the conflict arena. When U.S. tanks rolled into Baghdad in March 2003, they brought with them the largest army of private contractors ever deployed in modern war. Within three years, the numbers of private contractors on the ground in Iraq grew in numbers to an almost one-to-one ratio with active-duty American soldiers.

Much of this change stems from the vision of Donald Rumsfeld as Secretary of Defense. Rumsfeld felt that he could increase force readiness by decreasing the amount of self-contained supply required to maintain forces in the field. His vision called for light, mobile forces leveraging air power for muscle. Contemplating the invasion of Iraq, Rumsfeld reportedly favored a force of only 60,000 as opposed to the 400,000 desired by the American military.[5]

For Rumsfeld, running the Department of Defense seemed much like running a corporate business; accordingly, he made changes that ensured that the

---

5. *See* the autobiography of General Sir Mike Jackson, former Chief of General Staff, Armed Forces of the United Kingdom, *Soldier: The Autobiography of General Sir Mike Jackson*, Bantam, 2007. Referring to the messy post-conflict situation in Iraq, General Jackson faults Rumsfeld for rejecting the advice of his generals and discarding detailed post-conflict plans prepared by the State Department.

defense industry would be an integral part of any conflict in which the United States would be engaged. Before he resigned Rumsfeld classified private contractors as an official part of the U.S. war machine. In the Pentagon's 2006 Quadrennial Review (QDR), Rumsfeld outlined what he called a "road map for change" at the Department of Defense, which he said had begun to be implemented in 2001.

The QDR defined the "Department's Total Force" as "its' active and reserve military components, its civil servants, and its contractors—constitut[ing] its warfighting capability and capacity. Members of the Total Force serve in thousands of locations around the world, performing a vast array of duties to accomplish critical missions." Driven in part by Rumsfeld's vision for the Department of Defense, and in part by globalization and technological advances, contract employees, in short order, have become a major part of force projection. It requires but a brief glance at relevant statistics of conflict deployments over the past two decades to grasp the "sea change" that has occurred for doing business with private industry in time of conflict.

United States Contractors in Conflicts[6]

Conflict	Contractors	Military
1991 Gulf War	9,200	541,000
Bosnia	1,400	20,000
Kosovo	10,000–15,000	50,000 (KFOR total)
Iraq/OIF	100,000 [7]	140,000

These statistics are startling when viewed for the first time, but it would be well to remember that there are good and sufficient reasons for privatization. These include:

Surge Capacity: With military forces greatly reduced, the ability to respond quickly through civilian augmentation can help meet national security needs.

Speed: Government bureaucracy is frequently an impediment to fast and efficient movement of materials.

---

6. Numbers from: Merle, Renae. "Census Counts 100,000 Contractors in Iraq." *The Washington Post.* December 5, 2006, pg. D01; Avant, Deborah D. "The Privatization of Security: Lessons from Iraq." *Orbis,* Spring 2006, pp. 327–342. All numbers are estimates as there is no single point within the DoD or the Services that collects information on contractors supporting deployed troops.

7. Of the 100,000 contractors in Iraq, 48,000 work as private soldiers. (source: Scahill, Jeremy. "Bush's rent-an-army," *Los Angeles Times,* January 25, 2007, p. A23) No doubt a number of the remaining 52,000 are indigenous Iraqis employed in the reconstruction effort.

Skills: Skilled maintenance on modern weapons systems is frequently beyond the ability of government, and especially military personnel.

Cost: Certainly privatization comes with a price tag, but it can also come at a lower cost than some governmental capabilities.

Flexibility: Especially for short-term requirements, outsourcing may be faster, cheaper and more easily dispensed with than creating the capability within the government.

What drives much of the need for privatization is the changing nature of warfare. The United States is one of the few nations left with capacity for conventional warfare, but that fact drives another—unconventional and asymmetric warfare is the threat most likely to be faced simply because adversaries do not have a conventional capacity that can challenge United States capabilities. Asymmetry is precisely what we confront in fighting terrorism and insurgency. Increasingly, transnational threats of all types arise from non-state actors and standing military forces are primarily designed to engage state actors. Confounding the issues, in this environment, crime and war become blurred.[8] Even more problematic, foreign and domestic may become just as blurred, but that is a subject for another time.[9]

Increasingly, private players are assuming responsibilities previously managed exclusively by the uniformed military. Private corporations have penetrated Western warfare so deeply that they are now the second largest contributor to coalition forces in Iraq after the United States military.[10] Privatization has become a fact of life to meet military and diplomatic needs. Frequently these needs are being met by private military contractors whose employees are not far separated in function, and sometimes in appearance, from the military warrior; therein lays the potential for legal mischief.

Practical Issues of Privatization

The reasons to privatize are good ones, but the genesis of enhanced privatization was predicated, in part, on the notion that, even absent the Soviet

---

8. This has come to mean that civilian agencies of government, especially those with investigative skills, also have a focused mission in the conflict environment.

9. American jurisprudence distinguishes between foreign and domestic threats in a very real way. The techniques to investigate, surveil and disrupt are legally distinct. Even though the effect of terrorism may be the same whether it originates with Timothy McVeigh or Osama bin Laden, the law often does not permit them to be addressed the same way.

10. Ian Traynor, "The Privatization of War," *The Guardian*, December 10, 2003.

threat, if we had to fight the ensuing conflict would be relatively conventional—that certainly made sense when conflicts such as Kosovo/Bosnia erupted. Iraq and Afghanistan, however, proved to be very different. They are different because the threats are asymmetric; "winning" has little to do with military superiority and social issues are uppermost in the minds of military warriors. Just as importantly, however, providing for the welfare of the populace is a need that is difficult to meet when insurgents, terrorists and corrupt officials depend for their sustenance on getting the Americans out which, in turn, depends largely on their ability to show the Americans powerless by defeating reconstructions efforts. In this scenario privatized reconstruction efforts, on which winning the peace depends, have been unsatisfactory, both because of shoddy performance and because of insurgent attacks.

The Committee on Government Reform, U.S. House of Representatives, has been wrestling with privatization issues in Iraq since 2004. On September 28, 2006, the Committee held the fourth in a series of public hearings. The opening statement of Chairman Tom Davis included the following paragraph:

> The picture painted by our witnesses today will not be pretty, nor will their testimony necessarily tell the complete story of an evolving, dynamic sometimes dangerous process. But this much is clear: Poor security, an arcane, ill-suited management structure, and a dizzying cascade of set-backs have produced a succession of troubled acquisitions.[11]

Not merely the Congress has been involved in attempting to discern the effect of privatization in a conflict zone. In 2004 the Center for Media and Democracy found that, in Iraq:

- Despite over eight months of work and billions of dollars spent, key pieces of Iraq's infrastructure—power plants, telephone exchanges, and sewage and sanitation systems—have either not been repaired, or have been fixed so poorly that they don't function.
- San Francisco-based Bechtel has been given tens of millions to repair Iraq's schools. Yet many haven't been touched, and several schools that Bechtel claims to have repaired are in shambles. One 'repaired' school was overflowing with unflushed sewage; a teacher at the school also reported that 'the American contractors took away our Japanese fans and

---

11. Opening Statement of Chairman Tom Davis, Government Reform Committee Hearing, "Acquisition Under Duress: Reconstruction Contracting in Iraq," U.S. House of Representatives, September 28, 2006 (hereinafter, "Hearings").

replaced them with Syrian fans that don't work'—billing the U.S. government for the work.
- Inflated overhead costs and a Byzantine maze of sub-contracts have left little money for the everyday workers carrying out projects. In one contract for police operations, Iraqi guards received only 10% of the money allotted for their salaries; Indian cooks for Halliburton subsidiary Kellogg Brown and Root[12] reported making just three dollars a day.

The report also reveals further details of the controversial Halliburton contracts: for example, that of Halliburton's $2.2 billion in contracts, only about 10% has gone to meeting community needs—the rest being spent on servicing U.S. troops and rebuilding oil pipelines. Halliburton has also spent over $40 million in the unsuccessful search for weapons of mass destruction. The report concludes "'The politics and process behind these deals have always been questionable. Now we have first-hand evidence that they're not even doing their jobs.'"[13]

According to General Sir Mike Jackson, retired Chief of General Staff, Armed Forces of the United Kingdom, the United States Department of Defense, under Secretary Rumsfeld, paid little attention to reconstruction efforts.[14] The problem is that rebuilding a nation already in disrepair and further damaged by war requires reconstruction. Vexingly, in Iraq reconstruction called for levels of security not planned for under the Rumsfeld scheme.

However, the truly confounding issue for Iraq, and to a slightly lesser extent Afghanistan, has been security. The security environment in Iraq, which encompasses, insurgency, terrorism, organized crime and corruption, is of a magnitude not imagined in 2003. However, by 2004 the environment had become so hostile, that some 20,000 private security guards were in Iraq.[15] That statistic, startling in 2004, pales by comparison today. In 2006 the Government Accountability Offices very conservatively estimated that there were 181 private military firms supplying some 48,000 security personnel in Iraq[16] and

---

12. Kellogg Brown& Root performed so poorly in its work repairing pipelines that the contracts were let with other companies to finish their work. Chris Shumway, "U.S. Blames Own Contracting Rules for Iraq Reconstruction Failures," *The New Standard, available at* http://newstandardnews.net/content/index.cfm/items/1691.

13. "New Investigation Reveals 'Reconstruction Racket' in Iraq." January 21, 2004 press release (*available at* http://www.southernstudies.org/) by the *Institute for Southern Studies.*

14. General Jackson recollected Rumsfeld as saying "We don't do nation-building."

15. *Available at* http://www.pbs.org/wgbh/pages/frontline/shows/warriors/view/.

16. William Solis, Director Defense Capabilities and Management, Government Accountability Office before the Subcommittee on National Security, Emerging Threats, and International Relations, Committee on Government Reform, House of Representatives, June 13, 2006.

by October of 2007 the *New York Times* reported 160,000 private contractors in Iraq, some 50,000 of them being armed security operatives. Even so, it is not clear how many private contractors are in Iraq, nor is it clear how many have died there. Estimates vary considerably. Various non-military sources have counted at least 312 security contractors killed in Iraq.[17] In 2006 the Labor Department estimated 650 private contractors altogether had died in Iraq and counts approximately 100,000 in the workforce, but the numbers are soft and do not adequately account for Iraqi sub-contractors and employees.[18] Even so, these numbers are significant. What accounts for this rather startling number of contractors in a conflict arena is a direct, but inverse, correlation between the goals of reconstruction and the goals of the insurgency.

The security situation that developed in Iraq was largely unanticipated, but grew so serious that private security personnel quickly began to account for a significant amount of taxpayer expenditures in Iraq. Salaries for private security personnel can be as high as $33,000.00 per month. Additionally, there is clear evidence that accounting for security personnel is lacking—but it is lucrative. For example, in 2006 it was reported that Blackwater security personnel were paid $500.00 per day while Blackwater billed at between $815 and $1,075 per day, not counting food, housing and insurance.[19] In October of 2007 the New York Times reported that Blackwater was charging the government $1,222 per day per guard, six times the cost of an equivalent soldier.

In essence, the United States intended reconstruction to be a Marshall Plan for Iraq. Clean water, communications, sanitation and power were intended to win the hearts and minds of the people. However, the goal of the insurgents is to drive Western influence out of Iraq. A primary tactic adopted by the insurgents is to attack the infrastructure under construction, or newly completed, in order to convey a message that the people will never get the intended benefits as long as the allies are present. This is having a profound effect.

---

17. *See,* "Private Security workers Living on Edge in Iraq," *Washington Post*, April 23, 2005.

18. Renae Merle, "Census Counts 100,000 Contractors in Iraq," *Washington Post*, December 5, 2006.

19. Memorandum by the majority staff, House of Representatives, Committee on Oversight and Government Reform, dated February 7, 2007 and made part of the record, "Hearing on Reliance on Private Military Contractors in Iraq, Reconstruction," February 7, 2007. There are also suggestions that Blackwater has put its own employees at risk by not providing proper equipment, shorting manpower on dangerous missions and not properly training employees going into a foreign environment. *See, e.g.,* Tyson, Ann, "Pentagon Team to Study Oversight of Security Firms," *Washington Post*, September 27, 2007; A16.

Bechtel Corporation serves as an example. Bechtel got its first contract in 2003 with an assurance that it would have a safe working environment. In 2006 Bechtel, a corporation with significant experience working in hostile environments began to pull out. Dozens of Bechtel's employees and subcontractors had been killed, some were kidnapped and others marched out of their office and shot. Many others were wounded. The result is that huge amounts of contract money have gone into security that otherwise could have been spent on reconstruction projects—and that has been true with virtually all of the private contractors in Iraq.[20] Nor is it entirely clear, who the prime contractor is for many security personnel. On March 31, 2004, four Americans working as private security personnel for Blackwater were ambushed and killed in Fallujah. More than three years later we do not know, for sure, who the prime was. Blackwater initially believed it was KBR. ESS Support Services Worldwide told a House Committee it was Fluor Corporation but Fluor Corporation disputes that.[21]

Increasingly, money allocated by the United States for reconstruction has been diverted to security measures, thereby decreasing the amount of money available for private contracts. At the September 28, 2006 hearing before the Government Reform Committee,[22] Chairman Tom Davis, referring to uncompleted and poorly completed projects, remarked that "Obviously security is the critical factor driving costs and confounding contract management and oversight."

Beyond those challenges, however, is the challenge of dealing with so many civilians in the battle space. Add to that the armed populace, the insurgents who are indistinguishable from the populace and an often undisciplined set of armed security guards and the battle space becomes largely unmanageable. As this chapter was being written oversight of private security guards became a central issue as Iraqi authorities repeatedly clashed with armed guards over aggressive street tactics. The State Department allowed heavily armed teams to operate without an Interior Ministry license, even after the requirement became standard language in security contracts. These private military contractors are not subject to the military's restrictions on the use of offensive weapons, its procedures for reporting shooting incidents or a central tracking system that allows commanders to monitor the movements of security companies on the battlefield.

The issues became acute in September of 2007 when employees of Blackwater, a North Carolina-based security firm, killed 11 Iraqis in a sharply disputed

---

20. David R Baker, "Bechtel ends Iraq rebuilding after a rough three years," *San Francisco Chronicle*, November 1, 2006.

21. Opening Statement of Representative Henry A. Waxman, Chairman, Committee on Oversight and Government Reform for Hearings of February 7, 2007, *supra* n. 25.

22. *Supra*, n. 11.

chain of events. Blackwater officials denied wrongdoing. "Blackwater regrets any loss of life, but this convoy was violently attacked by armed insurgents, not civilians, and our people did their job to defend human life," spokeswoman Anne E. Tyrrell said. However, Iraqi Prime Minister al-Maliki said the company's description was "not accurate" and said the incident was the seventh violation of its kind by Blackwater.[23] In the end, an Army Quick Reaction Force had to mediate a residual disturbance that had, essentially, trapped a Blackwater team near the scene of the original incident.

At the time of that incident Blackwater was initially reported to have been involved in some fifty-six shooting incidents while on diplomatic guard duty, reportedly at least twice as many shooting incidents reported for other companies providing similar service. However, in October of 2007, the *Washington Post* reported that Blackwater had been involved in at least 195 "escalation of force" episodes. One result was a highly contentious dispute between a Congressional committee investigating Iraqi government corruption and the State Department, to include then-Secretary of State Condoleezza Rice. Additionally, the interests of military commanders in maintaining discipline in the battle space has put diplomats and the military at odds over private security firms.[24]

The issues quickly escalated to suspicions that the State Department had worked with Blackwater to play down these incidents.[25] Allegedly State Department employees argued against high compensation Iraqi high deaths for fear it would encourage "death by cop" scenarios to gain family financial security. In one case a State Department employee wrote "[W]e are all better off getting this case and any similar cases behind us quickly." One *New York Times* editorial noted that the dependence on "mercenaries" quickly became evident when American diplomatic efforts in Iraq ground to a halt during the few days that Blackwater had to stand down over these incidents. In the aftermath of this scandal, the Department of State installed video cameras in Blackwater vehicles and brought in many federal agents to ride with security contractors who guard diplomatic convoys.

Of course, security guards are not the only significant issue of privatization. Corruption apparently has been rampant throughout the reconstruction processes. The Kuwaiti company building the U.S. embassy in Baghdad was

---

23. *See, e.g.,* Sudarsan Raghavan and Steve Fainaru, "U.S. Repeatedly Rebuffed Iraq on Blackwater Complaints," *Washington Post*, September 28, 2007; A-18.

24. *See, e.g.,* Raghavan and Ricks, "Private Security Puts Diplomats, Military at Odds," *Washington Post*, September 26, 2007; A01.

25. *See, e.g.,* Warren Strobel, "State Dept., Blackwater cooperated to neutralize killings," *McChathy Newspapers*, October 1,2007, one of many similar allegations.

accused of agreeing to pay $200,000 in kickbacks in return for two unrelated Army contracts in Iraq.[26] The scheme, outlined in a now-sealed court document obtained by The Associated Press, allegedly involved First Kuwaiti General Trading & Contracting and a manager for Kellogg Brown & Root Inc. or KBR, a firm hired to handle logistics for the military in Iraq and Afghanistan.[27] An army major admitted taking more than one million dollars in bribes and two other officers similarly accused have committed suicide.

Legal and Regulatory Issues

The problems and issues raised by the burgeoning business of private military contractors have few, if any obvious solutions, but, assuming that privatization remains a cornerstone of United State military preparedness, there are regulatory and legal issues that need to be addressed. For these, unlike the more ephemeral problems of reconstruction and security, there are avenues of approach that hold promise. Those avenues exist for the government, but in an ideal world, private industry would step up to the plate and participate in crafting new regulatory processes. Private industry can do much to make its offerings more attractive and more responsive and the government can do much to focus responsible spending. In all likelihood, the most efficacious approach will be a combination of government and industry effort that involves regulation, a fresh look at contracting procedures and a new evaluation of the legal conventions that regulate status in combat situations.

Industry Regulation: This issue occupies several dimensions. While it would seem that a fresh look at the regulatory process is called for, especially regarding payment for services rather than goods, it would almost certainly be a mistake for the government to throw new regulations at the issues without considerable input from private industry. In all likelihood, it would also be a mistake for the government to assume a unilateral burden of regulating private military contractors. Rather, it seems logical that self-regulation by industry should be part of the solution. This could start with identification by private industry of "best practices" which would aid in adopting "standards." Additionally, as a measure of employee performance, private military contractors would

---

26. *See, e.g.,* "Graft in Military Contracts Spreads," *New York Times Online,* September 24, 2007.

27. Pete Yost, "Iraq Embassy Builder Tied to Kickbacks," Associated Press Writer, September 20, 2007.

benefit from adoption of a code of conduct that would be worked out between the government and private military contractors. Private industry should also have adequate mechanisms to oversee subcontractors.

Those recommendations for self-regulation, and, potentially for a code of conduct, are clearly ones that cannot be developed overnight, but they should be given encouragement and a chance to work. Private military contactors should be given the opportunity to begin the process before institutional changes are made. In the meantime, the government could, and should, work to solve the problems with the governmental system in a stair-step process.

On the government side, a first step would be to ensure that requests for proposal (RFPs) are both detailed and clearly articulated so that industry can know, and understand, exactly what will be required in performance of a contract. This should also entail a fresh look at contracting in general to account for the increasingly large number of RFPs for personal services rather than products.

A second measure would be to ensure that contracting and procurement personnel are part of both pre- and post-conflict planning. By involving these personnel in the planning processes the government would be including those personnel who are closest to private industry and who are likely to understand best the possibilities and problems of using private industry in a conflict environment.

Once private industry and government reflection have reached a level of maturity that indicates a logical path to follow, the government should develop an accreditation process for private military contractors. This is not substantially different from current practices which allow for pre-qualification of contractors for future, anticipated needs, but enhanced visibility would help to soften the image that developed early in the war of government agencies having let sweetheart, no bid contracts.[28] An accreditation process would also help by identifying the individual strengths of the increasingly large number of private military contractors and could also be a vehicle to track industry performance.

Government Regulatory Process: It is pretty clear that government stewardship of public money has not been satisfactory in Iraq. Part of the reason for that is probably the simple fact that the regulatory process was designed in a different era and for different deliverables.

Who Should Regulate: The interests of diplomats and military in the battle space are not always coincident. Department of Defense rules for licensing,

---

28. USAID Administrator Andrew Natsios refuted those charges on ABC Nightline, April 23, 2003, stating that the contracts were awarded by career officers based on the capabilities of the companies and their proven competence.

oversight and incident reporting are considerably more stringent than are those of the Department of State. Many believe the military should be the principle, perhaps exclusive, overseer for private, armed security guards. Absent intervention by Congress, however, that is unlikely to happen. The Department of Defense was, originally, reluctant to volunteer for that additional burden but is, reportedly, re-thinking the issue. However the Department of State is unlikely to relinquish a task assigned to the Department's Regional Security Officials that may have goals and means divergent from those of the Department of Defense.

Oversight: Every government and private study has concluded that, among the faults found by inspections and audits, there has been a lack of adequate oversight, both for expenditure of funds and for controlling private security guards.[29] Just as private industry should examine itself in light of a changing way of doing business for the government, the government should also examine its methodologies for overseeing expenditures of public funds. It is abundantly clear that the "business as usual" model has not been particularly successful in Iraq. The opportunity for graft is only just being recognized, but corruption within both military and civilian entities has been large scale.

Partnering with Private Industry: Recognizing that there are significant issues to involving private industry in the government planning processes—at least in advance of letting a contract—government should explore innovative ways to partner with private industry. It is logical to conclude that both government and industry would benefit from planning together. If nothing else it would make requirements and capabilities more transparent to both. Of course, competition requires that private industry guard certain of its information and processes so government and industry should work together to develop an "honest broker" methodology for private industry to follow in order to more fully bring together requirements and capacity.

Government should also periodically examine the effects and results of sole source and limited competition bidding. Similar to an accreditation process, a periodic re-examination of these contracts would help the government to a "best practices" methodology.

SIGIR Recommendations: The Special Inspector General for Iraq (SIGIR) came up with specific recommendations that he thought would be of benefit for a fast-paced environment like Iraq. These recommendations included creation of an enhanced Contingency Federal Acquisition Regulation (CFAR) cre-

---

29. An oversight committee of Congress reported that there is no evidence that the State Department sought to restrain Blackwater. Richard Lardner, "Blackwater portrayed as out of control," AP, October 1, 2007.

ated by an inter-agency working group and implemented by legislation. He also recommended legislation to institutionalize smaller scale contracting programs to ease the burdens of contracting for smaller projects. In general, his recommendations recognized that the world of the FAR and the world of conflict environments are different and that a regulatory process, along with a reserve of contingency personnel for contracting and oversight, that are intended to meets the needs of the conflict environment is needed.

A U.S. Government Mission: Beyond the contracting phase, the government also needs to engage all elements of government and private industry involved in stabilization and reconstruction projects to prioritize performance. In Iraq the military, the Coalition Provisional Authority and USAID all had major reconstruction projects but they did not coordinate or prioritize with each other. Moreover, an Iraqi complaint, likely valid, was that U.S. officials made decisions without engaging Iraqis "and the decisions were wrong."[30] Whatever the ground truth, it seems clear that a better means of coordinating and accounting for priorities is in order. In turn, that leads to one of the core legal issues of command and control, which, might be more appropriately styled as discipline in the battle space, and which tilts some critical privatization considerations away from regulation and toward firmer, and more serious, legal issues.

Legal Issues: Legal issues, as opposed to regulatory issues are, perhaps, the thorniest of the problems that need to be addressed.

Inherently Governmental: The first issue that needs attention is the very reason for contractor support. More specifically, what are the functions for which private contracting is appropriate? By definition, that which is "inherently governmental" is not amenable to privatizing.[31] Although not yet raised as a confounding issue, it seems logical that there should be some mechanism by which "inherently governmental" functions may be assessed.[32] Those functions which cannot be subjected to private decision-making clearly must be performed by government personnel. In a conflict zone that might mean delivery of food could be contracted but delivery of ammunition could not be, although in some circumstances food may mean survival and in others ammunition may

---

30. *See,* Shumway, *supra* at n. 12.

31. "Inherently governmental" is defined as activities related to "the act of governing" and "intimately related to the public interst." Office of Management and Budget, "Federal Acauisition Regulaton, Circular No. A-76," 4 August 1983 (rev. 1999).

32. Activities that are so important that they must be performed by government personnel and not made subject to the discretion of private contractors may vary by circumstances. What is considered appropriate for a contractor in one situation may not be in another so assessment, rather than identification, should be the requirement.

Types of Support	Examples
Support to military forces	Food preparation (Kellog Brown and Root), laundry, equipment maintenance
Restoration of services	Water, sewer, power, transportation, bridges, railways, airfields (Bechtel, Fluor)
Construction/reconstruction	Major facilities, hospitals, schools, oil refineries (Bechtel, Haliburton)
Civil affairs	Food distribution, training, election support, media (Fluor, DynCorp, Northrop Grumman)
Intelligence	Analysis of improvised explosive device attacks, attacks on officials, primary danger areas (Kroll)
Security	Protection of officials, construction sites, housing areas, convoys, other contractors (Blackwater, Kroll)
Miscellaneous	Interrogation, interpretation, judicial training, legal support (L-3, Global Linguistics, CACI, Systex)

not be associated with urgency. Similarly, collection and production of intelligence might be inherently governmental, but there is no reason why that should be so in all circumstances. In many circumstances, that which is "inherently governmental" will be situation and fact specific. At present there is little to guide one in determining what is "inherently governmental."

The fact that diplomatic efforts of the State Department ground to a halt when Blackwater was curtailed from operating for a few days raises significant questions of both propriety and law. Similarly, Blackwater, and all private contractor employees, have been allowed to function with impunity, exempt from Iraqi law, much as the military soldier or an accredited diplomat would be. In June of 2004, two days before the official end of United States military occupation of Iraq, the Coalition Provisional Authority (CPA) under Paul Bremmer revised a CPA order to provide immunity to foreign contractors from prosecution under Iraqi law.[33]

What this means is that standards for assessing "inherently governmental" need to be developed and applied against contracting for private services and geared to the precise environment in which services are needed. The Federal

---

33. The CEO of Blackwater has asserted that loss of immunity would drastically affect private security guard efforts because a fair trial in Iraqi courts would be dubious. *See, e.g.,* August Cole and Neil King, Jr., "Blackwater Furor May Alter Way U.S. Contractors do Business in Iraq," *The Wall Street Journal*, October 3, 2007.

Activities Inventory Reform (FAIR) Act of 1998 (P.L. 105-270) defines "inherently governmental" as activities "so intimately related to the public interest as to mandate performance by government personnel." These are generally considered activities that require the exercise of discretion in applying Federal Government authority or the making of value judgments in making decision for the Federal Government. Although helpful, this is necessarily incomplete. When it is clear that value judgment is part of the equation it is equally clear that there can be no definitive *a priori* determination of what is and is not "inherently governmental" that can serve future needs. The result is a critical need for a firm process that can evaluate what is and is not "inherently governmental;" a process that takes into account the specific needs and conditions of what we now know are sure to be unique situations.

Failure to Perform: Closely related, and sometimes co-extensive, is government contract law which is an arcane discipline to begin with. Historically, military contracting processes are predicated on an assumption that the contractor is providing a product, but much of what is contracted for today are personnel services. While contractors can generally be "fined" for failure to perform, that is a post-event remedy and one not well suited to needs of the commander in a conflict environment. In addition, failure to perform a required duty may be due to a perception of danger that is not shared by the military. It is not clear that there is a remedy for that situation but it is one that has arisen in Iraq.[34] Furthermore, in a case such as this, the importance of the function to the mission must be evaluated, and if found to be essential the question then arises as to whether it is properly one contracted out. Much like the issues arising from "inherently governmental," a process for working through performance issues needs to be in place before a crisis arises.

Contractor Conduct and Training: The next major issue is that of discipline on the battlefield and contractor conduct. Unregulated by the military, private military contractors often enter the battle space without coordinating, thereby exacerbating security issues in a constantly tense environment. Furthermore, allegations of misconduct, including rape and murder have been made against private military contractors. Video clips suggest that contractors for a British company fired at civilian vehicles. Private contractors are being used as interrogators but standards for proficiency do not exist. Many security per-

---

34. In one instance contractor personnel were to deliver supplies to a unit in a forward operating area. The military certified the route was safe to travel but contractor personnel disagreed and refused to make the delivery. The result was that soldiers in that forward area were denied hot showers and hot food for an extended period of time.

sonnel come from nations where information about them is difficult, even impossible to find.[35]

Additionally, many private security personnel are poorly trained; contractors have frequently had to replace security personnel for poor performance. Even Blackwater has had to fire some 122 employees for drug abuse, alcohol-related incidents and weapons violations. That figure is roughly 1/7th of the Blackwater force in Iraq, which spectacularly raises the question of training. The explosive growth of private contractors in Iraq was never contemplated years ago and begs for a series of regularized mechanisms to address it—conduct in the battle space is a critical one. At the very least standards for background investigations for individuals working directly for federal purposes need to be crafted. Moreover, the growth of private security personnel in conflict areas around the world fairly begs for international standards for training and experience.

A Failure of Civil Remedies: Another arena for legal concern is that of remediation—both civil and criminal. Clearly discipline in a conflict environment is necessary for effective management by the military commander, and the explosion of contractor personnel in his battle space must not interfere with that need.[36] Additionally, if the military commander is responsible for the safety of the contractor personnel, they should logically be responsive to his direction and accountable in some way for the commander's needs. Fines and ejection may be available remedies, but punitive measures may also be desirable for deterrent purposes. Secretary of Defense Gates reminded commanders that they have the authority to discipline contractor employees, but that authority is somewhat ephemeral and non-existent for sub-contractors. Then, too, there are multiple reports of failures to report incidents, even when death was involved.[37]

Of course if disciplinary measures were available that would seem to require, as well, a governmental mechanism for oversight. Exacerbating the problem is that the private security guards are often not subject to government contracts. Firms hired to perform reconstruction missions have hired many

---

35. For example, Global Risks Strategies employs armed Nepalese and Fijian soldiers, *see* Jim Krane, "AP Enterprise: A private army grows around the U.S. mission in Iraq and around the World," Associated Press, October 29, 2003.

36. To an indigenous population, the status of the soldier and that of the contractor will not be an appreciable distinction. Accordingly, the conduct of either may affect the ability of the commander to manage the environment.

37. *See, e.g.,* Daren DeYoung, "Other Killings By Blackwater Staff Detailed," *Washington Post*, October 2, 2007; A01.

thousands of armed guards, such as Blackwater, to guard their primary workers. These tend to be beyond the scope of military or State Department regulation. This would likely require legislative remedies as a starting point.

Inadequate Criminal Remedies: The so-called War on Terrorism has also placed new strains on traditional measures of criminal remediation. Even former Secretary of State Rice opined that a "hole" in United States law allowed private security guards to escape accountability for criminal acts. In providing immunity for civilian contractor in Iraq, the United States implicitly accepted responsibility investigating and prosecuting criminal activity, but what seems logical has been illusory. When the military is abroad, criminal accountability is governed by the Uniformed Code of Military Justice (UCMJ), the War Crimes Act and the Military Extraterritorial Jurisdiction Act of 2000 (MEJA). Of these, the only one over which the military commander exercises jurisdiction and competency is the UCMJ, and the UCMJ jurisdiction over civilians has Constitutional implications.[38]

These issues were considered in 1997 when Congress commissioned the "Overseas Jurisdiction Advisory Committee to "review historical experiences and current practices concerning the use, training, discipline and functions of civilians accompanying the Armed Forces in the field." That Committee found two jurisdictional gaps that it recommended be addressed by extending court-martial jurisdiction to cover civilians accompanying the force during contingency operations and by extending Article III federal jurisdiction to offenses committed by persons accompanying the armed forces overseas.[39]

Those recommendations were not implemented at the time, but the issues have become particularly important because contractors in Iraq have been accused of a wide range of abuse and violations of both domestic and interna-

---

38. *Reid v. Covert*, 354 U.S. 1 (1957), is a landmark case in which the United States Supreme Court ruled that the Constitution supersedes international treaties. According to the decision, "this Court has regularly and uniformly recognized the supremacy of the Constitution over a treaty," although the case itself was with regard to an executive agreement and the treaty has ever been ruled unconstitutional. The case involved Mrs. Covert, who had been convicted by a military tribunal of murdering her husband. At the time of Mrs. Covert's alleged offense, an executive agreement which permitted United States' military courts to exercise exclusive jurisdiction over offenses committed in Great Britain by American servicemen or their dependents. The Court found that "no agreement with a foreign nation can confer power on the Congress, or on any other branch of Government, which is free from the restraints of the Constitution." In particular, the Court found that Covert's right to trial by jury had been violated.

39. Report to the Secretary of Defense, The Attorney General and the Congress of the United States, April 18, 1997.

tional law.[40] As of October of 2007, no contractor had been convicted of a crime in Iraq, this in spite of the fact that one high-profile incident resulting in death was labeled as "murder" by another U.S.-contracted security firm. As noted previously, the Coalition Provisional Authority granted foreign contractors immunity from Iraqi law while working within the boundaries of their contracts, a rule which remains in effect today.[41]

The MEJA does provide for civilian court jurisdiction over significant offenses, but witnesses and evidence may be difficult to provide in a United States District Court thousands of miles from the locus of the activity. Not only that, MEJA applies only so long as the underlying contract "relates to supporting the mission of the Department of Defense overseas." As of October 2007, only one MEJA conviction has been obtained on a DOD contractor and that was for possession of child pornography. Furthermore, in a conflict environment discipline and interaction with the indigenous populace are important to the success of the mission and MEJA holds no remedy for social ills, insubordination, and absence from duty, etc. for civilians.[42]

One question is whether private industry can sufficiently regulate its personnel to accommodate military needs or whether limited legislation is needed to address such of those issues as have not been preempted by the Supreme Court. An Army brigadier general has commented that finding a way to prosecute security companies is more crucial than finding a way to regulate them. Moreover, it may be just as important for the ultimate mission that justice be seen, rather than promised as an event thousands of miles away.

At least some in Congress apparently believed that change in the law is necessary. Without fanfare, and largely unnoticed, a tiny clause was slipped in the Pentagon's fiscal year 2007 budget. One section of the UCMJ has, for many years, provided jurisdiction *in time of* war over persons "serving with or accompanying an armed force in the field. The addition of five little words may have altered the landscape considerably. Inserted, as section 522 out of a total of 3,510 sections, were the words "declared war or a contingency operation." The problem was recognized, but it is far from clear that the solution is an efficacious one. For one

---

40. Blackwater USA has been served notice that it faces investigations for war crimes as a result of alleged, unprovoked killing of 17 civilians. Department of the Army Field Manual FM 3-100.21 notes that such criminal activity is addressed by host-nation laws in the absence of international agreement to the contrary.

41. Memorandum cited *supra* n. 25.

42. As this chapter was being written, draft legislation was introduced to amend MEJA to expand jurisdiction to cover all United States Government contractors operating where the military is engaged in "contingency operations." It would also confer jurisdiction on the FBI to investigate.

thing, courts are likely to view "serving with or accompanying" the armed forces narrowly. Moreover, jurisdiction was extended only over those "in the field"—a term normally interpreted to mean areas where actual hostility is underway.

Under the UCMJ, commanders have wide latitude in deciding who should be prosecuted, but not all military crimes have civilian parallels—for example, disobeying an order, fraternization and adultery all may have consequences in civil society, but not criminal ones. Especially because winning hearts and minds is a reason for discipline on the battlefield, attempting to hold civilians to the same standards as U.S. troops will be messy and is likely to raise constitutional challenges. For one thing, civilians prosecuted in military court don't receive a grand jury hearing; moreover they would be tried by members of the military, rather than by a jury of their peers.

Historically, the Supreme Court has been quite hostile to trying civilians under military procedures, and no conviction of a civilian under the UCMJ has been upheld in more than half a century. On the other hand, considerable time has passed since this was an issue and the military justice system has more protections than it did fifty years ago—in fact, some matters, such as warning against self-incrimination, are more robust for military personnel than are Miranda warnings for civilians.

One of the most vexing issues that will surely arise from this will be determining to whom the new provision applies. Although it is intended only to hold contractors accountable, there are so many people on the battlefield today that it is unclear who, precisely, is serving with or accompanying the force. Contractors with the military seem an easy determination, but what about security guards hired not to perform service for the military, but to protect those who are providing those services. Then, too, what about contractors to other agencies who also occupy space in the battlefield; for example, USAID? Clearly there will be issues as to whether those five little words include employees of other government agencies, and if it does, what about reporters, some of whom are embedded with military units?

Christopher Anders, legislative counsel for the American Civil Liberties Union, feels the legislation was crafted so broadly that it could have negative consequences. As he puts it, "Soldiers subject themselves to a different system of criminal justice. That's a decision that's made by everyone who enlists," Anders said. "There may be some logic in applying military standards to civilian military contractors who are taking up arms. But it's a whole different thing when others are swept up."[43]

---

43. Griff Witte, "New Law Could Subject Civilians to Military Trial," *Washington Post*, January 15, 2007.

Discipline in the Battle Space: Following directly from the issue of the applicability of the UCMJ to civilians is the troublesome issue of control of a force nearly as large as that of the military which is not subject to military discipline. In other nations, making contractors subject to military discipline in a combat zone is not an uncommon practice, but that remedy has been at least partially foreclosed for the United States by the Supreme Court.[44] However, even if the modification to the UCMJ is effective for common crime, the most pressing issue for the military commander in Iraq well may be winning the hearts and minds of the populace. For that, discipline with respect to casual contact is necessary.

A soldier can be prosecuted for failing to follow a lawful order, for conduct bringing discredit on the service or for failure to follow a general regulation. Accordingly, a commander might reasonably prescribe the manner in which troops have contact with, talk to and communicate with the indigenous populace. It is far from clear, and even doubtful, that a civilian can be held to that sort of standard. If that is so, at least one logical first step might be a code of conduct developed by private industry and the Departments of Defense and Justice (which, again, raises the specter of training). It would also seem to call for an examination of the sufficiency of U.S. criminal laws in the conflict environment. While it is difficult to imagine a disciplinary remedy that will handle all the issues, a modification to MEJA, coupled with an agreed-upon code of conduct for civilians accompanying the force is probably a better option, in the long run, than use of the UCMJ for the issues arising in Iraq.

The Question of Status: An extremely vexing issue is the status of the contractor on the battlefield and status brings with it, issues of use of force, responsibility under the laws of armed conflict and jurisdiction. The law of war is clear in stating that civilians may not be military targets because they are not combatants. Civilians accompanying the force have never been considered "combatants," although, according to both the Hague and Geneva Conventions, they are entitled to prisoner of war status so long as they carry identification cards that certify their status. Today, however, when the Predator drone may be controlled by a civilian, when the contractor maintains the weapons systems on the battlefield, when agencies other than the military bring civilians to the battle space and when contractors hire their own armed security guards, lines begin to blur and authorities become deficient.

---

44. It should be noted, that this foreclosure is a Constitutional interpretation, which means that the option may not be foreclosed for other nations.

Additionally, there is no clear understanding of who may be armed in the conflict environment. Contracts generally provide that civilians must obtain explicit approval of the theater commander to be armed. However, two major contractors have taken the position that the restrictions do not apply to their subcontractors.[45] If contractors carry weapons on the battlefield they may be interpreted as combatants, but because they are not in uniform, operating under military discipline, they would not be "lawful combatants."[46] Even if not engaged in combat, wearing military-style clothing and body armor further blurs the perceptions. Furthermore, rules of engagement (ROE) are designed to be exercised under military discipline. Use of force by civilians, except in self defense, would seem to be controlled by criminal law—and that would be the criminal law of whatever jurisdiction has physical custody of the civilian. Additionally, if labeled an unlawful combatant because of lack of status, a civilian could be tried under international standards for war crimes.

The laws of war divide the world neatly into combatants and civilians, but in an era of non-state actors, some rules become blurred, if not meaningless. Clearly, contractors have been the targets of insurgents in Iraq. Confounding the issue is the puzzling claim made by Blackwater in a court appearance that it is immune from civil suit because they are operating in a war zone as an extension of the military.[47] Yet, if a Blackstone employee were to be prosecuted pursuant to MEJA, an immediately viable defense was that the statute does not apply because their primary mission is to protect State Department officials. If prosecution were attempted under the War Crimes Act the government would then have to prove that the war in Iraq is covered by the Geneva Conventions— a major policy issue. Nevertheless, if a contractor were to stray into the jurisdiction of another nation he would be subject to the perceptions and laws of that nation.

Adding to the conundrum, a United Nations Working Group on the Use of Mercenaries expressed grave concerns over the privatization and internation-

---

45. Memorandum cited *supra* n. 25.

46. Article 3 of the 4th Geneva conventions governs this arena. Basically, a lawful combatant is an individual authorized by governmental authority or the Law of Armed Conflict (LOAC) to engage in hostilities. A lawful combatant may be a member of a regular armed force or an irregular force. In either case, the lawful combatant must be commanded by a person responsible for subordinates; have fixed distinctive emblems recognizable at a distance, such as uniforms; carry arms openly; and conduct his or her combat operations according to the LOAC. The LOAC applies to lawful combatants who engage in the hostilities of armed conflict and provides combatant immunity for their lawful warlike acts during conflict, except for LOAC violations.

47. *See*, "Blackwater Blamed for Guard Deaths," AP, September 28, 2007.

alization of the used of violence.[48] In studying the issues with respect to the International Convention against the Recruitment, Use, Financing and Training of Mercenaries[49] the Group opined that the se of private security guards involved in the shooting deaths of Iraqi civilians amounted to a new form of mercenary activity—a view quickly rejected by the United States Mission to the United Nations offices in Geneva. Heretofore, mercenary has been commonly held to refer to the hiring of foreign soldiers by one country for use in another.

The United States needs to come to terms with the absence of a legal regime that accounts for armed contractors in a conflict environment. That well may call for national legislation—most likely an enabling statute for a regulatory scheme. However, national legislation is not binding on adversaries or even friendly governments with custody of such an armed contract employee. As noted above, under current international law, that contractor may not be considered a lawful combatant, and, depending on the circumstances, may even be found to be an unlawful combatant by other powers. The United States may have the largest proliferators of private military contractors, but other nations will find their practices changing as well. This issue deserves consideration at an international level and the United States should begin that dialogue—perhaps initially with the NATO nations since NATO now commands the Afghanistan engagement. Enabling national legislation and a regulatory framework could help to focus international discussion.

The Potential for a Constitutional Crisis: Finally, even aside from the issues of "inherently governmental" activity, there are two additional issues potentially of a Constitutional dimension that arise from the spate of privatization. These are accountability and separation of powers. For the first, it is simply a fact that the more common privatization becomes, the greater the distance between both Executive and Congressional oversight of both public money and the means to accomplish public goals. That fact alone begs for implementation of some of the SIGIR recommendations that would concentrate both oversight and process. As this chapter is being written there is an ongoing exchange between Congress and both the Department of Defense and the Department of State over issues of privatization. Several committees of Congress have expressed immense frustration over an inability to peer into activities that, in other circumstances, they would have had significant insight and oversight.

---

48. United Nations Press release, Geneva, September 25, 2007, *available at* www.ohchr.org/english/issues/mercenaries/index.htm.

49. General Assembly Resolution A/RES/44/34 of December 4, 1989. As of October 2007, only thirty nations, not including the United States or Iraq, have ratified.

Of somewhat greater concern, albeit a theoretical one, is the additional fact that use of private industry to accomplish military-related tasks has all the trappings of a shadow foreign policy mechanism. As of this writing, federally financed contractors were working in every United Nations-recognized nation except Bhutan, Nauru and San Marion. While the reasons for privatization are valid, visibility into the processes as they currently exist is muted at best, which inevitably generates suspicion and concern. At the very least, oversight by Congress of private industry activities is attenuated far beyond that of their capability to hold a government entity to account. At the far end of that issue is a separation of powers question where Executive accountability to Congress may yet be tested. Just as the war on terror is generating Constitutional tests for Executive authorities for detentions, interrogations and surveillance, it may yet test the Executive authority to outsource certain functions, some of which may be activities with which Congress might normally be heavily invested were they to be performed by a government entity.

Chapter 16

The Role of Immigration Policy in the Struggle Against Terror

*Lieutenant Colonel Margaret D. Stock**

Post September 11, U.S. policymakers have repeatedly asserted that immigration policy is a central part of the struggle against international terror. Yet immigration policy has two main and sometimes competing aspects: Most obviously, immigration controls are key to monitoring and preventing the travel of persons who intend to carry out international terrorist attacks. At the same time, immigration policy can enhance America's ability to fight international terrorism if that policy is used to support U.S. public diplomacy goals, strengthen the U.S. economy, and improve the U.S. capacity to fight terrorism by allowing into the United States those foreigners who can aid in the struggle against terrorism. After 9/11, however, immigration law and policy changes focused most heavily on restrictive travel controls; it has only been recently that American officials have begun to appreciate the larger and more positive role that immigration policy can play in the struggle.

Immigration Law as a National Security Tool

Since the founding of the American Republic, American leaders have claimed the right to use immigration policy to control the entry into the United States

---

* Lieutenant Colonel, Military Police Corps, US Army Reserve, currently assigned as a Drilling Individual Mobilization Augmentee (DIMA) (Associate Professor), Department of Social Sciences, US Military Academy, West Point, NY. The views expressed herein are those of the author, and are not necessarily the opinions of the United States Military Academy, the Department of the Army, the Department of Defense, or any other government agency.

of those non-citizens deemed to be national security threats. The first such example occurred when President John Adams signed into law the Alien and
Sedition Acts of 1798, which authorized the President to expel dangerous foreigners[1] and allowed enemy non-citizens to be detained or removed in time
of war. The latter authority still exists today.[2]

This early set of laws notwithstanding, immigration was relatively unrestricted throughout the early 1800s. In the late nineteenth century, however,
Congress began to tighten the laws substantially. An important development
was the announcement by the United States Supreme Court of the "plenary
power doctrine," a theory under which Congress would be permitted extraordinarily broad authority to exclude and remove non-citizens from the United
States. In The Chinese Exclusion Case,[3] the Court dealt with Chinese immigration
to California after the gold rush of the mid-1800s. California lawmakers asked
Congress to pass legislation excluding the Chinese immigrants, arguing that "the
presence of Chinese laborers had a baneful effect upon the material interests
of the State, and upon public morals; that their immigration was in numbers
approaching the character of an Oriental invasion, and was a menace to our
civilization ..."[4] The Supreme Court found that "if the government ... considers the presence of foreigners of a different race in this country, who will not
assimilate with us, to be dangerous to its peace and security," this "determination is conclusive upon the judiciary."[5] Congress's plenary power to control
immigration came not from an express provision of the Constitution, but from
powers incident to sovereignty.[6]

The plenary power doctrine would later allow significant restrictions on
non-citizens, even in cases where similar restrictions on citizens would be unconstitutional. Thus, after the McKinley assassination in 1901, amendments
to the immigration laws prohibited the entry of anarchists and other persons
deemed dangerous.[7] The onset of World War I led to immigration laws that
authorized the President to restrict the entry or departure of non-citizens in
time of war and allowed for non-citizens to be excluded on the basis of confidential information. Following World War II, non-citizens were barred from
the United States if they were Communists or Nazis. From the end of World

---

1. Alien Act, 1 Stat. 570 (1798).
2. 50 U.S.C. §§21–24 (Alien Enemies Act).
3. 130 U.S. 581 (1889).
4. 130 U.S. at 595.
5. 130 U.S. at 606.
6. The Chinese Exclusion Case, 130 U.S. at 609.
7. 32 Stat. 1213 (1903).

War II until September 11, the immigration code grew more and more complex, and grounds of inadmissibility and deportation were added to deny entry to anyone who was deemed to be a security threat to the United States. In 1996, Congress even created a special immigration court, the Alien Terrorist Removal Court, for deporting non-citizens accused of terrorist activity.

At the same time that immigration policies increasingly sought to bar persons deemed to be dangerous, less noted immigration policies allowed people into the United States who could assist in maintaining U.S. national security. Generous naturalization laws granted U.S. citizenship to non-citizens who had served honorably in the U.S. military. More obscure immigration laws sought to recruit Eastern Europeans during the Cold War, Russian nuclear scientists after the Cold War, and Filipinos who were willing to serve in the U.S. Navy. Thus, U.S. immigration law reflected a tension between policies designed to restrict those deemed dangerous from entering the United States and policies that allowed favorable treatment for those whose immigration could assist America in dealing with external threats. These trends have continued in the emerging security environment of the 21st century. Today, U.S. immigration laws continue to strike an uneasy balance between the need to keep dangerous non-citizens out of the United States and the desire to maintain American military, economic, and political dominance by allowing the free flow of people across U.S. borders.

In the past, America's open immigration policy has been an unacknowledged pillar of U.S. security, providing the United States with an advantage that no other nation has been able to match. Through relatively open immigration policies, the United States has attracted global talent to the United States, and assimilated this talent into the American melting pot, with significant security benefits to the United States. Yet after the 9/11 terrorist attacks, those relatively open immigration policies came under attack, as "immigration" and "terrorism" became conflated in the minds of many people.

Reaction to 9/11: Increased Enforcement and Travel Restrictions

Following the September 11 terrorist attacks on the World Trade Center and the Pentagon, many were quick to blame lax United States immigration policies. Because all nineteen terrorists were foreigners, such scrutiny was predictable, but inevitably resulted in overreaction. There were calls to halt immigration altogether; stop the issuance of student visas; close the borders with Canada and Mexico; eliminate the Diversity Lottery immigrant visa program, and draft ever harsher immigration laws. One commentator even suggested that the use of internment camps and profiling based on race and religion might be in order.[8] Typical was this comment from one Washington immigration policy organization: "September 11 exposed the serious breaches in our immigration policies and laws that could be exploited with relative ease and deadly consequences."[9]

All nineteen of the 9/11 hijackers were foreigners, and all had entered the United States by applying for visas overseas, boarding commercial aircraft, and passing inspection by U.S. immigration agents at airports in the United States.[10] Although U.S. immigration officials looked closely at some of the hijackers' paperwork, the hijackers were permitted to enter the United States. In reconstructing the attacks, the U.S National Commission on Terrorist Attacks Against the United States ("the 9/11 Commission") identified various vulnerabilities that the hijackers had exploited; they had used fraudulent passports, lied in order to obtain visas, and violated the terms of their visas. The Commission concluded that U.S. authorities missed abundant opportunities to intercept and arrest the hijackers.

Had the hijackers been barred from entering the United States, they could not have carried out their attacks. Thus, many people concluded that the way to stop future attacks was to stop future hijackers from getting to the United States in the first place. The most obvious way to achieve that goal seemed to be to tighten all immigration, on the theory that many immigrants were potential terrorists. In the months after September 11, the immense pressure on U.S. security officials caused immediate changes in U.S. immigration law and policy.

Among the immediate immigration initiatives were arrests of immigrants who met a certain profile; an enhanced emphasis on quick deportations of these immigrants through secret hearings; new security checks; enhanced tracking systems for foreigners who came to the United States; interviews and data collection affecting certain immigrants deemed "suspicious" because of their Middle Eastern origins; halting of the flow of refugees to the United States until new screening procedures could be implemented; and enactment of new laws making it harder to enter the United States and easier to deport those who

---

8. Michelle Malkin, *In Defense of Internment: The Case for Racial Profiling in World War II and the War on Terror* (2004).

9. Federation for American Immigration Reform, Invitation to Terror: *How Our Immigration System Still Leaves America At Risk—Executive Summary, available at* http://www.fairus.org/Research/Research.cfm?ID=2024&c=55.

10. For a detailed discussion of how the September 11 hijackers got into the United States, see National Commission on Terrorist Attacks on the United States, *The 9/11 Commission Report: Final Report Of The National Commission On Terrorist Attacks Upon The United States* at 168–69, 235 (Washington, D.C.: 2004).

do. Initially, however, there was little effort to consider how the immigrant community might be uniquely suited to assist in the effort to boost security, apart from a few initiatives to help immigrants who were serving in the U.S. military.

Mass Arrests

In the weeks following September 11, hundreds of people of Middle Eastern or South Asian origin were arrested as part of the investigation into the terrorist attacks. More than 500 were eventually deported, although the Department of Justice reported to the 9/11 Commission that only six had direct links to terrorist organizations. The U.S. Government initially released very little information about these people, but eventually some were able to tell their stories. According to various media reports, "the handling of Muslims arrested on immigration charges after September 11 [was] fraught with delay and sloppy bookkeeping and [] due process [was] shortchanged ..."[11] Immigrants were held for months without being charged. At least one detainee died while in custody, apparently as a result of the stress of his detention.[12] "[D]etainees the government suspects least end up being held longest since they are low on the list of priorities. In the meantime, reputations are ruined, jobs are lost, families are kept apart, and lives are turned upside down."[13] While being held in detention, some were abused. "As innocent Muslim men swept up in the post-September 11 dragnet begin to emerge after being held in custody, often in secret, for weeks and months, they [told] embarrassing and sometimes horrifying tales of official indifference and, occasionally, abuse."[14]

On September 21, 2001, in apparent reaction to the 9/11 attacks, immigration judges began to hold secret hearings whenever the Attorney General of the United States deemed an immigrant to be "of special interest."[15] Immigration judges closed thousands of immigration court hearings. When a hearing

---

11. Jim Edwards, "Data Show Shoddy Due Process for Post-September 11 Immigration Detainees," *New Jersey Law Journal*, Feb. 4, 2002.

12. Somini Sengupta, "Ill-Fated Path to America, Jail & Death," *N.Y. Times*, Nov. 5, 2001 (describing how a Pakistani detainee died of a heart attack after being inexplicably held in US jail after he agreed to depart the United States).

13. Tamara Audi, "Secrecy Veils Arrests, Jailings in Terror Probe," *Detroit Free Press*, Oct. 22, 2001, at 1A.

14. "Justice Kept in the Dark," *Newsweek*, Dec. 10, 2001, at 37.

15. Michael Creppy, Executive Office of Immigration Review, *Memo Regarding Cases Requiring Special Procedures*, Sept. 21, 2001.

was closed, the immigrant's family, the press, and the public were excluded. Moreover, the very existence of the hearing was kept secret, and no information about the case could be found on the public docket or the public information telephone line. In many cases, although the immigrants had attorneys, the Government refused to tell the attorneys their clients' whereabouts. Lawyers and family members reported that the "special interest" immigrants were being "denied legal counsel, held indefinitely without charges, suddenly moved to new locations, or kept in prison even after a judge" had ordered them released.[16]

The government did not define what it meant by a "special interest" case, but it was later revealed that "special interest" cases invariably involved persons from a selected set of countries, most of which were Middle Eastern, Muslim, or Arab.[17] The Attorney General claimed the sole discretion to determine when a hearing would be closed, and his criteria were also secret.

Detainees repeatedly told tales of abuse. In one highly-publicized case, Al-Badr Al-Hazmi, a doctor from Texas, answered his door one day to find armed federal agents. The agents arrested him, taking him to New York, where he was held in the Metropolitan Correctional Center. He was subjected to physical abuse, and not permitted to contact his family for more than a week. Finally, after twelve days in jail, he was released, without his glasses and wearing only prison clothing. His apparent transgression was to have the same last name as one of the September 11 hijackers—although that name is apparently as common in Saudi Arabia as "Smith" is common in the United States.[18] Eventually, the Department of Justice's own Inspector General issued a harsh report criticizing the mistreatment of these post 9/11 detainees.[19]

Temporary Halt to Refugee Processing

After September 11, the U.S. Government also called a temporary halt to all refugee admissions, regardless of the country of origin. When refugee ad-

---

16. Tamara Audi, "Secrecy Veils Arrests, Jailings in Terror Probe," *Detroit Free Press*, Oct. 22, 2001, at 1A.

17. *See, e.g.*, Matthew Purdy, "Their Right? To Remain Silenced," *N.Y. Times*, May 1, 2002 (recounting how an INS trial attorney told an immigration judge that a hearing was "special interest," and quoting a defense attorney saying "That's a long way of saying he's Arab."), *available at* http://www.nytimes.com/2002/05/01/nyregion/01TOWN.html.

18. "Justice Kept in the Dark," *Newsweek*, Dec. 10, 2001, at 37.

19. U.S. Dep't of Justice, Office of the Inspector General, "The September 11 Detainees: A Review of the Treatment of Aliens Held on Immigration Charges in Connection with the Investigation of the September 11 Attacks" (Apr. 2003).

missions began again, the number of admissions remained abnormally low. During fiscal year 2002, the United States admitted the lowest number of refugees in more than twenty years—only 27,500 of the 70,000 slots available.[20] Many said that the United States had "closed its doors" to refugees. By 2008, however, the Government had made a concerted effort to bring refugee admissions numbers back to a pre-9/11 level, and more than 60,000 refugees were admitted—although the United States did not come close to reaching the ceiling of 80,000 for that year. Of particular note, large numbers of Iraqi refugees were admitted during Fiscal Year 2008, and many found immediate employment working for the US Government as interpreters and translators.

USA PATRIOT Act and REAL ID Act

On October 26, 2001, President George W. Bush signed into law the "Uniting and Strengthening America by Providing Appropriate Tools Required to Intercept and Obstruct Terrorism ("USA PATRIOT")" Act of 2001.[21] The USA PATRIOT Act contained many uncontroversial sections designed to enhance border security and intelligence collection. At the same time, however, the Act made it possible to deport foreigners who engage in mere association with persons who turn out to be terrorists, and gave sweeping new power to immigration authorities to deport foreigners who were accused, but not convicted, of threatening a single person. The Secretary of State was given unreviewable authority to designate any group, foreign or domestic, as a terrorist organization, upon publication in the Federal Register; and the law made it a deportable offense to engage in any fundraising, solicitation for membership, or material support—even for humanitarian projects—of terrorist organizations, without regard to whether such activities furthered actual terrorist activity. The Act also redefined "terrorist activity" to include the threat to use, or the use of, any "dangerous device (other than for mere personal monetary gain), with intent to endanger, directly or indirectly, the safety of one or more individuals or to cause substantial damage to property." The USA PATRIOT Act and a later law, the REAL ID Act of 2005, together created a legislative scheme whereby

---

20. Mae M. Chang, "Security Roadblock to Refugees: US Admission Rate Looks to Remain Low," *N.Y. Newsday*, Sept. 26, 2002; George Lardner, Jr., "US Welcomes Fewer Refugees: '02 Admissions Had Ripple Effect in Post-9/11 World, Report Says," *Wash. Post*, May 30, 2003.

21. USA PATRIOT Act, Pub. L. No. 107-56, 115 Stat. 272 (2001).

the United States could deny visas—on security grounds—to any foreigners ever involved in a knife fight in a bar. The "material support to terrorism" provisions of these laws were eventually used to deny lawful permanent residence to Iraqis who had tried to overthrow Saddam Hussein. Concerned that the laws had created an illogical system that was harming core American national security interests, policymakers in early 2008 sought to reverse many of these restrictions by creating waivers for the laws' harshest provisions.

Enhanced Security Checks and NSEERS

In November 2001, the State Department implemented a new visa approval process for young men, age 16 through 45, from twenty-six Arab or Muslim countries.[22] The new checks, which were supposed to take about 20 days to process, sometimes took months. Visa applications from those countries dropped sharply. A State Department official admitted in October 2003 that although more than 125,000 visa applications had been screened using these checks, not a single application had been denied because of them.[23] The Department of State was eventually able to speed the processing of these checks through improved computer technology.

Other immigration initiatives after September 11 included the National Security Entry Exit System (NSEERS) and a related program called Special Registration. NSEERS required foreign men between 16 and 45 who came from certain countries to provide fingerprints, photographs, and substantial personal information to immigration authorities. They were also required to complete special checks upon entering and leaving the United States, and to report to immigration authorities at regular intervals while here. Billed as a way to locate terrorists, this program was implemented in several waves. More than a hundred thousand aliens complied with the program; when immigration authorities began to file deportation charges against some 13,800 who registered, however, many immigrants began leaving the United States rather than trying to comply.[24] After the program was roundly criticized for the poor way in which it had been implemented, Government officials suspended much of it in De-

---

22. Neil Lewis & Christopher Marquis, "Visa Approval Tightened for 26 Countries: FBI Scrutiny for Men from Arab, Muslim Nations," *S. F. Chronicle*, Nov. 10, 2001.

23. Edward Alden, "Security Screening Hurts US Interests," *Financial Times*, Oct. 24, 2003, at 13.

24. Sam Stanton & Emily Bazar, "Immigrants Flee From Fear in America," *Sacramento Bee*, Sept. 23, 2003.

cember 2003. DHS continued to deport persons who had not complied with it, however, and today, some foreigners are still subject to it.

In 2002, the Enhanced Border Security and Visa Entry Reform Act was enacted by Congress with the intent of improving controls over legal immigration. This law increased the number of border agents, mandated the completion of an entry and exit control system that had first been authorized in 1996, required more secure travel documents, and called for the enhanced tracking of some non-citizens.

Beginning in 2003, all U.S. institutions with foreign students or exchange visitors were required to comply with a new tracking system called the Student Exchange Visitor Information System (SEVIS). The system transmits electronic information about foreign students and exchange visitors to both the Department of Homeland Security and the State Department. American colleges and universities must now keep immigration officials constantly apprised of the whereabouts and status of their foreign students and exchange visitors, or risk losing the ability to enroll foreign students altogether. Although the SEVIS system was implemented with little fuss, many people have raised security concerns with its vulnerability to hackers, who have been able to steal valuable personal information from the SEVIS database.[25] It is also "inaccurate and chronically out of date."[26]

US VISIT

The Government also announced that it would move quickly to create US VISIT, a new centerpiece of efforts to improve national security through new immigration initiatives. Since 1996, the U.S. Government had repeatedly planned the creation of a system to track the entry and exit of all non-citizens, but these efforts had not yet come to fruition. The 9/11 attacks spurred new attention to this effort. An extremely expensive entry-exit system to track some—but not all—foreign visitors to the United States, US VISIT was implemented in 2004 at more than one hundred airports and seaports. The system allows the U.S. Government to compare fingerprints, photographs, and other identity information of persons entering the United States with matching information stored in government criminal and intelligence databases.

---

25. Michael Arnone, "Hacker Steals Personal Data on Foreign Students at U. of Kansas," *Chronicle of Higher Education*, Jan. 23, 2003.

26. Danielle Guichard-Ashbrook, "International Students at MIT Post 9/11," *MIT Faculty Newsletter*, Vol. XVIII, No. 4 (March/April 2006), at 10.

US VISIT was projected to cost in excess of $7 billion. Following its implementation, the Government Accountability Office (GAO) said that the program had significant problems and the true cost of the program was likely to be twice the Government estimate.[27] In 2007, DHS announced that it was unable to complete the land exit portion of US VISIT and was abandoning the attempt until further notice. At the same time, American officials hailed the system's ability to stop people from entering the United States with fraudulent documents and its usefulness in intercepting possible criminals and terrorists.

Expedited Removal

Immigration authorities also announced an expansion of the "expedited removal" program, whereby immigration officers can summarily return immigrants to their countries of origin.[28] Previously, expedited removal powers had only been exercised at ports-of-entry, but post-9/11, DHS announced the extension of expedited removal procedures to non-citizens, including asylum seekers, who were caught along the U.S.-Mexico border. The speed of the process meant that U.S. government authorities had very little time to collect information, verify facts, and exploit possible intelligence sources. Immigration authorities bragged about their newly-acquired ability to remove suspicious foreigners speedily, but others questioned why it made any sense to quickly release a suspected terrorist to his freedom in another country. In at least one case, a person removed expeditiously was released to commit a suicide attack in Iraq.

The exercise of these authorities was not without controversy. Perhaps the most disturbing case involved Canadian citizen Maher Arar, an engineer who was detained by U.S. immigration authorities in September 2002 after his flight from Tunisia to Canada stopped in New York during transit. Arar was taken off the flight, detained for more than a week, and then summarily deported to Syria, the country of his birth. He was held by the Syrians for nearly a year and tortured, after American authorities allegedly conveyed to the Syrians that he had ties to terrorists. The Syrians released Arar eventually, and he returned to Canada, where a Canadian Government commission cleared him of the ter-

---

27. Robert O'Harrow, Jr. and Scott Higham, "GAO Report Finds US VISIT Management Lacking," *Washington Post*, Feb. 24, 2005, at A22.

28. 69 Federal Register 48877, Aug. 11, 2004.

rorism charges, confirmed that he had been tortured, and agreed to pay him more than $10 million in damages because Canadian officials had assisted U.S. Government officials in effectuating his removal to Syria. Arar attempted to sue the United States government as well, but his lawsuit was dismissed on national security grounds, and he remains on a U.S. government watchlist today.

Construction of the Border Fence

For many years, some U.S. border security officials had sought to control unlawful immigration on the southern U.S. border by creating a system of fences and other barriers. The struggle against terror offered the opportunity to further these goals by linking the border fence concept—and the attempt to regulate unlawful immigration—to national security concerns. In 2005, the United States Congress passed Section 102 of the REAL ID Act as part of a measure funding the war on terrorism.[29] This highly unusual law granted the Secretary of Homeland Security the power to waive all local, state, and federal laws and regulations if he determined, in his sole discretion, that waiving those laws was necessary to achieving the national security goal of constructing a border fence. Congress also voted to allow only the narrowest possible court review of the decisions and actions of the Secretary. Following enactment of the law, Secretary of Homeland Security Michael Chertoff invoked its provisions to waive application of U.S. environmental and other laws to controversial sections of the border between the United States and Mexico—and the law remains a precedent that could be broadly applied to override other laws anywhere along the U.S. border.

The Congressional push to construct border fences continued after passage of the REAL ID Act, with both the House and Senate voting to construct additional fences. The U.S. trend tracks a similar trend worldwide, as countries such as Israel, India, and Saudi Arabia have constructed similar fences in an effort to enhance their security.[30] At the same time, property owners and others along the southern U.S. border sought to fight the law's provisions, arguing that they were unconstitutional delegations of Legislative authority to the Executive branch of the government.

---

29. Emergency Supplemental Appropriations Act for Defense, the Global War on Terror, and Tsunami Relief, Public Law 109-13, 109th Congress, 119 Stat. 231.

30. Martin Sieff, "Analysis: US Fence Follows Global Trend," United Press Int'l, May 24, 2006.

Increased Immigration Prosecutions and Detentions

Immigration authorities also sought generally to use U.S. immigration laws for anti-terrorism purposes when other legal systems—such as the criminal justice system—seemed inadequate to the task. Strict enforcement of U.S. immigration laws was viewed as a key tool to disrupt potential plots and uncover possible terrorist networks. In early 2002, U.S. Attorney General John Ashcroft was famously quoted "Let the terrorists among us be warned. If you overstay your visas, even by one day, we will arrest you." Government officials routinely linked national security concerns to immigration-related crimes that were previously viewed as minor and often not enforced, such as the use of false documents to work. DHS conducted investigations and mounted raids on employers, with a particular emphasis on employees at airports, military bases, power plants, and other "critical infrastructure" nodes. Critics of these efforts argued that the Government was harming security by focusing its efforts on people who were not a threat, alienating immigrant communities with a "war on immigrants," and exaggerating the numbers of terrorism-related prosecutions. Indeed, a General Accounting Office report found that three-quarters of all convictions labeled as terrorism were really for non-terrorist offenses. The report stated that the Government "does not have sufficient management oversight and internal controls in place, as required by federal internal control standards, to ensure the accuracy and reliability of its terrorism-related conviction statistics."[31]

Immigration detentions were deemed a particularly useful tool to disrupt potential terrorist plots. The complexity of immigration laws and the lesser procedural protections for defendants in administrative immigration proceedings made it relatively easy for the government to charge and detain non-citizens in connection with immigration violations. While it was difficult to keep an ordinary criminal defendant in jail beyond completion of his criminal sentence, immigration detentions could sometimes keep a non-citizen in government custody for years. Shortly before 9/11, however, the United States Supreme Court had ruled in the case of Zadvydas v. Davis[32] that certain immigration detainees must be granted a custody review every six months, and must be released if they could not be deported and did not pose a threat to Americans. The Court opined that preventive detention based on the need to

<hr>

31. General Accounting Office, Better Management Oversight and Internal Controls Needed to Ensure Accuracy of Terrorism-Related Statistics (Jan. 2003).
32. *Zadvydas v. Davis*, 533 U.S. 678 (2001).

protect the community—a justification that would be raised repeatedly in the struggle against terror—would be upheld "only when limited to specially dangerous individuals and subject to strong procedural protections." The Court left open, however, the possibility that preventive detention of non-citizens could be authorized in cases involving "terrorism or other special circumstances where special arguments might be made for forms of preventive detention and for heightened deference to the judgments of the political branches with respect to matters of national security."[33]

Enhanced Identification Measures

Congress and policymakers also sought to prevent terrorism through new identification measures that affected both citizens and immigrants alike. As part of the REAL ID Act of 2005, Congress imposed new federal mandates on State issuance of driver's licenses and identification cards. Several states resisted, calling the measure an unfunded and unconstitutional federal order. Under the new law, States were required to adopt new security features, check applicants' documents against federal databases, and deny licenses to non-citizens who were deemed to be unauthorized. Several States attempted to resist the federal mandate, and their outcries led to a delay in implementation of the program.

Congress also demanded reversal of previously lax border documentation requirements in North America. Beginning in 2008, U.S. border officials began requiring anyone traveling across borders in the Western Hemisphere to carry a passport under a program titled the Western Hemisphere Travel Initiative (WHTI). In response to WHTI, passport applications soared, and the Department of State scrambled to meet the sudden demand.

Creation of DHS

Yet the most dramatic immigration-related event following 9/11 was the demise of the Immigration and Naturalization Service and the creation of the Department of Homeland Security (DHS) in March 2003. With more than 200,000 employees, the new cabinet-level agency would take 22 agencies under its umbrella to become the third largest federal agency, behind the Department of Defense and the Department of Veterans Affairs. Immigration functions within DHS were split between three agencies—Customs and Border

---

33. 533 U.S. at 696.

Protection (CBP), Immigration and Customs Enforcement (ICE), and United States Citizenship and Immigration Services (USCIS). Lawmakers presumably thought that security would be enhanced through the reorganization of the immigration function, but oversight and coordination proved to be difficult, as more than eighty Congressional committees sought to control DHS, and the agencies within DHS found themselves developing conflicting and over-lapping policies.

Negative Impacts and a New Vision

Cumulatively, these post-September 11 immigration policies, intended to enhance U.S. national security, also had negative effects on security.

According to many experts, some of the broader measures implemented by the U.S. government after September 11—particularly the ones that focused on Muslims and Arabs—were too broad to enhance security effectively and fostered resentment among these groups both within the United States and abroad, hindering intelligence investigations.[34]

Many of the policies also harmed the U.S. economy. Inevitably, as the poli-cies and laws tightened in an attempt to keep terrorists out, they cast a much wider net. Many foreigners were excluded as "national security threats" al-though there was no reasonable probability that they truly were such threats. As word got out that the United States was behaving harshly towards foreign visitors, many simply stopped coming. Visa applications dropped substantially. Cross-border traffic fell. American businesses reported billions of dollars in losses as a result of the new, harsher security regime.[35]

Foreign students were significantly affected. Many of them, turned off by post-September 11 security measures, elected to study in more hospitable coun-tries.[36] Many said that the United States was no longer their destination of choice for higher education. The Institute of International Education, which tracks foreign students in the United States, noted that foreign student en-rollment in U.S. colleges and universities was flat after years of steady growth, with significant declines in 13 of the top 20 sending countries, including In-

34. John N. Paden & Peter W. Singer, "America Slams the Door (On Its Foot): Wash-ington's Destructive New Visa Policies," *Foreign Affairs*, May/June 2003.

35. Edward Alden, "Security Screening Hurts US Interests," *Financial Times*, Oct. 24, 2003, at 13.

36. Danielle Guichard-Ashbrook, "International Students at MIT Post 9/11," *MIT Fac-ulty Newsletter*, Vol. XVIII, No. 4 (March/April 2006), at 10–11.

donesia, Thailand, and Malaysia. A report by the Council of Graduate Schools found that nine in 10 U.S. graduate programs saw a significant drop in international applications, particularly in areas like engineering and science. In April 2004, Harvard president Lawrence Summers wrote a letter to U.S. Secretary of State Colin Powell, saying applications from Chinese students were down as much as 40 percent in certain Harvard departments.[37] "[W]e risk losing some of our most talented scientists and compromising our country's position at the forefront of technological innovation," he wrote. "If the next generation of foreign leaders are educated elsewhere, we also will have lost the incalculable benefits derived from their extended exposure to our country and its democratic values."[38]

Recognizing the negative impact that some post-9/11 immigration policies had had on the positive aspects of international travel, U.S. officials began to move toward a better balance. Announcing a new vision of "Secure Border, Open Doors," the Department of State and the Department of Homeland Security in 2006 jointly declared their desire to "to guide the current and future development of solutions that ensure the best use of new technologies and the most efficient processes—all of which will ensure that our joint facilitation and security objectives are met."[39] Following the declaration of this vision and significant concrete steps to restore the visa "welcome mat," there was some evidence that the negative trend was being reversed. Yet many argued that these measures were not enough; in the summer of 2008, well-respected New York Mayor Michael Bloomberg opined that America's immigration restrictions were "insane" and an attempt to commit "mass suicide" because they were hurting the U.S. economy and American competitiveness.

Efforts to Enhance Security through Immigration Policy

While many post-9/11 U.S. immigration policies were aimed at restricting foreigners from entering or remaining in the United States, there was one area

---

37. Letter from Lawrence H. Summers, President, Harvard University, to Colin Powell, U.S. Secretary of State (Apr. 19, 2004), *available at* http://www.president.harvard.edu/speeches/2004/powell.html.

38. *Ibid.* at 1.

39. Department of Homeland Security, "Factsheet: Secure Borders and Open Doors in the Information Age," January 17, 2006, *available at* http://www.dhs.gov/xnews/releases/press_release_0838.shtm.

LIEUTENANT COLONEL MARGARET D. STOCK

where restrictions were eased in an effort to enhance America's warfighting abilities. Once the nation was at war, immigrants in the armed forces were eligible for naturalization under the special wartime military naturalization statute. Section 329 of the Immigration & Nationality Act (INA) has long given the President authority to proclaim that, when the nation is engaged in armed conflict, immigrants who are in the military can obtain their U.S. citizenship regardless of their length of residency or immigration status.[40] President Bush invoked this statute on July 3, 2002, proclaiming that all immigrants who have served honorably on active duty in the armed forces after September 11, 2001, shall be eligible to apply for expedited U.S. citizenship.[41] Thousands of noncitizens took advantage of this provision to become U.S. citizens. President Bush's declaration that immigrants in the military were eligible for expedited naturalization also triggered the application of a statute allowing for posthumous U.S. citizenship to be granted to immigrants who die on active duty during periods of conflict. Congress also acted several times to improve the processing of military naturalization cases by allowing overseas citizenship ceremonies, waiving processing fees for military members, and pressuring DHS to expedite military applications.

In April 2005, the Center for Naval Analyses published a comprehensive report on immigrants in the military. The report noted that immigrants add valuable diversity to the armed forces and perform extremely well, often having significantly lower attrition rates than other recruits. The report also pointed out that "much of the growth in the recruitment-eligible population will come from immigration."[42] Similarly, the February 2006 Quadrennial Defense Review highlighted the key role that immigrants play in the Department of Defense and called for increased recruitment in all branches of the military of immigrants who are proficient in languages other than English—particularly Arabic, Farsi, and Chinese.[43]

Recognizing that immigrants could provide special assistance to the armed forces as translators, Congress in 2006 also passed a law providing for special immigrant visas for translators serving in Iraq and Afghanistan.[44]

---

40. Section 329 of the INA [8 U.S.C. § 1440].

41. Ex. Or. No. 13,269 of July 3, 2002, 67 Fed. Reg. 45, 287 (July 8, 2002).

42. Anita U. Hattiangadi, *et al.*, Non-Citizens in Today's Military: Final Report. Alexandria, VA: Center for Naval Analyses, April 2005, p. 5.

43. Department of Defense, Quadrennial Defense Review Report, February 6, 2006, p. 78–79.

44. National Defense Authorization Act of 2006, § 1059, Pub. L. 109-163, 119 Stat. 3136.

Despite the important contributions of immigrants to the military in the struggle against terrorism, Congress remained somewhat reluctant to increase their participation dramatically. One proposal that would have allowed more immigrants to serve in the armed forces made little headway since the start of the war, despite bipartisan support. The Development, Relief, and Education Act for Alien Minors (DREAM) Act would have legalized young undocumented immigrants in exchange for military service or college attendance. The Migration Policy Institute estimated that if the act had been signed into law "about 279,000 unauthorized youth would be newly eligible persons for college enrollment or the U.S. military."[45] Under current immigration law, they have no means of legalizing their status. Despite having attracted more than 200 cosponsors from both sides of the political aisle, DREAM Act bills repeatedly failed to pass in both the House and Senate after first being introduced in 2003. Supporters of the bill failed to convince opponents that deportation of such large numbers of American-educated youth could enhance the human intelligence capability of the countries to which they were deported at the same time that America would be deprived of their talents.

Unresolved Issues

The flurry of post-9/11 immigration-related policy changes was impressive in scope. At the same time, several major immigration issues remained unresolved. Although wartime needs and fears had driven many new initiatives, these pressures were not enough to solve several intractable and glaring immigration problems—in particular, what to do about the dysfunctional legal immigration system, and how to deal with the millions of unauthorized immigrants who resided within the United States.

Verdict Still Out on DHS Reorganization

It remains to be seen whether the massive reorganization of the federal government and the creation of DHS has helped or hurt the U.S. immigration system. DHS continues to be plagued with problems, including an inability to coordinate policy between sub-agencies, high personnel turnover, computer integration and security issues, and an inability to process immigration benefits

---

45. Jeanne Batalova & Michael Fix, New Estimates of Unauthorized Youth Eligible for Legal Status under the DREAM Act. Washington, DC: Migration Policy Institute, October 2006, p. 1.

packages in a timely or accurate manner. DHS has also been under fire for problems in its immigration detention system; detainees have complained of a lack of medical care (sometimes resulting in custodial deaths), slow processes for release, and lack of access to legal process. While there have been significant improvements in information sharing and the use of technology to collect information, the agency still appears to be suffering from growing pains that may impede its ability to provide optimal security. The complexity of the legal regime under which DHS operates also inhibits its efficient functioning.

Failure of Comprehensive Reform

Nor has the problem of illegal immigration been resolved. In 2005, there were thought to be somewhere between 8 and 20 million unauthorized aliens in the United States, and the numbers were growing daily.[46] The Department of Homeland Security admitted that it did not have the ability to stop them from coming, and it was also unable to deport them all. Policymakers feared that DHS's inability to control this flow could mean that a terrorist might slip into the United States through the same pathways taken by the unauthorized migrants who merely sought jobs. Others pointed out that mass illegal migration of people—whether Haitians fleeing the crime and poverty of their homeland or Mexicans coming to the United States for jobs—could threaten security if the migrants disrupted communities, overwhelmed social services, or perhaps—as Samuel Huntington alleged[47]—threatened national identity.

Many viewed this problem as primarily one that required strict enforcement of existing laws. Others argued that creating a system to legalize the unauthorized would enhance security by encouraging people to come forward to be fingerprinted, undergo security checks, pay taxes, and provide intelligence to authorities about their means of entry into the United States. They would no longer be the focus of wasted enforcement efforts. The conflict between these two opposing views came to a climax during the summer of 2007, when President Bush and key Congressional allies—most notably Senators Edward M. Kennedy (D-MA) and John McCain (R-AZ)—drafted a comprehensive immigration reform bill and sought to have it enacted. In what became something of an epic struggle, the bill underwent significant changes, eventually

---

46. Stephen Dinan, "Illegal Aliens Outpace Legals; Large Increase From '03 to '04," *Washington Times*, Sept. 28, 2005, A01.

47. Samuel Huntington, *Who Are We? The Challenges to America's National Identity* (New York: Simon & Schuster, 2004).

turning into a complicated compromise that failed to gain enough votes to pass. By the end, many of the original supporters of the bill were opposed to it. The bill's failure marked an abrupt end to legislative attempts to resolve the plight of the unauthorized with a legalization strategy. What was left was an "enforcement first" approach, which DHS began aggressively pursuing almost immediately after reform efforts failed. DHS worksite raids became a common news story. In nearly every case, DHS spokesmen argued that the increased enforcement was of direct benefit to U.S. national security. At the same time, DHS was criticized for spending so much time deporting hapless workers that it had no time or resources to intercept any terrorists.

Role of Immigration Policy in a Comprehensive National Security Strategy

Another area where the U.S. Government failed to make much progress was in the development of a comprehensive immigration-related national security strategy. Other nations continued to benefit directly from America's unwillingness to see the downside of harsher immigration rules. "The European Union overtook the United States as the most popular destination for the growing numbers of middle-class Chinese students seeking a Western high school or university education in 2002, and the trend continued to gain momentum through this fall semester," according to a report by the American Immigration Law Foundation.[48] The report also noted that Britain, Australia, and Canada—in stark contrast to the United States—had chosen to boost their foreign-student populations aggressively since September 11.[49]

Richard Florida, author of "The Rise of the Creative Class," argued that the harsher immigration regime helped spur an exodus of the best and brightest from the United States: "[F]ewer educated foreigners are choosing to come to the United States ... They now complain of being hounded by the immigration agencies as potential threats to security, and they worry that America is abandoning its standing as an open society."[50]

---

48. "America Closes Its Doors," *Newsweek*, Oct. 21, 2004 (discussing report by the American Immigration Law Foundation).

49. Immigration Policy Center, American Immigration Law Foundation, *Maintaining a Competitive Edge: The Role of the Foreign-Born & U.S. Immigration Policies in Science and Engineering*, Vol. 3, No. 3 (Aug. 2004).

50. Richard Florida, "America's Best and Brightest Are Leaving ... and Taking the Creative Economy With Them," Conference Board: Across the Board (Sept.–Oct. 2004), *avail-*

The complicated and time consuming security procedures for entering foreigners made it difficult for scientists, engineers, and even performing artists to
enter the U.S. in a timely fashion. As a result, many people chose to do business
elsewhere. The anti-immigrant climate after September 11 caused even American companies to shift their operations overseas. Unable to get foreign workers in the United States, they began to rely more heavily on overseas subsidiaries.
Americans desiring jobs in certain high tech sectors began to relocate overseas.[51]

In all the post 9/11 immigration measures, officials seemingly overlooked
the impact that tightened restrictions would have on the "soft power" of America's image.[52] Like the "goodwill" of a corporation, the image of America as a
land of freedom has been an invaluable national security asset. Preserving this
image has been a function of keeping America a country where the "rule of
law," fairness, and justice prevail. The U.S. approach to immigrants is thought
to be one of the overlooked "soft power" aspects of U.S. national security.
Those who perceive America as a land of opportunity and freedom are likely
to join with Americans in the war on terrorism; they are unlikely to cooperate with America if the United States is seen as xenophobic and isolationist.

Some of the post-9/11 "security" measures also had the potential to harm
American security more directly. For example, government attempts to create
huge databases on both foreigners and Americans—on the theory that collecting all of this data may help identify and locate terrorists—have backfired
when the newly collected data has been accessible to hackers or corrupt insid-
ers. The agency charged with creating the databases continues to have one of
the poorest computer security programs in government, and its vulnerability
to hackers has been well-publicized.[53] Employees of DHS have been caught
using its databases to engage in criminal acts.[54] As more and more sensitive

able at http://www.conference-board.org/articles/atb_article.cfm?id=269; *see also* Richard
Florida, *The Flight of the Creative Class* (New York: Harper Collins, 2005).

51. Jonathan Krim, "Intel Chairman Says U.S. Is Losing Edge," *Wash. Post*, Oct. 10,
2003, at E01 ("India's booming software industry, which is increasingly doing work for U.S.
companies, could surpass the United States in software and tech-service jobs by 2010, he
said.").

52. Joseph S. Nye is credited with having devised the concept of "soft power." *See, e.g.,*
Joseph S. Nye, *Soft Power: The Means to Success in World Politics* (2004).

53. Alfonso Chardy, "Miami International Airport System Revived After Big Delays,"
Miami Herald, Aug. 20, 2005, at 1 (describing how a computer virus had "disrupted critical databases" at US international airports).

54. "Customs Officials Accused in Drug Ring," *Associated Press*, Oct. 20, 2004 (describing
how customs agents involved in drug smuggling used law enforcement databases to determine if agents were investigating members of the drug ring).

personal data has been gathered in DHS databases, the likelihood that it will be abused or stolen—and the magnitude of harm resulting—has increased.

Lack of Cost-Benefit Analysis in Adopting Security Measures

There also has been no effort to do an overall cost-benefit analysis of U.S. national security immigration measures. Nor, beyond targeting the "types" of people who participated in the September 11 attacks, has there been any sort of comprehensive immigration strategy. A comprehensive strategy designed to enhance national security, rather than harming it, can provide the tools needed in the Global War on Terrorism. Yet the U.S. National Security Strategy,[55] the National Defense Strategy,[56] the National Military Strategy,[57] and the Homeland Security Strategy[58] do not recognize the role that immigration can play in enhancing American security. The first and only post-September 11 explicit recognition of the potential role was found in a few comments made by the 9/11 Commission in its Final Report:

"Our borders and immigration system, including law enforcement, ought to send a message of welcome, tolerance, and justice to members of immigrant communities in the United States and in their countries of origin. We should reach out to immigrant communities. Good immigration services are one way of doing so that is valuable in every way—including intelligence."[59]

"Our border screening system should check people efficiently and welcome friends. Admitting large numbers of students, scholars, businesspeople, and tourists fuels our economy, cultural vitality, and political reach."[60]

"The border and immigration system of the United States must remain a visible manifestation of our belief in freedom, democracy, global economic growth, and the rule of law, yet serve equally well as a vital element of counterterrorism."[61]

---

55. George W. Bush, *The National Security Strategy of the United States of America* (Washington, D.C.: The White House, Sept. 2002).

56. Donald H. Rumsfeld, *The National Defense Strategy of the United States of America* (Washington, D.C.: Office of the Secretary of Defense, Mar. 1, 2005).

57. Richard B. Myers, *The National Military Strategy of the United States of America* (Washington, D.C.: Joint Chiefs of Staff, 2004).

58. George W. Bush, *National Strategy for Homeland Security* (Washington, D.C.: Office of Homeland Security, July 2002).

59. *The 9/11 Commission Report* 12.4, page 390.

60. *The 9/11 Commission Report* 12.4, page 389.

61. *The 9/11 Commission Report* 12.4, page 387.

"[L]ong-term success demands the use of all elements of national power: diplomacy, intelligence, covert action, law enforcement, economic policy, foreign aid, public diplomacy, and homeland defense. If we favor one tool while neglecting the others, we leave ourselves vulnerable and weaken our national effort."[62]

These brief references by the 911 Commission point to the way ahead in using immigration law and policy as an asset in the struggle against terror.

Capitalizing on the Immigration Asset

The U.S. immigration system has an important role to play in a coordinated fight against terrorism. That role, however, is not entirely defensive. As the 9/11 commission implicitly recognized, immigrants can be an asset in a comprehensive national security strategy to fight terrorism. A comprehensive strategy would consider not only the possible threat posed by immigrants, but also the security benefits that immigrants can bring to the United States.

For example, immigrants play a vital role in the U.S. health care system, one of the foundations of American national security because it keeps the U.S. population healthy and is key to responding to national security emergencies such as terrorist attacks and natural disasters. The foreign born are 25.2 % of U.S. physicians; 17 % of nursing, psychiatric, and home health care workers; and 11.5 % of registered nurses.[63] The United States has a national shortage right now of 126,000 nurses[64]—a shortage that could be met by foreign nurses, except that restrictive immigration policies bar most of them from coming here legally. Health care workers are vital to American security, the United States is not producing enough of them among its native population, and yet the United States has not linked the immigration of health care workers to American national security.

Another critical national security asset are U.S. scientists and engineers.[65] The foreign-born are 11.1 % of the U.S. population, but 16.6 % of American scientists and engineers.[66] Foreign-born scientists and engineers comprise 38% of all scientists and engineers in the United States with a doctorate; they were

---

62. *The 9/11 Commission Report* 12.1, page 363–4.

63. Rob Paral, "Health Worker Shortages & the Potential of Immigration Policy," 3 *Immigration Policy in Focus* 1, at 1 (February 2004).

64. Id.

65. U.S. Commission on National Security/21st Century, *Road Map for National Security: Imperative For Change* (Phase III Report) (2001).

66. Rob Paral & Benjamin Johnson, "Maintaining a Competitive Edge: The Role of the Foreign-Born & US Immigration Policies in Science & Engineering," 3 *Immigration Policy in Focus* 3, at 1 (August 2004).

51% of engineers with a doctorate; 45% of life scientists, physical scientists, and mathematicians with a doctorate. Robert Paarlberg, a professor of political science at Wellesley College, published an article in an issue of International Security, entitled "Knowledge is Power: Science, Military Dominance, and U.S. Security."[67] Paarlberg pointed out that the United States dominates the world militarily because the United States is a net importer of scientific talent and knowledge from abroad. He argued that post-9/11 security measures aimed at immigrants have actually hurt American security because they have cut back significantly on the "vital net flow of scientific assets" that undergird U.S. military dominance. In his view, the United States should bring more talented foreigners into the United States in order to maintain its lead.

Furthermore, immigrants play a key role in military operations in the Global War on Terrorism. Thousands of immigrants serve in all branches of the military. Without them, the U.S. military could not meet its recruiting goals, and it could not fill the need for foreign language translators, interpreters, and cultural experts. Immigrants also enhance the Pentagon's ability to communicate with other countries and cultures, providing expertise that is not available in the native-born U.S. population.

Next, immigrants can serve as an intelligence tool in the war on terrorism. The 9/11 Commission identified two key intelligence shortcomings that immigrants could fill—the need for human intelligence sources who can infiltrate terrorist groups, and the need for translators who speak the language of the terrorists.

More than seven years after 9/11, the United States still lacks the human assets to analyze what intelligence about terrorists it does collect. To a great extent, America does not have enough people who speak the language.[68] Margaret Gulotta, chief of the FBI's Language Services Section, has said that most intelligence analysts may not recognize terrorist threats because of language barriers. Two years after 9/11, the FBI admitted that it had more than 100,000 intelligence intercepts that had gone untranslated because of a lack of interpreters.[69] "Warnings of terrorist attacks may not be translated in time unless more people are hired by the nation's defense and intelligence agencies," Gu-

---

67. Robert L. Paarlberg, "Knowledge as Power: Science, Military Dominance, and U.S. Security," 29 *International Security* 1, at 122–151 (Summer 2004).

68. Rowan Scarborough, "Troops Lack Intel Support," *Washington Times*, Sept. 4, 2002 ("agencies on which they depend to provide enemy locations, such as the Defense Intelligence Agency and the CIA, lack reliable human sources and enough foreign-language speakers").

69. Daniel Klaidman and Michael Isikoff, "Lost in Translation," *Newsweek*, Oct. 27, 2003, p.26 ("hundreds of hours of tapes from wiretaps and bugs pile up in secure lockers, waiting, sometimes for months on end, to be deciphered.").

lotta has said.[70] America simply does not produce enough native speakers of many critical languages.[71]

One can draw similar conclusions about human intelligence. Very few native-born Americans have the ability to infiltrate Al Qaeda camps. The few who have done so—John Walker Lindh and Jose Padilla, for example—have not been used as counterintelligence assets. It may take years to train native-born Americans to infiltrate terrorist organizations. In the meantime, America must recruit immigrants. But terrified immigrants who fear deportation are much less likely to cooperate with an intelligence or law enforcement investigation, or volunteer to work with the Central Intelligence Agency.

The Government has also summarily deported many who could have provided intelligence, or acted as counterintelligence agents. Rather than deporting immigrants to Somalia,[72] where they are likely to be killed or turned into future terrorists as a matter of survival, it might have been more effective to consider their value as intelligence sources and assets. Creating future terrorists—more angry people who have nothing to lose by attacking the United States—is not a logical strategy.[73]

Finally, the integration of immigrants into American society should be part of a coordinated strategy to fight terrorism. Recent events in Europe have affirmed the importance of immigrant integration to security. Focused integration efforts can help prevent a homegrown threat and enhance the ability of immigrant communities to contribute to the U.S. military, intelligence gathering, law enforcement, and other aspects of the struggle against terrorism.

---

70. Mark Niesse, "Translator Shortage Hampers Intelligence," *Associated Press*, Nov. 8, 2002.

71. *See* Richard D. Brecht & William AT Rivers, *Language & National Security in the 21st Century* at 119 (National Foreign Language Center, 2000) ("The nation's capacity in the so-called LCTLs [Less Commonly Taught Languages] is shockingly thin, particularly outside of Arabic, Chinese, Japanese, and Russian.").

72. *See, e.g.,* Janine di Giovanni, "How American Dream faded in downtown Mogadishu," *Times Newspapers Limited*, Feb. 26, 2002 (describing how the United States Government deported a group of men—including an Intel Corporation employee—to Mogadishu, Somalia, where there is no functioning government).

73. Ironically, the U.S. has also created a threat to other nations' security by deporting large numbers of American-trained criminals. *See., e.g.,* Randall Richard, "Criminal Deportees From U.S. Wreak Havoc Around World," *Chattanooga Times Free Press*, Oct. 26, 2003, at A10.

Conclusion

Immigration laws and policies are a logical part of any nation's national security apparatus, and can be an effective tool in the struggle against terror. After 9/11, however, U.S. immigration officials concentrated mainly on using immigration laws as a blunt instrument to restrict or remove non-citizens who may or may not have been dangerous. The history of the U.S. federal government's immigration response to the September 11 attacks has reflected a philosophy that stricter immigration policies will inevitably increase security, because keeping non-citizens out of the United States—or tightly restricting them—can prevent terrorism. While restricting immigration may have been a predictable reaction to the trauma of 9/11, a long term strategy to fight terror requires a more sophisticated use of immigration policy.

Restrictive immigration laws harm security if they cause the United States to exclude the wrong immigrants, deprive America of the human intelligence it needs to learn of the terrorist threat, waste resources by focusing on deporting people who are no threat to U.S. security, and lead Americans falsely to believe that the threat of terrorism can be solved by limiting the number of foreigners who come to American shores.[74] Tough immigration laws and policies alone cannot solve the security problems created by the struggle against terror.

The U.S. immigration system should not only prevent terrorists from entering the United States, but it should also allow the U.S. government to track terrorists, collect intelligence on terrorists, identify people who seek to enter the United States, focus its resources on high risks, integrate immigrants into U.S. society, and facilitate the entry of those who would serve America's interests.[75] In the past seven years, the United States has made some progress on each of these issues, but most of the attention has focused on terrorist travel. Yet in the struggle against terror, the United States is also in a global battle for people.[76] Current U.S. military and economic dominance is a direct result of

---

74. Many experts believe that the greatest terrorist threat to America now comes from "homegrown" terrorists, and emphasis on foreigners as the likely source of danger can be counterproductive. *See* Mitchell D. Silber & Arvin Bhatt, *Radicalization in the West: The Homegrown Threat* (New York City Police Department, 2007).

75. *See* Donald Kerwin & Margaret D. Stock, "National Security & Immigration Policy: Reclaiming Terms, Measuring Success, & Setting Priorities," *Homeland Security Review*, Vol. 1, No. 3, Fall 2007, at 131–203.

76. Stuart Anderson, "The Global Battle for Talent and People," 2 *Immigration Policy Focus* 2 (Sept. 2003).

the fact that the United States has historically been the destination of choice for immigrants. Immigration policymakers should be mindful that this historical trend may reverse if the United States does not take steps to maintain an atmosphere that welcomes talented immigrants.

Before enacting new and harsher immigration policies, U.S. policymakers should ask whether those policies will actually make Americans safer, and whether they will truly prevent future terrorism. In taking measures to enhance American security after the September 11 attacks, policies must be focused and effective, rather than a vast expenditure of resources to hit non-threatening targets. While 9/11 clearly revealed the need for improved counter-terrorism and security policies, post-9/11 events have illustrated that abandoning America's traditional openness to immigrants can hurt U.S. national security.

Chapter 17

Dealing with the Nuclear Threat in the Struggle Against Terror

Robert L. Pfaltzgraff, Jr.[1]

This chapter focuses on the threat and consequences of nuclear terrorism, together with what has been done, and what still needs to be done, to minimize the likelihood of such a catastrophic event. It addresses the question of how and why a terrorist might seek a nuclear weapon and the steps that have been taken especially since 9/11 to prevent nuclear terrorism. Remaining gaps are identified, together with proposals to help remedy them. The urgency of this problem is widely assumed. According to the 2007 *National Strategy for Homeland Security:* "Terrorists have declared their intention to acquire and use weapons of mass destruction (WMD) to inflict catastrophic attacks against the United States and our allies, partners, and other interests."[2] The *National Strategy for Combatting Terrorism* issued in September 2006 declares that terrorist use of WMD is one of the "gravest threats" confronting the United States against which a comprehensive approach is essential.[3]

Nuclear weapons represent only one type of capability within the overall category of weapons of mass destruction but all such weapons are considered to have grave consequences. The other WMD are biological and chemical

---

1. Dr. Robert L. Pfaltzgraff, Jr., is the founding president of the Institute for Foreign Policy Analysis and is the Shelby Cullom Davis Professor of International Security Studies at the Fletcher School of Law and Diplomacy, Tufts University.

2. Homeland Security Council, *National Strategy for Homeland Security,* October 2007, p. 6.

3. *National Strategy for Combatting Terrorism* (September 2006), p. 13. *See also National Military Strategy to Combat Weapons of Mass Destruction,* 13 February 2006, Chairman of the Joint Chiefs of Staff, Washington, D.C.

weapons. Next to nuclear weapons, biological agents are deemed to be the most deadly weapons, followed by chemical weapons. Biological warfare agents include living microorganisms that cause disease as well as toxins, which are nonliving organisms. Chemical weapons encompass toxic chemical compounds that can lead to lethal or injurious effects in humans, animals, or plants. Biological agents such as communicable disease, including for example smallpox, could inflict widespread effects which would vary depending on the incubation period for the disease. Chemical agents include anti-plant agents such as herbicides as well as blister, nerve, and choking agents. The level and radius of nuclear devastation depends on factors such as the size of the nuclear weapon and how it would be detonated. Biological weapons could spread communicable disease over a wide area. For example, a suicide bomber infected with smallpox aboard a commercial airliner could expose literally hundreds of people on the aircraft who would then have contact with thousands more as they moved from the aircraft to their respective destinations and only after an incubation period would the disease become apparent. A chemical weapon would possibly have the most concentrated effects against a target, for example, a crop field or combatants on a battlefield or civilian populations.

Deterrence and Nuclear Terrorism

During the Cold War there was a widespread assumption that nuclear weapons, because of their potential for unprecedented devastation, would induce caution in their possessors. The strategist Bernard Brodie went so far as to suggest that "Thus far the chief purpose of our military establishment has been to win wars. From now on its chief purpose must be to avert them. It can have almost no other useful purpose."[4] Although Brodie may have overstated his case, his essential point was that it was necessary to avoid nuclear war because of its devastating consequences. Such conflict could be prevented by deterrence strategies based on the premise that the gains to be achieved could never outweigh the costs of nuclear war. To some, nuclear weapons were seen as actually stabilizing in relationships between their possessors. According to Kenneth Waltz, nuclear weapons lower the probability that wars will break out because nuclear states will fear the possibility of nuclear war and therefore be unwilling to enter armed confrontation with other nuclear states. According to this strategic logic the United States might not have used nuclear weapons

---

4. Bernard Brodie, *The Absolute Weapon: Atomic Power and World Order* (New York: Harcourt Brace, 1946), p. 76.

against Japanese cities in order to end World War II if Japan had equivalent retaliatory capabilities.

Juxtaposed is the theory that additional nuclear possessors increase the likelihood of accidental war or that such nuclear states may not behave as rational actors.[5] Such entities might view nuclear weapons as first-use capabilities rather than as weapons of last resort whose purpose is to deter rather than to fight wars. They might also make such technologies available to terrorist groups who would be ideologically or religiously motivated to use them even if it meant that their societies would be sacrificed. The Brodie image is based on the assumption that mutual interest in societal preservation is the basis for mutual deterrence. In contrast, the suicide bomber rejects such a rational calculation in favor of the destruction of enemies who stand in the way of a more perfect society even if such action guarantees that the suicide bomber will perish. Nuclear weapons would become the justifiable means for eradicating the evil perceived by such fanatics. Nuclear weapons would be used to usher in a new era based on an apocalyptic vision in which the threat of mutual annihilation central to Cold War deterrence would be an incentive to martyrdom rather than a deterrent to nuclear use.[6]

In retrospect, Cold War deterrence was relatively simple compared to the problems of deterring terrorist use of nuclear weapons in the twenty-first century. We developed deterrence capabilities designed to place at risk those targets most valued by the Soviet leadership. Today, the potential list of nuclear adversaries is greater and they may not be deterred by the threat of retaliation for reasons already noted. As a result, there can be "no one size fits all" deterrence. Given the range of motivations that might lead a state or a terrorist to use nuclear weapons, deterrence must be tailored to the actor to be deterred.[7] Deterring terrorists imposes requirements that are not present in the case of states. Unlike states, which occupy known territory and have assets that could be targeted, terrorists may have no return address even though they are likely to train in bases established in locations that can be targeted when they become known.

---

5. For a discussion of this issue, *see* Scott D. Sagan and Kenneth N. Waltz, *The Spread of Nuclear Weapons: A Debate,* second edition, (New York/London: W.W. Norton, 2002/2003).

6. For an excellent treatment of these arguments, *see* William C. Martel, "Deterrence and Alternative Images of Nuclear Possession," T.V. Paul, Richard J. Harknett, and James V. Wirtz (eds.), *The Absolute Weapon Revisited: Nuclear Arms and the Emerging International Order* (Ann Arbor: The University of Michigan Press, 1998), esp. pp. 219–223. The idea of such nuclear use is explored in considerable detail in Noah Feldman, "Islam and the Bomb," *New York Times Magazine,* October 29, 2006, pp. 50–56, 72, 76–79.

7. *See* Keith B. Payne, *Deterrence in the Second Nuclear Age* (Lexington, KY, 1996), esp. chs. 2–4; 6.

In order to deter would-be nuclear terrorists, a multi-pronged strategy that contains psychological operations based in part on cyber warfare is considered to be essential.[8] It includes the ability to deny terrorist access to their potential targets and therefore embodies defensive elements, including the layered defenses set forth later in this chapter. It also includes disrupting terrorists' ability to communicate with each other. Access to cyberspace is necessary for terrorists to plan attacks, raise money, and recruit new members. In addition to denying terrorists access to cyberspace, the ability to inject into the communications process false information and messages designed to create confusion within and among terrorist groups is fundamental to such a strategy. Other psychological operations can be designed to shape the mindsets of would-be terrorists. These include systematic efforts to delegitimize suicide terrorism in general and nuclear terrorism in particular. Apparently there are theological splits within Islam that may be exploitable by encouraging debate about the acceptability of such terrorist acts. An effort would be made to substitute religious dishonor as the dubious reward that comes to those who embrace suicide terrorism in place of the alleged benefits of martyrdom, including the promised heavenly paradise. Yet another aspect of such deterrence may be found in the ability to target terrorist facilities to eliminate terrorists-in-training, and also to take aim at the suicide terrorist enabling network. This support system, if shown to be vulnerable, may not be prepared to sacrifice itself and, once identified, could become targetable as part of a deterrence concept. Finally, the ability to instill maximum uncertainty based simply on increased numbers of security forces that can move quickly and unexpectedly from one potential target to another provides an important dimension to deterrence designed to keep a would-be terrorist off balance as part of a comprehensive multi-tiered strategy against nuclear terrorism set forth in this chapter.

Steps Confronting Terrorists in Acquiring Nuclear Weapons

A terrorist might seek to build a nuclear weapon or to acquire one that was fully assembled. Except for a dirty bomb or radiological device, building a nu-

---

8. For an excellent survey of the evolution of this type of deterrence strategy since 9/11, see Eric Schmitt and Thom Shanker, "US Adapts Cold War Idea to Fight Terrorists," *New York Times*, March 18, 2008, p. 1. The points contained in this paragraph draw heavily on this article.

clear weapon would require a combination of capabilities for which a terror-ist would need assistance obtainable within or from an existing state. This would include access to plutonium or weapons-grade enriched uranium. It would also encompass technologies for a nuclear weapon—what is often termed weaponization and the means to transport such a weapon to its intended tar-get and to detonate it. It is difficult to envisage terrorist nuclear use without outside help that was traceable back to a state that willingly or inadvertently had aided in the building of a nuclear device such as an assembled nuclear weapon or even perhaps an improvised nuclear device. As discussed below, as such weapons decrease in overall sophistication as in the case of a dirty bomb, the need for outside help to the terrorist declines. Whether we can relax in the knowledge that there are major obstacles to terrorist nuclear acquisition is a ques-tionable proposition. We do know that the Aum Shinrikyo organization that released sarin gas, a chemical weapon, in the Tokyo subway in 1993 resulting in twelve deaths and as many as sixty causalities first tried but failed to obtain a nuclear device. That we have yet to experience nuclear terrorism provides little basis for optimism about the future.

In the event that terrorists succeed in acquiring a nuclear weapon, theo-retically an attack could be mounted by using a nuclear detonation with a wide area of impact or by a smaller device such as a dirty bomb with more restricted effects. In either case, populations would be exposed to radioac-tivity externally or internally. External exposure would result from contact with radioactive material outside the human body. Internal exposure would take place if the person breathed air, ate food, or drank water that had been contaminated with radioactive material. Exposure to high levels of radiation could result in death in days or perhaps months. Exposure to lower levels of radiation, whether external to the body or by eating food, drinking water, or breathing contaminated air would increase the risk of developing cancer and other health problems but would not necessarily be fatal. There could also be temporary or permanent eye damage and vision loss. In the event of a nuclear blast the result could be death or burns, depending on a person's proximity to the detonation. If the blast itself did not result in injury or death, debris released by the detonation would have such effects on sur-rounding populations. In the event of an electromagnetic pulse attack, de-scribed below, the effects on population would take place less immediately but with devastating consequences as the population lost access to essential services and sources of physical and economic survival and well-being.

The Forms of Nuclear Terrorism

Nuclear terrorism could take several forms, all of which would have potentially catastrophic consequences for those directly affected although some would have greater effects than others, as discussed below, and therefore are ranked in descending order based on greater or lesser consequences. Although the list is more extensive, the focus in this chapter is on five categories of nuclear terrorism, which are summarized and then discussed in greater detail:

1. Terrorists launch an attack with a nuclear missile that produces electromagnetic pulse high in the atmosphere disabling or destroying electronic systems;
2. Terrorists acquire an assembled nuclear weapon which they succeed in exploding in a major city;
3. Terrorists steal, buy, or are given fissile material that they then use to build an improvised nuclear device;
4. Terrorists launch attacks against a nuclear power plant leading to the release of large amounts of radioactivity; and
5. Terrorists gain access to radioactive materials that they would use to build a "dirty bomb" or radiological weapon that could be exploded.

An EMP Attack

First, a scenario is set forth in which a terrorist group had gained access to a nuclear warhead launched by a relatively unsophisticated missile such as a Soviet-era SCUD configured to detonate at an altitude of 40–400 kilometers above the Earth's surface. EMP (electromagnetic pulse) is generated by any nuclear weapon burst at any altitude above a few dozen kilometers, with the height-of-burst being significant in determining the area exposed to EMP. Such a launch could be mounted from a ship off our shores. According to the Congressionally mandated EMP Commission, such threats could be based on terrorist groups that have "no state identity, have only one or a few weapons, and are motivated to attack the United States without regard for their own safety."[9] Although profound consequences for populations would follow, the initial effects of an EMP attack would be to disable the infrastructure on which human life is heavily dependent. EMP would disrupt and destroy equipment rather

---

9. *Report of the Commission to Assess the Threat to the United States from Electromagnetic Pulse (EMP) Attack*, Vol 1: Executive Report 2004, p. 2.

than people. The rationale for such action would be the high political-military payoff in the form of devastating consequences.

A single nuclear weapon exploded above the Earth would produce electromagnetic pulse that would radiate back down to Earth. Electrical power systems, electronics, and information systems would be disrupted or destroyed. There would be cascading effects resulting in catastrophic damage to telecommunications, energy, and other key infrastructure and to the ability of the country to sustain its population, which would begin immediately after the attack to suffer the consequences. Transportation and banking systems, medical care, food supply, and manufacturing and service sectors would be heavily damaged, if not destroyed. The damage might be so widespread and protracted that recovery would be uncertain and difficult. According to the Commission, the cascading effects of an EMP attack might become so mutually reinforcing that the ability of the country to support its population would descend into a spiral of irreversibility. An EMP attack would represent the ultimate asymmetric strategy against a society as heavily dependent as the United States on electronics, energy, telecommunications networks, transportation systems, the movement of inventories in our manufacturing sector, and food processing and distribution capabilities. Given the interconnectedness of the United States and other economies in the global system, an EMP attack against the United States would have major international ramifications as well, just as a similar strike against other countries, for example Japan or in Europe, would spill over into the United States and elsewhere.

An Assembled Nuclear Weapon

Our second scenario is one in which there is terrorist acquisition and detonation of a nuclear weapon in a city in the United States or elsewhere. This would be a catastrophe beside which the devastation inflicted on lower Manhattan and against the Pentagon on 9/11 would pale by comparison. Instead of the three thousand who perished in the attacks on the World Trade Center, we would likely have casualties at least in the hundreds of thousands with extensive domestic and international ramifications as well. Depending on the size, or yield, of the nuclear weapon, the blast would produce temperatures possibly exceeding tens of millions of degrees Fahrenheit. In addition to heavy human casualties, a ten-kiloton warhead, comparable to the World War II nuclear detonations in Hiroshima and Nagasaki, would destroy every structure within a third of a mile from ground zero. There would be extensive damage in concentric circles extending over a radius of about one-and-a-half miles from the point of impact. Buildings would be destroyed or heavily damaged.

Many thousands would either be killed or injured by the effects of the blast itself or by collapsing buildings.

We need only superimpose on the map of any major city the coordinates for such an attack to visualize its devastating consequences. If the city was a port or financial center, for example, the cascading effects to surrounding and distant areas would be enormous. Electronic grids beyond the immediate blast area would be disrupted by the electromagnetic pulse generated by the blast. Although hospitals and emergency services would be overwhelmed with casualties, their equipment might not be able to function as a result of EMP effects. As in the case of Hiroshima and Nagasaki, there would also be lasting radiation effects on much of the population that survived the blast.[10] We may think of such an attack based on a nuclear weapon smuggled into a port within a cargo container or in the hold of a ship as discussed later in this chapter. Such a weapon could also be launched by missile from a ship such as a freighter or tanker off our shores. For example, a SCUD-type missile on board a ship with a range of up to 350 miles could carry a ten-kiloton warhead. Such a contingency was outlined in the 1998 Rumsfeld Commission Report.[11] As suggested later in this chapter, both contingencies must be addressed as part of a layered defense against nuclear terrorism.

An Improvised Nuclear Device

The third scenario is one in which terrorists acquire fissile material that is then used to build a crude nuclear weapon, or an improvised nuclear device. Here the terrorist would need to have access to highly enriched uranium (HEU) or to plutonium. HEU would be easier to obtain than plutonium. HEU is produced in facilities that contain centrifuges, gaseous diffusion, or lasers to achieve levels required for a nuclear explosion. There is a large global inventory of HEU in the hundreds of tons, much of which is dispersed at numerous sites, some of which may have less than adequate security arrangements. This situation, together with the fact that as little as 25 kilograms of HEU would be required for a crude nuclear weapon, heightens concern that a terrorist group could acquire this type of capability. The alternative to HEU lies in plutonium, which is produced by irradiating uranium fuel in a reactor and then reprocessing or separating the plutonium from unused uranium leading to weapons-grade plutonium. Global plutonium stocks have increased in the last decade. Although

---

10. *See* Graham Allison, *Nuclear Terrorism: The Ultimate Preventable Catastrophe* (New York: Henry Holt and Company, 2004), pp. 3–5.

11. Executive Summary of the Report of the Commission to Assess the Ballistic Missile Threat to the United States, July 15, 1998, pp. 12–13.

plutonium is used principally for nuclear weapons, it can be blended with uranium for nuclear power plant fuel. HEU and plutonium are located at literally hundreds of sites that are potential sources of fissile materials that could fall into terrorist hands. In addition to countries such as North Korea and Iran that could make fissile materials available, there are other possible sources. Russia has long been a country of concern because of the fact that large quantities of nuclear materials are stored at facilities that may not be sufficiently secure.

An Attack Against a Nuclear Power Plant

The fourth possibility is a scenario in which terrorists launch attacks designed to release radioactivity from a nuclear power plant. This might come about as a result of actions taken within the power plant or from an attack mounted by an aircraft comparable to 9/11 that would be crashed into the nuclear installation. The psychological effects on and beyond neighboring populations bring to mind the Chernobyl incident in the former Soviet Union and the accident at the Three Mile Island nuclear power plant near Harrisburg, Pennsylvania, that resulted in the release of radioactivity. Neither was the result of terrorist action but nevertheless generated great concern about nuclear power plant reliability and safety. In order to crash an aircraft into a nuclear power plant, it would first be necessary to execute successfully a hijacking or otherwise gain access to an appropriate airplane, which is obviously not beyond the capacity of a determined terrorist group. Nevertheless, this probably would be more difficult in the post-9/11 era than previously as a result of increased surveillance of flight training schools and airports. Nuclear power plant facilities are surrounded by a formidable security perimeter that would have to be penetrated in the event of a ground-based terrorist assault. Therefore, a frontal attack on such an installation could probably only be mounted with military precision and inside assistance in order to target those parts of the complex to generate release of radioactivity and assure the failure of safety systems.

Such an operation would be difficult but not impossible. The possibility of an attack against a nuclear power plant is heightened by the substantial number of such installations in countries around the world now exceeding 400 and located in more than 30 countries, including at least 100 nuclear reactors in the United States alone. Given increasing global demand for clean energy, it is likely that the number of nuclear reactors will increase at a rapid rate in the decades ahead, thus adding to the statistical possibility of such an attack and making more urgent the adoption of stringent international security standards that should be implemented on a global basis. Although the International Atomic Energy Agency (IAEA) has set standards for protecting nuclear reactors and power plants, they are not mandatory. This leads some facilities to be less adequately protected than others.

Added to this problem is the storage of spent fuel, which is often located next to the facility where it was produced. Several studies have assessed the vulnerability of stored spent fuel to terrorist attack, generally concluding, according to the Governmental Accountability Office (GAO), that because "spent fuel is hard to disperse and is stored in protective containers," there would be "little or no release of spent fuel, with little harm to public health."[12] Nevertheless, the GAO recommended that spent fuel storage be shipped in larger amounts with improved transportation security to reduce the potential for terrorist attacks to the Yucca Mountain, Nevada consolidated storage site.

A Dirty Bomb or Radiological Weapon

The fifth terrorist contingency is acquisition of radioactive materials to construct a "dirty bomb" or radiological weapon that would spread radioactivity without producing a nuclear explosion. Conventional explosives would be used to scatter radioactive material to the surrounding area. Such a capability would be produced from radioactive materials that are widely available in research reactors. Such reactors, where spent fuel is less radioactive than what is produced in nuclear power plants, are adequate for terrorist use in such a crude device as a "dirty bomb." Low-level radioactive waste is produced, for example, by hospitals, universities with research reactors, and by some companies.[13] There are several ways in which the radioactive ingredients of a dirty bomb might be obtained. This could include transfer from outside the United States by a state sponsor of terrorism, assistance from those having access to radioactive material, and purchase or theft of such material. However, radioactive ingredients of a dirty bomb, together with explosives, could be obtained within the country of use, especially the United States. Conventional explosives that are easily obtainable would be used to spread the radioactive material. Casualties from a dirty bomb might number in the hundreds, contrasted with the hundreds of thousands or more from a nuclear weapon described above. Depending on the level of exposure to radiation, there could be a range

12. General Accountability Office, *Spent Nuclear Fuel: Options Exist to Further Enhance Security,* Executive Summary, GAO-03-426, July 2003, Quoted in Charles D. Ferguson and William A. Potter, *The Four Faces of Nuclear Terrorism* (New York and London: Routledge, 2005), pp. 206–207.

13. Committee on Science and Technology for Countering Terrorism, National Research Council, "Nuclear and Radiological Threats," *Making the Nation Safer: The Role of Science and Technology in Countering Terrorism* (Washington, D.C., National Academy Press, 2002), pp. 48–49.

of short-term health effects such as nausea, organ damage, and burns. Longer-term effects would include cancers to those exposed that developed as a consequence of the terrorist detonation of a dirty bomb.

Such an act could be undertaken by a few terrorists with modest financial and other resources. They could probably acquire radioactive materials and the dispersal explosives for a few thousand dollars. The construction of such a radiological device could be relatively easy, especially to those knowledgeable about explosives. One or more dirty bombs could be brought into a public area to detonate at a time of day calculated to maximize casualties. Because the radioactive materials for such a bomb are available at many sites in the United States, it would not be necessary to import them from abroad or even to carry them across great distances. Although the damage from one dirty bomb would be far less than from a nuclear weapon, it is not difficult to envisage a terrorist detonation of multiple dirty bombs in one or several cities. Such a pattern would be fully in keeping with the al Qaeda 9/11 operation or the nearly simultaneous attacks against the U.S. embassies in Kenya and Tanzania in 1998. The explosion of only one dirty bomb would itself give rise to fear that other such weapons would be detonated, thus producing fear and precautionary measures that could have profound effects on activities in other cities, such as ports, financial centers, or government facilities. It would be necessary both to begin the recovery process and to plan for the contingency that other dirty bombs would be placed to explode elsewhere. The fact that the political, economic, and psychological consequences would probably be substantial could itself become a motivating factor for this type of nuclear terrorism.

Although the extent of damage would probably vary greatly within and among the five categories of nuclear terrorism, there are effects that are common to each. Each would lead to widespread panic among populations who have an ingrained (and justifiable) fear of nuclear weapons. The immediate reaction would be to attempt to flee the affected area. Efforts to escape would likely further expose people to dangers such as radiation that could be mitigated by the shielding provided by underground shelters, for example, basements, for several days until radiation levels had subsided.[14] If people panicked and attempted to leave the affected area, the result would be larger numbers of deaths. In the case of an EMP attack, the infrastructure, including transportation, needed to facilitate relocation might not be available, while large areas of the country would probably be affected, making fruitless most planned evacuation efforts.

14. Ashton B. Carter, Michael M. May, and William J. Perry, "The Day after a Nuclear Attack," *The Washington Quarterly,* Autumn 2007, p. 24.

Thus immediate diagnosis and communication with affected populations on all aspects of the situation would become an essential part of consequence management, discussed later in this chapter. Given the differences in effects among the five categories of nuclear terrorism, such consequence management is more easily stated as an essential requirement than carried out in practice. Each calls for detailed planning that includes key officials and first responders at all levels of government, together with cooperative arrangements between the public and private sectors.

Other Potential Types of Terrorist Nuclear Use

It is possible to identify other nuclear-related terrorist acts. They include situations of blackmail, in which a terrorist group would claim to have taken a particular action such as planting one or more nuclear devices at undisclosed locations timed to detonate if certain demands were not met. The terrorists would need to have a necessary level of credibility for their threat to be taken seriously. Depending on the sophistication of the capability, the terrorist group could instill sufficient apprehension to cause major disruption. Let us assume, for example, that dirty bombs were alleged to have been placed in cities such as New York and Washington, D.C., or major ports such as Long Beach and Norfolk. Whether or not the claim turned out to be real or simply a hoax, the disruption would have been extensive.

Another type of terrorist action could come in the form of radioactive contamination of food or water supplies. Chemical, biological, or radiological contaminants could be introduced into supplies of food or into drinking water systems. Although water is purified by a treatment process as it passes to the consumer, unexpected hazardous materials such as radiological contaminants would not necessarily be eliminated during a purification process that was not designed to remove this type of contaminant. Especially if terrorists had penetrated the facilities of a treatment system, they could transform the water supply into a radiological weapon against large populations. Another type of nuclear terrorism is related to wastewater treatment infrastructure where waste from nuclear power plants is filtered for further processing. A blast directed to such a facility, if it contained nuclear waste, could have the effects of a dirty bomb with radioactive particles being spread over a large area.[15]

---

15. For a discussion of this type of threat, *see* Jane A. Bullock, George D. Haddow, Damon Coppola, Erdem Ergin, Lissa Westerman, and Sarp Yeletaysi, *Introduction to Homeland Security* (New York: Elsevier, 2005), pp. 165–168.

Instability in a nuclear weapons state such as Pakistan provides other grounds for concern about terrorists gaining access to a nuclear weapon. Al Qaeda infiltration or disloyalty in the Pakistani nuclear weapons command and control structure might result in fissile material or even a nuclear warhead falling into terrorist hands. Pakistan is of special interest because of the A.Q. Khan network in which nuclear weapons technologies, including equipment of enrichment as well as designs for nuclear weapons, were sold to a variety of buyers, such as Libya, Iran, and North Korea.[16]

Russia and Nuclear Terrorism

Some analysts have pointed to the possibility that terrorists could use existing criminal networks and corruption to obtain nuclear material.[17] After the collapse of the Soviet Union, the state capacity to prevent nuclear smuggling declined, although Russia may have reasserted controls designed to prevent nuclear theft in more recent years. Russian organized crime is based on transnational criminal groups that could pose a threat to the security of nuclear facilities. Russia also contains Muslim groups who have been targeted by extremist recruiters. Terrorists could use a variety of criminals to gain access to nuclear material that could then be smuggled out of Russia with the complicity of corrupt officials and otherwise motivated groups—a combination of criminal and terrorist organizations. Moreover, a nuclear device might be hidden in the hold of a ship originating in a Russian port or elsewhere whose ultimate destination was the United States to be detonated in a U.S. port.

In the early 1990s after the collapse of the Soviet Union, it was feared that control of Moscow's vast nuclear weapons capabilities and the nuclear production complex would disintegrate. The Nunn-Lugar Cooperative Threat Reduction Legislation was passed at that time to facilitate the dismantling of nuclear weapons in the former Soviet Union, to provide for the safe custody

---

16. For a fascinating account of the A.Q. Khan network, *see* Gordon Corera, *Shopping for Bombs: Nuclear Proliferation, Global Insecurity, and the Rise and Fall of the A.Q. Khan Network* (Oxford University Press, 2006), especially chs. 3–5. Libya agreed in December 2003 to dismantle its nuclear weapons infrastructure.

17. Robert Orttung and Louise Shelley, "Linkages between Terrorist and Organized Crime Groups in Nuclear Smuggling: A Case Study of Chelyabinsk Oblast," PONARS Policy Memo No. 392, American University, December 2005, pp. 159–164.

of Russian nuclear weapons, and to help underemployed former Soviet scientists find suitable employment. Nuclear weapons that had been deployed during the Soviet era in republics of the former Soviet Union, including Ukraine, Belarus, and Kazakhstan, were returned to Russia at a time of great chaos, leading to questions about whether security was adequate to prevent illicit diversion. Despite the extensive efforts of the Nunn-Lugar program over the years, and more than a decade after the collapse of the Soviet Union, HEU and plutonium in quantities necessary to produce nuclear weapons may remain vulnerable to theft.[18]

How vulnerable are the various elements of the Russian nuclear weapons capability continues to be the object of controversy. Russia today is no longer the Russia of the years immediately following the collapse of the Soviet Union. The security surrounding nuclear weapons is said to have improved greatly as controls over access to nuclear storage facilities, including unauthorized access and surveillance have been strengthened.[19] Juxtaposed is the contention that Russia inherited from the Soviet Union a huge nuclear weapons infrastructure and capability that may remain less than fully secure. With the decline in conventional military power after the collapse of the Soviet Union, Russia retains a reduced but still formidable strategic nuclear force, together with a huge tactical nuclear weapons inventory. Nuclear weapons are considered to be an essential part of a Russian defense against invasion. However improbable such an event seems today, Russia's history and far-flung borders have led Russian strategic planners to continue to emphasize the importance of nuclear weapons. Reductions in strategic nuclear forces and the dismantling of nuclear warheads have produced quantities of fissile materials for which accounting standards may have been inadequate. The net effect is to create continuing uncertainty and concern about the possible acquisition of nuclear weapons know-how and hardware from Russian sources by a terrorist group determined to do so.

---

18. Graham Allison, *Nuclear Terrorism: The Ultimate Preventable Catastrophe* (New York: Henry Holt and Company, 2004), p. 147. In making this statement, Allison refers to Matthew Bunn, Anthony Wier, and John P. Holdren, *Controlling Nuclear Warheads and Materials: A Report Card and Action Plan* (Washington, D.C.: Nuclear Threat Initiative and the Project on Managing the Atom, Harvard University, 2003).

19. For a perspective that emphasizes the strengths of Russian controls over its nuclear capabilities, *see* Robin M. Frost, *Nuclear Terrorism after 9/11*, Adelphi Paper 378, International Institute for Strategic Studies 2005, pp. 12–23.

What Can Be Done: A Layered Approach to Defense Against Nuclear Terrorism

There is no simple single solution to the threat of nuclear terrorism. However, there is general agreement that a comprehensive, layered approach of synergistic elements should be designed to make terrorist acquisition and use of a nuclear device difficult and hopefully impossible by interposing a range of obstacles and difficulties between the terrorist and actual successful use of a nuclear weapon. Such a strategy starts with efforts to prevent terrorists from gaining access to the fissile material needed to produce a nuclear or radiation device as well as the components of a nuclear weapon, together with steps to prevent terrorists from using a weapon that they have acquired. It is obvious that nuclear terrorism is impossible if terrorists can be denied access to nuclear or radioactive materials or to assembled nuclear devices. We seek to cut off access and to deter or prevent use, and if this fails, to mitigate the consequences. A layered approach is designed to disrupt the chain of terrorist acquisition, development, deployment, and use of nuclear weapons. In the case of a nuclear suicide bomber, it may not be possible to deter use but instead to prevent enablers from getting a nuclear device to the potential user. Cutting off access to nuclear weapons is crucially important in the case of would-be suicide bombers. A suicide bomber does not act alone, but instead has necessarily had the help of an enabling network. If we could identify and target enablers who are not prepared to sacrifice themselves, as noted earlier in this chapter, we might succeed in dissuading them from providing necessary assistance to suicide bombers.

Central to a layered approach is the assumption that the greater the number of layers, the lower our confidence needs to be that any one of the layers will be adequate in itself. All of the layers may be necessary, but none in themselves are likely to be sufficient. In order to succeed, the terrorist must successfully overcome each of the layers. In order to thwart the terrorist, it is necessary for only one of the layers to succeed in stopping him.[20] A terrorist's effort to penetrate one layer may increase the difficulty of success in a subse-

---

20. For a detailed discussion of the layered defense concept, *see* Michael Levi, *On Nuclear Terrorism* (Cambridge, MA and London, England: Harvard University Press, 2007), p. 7. The author uses the analogy of the lottery ticket. The purchase of only one ticket represents a lower probability of winning the lottery than buying, say, one half of the total tickets available.

quent layer. For example, if we gathered intelligence indicating a nuclear theft overseas had taken place and possible perpetrators had been identified but not apprehended, we could alert those charged with protecting our borders and thwarting terrorist attacks. The net result would be obstacles to terrorist success that would not necessarily have been in place if the nuclear theft had not been detected.

To the probability factors inherent in a layered defense should be added the sometimes difficult steps that terrorist must take in acquiring, building, or actually detonating a nuclear weapon. In addition to whatever technical skills or knowledge may be needed to conduct or operate the device, these include the need to succeed in transporting an intact nuclear weapon to its intended target, the possibility that such a weapon will have codes and other features intended to prevent unauthorized use, and that terrorists would be unable for other technical reasons without state assistance to explode the nuclear device that they had acquired.

Therefore, a comprehensive strategy against nuclear terrorism includes several layers and components. First and foremost, it is designed to prevent nuclear hardware and know-how from falling into terrorist hands. A comprehensive layered strategy encompasses incentives to prevent nuclear proliferation from states with nuclear weapons programs as well as from other member states. It contains legal prohibitions as described in the discussion of the Nonproliferation Treaty (NPT) below, together with sanctions and other disincentives designed to penalize those who willingly aid terrorists to acquire nuclear weapons. Thus a layered strategy contains international legal and political components. Before discussing the other major layers of defenses against nuclear terrorism we turn to the non/counterproliferation legal framework.

Limitations of Non/Counterproliferation Regimes as Part of a Layered Approach

Since the end of World War II the United States has worked actively to forge an interlocking network of international treaties, bilateral agreements, national policies, and procedures designed to halt or prevent the spread of nuclear weapons. We have developed export-control and supplier arrangements whose overall goal has been to make impossible the proliferation of nuclear weapons while facilitating the peaceful uses of atomic energy. These international arrangements were developed as a result of U.S. post-World War II policies, and especially President Eisenhower's Atoms for Peace proposal of 1953. The United

States has sought to facilitate the peaceful uses of nuclear energy while at-tempting to prevent the proliferation of nuclear weapons. Except for the ac-knowledged nuclear weapons states, nations who became members agreed in the NPT of 1970 to forego the acquisition of nuclear weapons while holding open the option to develop peacetime nuclear energy. The NPT codified a widely held international norm against nuclear proliferation. This treaty is un-equal in that it recognizes as nuclear-weapons states the five states that existed at the time it came into force (the United States, the United Kingdom, the So-viet Union, China, and France), while requiring all other signatories to refrain from acquiring nuclear weapons. As of 2008, all but four of the world's 192 states have signed the NPT. This includes even North Korea and Iran, whose nuclear activities nevertheless provide ample evidence that international legal regimes themselves are woefully inadequate in preventing a state determined to acquire a nuclear capability from actually doing so. North Korea has several nuclear war-heads. Both North Korea and Iran have major missile programs. North Korea and Iran could be the tipping point for a cascade of other states determined to acquire their own nuclear weapons as Pyongyang and Tehran themselves gain nuclear weapons. States outside the NPT, notably India, Israel, and Pakistan, officially or otherwise possess nuclear weapons.

The NPT faces another major challenge from the growing demand for peace-ful uses of nuclear energy that will lead to a rapid expansion in the number of reactors in the next several decades as already noted. Article IV of the NPT refers to the "inalienable right of all the Parties to the Treaty to develop re-search, production, and use of nuclear energy for peaceful purposes without discrimination." In exchange for their agreement to forego nuclear weapons, non-nuclear weapons states are guaranteed the right to enrich uranium to levels necessary for peacetime uses. However, the capacity to enrich uranium for re-actor fuel for peaceful purposes provides a basis for a country then to engage in further enrichment to weapons-grade levels. Such enrichment moves a coun-try closer to nuclear weapons status. What remains is the ability to design, pro-duce, or acquire a warhead and delivery system. Having mastered the enrichment process, this final step is relatively easy. For example, Iran is developing a large enrichment capability that opens the way to weapons-grade production and to the emergence of Iran as a nuclear weapons state. Tehran's substantial ballis-tic missile program provides further compelling evidence that its goal is the acquisition of a nuclear weapons capability. To carry forward this strategic analysis, Iran is the chief enabler of terrorist organizations, such as Hezbol-lah. Iran has generously funded Hezbollah operations, including providing large quantities of weapons. A nuclear Iran might be prepared to make nu-clear weapons available to a terrorist organization such as Hezbollah. There would also be the danger that an Iranian nuclear capability could fall into the hands of an even more extremist regime that would be prepared either to threaten to use them or to make them available to Hezbollah.

Aside from the NPT there are other cooperative international efforts designed to prevent exports of nuclear technologies to non-nuclear weapon states. As long ago as 1974, a group called the NPT Exporters Committee agreed on a list of export items that would trigger a requirement for the application of IAEA standards. This list has been updated from time to time. There have also been other attempts, namely the Nuclear Suppliers Group, to expand the trigger list to include dual-use technologies and to assure that recipients accept IAEA inspections on their peaceful nuclear programs. Such approaches are useful, especially in the case of countries that adhere to an international norm against nuclear proliferation. They make it more difficult for undesired proliferation to take place, but they fall short of addressing adequately the problem of terrorist acquisition of nuclear weapons.

NPT Gaps

International treaty-based approaches in themselves fail to meet the challenges of nuclear terrorism for at least two reasons that can best be illustrated by reference to the NPT. First, there is the issue of noncompliance in which countries that agreed to international inspections as the condition for access to peacetime nuclear technologies nevertheless have developed clandestine programs leading to nuclear weapons. This was the case with Iraq as long ago as the 1970s and again in the years leading up to the first Gulf War in 1990–91. In 1981 Israel launched a successful air strike against the Iraqi nuclear reactor infrastructure in what became a successful effort to delay the acquisition by Baghdad of nuclear weapons. This raid was widely condemned even though it retarded by several years Iraq's nuclear efforts. Nevertheless, after the Gulf War, international inspectors uncovered a substantial Iraqi nuclear weapons program that had apparently largely been reconstituted in the decade after the Israeli attack. When they signed the NPT, the non-nuclear signatories, which included Iraq but not Israel, agreed to declare where their peacetime nuclear facilities were located and to open them to inspection by the IAEA, the inspection agency attached to the NPT and created under President Eisenhower's Atoms for Peace. With notable exceptions, all non-nuclear NPT members have done so. More than half of the NPT members have signed the Additional Protocol, which was introduced in the early 1990s in order to increase the number and types of facilities subject to international inspection, and to provide authority for the IAEA to conduct short-notice inspections at declared facilities as well as other sites.

Although the NPT cannot prevent a state determined to acquire a nuclear weapons capability from doing so, it can make such action more difficult. The bottom line, however, is that the success of the NPT depends ultimately on the willingness of its members to facilitate inspections of their declared nuclear installations rather than attempting to thwart such efforts. A state determined to gain a nuclear weapons capability would simply not sign the Additional Protocol or perhaps create a clandestine nuclear weapons capability beyond IAEA inspections as Iran and North Korea have done. If a member decided to acquire nuclear weapons, it could either withdraw from the NPT or possibly operate a secret nuclear weapons facility while still remaining a member. Iran remains an NPT member even though it continues nuclear programs that are widely believed to include development of nuclear weapons. It is not far fetched to suggest that a state that is prepared to develop its own nuclear weapons capability while remaining a member of the NPT would also be willing to transfer such capabilities to others, including terrorists.

The second major gap in the NPT relates to the fact that it cannot and should not include the terrorist actors most likely to acquire and use nuclear weapons outside the Treaty. By its very nature, nuclear terrorism would be committed by non-state actors who are not NPT members and therefore not subject to its restrictions. This is not a problem that can be remedied by changes in the NPT. The absurdity of a terrorist organization signing on to an international treaty is obvious, underscoring the limitations of treaty-based approaches in a world that contains terrorist groups such as al Qaeda, as well as states that, inside or outside the NPT, might be prepared to help them acquire nuclear capabilities. The 9/11 Commission explicitly warned that "al Qaeda remains extremely interested in conducting chemical, biological, radiological, or nuclear attacks."[21] Al Qaeda is reported also to have attempted to purchase intact nuclear systems as well as enriched uranium for nuclear weapons.[22] What can be done, of course, is to develop international cooperative measures designed to increase the difficulty of terrorist nuclear acquisition as part of layered defenses.

Yet another problem for which international treaties are largely deficient lies in the ability of terrorists to find materials for nuclear devices within a country of intended use rather than relying on international supply. Given the

---

21. Staff Statement, No. 15: "Overview of the Enemy," National Commission on Terrorist Attacks upon the United States, June 16, 2004, p. 12.

22. Graham Allison, *Nuclear Terrorism: The Ultimate Preventable Catastrophe* (New York: Henry Holt and Company, 2004), p. 27.

nature of the materials that would be needed to produce such a nuclear device, terrorists could possibly clandestinely acquire the means to build a weapon such as a dirty bomb from sources within states that are NPT members. As already noted, such materials might not have to be transported across borders or vast distances. Even NPT states may not have complete control over their nuclear capabilities or dual-use technologies from which a dirty bomb or radiological weapon could be constructed. The case of Russia as an NPT member again comes to mind.

Illicit Nuclear Export Networks: Another Challenge for the NPT

Whether or not a state is an NPT member, it is possible to develop clandestine networks for the export of nuclear know-how and hardware. A.Q. Khan developed his global nuclear proliferation network from Pakistan, which remains outside the NPT. However, his network also included scientists and engineers as well as other facilitators such as financiers and money launderers from diverse NPT-member countries such as Germany, Turkey, Malaysia, South Africa, and the United Kingdom.[23] Centrifuge enrichment technology, with some components manufactured in Malaysia, was transshipped through Dubai. State supporters of terrorism were among beneficiaries of the A.Q. Khan network. One such state was Libya, which decided to give up its nuclear weapons program in 2003. With its direct connections with a terrorist organization such as Hezbollah, Iran also gained important nuclear assistance from A.Q. Khan.

Pakistan is widely regarded as an unstable country with nuclear weapons. Pakistan contains a large number of terrorist groups as well as an ongoing armed insurrection in Balochistan. The central government does not exercise control over provinces in which the Taliban and al Qaeda are operating and Osama Bin Laden is believed to be hiding. Most attention has been focused on a scenario in which the Pakistani nuclear establishment was penetrated by, or even actually fell under the control of, al Qaeda. Having gained access to Pakistan's nuclear weapons arsenal and production facilities, as its new government, a regime controlled by, or sympathetic to, al Qaeda could not only threaten to use such weapons itself but also make them available to other ter-

---

23. Gordon Corera, *Shopping for Bombs: Nuclear Proliferation, Global Insecurity, and the Rise and Fall of the AQ Khan Network* (New York: Oxford University Press, 2006), see especially chs. 1, 2, and 10.

rorist operations on a global scale. However, another scenario also comes to mind. Pakistan has a nuclear power program that presently includes two operating power plants, together with one under construction, and others planned. Given the unstable security situation in Pakistan, the vulnerability of nuclear facilities to terrorist attack will probably grow. Such terrorist operations could be mounted with several possible motivations, including access to radioactive or fissile materials for construction of the types of nuclear devices described elsewhere in this chapter.[24] An attack might also be made in order to damage the nuclear power plant and to disperse radioactivity, as set forth in the nuclear power plant scenario earlier in this chapter.

Denying Terrorist Access to Nuclear Weapons: Detection and Attribution

A layered strategy against nuclear terrorism includes detection of where a nuclear weapon comes from. This forms the basis for establishing attribution.[25] Such a capability may be essential in some cases to reinforce the determination of an NPT member to take necessary steps to prevent illicit nuclear exports. In other cases the ability to determine the state of origin of a terrorist nuclear weapon could form an essential part of a deterrence strategy. A comprehensive nuclear counterproliferation strategy would include the ability to trace the material contained in a nuclear device to its source. It would also enhance our ability to verify compliance with an international treaty against nuclear proliferation if we could determine that an NPT member, for example, had transferred such a capability to terrorists. Ideally, attribution would have the advantage of making it possible to hold the country of origin responsible, under the assumption that terrorist acquisition of nuclear weapons would have had state origins, especially if the state had been responsible for the deliberate transfer of nuclear

24. For a detailed discussion of this type of threat *see* Chaim Braun, "Security Issues Related to Pakistan's Future Nuclear Power Program," in Henry D. Sokolski, ed., *Pakistan's Nuclear Future: Worries Beyond War,* U.S. Army War College, Strategic Studies Institute, 2008, p. 279.

25. For detailed discussions of nuclear weapons attribution and forensics, *see* Caitlin Talmadge, "Deterring a Nuclear 9/11," *The Washington Quarterly,* Spring 2007, pp. 21–34; Jay Davis, "The Attribution of WMD Events," http://homelandsecurity.org/Journal/Articles/Davis.html. April 2003; and "Trace a Detonated Nuclear Weapon to Its Source?" paper prepared for the 2006 American Political Science Association Annual Meeting, August 31, 2006.

weapons, contrasted with unauthorized terrorist nuclear weapons acquisition. Because nuclear reactors are needed to produce weapons-grade materials, it would be possible to establish signatures based on physical, chemical, and isotopic properties as well as the reprocessing techniques utilized. The differing amounts of organic compounds depending on the reactor in which it had been produced would yield clues about where it came from. Databases containing known weapons designs could be utilized or further developed for this purpose.

The difficulty of attribution would be much reduced if a terrorist nuclear weapon were to be captured before, rather than after it was detonated. After use, tracing a nuclear weapon back to its origins would present technical problems that distinguish a nuclear from a conventional explosion. In the case of conventional explosives, there are usually fragments remaining after the explosion that provide evidence of origin. A nuclear detonation would vaporize objects that would include actual evidence within a radius depending on the size of the weapon and how it was detonated. However, the detonation itself would provide an indication of the sophistication of the nuclear device which would limit the potential sources and furnish clues about where it came from. Airborne debris, or fall out, remaining after a nuclear explosion could be analyzed. This could reveal information about the efficiency of the bomb's design and thus its possible origin. Information about isotopic composition of weapons materials and weapons design might be available even after detonation. As already noted, terrorists on their own could probably only build a crude weapon such as a dirty bomb. If they detonated an improvised nuclear weapon, it might be based on a device using highly enriched uranium (HEU) or plutonium, or another weapons design that would provide clues about where it came from. The list of countries having nuclear weapons programs is short. In addition to the official nuclear weapons states, we may include four others (North Korea, India, Pakistan, and Iran). Although many other countries have weapons-usable material for nuclear reactors provided by the United States, markers could be placed on such nuclear material as a condition for international supply, thus providing additional clues about its origin.

Although we would want as quickly as possible after terrorist use to identify how much fissile material was utilized and where it came from, the sources of the material used in the weapon might not be forthcoming quickly enough to justify immediate retaliation. A major effort would be quickly mounted to determine the type of bomb design and to find out who provided the device, or the parts to make it. Let us assume that the origin of the fissile material was traced to a country from which it had been obtained by legal or by illegal means several years or even decades ago. For example, the fissile material may have been produced a generation ago in the Soviet Union, but may have been sold subsequently by an organized crime group to end up ultimately in terrorist hands. To say the least, there would be additional complicating circumstances in a U.S. decision to retaliate against the country of origin if it had its own nuclear deterrent. The case of Russia is the most extreme example. It would also be uncertain that the United States would want to hold accountable populations that had nothing to do with the incident. Would we wish to retaliate against the population of North Korea for the actions of the Pyongyang leadership? Yet it would be irresponsible in the extreme for the United States not to respond to a nuclear weapon attack on its own soil if we had conclusive evidence of its origin. Such inactivity might only embolden other terrorists and their state sponsors. Together with a declaratory policy clearly stating that such terrorists and their state sponsors would be held responsible, attribution represents one important means to deter nuclear terrorism by the ability to identify the source of a nuclear device.

Port and Border Security

Port and border security presents formidable detection problems in the case of nuclear terrorism. Much attention has been given to container security since 9/11. Detection includes the ability to monitor the millions of containers and other cargoes entering the United States by sea, aircraft, truck, and rail annually. Given the sheer volume of cross-border traffic, there are numerous potential avenues for smuggling an intact nuclear weapon or its components into the United States. Beginning in January 2002, therefore, the United States unveiled the Container Security Initiative (CSI) designed to operate in cooperation with host governments at the most important overseas ports to enhance maritime security from terrorist threats. Container cargoes are inspected and sealed before being loaded on ships bound for the United States. Some 58 ports in Europe, Asia, the Middle East, Africa, and the Americas are part of the CSI, with agreements between the United States and participating countries. An effort is made to identify high-risk containers that should be given detailed scrutiny. Both non-intrusive and physical inspections are utilized. The former include use of x-ray or gamma ray scanners to generate an image of the contents. Electronic seals, together with technologies that can track container shipments from point of origin to destination, are being utilized. Nuclear detection monitoring devices have also been developed that as yet are imperfect. The ability of such technology presently to detect a nuclear weapon or a lightly shielded dirty bomb as well as radioactivity from nuclear materials is questionable. If non-intrusive inspection raises suspicion about cargo contents, an intrusive examination can be undertaken. Unless the container had been regarded as "high risk," it might not even be subject to inspection by non-intrusive means. For example, terrorists determined to smuggle a nuclear weapon or its components into the United States could lessen the likelihood of detection by choosing a container from a company highly regarded for its procedures and therefore subject to minimal inspections, having nevertheless identified weak links in the chain of security, such as a disgruntled employee or a point in which security is lax.[26]

It is obvious that new-generation radiation detection and other technologies designed to identify containers carrying nuclear weapons or their components need to be developed and put into operation as soon as possible. However, a nuclear device configured to detonate in a port could have been placed aboard a ship as cargo but not necessarily in a container. In fact the stepped-up surveillance of containers provided by the CSI would give an incentive for terrorists to find other means to smuggle a nuclear weapon into a potential target area. The logical approach would be for the terrorist to load such a weapon aboard a ship, perhaps at an inland port that was not included in the CSI. A nuclear weapon in the hold of a ship, mostly surrounded by water, would not be easily detectable by current technologies and would fall outside CSI surveillance. In such a scenario, the weapon could be carried perhaps unobserved into a U.S. or allied port with devastating consequences. It should be of concern that Russia, with the uncertainties already noted about Russian controls over nuclear materials, is not a CSI member.

Border security and control forms an important dimension of a layered defense against nuclear terrorism. We face the dual problem of facilitating the movement of goods, services, and people while securing our borders from nuclear weapons and their components, as well as terrorists. This is a formidable problem. The United States has 5,525 miles of border with Canada as well as 1, 989 miles with Mexico. Our maritime border consists of 95,000 miles of shoreline counting the numerous inlets, harbors, and other indentations that shape our coastline from Maine on the Atlantic to Washington State on the Pacific. Although attention is often focused on formal points of entry, whether through major ports or at recognized border crossings, there are literally thousands of other places where U.S. borders can be crossed without detection, as

---

26. For a discussion of this possibility, *see* Stephen E. Flynn, "Port Security Is Still a House of Cards," *Far Eastern Economic Review,* January/February 2006, *available at* http://www.feer.com/articles1/2006/0601/free/p005.html.

we see especially in the controversy about securing the U.S.-Mexican border. Added to this situation is the fact that more than 500 million people are admitted to the United States each year, of whom more than 300 million are non-U.S. citizens.[27] To set forth these numbers is to point to the magnitude of the problem of reconciling the needs of commerce and those of security from terrorism, including nuclear terrorism. The formidable nature of the task provides further evidence of the requirement for a layered strategy that, among other things, pushes the borders out as far as possible, for example, by preventing terrorists from acquiring nuclear materials and inspecting containers and ships before they approach our ports and before they are loaded for shipment from overseas ports.

Among the post-9/11 efforts to detect WMD, including nuclear devices and their components, before they reach our ports and borders is the Proliferation Security Initiative (PSI), first announced by President Bush in 2003. This represents yet another layer in a comprehensive strategy. It is based on international partnerships to undertake interdictions at sea, in the air, or on land to prevent shipment of WMD, their delivery systems, and related materials. Participants work together to exchange intelligence, conduct maritime and other exercises planning for interdiction, and taking such action in the event that there is reasonable suspicion that such cargoes are being shipped to or from states or non-state actors "of proliferation concern."[28] As of 2009 the PSI consisted of 15 core members, including the United States, Russia, Japan, France, Germany, and the United Kingdom. An additional 60 countries have agreed to cooperate on a case-by-case basis.

Active Defenses

Another layer in our defense against nuclear terrorism consists of the deployment of defenses against missiles, including those that might be launched by terrorists. There has been discussion to the effect that a terrorist is more likely to attempt to smuggle a nuclear weapon into the United States than to

---

27. These numbers are set forth in Jane A. Bullock, George D. Haddow, Damon Coppola, Erdem Ergin, Lissa Westerman, Sarp Yeletaysi, *Introduction to Homeland Security* (New York: Elsevier, 2005), p. 146. *Available at* http://www.whitehouse.gov/homeland/book/sect3-1.pdf.

28. "The Proliferation Security Initiative," United States Department of State, *available at* http://fpc.state.gov/documents/organization/48624.pdf.

launch a missile with a nuclear warhead. Those who assert this likelihood do so without an empirical basis for their certainty. Is the EMP scenario outlined above more or less likely than the scenario in which assembled weapon is smuggled into a U.S. or allied port? The need to include missile defense is highlighted by the Israeli example. Israel has deployed the world's most extensive missile defense system, which it continues to upgrade. At the same time, Israel has experienced extensive attacks by suicide bombers, although of course not by suicide bombers with nuclear weapons. Israel has taken major steps to cope with both missile and suicide bomber threats. Although a terrorist attack could be mounted with various types of launchers, missiles are increasingly available as delivery systems. It is necessary to view the nuclear terrorist threat as encompassing smuggling operations that might be designed to bring nuclear weapons by land, air, or sea, as well as the possibility of the launch of missiles armed with nuclear or even conventional warheads from a ship off our shores.

A comprehensive defense includes steps to address both types of threat. The ship-based threat includes *both* container ships and other vessels that enter our ports *and* ships near the shore but likely outside our territorial waters from which SCUD-type missiles with 200–600-kilometer ranges could be launched with devastating effects against U.S. coastal cities as well as the urban areas of allies in Europe, Asia, and elsewhere, given the extent to which much of the world's population lives near a coastline. As noted earlier, a missile launched from off our shores to detonate a nuclear blast at an altitude between 40–400 kilometers would have catastrophic EMP effects on indispensable electronic systems. It is difficult to calculate the immense value of a capability that could intercept such a missile before it released its deadly nuclear payload.

As part of a layered defense against nuclear terrorism, missile defense would protect potential targets rather than relying on retaliation after an attack that would have inflicted widespread damage and generated probably hundreds of thousands of casualties. We would seek to deter such an attack by the ability to destroy the means by which it would be mounted. Assured survival would become the necessary alternative to assured destruction as a basis for deterrence. Deterrence would be based not on retaliation but instead by the ability to deny the enemy access to the target. In this sense, missile defense would contribute vitally to the layered defense concept against nuclear terrorism. A robust missile defense would incorporate capabilities providing multiple opportunities to destroy a missile, including in its ascent phase shortly after launch, as it traverses the midcourse phase, and finally as the missile or its payload descend to their target. Missile defense would also include the means to destroy a missile launched to detonate a nuclear payload intended to create EMP effects.[29]

Mitigating the Consequences

If all else fails, we are left with the need to mitigate the consequences of a terrorist nuclear weapon. Depending on the type of nuclear terrorist attack described earlier in this chapter, this task would be complex in even the case of a dirty bomb and far more demanding in the other scenarios. More than a decade ago the term consequence management was coined to encompass the comprehensive response that would be required in the event of a nuclear terrorist incident. In a study prepared in 1998 by TRADOC, the U.S. Army's training and doctrine command, noted a Defense Science Board 1997 study in which a nuclear device exploded at the World Trade Center Building in New York was hypothesized to generate about 100,000 casualties and vast physical damage to the core of the U.S. and global financial system.

In order to cope with the effects of such an event, comparable to the second scenario set forth earlier in this chapter, it would be necessary, it was suggested, to prepare in advance for a concerted response that brought together capabilities that previously had been seen as separate and unrelated to each other. The 1998 TRADOC Report referred to consequence management as consisting of interagency cooperation across the U.S. government and extending to the state and local levels. The TRADOC definition included "those measures necessary to restore essential government services, protect public health and safety, and provide emergency relief to government, businesses, and individuals affected by life-threatening or destructive events."[30] The definition went on to specify that: "Such services and activities may include population evacuation, decontamination, transportation, communications, public works and engineering, firefighting, information and planning mass care, resource support, health and medical services, urban search and rescue, hazardous materials, food, and energy."[31] Since most of the infrastructures affected

---

29. For a detailed assessment of missile defense, *see* Independent Working Group on *Missile Defense, the Space Relationship, and the Twenty-First Century*, 2007 Report, published by the Institute for Foreign Policy Analysis, Inc., 2006, *available at* http://www .ifpa.org/pdf/IWG2000.pdf.

30. Richard J. Rinaldo, *Consequence Management: The Mother of All MOOTWS* [Military Operations Other than Wars], *A Common Perspective, Joint Warfighting Center's Newsletter*, vol. 6, no 1, April 1998, p.11.

31. *Ibid.*

by a nuclear terrorist attack lie in the private sector, the dots to be connected were said to be numerous and unprecedented. Subsequent events, although fortunately not nuclear terrorist attacks, amply vindicated this assessment. The creation of the Department of Homeland Security and the various national strategies for homeland security, including extensive efforts at the state and local levels, although the result of 9/11, became essential parts of a comprehensive strategy against nuclear terrorism.

The ability to achieve necessary levels of coordination and cooperation within and among such entities will determine the effectiveness of the mitigation effort encompassed by consequence management. The TRADOC document recognized also the extent to which there is a commonality between the types of capabilities required in the event of a nuclear terrorist attack and those needed in the case of a natural disaster such as a hurricane or earthquake. This recognition opens the way to a capabilities-based approach. In the case of nuclear terrorism each of the categories of nuclear terrorism outlined earlier in this chapter would provide the basis for developing consequence management capabilities. Some would be common not only across all categories, but also vitally important in the case of natural disasters. For example, evacuation, food supplies, medical assistance, firefighting, and law enforcement come immediately to mind. In developing a capabilities-based approach, we ask what would be needed across all of the five categories and what might be unique to one or more.

Assessing the Risk of Nuclear Terrorism

In order to allocate finite resources for detecting, interdicting, or responding to nuclear terrorism, it is essential to assess the risk of one or another type of nuclear terrorism and to rely on accurate and timely intelligence to identify specific threats. Risk management is necessary as we act to prevent nuclear terrorism by detecting it beforehand and taking timely preventive action. Three basic questions must be addressed in determining nuclear terrorist risk: (1) what can happen? (2) how likely is it? and (3) what are the consequences?

In response to the question of what can happen we have the five categories of nuclear terrorism set forth earlier in this chapter, together with several other possibilities that were mentioned but not discussed in great detail. The level of probability attached to each category is inevitably related to the capabilities and motivations of a would-be terrorist. The answer to questions about terrorist capabilities and motivations lies in good intelligence and its timely analysis, together with its rapid dissemination to the community of users. A terrorist may be highly motivated but nevertheless lack the capabilities or the means to acquire them. Conversely, a terrorist may be sufficiently motivated to develop the political will to gain access to what is needed to carry out a nuclear act. The greater the capabilities available to a highly motivated terrorist organization, the greater becomes the likelihood of nuclear terrorism. It is axiomatic that only good intelligence will provide the basis for determining when, where, and how nuclear terrorism would take place. We may have strategic warning about the type of nuclear terrorist event that is planned, while we have little or no tactical warning about where or when it will take place. The security landscape is strewn with examples of intelligence failures, including most recently 9/11 itself. Given the range of nuclear terrorist possibilities set forth in this chapter, the effectiveness of a layered defense would depend on the quality of intelligence at each of the layers. The greater the number of layers that the terrorist must successfully penetrate, the higher the probability that a nuclear terrorist operation could be interdicted before it took place, based especially on timely and accurate intelligence. However, such action would depend on our ability to connect the dots in such a fashion as to focus resources on the appropriate target, as we clearly failed to do in the case of the 9/11 attacks.

Our third risk assessment question relates to consequences, including the impact of a nuclear terrorist act on the population, government, infrastructure, and economy. What is the likely effect of the loss of such assets? How devastating would the impact be and how long would it take to recover? Compared to the first two questions, this is easier to answer, provided we can identify accurately the types of targets likely to be attacked. Focusing on the five categories outlined earlier in the chapter, we would rank the consequences in descending order with the greatest flowing from an EMP attack and the least from a dirty bomb. However, a dirty bomb could be detonated at or near critically important infrastructure and the possibility exists, as noted earlier, that there would be multiple such incidents mounted at or near the same time. We can also estimate the likelihood of an EMP attack compared with the use of a dirty bomb as an input into our risk assessment. Although the prospects for an EMP attack may be ranked below those for a dirty bomb, the consequences of an EMP attack would be far greater. This in itself could increase its attractiveness to a terrorist group, especially if supported by a state such as Iran itself in possession of nuclear weapons. A lesson of 9/11 is that estimates of likelihood based on the past are possibly erroneous guides to the future. That which has been deemed to be least likely becomes the basis for strategic surprise for which we are least likely to be prepared because of a failure of creative thought.

To summarize, a risk assessment for nuclear terrorism would include estimates of threat and vulnerability. What is the priority attached to the asset by the terrorist and how vulnerable is the asset to nuclear terrorist acts? Such questions can help us to estimate likelihood, but they cannot fully remove uncertainty because the intelligence analyst and the policy maker may fail to "connect the dots" accurately. As part of our risk assessment we would ask whether there are sources of intelligence that could be utilized to provide insights into the types of targets likely to be chosen for nuclear terrorism based on previous terrorist activity. Again, however, the past may not be an accurate guide to the future, because strategic surprise could be maximized by terrorist action against unanticipated targets. Such targets are likely to be most vulnerable because they have not been considered to have highest priority in protection. There is a relationship between threat and vulnerability, combined with capabilities and motivation as well as the strategic creativity of a given terrorist group. A risk assessment represents an effort to address levels and types of threat and the extent of an asset's vulnerability in order to answer the questions set forth above as best we can.

When all is said and done, however, the possibilities for intelligence failure are numerous. Because the history of intelligence failures is extensive, the prospect for success in detecting nuclear terrorism is uncertain. As Thomas C. Schelling has pointed out: "There is a tendency in our planning to confuse the unfamiliar with the improbable. The contingency we have not considered seriously looks strange; what looks strange is thought improbable; what is improbable need not be considered seriously."[32] Schelling's commentary was part of his foreword to Roberta Wohlstetter's trenchant account of intelligence failures leading up to the Japanese attack on Pearl Harbor on December 7, 1941. Roberta Wohlstetter wrote that: "It is only to be expected that the relevant signals, so clearly audible after the event, will be partially obscured before the event by surrounding noise."[33]

As the 9/11 Commission Report set forth in some detail, the mindset described by Schelling and Wohlstetter remained in the period before 9/11. This is the basis for a failure of intelligence, whether in collection or in analysis. Even if tell-tale indicators are available, the dots are not connected because of the assumption that because something has not happened, its likelihood is low. In this respect, the findings of the 9/11 Commission are not reassuring: "With the important exception of analysis of al Qaeda efforts in chemical, radiological, and nuclear weapons, we did not find evidence that the methods to avoid

---

32. Foreword to Roberta Wohlstetter, *Pearl Harbor: Warning and Decision* (Palo Alto: Stanford University Press, 1962), p. vii.

33. *Ibid.*, p. 397.

surprise attack that had been to laboriously developed over the years were regularly applied" in the years preceding 9/11.[34] The authors of the 9/11 Commission Report were referring to the rigorous analytic methods that had been developed in the decades after Pearl Harbor in order to understand the problem of anticipating and forestalling another surprise attack. Whether such methods are utilized in the years ahead will have important implications for nuclear terrorism.

Conclusion

This chapter has surveyed the nuclear terrorist landscape, including the various types of terrorist acts. It discusses how and why they could be perpetrated. What is knowable is a range of general scenarios in which nuclear terrorism could take place. At the highest strategic level it is possible to set forth a spectrum of possibilities, while outlining the steps that terrorists would have to take in preparation for, as well as execution of, a nuclear attack. What cannot be known is the probability of nuclear terrorism in each of the categories set forth in this chapter as well as where or when such acts might take place. Given the potentially catastrophic consequences of nuclear terrorism, emphasis is placed on defenses designed to reduce, and perhaps deter, such an event. Therefore, a major focus has been layered defenses designed first to prevent terrorists from gaining access to nuclear weapons and then to make it difficult and hopefully impossible for such weapons to be used, and finally to mitigate the consequences of such use.

As indicated, much has already been done, especially since 9/11, although there remain substantial gaps, some of which may never be fully eliminated. The setting within which nuclear terrorism could take place is dynamic and therefore changing. Whether our ability to reinforce and expand a multi-tiered strategy against nuclear terrorism will keep pace with the threat remains to be seen. What is certain, however, is that we will need to maximize the uncertainty of success facing would-be nuclear terrorists, build capabilities

---

34. *The 9/11 Commission Report* (New York: W.W. Norton and Company, 2003), p. 346. According to the Commission: "The methods for detecting and then warning of surprise attack that the U.S. government had so painstakingly developed in the decades after Pearl Harbor did not fail; instead, they were not really tried. They were not employed to analyze the enemy that, as the twentieth century closed, was most likely to launch a surprise attack against the United States," pp. 347–348.

that are flexible and easily adaptable to complex and evolving threats, develop intelligence that enables us to allocate resources quickly and effectively, and thereby minimize, if not eliminate, the specter of nuclear terrorism.

Chapter 18

Bioviolence: Facing the Prevention Challenge

*Barry Kellman**

The most perplexing challenge, for both security policy and law, is an acute danger that has not yet happened. An urgent threat clarifies policy options and invokes well-honed principles concerning the legality of use of force. But a distant specter might never materialize; if it does, there might be ways to manage it at the time that are far better than what might now be envisioned. Moreover, it is wise to recognize that demagoguery thrives on dread of the unknown, and proponents of stronger security and law should both eschew such fear-mongering.

Yet, there are situations where willful blindness to evidence of a looming menace is irresponsible. To await the actual manifestation of a danger in these situations is to tragically ignore opportunities to prevent that danger and to suffer consequences that could have been avoided. Following a terrible event, of course, retrospective judgment will ask why preventive actions were not taken, even though at the time it is difficult for conscientious leaders to distinguish real and critical from inflated threats.

In today's strategic environment, the quandary about how to cope with inchoate dangers is especially crucial because any organized group can use advancing technology to inflict catastrophic harm anywhere in the world. In previous eras when commission of cataclysmic destruction required a military force that only a State might wield and when the amassing of that force obviously manifested a State's intentions, it was easier to put off preventive actions until a threat actually materialized. But this paradigm is outdated. In today's strategic environment, we are not likely to know that we are in dan-

* Professor and Director of the International Weapons Control Center, DePaul University College of Law; author, Bioviolence: Preventing Biological Terror and Crime (Cambridge University Press, 2007).

ger of an attack until it is too late to stop the death and destruction. Prevention is compulsory.

Bioviolence is the gravest manifestation of advancing technology's potential to cause widespread misery. While there have been small attacks involving biological weapons, notably the anthrax letters in late 2001, a true bioviolence catastrophe has not happened. It is precisely because bioviolence has not already taken a severe toll that there is no collective outrage about the systematic failure to implement preventive policies. Yet, capacities to do grievous harm are available to people who want to devote those capacities precisely to do harm. While it is difficult to judge when this danger will strike, there should be no doubt that we are vulnerable to a rupture.

Should preventive actions be taken now or should we hope that bioviolence continues forever to be only a hypothetical threat? The former option is complicated and has costs; the latter option is irresponsible. Today, however, too little is being done about the situation. National and international strategies for reducing the dangers of bioviolence are gap-ridden, often incoherent, and not globally observed. For most policy makers, this issue is too low a priority and too complicated. As a result, we are all facing unacceptable danger.

This essay advocates that the United States exercise a strategy which asserts that all States share a responsibility to prevent bioviolence. In addition to reducing dangers of bioviolence, this strategy would have the added benefit of strengthening the framework of international law.

Bioviolence: An Existential Danger

Even the most fanatical terrorists must realize that conventional attacks are not bringing modern society to its knees. The 9/11 strikes, the bombing of the Madrid and London subways, and numerous smaller attacks have all put civilization on edge, but history marches inexorably forward. A few thousand people can be killed, yet Western armies still traverse the world, and post-industrialized economies still determine winners and losers. From this perspective, the stakes must be raised.

A Doable Catastrophe

There are only two good options: a nuclear attack or a biological attack. Of course, detonation of a nuclear weapon in a major city would cause unquantifiable horror. It is unlikely, however, that a terrorist organization could make a nuclear weapon; it would have to buy or steal one. Then it would have to transport that weapon to the target site. None of this is impossible, but the difficulties are substantial and the likelihood of interdiction must be seriously considered.

While not as easy to make as the media might suggest, making a lethal bioweapon is certainly far easier than making a nuclear weapon where even a miniscule error could produce a dud. Refined seed stocks of potentially weaponizeable pathogens are found widely in laboratories around the world. Getting weapons grade nuclear material is, by contrast, extraordinarily difficult and far more expensive. The equipment necessary to produce nuclear weapons is far more tightly regulated than what biological weapons would require. Compared to nuclear weapons, bioweapons can be made in facilities that are far more difficult to detect. If a nuclear weapon has to be moved from its place of preparation to its place of use, the chances of detecting a heavy metal bomb surrounded by precision explosives and emitting radioactivity is incomparable to the chances of detecting a tiny vial full of an innocuous-looking gas or liquid. A single individual can transport bioweapons across borders by land, sea, or air and through airports and customs checks.

Fortunately, doing bioviolence is technically far more difficult than using conventional explosives. Natural pathogens like anthrax are difficult to weaponize. Smallpox remains unavailable (presumably); plague is readily treatable; Ebola kills too quickly to ignite a pandemic. But emerging scientific disciplines—notably genomics, nanotechnology, and other micro sciences—could alter these pathogens for use as weapons. These scientific disciplines offer profound benefits for humanity, yet there is an ominous security challenge in minimizing the danger of their hostile application.

For example, highly dangerous agents can be made resistant to vaccines or antibiotics. In Australia, scientists introduced a gene into mousepox (a cousin of smallpox) to reduce pest populations—it worked so well that it wiped out 100% of affected mice, even mice who had immunity against the disease. Various bacterial agents such as plague or tularemia (rabbit fever) could be altered to increase their lethality or to evade antibiotic treatment.

Diseases once thought to be eradicated can now be re-synthesized, enabling them to spread in regions where there is no natural immunity. The polio virus has been synthesized from scratch; its creators called it an "animate chemical." Soon, it may be resynthesized into a form that is contagious even among vaccinated populations. Recreation of long-eradicated livestock diseases could ravage herds severely lacking in genetic diversity, damage food supplies, and cause devastating economic losses.

Perhaps the direst bio-threat is manipulation of the flu or other highly contagious viruses such as Ebola. Today, scientists can change parts of a virus's

genetic material so that it can perform specific functions. The genomic sequence of the Spanish flu virus that killed upwards of 40 million people nearly
a century ago has been widely published; a savvy scientist could re-construct
it. The avian flu is even more lethal, albeit not readily contagious via casual aerosol
delivery. A malevolent bioscientist might augment its contagiousness. The
Ebola virus might be manipulated so that it kills more slowly, allowing it to be
spread farther before its debilitating effects altogether consume its carrier. A bit
further off is genetic manipulation of the measles virus—one of the great
killers in human history—rendering useless the immunizations that most of
us receive in early childhood. Soon, laboratory resynthesis of smallpox may
be possible.

Advanced drug delivery systems can be used to disseminate lethal agents
to broad populations. Bioregulators, small organic compounds that modify
body systems, could enhance targeted delivery technologies. Some experts
are concerned that new weapons could be aimed at the immune, neurologi-
cal, and neuroendocrine systems. Nanotechnology that lends itself to mechanisms for advanced disease detection and drug delivery—such as gold
nanotubes that can administer drugs directly into a tumor—could also deliver weaponized agents deep into the body, substantially raising the weapon's
effectiveness.

Altogether, techniques that were on the frontiers of science only a decade or
two ago are rapidly mutating as progress in the biological sciences enables new
ways to produce lethal catastrophe. Today, they are on the horizon. Within a
decade, they will be pedestrian. According to the National Academies of Science, "The threat spectrum is broad and evolving—in some ways predictably,
in other ways unexpectedly. In the future, genetic engineering and other technologies may lead to the development of pathogenic organisms with unique,
unpredictable characteristics."[1]

Rational Motivations

Some experts argue that terrorists and fanatics are not interested in bioviolence and that the danger might therefore be overblown. Since there have
been no catastrophic bioviolence attacks, these experts argue, terrorists lack
the intention to make bioweapons. Hopefully, they are correct. But an enormous amount of evidence suggests they are wrong. From the dawn of biol-

---

1. NATIONAL RESEARCH COUNCIL OF THE NATIONAL ACADEMIES, GLOBALIZATION, BIOSE-
CURITY, AND THE FUTURE OF THE LIFE SCIENCE, p. 49 (2006).

ogy's ability to isolate pathogens, people have pursued hostile applications of biological agents. It is perilous to ignore this extensive history by presuming that today's villains are not fervent about weaponizing disease.

Not a single State admits to having a bioweapons program, but U.S. intelligence officials assert that as many as 10 States might have active programs, including North Korea, Iran, and Syria. Moreover, many terrorist organizations have expressed interest in acquiring biological weapons. Whatever weight the taboo against inflicting disease might have for nation states, it is obviously irrelevant to terrorists, criminals, and lunatics. Deterrence by threat of retaliation is essentially meaningless for groups with suicidal inclinations likely to intermingle with innocent civilians.

Al Qaeda and affiliated Islamic Fundamentalist organizations have overtly proclaimed their intention to develop and use bioweapons. The 11th volume of al Qaeda's *Encyclopedia of Jihad* is devoted to chemical and biological weapons. Indeed, al Qaeda has acknowledged that "biological weapons are considered the least complicated and easiest to manufacture of all weapons of mass destruction."[2]

Al Qaeda is widely reported to have acquired legal pathogens via publicly available scientific sources. Before 9/11, al Qaeda operatives reportedly purchased anthrax and plague from arms dealers in Kazakhstan, and the group has repeatedly urged followers to recruit microbiology and biotechnology experts. Following the Taliban's fall, five al Qaeda biological weapons labs in Afghanistan tested positive for anthrax. Documents calculating aerial dispersal methods of anthrax via balloon were discovered in Kabul along with anthrax spore concentrate at a nearby vaccine laboratory.

According to a lengthy fatwa commissioned by Osama bin Laden, jihadists are entitled to use weapons of mass destruction against the infidels, even if it means killing innocent women, children, and Muslims. No matter that these weapons cannot be specifically targeted. "[N]othing is a greater duty, after faith itself, than repelling an enemy attacker who sows corruption to religion and the world." According to the fatwa "No conditions limit this: one repels the enemy however one can."[3]

The sentiment might be reprehensible, but it is certainly not irrational. Even the most passionate terrorists must realize that conventional attacks are not

---

2. Sammy Salama & Lydia Hansell, *Does Intent Equal Capability? Al Qaeda and Weapons of Mass Destruction*, NONPROLIFERATION REVIEW, Vol 12, No. 3, p. 631 (Nov. 2005), citing an article on *Biological Weapons* appearing in an al-Tawhid Wal Jihad website.

3. NASR B IN HAMD AL-FAHD, A TREATISE ON THE LEGAL STATUS OF USING WEAPONS OF MASS DESTRUCTION AGAINST INFIDELS (May 2003).

bringing the West to its knees. From that perspective, bioviolence is perhaps the direst, easiest to execute existential danger.

Envision a series of attacks against capitals of developing States that have close diplomatic linkages with the United States, perhaps timed to follow local officials' expressions of friendship to visiting U.S. dignitaries. The attacks would carry a well-publicized yet simple warning: "If you are a friend of the United States, receive its officials, or support its policies, thousands of your people will get sick." How many attacks in how many cities would it take before international diplomacy, to say nothing of international transit, comes to a crashing halt?

In comparison to use of conventional or chemical weapons, the potential death toll of a bioattack could be huge. Although the number of victims would depend on where an attack takes place, the type of pathogen, and the sophistication of the weapons maker, there is widespread consensus among experts that a high-end attack would inflict casualties exceedable only by all-out nuclear war. Various types of bioattacks could leave more than 100,000 casualties, perhaps far more.

Even more than the death toll, the truly unique characteristic of some bioweapons that distinguishes them from every other type of weapon is contagion. No other type of weapon can replicate itself and spread. Any other type of attack, no matter how severe, occurs at a certain moment in time at an identifiable place. If you aren't there, you are angry and upset but not physically injured by the attack. An attack with a contagious agent can uniquely spread, potentially imperiling target populations far from where the agents are released.

A bio-offender could infect his minions with a disease and send them across borders before symptoms are obvious. Carriers will then spread it to other unsuspecting victims who would themselves become extended bioweapons, carrying the disease indiscriminately. There are challenges in executing such an attack, but fanatical terrorist organizations seem to have an endless supply of willing suicide attackers.

All this leads to the most important characteristic of bioviolence: It raises incomparable levels of panic. Contagious bioviolence means that planes fly empty or perhaps don't fly at all. People cancel vacation and travel plans and refuse to interact with each other for fear of unseen affliction. Public entertainment events are canceled; even going to a movie becomes too dangerous. Ultimately, bioviolence is about hiding our children as everyone becomes vulnerable to our most fundamental terror: the fear of disease.

For people who seek to rattle the pillars of modern civilization and perhaps cause it to collapse, effective use of disease would set in motion political, economic, and health consequences so severe as to call into question the ability of existing governments to maintain their citizens' security. In an attack's wake, no one would know when it is over, and no government could credibly tell an anxious population where and when it is safe to resume normal life.

Just as planes flying into the Twin Towers on September 11, 2001 instantly became a historical marker dividing strategic perspectives before from after, the day that disease is effectively used as an instrument of hate will profoundly change everything. If you want to stop modern civilization in its tracks, bioviolence is the way to go. The notion that no one will ever commit catastrophic bioviolence is simply untenable.

The Internationalization of Security

Bioviolence prevention uniquely compels an international approach to security. These dangers are inherently global. Perpetrators from anywhere can get pathogens from virtually everywhere. Bioresearch labs that once were concentrated in about two dozen developed States are proliferating, expanding the risk that lethal agents could be diverted and misused. The knowledge needed to weaponize pathogens is available on the Internet. An attack can be prepared through easy networks of transnational communication. Once a bioweapon is prepared, terrorists or other perpetrators from anywhere can slide across national boundaries and release disease anonymously. Once released, a contagious agent would spread without regard for boundaries, race, religion, or nationality. Public health responses would have to be internationally coordinated. New modes of international legal cooperation would immediately be needed to investigate the crime.

Thus, bioviolence dangers shrink the planet into an interdependent neighborhood. It makes no sense for any particular country to try to insulate its homeland from these dangers. No missile defense system will protect us from bioviolence. Improved border security will not keep disease at bay. National efforts to enhance medical preparedness have virtues, but these defenses can be readily circumvented. To prevent bioviolence requires policies that focus on humanity as a species entity and that are implemented everywhere with centralized governance. Anti-bioviolence policies must be global.

Yet, advancing anti-bioviolence policies is what the international community does worst. Bioviolence dangers are unnecessarily high because national and international anti-bioviolence strategies are gap-ridden, often incoherent and not globally observed. As a result, we are all virtually naked in the face of unacceptable dangers. No other threat presents such a stark contrast between severity of harm and a failure of leadership to reduce risks.

The Extant (Outdated) Legal Framework

The Biological Weapons Convention (BWC) has ensconced a prohibition against bioweapons into international law, reflecting the centuries-held opprobrium against deliberate infliction of disease. Its entry into force thirty-five years ago was a nonproliferation landmark. For the first time, a treaty outlawed an entire class of weapons and compelled destruction of weapons stockpiles. It broadened the Geneva Protocol's prohibitions against use of bioweapons by outlawing their development, production, acquisition, or retention.

This normative prohibition against bioweapons has become more profoundly entrenched during the intervening decades. Most legal experts agree that the BWC's normative prohibition against bioweapons extends to all States, a position long avowed by the United States.[4] Yet, the BWC has been politically scorned and abused to a degree that is striking even in an environment that is pervasively disparaging of multilateral commitments. Today, in the broad scope of bioviolence prevention, the BWC has been relegated to the status of an infirm elderly relative worthy of affection and respect yet not really expected to provide meaningful answers to current challenges.

For nearly two decades, the BWC has been mired in a contentious debate about how to verify State compliance. In sharp contrast to analogous agreements to control nuclear or chemical weapons, the BWC has no mechanism to verify State compliance. In this context, *verification* includes: 1) State declaration of facilities that could constitute a prohibited weapons capability; 2) regular reports about each facility's activities to enable monitoring that critical items are not wrongfully produced or diverted; and 3) on-site inspections of those facilities to verify the reports' accuracy. As the BWC contains no verification system that is comparable to systems for chemical and nuclear weapons, the regime for preventing bioweapons proliferation is asserted to be uniquely deficient.

However, bioweapons do not neatly fit the nuclear or chemical nonproliferation paradigm where only a select number of uniquely specialized facilities have materials or equipment that, if diverted, could readily foster development of illegal weapons. A near-infinite number of biological facilities lacking distinctive features could readily produce offensive weapons. Few experts take seriously, therefore, the idea that States or non-State actors will produce bioweapons at select declared sites. More likely, if bioweapons emerge, their

---

4. *See* CASE STUDY: YELLOW RAIN, FACT SHEET, BUREAU OF VERIFICATION, COMPLIANCE AND IMPLEMENTATION. (October 1, 2005), *available at* http://www.state.gov/documents/organization/57428.pdf.

source will be any of the indistinguishable locales that are never declared or inspected. Therefore, verification modalities—declaration of critical facilities that must report on their activities and be inspected—would provide copious data about sites where bioweapons risks are negligible but would provide scant information about where bioweapons are being prepared.

More centrally, the BWC—as an archetypical arms control treaty—embodies a set of techniques that are designed to limit State weapons programs. It does not meaningfully address the two critical aspects of bioviolence: (1) bioviolence is by far the most powerful means of destruction and terror available to non-State actors; and (2) anti-bioviolence policies must focus on prevention, not just on accountability.

The BWC Article IV requires States Parties to enact domestic measures to prohibit persons within their jurisdiction from developing or acquiring biological weapons, but there is no content to this requirement. Does it mean that national laws must restrict possession of pathogens or weaponization equipment? Must access to sophisticated biolabs be curtailed? Must these laws prohibit certain types of advanced experimentation that might facilitate preparation of a bioweapon? Must trade of pathogens or equipment, domestically and internationally, be restricted? All of these questions, among many others, have no answers.

In operational terms, the BWC can at most require States to punish bioviolence perpetrators after the fact. That is, if there is a bioattack and if the perpetrators can be identified, then a State Party will be obligated to hold those perpetrators to account for their crime. This requirement is not insignificant, but it minimizes the implications of a biocatastrophe. In the wake of an attack that could inflict thousands or even millions of casualties, billions of dollars in losses, and global panic, the prosecution of perpetrators (who are likely to either have died or be beyond justice) is trifling solace.

None of this is to undervalue the power of the norm embodied in the BWC nor to diminish the prohibition of State bioweapons programs. States have unparalleled capacities for making bioweapons, and these capacities can be the source (wittingly or not) for non-State bioviolence. Also, State use of bioweapons is apt to be of a size and scale that exceeds what terrorists or fanatics can accomplish. No anti-bioviolence policy could be effective unless there is unequivocal denunciation of any State that develops or assists others in developing bioweapons, and any State that puts bioweapons to hostile use must know that it will suffer the harshest consequences permissible under international law.

Put simply, application of arms control mechanisms against bioviolence is absolutely necessary but substantially insufficient. Much more is needed.

The Emerging Legal Framework:
State Responsibility to Prevent

The doctrine of State responsibility posits that a State is legally accountable for its wrongful behavior and for the behavior of persons that can be imputed to it, either because those persons are agents of the State or because the State supports their wrongful conduct. Although constantly evolving, the doctrine is predominantly evoked in connection with a State's affirmative violation of explicitly recognized legal obligations. The doctrine has less application to situations where a State does not adopt legal or regulatory measures that might have prevented harm caused by a citizen of that State or by use of its territory. For many historical reasons, the doctrine focuses on what a State does or what it overtly tolerates, not on how it fails to establish and enforce preventive modalities.

It is a well-established principle of international law that every State is forbidden to allow its territory to be used in a way that causes injury to another State (*sic utere tuo ut alienum non laedas*). The International Court of Justice in the *Trail Smelter* decision,[5] applied this doctrine to transboundary pollution, and the principle has been a fixture of international environmental law since the Stockholm Declaration of 1972 which posits that States have "the responsibility to ensure that activities within their jurisdiction or control do not cause damage to the environment of other States or of areas beyond the limits of national jurisdiction."[6] A raft of environmental treaties which establish liability for transboundary pollution manifest commitment to this principle.[7] Thus, a State cannot escape responsibility for injury caused to a downwind or downstream State by asserting that it (the State) was not the active cause of harm.

---

5. The Trail Smelter Arbitration (United States and Canada), 3 UN Rep. Int'l Arbitration Awards 1911, 1938 (1941); reprinted in 35 Am J. Intl. L. 684 (1941).

6. *See* Declaration of the UN Conference on the Human Environment, June 16, 1972, princ. 21, UN Doc. A/CONF.48/14/Rev.1 (1973), reprinted in 11 I.L.M. 1416 (1972); UN ECE, Convention on Long Range Transboundary Air Pollution, Nov. 13, 1979, T.I.A.S. No. 10541, pmbl., reprinted in 18 I.L.M. 1442 (1979). The Principle was reiterated in the Declaration of Rio de Janeiro on Environment and Development adopted at the UN Earth Summit in 1992. *See also*, Non-Legally Binding Forest Principles princ. 2.

7. Recent environmental liability regimes include the Basel Convention on the Control of Transboundary Movements of Hazardous Wastes and their Disposal (1999 Protocol); the 2003 joint liability protocol to the 1992 UNECE Convention on the Protection and Use of Transboundary Watercourses; and the 1992 UNCED Convention on the Transboundary Effects of Industrial Accidents; the Protocol on Environmental Protection to the Antarctic Treaty; and the liability regime for the Biosafety Protocol.

There are two major qualifications to such responsibility. First, it applies only when the case is of serious consequence and the injury is established by clear and convincing evidence. This is important because, in contrast to more traditional invocations of State responsibility where the offensive behavior and the harm caused are manifest, to suggest that a State is responsible for ensuring that its territory not be used to cause transboundary harm could readily be abused by extension to relatively trivial matters or situations where the causal link between the critical activity and the harm is ambiguous. Indeed, extension of the doctrine of State responsibility to include a responsibility to prevent harm could collapse under its own weight if invoked with regard to any minor transgression.

Second, even with regard to major environmental damage, the principle of responsibility is usually invoked as a reactive measure after the damage has been done. A State might be responsible for having allowed pollution to cause harm, but the corollary obligation—to prevent the harm by adopting effective air or water pollution control measures—receives little if any attention. Thus, no matter how bad the pollution, if the wind or water flows the other way, there is no harm and therefore no responsibility. From this perspective, any State fortunate to have no downwind or downstream neighbors need not implement pollution control measures.

Even the recent expansions of concepts of State responsibility involving failure to interdict overtly criminal behavior, *e.g.* terrorism, presume at least constructive knowledge and passive acceptance of the wrongful conduct. Thus, the Taliban were widely viewed as responsible for the 9/11 attacks; the Taliban knew that al Qaeda was operating openly in Afghanistan and that the group was planning terror attacks. Yet, other States whose citizens were involved in al Qaeda or which became transit or meeting points in the execution of the plot were not deemed responsible—the link of responsibility was too attenuated to hold those States to account.

In this traditional conception, a State would of course be responsible for using or developing biological weapons. If that State hands those weapons to a private group which uses them malevolently, certainly that State would be responsible for the ensuing damage. But responsibility would not likely attach if a State has inadequate security surrounding its national biolab and someone infiltrates that lab, impermissibly steals a lethal pathogen strain, and covertly weaponizes that pathogen. Negligence in this context is insufficient to establish responsibility; there would have to be more evidence of State complicity in the wrongful infliction of disease. Even more certainly, if the theft is from a privately owned and operated biolab, it would profoundly stretch the concept of State responsibility to argue that the State should have required the private lab to adopt stricter security controls and that its failure to enforce such controls makes it responsible for the consequences of the theft.

But this is precisely the point. Bioviolence is an existential danger, one that can be readily wreaked by non-State actors, and one that if wreaked would almost definitely cause international suffering. If bioviolence happens, little weight should be given to a State's defense that it was not complicit in the crime, that its passive failure to prevent was not a contributing cause of the damage. The thesis here is that the danger of bioviolence compels expansion of the traditional conception of State responsibility to clarify that indeed a State behaves wrongfully if it fails to take reasonable measures to prevent bioviolence, and consequences should befall that State if its wrongful conduct is causally linked to a bioattack. More centrally, responsibility should apply preventively; consequences should befall a State that fails to take reasonable measures to prevent bioviolence now, without awaiting evidence that its failure to do so has led to a catastrophe.

United Nations Security Council Resolution 1540

The argument for State responsibility to prevent bioviolence starts with UN Security Council Resolution 1540,[8] adopted on 28 April 2004 under Chapter VII of the UN Charter. UNSCR 1540 was motivated by the concern that non-State actors "may acquire, develop, traffic in or use nuclear, chemical and biological weapons and their means of delivery." Recognizing "the need to enhance coordination of efforts on national, sub-regional, regional and international levels in order to strengthen a global response to this serious challenge and threat to international security," it requires all States to:

- [A]dopt and enforce appropriate effective laws which prohibit any non-State actor to manufacture, acquire, possess, develop, transport, transfer or use nuclear, chemical or biological weapons and their means of delivery, in particular for terrorist purposes (para. 2)
- [T]ake and enforce effective measures to establish domestic controls to prevent the proliferation of nuclear, chemical, or biological weapons and their means of delivery, including by establishing appropriate controls over related materials. These controls include: (a) measures to account

---

8. *Available at* http://ods-dds-ny.un.org/doc/UNDOC/GEN/N04/328/43/PDF/N0432843 .pdf?OpenElement.

for and secure such items; (b) effective physical protection measures; (c) effective border controls and law enforcement efforts; and (d) effective national export and trans-shipment controls over such items. (para. 3)

Moreover, UNSCR para. 7 invites States in a position to offer assistance in implementing the provisions of this resolution to offer appropriate assistance.

Four Requirements of State Responsibility to Prevent Bioviolence

With regard to prevention of bioviolence, it is useful to unravel UNSCR 1540's requirements into the following four categories. First, States must implement domestic measures to secure and protect especially dangerous pathogens and laboratories where those pathogens can be weaponized, and these measures must account for and enable tracking of those pathogens' location and movement. Second, States must criminalize preparations to commit bioviolence and must enable law enforcement detection and interdiction of wrongful bioviolence preparations. Third, States, within the limit of their capacity, should strengthen resilience to bioviolence and protect against an attack's trans-national spread. Fourth, States must enable the international community to have confidence that bioscience activities within its jurisdiction are not directed toward development of bioweapons.

Controlling Access and Accounting for Pathogens and Biolabs

It should be hard for a bio-offender to get the pathogens and technology needed to commit bioviolence. If he can obtain refined pathogens and readily weaponize them using advanced equipment and facilities, he will more likely succeed than if his preparations are unremittingly obstructed. National implementation of measures that impede the more straightforward ways to commit bioviolence will compel a bio-offender to pursue more precarious and expensive routes that raise the odds of botching his plans.

Most technologically advanced nations have effectively implemented mandatory standards for restricting access. In these nations, companies and academic institutions working with dangerous pathogens must be registered. Registration serves two purposes. First, lawful entities must comply with strict security safeguards for impeding misuse or diversion. Second, registration authoritatively distinguishes lawful possessors of select pathogens from out-law possessors: properly registered entities are presumptively legitimate; any-one having such pathogens without proper registration is presumptively a criminal.

Binding obligations to comply with denial measures have an additional ben-efit: implementing them generates a lot of information. To assess compliance with such measures for control access, legitimate bioscientists and their insti-tutions must report data about where laboratories are and where pathogens are kept. These reports will produce data flows that can generate a global con-sensus of biofacilities, location of pathogens, and the traffic in pathogens and equipment.

Today, too much critical information about bioscience is unknown. There is too much anarchy in bioscience about the location of particularly danger-ous pathogen strains. In far too many facilities worldwide, we do not know what disease pathogens might be stored. Moreover, there is no systematically institutionalized capability to track the movements of such strains globally. Neither is there any uniform, worldwide census of biological facilities that might be used for bioviolence preparations, and we have grossly inadequate capabilities of putting data together to give us the best chance to detect bio-of-fenders. Such data is essential for effective interdiction; without more com-prehensive and better-analyzed information, it is unlikely that illicit efforts to weaponize pathogens can be discerned among the cloud of legitimate bio-science going on around the world at an accelerating pace.

All nations should, therefore, enact regulations for bioscience that require legitimate bioscience practitioners and institutions working with weaponize-able pathogens strains to declare themselves, to implement globally accepted security measures, and to report basic information about their activities and the strains in their possession. However, most nations lack such regulations; the proliferation of bioscience is far outpacing the spread of appropriate se-curity standards. If measures to control access are not in place everywhere, then bio-offenders will exploit the gaps. Moreover, these measures must not only be legislated; officials must have authority and capability to actually en-force them.

There are hurdles to be sure. The first question is which pathogens should be controlled? Smallpox and anthrax would likely be on everyone's list; after that, there may be disagreement. Any list will have to be constantly evolving as new pathogens are discovered or synthesized. Similarly, which laboratories should be required to implement security measures? International organizations including the World Health Organization are recently accelerating efforts to harmonize standards for resolving these questions.

Enable Law Enforcement Interdiction

It is imperative to interdict illicit bio-preparations as well as transit of critical agents and ready-to-use weapons. Critically, interdiction must occur before an attack happens. In contrast to most criminal law enforcement where police await the crime before conduct an investigation, bioviolence entails a qualitative leap in devastation causing harm that could reverberate around the world well into the future. Prevention is imperative precisely because it is insufficient to punish bioviolence after it has been committed. Law enforcers must, therefore, identify bio-offenders as early as possible—well before their plans materialize. Throughout the vast majority of the world outside perhaps two dozen developed States, however, bioviolence preparations could proceed without substantial chance of detection.

The biggest problem here is the lack of comprehensive criminal legislation that authorizes police to focus on bioviolence preparations. Unfortunately, most States lack laws that criminalize unauthorized possession of lethal pathogens or building an amateur laboratory. Every nation must enact laws to criminalize not only the act of bioviolence but the preparations that are necessary to its accomplishment. If law enforcers have to await the completed attack, then bioviolence preparations can proceed without serious constraint. Accordingly, national laws should criminalize unauthorized possession of pathogens and access to laboratories. It must be a crime to: construct an unauthorized facility for working with select pathogens, divert pathogens from a facility, transfer pathogens or relevant equipment to someone who misuses them, or deliberately cause pathogens to be released. If the only legal way to possess controlled pathogens is to have a license, then possession of those pathogens without a license must be, in and of itself, a criminal offense.

Authorization must be backed up with training and equipment. Interpol has assumed responsibility for worldwide police training through a series of workshops, train-the-trainer programs, publications and guides, and promotion of stronger legislation. In only a few years, the Interpol Program has demonstrated the substantial benefits of specialized cooperation and organizational commitment. It will create a central information resource and reporting hub that raises awareness of bioviolence threats as it facilitates communication among experts and police officials in nations that might not otherwise draw on such expertise.

Moreover, law enforcers must be able to work with foreign counterparts by sharing information and conducting trans-national investigations. Again, the problem here is that States that do not appropriately criminalize behavior undermine such cooperation. This problem is especially pronounced in States where proliferation and terrorism are most worrisome. States must implement anti-bioviolence measures to ensure legal cooperation. Moreover, policies should promote international police training on detection and interdiction of bioviolence preparations including, as necessary: advocacy of national legislative measures to authorize law enforcement to execute necessary responsibilities; and enhancing capabilities for attributing responsibility for wrongful use/release of pathogens by enhancing bio-forensic methods.

Strengthen Resilience

Protecting targets and strengthening public health preparedness to cope with disease outbreaks can reduce vulnerabilities to bioviolence. A perpetrator is unlikely to inflict a disease against an effectively immunized population or try to spread it in a guarded site. It makes sense therefore to develop and stockpile vaccines and other medical counter-measures. It also makes sense to implement preparedness measures including rapid detection and post-attack commitment of public health resources to treat victims. An intentionally perpetrated disease will less catastrophically ruffle a community whose medical professionals can promptly apply countermeasures.

Effective disease surveillance is critical in this context so that outbreaks can be quickly and accurately identified and appropriate measures taken to stem its spread. Communication systems are essential to alert other national and international authorities and to coordinate response among key sectors including both public health and law enforcement. Preparedness must also take into account public confidence and willingness to cooperate with authorities in the event of a bioattack. Finally, preparedness measures include establishing quarantines to limit the spread of contagion.

In most nations, it is very unclear who should promote coordinated policies for selecting, developing, and distributing anti-bioviolence vaccines and medications. There is widespread recognition that national responses will likely be insufficient to address a major bioattack. More resources are needed to improve global cooperation among key sectors—health, law enforcement, environment, agriculture protection, and military—especially with regard to initiatives to strengthen food defense, promote cross-border cooperation and training, and develop rapid communications strategies.

The necessity of developing effective resilience and strengthening public health responses to bioviolence is indisputable, and the inadequacy of most nations' capabilities to meet these needs is similarly beyond controversy. To suggest, however, that States thereby violate their international obligations wholly ignores these States lack of capacity in general and, more specifically, the horrible toll that poverty and natural disease are taking throughout most nations. Put simply, it is illegitimate to say that States must devote scarce resources to building public health capabilities against bioviolence (which hasn't yet happened) in favor of confronting immediate health challenges.

Yet, neither is it legitimate to view bioviolence dangers as distractions from efforts to combat natural disease and therefore to put off beneficial measures until those afflictions are defeated. To do so would leave developing nations wholly vulnerable to a deliberate attack. More generally, this view frustrates forward movement even on limited and cost-effective initiatives that could help build an international security framework for advancing health. In this context, bioviolence prevention must be a facet of a broad commitment to prevent the spread of disease by enhancing public health and identify cures for disease by stimulating bioscience.

More specifically with regard to State responsibility to prevent, no State can be required to do more than it can to harden targets, stockpile vaccines, or establish preparedness capabilities. Yet, it is fair to suggest that every State must promptly report indications of any intentionally inflicted disease; notification of outbreaks to international organizations (*e.g.* the WHO) is required by the International Health Regulations.[9] Moreover, as rich nations and international organizations increasingly devote resources to preventing bioviolence, every State should be required to incorporate such assistance within the limits of its capacity.

Building Confidence Regarding Bioscience Activities

States need to have information that sustains confidence about each other's disinterest in developing bioviolence capabilities. As argued above, this is not an argument in favor of expending vast resources on superfluous verification systems. It is an argument for obligatory confidence building measures that reveal enough about bioscience activities to deflate suspicions that those activities are devoted to hostile purposes. Better information can: 1) lend credibility to States' claims that they are obeying their obligations, and 2) enhance legal cooperation to interdict criminal activity.

Confidence building measures are the one part of the traditional arms control agenda that continues to be vital; it is also the one part of the arms control agenda that has almost been entirely ignored. Throughout the 1990s, BWC States Parties agreed to provide information 1) bioscience activities including data on research scientists, biodefense programs, past offensive programs, and vaccine production facilities; 2) infectious disease outbreaks; and 3) their na-

---

9. International Health Regulations, 48th World Health Assembly, Articles 1, 6 and 7 (May 23, 2005). *Available at* http://www.who.int/csr/ihr/en/.

tional legal infrastructure relevant to preventing wrongful bioscience activity. However, most States do not provide this information; participation in the CBMs, never high, has been declining. Little political attention is paid to these measures so States have little incentive to report.

National biodefense programs present the greatest challenge to building mutual confidence that States are foregoing bioweapons. May a government engage in bioresearch in order to devise protective measures against biothreats if that research has direct and obvious potential for a bioweapons program? There is very little in the research that clearly reveals whether the State is pursuing a bioweapons capability or a defense from that capability. The dual-purpose problem makes it very difficult to draw a clear line between legitimate and illicit research; the distinction is often only a matter of intent.

No government should be castigated for trying to protect its people from biothreats. More accurately, the problem from the perspective of international security is not the research, it is keeping the research secret. The more tightly that research on lethal pathogens is kept secret, the more it suggests that it is contributing to hostile capabilities. Secret biodefense programs might amplify anxiety of hostile bioweapons capabilities shrouded from sight. The problem is that suspicions grow in darkness.

Conversely, the more that is known about a program, the easier it will be to distinguish offense from defense and to understand the intentions of the researcher. Open exchange of ideas encourages scientific progress and builds confidence that purported peaceful intentions are not a ruse. Accordingly, states should be responsible for providing information about what bioresearch activities are undertaken, where, and for what purpose.

Holding States Responsible for Preventing Bioviolence

State responsibility should not be viewed as an arcane doctrine of international law but as a powerful intellectual and political force that directs implementation of policies that converge States' efforts to combat global challenges. The doctrine posits not only that each State shares responsibility to address the challenge, it posits that all States must do what they can—within legal limits—to compel non-complying States to meet their responsibility.[10] Thus,

---

10. International Law Commission, Responsibility of States for Internationally Wrongful Acts, UN GAOR, 56th Sess. Supp. No. 10, UN Doc. A/56/10 (2001), Article 48.

State responsibility is a double-edged concept, holding States to account for how they comply with their responsibilities and authorizing other States to base foreign policy decisions, at least in part, on the basis of that compliance.[11] In that concept is a schema for preventing bioviolence.

There are profound implications here for the United States and other technologically advanced nations. Of course, these States must implement domestic bioviolence prevention measures; their compliance with these responsibilities is most critical because they have the most advanced bioscience sectors. No less important, under UNSCR 1540, these wealthy States have obligations to assist less developed States that are receptive to taking action but which lack capacity. Finally and perhaps most important, all States (especially those with the power to do so) should hold non-complying States to account.[12]

There is a model for how the United States should address State responsibility for bioviolence prevention. It is proposed that Congress enact a *Bioviolence Prevention Act* that is modeled on the Trafficking Victims Protection Act (TVPA).[13] At first glance, the dangers associated with bioviolence which have to do with security from terrorism and proliferation might seem altogether distinct from the human rights horrors of human trafficking. Yet in important respects, prevention of trafficking establishes an instructive framework for approaching the problem of bioviolence prevention.

Trafficking is an extraordinarily serious crime, arguably a crime against humanity. The definition of "crimes against humanity" in the Rome Statute of the International Criminal Court (the ICC Statute) includes, *inter alia*, "enslavement," "imprisonment or other severe deprivation of physical liberty in violation of fundamental rules of international law," and "rape, sexual slavery, enforced prostitution, forced pregnancy ... or any other form of sexual violence

---

11. Certain breaches of international law may be so grave as to trigger not only a right, but also a certain an obligation of States to foster compliance with the law by cooperating to end the breach through lawful means and a refusal to recognize that breach as lawful nor to render aid or assistance in maintaining that situation. The obligation to cooperate applies to States whether or not they are individually affected by the serious breach. *See generally* Articles on Responsibility of States for Internationally Wrongful Acts, arts 40–53, *in* Report of the International Law Commission on the Work of Its Fifty-third Session, UN GAOR, 56th Sess., Supp. No. 10, at 43, UN Doc. A/56/10 (2001), *reprinted in* JAMES CRAWFORD, THE INTERNATIONAL LAW COMMISSION'S ARTICLES ON STATE RESPONSIBILITY: INTRODUCTION, TEXT AND COMMENTARIES (2002).

12. *See generally,* Carsten Stahn, *Responsibility to Protect: Political Rhetoric or Emerging Legal Norm,* 101 A.J.I.L. 99 (2007).

13. 22 U.S.C. §§7101–7112.

of comparable gravity."[14] Bioviolence would also seem to fit the definition of a crime against humanity in that it is a widespread, systematic attack directed against a civilian population causing great suffering on a large scale. The importance of this characterization is that every State is obligated to combat this crime, not merely to refrain from committing it.

Trafficking is a truly global problem. Not only does it occur in many nations and involve illegal movement across nations; even nations where it does not occur can become involved if they fail to take preventive measures. The traffickers have no fixed commitment to operating only a few places; they will direct the traffic through whatever nations appear to have the weakest detection and interdiction capabilities. Thus, if trafficking is to be seriously fought, every State must accept responsibility for participating in global efforts to combat trafficking.[15]

Accordingly, the United Nations adopted the Protocol to Prevent, Suppress, and Punish Trafficking in Persons, Especially Women and Children,[16] setting forth a comprehensive approach to combating trafficking. The key elements are that every State must criminalize acts of trafficking with serious penalties and implement measures to prevent it. The UN Protocol provides that "State Parties shall establish comprehensive policies, programmes and other measures ... to prevent and combat trafficking in persons."[17] This includes an obligation to cooperate with other countries both in discouraging demand for trafficked persons and in prosecuting traffickers. Information exchange among States is essential to enable detection and interdiction of covert transnational criminal operations.[18]

Because no nation can wholly escape reasonable obligations to cooperate, every nation can legitimately adopt legal measures to impel implementation of these obligations. Put another way, "failure of a state to enact specific anti-trafficking legislation that provides for an appropriate sentence for trafficking,

---

14. *Rome Statute of the International Criminal Court*, 10 November 1998, 39 I.L.M. 999, Article 7.

15. *See generally*, Mohamed Y. Mattar, *State Responsibilities in Combating Trafficking in Persons in Central Asia*, 27 Loy. L.A. Int'l & Comp. L. Rev. 145 (2005).

16. United Nations, Protocol to Prevent, Suppress and Punish Trafficking in Persons, Especially Women and Children, Supplementing the United Nations Convention Against Transnational Organized Crime (2000). *Available at* http://www.uncjin.org/Documents/Conventions/dcatoc/ final_documents_2.

17. United Nations, Protocol to Prevent, Suppress and Punish Trafficking in Persons, Especially Women and Children, Supplementing the United Nations Convention Against Transnational Organized Crime, Article 9(1)(a) (2000).

18. *Id.* at Article 10(1).

in accordance with the UN Protocol, constitutes a violation of the state's international obligations."[19]

Because no nation can wholly escape reasonable obligations to cooperate, every nation can legitimately adopt legal measures to impel implementation of these obligations. Put another way, "failure of a state to enact specific anti-trafficking legislation that provides for an appropriate sentence for trafficking, in accordance with the UN Protocol, constitutes a violation of the state's international obligations."[20]

It is this premise that sets the foundation for the TVPA which authorizes the Department of State to evaluate the performance of governments in combating trafficking and generate annual reports on what other countries have done to criminalize trafficking, prevent it, and cooperate with other countries. The report ranks countries in four tiers: countries in full compliance with minimum standards for eliminating trafficking; countries that are making significant efforts to bring themselves into compliance; countries whose compliance needs to be watched; and countries that are not making progress.[21]

Countries in the middle two tiers may be provided assistance to help them meet standards such as assistance in drafting legislation, investigating and prosecuting offenders, and creating infrastructure and programs designed to combat trafficking. Countries in the bottom tier, by contrast, may have nonhumanitarian, nontrade-related foreign assistance withheld. This may include instructions to U.S. representatives within multilateral development banks and the IMF to deny the designated nations certain funds for the subsequent year. Notably, the sanctions referred to for these bottom tier countries are only optional; the President is allowed to decide that foreign aid to such countries should continue "in the national interest."

The TVPA is perhaps the clearest and strongest manifestation of expanding concepts of State responsibility to address extraordinarily serious global crimes. Why should the United States exercise its enormous economic and diplomatic power to reward and punish other States, not for what they do to or for the United States, but for what they do to address a global crisis? Isn't offering benefits or

---

19. Mohamed Y. Mattar, *State Responsibilities in Combating Trafficking in Persons in Central Asia*, 27 Loy. L.A. Int'l & Comp. L. Rev. 145 (2005).

20. Mohamed Y. Mattar, *State Responsibilities in Combating Trafficking in Persons in Central Asia*, 27 Loy. L.A. Int'l & Comp. L. Rev. 145 (2005).

21. *See* Trafficking Victims Protection Act, 22 U.S.C. 7107. *See also*, Congressional Research Service Report RL30545, Trafficking in Persons: U.S. Policy and Issues for Congress (June 20, 2007) at 13, 23. *Available at* http://www.fas.org/sgp/crs/misc/RL30545.pdf.

consequences to States on the basis of their adoption of preventive measures an intrusion of their sovereignty? Notably, U.S. legislators might have defended the TVPA on the grounds that since the United States is victimized by trafficking, there is a national interest in encouraging other countries to cooperate against trafficking; however, this argument of national self-interest is barely visible in the legislative history.

State Responsibility to Prevent—Application to Bioviolence

Bioviolence is a crime—quite literally, treason against humanity. For humans to pervert scientific progress into a catastrophic human loss is treachery most vile: members of our species using other species to devastate our species. It is a crime regardless of who the bio-offender is. It may not be even suggested that their used is justifiable in the name of self-determination. There are no legitimizing exceptions or national security justifications; no ideology or belief system can provide cause for ignoring the prohibition.

Setting clear norms and criminal prohibitions forces nations to choose: be a member of the global community or be a pariah. As global integration becomes ever more economically pivotal and as membership in regional associations depends on compliance with internationally recognized tenets of behavior, clear normative prescriptions gain weight. It means that law enforcers must cooperate worldwide to be watchful of bioviolence preparations and they must sustain vigilance for preventing those preparations' consequences. Ultimately, the status of "crime against humanity" means that every State has responsibilities. Every State must criminalize bioviolence under its national laws, attach strict penalties, develop mechanisms to detect illegal behavior, authorize law enforcers to interdict that activity, and cooperate to bring bio-offenders to justice. A State that refuses to conduct an investigation or request support to interdict criminal bioviolence in its jurisdiction will be signaling through its inaction that it condones the illegal conduct.

Most important, characterizing bioviolence as a crime against humanity means that bioviolence prevention must be a driver of national and international security policy. Accordingly, every State, in determining how it will regard and cooperate with other States, must assess how those other States are undertaking their responsibilities and must differentiate complying States from States that breach their responsibilities. The central premise of the proposed *Bioviolence Prevention Act* is that the United States should similarly impel all States to undertake bioviolence prevention responsibilities.

Conclusion

Our era is witnessing a scientific revolution that calls for a revolution in how we conceive national security policy. Historically, scientific revolutions that have prompted critical changes in the means and methods of executing violence have stimulated new security paradigms, but too often these paradigms were appreciated only when their obsolete predecessors had painfully failed. With regard to bioviolence, the consequences of learning through horrible experience are unacceptable.

Looking to the future of bioviolence and the mechanisms of its prevention is, ultimately, to open visions of an evolving paradigm of international law that is less centrally focused on treaties and deterrence and more focused on advancing global security under the rule of law. In the same sense that fortressed cities became obsolete when the security they offered became a mirage, today's security challenges erode the illusion that separate sovereign States can keep us safe by focusing only upon their own capabilities while effectively ignoring the enormous destructive capabilities available to non-State actors.

The need to prevent bioviolence has emerged from the confluence of radically accelerating progress in bioscience along with the post-2001 preeminence of non-State violence atop the world's strategic agenda. Thus, bioviolence prevention offers a new vision of how to globally organize strategic security under law whereby every governance organization, most definitely every State, has responsibilities to carry out. As bioviolence prevention is essential to humanity's advance, international pursuit of prevention responsibilities is a paramount priority.

Chapter 19

Cyberterrorism:
Legal and Policy Issues

*Jeffrey F. Addicott**

"We have learned from the tragedy of Sept 11 that our enemies will increasingly strike where they believe we are vulnerable ... our cyberspace infrastructure is ripe for attack today."

Senator Joseph Lieberman

Introduction

In the post-9-11 world, al Qaeda-styled terrorists, rouge totalitarian regimes and others are continuously expanding capabilities and techniques in their quest to spread fear and devastation. With its vast global network of interconnected computers, one area where society is particularly vulnerable is cyberspace. The malicious use of cyberspace to cause massive harm to the nation's critical infrastructure is so feared that a new term has been coined to describe the event: cyberterrorism.

The realm of cyberspace has become completely integrated into almost every aspect of the modern world so much so that civilized society is absolutely and totally dependent on the cyber world. The vast majority of Americans cannot go through a single day without being affected in some manner by its presence; over 80% of adults in the United States now use the Internet. Moreover, the explosion in commercial and consumer Internet use is not limited to the

* Distinguished Professor of Law and Director, Center for Terrorism Law, St. Mary's University School of Law. B.A. (with honors), University of Maryland, 1976; J.D., University of Alabama School of Law, 1979; L.L.M., The Judge Advocate General's School of Law, 1987; L.L.M., University of Virginia School of Law, 1992; S.J.D., University of Virginia School of Law, 1994.

United States. There are more than one billion Internet users across the planet, with the number predicted to pass two billion by 2011. Because the Internet is easily accessible, geographically unbounded and largely unregulated it is an ideal vehicle for communication and business. Globally, more and more businesses, consumers, government agencies and organizations of all kinds rely on cyberspace technology to enhance modernity. Not only does cyberspace provide unparallel opportunities for business transactions, communication, records storage and other personal uses, it also functions as the predominant tool for regulating all aspects of the nation's critical infrastructure to include water, electricity, banking, transportation, technology, agriculture, medical, nuclear facilities, waste management, government services, etc.

Unfortunately, the same qualities that promote the marvels of cyberspace also make the Internet extremely vulnerable to a variety of untoward activities, to include crime, terrorism and even armed conflict. As the cyber world expands, so has concern about security of and security on the Internet. In other words, society's dependency on the workings of cyberspace also provides unparallel opportunities for great harm. Apart from the ever present impact of common criminal activity through cyber crime—costing the American economy billions of dollars in losses each year—the specter of a cyberterrorist attack on one or more of the country's critical infrastructures hangs over the nation like the sword of Damocles.

The 2004 congressionally mandated 9/11 Commission Report strongly criticized the government for four kinds of failures in the context of the mega terror attacks of September 11, 2001(9/11). These failures were "in imagination, policy, capabilities, and management." Although the al Qaeda terrorist attacks of 9/11 caught the United States completely by surprise and resulted in the incineration of 3,000 people and billions of dollars in property loss, the emerging threat of cyberterrorism may prove to be even more devastating. Indeed, if terrorists can plan and execute large scale attacks on our physical world, a *fortiori*, our cyber world, which affects all aspects of modern society, is equally ripe for terrorist attack. When the attack comes, cyberterrorism will strike a heavy blow to the soft underbelly of the nation's critical infrastructure.

Until the April–May 2007 coordinated cyber attacks which shut down the entire nation of Estonia, the full destructive potential of cyberterrorism was something that the world had not adequately appreciated. When one considers that various Islamic terrorist organizations such as al Qaeda have been using the Internet to communicate, propagandize, finance and recruit new members for years, it is only logical to conclude that they are fully aware that cyberterrorism offers a low cost and easily masked method of inflicting major damage. It is simply naïve to believe that terrorists will fail to use cyberspace to conduct attacks against critical infrastructure. Accordingly, it is imperative that viable cybersecurity laws and policies be established to address cyberterrorism concerns prior to a mega cyber attack. Disturbingly, a survey of federal and private efforts to develop and implement cybersecurity measures reveals that the same lack of imagination cited in the 9/11 Commission Report may be mimicking itself in the sphere of cyberterrorism.

The question then turns to the matter of cybersecurity. Does a sufficient cybersecurity framework exist that can adequately protect cyberspace and the information it contains processes and transmits? While the government has embarked on a variety of initiatives with private and public entities to protect against the threat of cyberterrorism, a growing number of legal and policy issues remain unanswered. To be sure, the nation faces a variety of pressing challenges in addressing cyberterrorism. The purpose of this chapter is to provide a basic framework for understanding the threat of cyberterrorism and to explore the current state of preparedness from government and private industry perspectives.

Defining the Terms

With the phenomenal growth of the cyber world, dozens of new and unfamiliar terms have entered the lexicon. Before one can fully discuss the dangers associated with the threat of cyberterrorism, certain foundational terms require definition.

Cyberspace: The term cyberspace has many connotations and is used in a variety of contexts. Synonyms include the terms virtual space and cyber world (sometimes spelled cyberworld). In common understanding cyberspace refers to the entire function of computer-centric information technology—hardware and software—as it is created, stored and transmitted in the non-physical and physical terrain. A 2005 Congressional Research Service Report (CRS) (Creating a National Framework for Cybersecurity: An Analysis of Issues and Options), refers to cyberspace as "the combination of the virtual structure, the physical components that support it, the information it contains, and the flow of that information within it." As a global phenomenon, cyberspace is largely controlled by private companies.

Cyberterrorism: Similar to the problem of obtaining universal agreement on defining the term "terrorism," there is no generally accepted definition for cyberterrorism (sometimes spelled cyber terrorism). All attacks on a computer or computer network involve actions that are meant to disrupt, destroy, or deny information. These attacks may be motivated by monetary gain, vandalism, terrorism, or as acts of war. Thus, most cyber attacks may be categorized as cyber crimes, but not all cyber attacks are deemed to be an act of cyberterrorism or war. Clearly, the key difference between cyber crime and cyberterrorism is the concept of *terror*. If a universal definition of the term terrorism does not exist, one can at least list four key characteristics of terrorism that better reflect the nature of the activity:

1. The illegal use of violence directed at civilians to produce fear in a target group.
2. The continuing threat of additional future acts of violence.
3. A predominantly political or ideological character of the unlawful act.
4. The desire to mobilize or immobilize a given target group.

Combining these four key characteristics, then Secretary General of the United Nations, Kofi Annan, offered a succinct 2005 definition for terrorism:

[A]ny action constitutes terrorism if it is intended to cause death or serious bodily harm to civilians or non-combatants, with the purpose of intimidating a population or compelling a Government or an international organization to do or abstain from doing any act.

Adopting the general definitional theme of terrorism set out above, cyberterrorism is the improper use of various computing technology to engage in terrorist activity. Since the terror motivated cyber attack would most likely be against the critical infrastructure of a nation to intimidate or coerce another (usually a nation) in furtherance of specific political objectives, one commentator has defined cyberterrorism as "the premeditated, politically motivated attack against information, computer systems, computer programs, and data which results in violence against non combatant targets by sub-national groups or clandestine agents."[1] On the other hand, some commentators contend that the use of the term cyberterrorism to describe an attack on the critical infrastructure is inappropriate "because a widespread cyber attack may simply produce annoyances, not terror, as would a bomb, or other chemical, biological, radiological, or nuclear explosive (CBRN) weapon."[2]

Nevertheless, given the nation's complete dependency on cyberspace, if a cyber attack caused widespread damage to computer networks associated with the critical infrastructure, the level of fear from the resulting economic disas-

---

1. *See* Mark Pollit, *Cyberterrorism: Fact or Fancy?* PROCEEDINGS OF THE 20TH NATIONAL INFORMATION SYSTEMS SECURITY CONFERENCE, October 1997, at 285–289.

2. *See* John Rollins and Clay Wilson. *Terrorist Capabilities for Cyberattack: Overview and Policy Issues*, CRS Report RL33123. October 20, 2005.

ter and/or civilian fatalities would rapidly qualify as terrorism. Certainly the digital fears that emerged from the month-long denial of service (DDoS) cyber attack on the small Baltic country of Estonia (orchestrated from Russian sources apparently in response to the removal of a bronze statue of a World War II era Soviet soldier from a park) would qualify as cyberterrorism and perhaps, as some argued, as an act of war. The Estonian cyber attacks resulted in a digital infrastructure disaster as Web sites for government officials, government agencies, daily newspapers, and Estonia's biggest banks were overwhelmed and shut down due to the cyber onslaught of "unknown" digital information attacks.

Perhaps a more useful way to encapsulate the term cyberterrorism can be found in a 2005 CRS Report[3] where the authors present cyberterrorism in two related categories:

- Effects-based: Cyberterrorism exists when computer attacks result in effects that are disruptive enough to generate fear comparable to a traditional act of terrorism, even if done by criminals [as opposed to terrorists].
- Intent-based: Cyberterrorism exists when unlawful or politically motivated computer attacks are done to intimidate or coerce a government or people to further a political objective, or to cause grave harm or severe economic damage.

Critical Infrastructure: The predominant concern that most drives the discussion of cyberterrorism is that a cyber attack will target one or more of the nation's critical infrastructures. The term critical infrastructure is defined with more or less uniformity in a variety of documents and laws. The 2003 National Strategy for the Physical Protection of Critical Infrastructure and Key Assets provides a detailed list of assets of national importance and critical infrastructure to include: information technology; telecommunications; chemicals; transportation; emergency services; postal and shipping services; agriculture and food; public health and healthcare; drinking water/water treatment; energy; banking and finance; national monuments and icons; defense industrial base; key industry/technology sites; and large gathering sites. The Department of Homeland Security (DHS)[4] lists five general types of critical infrastructure:

1. production industries: energy, chemical, defense industrial base;
2. service industries: banking and finance, transportation, postal and shipping;

---

3. *Id.*
4. DHS/IAIP Daily Open Source Infrastructure Reports, *available at* http://www.dhs.gov/dhspublic/interapp/editorial-0542.xml.

3. sustenance and health: agriculture, food, water, public health;
4. federal and state: government, emergency services; and
5. Information Technology (IT) and cyber: information and telecommunications.

Section 1016(b)(2) of the Critical Infrastructures Protection Act (CIPA) of 2001 specifically identifies as critical infrastructures "telecommunications, energy, financial services, water, and transportation sectors," all of which have not only physical components, but cyber components as well. In addition, section 1016(e) of CIPA expands the concept of critical infrastructure to mean all "systems and assets, whether physical or virtual, so vital to the United States that the incapacity or destruction of such systems and assets would have a debilitating impact on security, national economic security, national public health or safety, or any combination of those matters." Both the Uniting and Strengthening America by Providing Appropriate Tools Required to Intercept and Obstruct Terrorism Act of 2001 (USA PATRIOT Act) (renewed in 2006) and the Homeland Security Act of 2002 adopt the same definition set out below:

SEC. 1016. CRITICAL INFRASTRUCTURES PROTECTION

(a) SHORT TITLE.—This section may be cited as the "Critical Infrastructures Protection Act of 2001."

(b) FINDINGS.—Congress makes the following findings:

(1) The information revolution has transformed the conduct of business and the operations of government as well as the infrastructure relied upon for the defense and national security of the United States.

(2) Private business, government, and the national security apparatus increasingly depend on an interdependent network of critical physical and information infrastructures, including telecommunications, energy, financial services, water, and transportation sectors.

(3) A continuous national effort is required to ensure the reliable provision of cyber and physical infrastructure services critical to maintaining the national defense, continuity of government, economic prosperity, and quality of life in the United States.

(4) This national effort requires extensive modeling and analytic capabilities for purposes of evaluating appropriate mechanisms to ensure the stability of these complex and interdependent systems, and to underpin policy recommendations, so as to achieve the continuous viability and adequate protection of the critical infrastructure of the Nation.

(c) POLICY OF THE UNITED STATES.—It is the policy of the United States—

(1) that any physical or virtual disruption of the operation of the critical infrastructures of the United States be rare, brief, geographically limited in effect, manageable, and minimally detrimental to the economy, human and government services, and national security of the United States;

(2) that actions necessary to achieve the policy stated in paragraph (1) be carried out in a public-private partnership involving corporate and non-governmental organizations; and

(3) to have in place a comprehensive and effective program to ensure the continuity of essential Federal Government functions under all circumstances.

(d) ESTABLISHMENT OF NATIONAL COMPETENCE FOR CRITICAL INFRASTRUCTURE PROTECTION.

(1) SUPPORT OF CRITICAL INFRASTRUCTURE PROTECTION AND CONTINUITY BY NATIONAL INFRASTRUCTURE SIMULATION AND ANALYSIS CENTER.—There shall be established the National Infrastructure Simulation and Analysis Center (NISAC) to serve as a source of national competence to address critical infrastructure protection and continuity through support for activities related to counterterrorism, threat assessment, and risk mitigation.

(2) PARTICULAR SUPPORT.—The support provided under paragraph (1) shall include the following:

(A) Modeling, simulation, and analysis of the systems comprising critical infrastructures, including cyber infrastructure, telecommunications infrastructure, and physical infrastructure, in order to enhance understanding of the large-scale complexity of such systems and to facilitate modification of such systems to mitigate the threats to such systems and to critical infrastructures generally.

(B) Acquisition from State and local governments and the private sector of data necessary to create and maintain models of such systems and of critical infrastructures generally.

(C) Utilization of modeling, simulation, and analysis under subparagraph (A) to provide education and training to policymakers on matters relating to—

(i) the analysis conducted under that subparagraph;

(ii) the implications of unintended or unintentional disturbances to critical infrastructures; and

(iii) responses to incidents or crises involving critical infrastructures, including the continuity of government and private sector activities through and after such incidents or crises.

(D) Utilization of modeling, simulation, and analysis under subparagraph (A) to provide recommendations to policymakers, and to departments and agencies of the Federal Government and private sector persons and entities upon request, regarding means of enhancing the stability of, and preserving, critical infrastructures.

(3) RECIPIENT OF CERTAIN SUPPORT.—Modeling, simulation, and analysis provided under this subsection shall be provided, in particular, to relevant Federal, State, and local entities responsible for critical infrastructure protection and policy.

(e) CRITICAL INFRASTRUCTURE DEFINED.—In this section, the term "critical infrastructure" means systems and assets, whether physical or virtual, so vital to the United States that the incapacity or destruction of such systems and assets would have a debilitating impact on security, national economic security, national public health or safety, or any combination of those matters.

SCADA: Cyberterrorism is not simply an attack on the Internet. As previously stated, the primary concern is that a cyberterrorist attack will target the electronic control systems that regulate the operational functions of a critical infrastructure so that the flow of essential services is disrupted. Such a scenario is possible because the thousands of interconnected computers, servers, routers, and switches associated with the myriad physical and virtual tasks inherent in operating and maintaining the nation's most important critical infrastructures, such as defense systems, chemical and hazardous materials, water supply systems, transportation, energy, finance systems and emergency services are no longer predominantly handled by people, but are rather electronically monitored and controlled by centralized computer networks called Supervisory Control and Data Acquisition (SCADA) systems (a term that also applies to systems that are equivalent in function such as distributed control systems or programmable logic control systems).

SCADA systems, or their equivalent, digitize and automate almost every imaginable task associated with a given critical infrastructure—from opening and closing valves in nuclear facilities, to operating circuit breakers on electrical power grids, to managing air traffic in the sky. Since SCADA systems provide the "brain power" to manage critical infrastructures a successful cyberterrorist attack on even a single SCADA could cause massive economic and physical damage across broad sections of the country.

Approximately, 85% of the nation's critical infrastructures are owned and operated by private business where the predominant emphasis for SCADA is on maintaining system reliability and efficiency, not cybersecurity. In most cases, the SCADAs are connected to their associated private corporate networks which are in turn primarily connected directly or indirectly to the Internet. This cyberspace vulnerability presents an open door for a terrorist with the necessary skills to hack into a SCADA and, for example, disable the valves at the nuclear facility, shut down an entire electrical power grid, or redirect air traffic to harmful flight patterns.

Techniques Employed in Cyber Attacks: Not all disruptions of an information system's confidentiality, integrity, or availability (CIA) constitute a cyber attack. In fact, most disruptions of information systems are caused by unintentional human error and called cyber incidents. A cyber attack refers only to the intentional disruption of an information system's CIA. The National Institute of Standards and Technology Federal Information Processing Standards Publication 200, *Minimum Security Requirements for Federal Information and Information Systems*, March 2006 defines a cyber incident as:

> An occurrence that actually or potentially jeopardizes the confidentiality, integrity, or availability (CIA) of an information system or the information the system processes, stores, or transmits or that constitutes a violation or imminent threat of violation of security policies,

security procedures, or acceptable use policies. Incidents may be intentional or unintentional.

Taken from a Government Accountability Office Report, GAO-07-705, dated
June 2007, the chart below lists the most common techniques employed in
conducting a cyber attack, along with a brief description. The individuals making such attacks range from juveniles (so-called "script-kiddies"), to disgruntled ex-employees, to thieves, to competitors, to terrorists, to agents of foreign
governments. Terrorists wishing to launch a cyberterror attack would employ
one or more of the tools listed below:

Type	Description
Spamming	Sending unsolicited commercial e-mail advertising for products, serv-ices, and Web sites. Spam can also be used as a delivery mechanism for malware and other cyber threats.
Phishing	A high-tech scam that frequently uses spam or pop-up messages to deceive people into disclosing their credit card numbers, bank ac-count information, Social Security numbers, passwords, or other sen-sitive information. Internet scammers use e-mail bait to "phish" for passwords and financial data from the sea of Internet users.
Spoofing	Creating a fraudulent Web site to mimic an actual, well-known Web site run by another party. E-mail spoofing occurs when the sender address and other parts of an e-mail header are altered to appear as though the e-mail originated from a different source. Spoofing hides the origin of an e-mail message.
Pharming	A method used by phishers to deceive users into believing that they are communicating with a legitimate Web site. Pharming uses a va-riety of technical methods to redirect a user to a fraudulent or spoofed Web site when the user types in a legitimate Web address. For exam-ple, one pharming technique is to redirect users—without their knowl-edge—to a different Web site from the one they intended to access. Also, software vulnerabilities may be exploited or malware employed to redirect the user to a fraudulent Web site when the user types in a legitimate address.
Denial-of-service attack	An attack in which one user takes up so much of a shared resource that none of the resource is left for other users. Denial-of-service at-tacks compromise the availability of the resource.
Distributed denial-of-service	A variant of the denial-of-service attack that uses a coordinated attack from a distributed system of computers rather than from a sin-gle source. It often makes use of worms to spread to multiple computers that can then attack the target.
Viruses	A program that "infects" computer files, usually executable programs, by inserting a copy of itself into the file. These copies are usually ex-ecuted when the infected file is loaded into memory, allowing the

	virus to infect other files. A virus requires human involvement (usually unwitting) to propagate.
Trojan horse	A computer program that conceals harmful code. It usually masquerades as a useful program that a user would wish to execute.
Worm	An independent computer program that reproduces by copying itself from one system to another across a network. Unlike computer viruses, worms do not require human involvement to propagate.
Malware	Malicious software designed to carry out annoying or harmful actions. Malware often masquerades as useful programs or is embedded into useful programs so that users are induced into activating them. Malware can include viruses, worms, and spyware.
Spyware	Malware installed without the user's knowledge to surreptitiously track and/or transmit data to an unauthorized third party.
Botnet	A network of remotely controlled systems used to coordinate attacks and distribute malware, spam, and phishing scams. Bots (short for "robots") are programs that are covertly installed on a targeted system allowing an unauthorized user to remotely control the compromised computer for a variety of malicious purposes.

A review of the listed techniques point to four general types of attack. First, the most common type of cyber attack is service disruption or the distributed denial of service (DDoS) attack,[5] which aims to flood the target computer with data packets or connection requests, thereby making it unavailable to the user or, in the case of a website, unavailable to the website's visitors. DDoS attacks are often conducted utilizing "zombies"—computer systems controlled by a "master" through the utilization of "bots" or "botnets." Service disruption could directly affect any aspect of the critical infrastructure causing regional or even global damage. A second, but related, type of cyber attack is designed to capture and then control certain elements of cyberspace in order to use them as actual weapons. The third category of cyber attack is aimed at theft of assets from, for example, financial institutions. This activity not only includes theft, but also extortion and fraud. Finally, a cyber attack can also manifest itself in a conventional explosive attack on a physical structure, such as a building that houses a SCADA.

---

5. *See* Mindi McDowell, *Understanding Denial-of-Service Attacks*, US-CERT Cyber Security Tip ST04-015 (2004), *at* http://www.us-cert.gov/cas/tips/ST04-015.html.

In a distributed denial-of-service (DDoS) attack, an attacker may use your computer to attack another computer. By taking advantage of security vulnerabilities or weaknesses, an attacker could take control of your computer. He or she could then force your computer to send huge amounts of data to a web site or send spam to particular email addresses. The attack is "distributed" because the attacker is using multiple computers, including yours, to launch the denial-of-service attack.

Id.

Cybersecurity: There is no commonly accepted definition for the term cybersecurity (sometimes spelled cyber security). Obviously, responding to the task of protecting cyberspace requires, as a minimum, the adoption of a unified government definition. Different uses of the term cybersecurity can be found in a wide variety of federal laws, executive orders, presidential directives, and other agency directives. Taken together, cybersecurity is concerned with protecting the basic security of computerized systems from unauthorized access. The central focus of cybersecurity is protection of an information system's CIA. According to the 2005 CRS Report, Creating a National Framework for Cybersecurity: An Analysis of Issues and Options, cybersecurity refers to:

> a set of activities and other measures intended to protect—from attack, disruption, or other threats—computers, computer networks, related hardware and devices software [sic], and the information they contain and communicate, including software data, as well as other elements of cyberspace. The activities can include security audits, patch management, authentication procedures, access management, and so forth. They can involve, for example, examining and evaluating the strengths and vulnerabilities of the hardware and software used in the country's political and economic electronic infrastructure. They also involve detection and reaction to security events, mitigation of impacts, and recovery of affected components. Other measures can include such things as hardware and software firewalls, physical security such as hardened facilitates, and personnel training and responsibilities.

The Threat of Cyberterrorism

Along with the growth in cyberspace is a growth in cyber attacks. The almost seamless interconnectivity of the Internet presents a readily available and inexpensive opportunity for computer network cyber attack. Each day uncountable numbers of people gain access, or attempt to gain access, without authorization to computers in order to read, modify, or destroy information. Although the vast majority of harmful cyber attacks on U.S. interests to date—both government and private—have involved criminal activity, common sense and reason dictate that cybersecurity must better prepare for the real possibility of an Estonian-styled cyberterror attack. New forms of digital attacks are constantly emerging so that future cyber attacks will result from vulnerabilities in software that hackers find and exploit. During the week of July 17, 2006, alone, the United States Computer Emergency Response Team (US-CERT) listed more than 30 new vulnerabilities in cyberspace that fell in what they deemed a "high risk" category. Some of the security breaches that actually caused widespread damage received much publicity and still linger in the collective memory of society, e.g., computer worms such as the Love Bug, Slammer and Blaster. The Log Bug virus, which caused billions of dollars in losses, was caused by a single university student in the Philippines.

Former FBI Director Louis Freech claimed that "the FBI believes cyber-terrorism, the use of cyber-tools to shut down, degrade, or deny critical national infrastructures, such as energy, transportation, communications, or government services, for the purpose of coercing or intimidating a government or civilian population, is clearly an emerging threat." Militant Islam's goal of global war fits perfectly with the Internet's anonymity and ability to reach millions. The terror groups need not even use fixed Internet sites that can be monitored, since discussion boards and encrypted messages are nearly impossible to break. By extrapolation, it is inevitable that they will sooner or later graduate to full fledged acts of cyberterroirsm.

To be sure, there are numerous instances of Islamic terrorists using the Internet to commit cyber crime and to further logistical support activities for terror initiatives. It is common knowledge that al Qaeda-styled terrorists are especially attracted to banking and other financial institutions where they can steal funds, disrupt day-to-day business, or even launch a major cyber attack to cause panic. A successful breach of security could mean far more than the inconvenience of shutting down an ATM machine. A sudden loss of millions of dollars from banking accounts would create mass panic.

Representing the tip of the cyber jihad iceberg, one recent case from England illustrates what is occurring across the world in growing intensity. In 2007, a 21-year-old biochemistry student named Tariq al-Daour, a 24-year-old law student named Waseem Mughal and 23-year-old Younes Tsouli were convicted in the United Kingdom of using the Internet to incite murder. These Islamic terrorists employed a wide range of computer viruses and stolen credit card accounts to set up a sophisticated network of communication links and Web sites that hosted videos of al Qaeda suicide bombings, beheadings and detailed tutorials on computer hacking and bomb-making. Tsouli was the administrator of the online jihadist Web site "Muntada al-Ansar al-Islami," the once main Internet propaganda outlet for Abu Musab al-Zaraqwi, al Qaeda's notorious chief lieutenant in Iraq (Zaraqwi was killed by American forces in 2006). According to British investigators, the trio used scores of stolen credit card accounts to register more almost 200 Web site domains at 95 different Web service providers in the U.S. and Europe. A single computer found in the London apartment of al-Daour had 37,000 stolen credit card numbers with detailed personal information cross-referenced for each holder.

In 2002 American military raids in Afghanistan uncovered the fact that al Qaeda operatives had scoured the Internet for information regarding how to attack SCADA networks to include American domestic water supplies and electrical grids. Also, in 2002 the FBI pursued information emanating out of the Middle East that hackers were studying the electrical generation, transmission, water storage, distribution and gas facilities of SCADA digital systems used to control major utilities in California's San Francisco Bay area. Although the exact details of the threat were never revealed, the ever present fear is that hackers could disrupt a SCADA or even take command of the system in order to disable the flood gates or control hundreds of thousands of volts of electric energy.

Of course, to those familiar with the 2000 cyber attack on the SCADA of an Australian sewage and water treatment plant, such a scenario has already taken place. On April 23, 2000, a disgruntled (ex) employee by the name of Vitek Boden was arrested in Queensland, Australia, in possession of a stolen computer and radio transmitter which he had used to breach the SCADA system of an Australian water and sewage treatment plant off Australia's Sunshine Coast. Boden had cyber attacked the SCADA system on 46 separate occasions and had caused one million liters of raw sewage to be pumped into the local community. While this was not the first reported instance of a hacker successfully breaking into a SCADA—a malicious control system breach occurred in 1997 at the Worcester, Massachusetts Regional Airport that shut down the control tower—it was the first incident that resulted in widespread damages. Many believe it is a harbinger of things to come.

In addition to the threat of a stand alone cyber attack, the government has long predicted a scenario in which terrorists conduct a conventional explosives attack on a SCADA or its equivalent, perhaps in conjunction with a cyber attack. In testimony before the United States Senate in 2004, the Deputy Director of the FBI's cyberterrorism division stated: "The FBI predicts that terrorist groups will either develop or hire hackers, particularly for the purpose of complementing large scale attacks with cyberattacks." There is no doubt that al Qaeda-styled terrorists are studying a variety of means to attack the West's critical infrastructure by means of cyberspace. If they are successful, the world could suffer an "electronic Pearl Harbor."

Numerous reports indicate that Islamic extremists are looking to develop a hackers' Army to plan cyber attacks against the United States. The so-called "Electronic Jihad Program," a recent enterprise of the jihadi Web site Al-jihan.org, desires to instigate what it calls electronic jihad. The jihadi desire is to conduct a focused mega attack on a targeted network to cause havoc. With the expanding use of the Internet in the Islamic world, the number of users who desire to engage in some form of electronic jihad is likely to increase substantially. Not only do militant Islamic groups routinely depend on the Internet for organizational issues but according to those who monitor jihadist terror Web sites, the number of such Web sites has risen from 12, just fifteen years ago, to more than 4,500 as of 2005.

As al Qaeda-styled terror groups expand their reach into cyberspace, it is certain that they will soon engage in significant cyberterrorism attacks to disrupt entire networks that control vital infrastructure. In fact, the probability of a cyber attack on a SCADA system is more likely than not because almost every government agency as well as practically every component of the private sector uses the so-called information superhighway of the Internet to communicate and conduct day-to-day activities. Not only is ease of communication a significant factor, but the appeal of cheap off-the-shelf software operating packages from, e.g., Microsoft, has proven irresistible to public and private entities when measured against the cost of developing and maintaining in-house proprietary software. In terms of cybersecurity, when one realizes that SCADA systems, or their equivalent, are no longer operated on more secure in-house special purpose software, but rather on off-the-shelf commercial software and hardware connected directly to the Internet, the probability of a successful mega cyber attack via a DDoS attack or virus is only a question of time.

Prosecuting Cyber Attacks

To even the cursory viewer, the expansion of law enforcement techniques in the post-9/11 world is stretching the protections of the Constitution's Fourth Amendment (unreasonable searches and seizures). This debate is healthy and must continue as Congress and the Executive take steps to increase security measures. Early on the Congress expressed concern with cyber attacks conducted by hackers. The primary tool to criminalize such acts is found in the 1984 Counterfeit Access Device & Computer Fraud and Abuse Act (18 U.S.C. § 1030). It was amended in 1994, 1996 and in 2001 by the USA PATRIOT Act. The Counterfeit Access Device & Computer Fraud and Abuse Act makes it a federal crime to gain unauthorized access to, damage, or use illegally, certain "protected" computers and computer systems. The term protected applies to those computer systems used by the nation's financial institutions, a federal government entity, or for interstate and foreign commerce. In addition to addressing acts of trafficking in passwords, espionage and fraud, the Counterfeit Access Device & Computer Fraud and Abuse Act also covers damage to such protected computers by the use of a virus, worm, or other device. The seven areas of interest in 18 U.S.C. § 1030(a) include:

- computer trespassing, e.g., hacking, associated with a government computer § 1030(a)(3);
- computer trespassing resulting in exposure to certain governmental, credit, financial, or commercial information, § 1030(a)(2);
- damaging a either a government computer, a bank computer, or a computer that is used in interstate or foreign commerce, § 1030(a)(5);
- committing fraud where an integral part involves unauthorized access to a government computer, a bank computer, or a computer used in interstate or foreign commerce, § 1030(a)(4);
- threatening to damage a government computer, a bank computer, or a computer used in interstate or foreign commerce, § 1030(a)(7);
- trafficking in passwords used for a government computer, a bank computer, or a computer used in interstate or foreign commerce, § 1030(a)(6); and
- accessing a computer to commit espionage, § 1030(a)(1).

Section 1030(b) makes it a crime to attempt to commit any of the offenses in § 1030(a). Section 1030(c) sets out the penalties, which range from imprisonment for not more than a year for simple violations to a maximum of life imprisonment should death result from intentional computer damage. Section 1030(g) creates a separate civil cause of action for victims.

Under § 218, the USA PATRIOT Act increased the scope and penalties associated with hackers where violators only need to intend to cause damage generally, and a second offense is punishable by up to a 20 year prison sentence. The USA PATRIOT Act also enlarged the definition for criminal acts associated with terrorism, 18 U.S.C. § 2332b(g)(5)(B), to include intentionally damaging a protected computer if the offense involves either impairing medical care, causing physical injury, threatening public health or safety, or damaging a governmental justice, national defense, or national security computer system.

Other federal statutes address illegal wire fraud, 18 U.S.C. § 1343; aggravated identity theft, 18 U.S.C. § 1028A; fraud in connection with identification documents, authentication features and information, 18 U.S.C. § 1028; intentional interference with computer-related systems used in interstate commerce, 18 U.S.C. § 1030(a)(5); deceptive practices affecting commerce, 15 U.S.C. § 45(a)(1); and installing "sniffer" software to record keystroke and computer traffic, 18 U.S.C. § 2510-2421.

The case of *U.S. v. Mitra*, 405 F.3d 492 (2005), United States District Court for the Western District of Wisconsin, serves as a good illustration of the application of the Counterfeit Access Device & Computer Fraud and Abuse Act in terms of defining offenses that fall under its umbrella. In *Mitra* the defendant was convicted of two counts of intentional interference with computer-related systems used in interstate commerce, in violation of 18 U.S.C. § 1030(a)(5). The judge in the case noted that even though the statute violated does not directly address the acts committed by the defendant, that Congress had written a general statute not intended to list each and every particular forbidden act. The judge rightly explained that "[e]lectronics and communication change rapidly, while each legislator's imagination is limited." The conviction was upheld on appeal.

UNITED STATES v. MITRA
United States Court of Appeals, Seventh Circuit
405 F.3d 492 (2005)

EASTERBROOK, Circuit Judge. Wisconsin's capital city uses a computer-based radio system for police, fire, ambulance, and other emergency communications. The Smartnet II, made by Motorola, spreads traffic across 20 frequencies. One is designated for control. A radio unit (mobile or base) uses the control channel to initiate a conversation. Computer hardware and software assigns the conversation to an open channel, and it can link multiple roaming units into "talk groups" so that officers in the field can hold joint conversations. This is known as a "trunking system" and makes efficient use of radio spectrum, so that 20 channels can support hundreds of users. If the control channel is interfered with, however, remote units will show the message "no system" and communication will be impossible.

Between January and August 2003 mobile units in Madison encountered occasional puzzling "no signal" conditions. On Halloween of that year the "no system" condition spread citywide; a powerful signal had blanketed all of the City's communications towers and prevented the computer from receiving, on the control channel, data essential to parcel traffic among the other 19 channels. Madison was hosting between 50,000 and 100,000 visitors that day. When disturbances erupted, public safety departments were unable to coordinate their activities because the radio system was down. Although the City repeatedly switched the control channel for the Smartnet system, a step that temporarily restored service, the interfering signal changed channels too and again blocked the system's use. On November 11, 2003, the attacker changed tactics. Instead of blocking the system's use, he sent signals directing the Smartnet base station to keep channels open, and at the end of each communication the attacker appended a sound, such as a woman's sexual moan.

By then the City had used radio direction finders to pin down the source of the intruding signals. Police arrested Rajib Mitra, a student in the University of Wisconsin's graduate business school. They found the radio hardware and computer gear that he had used to monitor communications over the Smart-net system, analyze how it operated, and send the signals that took control of the system. Mitra, who in 2000 had received a B.S. in computer science from the University, possessed two other credentials for this kind of work: criminal convictions (in 1996 and 1998) for hacking into computers in order to perform malicious mischief. A jury convicted Mitra of two counts of intentional interference with computer-related systems used in interstate commerce. See *18 U.S.C. § 1030(a)(5)*. He has been sentenced to 96 months' imprisonment. On appeal he says that his conduct does not violate *§ 1030*—and that, if it does, the statute exceeds Congress's commerce power.

Section 1030(a)(5) provides that whoever

(A)

(i) knowingly causes the transmission of a program, information, code, or command, and as a result of such conduct, intentionally causes damage without authorization, to a protected computer;

(ii) intentionally accesses a protected computer without authorization, and as a result of such conduct, recklessly causes damage; or

(iii) intentionally accesses a protected computer without authorization, and as a result of such conduct, causes damage; and

(B) by conduct described in clause (i), (ii), or (iii) of subparagraph (A), caused (or, in the case of an attempted offense, would, if completed, have caused)—

(i) loss to 1 or more persons during any 1-year period (and, for purposes of an investigation, prosecution, or other proceeding brought by the United States only, loss resulting from a related course of conduct affecting 1 or more other protected computers) aggregating at least $5,000 in value;

(ii) the modification or impairment, or potential modification or impairment, of the medical examination, diagnosis, treatment, or care of 1 or more individuals;

(iii) physical injury to any person;

(iv) a threat to public health or safety; or

(v) damage affecting a computer system used by or for a government entity in furtherance of the administration of justice, national defense, or national security ... shall be punished as provided in subsection (c) of this section.

Subsection (e)(1) defines "computer" as "an electronic, magnetic, optical, electrochemical, or other high speed data processing device performing logical, arithmetic, or storage functions, and includes any data storage facility or communications facility directly related to or operating in conjunction with such device, but such term does not include an automated typewriter or typesetter, a portable hand held calculator, or other similar device." Subsection (e)(2)(B) defines a "protected computer" to include any computer "used in interstate or foreign commerce or communication." Finally, subsection (e)(8) defines "damage" to mean "any impairment to the integrity or availability of data, a program, a system, or information."

The prosecutor's theory is that Smartnet II is a "computer" because it contains a chip that performs high-speed processing in response to signals received on the control channel, and as a whole is a "communications facility directly related to or operating in conjunction" with that computer chip. It is a "protected computer" because it is used in "interstate … communication;" the frequencies it uses have been allocated by the Federal Communications Commission for police, fire, and other public-health services. Mitra's transmissions on Halloween included "information" that was received by the Smartnet. Data that Mitra sent interfered with the way the computer allocated communications to the other 19 channels and stopped the flow of information among public-safety officers. This led to "damage" by causing a "no system" condition citywide, impairing the "availability of … a system, or information" and creating "a threat to public health or safety" by knocking out police, fire, and emergency communications. *See § 1030(a)(5)(A)(i), (B)(iv)*. The extraneous sounds tacked onto conversations on November 11 also are "information" sent to the "protected computer," and produce "damage" because they impair the "integrity" of the official communications. This time subsection *§1030(a)(5)(B)(v)* is what makes the meddling a crime, because Mitra hacked into a governmental safety-related communications system.

Mitra concedes that he is guilty if the statute is parsed as we have done. But he submits that Congress could not have intended the statute to work this way. Mitra did not invade a bank's system to steal financial information, or erase data on an ex-employer's system, see *United States v. Lloyd, 269 F.3d 228 (3d Cir.2001)*, or plaster a corporation's web site with obscenities that drove away customers, or unleash a worm that slowed and crashed computers across the world, see *United States v. Morris, 928 F.2d 504 (2d Cir.1991)*, or break into military computers to scramble a flight of interceptors to meet a nonexistent threat, or plant covert programs in computers so that they would send spam without the owners' knowledge. All he did was gum up a radio system. Surely that cannot be a federal crime, Mitra insists, even if the radio system contains a computer. Every cell phone and cell tower is a "computer" under this statute's definition; so is every iPod, every wireless base station in the corner coffee shop, and many another gadget. Reading *§ 1030* to cover all of these, and police radio too, would give the statute wide coverage, which by Mitra's lights means that Congress cannot have contemplated such breadth.

Well of course Congress did not contemplate or intend this particular application of the statute. Congress is a "they" and not an "it"; a committee lacks a brain (or, rather, has so many brains with so many different objectives that it is almost facetious to impute a joint goal or purpose to the collectivity). See Kenneth A. Shepsle, *Congress is a "They," Not an "It": Legislative Intent as Oxymoron, 12 Int'l Rev. L. & Econ. 239 (1992)*. Legislation is an objective text approved in constitutionally prescribed ways; its scope is not limited by the cerebrations of those who voted for or signed it into law.

Electronics and communications change rapidly, while each legislator's imagination is limited. Trunking communications systems came to market after 1984, when the first version of *§ 1030* was enacted, and none of the many amendments to this statute directly addresses them. But although legislators may not know about trunking communications systems, they *do* know that complexity is endemic in the modern world and that each passing year sees new developments. That's why they write general statutes rather than enacting a list of particular forbidden acts. And it is the statutes they enacted—not the thoughts they did or didn't have—that courts must apply. What Congress would have done about trunking systems, had they been present to the mind of any Senator or Representative, is neither here nor there. For instance, one may look at *West Virginia University Hospitals, Inc. v. Casey, 499 U.S. 83, 100–01, 111 S.Ct. 1138, 113 L.Ed.2d 68 (1991)*.

Section 1030 is general. Exclusions show just *how* general. Subsection (e)(1) carves out automatic typewriters, typesetters, and handheld calculators; this shows that other devices with embedded processors and software are covered. As more devices come to have built-in intelligence, the effective scope of the statute grows. This might prompt Congress to amend the statute but does not authorize the judiciary to give the existing version less coverage than its language portends. See *National Broiler Marketing Ass'n v. United States, 436 U.S. 816, 98 S.Ct. 2122, 56 L.Ed.2d 728 (1978)*. What protects people who accidentally erase songs on an iPod, trip over (and thus disable) a wireless base station, or rear-end a car and set off a computerized airbag, is not judicial creativity but the requirements of the statute itself: the damage must be intentional, it must be substantial (at least $5,000 or bodily injury or danger to public safety), and the computer must operate in interstate or foreign commerce.

Let us turn, then, to the commerce requirement. The system operated on spectrum licensed by the FCC. It met the statutory definition because the interference affected "communication." Mitra observes that his interference did not affect any radio system on the other side of a state line, yet this is true of many cell-phone calls, all of which are part of interstate commerce because the electromagnetic spectrum is securely within the federal regulatory domain. See, e.g., *Radovich v. National Football League, 352 U.S. 445, 453, 77 S.Ct. 390, 1 L.Ed.2d 456 (1957); Federal Radio Commission v. Nelson Brothers Bond & Mortgage Co., 289 U.S. 266, 279, 53 S.Ct. 627, 77 L.Ed. 1166 (1933)*. Congress may regulate all channels of interstate commerce; the spectrum is one of them. See *United States v. Lopez, 514 U.S. 549, 558, 115 S.Ct. 1624, 131 L.Ed.2d 626 (1995); United States v. Morrison, 529 U.S. 598, 608–09, 120 S.Ct. 1740, 146 L.Ed.2d 658 (2000)*. Mitra's apparatus was more powerful than the Huygens probe that recently returned pictures and other data from Saturn's moon Titan. Anyway, the statute does not ask whether the person who caused the damage acted in interstate commerce; it protects computers (and computerized communication systems) used in such commerce, no matter how the harm is inflicted. Once the *computer* is used in interstate commerce, Congress has the power to protect it from a local hammer blow, or from a local data packet that sends it haywire. (Indeed, Mitra concedes that he could have been prosecuted, consistent with the Constitution, for broadcasting an unauthorized signal. See *47 U.S.C. §301, §401(c)*.) Section 1030 is within the national power as applied to computer-based channel-switching communications systems.

Mitra offers a fallback argument that application of *§1030* to his activities is so unexpected that it offends the due process clause. But what cases such as *Bouie v. Columbia, 378 U.S. 347, 84 S.Ct. 1697, 12 L.Ed.2d 894 (1964)*, hold is that a court may not apply a clear criminal statute in a way that a reader could not anticipate, or put a vague criminal statute to a new and unexpected use. Mitra's problem is not that *§1030* has been turned in a direction that would have surprised reasonable people; it is that a broad statute has been applied *exactly as written*, while he wishes that it had not been. There is no constitutional obstacle to enforcing broad but clear statutes. See *Rogers v. Tennessee, 532 U.S. 451, 458–62, 121 S.Ct. 1693, 149 L.Ed.2d 697 (2001)* (discussing *Bouie's* rationale and limits). The statute itself gives all the notice that the Constitution requires.

The most well known piece of legislation associated with the terror attacks of September 11, 2001, is the USA PATRIOT Act. Designed as a tool to assist law enforcement to disrupt terrorist cells and their bases of operation, the USA PATRIOT Act was passed by an overwhelming majority of the Congress and signed into law by President Bush on October 26, 2001, and renewed with amendments on March 26, 2006.

The USA PATRIOT Act consists of a mixed variety of provisions aimed at both the investigation of suspected terrorists and the disruption of the sources of funding and support for terrorist organizations. Almost all of the provisions in the USA PATRIOT Act amend or add language to existing federal statutes. In terms of cyberterrorism, a number of changes have expanded the ability of both law enforcement and intelligence agencies (there are a variety of federal entities involved in the collection of foreign intelligence which include the National Security Agency, the Federal Bureau of Investigations, the Central Intelligence Agency, the Department of Defense, and the Department of Homeland Security) regarding surveillance and investigative powers. The intelligence community can now better monitor the Internet and share information with other federal and state entities.

Sections § 201 and § 202 of the USA PATRIOT Act authorizes interception of certain electronic communications for the collection of evidence related to terrorism, computer fraud and abuse. The USA PATRIOT Act at § 214 ("Pen Register and Trap and Trace Authority under FISA") also expands the ability of law enforcement agents to employ "pen registers," "trap and trace" devices, "sneak and peek" searches and "roving wiretaps" (which permits surveillance on the person and not, for example, on the phone or phone number). This section expands the scope of the Foreign Intelligence Surveillance Act of 1978 (FISA) and provides more powers to the FISA courts to grant court orders.

Section 217 sets out precise definitions regarding interception of computer trespasser communications. Among other things it clearly defines "wire communications," "electronic communications," "user" and "computer trespasser." For instance, a computer trespasser "means any person who accesses a protected computer without authorization and thus has no reasonable expectation of privacy in any communication transmitted to, through, or from the protected computer."

In addition, both the USA PATRIOT Act at § 214 and the Cyber Security and Enhancement Act (CSEA) have eased the warrant and subpoena requirements under the old Electronic Communications Privacy Act of 1986 (ECPA) in cases requiring immediate action. Under the CSEA, the government official need not obtain a warrant if he has a "good faith" belief regarding the prevention of death or serious bodily harm. In addition, the CSEA amends 18 U.S.C. § 3125(a)(1) to allow a government official to use a pen register or a trap and trace device without a warrant or a court order if there is a "threat to national security and an ongoing attack on a protected computer system."

Under § 506(a) of the USA PATRIOT Act, the Federal Bureau of Investigation (FBI) was given primary authority to investigate offenses associated with espionage or national security, expect those cases under the Secret Service. The USA PATRIOT Act authorizes the Director of the Secret Service to establish nationwide electronic crimes task forces (ECTF) to assist law enforcement, the private sector and academia in detecting and suppressing computer-based crime, and allows enforcement action to be taken to protect financial payment systems while combating transnational financial crimes directed by terrorists or other criminals. Since combating cyberterrorism as a partnership effort is imperative, the Secret Service encourages the private sector to bring issues to the ECTF that affect their particular industry and to learn how to protect their own corporate security. One of the many perks for the government is that it is able to connect with private companies that have a particular expertise and resources that many law enforcement agencies are lacking. For instance, AT&T is able to break encryption codes with greater speed than most law enforcement entities.

A 2007 report issued by the Government Accountability Office (GA0) noted that government and private sectors face a number of serious obstacles in securing cyberspace particularly in the context of law enforcement and operational security. The four main categories of concern in the GAO report touched on cyber crime, but would also be equally pertinent in regards to any type of cyber attack to include cyberterrorism:

> (1) accurately reporting cyber crime to law enforcement;
> (2) ensuring adequate law enforcement analytical and technical capabilities: obtaining and retaining investigators, prosecutors, and cyber forensics examiners & keeping up to date with current technology and criminal techniques;
> (3) working in a borderless environment with laws of multiple jurisdictions; and
> (4) protecting information and information systems & raising awareness about criminal behavior.)

Individual states have also enacted laws associated with cyberterrorism concerns. These laws address a wide range of issues from improving security measures for wireless networks to criminalizing the installation of software on another's computer which is then used in deceptive methods. In addition to criminal laws, civil actions based on commercial code unfair competition prohibitions can also serve to punish hackers.

The fear of cyberterrorism as a destructive force has caused at least 48 states to pass non-release provisions to their state open government laws—state freedom of information laws (patterned after the federal Freedom of Information Act) and state Sunshine laws (providing for public access to government meetings). An examination of the legislative thrust of most of these non-release provisions is to deny potential terrorists access to certain information that could aid them in conducting a disabling physical or cyber attack on the critical infrastructure. For instance, the Ohio Revised Code makes specific exceptions to the Ohio Open Government law regarding non-release of information related to *acts of terrorism*, *critical infrastructures*, and *security records*. Under § 149.433(B): "A record kept by a public office that is a security record or an infrastructure record is not a public record under § 149.433 of the Revised Code and is not subject to mandatory release or disclosure under that section." Under § 149.433(A)(3), the term "security records" is broadly construed to include:

(a) Any record that contains information directly used for protecting or maintaining the security of a public office against attack, interference, or sabotage, and

(b) Any record assembled, prepared, or maintained by a public office or public body to prevent, mitigate, or respond to acts of terrorism, to include any of the following:

(i) Those portions of records containing specific and unique vulnerability assessments or specific and unique response plans either of which is intended to prevent or mitigate acts of terrorism, and communication codes or deployment plans of law enforcement or emergency response personnel;

(ii) Specific intelligence information and specific investigative records shared by federal and international law enforcement agencies with state and local law enforcement and public safety agencies; and

(iii) National security records classified under federal executive order and not subject to public disclosure under federal law that are shared by federal agencies, and other records related to national security briefings to assist state and local government with domestic preparedness for acts of terrorism.

The term "infrastructure record" under the Ohio Revised Code § 149.433(A)(2) means:

Any record that discloses the configuration of a public office's critical systems including, but not limited to, communication, computer, electrical, mechanical, ventilation, water, and plumbing systems, security codes, or the infrastructure or structural configuration of the building in which a public office is located." However, the term infrastructure record "does not mean a simple floor plan that discloses only the spatial relationship of components of a public office or the building in which a public office is located.

The term "act of terrorism" under the Ohio Revised Code § 149.433(A)(1) has the same statutory meaning as is found in Ohio Revised Code § 2909.21:

> 'Act of terrorism' means an act that is committed within or outside the territorial jurisdiction of this state or the United States, that constitutes a specified offense if committed in this state or constitutes an offense in any jurisdiction within or outside the territorial jurisdiction of the United States containing all of the essential elements of a specified offense, and that is intended to do one or more of the following:
> (1) Intimidate or coerce a civilian population;
> (2) Influence the policy of any government by intimidation or coercion; or
> (3) Affect the conduct of any government by the act that constitutes the offence.

Government Responses to Cyberterrorism

Starting with the Clinton Administration and continuing to date, the government's approach to cybersecurity for owners/operators of private computer systems has been one of cooperative engagement and not mandatory regulation. In short, despite the rapidly expanding reliance on the Internet by American businesses, consumers and government agencies, the government provides extremely little affirmative regulatory laws in terms of cybersecurity functions for non-government computer systems. Instead, the concept of engagement stresses the promotion of voluntary public-private alliances to combat cyber attacks of all kinds with particular regard to protecting the nation's critical infrastructure. With but minor exceptions, aimed at government computer systems, the theme of engagement predominates all of the federal laws, executive orders and presidential directives associated with cyberspace. These include the following: Internet Integrity and Critical Infrastructure Protection Act (2000); Cyber Security Research and Development Act; National Strategy to Secure Cyberspace (2003); National Strategy for the Physical Protection of Critical Infrastructures and Key Assets (2003); Presidential Decision Directive (PDD) 63; Executive Order 13821, Critical Infrastructure Protection in the Information Age; and Homeland Security Presidential Directive No. 7 (HSPD-7). The two strategies are designed to help America secure the cyber world by establishing three main objectives: (1) prevent cyber attacks against America's critical infrastructure; (2) reduce national vulnerability to cyber attacks; and (3) reduce damage and recovery time from cyber attacks when they do occur.

The National Strategy to Secure Cyberspace specifically recognizes that cyberspace constitutes "the control system of our country." In addition, the document recognizes that a comprehensive national strategy must protect against such cyber attacks which "can have serious consequences such as disrupting critical operations, causing loss of revenue and intellectual property, or loss of life." The main goal of the National Strategy to Secure Cyberspace calls of the entire society—the federal government, state and local government, private industry and the American public—to engage in coordinated and focused efforts to secure cyberspace. To expedite this goal, the primary focus of the National Strategy to Secure Cyberspace is the establishment of a national cyber space security response system consisting of federal, state and local governments as well as the private sector. Thus, not only does the National Strategy to Secure Cyberspace reinforce the private sector's involvement in critical infrastructure protection, it also expands on the Clinton era 1998 PDD 63. PDD 63 recognizes that addressing cyber risks to the nation's critical infrastructures requires close coordination and cooperation across federal agencies and among the private sector. Since the policy of engagement depends on public and private sector coordination, research and preparation to repel a cyber attack, PDD 63 specifically tasks federal agencies with developing critical infrastructure protection plans (CIP) and establishing relationships with private industry sectors. It calls for those private commercial enterprises working in any of the identified 14 vertical industries such as banking, commerce, telecommunications, power, water, utilities and transportation, to have assessments conducted of their network infrastructure.

In 2001, President Bush expanded this effort with Executive Order 13821, Critical Infrastructure Protection in the Information Age, which continues many of the initiatives begun by PDD 63 to include the creation of the President's Critical Infrastructure Protection Board to better coordinate all federal cyber security efforts. In addition, the 2003 HSPD-7 designates certain federal agencies to work with private sector counterparts; designates the DHS as the lead agency for information and telecommunications critical infrastructure; and assigns the Secretary of Homeland Security with the task of coordinating all matters dealing with protecting the nation's critical infrastructure. In fact, numerous public entities have individual and collaborative responsibilities to ensure that the cyber world is protected. For example, DHS established the National Cyber Security Division as part of its Information Analysis and Infrastructure Protection Directorate to better fulfill its oversight responsibilities. One of DHS's main objectives is to structure a response system that fully joins the government and the private sector together in order to promote the creation of a viable crisis management response in the event of a major cyber attack. In addition, DHS seeks to identify and remediate existing vulnerabilities by developing new security systems and technologies. Along with DHS, the Department of Justice (DOJ), the Federal Trade Commission (FTC), and the Department of Defense (DOD) are all focused on responding to intentional, unlawful cyber attacks that threaten the confidentiality, integrity and availability of information networks.

DHS also encourages the development of voluntary partnerships with the private sector through information sharing and analysis centers (ISACs). Currently DHS lists 14 ISACs across the nation. The Cyber Security Research and Development Act authorizes a multi-year grant effort to promote computer security measures from private sources as well as universities and the establishment of multi-disciplinary Centers for Computer and Network Security Research. US-CERT is another joint endeavor between DHS and the public and private sectors. It is charged generally with protecting the nation's infrastructure and is responsible for coordinating defense and response against cyber attacks nationwide.

The development of effective tools to protect cyberspace is of paramount importance. Realizing that the superhighway of the cyber world is composed of hundreds of thousands of interconnected computers, servers, switches and fiber optics that allow our critical infrastructures to function, the threat of cyberterrorism requires urgent cybersecurity measures. As demonstrated by the cyber attack on Estonia in 2007, the threat is no longer a topic of academic debate. Considering that approximately 85 percent of America's critical infrastructure is privately owned and operates via control systems that are largely connected to the Internet, it is imperative that the government—law enforcement and military—not only partner with private industry in a unified manner to establish both reactive and proactive strategies, but also conduct realistic training exercises. Unfortunately, the pace of progress in this regard is slow.

February 2006, DHS hosted the first ever government-led real world cyber exercise called Cyber Storm (Cyber Storm 2 was held in 2008). Costing over 3 million dollars, this invitation only exercise provided over 100 public and private agencies from over 60 locations in five countries with a platform to address a variety of technical and cooperative issues associated with a realistic "staged" mega cyber attack against large-scale critical infrastructure elements to include energy, transportation and information technology. Considering that reviews of the exercise showed that many of the participants did not even know of the existence of the National Cyber Response Coordination Group, which serves as the primary federal organization to respond to major cyber attacks, it is evident that a key component of the engagement strategy demands increased training exercise. In addition, considering that 90 percent of the threat from cyberterrorism exists in the private sector, it is equally evident that relying on voluntary engagement practices may not be adequate—regulatory mandates are needed.

There can be absolutely no question that the threat of cyberterrorism is a grave concern that has the potential for significant damage to vast areas of the public domain. Indeed, because of cyberterrorism's great potential for harm to the basic pillars of society many commentators argue that cyberspace has passed into the realm of a societal "commons" that obliges the government to exert greater protection. If cyberspace is considered a commons, *a fortiori*, cybersecurity demands that the government provide solid protection and regulation for the common good of the general public. From this perspective many question the wisdom of a federal policy to secure cyberspace that fails to incorporate strict security cybersecurity standards or regulations on the private sector as part of the strategy.

Because it is impossible to immediately determine the source of a cyber attack—it may be an amateur "script kiddie," a terrorist, or even a nation-state— the so-called "response baton" will originate with the private sector and then may be passed to law enforcement and next, perhaps, to the military. Clearly, the main thrust of a commons oriented cybersecurity strategy would involve two key elements: (1) a program that required the sharing of timely and accurate information all along the continuum from private to government and (2) the adoption of industry specific cybersecurity standards and certification for all information systems.

The concept of "standards" is defined by the National Standards Policy Advisory Committee as: "a prescribed set of rules, conditions, or requirements concerning definitions of terms; classification of components; specification of materials, performance, or operations; delineation of procedures; or measurement of quantity and quality in describing materials, products, systems, services, or practices." As suggested by the government's current engagement strategy, the federal government only promulgates cybersecurity standards for federal computer systems, except national security systems. The federal standards are developed by the National Institute of Standards and Technology (NIST) and set out as Federal Information Processing Standards (FIPS). FIPS are promulgated under the simple rule-making procedures (notice and comment) of the Administrative Procedure Act.

In accordance with National Security Directive 42, standards regarding national security systems are developed and controlled by the Committee on National Security Systems. The Federal Information Security Act of 2002, defines a national security system as:

Any computer system (including any telecommunications system, used or operated by an agency or by a contractor of an agency, or other organization on behalf of an agency ...

(i) the function of which—

(I) involves intelligence activities;

(II) involves cryptologic activities related to national security;

(III) involves command and control of military forces;

(IV) involves equipment that is an integral part of a weapon or weapons system;

(V) ... is critical to the direct fulfillment of military or intelligence missions; or

(ii) is protected at all times by procedures established for information that have been specially authorized under criteria established by an Executive Order or an Act of Congress to be kept classified in the interest of national defense or foreign policy.

In 2008, President Bush signed National Security Presidential Directive 54 and Homeland Security Presidential Directive 23. The classified directives expand the intelligence communities' role in cybersecurity for federal agencies' computer systems and expand DHS's ability to work with the DOD on cybersecurity threats.

To be sure, numerous public and private studies offer various proposals for sound security and best practices needed to reduce vulnerabilities from cyber attack. The studies usually prescribe a standardized integration of cybersecurity technology associated with all critical infrastructure systems in order to ensure an acceptable national level of cybersecurity. While various approaches have been advanced, the 2005 CRS report RL32777, observed that none of them are "likely to be widely adopted in the absence of sufficient economic incentives for cybersecurity."

Those who believe that the federal government should not require the development and enforcement of mandatory cybersecurity standards in the private sector, often argue that apart from issues of intrusiveness and technical feasibility, that such requirements would simply be too costly. Although the argument related to cost would be dwarfed into insignificance when measured against the monetary damage incurred in the event of a mega cyberterrorist attack, technical matters ranging from how to develop said standards in the rapidly changing world of cyberspace to how the government would measure compliance pose significant challenges.

Those who critique the engagement strategy argue that absent the impetus that would be provided by a massive cyberterrorist attack on the nation's critical infrastructure, efforts to actually create a meaningful cooperative proactive and reactive strategy between the government and private industry are piecemeal. Even the more immediate negative consequences to businesses caused by the impact of cyber crime (which drains billions of dollars from consumers and private industry each year) have not resulted in the necessary strides to produce stronger and more secure computer networks.

The basic reason for the lack of cooperation is that private companies are largely unwilling to share information about security breaches with other companies or the government. First, they are concerned that competitors might gain access to exclusive company data that is shared with the government through a public Freedom of Information Act (FOIA) request or by means of other sources (the Critical Infrastructure Protect Act exempts such revelations to the government from FOIA). Second, because the private sector operates in a competitive market-based economy, public revelations about security breaches at the company could have serious negative responses from stockholders or consumers.

Unfortunately, it is a hard fact that very few private companies have exhibited interest in joining the cybersecurity effort to the degree that the various government strategies so strongly desire. The frustration is that without a cooperative effort to identify breaches and the possible weak points of security systems, the vulnerabilities to cyber attack are magnified and countermeasures remain far behind. For certain, when the West suffers its first "Pearl Harbor cyber attack," the government will adopt a more draconian stance in order to force private industry to share information and to develop better cybersecurity systems. For the time being, apart from suffering economic loss, there are no driving incentives for private industry to work together to combat cyberterrorism.

Cyber Attacks as an Act of War

A number of nation-states, including the United States, are rapidly developing the operational doctrine and functional tools necessary to conduct cyber warfare. There is no doubt that cyber warfare with its non-kinetic use of force will be the next area for weapon development by militaries around the world. In fact, according to a variety of open source documents to include, the Peoples Republic of China openly boasts that it intends to develop the capability to win an information cyber war by the mid-21st century. Cyber warfare involves the action of conducting a cyber information attack on the computer network of an adversary in order to limit their ability to obtain or use information. Of course, this matter is not restricted to the activity of nation-states—hackers and terrorists are not constrained by any rule of law and might engage in coordinated cyber attacks that could equally disrupt a nation's computer network system. Nevertheless, since the rule of law would certainly encompass the use of cyber information activity conducted by a nation-state, it is necessary to examine the law and policy issues related to cyber warfare.

The use of "information warfare" or cyber warfare is a new concept; the use of cyber tactics is emerging as a key component of 21st century warfighting. For instance, the U.S. military conducted successful cyber attacks in both the 1991 Gulf War and the 2003 Iraq War (to a lesser degree) to disrupt Iraqi command and control networks and the operation of other essential physical facilities. Currently, the Joint Functional Component Command for Network Warfare (JFCCNW) functions under the United States Strategic Command (STRATCOM), to coordinate cyber information actions for the DOD. In 2008, the U.S. Air Force established a Cyber Command to prepare its forces for fighting wars in cyberspace by protecting those information systems which operate U.S. critical infrastructures and to be able, if tasked, to attack an adversaries computer networks. The U.S. Navy has the Naval Network Warfare Command in Norfolk, Virginia. In short, DOD is developing both offensive and defensive capabilities to conduct war in cyberspace.

Like a number of legal issues that have emerged in the post-9/11 world, the question of addressing cyber attacks from an international law of war perspective remains unsettled. The central legal issue poses the following question: Does the use a of cyber attack constitute a sufficient "use of force" in the context of the law of war to be deemed an "armed attack" or an "act of war?"

The use of the term act of war traditionally refers to the use of aggressive force against a sovereign State by another State in violation of the United Nations (U.N.) Charter and/or customary international law. In almost every instance in the modern era, such illegal acts occur without a formal declaration of war and the aggressive act itself triggers the ensuing armed conflict, i.e., war. The application of the traditional law of war principles (also known as the law of armed conflict) was developed by the international community in response to readily recognized deliberate armed attacks by soldiers, aircraft, or vessels on the military, citizens, or territory of another nation-state. At the time of the development of the law of war, cyberspace did not exist. Thus, the question of whether or not a computer network attack is an act of war requires extrapolation from the existing norms related to the law of war.

Any analysis of the matter must begin with the U.N. Charter. The goal of the U.N. Charter is to restrict the unfettered power of member States to pursue activities and policies that threatened international peace and security. Understanding that the U.N. Charter does not outlaw the use of force—it only outlaws the use of *aggressive* force—there are four primary provisions of the U.N. Charter under which the use of force is analyzed.

First, Articles 2(3) and (4) set out the general obligations of all member States to settle disputes in a peaceful manner and to refrain from "the threat or use of force." U.N. Charter Article 2(3) requires that, "[a]ll Members shall settle their international disputes by peaceful means in such a manner that international peace and security, and justice are not endangered." U.N. Charter Article 2(4) states, "[a]ll Members shall refrain in their international relations from the threat or use of force against the territorial integrity or political independence of any State, or in any other manner inconsistent with the purposes of the United Nations." In 1970, the General Assembly elaborated on Article 2(4), with U.N. General Assembly Resolution 2625, Declaration on Principles of International Law Concerning Friendly Relations and Cooperation among States in Accordance with the Charter of the United Nations. Although General Assembly resolutions are considered as non-binding recommendations they often prove useful, particularly to the extent that they contain authoritative restatements of customary international law. General Assembly Resolution 2625 states:

> Every State has the duty to refrain from organizing, instigating, assisting, or participating in acts of civil strife or terrorist acts in another State or acquiescing in organized activities within its territory directed towards the commission of such acts, when the acts referred to in the present paragraph involve a threat or use of force.

Second, if a State engages in the use of aggressive force, Article 24 of the U.N. Charter gives the Security Council the "primary responsibility for the maintenance of international peace and security." Article 27 requires that all permanent members of the U.N. Security Council (China, France, Russia, the United States and Britain) must agree on enforcement provisions, e.g., authorizing member States to engage in the defensive use of armed force.

The third element in the analytical framework is Article 51 of the U.N. Charter, which expresses the "inherent right of self-defense" in the case of an armed attack. The inherent right of self-defense refers to the ancient customary right of a country to unilaterally engage in acts of self-defense in response to an armed attack regardless of what any other nation or organization, to include the United Nations, may or may not do. Article 51 of the U.N. Charter states:

> Nothing in the present Charter shall impair the inherent right of individual or collective self-defense if an armed attack occurs against a Member of the United Nations, until the Security Council has taken measures to maintain international peace and security. Measures taken by Members in the exercise of the right of self-defense shall be immediately reported to the Security Council and shall not in any way

affect the authority and responsibility of the Security Council under
the present Charter to take at any time such action as it deems necessary in order to maintain or restore international peace and security.

While a cyber attack has the potential to do great harm to the critical infrastructure of a given nation-state, would such an action rise to the level of
what Article 51 deems as an "armed attack?" Clearly, a cyber attack of sufficient scope on either the military network or the critical infrastructure could
constitute a violation of Article 2(3) and 2(4), but would that be considered enough
to constitute an armed attack triggering the customary right of self-defense
now codified under Article 51 of the U.N. Charter?

Common sense would dictate that a cyber attack of sufficient magnitude
should be considered an armed attack, but when the U.N. Charter was drafted
in 1945, the founders clearly did not foresee the potential for devastation that
could come from cyberspace. For instance, Article 41 of the U.N. Charter
views the "complete or partial interruption of … telegraphic, radio, and other
means of communication" as measures not rising to the level of the use of
armed force. In turn, the definition of aggression as adopted by the 1974
General Assembly Resolution 3314, excludes the concept of cyber attacks as
an act of aggression that would constitute an armed attack. According to the
U.N. Definition of Aggression, a State engages in aggression in the following ways:

Article 1
Aggression is the use of armed force by a State against the sovereignty,
territorial integrity, or political independence of another State, or in
any manner inconsistent with the Charter of the United Nations....

Article 2
The first use of armed force by a State in contravention of the Charter shall constitute prima facie evidence of an act of aggression....

Article 3
Any of the following acts, regardless of a declaration of war, shall …
qualify as an act of aggression:
(a) The invasion or attack by the armed forces of a State … of an-
    other State or part thereof;
(b) Bombardment by the armed forces of a State against the territory
    of another State …
(c) The blockade of the ports or coasts of a State by the armed forces
    of another State;
(d) An attack by the armed forces of a State on the land, sea, or air
    forces, or marine and air fleets of another State;

(e) The use of armed forces of one State ... in contravention of the conditions provided for in the agreement or any extension of their presence in such territory beyond the termination of the agreement;

(f) The action of a State in allowing its territory, which it has placed at the disposal of another State, to be used by that other State for perpetrating an act of aggression against a third State;

(g) The sending by or on behalf of a State of armed bands, groups, irregulars, or mercenaries, which carry out acts of armed force against another State of such gravity as to amount to the acts listed above, or its substantial involvement therein.

Finally, because there is no absolute requirement that a "threat to the peace, breach of the peace, or act of aggression," take the form of a traditional styled armed attack, Article 39 of the U.N. Charter ultimately provides the Security Council with the final authority to determine whether a particular cyber attack would constitute a breach of the peace, and to what degree. Obviously, for the Security Council to take action, the cyber attack would have to be extensive in nature. In other words, the consequences of a cyber attack would be a central ingredient in their decision making process. Article 39 of the U.N. Charter states:

> The Security Council shall determine the existence of any threat to the peace, breach of the peace, or act of aggression and shall make recommendations, or decide what measures shall be taken in accordance with Articles 41 and 42, to maintain or restore international peace and security.

A related issue in the analysis is the issue of State-sponsorship. The law of war recognizes acts of self defense in the context of the acts of a hostile nation-state, not of individual actors or groups of individuals that act in their private capacity. The expectation is that the aggrieved State will notify the nation-state where the private actors are located and then request assistance and cooperation. If the host nation is unwilling or unable to provide assistance and cooperation, then the aggrieved State may be justified to use force as was the case with the United States *vis a vis* the Taliban's support for the terrorist al Qaeda network in Afghanistan. On the other hand, if the cyber attack cannot be traced to a nation-state, the matter of retaliation is greatly limited.

Clearly, the international laws associated with the use of force are woefully inadequate in terms of addressing the threat of cyber warfare. Without a clear set of rules addressing cyber warfare, individual nation-states will no doubt operate within the framework of existing legal norms by extrapolation, much like the North Atlantic Treaty Organization (NATO) did when it invoked the NATO collective self-defense clause under Article 5 of its Charter, declaring that the terror attacks of 9/11 constituted an "armed attack" under international law despite the fact that al Qaeda is not a nation-state.

The international community needs to agree on the application of cyber warfare to the international rules of armed conflict. To date, however, periodic calls for the development of international rules dealing with information warfare have gone unanswered. In 1998 and 1999, for example, Russia was unsuccessful in its bid to get the United Nations to explore the need for an information warfare weapons arms control protocol. The Russian resolution asked member States to provide input on the "advisability of elaborating international legal regimes to ban the development, production and use of particularly dangerous information weapons."

The only real significant international agreement on cyber matters to date is the Council of Europe Convention on Cybercrime, which was ratified by five nations, including the United States, on July 1, 2004. There is hope that this convention, which focuses on cyber crime and not cyber warfare, may at least present a starting point for future efforts in the realm of cyber warfare.

Currently, DOD views the use of cyber technology in military operations as a part of what is termed Information Operations (IO). IO consists of five subcategories: Psychological Operations (PSYOP); Military Deception (MILDEC); Operations Security (OPSEC); Computer Network Operations (CNO); and Electronic Warfare (EW). While the domestic guidelines that detail how and when the United States would conduct a computer network attack is classified information in National Security Presidential Directive 16 (February 2003), there are a number of unclassified DOD policy directives that speak to IO operations which would certainly have impact on cyber warfare. For instance, in regard to PSYOP, only non-domestic audiences can be targeted. This restriction would certainly apply to electronic warfare.

From a military perspective, the use of cyber technology in warfare is something that is clearly viewed as a new and powerful weapon. Cyber warfare offers a cheap method of employing targeted force against an adversary—it requires no deployment of soldiers, vehicles, or vessels. As is the case for all weapons, however, the American military command structure responds to lawful commands from the government and uses force in accordance with Standing Rules of Engagement (SROE). Depending on the objective of the military operation, the SROE are further amplified by multiple levels of Rules of Engagement (ROE) which are developed by commanders and their lawyers. Designed for offensive and defensive uses of force, these rules ensure compliance with the law of war as well as domestic law. Even though no review has yet been produced, the DOD has recommended a legal review to determine what level of data manipulation constitutes an attack.

At the end of the day, if directed by lawful authority, DOD can and will attack an adversary's computer system—private or government. The unresolved issue that is seldom discussed centers on the mechanics—the U.S. military relies significantly on the computer systems of the private sector and would presumably have to use those private assets in any large scale cyber attack.

Legal Issues in the Private Sector

From the viewpoint of the private sector, there are a variety of cyberspace related legal issues that require close attention. At the forefront of most Internet users' minds is the question of privacy. As they venture online, users and consumers look for reassurance that the personal information they submit will remain protected by their own computer, their Internet service provider (ISP) and the Web site they are visiting. Conversely, the chief concern of technology developers, manufacturers and owner/operators is the question of legal responsibility regarding the type and level of cybersecurity protection.

As noted in the discussion on the government's overall cybersecurity strategy in the private sector, the understated theme of engagement continues to characterize the approach for user privacy and cyber system integrity. The matter of cybersecurity in general and security standards in particular are left in the hands of civilian technology developers, manufacturers and owner/operators.

Federal legislation mandating protective measures in terms of computer security is restricted to federal agencies only, e.g., the Federal Information Security Management Act of 2002. Apart from a few specific laws associated with protecting financial and health-related information from disclosure, government efforts to set security standards or make private entities responsible for protecting their computer systems has not yet come of age. A brief survey of federal involvement in this area reveals only two major pieces of legislation—one in health and one in financial reporting—and even those two indirectly address cybersecurity concerns. The Health Insurance Portability and Accountability Act of 1996 requires certain private entities to establish security programs that protect the health-related information in their possession and the Sarbanes-Oxley Act of 2002, requires corporate executives of publicly held companies to annually certify the integrity of their financial reporting under penalty of fines or imprisonment. While the Sarbanes-Oxley Act was passed in the wake of the accounting scandals at Enron and WorldCom, it spurred a massive increase in cybersecurity spending by private companies now concerned about the operating effectiveness of computerized internal controls and fraud prevention.

Liability issues associated with breaches of computer security rubricate cyber discussions from both ISPs and private companies. Liability for failure to protect customers from cyber attacks and liability for (unknowingly) hosting a DDoS attacker are two significant concerns that will soon find their way into court as civil actions in tort or product liability claims. Currently, however, there are no federal laws holding a technology developer, manufacturer, or owner/operator liable if they sell or offer a product that has inadequate cybersecurity protections or design flaws. As a practical matter, licensing agreements or terms of service agreements include disclaimer protections.

In tandem with these cyber "defensive" concerns, i.e., responsibility for damage done to third parties as a result of inadequately providing security protection as a technology developer, manufacturer, or owner/operator, is the emerging issue of the increased use of "offensive" or self-defense responses to a cyber attack, e.g., actions employed by private network security personnel in response to a cyber attack on their system. Known as hackback—an offensive response against a cyber attacker—this offensive process may also damage the computer networks of innocent third parties used by the attacker. While hackback illustrates a desire by some in the civilian sector to take cybersecurity matters into their own hands, it also raises a number of legal issues.

Identification of the source(s) of a cyber attack, including the Internet Protocol (IP) address of the attacker, is vital to the identification of the attacker, the deployment of effective countermeasures and the development of new cybersecurity defense tools. However, due to a number of techniques that can be used to hide the identity of an attacker, manually tracing the multiple sources of a DDoS attack generally proves overly burdensome and requires more time to conduct than the actual attack itself. As a practical matter, then, the best way to identify the source of an attack is through an automated process. One such program is known as "IP Traceback." Southwest Research Institute (SwRI), San Antonio, Texas is currently working on a project to develop an Autonomous System Traceback (AST) solution to combat cyber attacks, including DDoS attacks. As such, AST provides a useful platform in the discussion of a variety of legal issues that are not only integral in the context of developing and deploying the AST solution, but in dealing with liability and privacy issues associated with both defensive and offensive cybersecurity actions.

Experts correctly refer to the IP traceback concept as a problem because tracing an attack to its source is complicated by the fact that attackers typically forge, or "spoof," the IP address from which the attack packet is sent. Spoofed packets will contain an invalid or false IP address in the packet header making the packet appear as though it originated from the "spoofed" IP address. To complicate matters further, the traditional method of tracing the source of an attack is largely a manual process that must be conducted during the course of an attack (this is further aggravated because the attack can be carried out from a multitude of sources). The complexity of such attacks thereby renders traditional tracing of IP addresses impractical for commercial networks in terms of cost effectiveness.

Four main types of IP traceback exist: packet marking; packet or hash-based logging; link testing; and Internet Control Message Protocol (ICMP) traceback.[6] In general, each of these approaches has suffered technical, policy and legal restrictions. The need for additional hardware, software upgrades, modifications to network configurations and filtering the enormous amount of data processed on computer networks have presented technical obstacles. Further, one of the key limitations to successful deployment of IP traceback systems is the necessity for cooperation among ISPs. According to one report on the matter:

> Tracking an anonymous attack is not a trivial task. An individual or organization would find this task difficult, if not impossible, without involving their upstream ISPs. Today, tracing an anonymous attack even within a single ISP remains a manual task. ISPs and enterprise networks do not have incentives to monitor for attack packets.... The lack of incentives comes from the fact that monitoring for such packets has no immediate benefit to the ISP itself or its subscribers. Furthermore, participating in traceback may mean disclosure of internal topology, investment in additional equipment, upgrades to existing equipment and additional operational costs for the ISP. Consequently, IP traceback solutions should not assume complete cooperation of ISPs.[7]

Looking at the final goal of the traceback process—identifying and blocking the source of the attack—the AST method of IP traceback focuses not on identifying a specific computer as the attack source but rather locating the Autonomous System (AS)[8] from which the attack originated. AST monitors record

---

6. Andrey Belenky & Nirwan Ansari, *On IP Traceback*, IEEE Communications Magazine, vol. 41, no.7, 142–153 (July 2003) (analyzing the technical details of the various approaches to IP Traceback.); Chun He, Formal Specifications of Traceback Marking Protocols, (May 2002) (unpublished honors thesis, University of Texas at Austin), *available at* http://www.cs.utexas.edu/ftp/pub/techreports/tr02-42.pdf (summarizing the four named techniques).

7. *Id.* at 152.

8. An autonomous system (AS) is defined as: "A network that is administered by a single set of management rules that are controlled by one person, group or organization. Autonomous systems often use only one routing protocol, although multiple protocols can be used. The core of the Internet is made up of many autonomous systems." Scalable IP Trace-

hashes of the packet signature—in this case, specific fields in the packet header—for each packet that crosses their borders. The route of an attack packet may then be traced back by identifying each AS it crossed, without the need to examine internal network paths. Additionally, and most importantly for privacy concerns, the contents of the traffic are never viewed or stored. Only a hash of the packet's header information is stored by the AST. In other words, no internal network topology is disclosed to the AST, only whether an AS saw the packet and where it received the packet from. Since AST does not utilize any of the active traceback techniques such as "active defense" or hackback, an AST model remains within the passive realm. Because there is no expectation of privacy from routing information, the Electronic Communications Privacy Act (ECPA), which generally prohibits the interception, use, or disclosure of email contents while they are being transmitted, does not protect packet headers which are used to route information from point A to point Z.

Accordingly, AST developers express two specific concerns in the area of liability: (1) what liability might a company or ISP have for failing to use AST technology (if it were one day viewed as an industry standard practice, for instance) in its network cybersecurity program, and (2) what liability might attach if a company or ISP became host to a DDoS attacker?

Answering the first question, without the benefit of significant judicial case law on the subject, mandates reference to traditional notions of common law tort liability. For an ISP, or other commercial firm, to be liable under tort law requires that the provider breach a legal duty to exercise a level of care imposed by either statute or common law.

Sources for common law tort liability require consideration as to the developing legal standard for information security, which in this case would be discovered by reviewing trends in the area of cybersecurity. At a minimum, there exists at least a general obligation to provide some level of cybersecurity. Specifically, legal obligations for technology developers, manufacturers and owner/operators regarding information security derive from multiple sources— enacted federal and state laws; regulations and government enforcement actions; and common law fiduciary duties and obligations to provide reasonable care. The legal obligation to implement cybersecurity measures can be classified as either industry-specific, data-specific, or focused on public companies.

As previously noted, a handful of federal laws have been enacted in order to protect personal data and financial reporting of individuals, customers, or

---

back for Internet Attack Attribution," *available at* http://www.SwRI.org/3pubs/ird2005/Synopses/109446.htm.

prospects held by certain private companies. The Sarbanes-Oxley Act and the Gramm-Leach-Bliley Act require the integrity of financial reporting and the Health Insurance Portability and Accountability Act mandates cybersecurity protections for personal information. The Children's Online Privacy Protection Act of 1998 requires protection of personal information regarding children. The Securities Exchange Commission (SEC) also imposes regulations regarding cybersecurity standards for internal financial controls over information systems.

The Federal Trade Commission (FTC) possesses a series of enforcement actions and consent decrees which extend security obligations to non-regulated industries. Originally, the FTC facilitated cases based on the alleged failure by companies to provide adequate information security contrary to representations they made to customers (deceptive trade practices claims). In June 2005, the FTC significantly broadened the scope of its enforcement by asserting that a failure to provide appropriate information security was, itself, an unfair trade practice—even in the absence of any false representations by the defendant as to the state of its security.

A variety of federal and state E-transaction laws (E-SIGN and UETA) now require all companies to provide security for storage of electronic records relating to online transactions. In addition, sector-specific regulations are experiencing proliferation. This includes the Internal Revenue Service's (IRS) requirement for companies to implement information security to protect electronic tax records and SEC regulations on cybersecurity concerns as a condition to engage in certain E-transactions. The Food and Drug Agency (FDA) also has agency regulations that require security for certain types of records.

Many legal commentators suggest that corporate directors have a duty of care rooted in a fiduciary obligation that includes responsibility for the security of the company's information systems. They also argue that there may be a common law duty to provide cybersecurity, the breach of which constitutes a tort.

State laws also impose certain cybersecurity obligations to ensure the security of personal information. These laws are known as security breach laws. In 2003, California enacted the California Database Protection Act, Cal. Civil Code § 1798.82 (2006), becoming the first state in the nation to enact legislation requiring any government or private entity that possessed confidential personal information (e.g., Social Security numbers) to notify the owners of said information in the event of a disclosure to an unauthorized person resulting from a security breach. Additionally, § 1798.81.5 (2006) of the Act added an unprecedented statutory duty on businesses that own or authorize the use of personal information to "implement and maintain reasonable security procedures and practices appropriate to the nature of the information, to protect the personal information from unauthorized access, destruction, use, modification, or disclosure." Thus, businesses obtaining the personal or confidential information of California customers now have a statutory duty to not only provide notification to individuals regarding security breaches but must also provide reasonable care for securing such data. California's approach has served as a model for statutes in dozens of other states to include:

> Arkansas (Ark. Code Ann. §4-110-101 *et seq.*)
> California (Cal. Civ Code §1798.82)
> Connecticut (2005 Conn. Acts 148)
> Delaware (De. Code Ann. tit. 6, 12B-101 *et seq.*)
> Florida (Fla. Stat. Ann. §817.5681)
> Georgia (Ga. Code Ann, §10-1-910 *et seq.*)
> Illinois (815 Ill. Comp. Stat. 530-1 *et seq.*)
> Indiana (Ind. Code §1.IC 4-1-10)
> Louisiana (La. Rev. Stat. Ann. §51.3071 *et seq.*)
> Maine (Me. Rev. Stat. Ann. tit. 10, §1346 *et seq.*)
> Minnesota (Minn. Stat. §325E.61 and §609.891)
> Montana (Mont. Code Ann. §30-14-1701 *et seq.*)
> Nevada (2005 Nev. Stat. 485)
> New Jersey (A. 4001, 2005 Leg. 211th Sess. (N.J. 2005))
> New York (A. 04254, 228th Gen. Assem., Reg. Sess. (N.Y. 2005))
> North Carolina (N.C. Gen. Stat. §75-65)
> North Dakota (N.D. Cent. Code §51-30-01 *et seq.*)
> Ohio (Ohio Rev. Code §1349.19)
> Pennsylvania (S.B. 712)
> Rhode Island (R.I. Gen. Laws §11-49.2-1 *et seq.*)
> Tennessee (2005 Tenn. Pub. Acts 473)
> Texas (Tex. Bus. & Com. Code Ann. §48.001 *et seq.*)
> Washington (Wash. Rev. Code §19.255.010)

For instance, in 2005, the Texas legislature passed Senate Bill 122, which amended the Texas Code of Criminal Procedure and Texas Business and Commerce Code. The relevant portion of the Texas Business and Commerce Code, §48.102(a) (2006) reads: "A business shall implement and maintain reasonable procedures, including taking any appropriate corrective action, to protect and safeguard from unlawful use or disclosure any sensitive personal information collected or maintained by the business in the regular course of business." Like the approach in California, the Texas legislature statutorily defined that businesses within the state owe a duty to their customers to implement reasonable procedures to safeguard personal data.

What, then, is considered reasonable care in the context of cybersecurity protection? Some analysts argue that the very fact that a security breach occurs indicates a breach of a common law duty owed by the ISP or a commercial firm to provide reasonable security for its customers' personal information. The more reasoned approach is to look at industry standards. In fact, in various cyberspace arenas a number of standards, best-practices and guidelines have been developed. While adherence to an existing industry standard is not dispositive to the determination of reasonable care owed, it is relevant.[9] Indeed, a given court could determine that a party was negligent and did not take reasonable security precautions even if the industry standard was met.[10] Accordingly, although implementation of IP traceback technology is not yet an industry custom, the availability of the AST technology may help determine a new standard of reasonable care owed to protect customer data from intruders. Of course, other factors would also be relevant, such as the cost of using the technology, the availability of alternative technologies and any evidence of problems with the technology (e.g., security breaches in networks using IP traceback methods).

Another approach would be for the federal or state government to allow plaintiffs to sue manufacturers under various product liability laws. This has not occurred at the federal level.

The second question regarding liability issues for hosting a DDoS attacker poses a more difficult challenge. No court has thus far held an ISP liable for the actions of its users.[11] Most cases involving ISP liability have involved questions of copyright and trademark infringement or responsibility for offensive content posted on the Internet. In fact, many of the court decisions find that ISPs are statutorily immune from liability for the actions of their customers under, for example, the Communications Decency Act. The Communications Decency Act states that "no provider or user of an interactive computer serv-

---

9. *See Coats & Clark, Inc. v. Gay*, 755 F.2d 1506, 1511 (11th Cir. 1985) (holding that evidence of industry custom is admissible to determine negligent care); *Rossell v. Volkswagen of America*, 709 P.2d 517, 523–34 (Ariz. 1985) (finding that, under Arizona law, industry custom is admissible evidence to establish defendant's conduct as reasonable under the circumstances).

10. *See* The T.J. Hooper, 60 F.2d 737 (2d Cir. 1932) (holding that failure to equip tug boats with radios that could receive weather broadcasts was negligent, even though it was not yet industry custom to install such radios).

11. *See* limitations on liability relating to material online, 17 U.S.C.A. §512 (1999) (providing a "safe harbor" for Internet Service Providers that unknowingly host copyrighted material).

ice shall be treated as the publisher or speaker of any information provided by another information content provider."[12]

Do ISPs enjoy the same protection in the case of security breaches by intruders that harm ISP customers? While it may seem a stretch to extend the Communications Decency Act to this area, at least one court has already done so. In *Green v. America Online, Inc.*, 318 F.3d at 471 (3rd Cir. 2003) the court extended the language of the Communications Decency Act to a "punter" program. The court first "not[ed] that the dictionary includes 'signal' as a definition of 'information'," and it then asserted that the punter program was in fact a signal; therefore, it was information.

The current approach of some courts to provide immunity is consistent with the way ISPs view their role. Universally, ISPs take the position that they are only providing a "pipe" through which customers connect and information flows. Additionally, most ISPs have a "Terms of Use" agreement with their customers in which the customer agrees not to engage in certain prohibited or criminal activities. In *Green v. America Online, Inc.*, the court held that an ISP was not liable for the actions of two of its subscribers, including posting offensive messages about the plaintiff in a chat room. The *Green* opinion was in line with a 1997 ruling from the 4th Circuit in *Zeran v. America Online, Inc.*, 129 F.3d 328 (4th Cir. 1997). The court in *Zeran* ruled that the defendant was not liable for damages caused by the defamatory messages posted by an unidentified third party. In *Noah v. AOL Time Warner*, 261 F. Supp.2d 532 (E.D. Va. 2003), the district court held that a "chat room" was not a place of public accommodation under the Civil Rights Act and that the ISP was not liable for defamatory messages posted in the chat room.

Aside from the limited amount of firm case law, new distinctions in terminology will certainly impact on future regulatory issues. In *Nat'l Cable & Telecomm. Assoc. v. Brand X Internet Serv.*, 125 S.Ct. 2688, 2711–12 (2005), the Supreme Court held that broadband cable companies provided "information services" rather than "telecommunication services." This means that cable companies, functioning as ISPs, are not common carriers, yet, telecommunication companies, which function as ISPs, are common carriers and subject to regulation under the Telecommunications Act of 1996. While the Telecommunications Act focuses almost exclusively on rates of service and interchange between carriers, any future legislation that affects one industry, should be carefully worded to include both telecommunication and information providers.

---

12. *Id* at §230 (c) (1). The term "information content provider" means any person or entity that is responsible, in whole or in part, for the creation or development of information provided through the Internet or any other interactive computer service. *Id.* at §230(f)(3).

In a DDos attack, the actual attacker is the immediate wrongdoer, but courts may extend liability to other tortfeasors who have contributed to the attacks. The most common civil action following a DDoS cyberattack will most likely be under a negligence theory of some sort. In this vein, an emerging negligence theory is the so-called "Encourage Free Radicals" (EFR) doctrine. The EFR doctrine preserves the liability of an original tortfeasor if the second tortfeasor is a "free radical" and the case exhibits factors that influence the courts to hold the original tortfeasor liable for encouraging free radicals.[13] Free radicals are "those individuals who are shielded from liability by anonymity, insufficient assets, lack of mental capacity, or a lack of good judgment."[14] Cyber criminals clearly fit the description of free radicals because they are judgment-proof, elusive and protected by anonymity. Cyberterrorists, in particular DDoS attackers, exemplify free radicals because their judgment is blinded by ideological or religious motivations. Additionally, a DDoS attacker spoofs or hides the true origin of the attack, making identification of the attacker difficult.

The second factor necessary for applying the EFR doctrine is that the original tortfeasor's encouragement of the free radical constituted negligent behavior. Liability in a negligence action requires that the victim of a DDoS prove: (1) that the defendant had a duty to the plaintiff to take reasonable care to avoid the attack or reduce its risk; (2) that defendant breached this duty; (3) that the breach was the actual and legal cause of the attack; and (4) that the breach resulted in actual harm. While courts have not explicitly identified a duty of care for Internet cybersecurity a willingness to recognize such a duty is developing. For instance, some courts have recognized that in certain circumstances a failure to apply a security patch constitutes a breach of duty.[15] The AST system is

---

13. *See* Meiring de Villiers, *Free Radicals in Cyberspace: Complex Liability Issues in Information Warfare*, 4 Nw. J. Tech. & Intell. Prop. 13 (2005) (discussing the policy rationale behind the EFR doctrine is that solvent defendants should not be allowed to escape judgment by shifting liability to judgment-proof and undeterrable individuals because the deterrence rationale of tort law would be defeated and plaintiffs left without compensation).

14. Mark F. Grady, *Proximate Cause Decoded*, 50 UCLA L. Rev. 293, 306–12 (2002) (The EFR Doctrine was pioneered by Mark Grady. *See* Mark F. Grady, The Free Radicals of Tort, Supreme Court Economic Review, 2004, 189 discussing that the EFR doctrine's long history developed primarily during the nineteenth century alongside negligence cases generally).

15. *See id.* citing Maine Public Utilities Commission, Docket No. 2000-849, Inquiry Regarding the Entry of Verizon-Maine Into the InterLATA Telephone Market Pursuant to Section 271 of Telecommunications Act of 1996 (2003) (Maine Public Utilities Commission concluded that Verizon acted unreasonably by failing to apply a security patch issued six months prior by Microsoft). *See also* Guess?, Inc., F.T.C. Docket C-4091 (2003) Com-

a logical and cost-effective precaution to protect against DDoS because if implemented by ISPs, it operates as a central element of the ISP's information security protocol by mitigating or preventing the attack and resulting damage.

The court will consider other factors in holding the original tortfeasor liable for damage caused to third parties by encouraging free radicals. These factors include such things as whether the defendant (ISP) by lax cybersecurity measures, created an opportunity for the free radical; whether the free radical's behavior was foreseeable; whether the foreseeable harm was serious; the deliberateness of the defendant's behavior; and whether a special relationship existed between the defendant, the third party victim, or both (a defendant who encourages a free radical through a nonfeasance as opposed to a misfeasance will not be liable unless there was a special relationship). The court also factors in the seriousness of the harm as measured by the economic impact of the cyber attack.

While the law is currently in the early stages of development, ISPs and others need to anticipate developments and implement risk management strategies for cyber attacks. Clearly, advancements in DDoS fighting technologies will shape the future of ISP tort liability.

Another statute warranting attention in the context of the AST and other new cybersecurity tools is the federal Support Anti-Terrorism by Fostering Effective Technologies Act (SAFETY Act). The SAFETY Act provides a legal liability shield to designated anti-terrorism technologies thereby encouraging the adoption of innovative technologies that will help protect cyberspace. Under the terms of the SAFETY Act, "sellers" of a technology that would "be effective in facilitating the defense against acts of terrorism, including technologies that prevent defeat or respond to such acts" can petition the Secretary of Homeland Security to designate the technology as a Qualified Anti-Terrorism Technology (QATT).[16] Specifically, the sellers of "any product, equipment, service, device, or technology designed, developed, modified, or procured for the specific purpose of preventing, detecting, identifying, or deterring acts of terrorism" can apply for government certification from DHS. Once the Secretary has cer-

---

plaint, at http://www.ftc.gov/os/caselist/0223260.htm. (FTC held that Guess?, Inc. failed to patch a website vulnerability that made it susceptible to SQL injection attacks. The FTC explained that Guess had been vulnerable to commonly known or reasonably foreseeable attacks and that the vulnerability was successfully exploited resulting into the loss of 191,000 customer credit card numbers. Further, Guess had known of the vulnerability and the fix was relatively cheap and easy.)

16. Homeland Security Act of 2002, Pub. L. No. 107-296, §862 (2002) (defining the term "technology" to include products, equipment, services and devices) *id.* at §865(1).

tified that the proposed "goods" conform to the seller's specifications, a re-buttable presumption is established that can "only be overcome by evidence showing that the seller acted fraudulently or with willful misconduct in submitting information to the Secretary during the course of the Secretary's consideration of such technology." A cybersecurity technology certified as a QATT, means that any liability actions regarding the use of the QATT must be brought in federal court. The SAFETY Act also restricts the legal claim to actual damages, removing punitive or exemplary damages from the claim.

Furthermore, the SAFETY Act approach departs from the government contractor's defense set out in *Boyle v. United Technologies Corp*,[17] where the private party contractor obtained immunity only if he conformed to the "government's specifications." Not only does the SAFETY Act provide the designer of a QATT certified technology the ability to raise a government contractor defense (which absolves the manufacturer of liability outright), but it actually departs from the criteria that such a defense can only be raised in products liability where the product was developed and manufactured according to government contract and specifications required by such contract. Again, the SAFETY Act standard is simply that the goods conform to the seller's specifications. This presumption may only be rebutted by a showing of evidence that the seller acted fraudulently or with willful misconduct in submitting information to the Secretary during the QATT application process. Moreover, it should be noted that this presumption follows the QATT no matter where the customer is located. Therefore, the defense would be viable in situations where the technology was sold to non-federal government customers, in addition to instances where the federal government is the customer.

Finally, sellers of QATTs are required to obtain liability insurance for themselves, "contractors, subcontractors, suppliers, vendors, customers of the seller" and vendors of those customers. Thus, if the AST, or any new cybersecurity technology, could be certified as a QATT, potential customers would certainly be more inclined to adopt the technology.

At a minimum, technology developers, manufacturers and owner/operators should ensure that they craft judicious licensing agreements or terms of service agreements that make clear to potential customers the following: (1) they (ISPs in particular) are not liable for the actions of third parties which result in damages; (2) they will use network monitoring technologies for performance and security purposes; and (3) they reserve the right to terminate connections that threaten their customers. Acceptance of such an agreement could signify approval of the technology's use.

---

17. Boyle v. United Technologies Corp., 487 U.S. 500 (1988).

From a defensive perspective, the issue of liability to customers in the context of safeguarding private information and securing networks against cyber attack is of great concern. Unfortunately, from a legal perspective, because of the rapid pace at which technological developments occur, the law in this area is substantially behind.

Conclusion

The use of SCADA systems and the Internet to digitize and automate almost every aspect of the workings of electric utilities; chemical, gas and oil refineries; public transportation; or hospital services makes them a tempting target for cyber terrorists who desire to cripple some component(s) of the nation's critical infrastructure. Since American SCADA systems are designed for efficiency not security—SCADAs are predominately linked to the Internet—the opportunity for a significant cyber attack is greatly enhanced. Making SCADA systems safe and secure is further frustrated by the absence of a strong federal strategy that mandates information sharing and cybersecurity standards. In addition, the widespread technical ignorance of security managers and the false sense of security due to the absence of a major cyberterrorist incident on America's infrastructure contribute to the vulnerability equation.

If the threat of cyberterrorism is not met with the same recognition and gravity as a physical terrorist attack, it is only a matter of time before a computer savvy jihadist will deal a devastating blow to the United States. To date, private industry has expressed great opposition to increased government management of cyberspace and has lobbied hard against mandatory cybersecurity standards and regulations regarding, for example, legal liability (product liability law suits) for security failures.

Clearly, meaningful federal action is needed to elevate cybersecurity to a national priority. At a minimum, this means instituting mandatory reporting requirements to the government for cyber attacks directed towards private industry and increasing the partnering of private industry with the government to develop long-term research and development in cybersecurity standards.

Selected Bibliography

Mark Pollit, *Cyberterrorism: Fact or Fancy?* PROCEEDINGS OF THE 20TH NATIONAL INFORMATION SYSTEMS SECURITY CONFERENCE, October 1997, at 285–289.

John Rollins and Clay Wilson, *Terrorist Capabilities for Cyberattack: Overview and Policy Issues*, CRS Report RL33123, Oct. 20, 2005.

Peiter Zatko, *Inside the Insider Threat*, COMPUTER WORLD, June 10, 2004.

CYBERCRIME LAW REPORT, *On the Hill Hacking for Terror*, March 8, 2004.

Dan Verton, BLACK ICE: THE INVISIBLE THREAT OF TERRORISM (2003).

John Malcolm, *Virtual Threat, Real Terror: Cyberterrorism in the 21st Century*, Testimony of the Deputy Assistant Attorney General John G. Malcolm on Cyberterrorism, Senate Judiciary Committee, Subcommittee on Terrorism, Technology and Homeland Security, February 24, 2004.

Brett Stohs, *Protecting the Homeland Exemption: Why the Critical Infrastructure Information Act of 2002 will Degrade the Freedom of Information Act*, BERKELEY TECHNOLOGY LAW JOURNAL, Summer 2003.

Index

Abdel-Rahman, Omar: 51

Abdulmutallab, Umar (underwear Christmas bomber): 281

Abu Ghraib: 13n., 19, 22, 31, 149n., 222, 226, 266, 267

Abu Omar: 257

ACLU v. NSA: 154n.

Acree v. Republic of Iraq: 197n., 202n., 221

Adams, President John: 89, 438

Addicott, Dr. Jeffrey: xviii, 519

Afghanistan: xii, 8, 10, 11, 12, 13, 14, 16n., 17, 20, 21, 30, 36, 55n., 56, 65, 72, 79, 104, 125, 174, 175, 237, 240, 248, 256, 257, 264, 267, 270, 273, 282, 316, 350–53, 386, 388n., 391, 394n., 396, 399, 404, 417, 418, 422, 434, 452, 499, 505, 531, 551

Africa Command (AFRICOM): xvi, 300n.

Ahrens v. Clark: 70

Al-Banna, Ra'ed: 277, 278

Al-Haramain Islamic Foundation, Inc. v. Bush: 123, 131n.

Al-Hazmi, Al-Badr: 442

Al-Hazmi, Nawaf (9/11 terrorist): 281

Al-Jezeera: 173

Al-Manar Television (Hezbollah): 173

Al-Midhar, Khalid (9/11 terrorist): 281–82

Al Odah v. United States: 70, 71

Al Qaeda (Al Qa'eda): ix, xi, xv, 3, 7–18, 20, 25n., 26, 28, 29, 30, 36, 51, 65, 104, 106, 122, 123, 124, 175, 235, 239, 240, 241, 245, 255, 256, 257, 264, 265, 267, 269, 273, 280, 293, 309, 310, 331, 359, 376, 378, 380n., 381, 386–90, 391n., 394n., 396, 399, 400, 403, 404, 460, 473, 475, 481, 482, 492, 499, 505, 519, 520, 530, 531, 532, 551, 552
Declaration of War Against America: 36

Altenburg, Maj Gen. John: xii, 35

Alvarez-Machain, Humberto: 253

Alvarez-Machain, United States v.: 254n.

Amendments, Constitutional, (see Constitutional Amendments)

American Bar Association
House of Delegates on "Signing Statements": 106, 126
Section on International Law and Practice: xviii
Standing Committee on Law and National Security: xiv, 197n., 198n.

Ames, Aldrich: 235n.

Anti-Terrorism and Effective Death Penalty Act of 1996: 203

Arar, Maher: 168n., 267, 268, 446

Armed Forces (see Military)

Army Field Manual (FM): 3, 4, 7n., 32, 34–52, 430n.

Army Judge Advocate General's Legal Center and School: xii, 3n., 4n., 11n., 333n., 343n.

Articles of War: 37n., 38, 40, 41, 45

Atta, Mohamed (9/11 terrorist): 282

Authorization for the Use of Military Force (AUMF): 8, 29, 142, 148, 159, 314–19

Automated Targeting System (ATS): 281n.

Baker, Stewart: xv, 277, 282n.

Ballistic Missile Defense (BMD): 487–89

Bay of Pigs: 236

Beauharnais v. Illinois: 178

Bechtel Corporation: 417, 420, 426

Bell, Attorney General Griffin: 103–04

Biagase, United States v.: 45

Bin Laden, Osama: 51, 239, 240, 254n., 269, 314, 350, 351, 352, 353, 388n., 416n., 482, 499

Biological Warfare (see Bioviolence)

Biological Weapons Convention: 502

Bioviolence: xviii, 463, 464, 474, 481, 495–517
 Need for International Approach: 501

Blackstone, Sir William: 85

Blackwater (Xe Services): 419–21, 424n., 426, 428–30, 433

Bollman, Ex Parte: 67n.

Bouie v. Columbia: 538

Boumediene v. Bush: 3n., 21n., 33, 70, 74, 75, 77, 78, 79

Bowman, M. E. "Spike": xvii, 411

Boyle v. United Technologies Corp.: 563

Brandenburg v. Ohio: 180–82, 185–89, 192–95

Bridges v. California: 188n.

Burger, Chief Justice Warren: 101, 180

Burr, United States v.: 115n., 116

Burrow-Giles Lithographic Co. v. Sarony: 93

Bush, President George H.W. (served 1989–1993): 221

Bush, President George W. (served 2001–2009): xii, 3, 8, 11, 13n., 29, 44, 49, 50, 66, 70, 72, 108, 109, 121, 159, 170, 206, 217, 222–25, 227, 228n., 235, 236, 240, 241, 244–46, 248, 252, 254, 257, 258, 261, 264, 266, 270, 273, 274, 301, 388, 443, 452, 454, 457n., 487, 538, 543, 546

Bushell's Case: 68n.

Bybee, Jay S.: 11n., 13n., 14n.

Camarena Salazar, Enrique: 253

Cambodia: 94, 95

Canadian Human Rights Tribunal: 173

Carter, President James Earl "Jimmy": 101, 103, 104, 238

Carthage: vii

Center for National Security Law: xi, xv, xix, 81n., 197n., 198n., 199n., 235n., 411n.

Central Intelligence Agency (CIA): xii, xiv, xv, 26, 27, 28, 33, 34, 125, 147n., 150, 154n., 163, 235–50, 251–57, 259–62, 264, 265, 267–70, 273, 459n.

Chaplinsky v. New Hampshire: 177n., 190

Charter of Fundamental Rights of the European Union: 286n.

Chemical Weapons: 246, 351, 464, 500, 502

Chesney, Professor Robert M.: xiii, 113

Chicago Convention on International Civil Aviation (1944): 284, 285n., 289n.

Chicago & Southern Airlines v. Waterman: 93n.

China, People's Republic of: 143n., 248, 371n., 479, 547, 549

Chinese Exclusion Case: 438

Church Committee: 147n., 163n., 235n.

Cicippio-Puleo v. Islamic Republic of Iran: 202n., 204, 205n.

Cieply, Professor Kevin: xvi, 299

Citizen Publishing Co. v. Miller: 174n.

Civil Liberties: xiii, 106, 141–70, 172, 173, 303, 309, 323, 334

Civil Litigation Against Terrorists: xiv, 197–234

Civilians Performing Military Functions in Wartime: 411–36

Classified Information Procedures Act (CIPA): 132n., 134n., 153

Clay, Rep. Henry: 102

Clinton, President William "Bill" Jefferson: 51, 109, 239, 240, 241, 254, 351, 388n., 542, 543

Coalition Provisional Authority (CPA) (Iraq): 425, 426, 430

Coats & Clark, Inc. v. Gay: 559n.

Cohen v. California: 186

COINTELPRO: 163n.

Cole, U.S.S. (attack on): 7, 240, 387

Collin v. Smith: 184n.

Combatant Status Review Tribunals (CSRT): 21

Combatant's Privilege: xvi, 362, 363, 368, 393, 397, 400

Communist Party of Indiana v. Whitcomb: 187n.

Computer Attacks by Terrorists (see Cyberterrorism)

Constitutional Amendments (U.S.)
    First Amendment: viii, xiv, 171–98, 156, 162, 169, 171–172, 174, 176, 178, 180–96
    Hate Propaganda and First Amendment: 171–98
    Second Amendment: 311
    Third Amendment: 100
    Fourth Amendment: xiv, xix, 48, 59n., 103–06, 110, 122, 156–59, 157, 162n., 282–84, 532
    Fifth Amendment: 23, 24n., 27, 48, 49, 59n., 71, 99, 125, 153, 211, 262, 263
    Sixth Amendment: 59n., 60, 153
    Eighth Amendment: 23, 24n., 27
    Tenth Amendment: 304, 311, 324
    Fourteenth Amendment: 23, 24n., 27, 290

Constitutional Issues (U.S.): 81–112
    Cases or Controversies Requirement: 109
    Commander in Chief Power: 82, 105, 159
    Convention of 1787: 86n.
    Declare War Power: xiii, 82, 303, 311, 312, 361n.
    Due Process: 20, 21, 24n., 31, 33, 59n., 72, 99, 125, 144, 145n., 153, 214, 215, 232, 233, 258, 262–64, 441, 538
    Duty to see Laws "Faithfully Executed": 83, 96, 107, 109, 110, 311

Constitutional Issues (U.S.), *continued*
  Exclusive Presidential Powers:
    91–93
  "Executive Power" Clause: 87
  Foreign Affairs Power: 89
  Original Understanding: 110
  "Political Bibles" of Framers: 85
  Power to Negotiate: 92
  Power of the Purse: 82
  Religious Tolerance: viii, 81–112
  Separation of Powers - Competing
    Theories: 82
  "Shared Powers" Paradigm: 83
  Suspension Clause: 75, 77
  Treaty Powers: 84

Convention Against Torture (CAT):
  18n., 62, 109, 218, 258, 346

Cornyn, Sen. John: 74n.

Corwin, Professor Edwin S.: 82

Court of Military Appeals (CMA): 46,
  47

Courts Martial: xvii, 37–38, 42, 45,
  46, 47, 48, 52, 53, 57, 59

Courts of Inquiry: 37, 38, 41, 62

*Curtiss-Wright Export Corp., United
  States v.*: 89n., 91, 92, 96, 97, 98,
  99, 101, 102, 104n.

Customary International Law: 18,
  125, 258, 263, 338, 340, 341, 342,
  343, 346, 360n., 379, 384n., 548,
  549

Cyber Security and Enhancement Act
  (CSEA): 539

Cyberspace defined: 521

Cyberterrorism: xviii, 173, 519–65

Dames & Moore v. Regan: 93, 211n.

Declaration of War (see Constitution)
  by Al Qaeda against America (1996)
  36

Defense Intelligence Agency: 163,
  459n.

Dennis v. United States: 179n., 187,
  188, 189

Department of Homeland Security:
  xv, 145, 147, 152, 161, 243, 259,
  277n., 279, 288, 291n., 306, 317,
  320, 325, 445, 449, 451, 454, 490,
  523, 539

Department of Justice Office of Legal
  Counsel: 19n.

Department of the Navy v. Egan: 93n.

Detainees: 3–80
  Definition: 4
  (see also Prisoners of War)

Detainee Treatment Act (2005): xii,
  22, 27, 31, 72, 73, 74n., 76, 78, 79,
  108, 266n.

Director of National Intelligence
  (DNI): 123, 129n., 135, 237, 242,
  261

"Dirty Bomb" Attack: xvii, 154n., 466,
  467, 468, 472, 473, 474, 482, 484,
  485, 489, 491

Doe v. University of Michigan: 187n.

Domestic Role of Military: 299–332

Duncan v. Cammell, Laird, & Co.: 117

Duncan v. Kahanamoku: 69n.

Eisenhower, Gen. Dwight David: 209,
  478, 480

Electromagnetic Pulse Attack (EMP):
  467–69

Electronic Communications Privacy
  Act: 165n., 167, 539, 556

Electronic Crimes Task Forces (ECTF):
  539–40

Electronic Surveillance: xiii, 94, 104,
  159, 164n., 169, 279, 287

Data Mining Telephone Records: 105, 164, 168, 169
NSA Surveillance Litigation: 122
Use of "pen register": 106, 282, 539
(see also Foreign Intelligence Surveillance Act)

El-Masri, Khaled: 125, 267

El-Masri v. Tenet: 125

Ely, Dean John Hart: 83

Enemy Combatant Cases of 2004: 70–75

Espionage Act of 1917: 42

European Command (EUCOM): xvi, 300

European Union (EU): 213, 278, 286, 288–92

Ex Parte (see name of party)

Executive Order No. 13223: 8

Executive Order No. 13440: 26

Executive Power (See Constitutional Issues)

Extradition: xv, 89, 251–76, 390

Federal Activities Inventory Reform (FAIR) Act of 1998: 426–27

Federal Emergency Management Agency (FEMA): 243, 306, 307, 317, 325

Federal Radio Commission v. Nelson Brothers Bond & Mortgage: 538

Federal Rules of Evidence: 38, 48, 120

Federal Tort Claims Act: 117, 201

Federalist Papers: 105

Field, Justice Stephen: 116

Fifth Amendment (see Constitutional Amendments)

First Amendment (see Constitutional Amendments)

First Nat'l City Bank v. Banco Para el Comercio Exterior de Cuba: 202n.

Firth Sterling Steel Co. v. Bethelehem Steel Co.: 116, 117n., 118–20

Flatow v. Islamic Republic of Iran: 198n.

Florida, United States. v.: 320n.

Foreign Corrupt Practices Act: 272

Foreign Intelligence Surveillance Act (FISA): xiii, 94, 102–05, 122, 124, 151n., 158–62, 169n., 201n., 202n., 208n., 244, 245, 274

Foreign Intelligence Surveillance Court: 149n., 151n.

Foreign Sovereign Immunities Act (FSIA): 202–04, 205n., 214, 216, 220–22, 228, 229
Flatow Amendment, 203–04

Foundation for Defense of Democracies: 174n.

Fourth Amendment (see Constitutional Amendments)

Frankfurter, Justice Felix: 93, 94, 178, 187

Freedom House: 172n.

Freedom of Information Act (FOIA): 540, 547, 565n., 224

Fulbright, Senator J. William: 90, 95n.

Gallatin, Secretary of the Treasury Albert: 90

Gates, Secretary of Defense Robert M.: 199n., 206, 428

Geneva Conventions (1949): xvii, 6, 10, 11–14, 18, 24–26, 27n., 30–34, 109, 155n., 214, 218, 219, 256, 344, 372, 373n., 374–76, 379, 380, 384n., 385, 386n., 389, 391, 392, 395, 397, 401, 406, 407, 408n., 409, 432, 433

Geneva Conventions (1949), *continued*
  Additional Protocol I: 344n., 364n.,
    380–85, 389, 391, 393n., 397,
    399, 401, 405, 407n.
  Commentary (Pictet) on: 15
  Common Article 3: 12, 16, 18,
    24–27, 32, 33, 109, 256n., 309n.,
    374, 375, 376n., 385, 395, 401,
    406, 407
  Third Geneva Convention Relative
    to the Treatment of Prisoners of
    War: 10
    Article 4: 13n., 372, 373, 379,
      382, 383, 401
    Article 5: 15, 55, 56, 230, 374
    Article 6: 56
  Fourth Convention Relative to the
    Protection of Civilian Persons in
    Time of War: 18
Global War on Terrorism (Global War
  on Terror): 3, 20, 24n., 29, 30, 65,
  70, 72, 388–91, 447n., 457, 459
Goebbels, Josef: 179
Goldberg v. Kelly: 262n.
Goldwater v. Carter: 101n.
Gonzales, Alberto: 11n., 14n., 224
Graham, David: xii, 3, 362n., 409
Graham, Sen. Lindsay: 74
Gray v. United States: 211n.
Graymail: 52
Green v. America Online, Inc.: 560
GTMO (see Guantanamo Bay)
Guantanamo Bay, Cuba: xii, xiii,
  17–21, 30–33, 37, 49, 53–55, 62,
  63, 66, 68, 69, 70, 71, 73, 74n., 75,
  77–79, 102, 141n., 144n., 149n.,
  154n., 155n., 169n., 255, 258, 259,
  264, 266, 267, 408n.
Guillot v. France: 287n.
Gulf of Tonkin Resolution: 95n.

Habeas Corpus: xiii, 23, 32, 65–80,
  141n., 143n., 153n., 155n.
Hague Convention III of 1907: 337
Hague Peace Conferences: 337, 367,
  370
Haig v. Agee: 92n., 93n., 308n.
Halkin v. Helms: 120
Halliburton: 414, 418
Hamdan v. Rumsfeld: xii, 24, 25n., 32,
  36, 40, 41, 49–51, 53, 54, 61–63,
  73, 74, 144n., 154n., 255, 266,
  308n., 309n., 315, 408n.
*Hamdan, Salim Ahmed, United States
  v.*: 35
Hamdi v. Rumsfeld: 20, 70n., 71–73,
  79, 144, 155n., 266, 390n., 408n.
Hamilton, Alexander: 88–89, 90, 197
Harman, Representative Jane: 172
Hate Propaganda: xiv, 171–98
Haynes, Hon. William J. II: 11n., 19n.,
  398n.
Hearsay Evidence: 59, 61, 62
Henkin, Professor Louis: 89, 101,
  219n.
Hepting v. AT&T: 123, 154n.
Hess v. Indiana: 180–82, 185–89,
  192–95
Hezbollah: 173, 381, 479, 480, 482
Hill, General James T.: 17n.
Hitz, Professor Frederick P.: xv, 235
Ho Chi Minh Trail: 95
Holmes, Justice Oliver Wendell Jr.:
  189, 192, 228, 296
Homeland Security: xv, 244, 277–98,
  304, 490
Homeland Security Act of 2002: 279,
  325, 328n., 524, 562n.
Hugo Princz v. Federal Republic of Germany: 217n.

Human Rights Watch: 149n.

Human Trafficking: 251, 513

Hussein, Saddam: 220–23, 246, 247, 277, 345n., 380n., 403, 405n., 444

Immigration Policy: xvii, 437–62
Border Fence: 447

Improvised Explosive Devices (IEDs): 282

Information Operations: 552

Information Policy: 277–98

INS v. St. Cyr: 77n.

Intelligence: xv, 5, 51, 53, 59, 85, 90, 93, 102–05, 113, 124, 129, 142, 147, 148–50, 151n., 152, 153, 155–58, 159n., 160–63, 165, 169, 170, 209, 235–50, 251, 252, 256, 260–62, 265, 266, 269, 270–73, 279, 280, 289, 328–31, 347, 349, 356, 389, 393, 402, 406, 407, 426, 443, 445, 446, 450, 453, 454, 457–61, 478, 487, 490–92, 494, 499, 537, 539, 541, 546

Intelligence Community: 51, 59, 94, 111, 114, 120, 124, 152, 156, 157, 235, 241, 247, 279, 539

Intelligence Reform and Terrorism Prevention Act of 2005: 237

International Committee of the Red Cross (ICRC): 262, 374, 379, 386, 389, 408n., 409

International Court of Justice (ICJ): 208, 319, 345, 346, 350, 504

International Covenant on Civil and Political Rights: 18, 258

International Criminal Court: 48, 219n., 513, 514n.

International Criminal Tribunal for the Former Yugoslavia (ICTY): 48, 49, 59, 389, 391, 392

International Criminal Tribunal for Rwanda (ICTR): 48, 59

International Law of War: 48, 548

Iraq: 11n., 19, 31, 65, 79, 82, 169n., 174, 197n., 202n., 204n., 208n., 217, 220–27, 240, 246, 247, 256, 257, 264, 270, 277, 278, 282, 324n., 345n., 359n., 403, 414–34, 443, 444, 446, 452, 480

Jackson, Justice Robert: 98–101, 145n., 179, 180, 182, 187, 188, 195, 273, 316, 317

Jay, Chief Justice John: 88

Jay Treaty of 1794: 89

Jefferson, President Thomas: xiv, 85, 88, 90, 92, 107, 109, 115, 213, 299, 324

Johnson, Kurt: xvi, 299

Johnson v. Eisentrager: 66, 67, 73, 76, 78, 92n., 99, 143n.

Just War Tradition: 361, 376

Katz v. United States: 103, 157, 158, 282n.

Keith Case (see United States District Court)

Kellman, Professor Barry: xviii, 495

Kellogg-Briand Pact (1928): 338

Kellogg Brown & Root: 422

Kennedy, Senator Edward "Ted": 126, 454

Kenya: 7, 240, 350, 352, 387, 395, 396, 407n., 473

Khalid Sheikh Mohammed (KSM): 51, 242, 281

Kilburn v. Socialist People's Libyan Arab Jamahiriya: 202n.

Kim Jong-Il: 313

Koh, Dean Harold Hongju: 83–85, 96–99, 101

Korea, Democratic People's Republic of (North): 200n., 212, 248, 313, 400, 471, 475, 479, 481, 484, 485, 499

Korean War: 95, 99, 145

Ku Klux Klan: 180, 212

Ku Klux Klan Act (1871): 68–69

Lackawanna Six: 175

Laos: 94

Lautenberg Amendment: 198, 204–06, 215, 228

Law of Armed Conflict (see also Law of War): xvi, xvii, 50, 360n., 433n., 548

Law of War (*jus ad bellum*—law governing initiation of coercion): xvi, 333–58, 361n.

Law of War (*jus in bello*): xvi, 337, 342, 343, 359–410
　Origins: 360
　Sources: 396
　(see also Law of Armed Conflict)

Leahy, Senator Patrick: 74, 106

Legislative Tyranny (fear of): 110

Levi, Attorney General Edward: 113n.

"Liberty City Seven": 175

Lieber Code (U.S. Civil War): 318, 365, 367n., 369, 397, 406

Lin Biao: 95

Lincoln, President Abraham: 273, 318

Lindh, John Walker: 460

Lindh, United States v.: 362n., 386

Litigation
　Civil, Against Terrorists: xiv, 197–234
　of National Security Cases: 113–41, 154n.

Lloyd, United States v.: 536

Locke, John: 85, 86n.

Lockington's Case: 77n.

Lopez, United States v.: 538

Louisiana, United States v.: 320, 558

Lovett, United States v.: 107n.

Madden, Thomas F.: vii

Madison, President James: 86, 87, 265n., 312

Marbury v. Madison: 91, 256

Marshall, Chief Justice John: 89, 91, 201, 299n.

Martens Clause: 369, 370, 373, 393, 396, 398

Material Witness Warrants: 148

Mathews v. Eldridge: 263n.

McKinley, President William: 69, 438

Meyer, Lt. Col. Jeanne: xvi, 299

Military: xvi, 10, 33, 65, 72, 313, 351, 359, 380n., 387n., 392, 393, 396, 399, 400, 403, 408n., 414, 439, 441, 453, 459, 460, 461, 548, 553
　Courts (see also Courts Martial, and under Court): xvii, 47, 429
　Detention Order: 9
　Geographic Combatant Commands (see by name)
　Use within United States: 299–333

Military Commissions: xii, 9, 40–41
　Presidential Order (2001): 9, 16, 30, 32, 45

Military Commissions Act: xii, 23, 24, 27, 32, 40, 54, 74, 75, 78, 79, 266

Military Commissions, Office of: xii, 49, 50, 54

Military Justice Act of 1950: 38, 45

Military Justice Act of 1968: 46, 56

Military Law: xii, 35–64

Military Rules of Evidence: 38, 48

Miller, United States v.: 283n.

Miranda v. Arizona: 45

Missouri v. Holland: 295

Mitra, United States v.: 533–36

Monroe, President James: 107

Montesquieu, Baron de: 85, 86, 87, 89

Moore, Professor John Norton: xi, xiv,
     81, 197, 198, 199, 210n., 221,
     229n., 337n., 343n., 355n.
     Proposed Draft Protocol to the
          United Nations Anti-Terrorism
          Conventions: 231

Moqed, Majed (9/11 terrorist): 282,
     288

Morris, United States v.: 536

Morrison, United States v.: 538

Moussaoui, Zacarias: 53, 155
     United States v. Zacarias Moussaoui:
          155n.

Mueller, FBI Director Robert: 243

Mutual Legal Assistance Agreements
     (MLATs): 251

Myers, General Richard B.: 17, 457n.

*National Broiler Marketing Ass'n v.
     United States*: 537

*Nat'l Cable & Telecomm. Assoc. v.
     Brand X Internet Serv.*: 560

National Counterterrorist Center
     (NCTC): 242–43

National Decision Directive: 39, 254

National Liberation Movements: 94,
     364, 377, 379–81, 395

National Reconnaissance Office
     (NRO): 237, 239, 243

National Security Act of 1947: 97,
     165n., 236

National Security Agency (NSA): 81,
     105, 154n., 159, 237, 539
     SHAMROCK Program: 121
     Surveillance Litigation: 122–24

National Security Concerns: 49, 52,
     61, 194, 447, 448

National Security Entry Exit System
     (NSEERS): 444

National Security Law (History as Aca-
     demic Field): xi

National Security Law Institute at
     UVA: xi

National Security Letters: 142, 165,
     167n.

New York Times v. Sullivan: 190

Noah v. AOL Time Warner: 174n., 560

North Atlantic Treaty Organization
     (NATO): 390, 392, 434, 552

Northern Command (NORTHCOM):
     xvi, 300–24

Nuclear Non-Proliferation Treaty
     (NPT): 478–83

Nuclear Threat and Terrorism: xvii,
     301, 312, 313, 319, 326, 331,
     463–94
     Assessing the Risks: 490
     Defenses: 477
     Deterrence: 464
     Forms of Nuclear Threats: 468

O'Callahan v. Parker: 46

O'Connor, Justice Sandra Day: 55, 56,
     144, 183

Office of Legal Counsel (see Depart-
     ment of Justice)

Office of Military Commissions (see
     Military Commissions, Office of)

Oklahoma City Bombing (Murrah
     Federal Building): 203, 205n., 239

O'Neil, Professor Robert M.: xiv, 171

Operation JUST CAUSE (Panama): 393

Operation URGENT FURY (Grenada): 392

Orwell, George: ix-x

Osama Bin Laden (see Bin Laden)

Outsourcing Military Functions in Wartime: xvi, 411–36

Pacific Command (PACOM): xvi, 300, 309

Padilla, Jose: 20, 154, 155, 460

Padilla v. Hanft: 154

Padilla v. Rumsfeld: 70–72, 79, 144, 154

Paine, Thomas: 197, 220

Pan Am Flight 103: xiv, 203

Parker, Dean Elizabeth Rindskopf: xiii, 141

Parks, Professor W. Hays: xvi, 359, 398n., 399n.

Passenger Name Records (PNR): 279–98

Peace of Westphalia: 200, 413

Pearl Harbor: 69, 313, 400, 492, 493, 531, 547

Peyton v. Rowe: 67n.

Pfaltzgraff, Dr. Robert L. Jr.: xvii, 463

Philippines: 43, 69, 377, 408, 530

Pictet, Jean – *Commentary* (see also Geneva Conventions): 15n., 375n.

Pierce v. Society of Sisters: 287n.

Pinochet, Augusto: 272

Planned Parenthood of Southeastern Pa. v. Casey: 76

Pollen v. Ford Instrument Co., Inc.: 117

Port and Border Security: 485–87

Posse Comitatus Act: 146n., 327n., 328–31

Powell, Hon. Colin L.: 13, 246, 247, 451

POWs (see Prisoners of War)

Preiser v. Rodriguez: 67

President, Above the Law: 83, 91–92, 109

Presidential Constitutional Powers (see Constitutional Issues)

Presidential Decision Directive (PDD) 35: 239

Presidential Decision Directive (PDD) 39: 317, 319

Presidential Signing Statements: 82, 106–10

President's Intelligence Oversight Board (PIOB): 150

Prisoners of War—POWs (see also Detainees; *Acree v. Republic of Iraq*): xiii, 4, 5, 10, 13, 14, 15, 17, 19, 26, 37, 214, 218, 220–27, 229, 309n., 366, 367, 368, 371, 372, 380, 382, 385, 393, 406, 408, 409

Provost Courts: 37, 39, 41

Quirin, Ex parte: 41, 42, 44, 47, 49, 56, 69, 143, 153

R. v. Keegstra: 173

Radiological Weapons: xvii, 301, 326, 466, 468, 472–74, 481, 482, 492, 522

Radovich v. National Football League: 538

Radsan, Professor John: xv, 251

Rasul v. Bush: 21, 36n., 70n., 71, 72, 74n., 144n., 155n., 258n., 266, 390n.

R.A.V. v. St. Paul: 183n.

REAL ID Act of 2005: 443, 447, 449

Reid, Richard (shoe bomber): 155n., 386n., 387

Reid v. Covert: 429

Rendition: xv, 114, 122, 136, 149, 154, 168, 248, 251–76
Litigation: 124

Republic of Iraq v. ABB AG: 217

Rex v. Cowle: 77

Rex v. Schiever: 77n.

Rex v. Watson: 115

Reynolds, United States v.: 117–20, 127–30, 135

Rezaq, United States v.: 146

RICO Act: 199

Riesman, Professor David: 176–78, 191

Right to Financial Privacy Act: 165

Rives, Maj. Gen. Jack: 63

Roberts, Chief Justice John: 75, 76

Rogers v. Tennessee: 538

Roosevelt, President Franklin D.: 42, 44, 45, 47, 56, 69, 107, 228,

Rule of Law: viii, xiv, 34, 77, 83, 106, 109, 173, 198, 199, 200, 207, 208, 210–14, 217–20, 223, 224, 226–28, 230, 231, 252, 256, 258, 270, 343n., 360, 394, 456, 457, 517, 547, 548

Rules of Engagement (ROE): 321, n.343, 406, 433, 552

Rumsfeld v. Padilla: 20, 144n.

Russia and Nuclear Terrorism: 471, 475–76, 486

Rwanda Tribunal (See International Criminal Tribunal for Rwanda)

Salameh, United States v.: 153

Sales, Professor Nathan: xv, 277

Scalia, Justice Antonin: 75, 76, 79n., 110n.

Schenck v. United States: 192n.

Schooner Exchange, The: 201

Scott, General Winfield: 43, 68

Sealed Case, *In re*: 151, 159, 279

SEATO Treaty: 94, 95

Second Punic War: vii

Senate Committee on Foreign Relations: 81n., 90, 95n., 124n.

Separation of Powers (see Constitutional Issues)

Sharp, Dr. Walter Gary: xvi, 333, 339n., 340n., 361n.

Sherman, Roger: 87

Sierra Leone Tribunal: 48, 59

Signing Statements (see Presidential Signing Statements)

Simon v. Republic of Iraq: 204

Smith Act: 179, 188

Smith v. Libya: 205n.

Smith v. Maryland: 105, 283n.

Society for Worldwide Interbank Financial Telecommunication (SWIFT): 293

Southern Command (SOUTHCOM): xvi, 17, 19, 300, 302

Sovereign Immunity: 198, 200, 201, 204, 206, 208, 217, 220, 232

Sovereignty: 70, 257, 302, 313, 316, 318, 319, 320, 333, 334, 335, 336, 345, 347, 349, 350, 353, 354, 356, 357, 358, 404, 413, 438, 516, 550

Spanish American War: 43, 69

Spanish Inquisition: viii, ix

Specter, Senator Arlen: 126, 204n.

Starkie, Thomas: 115

State Responsibility: 345
and Bioviolence: 504–507, 511–13, 515, 516

State Secrets Privilege: 57, 113–41, 256, 267, 268,

State Secrets Protection Act (SSPA): 126–140
(See also names of individual cases and Justices)

Steel Seizure Case (see *Youngstown*)

Stock, Professor Margaret: xvii, 437

Stockholm Declaration of 1972: 504

Supervisory Control and Data Acquisition (SCADA) Systems: 525, 526, 528, 531, 532, 564

Support Anti-Terrorism by Fostering Effective Technologies Act (SAFETY Act): 561–63

Supreme Court, U.S.: xii, xiii, xiv, 12, 20, 22–25, 31–33, 36, 38, 42–44, 46, 47, 49, 50, 51, 59, 62, 66, 69, 70–75, 77, 78, 89, 90–93, 97, 98, 101–110, 114, 116–19, 128, 130, 144, 145, 150, 153, 154, 158, 159, 161, 162, 173, 174, 177–82, 186, 187, 190, 193, 202, 208, 211, 222, 254, 258, 266, 268, 282–84, 290, 292, 304, 309, 311, 314, 315, 316, 389, 390, 402, 408, 429–32, 438, 448, 560, 561
(See also names of cases)

Syria: 168, 261, 262, 268, 269, 273, 377, 388, 418, 446, 447, 499

Taepo Dong 2 (North Korean Missile): 313

Taliban: xv, 10, 11–20, 26, 28–30, 36, 264, 316, 351, 386, 390, 404, 405, 482, 499, 505, 551

TALON (Threat And Local Observation Notice): 149

Tanzania: 7, 240, 350, 352, 387, 396, 473

Telephone Records, Data-Mining (see Electronic Surveillance)

Tenet v. Doe: 118

Terkel v. AT&T Corp: 154

Terminiello v. Chicago: 178

Terrorism:
Non-State Sponsored: 333, 340, 346–49, 356–58
State Sponsored: 200, 203, 208, 225, 333, 340, 341, 343, 348–50, 357, 358, 372, 377
Transnational: 7, 9, 200n., 288, 291, 292, 300, 314, 362, 374, 376–78, 381, 387, 389, 391–406, 412, 413, 416, 475, 501, 514, 540

Terrorist Surveillance Program (NSA): 106, 120–24, 126, 129, 136, 147, 149, 154, 159n., 237, 239, 243, 245

Terrorist Threat Integration Center (TTIC): 242

Terry, Dr. James: xiii

Thach, Dr. Charles: 87

Third Geneva Convention Relative to the Treatment of Prisoners of War (See Geneva Conventions)

Thomas Jefferson Center for the Protection of Free Expression: xiv

Three Spanish Sailors, Case of: 77

T.J. Hooper, The: 559

Torture: vii, 5–6, 13, 25, 27, 58, 62, 109, 124, 125, 141n., 149, 168, 202n., 203, 208n., 209, 214–18, 220–27, 248, 253–55, 257–60, 264, 268, 269, 272, 274, 346, 402, 409, 446, 447
Convention Against (CAT): 109
U.S. Torture Statute: 17–19

Total Information Awareness Program: 149

Totten v. United States: 116

Transatlantic Alliance: 277–98

Treason: 115, 375n., 516

Treaties, Does Senate "Ratify"?: 84

Truman, President Harry: 95, 96n., 99, 145n., 237

Truong Dinh Hung v. United States: 105

Tsesis, Professor Alexander: 172, 193n.

Turner, Professor Robert F.: xiii, 81, 96n., 390n.

UN (see United Nations)

Uniform Code of Military Justice (UCMJ): 6, 7, 16, 37–41, 45, 46, 48, 51, 52, 62, 63, 429, 430, 431, 432

Unitary Executive (see Executive Power)

United Nations: 7, 84, 197n., 198, 207, 208, 212, 215, 218, 219, 229–234, 246, 318, 319, 334, 336–338, 339, 340, 343, 346, 348n., 350, 352n., 380, 388, 390, 392, 404, 405n., 413, 433, 434, 435, 506, 514, 522, 548, 549, 550, 552
    Charter: 7, 95n., 231, 318–19, 334–43, 346, 348, 350, 380, 413, 506, 548, 550
        Article 1: 338n.
        Article 2(4): 336n., 338–41, 345, 348, 354, 357, 549
        Article 24: 549
        Article 25: 335n., 340n., 348n.
        Article 27: 549
        Article 39: 338, 339, 340, 551
        Article 41: 336n., 550
        Article 42: 369n.
        Article 51: 318–319, 338–41, 348, 364n., 388, 390, 401, 404, 405n., 549, 550
        Article 59: 346
        Article 103: 336n.
    Definition of Aggression: 550–51

Security Council: 7, 197n., 236, 306, 334, 335, 339, 340, 341, 343, 348, 349, 350, 352, 356, 390, 392, 403, 463n., 506, 549, 550, 551
    Resolution 1368: 8, 390
    Resolution 1373: 8
    Resolution 1540: 506, 507, 513

Unlawful Combatants: 4, 7, 12, 15, 16, 18, 19n., 23n., 24n., 30, 367n.

Unprivileged Belligerents: 4, 49, 61, 363–409

USA PATRIOT Act: 142n., 148, 151, 161, 163, 165, 166, 244, 266n., 278, 279, 287, 443, 524, 532, 533, 538, 539

U.S. Constitution (see Constitutional Amendments, Constitutional Issues)

U.S. Convention Against the Spread of Terrorism: 197

U.S. Court of Appeals for the Armed Forces (CAAF): 47, 48

U.S. Military (see Military)

"U.S. Person" (defined): 159

U.S. Supreme Court (see Supreme Court)

United States District Court, United States v.: 103

United States v. (see name of other party)

Universal Declaration of Human Rights: 18

University of Virginia: xi, xiv, xv, 3, 197, 199, 219n., 235

Unlawful Combatants: 4, 7, 12, 15, 16, 18, 19, 23, 24, 30, 367

Viet Cong: 94, 364n., 401

Vietnam War: 93, 94, 96, 107, 108, 181, 182, 187, 238

Vietnam War, *continued*
Assassinations During: 364

Violent Radicalization and Home-grown Terrorism Prevention Act: 172

Wall (Separating Intelligence from Law Enforcement): 151, 266, 279, 289

War:
Can Cyber Attacks Be an "Armed Attack"?: xvii, 520, 522, 523, 526, 529, 531, 532, 542, 543, 544, 547, 548, 550, 554, 562, 564
Declaration of (see Declaration of War)
Is America at "War" with Terrorists?: viii, 8, 9, 51, 387

War Crimes Act: 25, 27, 32, 429, 433

War Powers Resolution: 93, 97, 108, 216, 311n., 315, 317n.

Warrantless Wiretaps (see Electronic Surveillance)

Warren, Professor Charles: 110

Washington, President George: 43, 84, 88, 99, 102

Watergate: 97n., 147n.

Watts v. United States: 182n.

Weapons of Mass Destruction: xvii, xix, 141, 146n., 230, 239, 246, 255, 273, 307, 314, 319, 327, 328n., 335, 345n., 418, 463, 499
(see also Nuclear, Bioviolence, Chemical)

West Virginia University Hospitals, Inc. v. Casey: 537

Whitney v. California: 182

Wilson, James: 86

Winthrop, William: 38n., 41, 42, 43n., 46,

Woolsey: Hon. R. James, vii

World Trade Center: 3, 7, 36, 51, 53, 65, 153n., 171, 192, 239, 243, 251, 299, 359, 387, 390, 439, 469, 489

Wright, Lawrence: ix

Wright, Professor Quincy: 89

Yemen: 7, 175, 239, 240, 387, 388, 404

Yoo, Professor John: 258n., 273, 390

Youngstown Sheet & Tube Co. v. Sawyer: 93–94, 97, 145n., 316n.

Yousef, Ramsi: 51, 153n., 239, 240

Yunis, Fawaz: 253, 254, 272, 386n., 395, 396n.

Yunis, United States v.: 146n., 328n., 386n., 396n.

Zelikow, Professor Philip: 124n., 313n.